Fundamentals of
BUSINESS ANALYSIS

Fundamentals of
BUSINESS ANALYSIS

HOWARD B. BALTZ
*Associate Professor of Statistics
and Quantitative Management Science
University of Missouri—St. Louis*

RICHARD B. BALTZ
*Chairman, Department of Economics
and Business Administration
Millsaps College*

PRENTICE-HALL, INC.

Englewood Cliffs, New Jersey

PRENTICE-HALL INTERNATIONAL, INC., London
PRENTICE-HALL OF AUSTRALIA, PTY. LTD., Sydney
PRENTICE-HALL OF CANADA, LTD., Toronto
PRENTICE-HALL OF INDIA (PRIVATE) LTD., New Delhi
PRENTICE-HALL OF JAPAN, INC., Tokyo

This book is dedicated to
Dr. William J. Thomas for the
professional and educational
inspiration he gave us.

ACKNOWLEDGMENTS

We wish to acknowledge the assistance and suggestions of those who have given us both their time and advice. We are indebted to William J. Thomas of Midwestern University for providing the initial stimulation for developing a text of this nature. He has been most helpful at various stages in this enterprise in providing general impressions and suggestions. Robert E. Harrison of Texas Technological College and Samuel Nicholas, Jr., of Millsaps College each were kind enough to read a specific section and present comments. Our appreciation for the typing of the text and supplementary material at various stages is extended to Brenda Smith, Marilyn Brinkman, Virginia Stehling, and especially Margaret Cavin for her very able and accurate assistance. We also thank our wives for their patience during the writing of the book and especially Mrs. Sylvia Baltz who proofread the entire manuscript during the editing stage and who was instrumental in suggesting many significant improvements.

CONTENTS

PART FIVE

Statistical Methods for Decision Making

PART SIX

Computer Concepts for Business

1

ECONOMIC, SOCIAL,

AND LEGAL DIMENSIONS

The objective of this chapter is to introduce the reader to some fundamental characteristics of the environment in which modern business operates.
This objective will be achieved by considering the economic, social, and legal
dimensions of the business environment in the United States. In the annex to
this chapter a brief description of the evolution of business is provided.

ECONOMIC ENVIRONMENT

The economic environment in which business enterprise operates in
the United States is a factor which has contributed heavily to the success
story of the American economy, a success story that is reflected by the high
per capita income enjoyed by citizens of the United States compared with
other nations of the world. The average per capita income of an American is
approximately twice that of most Europeans and 10 to 20 times greater than
the average income of an African, Asian, or Latin American. Business enterprise has been instrumental in making this story come true.

The economic environment in which business enterprise operates is
conditioned by man's struggle for material survival and by the scarcity of
nature. While man does not live by bread alone, neither can he live without
it. He necessarily must devote his effort to the activity of providing for the
material necessities of life: food, clothing, and shelter. Because of scarcity
he must devote a substantial amount of effort to maintaining or improving
his material well-being. However, man has learned to apply himself and has
been able to offset the meagerness of nature by specializing his effort. Your

1

attention will first be directed to the three basic characteristics of the economic environment—survival, scarcity, and specialization. The dynamic characteristics of the economic environment, which are freedom, self-interest, competition, flexibility, and the mixture of centralized and decentralized decisions, will then be discussed.

Basic Characteristics

Man's struggle for *survival* has required him to come face to face with nature and with himself. For a long time he did not understand much about his physical environment. Literature about the ancient history of man is abundant with descriptions of man worshipping the elements—fire, earth, and water. He usually feared or worshipped whatever he did not understand.

Even when he understood his physical surroundings better, man still struggled with nature for survival; this struggle goes on today. The ravages of nature have been a constant threat to man. Floods, earthquakes, tornadoes, droughts, volcanic eruptions, lightning, and disease are examples of nature on the rampage. Even in today's modern world, man's attempts to impose controls have not freed him from nature's whims, although he has devised many ways to protect himself, such as building dams for flood control, developing better irrigation methods, and experimenting with new medicines to fight disease.

In addition to protecting himself from nature, man has worked continuously to make his environment more comfortable. Clothing and shelter are basic requirements of man's physical well-being; medical science contributes to his ultimate survival and extends his lifetime. But he is also trying to improve his physical comforts by building better houses, faster airplanes, and safer factories.   He devotes much of his time to finding better and easier ways to do things.

As important as man's struggle with his environment has been his struggle with his fellow men. War is a serious threat to man's survival, which expresses his inability to get along with other men and destroys man himself. It is also a waste of resources. Both private wants and public needs could be better accomplished if resources did not have to be diverted to defense projects.

Man's psychological nature may also explain his behavior.   Pleasure and pain, reward and penalty are strong motivations for human effort. The desire for the power to manipulate men and machines has motivated many a man to action, as have compassion, sympathy, and concern for others.

The mere fact that man exists is evidence of the success of his material survival. His material substance has been adequate to place him in the twentieth century. The fact that man has survived, however, is not necessarily a testimonial to how "well" he has survived. His material survival may be evidence only of a minimum standard of well-being. In some of the underdeveloped parts of the world, such is the case. In other parts of the world, a high standard of living is evidence of greater success.

Man's struggle for material survival suggests the *scarcity* of resources. Economic resources can be divided into three categories—natural, human, and produced. Natural resources include such endowments of nature as land, forests, minerals, and water. Human resources refer to those mental and physical skills, talents, and abilities which man uses to produce goods and services, including skilled and unskilled labor, managerial and entrepreneurial skills, and professional and scientific talents. Produced resources result from the combination of natural and human resources. Natural and human resources are used to make tools, machinery, equipment, and buildings, all of which are examples of produced resources.

The nature of scarcity depends upon two quite different characteristics. Scarcity can be considered as being *absolute* or *relative*. The absolute nature of scarcity pertains to the physical availability of resources; the relative nature constitutes the demands and requirements man places upon his physical environment. Each of these concepts will be discussed at length and the absolute scarcity of natural, human, and produced resources will be explained individually. Finally, we will indicate how scarcity imposes the need to make choices.

Natural resources are limited on two accounts. First of all, the earth is fixed, absolute, and limited in size, although the potential supply of natural resources on the earth can be considered enormous. Man may have only scratched the surface, so to speak, of his physical world, but he cannot escape the fact that natural resources are limited. Even air becomes limited as man reaches the higher altitudes. In the second place, much of the potential supply is inaccessible to man. He must go deep into the surface of the earth, for example, to acquire oil and other minerals. The more remote the resource, the more expensive it is to obtain. Although a vast reservoir of resources may exist, if it is as yet unknown or unavailable to man it must be considered scarce. A resource may be thought of as remote even if it is geographically available, if it is too expensive to process into a form usable by man. Oil, for example, may be available on the earth's surface in the form of rocks, but may be too expensive to extract because of its low concentration.

Human resources are scarce to the extent that skills, talents, and abilities take time to develop and must be properly directed before they can be applied to man's efforts to enhance his material existence. Years of study and training may be required in certain scientific and engineering fields; the art of management requires, in addition, years of practice. As a matter of fact, continued experience in any particular field can be considered as further development of human resources and, in a very extreme sense, the time required to develop a human resource may be a lifetime.

There are several characteristics of *produced resources* related to scarcity which require special attention. First, capital goods contribute to man's material survival because they enable him to produce more. With such aids to production as screwdrivers, drill presses, and steel girders, more can be produced in a given time. One can then eventually expect to have available more potatoes, shoes, and curtain rods. Second, produced resources are dependent upon a combination of natural and human resources. They are not merely extracted, but are transformed by human effort from natural resources. Third, produced resources require immediate and permanent diversion of both natural and human resources from other production activities. This diversion necessarily means a delay, initially, in the production of potatoes, shoes, and curtain rods. For these reasons, human and natural resources become even more scarce because they are not available for direct production of consumer goods.

Finally, it must be emphasized that a growing stock of produced resources eventually offsets any of the scarcity that it initially created by diversion and delay. Because human resources become more productive, they can be released from one activity and made available to another productive or useful activity. For example, as factory workers become more productive, some manpower can be channeled into the arts, or social work, or medical services. In summary, scarcity is reduced as more aids to production become available. Produced resources require diversion of resources and delay of some consumption, all of which eventually result in more production and less scarcity. It takes little imagination to see the value of this to man's struggle for survival.

So far we have discussed the absolute nature of scarcity, particularly the fact that resources are limited. Scarcity can also be explained as being relative in nature. Man's own appetite to consume provides one principal explanation for this. For example, meat and potatoes, ballpoint pens, raincoats, shaving lotion, refrigerators, radios, automobiles, and houses all provide various kinds and degrees of satisfaction, as do services. The butcher trims your meat, the jeweler repairs your pen, the doctor prescribes medicine, a repairman fixes your appliances, and the lawyer assists in transferring a house title. Scarcity is relative, then, because the wants that must be satisfied are varied and ever-changing. The specific kinds of goods and services that man consumes are influenced by his basic needs and environment and by changes in his appetite that occur over time.

Man's material wants fall into two categories. The first is based upon *biological needs*. There is no way to avoid such demands. Food is necessary for human energy, and clothing and shelter are protection against the elements. Man consumes enormous quantities of foodstuffs, covers himself with all kinds of garments, and isolates himself from rain, wind, and the cold by building both simple and elaborate structures.

The second category of wants is known as *contrived wants*, in the sense that they are the result of man's conditioning by his environment. Advertising tries to influence us to consume goods which would normally go unnoticed, and the introduction of new products expands our appetites to consume goods which never existed before. Not too long ago, desires for such things as electric carving knives and toothbrushes, room air-conditioners, color television, snow tires, and stereo phonographs were nonexistent. Then too, we usually are not content unless we imitate others. Observing the consumption patterns of higher-income receivers alters the appetites of those who try to emulate them. The Chevrolet owner perhaps looks forward to the day when he can own a Cadillac.

The other principal explanation for the relative nature of scarcity is the fact that human wants are generally considered to be unlimited. This means that it is impossible for man to completely satisfy his demands for goods and services. Verification of this point can be achieved merely by compiling a list of those goods and services you would like to have. It will become apparent that such a list can go on and on. New products and opportunities continue to expand the possibilities from which man might seek satisfaction. It must not be forgotten, however, that some desires, such as food, can be satisfied temporarily. Such items as sport shirts are sufficient for a while but must be replaced with the passing of time because of wear and tear.

In conclusion, scarcity requires man to continually make choices if he is to do the best he can with what he has. Maximum satisfaction requires consumers to make the best possible choices. Although we cannot satisfy all of our wants, each consumer has a notion of the relative priorities he attaches to the wide range of goods and services that are available to him. By comparing the relative prices of goods and services and the ability of each to contribute to his total satisfaction, the consumer makes up his basket of goods and services, taking into account the limits of his income.

Maximum output also requires producers to make optimum choices. Economic resources are limited. Once a producer has decided what to produce and how much to produce, he must seek the best combination of resources available. By comparing the relative prices of all resources and the ability of each to contribute to the production of the final product, the producer chooses that combination of resources which achieves the desired output.

In essence, what we have been trying to do is to explain a simple law of economics. As producers and consumers we can do or have anything we want, as long as it is not everything. This is a direct way of saying that the conflict between ends and means imposed by scarcity must be satisfied by choosing from among various alternatives. Scarcity forces upon each and every one of us—individual, business, and government alike—the need to make economic decisions.

Specialization of effort is a means by which the productive efforts of modern society are mobilized to cope with the constraints imposed by scarcity. Individual consumers in a modern society seldom, if ever, consume directly the goods and services they themselves produce. The assembly-line worker who installs headlights in Pontiacs all day may drive a Plymouth. Even the wheat farmer in Kansas probably purchases his bread from the local grocer instead of baking it himself.

In some less developed areas of the world, however, direct forms of production and consumption still exist. It is for this precise reason that these areas are still underdeveloped economically. As a matter of fact, a very large proportion of the world's population probably still lives in small, self-contained communities and villages, having little contact with other parts of the world. Because of their size and isolation, the extent to which they can specialize is also severely limited. In such an environment there is insufficient demand for one person to devote all of his working hours to one task.

Specialization is also practiced on a regional basis; the quality of the land, the climate, and the abundance of certain minerals help to explain geographical specialization. Coffee is grown in Brazil, movies are produced in California, chickens are raised in Arkansas, petroleum is shipped from Arabia, and fine wool is processed in England. Geographical specialization is essential to the efficient use of resources. Consequently, each area produces those products for which it is best adapted.

Whether specialization of effort is applied to the production of "pins" or Pontiacs, the result is the same—*greater total output*. There are several ways in which specialization contributes to production. The person who performs a specific task eventually develops a skill for that task. If complex tasks are divided into simple operations and each operation is assigned to a specific individual, that individual gradually increases both the quantity and the quality of his work. The second contribution of specialization is the saving of time. Less movement of the worker from operation to operation is required, continuous attention is devoted to each operation, and there is no loss of motion. The opportunity to apply innate abilities may also exist. Some individuals who have keener senses, for example, may be able to contribute more to production than others can.

Besides greater production, there are *other consequences* that are associated with specialization. For one thing, an efficient *system of exchange* is developed. For another, individuals become extremely *dependent* upon each other. Furthermore, the many individual economic activities resulting from specialization suggest the need for some sort of mechanism to *coordinate* all this effort. Each of these effects requires additional comments.

It would do little good to specialize production if producers were unable to trade with each other. It becomes important therefore to consider a system of exchange. Trade could be achieved by a system known as *barter*, in which goods and services are exchanged for other goods and services. However, barter is not considered to be efficient; therefore, modern society depends upon money to facilitate the exchange of goods and services.

Money is necessary because of the *noncoincidence* of wants. For example, if Smith is a dentist and Jones is a dairy farmer, it is very probable that their wants will not coincide. Perhaps Jones has perfect teeth and no decays. However, Smith, the dentist, has ten growing children. How is he going to trade for the necessary milk? Even if Jones did require a filling occasionally, it would indeed be a coincidence if his ten children consumed exactly enough milk to exchange for a filling. Perhaps the dentist would have to pay in some other way, such as helping to milk the cows every other day. But then, he would not be specializing his effort any more.

There are other reasons why modern societies depend upon an efficient system of exchange. A system which uses a medium of exchange, such as money, provides several advantages. First, the holders of money possess three important options: they can buy what they want, from whom they want, and when they want. Not only are the obstacles resulting from a non-coincidence of wants eliminated, but the holder can obtain a better bargain. If he had to trade his labor each month for goods and services at the "company store," he might indeed end up "deeper in debt." But if his labor efforts for the month are converted into money, he is in a much better position. He can trade where he wants and buy what he wants. And by being able to space his consumption, he can store up buying power for later purchases or purchase goods and services when he believes prices are more favorable.

There is still another advantage to using money as a medium of exchange. Goods and services are more readily compared when the value of each is expressed in terms of a common denominator. This eliminates the need for an extensive and complex price list.

Take the example of two commodities, Product A and Product B, where Product A is expressed in terms of Product B, and Product B in terms of Product A. There will be two products and two prices. If three commodities existed, the number of prices would increase not to three, but to six. If there were four commodities, the number of prices would be twelve. This progression in the number of prices is illustrated in Fig. 1–1. Each arrow represents the price of one product in terms of another.

It becomes apparent that an impossible situation would exist if the prices of all the goods and services of today's modern world had to be expressed in terms of each other. One item might have several million prices— that is, its value would be expressed in terms of several million other items. Adopting the use of money, however, eliminates the need for such a situation. The value of each item is expressed in terms of one common denominator— money.

The second consequence of specialization is that individuals become

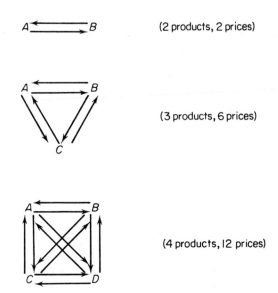

FIGURE 1-1.   **Progression in prices as number of commodities increases.**

dependent upon each other. As a result, the members of a modern society are bound to each other for their own common good. Each contributes in his own way to the material well-being of the others. The individual usually does not benefit directly from his own efforts; instead, he depends upon others for his material survival. This fact is vividly portrayed when attention is directed toward any large metropolitan area, such as New York City, Chicago, or Los Angeles. The individuals in these areas are practically helpless. Each makes his specialized contribution, but in turn he depends upon the efforts of thousands like himself for his existence. Whether one lives in a large city, in rural America, or in something in between, such as a medium-sized city or a small town, dependence will vary only slightly, according to the individual's own circumstances.

By contrast, the inhabitants of isolated or remote areas in Africa, Asia, South America, or the South Pacific are *independent*, in the sense that each one can scratch out of the earth or depend upon animal prey for his minimum survival requirements.

The third and final consequence of specialization that we will consider is the emergence of *coordination*. The essence of coordination is having the right goods in the right amount at the right time. A vast number of occupations, professions, trades, and specialities exist in the American economy. These and other activities, such as manufacturing, agriculture, mining, construction, and services, are organized into several million business and professional enterprises, governmental units, and nonprofit institutions. All of these economic activities and organizations require coordination of their diversified efforts.

When one visits a hardware store to buy a certain size and type of screw, he expects this desire to be satisfied. Most of the time this simple transaction is accomplished with little fuss and bother. The same goes for the items of food and clothing consumers purchase every day. Even the services of the repairman, the plumber, the surgeon, the butcher, the baker, and the modern-day counterpart of the candlestick-maker are available when needed. We take the coordination of all these activities for granted. More careful consideration, however, awakens our sense of accomplishment when we recognize the difficulties of coordination in a world of specialists.

The coordination of economic activities can be achieved in two ways: depending upon the decisions of economic units as they are expressed in the marketplace, or depending upon the decisions of a central planning authority. These decisions, for the purpose of allocating resources to production and goods and services to consumption, are the essence of the next chapter.

Dynamic Characteristics

In addition to basic characteristics, there are certain dynamic characteristics which also influence the economic environment. *Economic freedom* is one of these characteristics. Freedom of individual consumer choice has been immensely helpful in directing economic efforts toward desired goals. Determining what to produce and how much, what will be bought and sold, depends essentially on the decisions the individual consumer makes when he spends his income. Freedom of choice also applies to resource owners. Owners of property and money capital can employ these resources as they please. Laborers are free to enter occupations and employments for which they are best suited. Business establishments also have freedom of enterprise, which allows them to acquire economic resources, organize these resources into the production of a product, and sell the product as they see fit. Freedom of choice and freedom of enterprise are closely related to private property or ownership. The rights and responsibilities associated with ownership make meaningful choices possible. Without ownership choices by consumers, businesses and resource owners would be without authority.

Freedom of choice and freedom of enterprise, however, are not without limitations. The economic role of government is broad in scope; it is justified mainly on the basis that its actions are intended to strengthen the free enterprise system and to improve the general welfare. The government also establishes legal "rules of the game" to govern the relationships of businesses, resource owners, and consumers with one another. It provides social goods and services, influences the use of resources, and alters the distribution of private goods and services. The government is keenly interested in controlling unemployment, inflation, and the instability caused by business cycles and in promoting economic growth and satisfactory international relations.

Self-interest is another important ingredient of the economic environment in which business enterprise exists; it probably best describes the behavior of the various types of economic units. In old-fashioned terms, self-interest provides the economy with incentive and initiative, as each economic unit tries to do the best it can for itself. Business enterprises and the owners of the various types of resources—land, labor, and capital—try to get the best price for the use or from the sale of their respective contributions. Likewise, consumers concerned with a certain standard of living try to pay the lowest prices possible for goods and services.

Competition is also an important feature of the American economic environment that has taken on many dimensions in the modern world. It is reflected by the interactions of the individual and corporate buyers and sellers who operate in the marketplace for any particular product or resource. Competition also exists between sellers in different industries, such as steel and aluminum or plastics and paper. Competition involves not only prices but also the characteristics of the product itself, its promotion, its package, and the conditions under which it is sold, including various services such as credit and delivery. The essence of competition is that economic power either is diffused among the many or is counterbalanced by an equal opponent or group of opponents. Competition depends upon the freedom of entry of the participants in the marketplace. When new participants are restricted by legal devices or institutional obstacles from entering a particular industry, competition has been abridged.

Another characteristic of the economic environment of a market economy is the *role of prices*. The decisions of consumers and producers are reflected by product and resource prices, which perform an organizing function: by the price system, resources are allocated to production and products are allocated to various uses. The market economy, with the aid of prices, also signals the need to change, for example, from producing buggy whips to producing auto seat belts. Profits resulting from high prices for a new product signal the need for more production and the entry of new producers. In this way resources are attracted from other, less desirable production. Over a period of time the economy adjusts its production from the old to the new. Competition simply expedites the system's ability to adapt or change.

The economic environment in the United States is represented by *decentralized and centralized economic decisions*. Individual consumers, producers, and resource owners make the decentralized decisions which add freedom and flexibility to the economic environment. The various government units make the centralized decisions, influencing, directing, stimulating, and stabilizing economic activities. Centralized government decisions are most relevant to the overall economic performance of the economy. See Chapter 3 for more on economic performance providing purpose and power to society's economic efforts.

The importance of both decentralized and centralized decisions was recognized in the Economic Report of the President transmitted to the Congress in January, 1965. The Report refers to the centralized influences of Federal fiscal and monetary policies in recent years as follows:

> Federal policies have made a major and continuing contribution to the great achievements of the American economy during the past four years.[1]

In a similar manner, emphasis is directed to decentralized decisions when the Report refers to competition and regulation for a flexible market economy as follows:

> Decentralization of economic power has long beenconsidered desirable for social and political reasons, as well as for its contribution to an efficient economy."[2]

To summarize, freedom, self-interest, and competition are important factors contributing to the economic environment of business enterprise in the United States. These three factors are also interrelated in a special sense. Freedom allows individual economic units to protect their own self-interest, providing the tremendous drive that is so apparent in the American economy. Self-interest, however, may sometimes bring out the worst in people, who will take advantage of each other in the marketplace if the opportunity arises. But if competition is allowed to be operative, there is little chance for this to happen. Competition provides a check against this side of self-interest by encouraging someone else to make a better or similar product. Self-interest, then, is allowed to bring out the best in man, while competition tends to restrict the worst in him.

In summarizing, competition and the market economy provide flexibility and adaptability in the use of our economic resources. The economic environment is also a mixture of centralized and decentralized decisions. Such a mixture recognizes the merits associated with individual and collective actions, each of which is necessary to promote the well-being of mankind.

SOCIAL ENVIRONMENT

The American society is a mixture of many groups and influences. It is made up of households, businesses, and governments; consumers, managers, workers, and stockholders; schools, hospitals, churches, and as-

[1]Executive Office of the President, *Economic Report of the President* (Washington, D. C.: Government Printing Office, 1965), p. 61.
[2]*Ibid.*, p. 131.

sociations; teachers, doctors, and preachers; lawyers, judges, and public servants; and many others. Business establishments make up an integral part of this picture.

Business activities have a far-reaching effect upon American society. On the one hand, business produces the bulk of goods and services that consumers enjoy, that governments purchase and distribute, and that other businesses use. On the other hand, business accomplishes this production by purchasing or hiring the available supply of the economy's resources and thus provides employment and income to many resource owners.

Because of this dominant economic position, business enterprise has a responsibility to society. Recognition of this responsibility varies among firms; some are more conscious of it than others. There is no doubt, however, that as a whole the "public be damned" attitude of business during the late nineteenth century has been replaced by a more responsible outlook. Businessmen use ethics and standards of conduct to guide their decisions and actions. They behave in a more ethical manner, not for the sake of ethics alone, but also to make higher profits. Today the business establishment exercises a citizenship role by recognizing its responsibilities to consumers, employees, governments, and communities, as well as responsibilities to creditors and stockholders.

The social environment of business is reflected by the evolutionary changes in society and in business itself, by the increased significance of employee relations and labor organizations, and by the ever-expanding influence of public opinion. We now will discuss in more detail these factors, which have imposed upon business an attitude toward its social responsibilities that has had a far-reaching effect on business practices.

Evolutionary Change

Change is, without doubt, a part of the American way of life. Time itself has brought about evolutionary changes in our society. The nation has lived through difficult and unstable times. Scientific advances, two decades of war, expansion of the public sector, the experience of affluence by many, greater leisure, the attempts to fight poverty, and the erupting demands of oppressed minorities all reflect the extent of massive social change. It cannot be ignored. Change is probably the only element of the business environment that can be considered permanent.

In addition to the changes of society, the nature and structure of business have changed. Three of these important changes are (1) the growth of business giants, (2) a shift in the ownership of American business, and (3) the emergence of the professional manager. Mass production, consumer credit, rapid transportation, and other factors contributed to the evolution of large corporations. With this growth has come social, economic, and even political power, which is capable of affecting a community, a region, or the world. But such power can and has been abused, and therefore it demands responsible business attitudes and actions.

Another change has been the shift of ownership in American enterprise. Generally, the owners of today's big giants do not control company operations; management is in the hands of salaried employees. Thus, the professional business manager has emerged. These men have come to recognize that their business firms must be responsible citizens and now place importance on the human factor in the operations as well as on the scientific approach to management. They have become aware of their responsibilities to consumers, employees, and stockholders and of the fact that corporate policies involving salaries, benefits, purchasing, and expansion have a major impact upon the community. This responsibility has gone so far that many corporations interested in encouraging and preserving American culture have acquired fine arts collections. Area development, support of education, funds for hospitals, and the reduction of poverty are other activities in which the modern business enterprise engages.

Labor Relations

Employee relations and labor organizations represent another important reflection of the social environment. The human factor receives keen attention in today's business setting, since individual attitudes and group behavior can have a direct bearing on production results. Both on the job and off, the contact and relationships between people and groups of people continuously affect the environment in which we live and work. Legislation and union activities have been instrumental in improving employee relations and working conditions, in providing a vehicle by which the voice of labor is recognized and respected, and in drawing attention to the human factor. Labor and management have come a long way in recognizing that they derive mutual benefit from each other's association.

Public Opinion

Public opinion also plays a vital role in the social environment of business. The acceptance or rejection of a firm's product eventually depends upon public opinion. If the product is satisfactory, the firm will receive votes of confidence in the form of purchases in the marketplace; poor sales will register dissatisfaction. Public opinion also has been instrumental in bringing about changes in business practices. Hostile public reactions to business practices can lead to governmental control if corrections are not self-imposed. Public opinion in a democracy is revealed by letters, editorials, pamphlets, books, elections, surveys, and spontaneous boycotts, all of which bring pressure upon the business community. Business itself also examines at length the effect of its policies on the general public and may sponsor educational and informational programs to acquaint the public with its problems and viewpoint. Business is not and cannot be ignorant of public opinion.

LEGAL ENVIRONMENT

Laws represent the rules of conduct necessary for the proper behavior of the members of society, as well as indicate the rights and responsibilities of each member. In essence, the nature of law is to regulate or control individual and group activities. Some laws depend upon tradition and custom and are the result of past court decisions. Others known as statutory laws are enacted by duly authorized governmental bodies, such as the U.S. Congress, a state legislature, or a city government.

Legal Jurisdictions

Legal jurisdiction in the United States is divided between the Federal government and the various state governments. Activities involving interstate commerce, for example, are subject to Federal control, while certain business activities that occur within a state are under the jurisdiction of the state government. The U.S. Constitution specifically divides legal jurisdiction between the states and the Federal government. Transportation, communications, insurance, agriculture, banking, foods, and drugs are a few of the business areas controlled by the Federal government. Wholesaling, real estate, amusements, and construction are relatively free of Federal regulation.

The Federal government and the various states also have separate court systems. Courts have been established to determine if a law has been violated and to issue judgments. In both the Federal and state systems, agencies, commissions, and administrative boards have been established to perform many of the duties of the courts, and have been given the authority to investigate and issue orders within their limited areas. Such agencies as the Federal Trade Commission, the Securities and Exchange Commission, the National Labor Relations Board, and the Federal Communications Commission are well known to the business community. State agencies and commissions that deal with utility companies, commodity pricing boards, and liquor control commissions are also active.

Many business activities are subject to law. A brief discussion of business law will be offered here for the purpose of indicating to the reader the important relationship of law to the business environment. Business activities and transactions, first of all, depend upon certain legal arrangements, pertaining to such things as contracts, agency relationships, property, negotiable instruments, and bankruptcy. Business activities and transactions are also affected by laws which regulate commerce and competition, impose taxes, and influence labor relations. Each of these items will be discussed in turn.

Legal Requirements

Virtually every business transaction is affected by the *law of contracts*. In essence, a contract is an agreement between two or more parties, which can be either oral or written. State statutes specify whether or not the contract should be in writing to be valid; this depends upon the nature of the transaction, its magnitude, and the time involved.

For a contract to be binding, it must satisfy certain requirements. First of all, there must be an offer and an acceptance, as when a retailer encourages customers to come into his establishment and make an offer for his goods, which the retailer can accept or reject. To be binding, a contract also requires a common understanding between the parties. Very obvious errors are usually not enforceable. The parties to a contract normally must be competent—that is, sane, sober, adult, free, and so on. There are several exceptions to this requirement; for example, a contract with a minor for necessities is enforceable. Another essential requirement of a binding contract is consideration. Something of value must be given in return for something else. And finally, contracts are unenforceable if they involve an unlawful act. When one party to a contract fails to perform any part of the agreement, a *breach of contract* occurs. These and other matters pertaining to contracts are provided for in the laws of contracts. It thus is apparent that the laws of contracts are vital to the responsible conduct of business activities.

Business transactions and activities are also affected by *agency laws*. An agent is one who is authorized to act in behalf of another. Many business transactions involve an agency relationship, where the owner of a business establishment hires a manager whom he empowers to represent him in buying and selling activities and in other contractual duties. Such a relationship is usually well defined and publicized, insuring that everyone concerned knows the exact limits of the agent's authority. If such limits are not specified, the law normally depends upon what is typical of similar agents. For example, a contract between the manager of a retail shoe store and a distributor of men's socks is binding if this transaction is typical for other shoe store managers. Even if the principal (store owner) did not intend his agent to buy socks but failed to specify such to his suppliers, the purchase of men's socks would be binding.

Agency laws also cover the activities of an employee who does not initially have agency authority. If the businessman pays for goods he permitted a servant (the legal term for an employee who is not an agent) to buy in his name, he has made the servant an agent by implication. An agent is usually authorized by a written document known as a *power of attorney*. It is again apparent that law provides important guidelines to various business arrangements and activities.

Property or private ownership is a fundamental characteristic of American society. Property is commonly classified as *real* or *personal*. Real property is land, including everything above and below its surface and all improvements such as buildings that are firmly attached to the land. Personal property is generally not as fixed; it is all other property which is not real property. Automobiles, equipment, furniture, and fixtures are examples of personal property. The business establishment must be concerned with laws pertaining to property, since the most common of all business transactions involves the buying and selling of goods. There are specific laws including the Uniform Sales Act which govern the *sale of property*, real and personal. Determination of the actual sale, transfer of title, warranties, ownership arrangements, conditional sales, and bailments are just a few of the specific areas governed by the statutes.

Most business activities depend upon some sort of arrangement that allows for the delay of payment. Extension of credit, as it is called, is made possible through the use of *negotiable instruments*, which can be either written promises to pay, known as promissory notes, or written orders to pay, known as bills of exchange. For example, an I.O.U. is a simple promissory note. A bond is a more complicated debt instrument. A personal check is a good example of a bill of exchange; it is a written order for a bank to pay a certain sum of money to another party. A negotiable instrument is a contractual obligation that can be transferred by delivery or by endorsement. The various classifications and specific provisions governing negotiable instruments are contained in the Uniform Negotiable Instruments Law. Negotiable instruments and the law facilitate the many transactions without which a business community could not possibly survive.

One other area of business law which is particularly relevant to the business environment is the act of *bankruptcy*. Most businesses are started with the hope that they will be successful. However, in a competitive system, not all business enterprises survive. When failure occurs, the owner of the business often has debts he is unable to pay. The Federal government has instituted the Federal Bankruptcy Act, which governs the distribution of the assets of a business (or individual) when insolvency occurs. Bankruptcy can be declared voluntarily by the debtor, or it can be requested by the creditors. The purpose of the law is to protect the public in the distribution of the remaining assets.

Legal Constraints

The legal environment of business also depends on laws which *regulate* and *control* business activities. The U.S. Constitution provides the Congress with the power to regulate commerce. State governments complement the Federal government's power, and local governments use the police power which has been delegated to them by the states to regulate business within their respective areas. The various levels of government have the authority to regulate a vast range of business activities, using such tools as the so-called *antitrust laws*, which were designed to promote competition, and *labor laws*, which were enacted to insure proper and equitable relationships between labor and business. This authority includes state and local intervention in the form of licensing laws, pricing boards, and zoning laws.

Most of the costs of maintaining the government are met eventually by its *power to tax*, although some of the services provided by government (Federal, state, and local) are financed by bond issues that are repaid from proceeds collected from users. Other services, such as postal delivery, are purchased directly by the user. The imposition and collection of taxes establish a legal environment whereby business firms must conform to certain tax requirements. A by-product of taxation has been the need for business establishments to keep proper and adequate records. The business establishment also has been commissioned indirectly to be the nation's tax collector, by collecting sales taxes and deducting employees' payroll taxes. Various types of taxes are imposed by government, many of which are familiar to the reader. Some of the more important categories are: income tax, property tax, sales tax, excise tax, import duty, incorporation tax, severance tax, license fees, and stock transfer tax.

Government taxation is without a doubt a part of the legal environment of business enterprise. The imposition and collection of taxes allows government intervention into business affairs; taxation also may affect business decisions and activities. The expectation of a change may encourage or delay certain business activities, as when the possible reduction of an import duty encourages a business firm to delay foreign purchases. Taxes which affect profits may also affect business decisions. Investment spending for new buildings and equipment may be affected by various taxes and tax credits. Property taxes have been instrumental in encouraging plant relocation; when they are high relative to other locations, they may become an important factor in a decision to move the business establishment. Taxation therefore is an important element in the legal framework that affects the business environment.

In summarizing this chapter, one can say that business does not operate in a vacuum; there are many influences which operate continuously. Through the years, the business environment has been determined by certain economic conditions. Business enterprise, fully aware of its legal, economic, and social environment, provides a dynamic force in our society. The maturity of American business is evidenced by the decisions it makes. In addition to business decisions, moral and ethical decisions must be made which require an attitude of responsibility. The business enterprise that recognizes this challenge makes a vital contribution to the survival of man and the improvement of our modern way of life.

ANNEX : EVOLUTION OF BUSINESS ENTERPRISE

The importance of the economic, social, and legal dimensions of business can be illustrated by a brief description of the evolution of business enterprise in the United States. Business enterprise has developed from a dependence on home production in the early American Colonies to the dominance of big business in today's space age, from a concentration of human effort and simple tasks to the employment of automation and mass production.

When the desire to specialize effort and to exchange or trade appeared in the Colonies, it first showed itself in exchanges with the mother country. The Colonies traded raw materials for certain manufactured products they could not obtain otherwise. Families in the Colonies were forced to depend upon their own efforts for such items as shoes, cooking utensils, furniture, food, and clothing. Later on, some of the men gained a reputation for being experts in making shoes, utensils, or furniture. They traveled around to "drum up business" by bartering their wares and services for subsistence and other goods. Eventually, the craftsman established himself in a small shop to which customers came. At this stage, transactions were essentially between the producer and the consumer.

The next phase in the evolution of business enterprise was marked by the emergence of merchants or storekeepers. The storekeeper would assemble the wares of others, including imports, and offer these items for sale. In this way, he became dependent upon an adequate inventory. To insure control over his sources of supply, the merchant eventually assembled the scattered craftsmen under one roof and supplied them with materials. This concentration of workers in a factory allowed for further specialization. Workers were grouped and assembled according to particular skills and tasks.

Machinery was introduced to production processes as a result of the industrial revolution, which began in England early in the eighteenth century. The use of inventions such as textile-producing machinery and the steam engine required the accumulation of capital (money). The existence of vast natural resources, the pooling of financial resources, and the concept of free enterprise made the United States an ideal setting for industrial development.

The age of big business was undoubtedly prompted by a desire to take advantage of certain economies of large-scale production. Machinery and production processes had developed to the point where the cost of producing steel, for example, on a grand or massive scale was reduced to a fraction of the cost associated with old methods. Small-scale production gradually disappeared. The development of large markets, improved techniques of production, and efficient management techniques gave impetus to the mass production of many products. This merely accentuated the movement toward big business.

The desire for power and growth encouraged combinations, mergers, and other forms of business concentration, and the economy that had relied upon competition as a regulating device was soon threatened by declining competition. Some of the mergers and combinations, however, were not in the public's best interest. When control over markets, prices, and production caused serious damage to the consumer, it became necessary for the government to step in and act on behalf of the public interest.

In summary, the trend toward specialization, mass production, automation, and industry concentration (see Chapter 4) has been under way for some time. The nature of such trends, their possible consequences, and their apparent continuance are of great concern to the consumer, business, and government.

PROBLEMS AND PROJECTS

1. Familiarize yourself with the *Standard Industrial Classification Manual* published by the Office of Statistical Standards, Bureau of the Budget (Washington D.C.: Government Printing Office, 1967). How does the Bureau define establishment? What are the major divisions into which all economic activities are classified?

SELECTED REFERENCES

Cheit, Earl F., ed., *The Business Establishment*. New York: John Wiley & Sons, Inc., 1964.

Corley, R.B., and R.B. Black, *Legal Environment of Business*. New York: McGraw-Hill Book Company, 1963.

McGuire, Joseph W., *Business and Society*. New York: McGraw-Hill Book Company, 1963.

Smith, Adam, *The Wealth of Nations*. Chaps. 1–3. Originally published in 1776.

Walton, Scott D., *American Business and Its Environment*. New York: The Macmillan Company, 1966.

2

DYNAMICS OF

ECONOMIC ALLOCATION

As individuals or as members of society, we all have common problems. In Chapter 1, we explored the problems caused by the fact that only limited resources are available to satisfy unlimited ends. We are required to make choices constantly when we allocate these resources. It is this concept of allocation to which our attention will now be directed. Before proceeding, however, a definition is in order. Economic allocation essentially refers to the process by which society decides how to use its resources—natural, human, and produced—and how to implement these decisions to satisfy human needs.

The process of allocation is particularly relevant to two basic economic activities. As a matter of fact, the term "allocation" may be a good, concise definition of production and distribution. Production involves the allocation of resources; distribution involves the allocation of goods and services. Society has three decisions to make concerning allocation. It has to decide *what* goods and services are going to be produced, *how* they are going to be produced, and *for whom* they are to be produced. Production provides the substance of the first two decisions—*what* and *how*. Distribution provides the resolution of the third decision—*for whom*.

There are basically two methods by which allocation is achieved. One method is for production and distribution to proceed according to the intentional direction of a central authority. Another method is for households and businesses to make independent decisions.

To begin with, we will investigate and describe some basic elements of production and distribution. Then a few comments about the different methods of accomplishing production and distribution will be presented.

Finally, we will take a glimpse at the American economy to see how it accomplishes the task of allocation.

BASIC ALLOCATION ACTIVITIES

The allocation of resources for the benefit of society involves two distinct activities. First of all, resources must be used to produce goods and services; and second, the fruits of production must be distributed among the members of society.

The process of allocation is illustrated briefly in Fig. 2–1. Resources are allocated to production and combined to produce goods and services. These goods and services are in turn allocated to households. In each of these situations important decisions must be made, either by a central authority such as government or by independent economic units such as households and businesses.

Production and *distribution* are the two basic activities that must be performed by any society. At first glance, these two activities seem simple. However, they are actually quite complex, particularly when the members of society are dependent upon each other because of specialization. Producing the right amount of the right goods at the right time for the right people is no easy task.

We will first take a look at *production*, which is a process that requires the mobilization of human effort. Mobilizing human energy for productive purposes is not difficult, since the desire to survive induces most men to work. In addition, in our modern day a man who is not employed may fall into disrepute. It would be safe to say that most men want to work; the real task, therefore, is to get them to put forth their best effort. This requires training, education, and well-developed skills. The success or failure of an economic society depends upon the *quality* of its human effort. Providing the proper environment and the social institutions that will motivate this effort is the real challenge. It is the old-fashioned concept of initiative and incentive that provides the positive motivation for well-trained human effort.

At times, although motivation is not lacking, an inadequate *quantity* of effort is mobilized. Men are unemployed, machines stand idle, and the total effort falls far short of its potential. There seems to be what we will elect to call a *breakdown* in the economic processes that are necessary to achieve a satisfactory level of overall economic performance; an insufficient amount of effort is mobilized for productive purposes. For example, in the United States during the great depression of the 1930's, nearly one-fourth of the work force was idle. The need for goods and services still existed, but there was a partial collapse or breakdown of the production and distribution processes. To avoid a recurrence of this situation, certain devices have been inaugurated

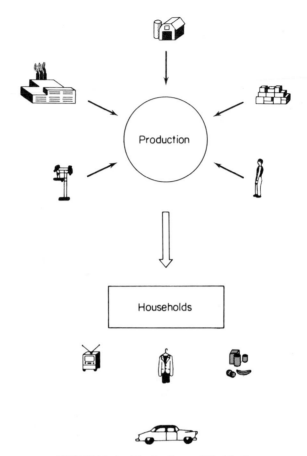

FIGURE 2–1.   Production and distribution.

by the government to check and to compensate for such a breakdown. A closer look at overall economic performance will be provided in Chapter 3.

Sufficient motivation and the avoidance of an economic breakdown represent only one part of the production problem. To achieve *effective* production, men and machines must be put to work *doing the right things;* they must produce what society wants. Resources should be directed into the activities which accomplish this end. Even in supplying screws for hardware stores, society must allocate its efforts properly: it may produce too many screws, or too few, or none of the right size. Society may produce too many automobiles, but not enough tires; too many diamond rings, but not enough shoes. Or it may not devote enough effort to research or education, or to new fields such as space exploration.

Effective production in the economy is reflected by the extent to which the price paid by consumers matches the cost of the last unit produced. When the price exceeds this cost, society is paying more for that last unit than the cost necessary to attract resources to the production of that particular product. In essence, consumers are saying that the economy should divert more resources to that particular production activity. The more competitive markets are, the more likely it is that effective production will be achieved. In non-competitive markets where there is only one seller (monopoly), prices can be regulated by a public authority to encourage adequate utilization of resources.

The wants of society as a whole are the collective reflection of individual desires and preferences. In this sense, individuals may determine to a large extent *what* is to be produced. Whether or not this is the case depends upon whether an authoritarian or a market system is in operation.

Finally, resources should be utilized in an *efficient* manner. The efficient combination of resources, for a particular level of production depends upon two important requirements: the engineering or physical techniques of production must be recognized, and the relative value of resources must be considered. The following explanation and examples concerning the combination of resources illustrate the decision *how* goods and services are to be produced.

For example, suppose that the available engineering information suggests the existence of several different combinations of resources to achieve a particular amount of production. Our task would be to choose the combination of resources that would make the greatest use of the abundant resources and the least use of the scarce resources. In a market economy, scarce resources will command higher prices than the more abundant resources. The most efficient combination will be that one which is reflected by the lowest money outlay when compared to the other alternatives. In the case of an authoritarian system, if market prices are not available, some other device must be used to judge the relative abundance and scarcity of the available resources.

In either case, production efficiency demands greater use of abundant resources and less use of scarcer resources. For example, if a region is abundant with trees, much of the construction in that area will probably be of wood. The more abundant labor is relative to tools and machinery, the more likely it is that production will be achieved by using more human resources than produced resources. In underdeveloped countries, roads are constructed with the use of much human labor and very little machinery because of the relatively higher cost of the machinery; in the United States, roads are built with a greater proportion of machinery to labor.

Electricity can also be generated by more than one method: hydro-electric production represents a very large fixed plant—a dam—and small amounts of other resources such as manpower; with steam-generated electricity, the plant is small when compared to the large amounts of other resources

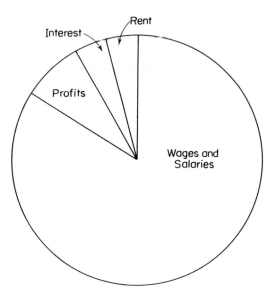

FIGURE 2–2.   Functional distribution of income.

such as coal or gas. All of these examples illustrate that economic efficiency depends upon the relative availability of resources.

So far we have only told half the story of allocation. Production is one part; *distribution* is the other. Distribution is the allocation of goods and services to the members of society and represents the *for whom* decision. Having mobilized resources to produce the right goods in an efficient manner, society must now set itself the task of distributing those goods. In other words, now that the pie has been baked, it must be cut up.

Money income is a basic determinant of distribution. Figure 2–2 is a pie-shaped diagram illustrating how the results of production might be distributed according to different kinds of money incomes. The money incomes are closely related to different types of resources. For example, wages and salaries represent payment to human resources. Rents represent payment to owners of land, which is a natural resource. Interest is payment to those who have claims on produced resources, such as machines and buildings. Profits represent a special kind of income: the payment of money income for those who are willing to take business risks. Economists classify and arrange this type of information in a way to represent the relative contributions made by the different types of resources to the production process and call it the "functional distribution of income." In Fig. 2–2, the circle or pie might represent the total amount of production in an economy for one year; the pie is dissected according to a functional distribution of income for the economy in that year.

In this way the claims of individuals or households on society's production are reflected by the different kinds of money incomes received. This is not a reflection of goods and services distributed per household or individual. That would have to be accomplished by dissecting the pie into several million sections, each section representing one household. Some sections would be very large, some about average, and some very small, depending upon the size of the income earned by each household.

Under an authoritarian system, where production is accomplished according to a plan, each individual's share of society's product would probably be parceled out by the central authority. It is also probable that money income would be the main vehicle for facilitating distribution; specialization and an efficient system of exchange would require it. However, the money incomes would be dependent upon the dictates of the planning authority. Whether or not there existed a functional distribution of income according to the different types of resources would depend upon whether or not private ownership of the means of production, machines, and land were allowed. An authoritarian system can exist, for example, with or without private ownership of property.

The extent of an individual's *ability* to participate in the process of distribution depends upon the *size* of his money income, which reflects his claim upon society's production. He receives this claim in return for the time and effort he contributes to production. The size of the claim depends upon several factors: the *type*, the *quantity*, and the *price* of the resources he commands.

Each household may own a different type of resource. Some may own all three types—natural, human, and produced. That is, they have title to land, ownership in a business, and command over their own mental and physical abilities, all of which are available for hire. Other households may have possession of only one type; for example, they may be able to offer only labor resources. The quantities of each of these types would naturally have a direct bearing on the size of the household's income. A person who owns vast amounts of land or a large quantity of stocks and bonds would have a larger income than one who does not. A disabled or underemployed person would be likely to earn low wages.

The price of each type of resource plays an additional role in determining size of income. Some resources command a higher price than others. This may reflect relative scarcities, strong preferences, or an unusual market condition that allows the seller of the resource to capture a high price. It may also reflect the wishes or influence of a central planning authority which sets the prices for various resources.

An individual's *willingness* to participate in a particular pattern of distribution depends upon *product prices*. Constrained by a certain amount of income, the individual decides whether or not he is willing to pay the price for, let us say, a cashmere sweater. The price of the sweater and his judgment of its worth determine whether or not the sweater will be distributed to him. His willingness to buy the sweater also depends upon his desire to have a sweater as opposed to, for instance, a Dacron jacket or a fancy fishing rod. By comparing these alternative preferences and their relative prices, the consumer determines what combination of goods and services will be distributed to him.

A hypothetical situation may clarify this point. Let us say that our consumer has a "preference counter," similar to a Geiger counter, which he uses to measure the satisfaction he can obtain from different items. When pointed at an item, it would give a certain number of "clicks" or register some value of satisfaction on a visual meter. In reality, the individual does this in his own mind; we call it human judgment. Continuing, then, let us say that his "preference counter" registers 40 clicks for the cashmere sweater and 20 clicks for the Dacron jacket. Suppose also that the price of the sweater is $20 and that the price of the jacket is $5. Would he be better off owning the sweater or the jacket? By comparing the values of satisfaction and the prices of the two goods, the answer becomes obvious. This comparison is illustrated as follows:

$$\frac{\text{satisfaction from sweater expressed in "clicks"}}{\text{price of sweater}} \quad \text{compared to} \quad \frac{\text{satisfaction from jacket expressed in "clicks"}}{\text{price of jacket}}$$

Substituting the numerical data, the comparison becomes:

$$\frac{40 \text{ "clicks"}}{\$20} \quad \text{compared to} \quad \frac{20 \text{ "clicks"}}{\$5}$$

Reduced to a common denominator of $1, the comparison is:

$$\frac{2 \text{ "clicks"}}{\$1} \quad \text{compared to} \quad \frac{4 \text{ "clicks"}}{\$1}$$

And stated another way, it becomes:

2 clicks per dollar compared to 4 clicks per dollar.

It is apparent that our consumer would get more satisfaction or usefulness per dollar spent if he bought the Dacron jacket. He would get four "clicks" of satisfaction per dollar instead of just two. Because preference values and prices may change, the process of selection is based upon marginal considerations.

This illustration would also be applicable to an authoritarian system. The only difference is that the central planning authority would influence the decision by setting the price. If, for example, the central authority wanted to discourage the purchase of Dacron jackets, it would only have to lower the price of cashmere sweaters or raise the price of Dacron jackets. If the price of jackets were raised above, say, $10, consumers would buy sweaters instead of jackets because they could obtain more satisfaction per dollar doing so.

So far, we have said that money income is the main determinant of distribution in both authoritarian and market systems, and that each household allocates this money income among the many goods and services that are available. There is, however, an important difference between authoritarian and market systems on this issue; that is, the authoritarian system directly and to a great extent determines incomes and sets prices. It therefore plays a vital role in deciding *for whom* goods and services are to be produced. In a market system, the prices of resources, which determine money incomes, and the prices of products, which affect consumer choices, are influenced by market conditions. Society and not a planning authority decides *for whom* goods and services will be produced.

Our attention will now be directed to an interesting aspect of distribution. A pattern of different annual incomes per household (consumer unit) is usually typical for a nation. In a nation with a large middle class a pattern emerges where a relatively small number of households exist at both very low and very high levels of income, the bulk falling in the middle ranges. This pattern of different incomes (income dispersion) can illustrate to what extent an uneven or unequal distribution of goods and services occurs by comparing the percentage of total income received to the percentage of total recipients according to specified income classes. For purposes of illustration, a hypothetical dispersion of income is given in Fig. 2–3 to clarify this further. The shaded bars in the graph indicate the percentage of consumer units in a particular income class, and the unshaded bars the percentage of total personal income received by all the consumer units in that particular income class. There are four income classes. It is obvious that consumer units earning less than $4,000 a year represented 30 per cent of the consumer units and that they received 15 per cent of the total personal income. Those in the $4,000–$8,000 class represented 35 per cent of the consumer units and received 30 per cent of the total personal income. Those in the $8,000–$12,000 class represented 20 per cent and received 30 per cent of the income. The $12,000-and-over group represented the remaining 15 per cent and received 25 per cent of the total income.

Whether or not income dispersion should exist is a controversial matter to which economists devote a great deal of attention. However, any attempt to alter the dispersion of income, by either public or private means, may change the final distribution of goods and services. For this reason, some of the causes and remedies of income dispersion will be cited.

There are several reasons why income dispersion exists. Some individuals are more capable, physically or mentally. Some are more fortunate than others, or have command over more resources. Some individuals may be in a position to take advantage of others, while some may be handicapped or disabled. Finally, different individuals have varied attitudes toward work.

Several devices are available to remedy income dispersion. Government

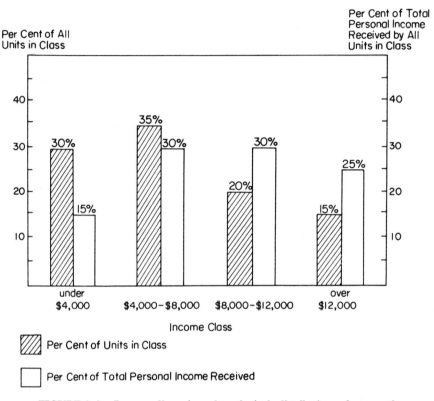

FIGURE 2–3.   Income dispersion: hypothetical distribution of personal income by consumer units.

programs can redistribute money income from one person to another by way of taxes and expenditures. The government also can assist in the training and education of the less fortunate and can provide relief to those who become disabled, have an accident, or become ill. It can alter conditions where certain individuals take advantage of others—for example, by regulating monopolies—and it can redistribute income from working groups to those too young or too old to work.

Private means are also available to remedy income dispersion. The United Fund is a community effort to redistribute income. Benevolent contributions channeled through churches provide another example. The support of elderly parents by their children is a very direct form of redistribution. And a gift of $1,000,000 by a private citizen or foundation to cancer research or to a hospital is a shift of resources from which many members of society can benefit. These various methods change the final distribution of goods and services.

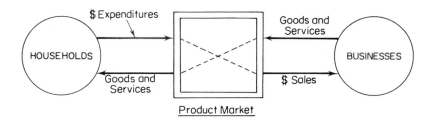

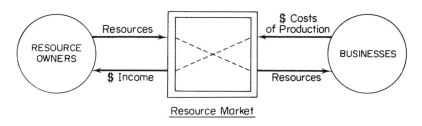

FIGURE 2–4.   Two fundamental markets.

METHODS OF ACHIEVING ALLOCATION

In the modern world, production and distribution are achieved primarily by two basic methods; that is, goods and services are produced and distributed according to the dictates of the market or according to the dictates of some central authority. Each of these methods offers a means whereby the basic social decisions concerning *what, how,* and *for whom* are resolved.

Economists devote much time and effort to explaining how markets perform the vital processes of allocation. There are basically two fundamental markets in which this activity takes place: *product markets* and *resource markets.* These two markets are illustrated in Fig. 2–4. In the product market, dollars are spent by households to buy goods and services from businesses. In the resource market, they are spent by businesses to acquire the resources necessary for production. The structure of a market depends upon certain conditions or characteristics, such as the number of buyers and sellers, the similarity of the products or resources, and the extent to which there are barriers to entering or leaving the market. This will be developed further in Chapter 4.

In the market system, emphasis is put upon independent economic units and decisions. The consumers and producers make the choices which seem most appropriate in solving their own economic problems. In some mysterious way, these wishes and actions are channeled into the vast network of markets. Producers then react by going about their business of acquiring resources, making decisions, and producing the goods and services consumers want. In this manner, the "wants" of society are determined and satisfied by independent units.

Producers are believed to behave in a way that is generally beneficial to society. The forces of incentive, initiative, and self-interest usually prompt man to perform mainly because he expects to benefit directly from his own efforts. However, competition restrains these same efforts when they take advantage of someone else. If a seller tries to charge too much or pass on goods of inferior quality, he inevitably comes face to face with the fact that others may replace him. In essence, the market may bring out the best and restrain the worst in man. This, of course, will depend upon the extent to which competition is present.

The market system as we know it today is actually a very recent development. It is the result of the evolution from medieval feudalism through seventeenth-century mercantilism to present-day capitalism. The breakdown of feudalism was brought on by the emergence of the traveling merchant, gradual urbanization, travel to other parts of the world (for religious reasons), and the development of national states.

Two other important forces of change may not be quite as obvious from historical investigation. One of these was the change in religious attitudes that made virtues of thrift, human effort, and the constructive use of wealth. These changing attitudes encouraged the accumulation of capital, an increase in production, and respect for work. The other less visible force was the development and use of money as a medium of exchange, which allowed factors of production (economic resources) to become more mobile. Labor, for example, became a commodity that could be bought and sold, which broke the ties to the manorial lords. In a like manner, property became more flexible. Instead of being represented by tangible objects, a man's worth was represented by his bank account or claims on productive property. Thus the groundwork was laid to support that important ingredient of a market economy—competition. Men were free, socially and religiously, to do the best they could with what they had in order to enhance their station in life. Since capital no longer remained inert or static, it could be put to the most rewarding use.

Before the market evolution could be completed, the social, legal, and political structure had to be altered. For example, a market economy as we know it today could not exist under a legal system that did not recognize certain standards and guidelines for human behavior. Nor could it develop under conditions where economic power was reserved to a privileged class by political means.

The other major method of accomplishing production and distribution is to use an authoritarian system. Advocates of such a system see in the market system chaos and an inefficient use of resources. In its extreme form, the authoritarian system centrally plans, directs, and coordinates all production and distribution activities. The wants of society are determined not by individual units but by the planners, and the allocation of resources and products is accomplished according to a formal plan. Such plans look impressive on the drawing board, but it is often quite a different matter to accomplish them. One vital ingredient that is usually missing in such an arrangement is human motivation. The plans are available but the proper incentive is missing. This is not to say, however, that planning cannot have any degree of success. Economic achievement often has been accomplished by this method.

Authoritarian economic programs can be found in many of the civilizations of the world, past and present. The Egyptian pharaohs built massive monuments; the Roman emperors commanded slaves to construct their public projects. The pages of history contain many more instances where a select few have commanded the efforts of many to achieve certain economic objectives. In the present world, we find this situation in countries run by dictators. Even in democratic societies, central authority is evidenced by the collection of taxes by the government for public purposes.

In a democratic society, central authority may be used to direct or influence some aspects of production and distribution; it also may be the best way to administer certain economic goods such as public health, defense, and highways. A central authority can provide proper goals for a democratic society and, with the proper financial framework, it can foster the maximum utilization of resources and economic growth.

Two facts should not be overlooked when bureaucratic or central authority exists. First, a mistake in planning can be very costly. The whole system depends upon good judgment; if the central authority is not right, society will suffer. The consequences of an error in judgment can be far more serious to society than the decisions of a single business firm, even though the central authority is made up of people who are also members of the fallible human race. The second fact is that bureaucratic systems usually contain within themselves the seeds of corruption and abuse. Unscrupulous public officials have been known to squander public funds, to abuse their authority, and to use their office for private gain. By the same token, there are also many very responsible public officials. Moreover, bureaucracy can also be a problem in large, private organizations or enterprises.

Although there are undesirable conditions associated with central authority, at times it is very necessary. In an emergency, martial law may be the only preserver of law and order; after a tornado or flood, it is often exercised to prevent pilferage and a deterioration of the social order. In defending his nation against attack, a commander-in-chief may require unusual political and economic authority in order to bring the conflict to a successful end.

A variant of the authoritarian method is one in which production and distribution are prescribed according to tradition and custom. At first glance, economic activity appears to be the result of some definite or intentional authority. Further exploration will usually reveal, however, that it has developed by trial and error and long-standing experience. Once all activities become balanced, the system tends to perpetuate itself; its very obvious order is not the result of some central authority but the product of an unintentional authority—the static nature of the system itself.

Such a system was prevalent during the Middle Ages, when tasks were assigned according to the station in life in which one was born. A son followed in his father's footsteps; if his father was a shoemaker, he also would be a shoemaker. To do otherwise would upset the order of things. Thus a continuous chain was established from generation to generation to assure that skills would be passed on and that production would be accomplished in an orderly fashion. In like manner, distribution of goods also followed the accepted, established scheme of things. It too was the result of long-standing experience.

One does not need to return to history to find evidence of economic activity being determined by tradition or custom. In many parts of the world, particularly in the less developed areas, tradition plays an important role in production and distribution. This was true in India until very recently as a result of the caste system; in Africa and isolated areas of the South Pacific, such systems still exist today.

Even in the more advanced economies of the West, tradition and custom have not wholly disappeared. This is less evident in determining distribution, but it can be observed, for example, in the tips we pay for services. One usually feels compelled to tip because it is the right thing to do; it is the custom. Tips represent money income to the receiver which can be used to obtain a part of the social product. There is also evidence that tradition and custom are still being used in America as a means of allocating production tasks; many sons still follow in their fathers' footsteps. Social attitudes and customs can limit the integration of races into some occupations, and personal appearance can determine whether or not an individual is thought suitable for employment. It is customary for conductors on trains to be men, not women; the opposite is true of airline stewardesses.

Let us compare the two major countries in the world, the Soviet Union and the United States. The Soviet Union uses a planning mechanism that is highly but not completely centralized. They recently have been experimenting more and more with market mechanisms, after discovering that they cannot rely on a totally planned economy. However, even though they use planning very heavily, they have been able to achieve the necessary economic activities of production and distribution.

In the American economy, more reliance is placed upon the market mechanism, although some central planning also is used. The United States has not depended completely upon free markets or entirely rejected planning. In the United States, the greater proportion of economic activity is directed according to a market system. In the case of some products, however, there is interference with the market mechanism. For example, government price supports hold up the price of some agricultural commodities. There are many reasons for doing this, not all of which are economic. In the case of natural monopolies such as telephone companies and electric utilities, government restrictions and regulations are administered in the best interests of consumers.

In other cases, experience has indicated that there are some things which may be provided more efficiently by government allocation than by market forces. For example, ambulance service, education, and highways may fall into this category. In still other instances there may be no alternative to government allocation. The case of fire protection is not very controversial. Most people agree that this service ought to be provided by the government. National defense is another case where private enterprise does not plan the allocation of resources. This is within the government sector. Note, however, that while the government allocates dollars for defense, private firms operating through markets provide the goods and services necessary to maintain the defense establishment.

In essence, the American economy represents an attempt to combine the best of two worlds. That is, it adds a certain amount of planning to a market system and allocates some resources through a government mechanism. This is true not only on a national level but also on the state and local levels. Remember too that these modifications were made as a result of a democratic process. In other words, both political decisions and economic decisions are used to decide how to allocate the nation's resources.

PROBLEMS AND PROJECTS

1. Read Chapters 2, 3, and 4 of *The Making of Economic Society*, by Robert L. Heilbroner (Englewood Cliffs, N. J.: Prentice-Hall, Inc., 1962). These chapters contain a delightful account of economic history and the dawn of the market system.

2. Secure from any issue of *Survey of Current Business*, by the U.S. Department of Commerce, Office of Business Economics (Washington, D.C.: U.S. Government Printing Office), for the current year, national income data by type of income. Construct from these data a table or a pie-chart illustrating the functional distribution of income for the United States. (Instructions on constructing a pie-chart are available in Chapter 18 of this book.)

3. For an interesting and brief description of an authoritarian system, read "New Trend in Russia: 'Creeping Capitalism,'" *U.S. News and World Report* (September 28, 1964), pp. 119–120. Briefly summarize the new trend.

4. The following combinations of resources are available to produce a given quantity of a product in Country *A*, where resource prices are as follows: Land is $5 per unit, labor is $10 per unit, and capital is $4 per unit.

COUNTRY A

	COMBINATION 1		COMBINATION 2		COMBINATION 3	
	Quantity of Resource Required	Money Outlay	Quantity of Resource Required	Money Outlay	Quantity of Resource Required	Money Outlay
Land	1		1		1	
Labor	3		4		5	
Capital	6		4		2	
Total Money Outlay						

a. Complete the first table by calculating the total money outlay for each combination; then select the most efficient combination, which is

_____.

b. Assume now that the same combinations of resources are applicable in Country *B* except that resource prices are as follows: Land is $5 per unit, labor is $8 per unit, and capital is $5 per unit. Complete the second table. Then select the most efficient combination, which is

_____.

COUNTRY B

	COMBINATION 1		COMBINATION 2		COMBINATION 3	
	Quantity of Resource Required	Money Outlay	Quantity of Resource Required	Money Outlay	Quantity of Resource Required	Money Outlay
Land	1		1		1	
Labor	3		4		5	
Capital	6		4		2	
Total Money Outlay						

c. Even though the price of labor is still greater than the price of capital in Country *B*, compare the combination used in Country *A* with the combination used in Country *B* and comment on them.

d. Comment on how this example illustrates the way in which prices guide production by encouraging more use of the abundant resources and less of the scarce resources.

SELECTED REFERENCES

Heilbroner, Robert L., *The Making of Economic Society*. Englewood Cliffs, N. J.: Prentice-Hall, Inc., 1962.

Leftwich, Richard H., *The Price System And Resource Allocation*. New York: Holt, Rinehart & Winston, Inc., 1966.

McConnell, Campbell R., *Economics: Principles, Problems, and Policies*, New York: McGraw-Hill Book Company, 1966. Chaps 5, 6, 24.

U. S. Department of Commerce, *Profits and the American Economy*. Washington, D.C.: U.S. Government Printing Office, 1965.

3

PERFORMANCE OF

THE ECONOMY

While Chapter 2 deals with economic allocation, it ignores the importance of overall economic performance. This chapter will direct attention to this equally important aspect of the economic environment. It is desirable not only to use resources efficiently, but also to provide for the full employment of all available resources. Thus, economic performance can be thought of as the level of economic activity that determines the extent to which resources are being utilized. More specifically, this chapter will deal with the measurement of economic performance, with some of its determinants, with reflections of its power and purpose and with its management.

Business enterprise cannot be divorced from economic performance any more than it can be separated from economic allocation; it is the primary organizer of economic resources, accounting for the bulk of production in the United States. It brings together the varied resource groups, assembles them, assigns tasks, and directs their activities in an effort to achieve production results. At the same time, resource owners allocate the incomes they receive toward the purchase of the goods and services produced by business enterprise. Governments also take a hand in these processes, by purchasing goods and services with the revenues they acquire as taxes. All of these separate activities eventually combine into markets and finally into totals or aggregates; these totals or aggregates condition the business environment and have a direct bearing on business analysis and business decisions.

THE MEASUREMENT OF ECONOMIC
PERFORMANCE

There are several important reasons for measuring economic performance. First, it helps us to understand what is meant by the term "economic performance." Second, it is necessary if some sort of comparison of performance is to be made over a period of time. And third, measuring performance and making comparisons provide a basis for predictions and a justification for policies designed to alter future performance. The measure of economic performance represents, in essence, an indicator of the economy's health. It helps us answer the question; "How is our economy doing?"

Gross National Product

The most widely used indicator of an economy's health is the total dollar value of all goods and services produced for final use in a given period, usually a year. This indicator is known as the *gross national product* (GNP). It measures the physical output of such widely diversified products and services as canned beans, cashmere sweaters, window frames, mailboxes, dentists' services, drill presses, smokestacks, and public libraries. By converting all of this output into dollar amounts, GNP expresses economic performance in terms of market value.

Gross national product measures the value of *final* goods and services; it does not include goods and services that are purchased for resale or for further processing—in other words, those that are still involved in the various stages of production. Since consumers are generally considered final users, most of their purchases are counted. Business firms and government agencies are also final users. A business firm that buys a truck to make deliveries has bought it for final use, although a purchase of raw materials is not considered to be for final use. The purchase of paper and office equipment by a government agency qualifies as a final use. Government-provided goods and services are also counted; however, those that are not sold are calculated at cost rather than at market price.

Since GNP is a measure of production, it necessarily would exclude such transactions as a sale of General Motors stocks. It also excludes public and private gifts, such as Social Security payments or Christmas presents, and such things as the secondhand sale of an automobile or an artist's masterpiece. Gross national product, then, excludes *transfers* and items which are not *currently* produced.

Several shortcomings of GNP as a measure of economic performance deserve brief mention. First, many productive activities are not measured by GNP, including the activities of the housewife and the "do-it-yourself" projects and house repairs made by the home owner. A second shortcoming of GNP is that it does not reflect accurately improvements in the quality of goods and services over time: a 1965 Chevrolet is different in quality from a 1955 model. Third, since GNP is an *aggregate* measure of performance, it says little about the composition or distribution of output. Are the "right" goods being produced? Just how are individual consumers participating in the economy's output?

Real GNP

One other important characteristic of GNP requires consideration. If GNP is to be used to compare economic performance from year to year or from decade to decade, it must be adjusted for changes in price. Gross national product measures the physical quantity of output each year in terms of that year's prices; inflation, on the other hand, refers simply to the increase in prices over a period of time. Therefore, GNP for a particular year cannot be compared accurately with another year, since the "measuring stick" (prices) varies over time. For example, using hypothetical data, if GNP was $100 billion one year and $300 billion ten years later, it would appear to have tripled during that decade. However, if the prices of most goods and services had increased 100 per cent (doubled) during this period, it would be more accurate to compare each year's performance in terms of some common denominator, a common level of prices. The $300 billion GNP, for example, could be expressed in terms of the earlier year's prices by dividing $300 billion by 2, which would reflect the doubling of prices. In terms of the earlier period's prices, the $300 billion GNP would be $150 billion. It is apparent that GNP *really* increased by only 50 per cent, not 300 per cent. The process illustrated here is called *deflating*. Another approach is to *inflate* the earlier period's GNP ($100 billion) by expressing it in terms of present

TABLE 3–1

UNITED STATES GNP, SELECTED YEARS

Year	GNP in Dollars of the Given Year (billions)	GNP in 1958 Dollars (billions)
1929	103	203
1933	55	141
1941	124	263
1950	284	355
1961	520	497
1962	560	529
1963	590	551
1964	631	580
1965	681	614

Source: *Federal Reserve Bulletin* (September 1965), 1337.

prices. The $100 billion GNP in present prices would be $200 billion ($100/ 0.5). The previous GNP is divided by a factor of 0.5 because prices in the pre- vious period were half those of the current period. The increase from $200 billion to $300 billion reflects the same 50 per cent increase in GNP as the deflating process revealed. When GNP is adjusted for changes in price it is referred to as *real* GNP.

Table 3–1 shows the United States GNP for selected years in both 1958 dollars and dollars of the actual year. The same type of information is illustrated graphically in Fig. 3–1 for a longer period of time.

Two important factors are revealed by Fig. 3–1: first, that there has been spectacular *growth* in GNP over the years, and second, that this growth has been *uneven* or erratic. Additional considerations concerning prices,

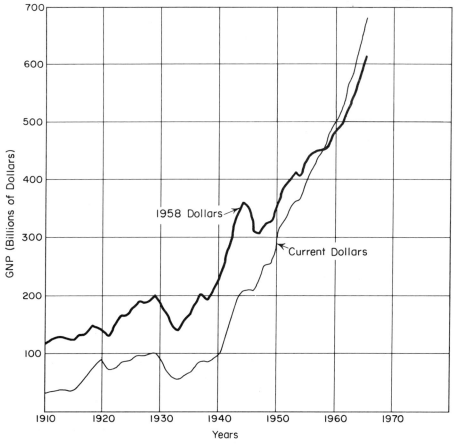

Source: Bureau of the Census, *Long Term Economic Growth, 1860–1965* (Washington, D. C.: U. S. Department of Commerce, October, 1966), pp. 166–167.

FIGURE 3–1.   Gross National Product (billions of dollars).

output, and employment are not directly revealed from the chart but are inherent in the GNP figures. These reflections of economic performance will be dealt with later in this chapter.

The Office of Business Economics of the Department of Commerce records GNP figures. This office estimates GNP by means of careful and accurate statistical sampling processes. The information is made available through the Department's monthly publication, the *Survey of Current Business*.

Two Approaches to GNP

So far we have discovered that GNP is nothing more than a summing up of the goods and services that are produced in a given period. There are two ways of achieving this summing-up process, by simply adding up all the purchases for final use that occur within a year or by adding up all the incomes created in the production of these purchases. The former is known as the *product* or *expenditure approach* to GNP; the latter is the *income approach*. These are indeed two ways of looking at the same thing. What is spent on goods and services is received as income by the resource owners who produce the goods and services.

These two sides to GNP are illustrated in Fig. 3–2 as flows of expenditures and flows of incomes between two important segments of the economy—households and businesses. The flows between these two groups pinpoint the fact that one man's expense is another man's income. The top flows indicate households spending dollars to purchase goods and services from businesses. The bottom flows indicate households receiving dollar incomes in the form of wages, interest, rent, and profits for the resources they have made available to businesses.

Economic performance can be reflected by measuring either type of flow: expenditures from households or income received by households. Expenditures or purchases would measure the upper flow in Fig. 3–2; income, the bottom flow.

Expenditure Approach

A closer look at the expenditure side of GNP reveals four important groups that purchase the economy's output. Three of these are groups within our own country: individual consumers, businesses, and government. The U.S. Department of Commerce records the expenditures of these three groups as personal consumption expenditures, gross private domestic investment, and government purchases of goods and services. The fourth group of purchasers consists of foreigners. However, since we buy from foreigners also, only the *net* or difference between what we buy and what they buy is recorded. Net foreign investment, as it is called, would be *positive* if they purchased

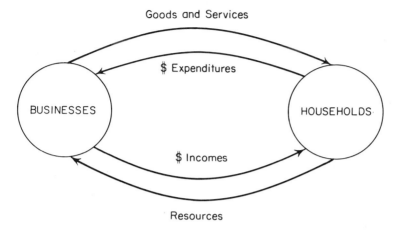

Figure 3–2. Flows of income and expenditures.

more from us and *negative* if we purchased more from them. For example, if they purchased $5 billion worth of goods and services from us and we purchased $3 billion worth from them, net exports would be recorded as a *positive* $2 billion. In this way, GNP would include what we produced for domestic use plus the excess of exports produced for foreigners over imports. The actual expenditures for imports are already included in the other components of GNP.

Of the total GNP of $681 billion produced in 1965, consumers purchased the largest portion, a whopping $431 billion. This amount as well as the other components of GNP are illustrated by the pie-chart in Fig. 3–3.

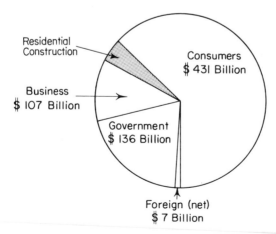

FIGURE 3–3. GNP components for 1965. The shaded part of the Business sector represents residential spending.

All amounts are in current dollars—that is, in 1965 dollars. Gross private domestic investment was $107 billion, government purchase of goods and services amounted to $136 billion, and net export figures stood at $7 billion.

Consumer spending can be further divided into such categories as durable goods, nondurable goods, and services. Durables consist of such things as automobiles, furniture, and household appliances. Nondurables include, among other items, such things as food, clothing, gasoline, and oil. Services cover a wide range, including rents, recreation, haircuts, medical services, car repairs, dry cleaning, bridge tolls, and bus fares.

Gross private domestic investment involves what is generally referred to as business spending—the purchase of goods and services that are used to produce other goods. Business purchases of GNP are divided into three main categories: new construction, producers' durables, and inventories. The figure for new construction includes the construction of factory buildings, shopping centers, and public utility plants; it also counts residential construction, which amounted to $28 billion in 1965. Business spending in 1965 actually amounted to $79 billion, if residential construction is subtracted from gross private domestic investment. Businesses also spend money for durables, such as factory machinery, machine tolls, drill presses, and vehicles.

The inventory figure in business spending is *not* a total of purchases put into the firm's inventory during the year. Rather it reflects the *change* in inventories from the beginning to the end of that period. For example, if the inventories held by businesses at the end of a period were $2 billion greater than at the beginning, then the businesses evidently added to their investment in inventories. This may have been either intentional or unintentional. A decrease in inventories of $2 billion would have reduced total business spending by that amount.

Governments—Federal, state, and local—also purchased some of the economy's output. The Federal government's expenditures for goods and services include such things as tanks, ships, missiles, health services, education, veterans' services, and conservation. There are other items in the Federal government's budget that do not represent purchases of goods and services, such as interest on the national debt. State and local government purchases of goods and services include such items as highways, education, police protection, and fire protection. Only purchases of goods and services by the government, and not total budget expenditures, are counted in GNP.

Income Approach

So far, we have been looking only at the expenditure approach to GNP. Now we will look briefly at the income approach. Income is received by resource owners for their efforts and their contributions to production. National income, as it is often called, is the summation of all types of income;

it is the income received (before income taxes) by resource owners. There are five major components of national income as recorded by the U.S. Department of Commerce. For 1965 national income totaled $559 billion and was broken down as follows:

Type of Income	Income (Billions)
Compensation of employees	$393
Proprietors' income	56
Rental income of persons	18
Corporate profits	74
Net interest	18
National income total	$559

A comparison of this national income figure and the GNP of $681 billion for 1965 reveals a discrepancy of $122 billion. The reason for this is that since GNP reflects purchases of final products at market prices, it includes two important items which do not reflect income received during the current period. For national income to be reconciled to GNP, it must be adjusted for *depreciation* and *indirect business taxes.*

Depreciation estimates (also called capital consumption) for each year wind up in GNP because the market value of final products is made up of the costs of production. The latter include an estimate of wear and tear on plant and equipment that has been produced and purchased in some previous period. For example, a manufacturer of mailboxes may have produced $100,000 worth of mailboxes during the year. If $10,000 represents the estimate of wear and tear on the firm's facilities, then $90,000 would represent income to resource owners. In this case the market value of mailboxes exceeds income receipts by an amount equal to depreciation or capital consumption. Only $90,000 represents income that has been earned during the current period. For the economy as a whole, capital consumption in 1965 amounted to almost $60 billion, nearly 9 per cent of GNP.

Indirect business taxes are a nonincome cost component of GNP. There are certain taxes a producer pays to the government before he offers his product for sale. The excise tax on a bottle of liquor, for example, is paid by the manufacturer before it is sold. The business firm treats such a tax as a production cost and adds it to the price of the product. Other taxes that are handled in a similar manner are general sales taxes, license fees, property taxes, and customs duties. Indirect business taxes become a part of GNP but do not represent income earned for a productive activity; thus, GNP will be that much large than national income. In 1965, indirect business taxes amounted to just under $63 billion, slightly greater than the capital consumption allowance. Gross national product and national income are reconciled in Table 3-2 by adding these two nonincome components of GNP to the income accounts.

TABLE 3–2

COMPONENTS OF GNP

Expenditures		Income
Personal consumption expenditures		Wages and Salaries
plus		plus
Government purchase of goods and services		Rental Income
plus		plus
Gross private domestic investment	GNP	Interest
plus		plus
Expenditures by foreigners		Profits
		plus
		Depreciation and indirect business taxes

Certain elements of national income can be segregated to emphasize certain segments of the social income accounts, such as personal income and disposable personal income. Such items as social security contributions, corporate income taxes, undistributed profits, transfer payments, and personal taxes distinguish the social income accounts from each other.

DETERMINANTS OF ECONOMIC PERFORMANCE

Now that the components of GNP have been established and defined, it would seem natural to direct attention to the determinants of economic performance. Overall economic activity has been represented by a flow of expenditures and income between the various sectors of the economy (Fig. 3–2). Gross national product, which measures this flow, is determined by an interplay of the economic activities of consumers, businesses, and government. It will be our aim (1) to consider what determines spending, (2) to consider how the flow of spending determines the level of economic performance, and (3) to consider how changes in spending affect income.

Determinants of Spending

An examination of spending can conveniently proceed according to the three major components of GNP: consumption (C), investment (I), and government spending for goods and services (G). The personal consumption expenditures for 1965 of $431 billion represent 63 per cent of GNP, by far the largest component. When residential construction of $28 billion is included, C approaches 68 per cent of GNP. Because of its relative magnitude, consumption deserves the primary position in this investigation.

Consumption spending. As a percentage of income in the United States, consumption spending has been fairly stable over the long run. Since

TABLE 3–3

**DISPOSABLE PERSONAL INCOME AND
PERSONAL CONSUMPTION EXPENDITURES, 1948–1965
(BILLIONS OF 1958 DOLLARS)**

(1) Year	(2) Disposable Personal Income	(3) Personal Consumption Expenditures	(4) Average Propensity to Consume
1948	229.8	210.8	0.917
1949	230.8	216.5	0.938
1950	249.6	230.5	0.923
1951	255.7	232.8	0.910
1952	263.3	239.4	0.909
1953	275.4	250.8	0.911
1954	278.3	255.7	0.919
1955	296.7	274.2	0.924
1956	309.3	281.4	0.910
1957	315.8	288.2	0.913
1958	318.8	290.1	0.910
1959	333.0	307.3	0.923
1960	340.2	316.2	0.929
1961	350.7	322.6	0.920
1962	367.6	338.6	0.921
1963	380.6	352.4	0.926
1964	406.5	372.1	0.915
1965	428.1	394.1	0.920

Source: *Economic Report of the President 1966, p.* 227.

1948, personal consumption expenditures have accounted for roughly 92 per cent of disposable personal income (after-tax income), with the rest going into savings. This long-run characteristic of consumption spending is illustrated in Table 3–3. The *average propensity to consume,* as is shown by the calculated figures in column 4 of Table 3–3, merely expresses the *proportion* of income that is spent. These figures could be converted to percentages by multiplying each of them by 100 and adding a percentage sign (%). The average propensity to consume, then, is nothing more than a percentage converted to its decimal counterpart which represents some proportion of income that is spent. "Propensity" merely clarifies the concept because it denotes inclination or tendency and "average" denotes just that, i.e., the average of all the amounts spent out of each dollar of income.

Average propensity to consume (APC) can be related to family income as well. For example, a family earning $8,000 per year after taxes might spend $7,200 and save $800. This family then would have an APC of 90 per cent or 0.90.

Suppose now that this family experiences a $1,000 increase in income (after taxes). This additional $1,000 might have come about as a result of winning at the track, a surprise Christmas bonus, unexpected overtime pay, or unusually large sales commissions. Since it is regarded as *extra* income, it will probably receive special treatment. Most people would spend a *smaller* percentage of this extra income than their long-run average propensity to consume of, say, 90 per cent. Some of the extra income might go to buy a new stereo phonograph, but a larger than normal amount would probably go into savings. Thus the family might spend only three-fourths of the $1,000, which represents the propensity or proportion of the *extra* income that is spent. In this case, the family's *marginal propensity to consume* (MPC) is 0.75. This concept is also appropriate to the spending in the economy as a whole as is the average propensity to consume.

Short-run changes in income, then, are subject to MPC rather than to the long-run APC. One very likely reason for this is that man is by nature a creature of habit, especially in his spending patterns. If he considers extra income as temporary, he is not likely to make any substantial changes in his pattern of spending.

So far we have seen that consumption spending is closely related to income. The economist would say that consumption is a *function* of income. However, this is not the complete story. Consumption on a family basis or an aggregate basis experiences changes or shifts that are not related to income. These changes are explained by what are called *nonincome* determinants of consumption. Some of these determinants are temporary and some are permanent; in any event, they reflect spending out of given levels of income. Over the long run, it is these nonincome determinants that keep the economy's APC around the 92 per cent level. Several of these determinants have been selected for discussion. Normally, APC will decrease as income increases. This is easily explained by an example. If a family's MPC is 0.70 and its APC is 0.90, a change of income from $8,000 to $9,000 will yield an APC of roughly 0.88 at the $9,000 level of income ($7,900[1] divided by $9,000). Consumption would have to increase by $900 to $8,100 for the APC to remain at 0.90. The MPC of 0.70 indicates that it will increase by only $700.

Consumers' desires and preferences may change from time to time. Sales of new cars often undergo unusual deviations from established patterns as consumers show preferences for either economy or luxury in automobiles. For example, people living in crowded urban areas may prefer compact, economical automobiles. On the other hand, the interstate highway system may stimulate a demand for larger, more luxurious cars. Since the price tags on luxury and compact cars are quite different, spending out of income will be affected by this type of consumer behavior.

Closely related to consumer preferences is the attitude of consumers toward essentials. Many household appliances fall into this category. The electric dryer, electric toaster, electric can opener, and television set are considered essential in many homes. As other new products are introduced, they

[1] The $7,900 represents 90 per cent of $8,000 + 70 per cent of $1,000.

too may eventually move into this category. More and more essentials increase the propensity to consume.

As consumers experience prolonged prosperity, they accumulate a greater stock of wealth and become more confident about the future. This enhances the individual's feeling of security and usually causes him to spend more freely.

Expectations concerning future prices, future income, or the availability of goods also affect present spending. If consumers expect prices to rise, incomes to increase, or goods to be in short supply, they are likely to increase their spending. At the beginning of the Korean conflict, for example, there was a sudden rise in consumer spending based upon such expectations. After World War II, consumer spending was at unusually high levels chiefly because there had been a shortage of durables, and people were were simply trying to catch up on their spending.

Credit and consumer indebtedness also play important roles in the pattern of spending. When credit is available, it is easier for purchases of durables to take place, not only because funds can be obtained, but because these times usually are reflected by low down payments and long repayment periods. In addition, consumers usually follow a pattern of adjusting to their level of indebtedness. When the burden of debt in the form of monthly payments increases, consumers go through a catching-up period. Some purchases may be delayed or a tighter budget may reduce other nonessential spending. The consumer's reappraisal of his spending patterns and debt level may cause him to alter his propensity to spend.

Urbanization of American society has tended to raise the overall spending levels of consumers, since city dwellers usually have a higher propensity to consume. As a greater and greater proportion of the American population becomes urbanized, the nation's APC will become still higher.

The relative importance of different age groups in American society would also seem to affect the nation's APC. As medicines are improved and health services expand, life is prolonged, increasing the percentage of retired people in our total population. Members of this group are typically spenders, not savers. Teenagers are also typical spenders. If the proportion of teenagers and college students increases, it may also cause the nation's APC to increase.

The all-important component of GNP, consumption, is subject to many influences; its income and nonincome determinants are not always easy to predict. Consumption spending is also partly affected by previous income, since income generally must be earned before it is spent. Consequently there is some lag effect between income and consumption.

Investment Spending. Investment spending by business is the second component of spending that requires attention. In 1965, business spent almost $70 billion on new plant and equipment and $9 billion on additional inventories. Sometimes inventories may decrease during the year; economists call this *disinvestment*. Residential construction is not included in the category of investment spending *here*, even though it is included in gross private domestic investment, which was discussed earlier. The reason for this is obvious when one considers the quite different determinants of business and consumer spending. As a total, investment spending by business in 1965 accounted for almost 12 per cent of GNP. Since replacement of plant and equipment accounted for $60 billion (capital consumption allowance), *net* investment spending by businesses was $19 billion.

The single most important determinant of business investment is profits. The expectation and realization of profits play an important role in this business decision. Expected net profits are the profits businesses hope to realize from investment spending. The firm chooses among alternative projects by selecting those which offer the greatest potential. In addition, businesses pay for a substantial amount of investment in plant and equipment with retained earning—profits that are not paid out to owners. The Department of Commerce recorded $25 billion in undistributed profits in 1965. Expected profits reflect the willingness to invest while realized profits provide the means; together, they make possible the investment in plant and equipment that will produce more goods in the future.

Besides retained earnings and the internal generation of funds from capital consumption allowances, business firms also obtain investment money from outsiders. A substantial amount of borrowed funds is acquired by selling bonds to individuals and financial institutions. Sometimes business firms sell new stock (ownership claims) to the public to acquire funds. These funds flow from suppliers to businesses through financial markets and financial institutions.

Businesses attract borrowed capital by offering to pay interest on it; in this way the users and suppliers of money capital are brought together in financial markets. The interest rate in the market reflects the supply and demand conditions of loanable funds. Stocks and bonds are also *traded* in these financial markets. Such trading, however, involves claims that have already been issued and does not represent new investment in capital goods.

Rate of interest is another factor which determines the level of investment spending. A low rate of interest is generally believed to encourage investment spending because it represents the cost of using money capital regardless of whether it is generated internally or externally. In essence, the business manager compares the net expected rate of return of an investment project with the cost of capital. In this way he is provided with guidelines for accepting or rejecting the project. If the net expected rate of return exceeds the cost of capital, the project should be worthwhile. A higher rate of interest generally is believed to discourage investment spending by causing the cost of capital to exceed the net expected rate of return. The process of financing business operations is explained in Chapter 11.

Expectations of profits are affected by other important factors. Technological innovations reduce production costs, improve profit margins, and encourage investment spending. The state of existing capacity also has a direct bearing. If idle resources exist, new investment in plant and equipment will first require the absorption of the existing facilities into production activities. Also important are taxes on corporate profits. Since these taxes are usually around the 50 per cent level, any changes—even of 2 or 3 per cent—will affect profit margins. An increase in the rate will discourage investment spending; a reduction will stimulate investment. The government also uses other taxing devices which can affect investment, such as the tax credit used in recent years. Finally, businessmen's investment decisions are affected by consumer spending because it alters investment prospects. Since consumer spending depends upon income, investment spending is also related to income. Investment that is directly caused by consumer spending is called *induced investment*. The opposite of induced investment is *autonomous investment*—the investment caused by nonincome determinants.

In summary, investment spending depends upon many considerations and activities. It is closely tied to the probable level of future profits, the availability of funds, interest rates, improved production techniques, new products, the level of taxes, government policy, and the level of consumer incomes.

Government Spending.   This is the third major component of GNP. Federal, state, and local government spending account for about 20 per cent of GNP. In 1965, government spending for goods and services amounted to $136 billion. Such spending is the result of the desire among consumers for certain public services and the willingness of voting citizens to allocate funds by taxes to the public sector of the economy. Spending by the various levels of government is arranged by elected officials, who supposedly carry out the wishes of the voters. The actual amount of spending is determined by extensive planning for such needs as national defense, highways, education, and health services.

Flow of Spending

The actual level of economic performance at any time is reflected by the total amount of spending in all sectors of the economy. This level of spending, stated in the form of GNP, is obtained by combining consumption spending (C), investment spending (I), and government spending (G) for goods and services. In other words, $C + I + G = $ GNP. If these spending components were higher, GNP would increase; if they were lower, it would decrease. However, this is an oversimplification of how the level of economic performance is determined.

The level of economic performance depends upon an interplay of the

various spending activities; it is determined in a special way by the flow of
spending among the economic units in these categories. A simple flow of
spending between business and households was illustrated earlier in Fig. 3–2.
At that point two flows were apparent: a flow of income and a flow of expenditures. This is a very important relationship because it is these flows
which account for the interplay among the various spending units in the
economy.

Fig. 3–4 is more complete than Fig. 3–2, since it also includes the government sector. This diagram shows a flow of tax income from businesses and
households to government in return for a flow of government services; it
also shows a flow of government expenditures in return for goods and services purchased from businesses and resources purchased from households.
Note that there is a flow of income and a flow of expenditures between each
segment.

The interplay between C, I, and G depends upon the flow of income

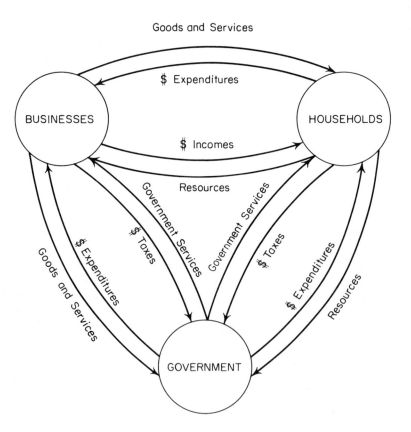

FIGURE 3–4.   Flows of income and expenditures.

and the flow of expenditures. In simple terms, this interplay is expressed as follows: What is one man's expense is another man's income.

The relationship of income to expenditure and the interplay of the spending units in the economy can be explained by tracing through a simple example. When a household purchases a television set, the expenditure represents income to the retail outlet. But the retail store has expenses too, such as the payment of salaries to its help. Its expenditures become income for the employees. Going further back, the purchase of the television set from a wholesaler represented income to the supplier. This process reaches back through the stages of production to the initial manufacturer who has expenditures for raw materials, plant, and equipment. These expenditures represent income to other resource owners and to households. And this is where the example started—with a particular household. To generalize, we can say that expenditures by consumers, businesses, and governments become income to consumers, businesses, and governments. Thus there is a direct relationship between income and expenditure.

The actual flow of spending or level of income at any particular time is the result of the income-expenditure relationship. In essence, the level of economic performance depends upon an equality between income and expenditure. The economy is always adjusting expenditure and income patterns in an attempt to bring about this equality; economists call this process the tendency for the economy to seek an *equilibrium* level of income.

Equality of income and expenditure is also significant in respect to the levels of employment it may support. At times it may provide an insufficient amount of expenditures to support full employment of the economy's resources, with particular reference to labor. Equality can also be misleading because expenditures may exceed the economy's ability to satisfy them. This is reflected by inflation. Reflections of economic performance in terms of such things as employment and price levels will be considered in the next section of this chapter. First, however, we will consider ways in which changes in spending affect income.

Changes in Spending

There are two important economic concepts which are particularly relevant to the level of economic performance. First, a change in any one of the spending categories of GNP can alter the equality between income and spending. This will cause the level of economic performance to either increase or decrease. Second, a one-dollar change in spending does not merely affect the level of economic performance by one dollar; it changes GNP by more than one dollar. In essence, a one-dollar change has a multiplied effect on the economy.

Changes in the level of economic performance are set into motion by changes in any of the spending categories of GNP. A change in any one category may cause an inequality between income and expenditure; this sets in motion forces that alter the flows of spending and economic activity in the direction of equality. For example, when businesses experience reduced sales, they cut back their expenditures on inventory and reduce the number of sales personnel until what they spend is more in harmony with what they receive. The economy then experiences a contraction in the flows of income and spending among the various sectors. On the other hand, if consumers step up their spending for some reason, the economy experiences an expansion in the flows among the various sectors. The economy therefore is continuously adjusting to changing income and expenditure patterns.

There are basically two phenomena that cause the economy to experience multiplied effects. One has come to be known as the *multiplier*; it is triggered by changes in expenditures. The other is known as the *accelerator*; it is set in motion by changes in income. Furthermore, since the flows of income and expenditure are interconnected, the multiplier and accelerator also interact with each other.

The Multiplier.   The *multiplier*, as just stated, is sparked by a change in spending. This change can be due to a spurt in autonomous investment, additional government spending, or the willingness of consumers to spend more out of given levels of income. The multiplier permeates the economy much like the ripples caused by a rock thrown into a body of water. The rock stirs up ripples which at first are large in size, but then diminish as they move away from the point of entry. The same effect is noticed when substantial amounts of autonomous investment spending "rock" a local community. Boom towns, as they have been called, have depended, in the past, upon investment spending in gold or silver mining, oil wells, or railroad construction. Today, boom conditions may be caused by investment spending in a new paper mill, assembly plant, or space project. Some of this investment spending spreads to other segments of the economy as materials, supplies, and equipment are shipped in from other production centers. Such purchases also inject new spending into these other areas, and the economy experiences ripples of spending.

The extent of the multiplier effect can be calculated more precisely. If *extra* income is generated by the original spurt in investment, then the spending out of this extra income can provide a basis for quantifying the multiplier effect.   The amount of consumption spending resulting from extra or additional income has already been expressed as MPC.   If people spend three-fifths of their additional income on consumption and save two-fifths, consumption spending will spread through the economy in a way that increases GNP. Each time someone spends three-fifths of his extra income, it becomes extra income to someone else. The marginal propensity to consume is very important to the multiplier effect because it indicates how much of one man's extra income will be spent.

TABLE 3–4

MULTIPLIER

Alworth receives	$100.00	3/5 of which is spent with
Bentley who receives	60.00	3/5 of which is spent with
Caldwell who receives	36.00	3/5 of which is spent with
Donnelly who receives	21.60	3/5 of which is spent with
Evans who receives	12.96	3/5 of which is spent with
Fuller who receives	7.78	3/5 of which is spent with
Gavin who receives	4.67	3/5 of which is spent with
Hall who receives	2.60	3/5 of which is spent with
Isen who receives	1.56	3/5 of which is spent with
Jacobs who receives	0.94	3/5 of which is spent with
Kullen who receives	0.56	3/5 of which is spent with
Lamb who receives	0.34	3/5 of which is spent with
Murphy who receives	0.20	3/5 of which is spent with
Nollen who receives	0.12	3/5 of which is spent with
Owens who receives	0.07	3/5 of which is spent with
Porter who receives	0.04	3/5 of which is spent with
Quinner who receives	0.02	3/5 of which is spent with
Roberts who receives	0.01	
Total receive	$249.47	

Let us trace through the effect of the multiplier by using a simple illustration. If Alworth, one of the construction workers on a new plant site, receives $100, his income is the result of investment spending. If everyone in the economy has an MPC of $\frac{3}{5}$, Alworth will spend $60 of his income. He gives this money to Mrs. Bentley for room and board, so that it becomes income for her. She spends three-fifths of this income on her needs, which in this instance might be a new dress. Her seamstress, Mrs. Caldwell, would receive $36, out of which she would spend $21.60, and so on. The entire series of incomes and expenditures appears in Table 3–4. (Some figures are rounded.)

Because of the multiplier, the $100 has become almost $250. This seems to indicate a multiplier of $2\frac{1}{2}$. If the MPC were larger, the multiplier would be larger, and vice versa. The multiplier can be calculated by a simple formula:

$$\text{Multiplier} = \frac{1}{1-\text{MPC}}$$

In our example the MPC was $\frac{3}{5}$, so the calculations are as follows:

$$\text{Multiplier} = \frac{1}{1-\frac{3}{5}}$$
$$= \frac{1}{\frac{2}{5}}$$
$$= 2\frac{1}{2}$$

If the MPC were $\frac{4}{5}$, the multiplier would be 5. The multiplier for the American economy has been estimated to be between 2 and 3. Therefore, every extra dollar of spending will raise GNP by $2 or $3. A reduction in spending will cause the process to reverse itself and lower GNP by a multiple.

The Accelerator.   This refers to the effect on economic performance of changes in income. More specifically, changes in income that increase consumption may substantially alter investment spending by business firms. For example, let us assume that a small manufacturing firm which makes mailboxes does a volume of 50,000 mailboxes a year. Let us also assume that there are ten stamping machines in operation in the stamping department, each of which can turn out 5,000 mailboxes a year, and that one machine wears out each year. If the firm experiences what appears to be a permanent increase in sales of 5,000 mailboxes (10 per cent), a new stamping machine will be needed, making a total of eleven. Since one machine also must be replaced, the firm will have invested this year in two machines. Thus a 10 per cent increase in sales has caused a 100 per cent increase in investment spending. By the action of the accelerator, an increase in income which caused more consumer spending on mailboxes has induced investment spending to increase by an even larger amount. The existence of idle capacity, the overtime employment of facilities, and the machine's lifetime all affect the extent of the accelerator.

The accelerator also works in reverse. For example, if mailbox sales fall back to 50,000 next year, the firm will not buy any machines—a drop in investment spending to zero. If the firm has eleven stamping machines and only needs ten, no replacement purchase will be required next year when one wears out. As a matter of fact, if mailbox sales remain at the new higher output level of 55,000, investment spending would still experience a 50 per cent drop. With a requirement of eleven machines, investment spending would return to the annual replacement requirement of one machine.

There is also interaction between the multiplier and the accelerator. The extent of this interaction depends upon a variety of conditions that have a bearing on the size of the multiplier and the accelerator. Briefly, the interaction proceeds in the following manner. An increase in investment spending increases income and consumer spending, which stimulates sales. The increase in sales makes investment appear more profitable and leads to an increase in investment spending. In this way, expenditures and incomes interact with each other to provide cumulative effects on economic performance.

REFLECTIONS OF ECONOMIC PERFORMANCE

Now that economic performance has been defined, its measurement explained in terms of GNP, and its determinants analyzed, it is appropriate to attend to certain manifestations of economic performance. In essence, they reveal the real power and purpose of the economy and can be expressed in terms of the effects on: (1) employment, (2) the prices we pay for goods and services, (3) the growth we experience from year to year, (4) the fluctuations in growth that occur, and (5) the rate of flow of our receipts and payments with the rest of the world. Not only does the use of these more specific terms make the expression of economic performance more meaningful, the terms also provide the basis for establishing goals to which the power and purpose of the economy can be directed.

Employment

Employment of resources in the American economy is measured primarily in terms of labor. Other resources (natural and produced) are important but do not account for nearly as large a portion of the income earned in the economy. This was revealed by the breakdown of income listed on page 43: compensation of employees accounted for $393 billion of the $559 billion national income, or approximately 70 per cent. In addition, it is easier to measure the extent of employment of the labor resource than that of the other resources.

Figures are also readily available concerning capacity utilization in manufacturing; this reflects the utilization of produced resources in a large segment of the economy. The utilization of plant capacity in manufacturing can be expressed as a percentage of total capacity. In recent years unused capacity in manufacturing has ranged from over 20 per cent to less than 7 per cent. Naturally, a low percentage of unused capacity is more desirable than a high one.

Total employment generally rises from year to year; nearly every year it sets new records. On the other hand, unemployment figures vary from year to year. In some years, total employment and unemployment may even rise together. At first glance this may seem puzzling—more jobs while there are more jobless workers. The explanation, of course, is that the total labor force at times increases faster than the number of jobs. For this reason, it is better to consider employment and unemployment as a percentage of the total labor force.

Unemployment has fluctuated at around 5 per cent of the total labor force since 1948. This is not a very large figure compared to the level of 25 per cent during the depression in the 1930's, when one in every four people in the labor force was unemployed. Although at times unemployment drops below 5 per cent, and although it may even break through the 4 per cent level occasionally, the economy will always experience some unemployment. In a free society a certain amount is inevitable because some jobs are seasonal, a portion of the labor force is always in the process of changing jobs, and some people only seek employment periodically. This is what is known as *frictional unemployment*.

A closer look at the unemployment rolls will reveal that the percentage of unemployment is often higher for certain regions of the economy, occupations, age groups, minority groups, and educational levels. This pattern of unemployment has many explanations. An uneven composition of unemployment is more difficult to correct than is an overall high percentage of unemployment.

Explanations of why an acceptable level of frictional unemployment may be exceeded fall into two broad categories; one involves the overall *level of spending* in the economy, and the other involves *inflexibility* in the economy.

Spending by consumers, businesses, and governments can be lumped together and called *aggregate spending*. Sometimes aggregate spending is insufficient to provide full utilization of available resources, even though the economy is approaching an equality between income and spending. Insufficient aggregate spending probably represents the single most important reason for serious unemployment that occurs during depressions and recessions.

The economy may experience substantial unemployment even in prosperous times; that is, when aggregate spending is strong. Under these circumstances, it usually is due to *inflexibility* in the economy. Changes in spending habits often bring out this inflexibility; for example, when consumers buy clothing made of synthetics instead of wool or cotton, the sheepherder and cotton picker find themselves out of jobs. Likewise, as incomes rise, more money is available for what is called *discretionary spending*. This type of spending pays for stereo systems or tape recorders, fancy boats or extensive travel. Both new products and changes in discretionary buying cause unemployment when labor does not adjust quickly enough to the new situation.

Still another reason for unemployment due to inflexibility is the inability of labor to adjust fast enough to new foreign competition. The unemployment is due to an inability of resources to shift to other activities. Foreign trade creates more jobs than it takes away for an economy such as the United States when it exports more than it imports. Disruptions in employment may also be caused by automation. When labor is suddenly replaced by a machine, it takes time to learn a new skill or to find a similar job. The consequence is usually temporary unemployment.

Unemployment may result from rigidity in prices and wages. Big business, labor unions, and legislative control of prices tend to make the economy less adaptable. When prices and wages do not adjust readily to changes in spending, the slack often results in unemployment. With more flexible prices and wages, business activity and employment would remain more stable because sales could be stimulated by lower prices and cost pressures could be relieved by lower wages. (The danger in carrying this analysis too far is that aggregate spending may be affected by lower wages.) Recently, business and labor have come to expect the government to "do something" when demand slackens, and to compensate for any drops in private spending; consequently, they are not likely to reduce prices and wages themselves.

While there are still other causes of unemployment that could be cited, it is apparent by now that there is no one cure for it. Increasing the level of spending may at times be the answer; however, when unemployment exists during prosperous times, this policy is not particularly applicable.

In any event, a goal of full employment for the economy can be established in terms of some acceptable level of unemployment expressed as a percentage of the labor force. This acceptable level can take into account a certain amount of frictional unemployment. Expressing a goal in these terms is useful because it recognizes changes in both the level of employment and the size of the total force, indicating when something must be done to provide for full utilization of available resources.

Prices

Economic performance is also reflected by the prices we pay for goods and services. This is important because prices directly affect what and how much we can buy. We care about the price of housing, furniture, groceries, and medical services. These are things which are close to us all. Prices determine *what* we buy because we allocate our income among various goods and services according to the individual prices of specific items. *How much* a household is able to buy from a given income also depends upon prices. For example, if the prices of most goods and services are generally higher now than they were a decade ago, a family with the same income would not be able to buy as much today. Thus, individual prices affect the allocation of income and the overall level of prices influence a family's economic status.

A price index is a convenient way to look at prices; it can be used to sum up changes in the prices of everything we buy. The Department of Commerce calculates several price indexes. A very common one is the *consumer price index*, which is computed from the prices of a selection of many consumer products and published each month. A *wholesale price index* is also published by the Department. Strict statistical techniques are used in constructing both indexes. An explanation of index numbers is provided in Chapter 20. The change in prices from year to year can be seen conveniently by looking at the consumer price index. For example, at the end of 1965, the index stood at 109.9. This means that in terms of prices during the base period, 1957–1959, the average prices of consumer goods and services had increased 9.9 per cent. Other base periods can be used to construct a price index, but it will always reflect the change of prices in terms of prices for the base period selected.

A price index reflects economic performance by indicating whether or not an imbalance exists between what the economy wants to produce and what it is able to produce. When spending in the economy exceeds the actual output of goods and services, the excess will be reflected in higher income and higher prices. Another way to look at this is to consider the flow of dollars in Fig. 3-4. If the flow of dollars to businesses and households (inner flow) increases while the flow of goods and services and the flow of resources remain constant, the economy will experience rising prices or what has come to be known as *inflation*.

Inflation varies; sometimes it is mild, sometimes rampant. The difference depends upon the rate at which prices change. Mild inflation of 1 to $1\frac{1}{2}$ per cent a year is considered acceptable because it may merely reflect the improved quality of goods and services from year to year. A somewhat more rapid increase would indicate that some serious imbalances have developed in the economy.

It is not always easy to determine exactly what causes inflation. However, two basic explanations have emerged. One has been termed *demand pull*; the other is called *cost push*. At times only one of these causes may be evident, but it is usually a combination of the two that results in serious inflation. Demand-pull inflation is the result of excessive spending, which can be caused by any one sector of the economy—consumers, business, or government—or a combination of sectors. Cost-push inflation may creep into the economy when resource owners demand higher prices for their land, labor, or capital; if such demands exceed productivity improvements, they will increase the costs of production. These increases may be passed on to consumers in the form of higher prices.

Inflation has several serious consequences. First, persons who live on fixed incomes, such as pensions, are not able to compensate for higher prices; they experience a decline in living standards because their fixed incomes buy less as time goes on. Persons who have their money in savings accounts and government bonds also feel the impact of inflation. Their savings are worth less and less as time passes. On the other hand, people who borrow money benefit from inflation because they pay off their debts with dollars which are easier to come by, especially if they do not live on fixed incomes.

The impact of inflation is expanded through the economy by expectations. When households and businesses anticipate higher prices, they may increase spending rather than delay until prices are higher. In this way inflation feeds upon itself. It may also set into motion cost-push forces which further complicate the situation. If inflation is not controlled, such excesses may cause a serious economic collapse from which the economy will find it difficult to recover.

It should be apparent by now that price stability is an important goal of economic performance, which itself may be affected by what is happening to prices. A lack of stability may affect the behavior of economic units and disrupt economic activity.

Economic Growth

The American economy has grown in many dimensions: GNP, total population, total employment, plant and equipment, social goods, and new products, services, and occupations. Let us look at this record of growth and at the requirements of economic growth.

The nation's *record of economic growth* over the years is only another reflection of economic performance. The pattern of growth in terms of *real GNP* (GNP adjusted for changes in price) was depicted in Fig. 3–1. Estimates of the real GNP at the turn of the century indicate that the value of the nation's output today is roughly eight times what it was then. Moreover, GNP has approximately doubled every 20 years. This tells us that the economy is bigger now than it was at the beginning of this century. Growth can be measured for any period of time merely by comparing the real GNP's at the beginning and end of the period.

Another way of looking at growth is to take into account the size of the population. The growth in real GNP that is accompanied by an increase in population may not have allowed us as individuals to be any better off economically. The significance of growth to us as individuals is often referred to as the *standard of living*. If we eat more, dress better, and have more home furnishings and more living space, our standard of living has improved. Besides the basic items of food, clothing, and shelter, the standard of living is reflected by what we spend on conveniences, luxuries, and services. For these reasons, it is also worthwhile to consider another means of measuring growth—*real national product per person*. Dividing GNP for one year by the nation's population for that year provides a figure that measures output per capita. For example, if GNP is $800 billion and the population is 200 million, then real GNP per capita would be $4,000; this would be a good measure of our individual standard of living. Real GNP per capita has increased approximately threefold since the beginning of this century. This is somewhat less than the eightfold increase in real GNP; the difference is accounted for by the increase in population.

Income after taxes and income per family are two other useful ways to measure growth. Taxes and government expenditures have grown over the years, and disposable income (income after taxes have been paid) may now be more relevant as a measure of growth in terms of private goods. In addition, we earn income and spend money primarily as families and not as individuals, making family income and family size more meaningful as a guide to the patterns of spending and growth.

The *requirements of economic growth* can be considered in two respects:

first, growth is concerned with the achievement of full employment, especially when slack exists in the economy; and second, growth is concerned with the economy's overall ability to produce. In the first case, growth is achieved by making full utilization of available capacity in terms of both men and machines. In the second, growth is achieved by adding to capacity. The economy probably grows in both respects, at times more in one than in the other.

When the economy experiences a significant underutilization of existing capacity, factories and machines stand idle and unemployment is high. There is adequate room for the economy to grow because of the gap that exists between its potential and its actual performance. Expanding to full employment levels would increase the economy's performance. Thus more goods and services would be produced and would be available for distribution, and each person's standard of living would be improved. Growth in this regard depends upon an increase in the demand for goods and services, which can be accomplished by increasing spending in the economy. Since the three major components of GNP are consumer spending, investment spending, and government spending for goods and services, an increase in one or more of these would suffice. As a matter of fact, any initial increase in spending sets the multiplier and accelerator into motion to generate more spending.

The other basic requirement for growth is that the economy expand its ability or capacity to produce goods and services. This ultimately means that workers must be able to produce more. Workers in this sense include managers, scientists, and clerks as well as production workers. Growth can be accomplished if workers work harder, work longer hours, or become more efficient. In a day and age when we seek shorter hours and less strenuous activities, the first two choices do not seem relevant. On the other hand, improvements in efficiency may be sufficient to provide both growth and shorter hours. The various factors that determine the level of efficiency can be grouped under four main headings: (1) skill, (2) attitude, (3) innovation, and (4) capital goods.

1. Workers' *skills* and dexterity can make a tremendous difference in the amount of output obtainable with existing plant and equipment. Education, training, and health are the most important factors in determining the output per individual worker. The worker and his employer both are interested in improving productivity: the worker benefits by higher income and a higher standard of living, the employer by lower production costs. For these reasons, self-improvement and company training programs are quite common. Medical benefits and services are also important to productivity; a healthy worker can do more than one who has been sapped of his strength, and absenteeism because of poor health can be costly.

2. The *attitudes* of the workers also can affect production. Morale and ambition are two reflections of worker attitudes. When poor labor-management relations exist, worker morale is low. Workers who do not participate in wage incentive plans and bonus programs are not likely to show much

ambition. On a nation-wide basis, even taxes must be considered carefully lest they affect ambition and incentive. Working conditions are also an important determinant of attitude and productivity. Pleasant surroundings and safety measures should improve workers' attitudes.

3. *Innovation* simply means the development of new products and processes. By devoting resources to research and technology, business and government explore and test new ideas; for example, atomic energy and aerospace technology have opened many new avenues of endeavor. An environment of freedom in thought and action is believed to be a vital ingredient of innovation for individual organizations as well as for nations. Therefore, not all of the growth in GNP can be accounted for by increases in the work force or the nation's stock of capital goods; some is due to the impact of new technology.

4. *Investment* in *capital goods*, such as production facilities and equipment, can contribute to growth in two ways: by representing business spending and by increasing worker efficiency. Whether or not efficiency is affected by a capital expenditure will depend upon the extent to which capital per worker is altered. Investment may merely represent the extension of given facilities, as when new workers are equipped with the same type and amount of equipment already in use by everyone else. While this represents spending and may contribute to growth when unemployment exists, it does not represent growth in terms of increased efficiency; to enhance the efficiency or productivity of workers, more equipment per worker will be required. For example, an auto mechanic in a well-equipped garage is more productive than one who must depend upon a limited amount of equipment. Growth resulting from new technology or an innovation, which has been discussed, also increases worker output. Investment that increases capital per worker is, and will probably continue to be, one of the most effective ways to raise output per worker.

As is apparent by now, growth does not depend on any one single factor, but rather is a combination of various forces at work. For instance, better equipment requires better-trained personnel. Understanding the effect of automation on productivity and income will have a direct bearing on workers' attitudes. When unemployment exists, growth can be achieved by increased spending; when the economy is fully employed, growth depends upon an increase in the labor force, innovation, and the extent to which consumers are willing to sacrifice present consumption for future consumption. When consumers save more out of their income, the economy is able to direct resources to the production of more capital goods and fewer consumer goods.

Stability

Stability is applicable to economic performance in terms of both prices and growth. Fluctuations in overall prices reveal imbalances between money flows and physical flows within the economy. Over the years, fluctuations in growth reveal irregular patterns in the spending components of GNP. Several of the GNP components are notorious for their cyclical swings. These include business investment in plant and equipment, homebuilding, changes in business inventories, and consumer durable goods. They decline sharply and bounce up abruptly; altogether they account for about one-fourth of GNP.

In general, consumer spending on nondurables (food and clothing) tends to be fairly stable year after year. On the other hand, investment spending and consumer expenditures on durables (automobiles and refrigerators) tend to be unstable. This is partially explained by the fact that both investment spending and spending on consumer durables are postponable. If a businessman is pessimistic about future sales, he will postpone buying new equipment to expand, while expectations of growing sales will cause him to increase investment spending. Likewise, the consumer can postpone or expand his purchase of durables. In addition, interaction between the multiplier and the accelerator may contribute to the expansion or contraction of economic activity. Attempts to stabilize the economy apparently must concentrate on business investment and on consumer spending for durables.

A simplified picture of economic fluctuations is depicted in Fig. 3–5. When spending, production, employment, prices, and even wages move downward, the economy experiences a recession. At other times, spending, employment, prices, and wages move upward. So it goes, with the economy rocking up and down from year to year.

The search for stability is really an attempt to make these ups and downs less severe. For example, the dotted line in Fig. 3–6 represents greater stability; the fluctuations have been reduced. The tools of public policy that can be used to achieve this aim will be discussed later in the chapter.

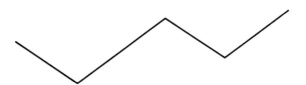

FIGURE 3–5.   Economic fluctuations.

FIGURE 3–6.   Economic fluctuations.

International Equilibrium

International relations provide another way to look at a nation's economic performance: that is, by comparing the economic and financial flows of the nation with the rest of the world. Such flows are reflected in what is known as the *balance of payments account*, which merely shows the money flows that result from economic activities with other nations. When a nation buys goods, these imports are recorded as payments. The United States usually ends up exporting more than it imports every year, and is primarily an importer of raw materials and an exporter of manufactured goods such as industrial machinery, computers, and electrical apparatus. Our exports in 1965 were approximately $27 billion as compared to imports of $21 billion.

Some other items, such as transportation, financial services, the tourist trade, investments, and income on investments, will also appear in the balance of payments account for the year. When shipping and insurance services are provided by American firms, they represent receipts; performed by foreign companies, they show up as payments. Also, when Americans travel abroad, they make payments there. When foreigners travel in the United States, we become the recipients of money. Money invested overseas by directly buying or building a plant there, buying stocks and bonds of foreign firms or governments, or buying short-term (less than a year) obligations will show up as payments because the money is going out of the United States; investments in the United States by foreigners will show up as receipts. The income on investments (dividends and interest) paid during the current year will be a receipt to the receiving nation.

Activities of the U. S. government abroad also enter the balance of payments account. When Washington maintains America's armed forces in foreign countries, military expenditures are made abroad. When the United States grants certain nations money under foreign aid programs or makes loans, largely to underdeveloped countries, it is making payments abroad. Add in a few miscellaneous items, total the receipts and payments, and the difference will be a deficit or a surplus depending on whether payments or receipts are larger. In essence, our balance of payments is a record of all monetary receipts from and payments to the rest of the world. Differences are settled by gold payments.

The U. S. Department of Commerce is responsible for keeping track of our international accounts. Four times a year its monthly *Survey of Current Business* shows detailed figures on the international transactions of the United States. A balance of payments account for the United States summarizing these data for 1965 is illustrated in Fig. 3–7.

The international activities revealed by the balance of payments account can be a reflection of economic performance. The account may indicate

Receipts (Billions of Dollars)		Payments (Billions of Dollars)	
Exports	$ 27	Imports	$ 21
Transportation, Tourist Services, etc.	6	Transportation, Tourist Services, etc.	6
Income on U.S. Investments Abroad	6	Income on Foreign Investments in U.S.	2
		Military Expenditures	3
		U.S. Government Grants and Aid	4
Investments in U.S. by Foreigners	—	Investments Abroad by Americans	5
Miscellaneous	—	Miscellaneous	—
	$ 38		$ 41
Deficit (Gold Outflow)	3		
Total	$ 41	Total	$ 41

FIGURE. 3–7. U. S. balance of international payments (1965). Figures have been rounded and amounts less than $1 billion have not been shown.

whether or not we sell more goods and services than we buy abroad. If we have higher prices or experience more inflation relative to other world markets, then we are not performing adequately. If markets and growth prospects appear more optimistic abroad, Americans will seize the opportunity to invest or lend money there; these money flows will show up in the account. Military and political commitments, however, often obscure the reflections of economic performance. Therefore, an analysis of the account should proceed with caution.

THE MANAGEMENT OF ECONOMIC PERFORMANCE

The management of economic performance concerns itself primarily with the tools of public policy that can be used to direct the power and purpose of the economy. The economy is more likely to achieve its purpose if it is not left entirely to itself. Conflicts of goals also require responsible public policy and proper direction of economic activity. The American people should never be expected to tolerate anything like the depression of the 1930's. Public policy, if properly administered, can be used to avoid such a situation, We will briefly explore two tools of public policy—*monetary policy* and *fiscal policy*—and will discuss ways in which they can even out fluctuations in the economy.

Monetary Policy

Federal monetary policy influences the economy by affecting the amount of money and credit available. The Federal Reserve System (Fed) has been commissioned by Congress to perform this responsibility. Since it is a centralized banking system, the Fed can alter the supply of money at its discretion; therefore, we are on what is called a "managed money system." The Fed influences the supply of money and credit primarily by altering the reserves of commercial banks. These commercial banks, called "member banks," are required to maintain a reserve balance or minimum deposit at the Fed, imposed by law, which is stated as a percentage of the commercial banks' own customer deposits.

The commercial banks invest in securities and make loans when they have an excess balance in their deposit at the Fed; by doing this, they usually create demand deposits. Since demand deposits[2] make up approximately 80 per cent of the money supply (coins and currency make up the remaining 20 per cent), the Fed can alter the supply of money (demand deposits) by changing member bank reserves (deposits at the Fed). There are several devices the Fed can use to do this. It can change the reserve requirement, let banks borrow reserves, or engage in open-market operations, the latter of which is simply the buying and selling of securities by the Fed arranged with individuals, institutions, or commercial banks.

Changes in the money supply also affect interest rates. When excess reserves are available, the banks have more funds to lend and may offer these funds at lower interest rates to make them attractive to potential borrowers. Interest rates on securities will also tend to fall when the Fed buys them in the open market and when commercial banks acquire additional securities with some of their excess reserves. More loanable funds and lower interest rates influence investment spending, output, employment, and prices. Businesses willing to expand will borrow more at lower interest rates, more investment spending will activate the multiplier, employment and output will rise, and prices may experience upward pressures.

When the economy experiences a recession, we are at a trough in the business cycle. In Fig. 3–8 this is labeled "t" for trough. At this point in the business cycle the Fed increases the amount of money in the banks. The banks in turn make these funds available at lower interest rates. Businessmen are encouraged to expand and thereby to speed up the total level of spending. The economy may then move into an upswing.

As the economy's spending approaches a peak in the business cycle

---

[2] *Demand deposits* are simply checking accounts at commercial banks.

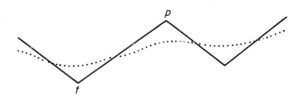

FIGURE 3–8.   Fluctuations and monetary policy.

("p" in Fig. 3–8), the Fed may feel that there is too much spending going on; it then decreases member bank reserves and makes money "tight." It becomes harder for businessmen to get loans. Higher interest rates make investment less attractive and some projects are postponed. This helps to avoid inflation.

By stimulating spending at the troughs and restraining it at the peaks with changes in the money supply, the Fed can even out the business cycle so that the economy follows more closely the dotted line of spending How-ever, since monetary policy cannot be completely effective in bringing about stability, most economists today are convinced that the government must also use its powers in the areas of taxation and spending.

Fiscal Policy

The government can play a direct role in the achievement of stability. Since government expenditures for goods and services represent one of the major components of GNP, its spending activities cannot be disregarded. The government also collects taxes to finance these expenditures. The process of taxing and spending by the government to stabilize the economy is called *fiscal policy*.

Looking first at spending by the government, we can see that when we are in a trough of the business cycle, more spending by the government can boost the economy. This can be accomplished by public investment projects such as the building of post offices which can be planned ahead and undertaken when the economy needs a boost. Government spending starts the multiplier working; it can lead the economy back to recovery from a trough ("t" in Fig. 3–9). At a peak of the business cycle, government spending is decreased. Nonessential programs are cut back or postponed.

Another aspect of fiscal policy to consider is taxation. The right policy to stabilize the economy would seem to be to lower taxes in a trough and to raise taxes at a peak. With lower taxes, the private sector—consumers and businesses—will be able to spend more; higher tax rates discourage private spending.

The fiscal policy that seems most appropriate in a trough is increased government spending and lower taxes. This may very well cause *deficit spend-ing*, where expenditures exceed Treasury receipts. On the other hand, at peaks,

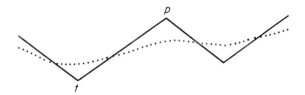

FIGURE 3–9. Fluctuations and fiscal policy.

we have suggested raising taxes and reducing spending, which causes a surplus in the Treasury's accounts. To some extent, deficits and surpluses offset each other over time. In any event, economists are primarily concerned with the effects of fiscal policy on income and employment.

In conclusion, it must be pointed out that both monetary and fiscal policy should be applied gradually, and preferably in anticipation of troughs and peaks, rather than after they have been reached. In this way the dotted line of spending will be followed. Several leading indicators are available which provide early signals of change in the economy. Close surveillance of these indicators can be very helpful to the authorities.

There are also certain lag effects in both monetary and fiscal policy. Monetary policy, for example, affects spending indirectly and may take a little time to have an influence on it. Fiscal policy, on the other hand, has more direct effects on spending. However, it may lag when it is dependent upon legislative action; monetary policy does not require such action and can usually be applied immediately. Some taxes and spending by the government, however, escape this legislative lag because they occur automatically, setting into motion changes in income and employment that do not depend upon continuous decisions. There are two principal *non-discretionary* tools, as they are called, that are always at work in the economy. One is income taxes, which increase proportionately more than income does and thus tend to stabilize spending. The other is unemployment compensation or payments, which automatically offset changes in income due to unemployment.

Stabilizing the economy requires the use of both monetary and fiscal policy. Fiscal policy is believed to be more reliable in a trough; monetary policy, at a peak. At times, however, dependence on one or the other may cause some distortions in the economy. Reliance on monetary policy to slow up spending may affect the construction and building sector more strongly than is necessary because spending in that sector is responsive to interest rates and changes in the credit markets.

Public policy directed toward stabilization requires a proper mixture of monetary and fiscal policy. The proper use of public policy to direct the power and purpose of the economy is strongly justified on the basis that it helps the private sector to achieve its fullest potential and thus strengthens the free enterprise system.

PROBLEMS AND PROJECTS

1. Obtain from the *Survey of Current Business* for the last complete year the gross national product in current and constant dollars. What accounts for the difference? Note that GNP's for the quarters of the year are stated in terms of annual rates. Record the GNP (current dollars) and the percentage of GNP that each major component represents.

Gross National Product (current $) _____
Gross National Product (constant $) _____

Major Components	GNP in Current Dollars (billions)	Per cent of GNP
Personal consumption expenditures		
Gross private domestic investment		
Government purchases of goods and services		
Net exports of goods and services		

2. Outline a proposal of various monetary and fiscal policy measures to pull the economy out of a slump.
3. An individual's (or family's) propensity to consume can be illustrated by a problem using hypothetical figures.
   a. On graph paper, plot the data in the table, using consumption expenditures and income as axes. Calculate the APC and MPC at each hypothetical level of income.

HYPOTHETICAL FAMILY CONSUMPTION AND INCOME

Income	Consumption Expenditures	APC	MPC
3,000	3,000		
4,000	3,800		
5,000	4,600		
6,000	5,400		
7,000	6,200		
8,000	7,000		
9,000	7,800		
10,000	8,600		

   b. The data represent the amounts that are likely to be spent at different levels of income. A family would be at only one of these alternatives at a given time. Suppose that the family's income were unexpectedly increased from $6,000 to $7,000. Consumption would increase by $_____. When expressed as a fraction of the change in income this is called the _____. What is not spent is _____.

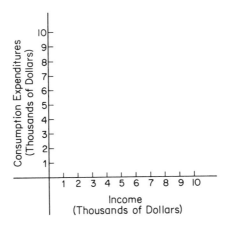

SELECTED REFERENCES

McConnell, Campbell R., *Economics: Principles, Problems, and Policies*, Parts II, III. New York: McGraw-Hill Book Company, 1966.

McKenna, Joseph P., *Aggregate Economic Analysis*. New York: Holt, Rinehart & Winston, Inc., 1965.

U.S. Department of Commerce, *Do You Know Your Economic ABC's?* Washington, D.C.: U.S. Government Printing Office, 1966.

————, *U.S. Balance of Payments*. Washington, D.C.: U.S. Government Printing Office, 1964.

————, *U.S. Economic Growth*. Washington, D.C.: U.S. Government Printing Office, 1966.

4

THE BUSINESS

ESTABLISHMENT

The role of business enterprise is far-reaching in a free enterprise, price-directed economy like the United States. The principal forms of business ownership in the United States are the single proprietorship, the partnership, and the corporation. The two basic financial statements which summarize a firm's activities are the balance sheet and the income statement. Business combinations are quite prevalent on the American scene. The market structures of American industry explain the behavior and the performance of business enterprise. Each of these aspects will be discussed separately in this chapter.

ROLE OF BUSINESS

Business establishments make an indispensable economic contribution to our material survival. For one thing, most of our goods and services result from their efforts. Moreover, businesses employ and organize the economy's resources, thereby generating the income that supports consumption. They also make substantial tax contributions, which finance government activities. Business consequently plays an important and continuous role, satisfying the needs of many groups. Consumers buy and use its output, workers are provided the employment and income necessary for survival in a modern society, and government can obtain the goods and services it needs as well as funds to pay for its operations.

More specific contributions of business establishments can be identified depending upon whether the firms produce raw materials, process these materials, distribute products, or provide services. For example, mining and quarrying provide the economy with important resources. Construction is responsible for much of the economy's tangible wealth. Manufacturing is devoted to the production of many industrial and consumer products. Transportation, communication, and other utilities facilitate the operation of other businesses. Wholesaling helps to deliver the goods to the retailer. Retailing is well known to most citizens because it represents the final transfer of goods to the consumer. Finance, real estate, and insurance are related to the transfer, control, and protection of assets. Service industries provide the intangibles which are so important to our survival. Agriculture, of course, is devoted to the production of food, feed, and fiber. Government activities also play a vital role in the modern society.

The employment and income generated by business establishments annually is very substantial. Such data are provided by the U. S. Department of Commerce according to a convenient and commonly used classification of industry. The number of civilians employed in each industry is given in the *Survey of Current Business*. Such data for 1966 are provided in Table 4–1. The dollar amount of national income attributed to each industry is provided in Table 4–2. Table 4–1 shows that manufacturing accounts for the largest number of employees, almost 29 per cent. Wholesale and retail trade ranks second, with government employment trailing close behind. As would be expected, manufacturing also accounts for the largest share of national income generated, slightly over 28 per cent (Table 4–2).

TABLE 4–1

**EMPLOYMENT BY MAJOR INDUSTRY AS OF NOVEMBER 30, 1966
(ANNUAL RATE)**

Industry	Number Employed (thousands)
Agriculture	3,969
Manufacturing	19,532
Mining	627
Contract construction	3,318
Transportation and public utilities	4,206
Wholesale and retail	13,586
Finance, insurance, and real estate	3,097
Services and miscellaneous	9,741
Government	11,280

Source: Survey of Current Business (January 1967), S-13.

TABLE 4–2

NATIONAL INCOME BY INDUSTRY FOR THIRD QUARTER, 1966
(ANNUAL RATE)

Industry	Income (billions of dollars)
Agriculture, forestry, and fisheries	$ 21.6
Mining and construction	37.9
Manufacturing	188.6
Transportation	24.7
Communication	12.5
Electric, gas, and sanitary services	12.7
Wholesale and retail trade	89.6
Finance, insurance, and real estate	66.0
Services	69.8
Government and government enterprise	85.8

Source: Ibid., p. 15.

FORMS OF BUSINESS OWNERSHIP

Identification

There are three principal forms of ownership in modern business establishments: *individual proprietorships*, *general partnerships*, and *corporations;* there are also other special forms of partnership, which will not be included in this brief discussion.

The *sole proprietorship* has only one owner. It is usually representative of very small business enterprises. Excluding agriculture, the proprietorship can be associated with such enterprises as the small-town restaurant, the auto repair shop, the barber shop, the clothing store, the local tavern, and the local drugstore. The sole proprietorship is the easiest form of business to establish and the simplest to manage. There is usually only one boss, who is the owner and manager. Generally, no complicated reports or requirements are imposed upon this form of business establishment.

The *partnership* consists of two or more owners; some even exceed 100 members. Like the single proprietorship, the partnership can be associated with the wholesale and retail trade as well as with service institutions. However, in contrast to the sole proprietorship, it is used more by security brokers, insurance agencies, and real estate brokers than by the service institutions such as barber shops and restaurants. The larger partnerships, in terms of members, are usually in such professions as law and public accounting.

The *corporation* is a form of business ownership which depends upon a more formal structure than either the proprietorship or the partnership. It is established as a *legal entity* when a state authorizes its formation and issues a *charter.*The owners are called *stockholders;* they in turn elect a *board of direc-*

TABLE 4-3

SOLE PROPRIETORSHIPS, PARTNERSHIPS, AND CORPORATIONS: NUMBER, RECEIPTS, AND NET PROFIT, 1963 (numbers in thousands, money figures in millions of dollars)*

Industry	Number			Receipts			Net Profit		
	Sole Prop.	Part-nership	Corpor-ation	Sole Prop.	Part-nership	Corpor-ation	Sole Prop.	Part-nership	Corpor-ation
Agriculture, forestry, and fisheries	3,338	130	23	$ 30,050	$ 4,690	$ 7,493	$ 3,048	$ 567	$ 96
Mining	34	14	15	1,049	894	12,448	10	9	1,210
Construction	692	60	96	16,345	6,895	44,731	2,171	625	643
Manufacturing	187	39	182	6,369	6,107	419,324	678	543	28,776
Transportation, communication, electricity, and gas	307	17	56	4,969	1,122	75,711	694	143	8,925
Wholesale and retail trade	1,837	257	403	89,775	35,471	302,904	5,807	2,157	5,350
Finance, insurance, and real estate	506	234	375	5,467	5,469	56,045	1,782	932	8,255
Services	2,185	172	164	27,095	11,106	30,018	9,529	3,710	901
Totals	9,136	924	1,323	$181,551	$71,762	$948,790	$23,771	$8,668	$54,147

*Based on a sample of unaudited tax returns filed for accounting periods ending between July 1, 1962, and June 30, 1963 (totals as reported differ due to rounding). Figures pertain to active partnerships and corporations. Inactive organizations were not included because they were accounted for by tax returns, which showed no income or deductions but represented firms that were required to file a return.

Source: Statistical Abstract of the United States (1966).

tors to guide the firm's activities. Officers such as a president, vice presidents, a secretary, and a treasurer are selected by the board of directors to manage the firm's operations. A corporation may have hundreds of thousands of owners; Standard Oil of New Jersey reported 728,000 shareholders at the end of 1965. Corporations vary widely in asset size and are ranked in the *Statistical Abstract of the United States* according to several categories ranging from "less than $100,000" to "over $250 million." Standard Oil falls into the latter category and reported over $13 billion in assets at the end of 1965. Some of the other big giants are General Motors, American Telephone and Telegraph, Sears, Roebuck and Co., and the Bank of America. The corporate form of ownership is associated with national business firms that engage principally in trade, finance, and manufacturing.

Comparisons

Certain characteristics of business establishments are revealed by comparing the forms of business ownership in terms of available quantitative data. This comparison is accomplished by analyzing the kind of data that has been reproduced in Table 4–3. First, the number of sole proprietorships far exceeds the number of partnerships and corporations. There were over nine million sole proprietorships (including farms) operating in the United States according to income tax returns filed during the 12-month period ending June 30, 1963. There were only $1\frac{1}{3}$ million corporations and less than a million partnerships.

In terms of business receipts, the story is entirely different. Corporations accounted for over $948 billion in receipts, sole proprietorships for $181 billion, and partnerships for only $71 billion. Corporations were responsible for almost 80 per cent of business receipts. Corporations also reported larger profits than the other two types of business firms. The relative importance of the total number of firms and the total dollar volume of receipts are illustrated in Fig. 4–1. This information shows that in summary, sole proprietorships are larger in number but smaller in terms of receipts and economic contributions than corporations as a group. Expressed in general terms, sole proprietorships are usually thought of as small business establishments and corporations as large business establishments.

More careful perusal of Table 4–3 reveals additional information about the characteristics of business establishments in the United States. The table shows that for sole proprietorships (excluding agriculture), the largest number are engaged in services, although most receipts are generated by wholesale and retail trade establishments, and net profits are larger for the services. Such figures may be misleading when one realizes that profits for small business firms are a mixture of wages, interest, rent, and profits. Even though the number of partnerships in wholesale and retail trade was just slightly larger than in

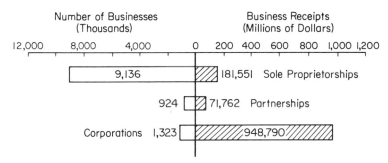

FIGURE 4-1. Number of units and volume of business receipts for sole proprietorships, partnerships, and corporations (based on tax returns for 12-month period ending June 30, 1963).

finance, insurance, and real estate, receipts were substantially larger, while profits were highest for services.

At a glance, the data for corporations may seem a little confusing. Table 4-3 reveals that the largest number of corporations are engaged in the wholesale and retail trades. When these trades are considered separately, finance accounts for the largest number. However, manufacturing is responsible for the largest portion of corporate receipts. Corporate profits in manufacturing also far exceed those of any of the other industry classifications and alone is almost as large as the total profits of sole proprietorships and partnerships combined.

Determinants

Obviously, there must be sound reasons to explain the existence of these three principal forms of business ownership in the United States. Choosing the most appropriate form must of necessity depend upon the merits of each in relation to the given circumstances. For this reason, thorough coverage of the advantages and disadvantages of each type will not be attempted here. Instead, a few of the most important determinants will be suggested and discussed.

Liability of ownership is one very important determinant. In the case of both sole proprietorships and general partnerships, the liability of the owners for business debts is described as unlimited. In corporations, however, stockholders hold the enviable position of having limited liability for business debts. Under certain forms of partnership, some partners have limited-liability privileges as long as at least one partner has unlimited liability. In the event of business failure, this matter of liability becomes very important; with sole proprietorships and partnerships the creditors may look to the personal assets of the owners to satisfy their claims. This is not true for corporations, however. There the stockholder is usually only liable for the monetary contribution or stipulated value of the stock certificate.

The *continuity* of a business establishment is automatically terminated by the death, withdrawal, or bankruptcy of a single owner or single partner, although the transfer of ownership in a corporation does not alter its status.

As a matter of fact, every business day, the ownership of the nation's giant corporations is transferred by sales of stock. This transfer is facilitated by the nation's organized securities exchanges and the vast network of investment bankers, dealers, and brokers. If a partnership wishes to expand by inviting in another partner, the old arrangement must be terminated. In the case of the corporation, new owners can be acquired simply by issuing additional shares of stock.

The *capital* requirements of a growing or large-scale enterprise can be most easily satisfied by the corporate form of business enterprise. This is probably the principal justification for this form of ownership. It takes vast sums of money to establish, maintain, and operate large-scale, mass-production industry. Although in some cases, individual wealth may be sufficient, today it is generally recognized that capital must be pooled for a free society to benefit from the economies of large-scale production. Steel, for example, simply cannot be produced in a "bathtub"; it requires large amounts of complicated equipment. Incidentally, the limited-liability feature helps to satisfy this need for vast sums of money because it attracts ownership capital that otherwise would not become available.

Tax considerations also have a bearing on the form of business ownership adopted. Corporations are often subject to taxes which the sole proprietorship and partnership escape. In addition, unless individual income is very high, proprietorships and partnerships generally have an advantage over corporations in regard to income taxes. In recent years, taxes on corporate profits have averaged about 22 per cent of the first $25,000 and 50 per cent of profits above this amount. For many large corporations, taxes amount to one-half of the profits. And if the remaining profits are distributed as dividends, they are subject to personal income taxes as well.

There are still other determinants that may be important in selecting the appropriate form of business ownership. For example, the single proprietor or partner is closely attached to the business enterprise; profits are more closely identified with his individual effort and initiative. There also is relatively greater ease of entry and exit for proprietorships and partnerships. In conclusion, the reader is reminded that many business establishments evolve from a sole proprietorship through a partnership to a corporation. The circumstances associated with this evolutionary process dictate the most desirable form of ownership.

FINANCIAL STATEMENTS

Two basic financial statements are used to summarize the activities of a business establishment. The money that flows through a business enterprise is reflected by the *income statement*, and the financial condition of the enterprise is reflected by the *balance sheet*. Both of these statements are useful in business analysis, providing a basis for analysis and the data for comparison of performance.

Income Statement

The income statement is a detailed summary of business operations over a specified period of time. Income statements are prepared monthly, quarterly, and annually. Businessmen must keep accurate records of income and expenses in order to determine how much net income or profit they are making. The income statement shows the sources of a business firm's income and the manner in which these funds are disbursed during a given period. Generally the statement will show receipts from sales of goods and services and the apportionment of these receipts among the various costs, taxes, and profits.

TABLE 4-4

HYPOTHETICAL INCOME STATEMENT

Items			Items as Per cent of Net Sales
Revenue from sales:			
Sales		$101,000	101.0
Less sales returns and allowances		1,000	1.0
Net sales		$100,000	100.0
Cost of goods sold:			
Beginning inventory	$ 1,000		1.0
Purchases	19,000		19.0
Goods available	$20,000		20.0
Less ending inventory	1,500		1.5
Cost of goods sold		18,500	18.5
Gross profit on sales		81,500	81.5
Operating expenses:			
Wages and salaries	$30,000		30.0
Rent	3,000		3.0
Interest	8,000		8.0
Depreciation	1,000		1.0
Taxes	9,000		9.0
Total operating expenses		51,000	51.0
Net profit		$ 29,500	29.5

A simplified income statement is presented in Table 4-4 for a company with material costs amounting to $18,500. The statement summarizes payments to employees, interest and rent charges, depreciation, taxes, and net profits available to the owners. Most of the items are self-explanatory. Interest, of course, consists of payments for the use of borrowed money. Payroll, sales, and profits taxes are lumped together into one item.

Most of the expenses reported during the accounting period represent actual money outlays for labor, materials, and supplies during that period.

By contrast, some building, equipment, and tools that contribute to production may have been purchased in a previous period; production costs would be understated if no allowance were made for that fact. A convenient device has been developed by accountants whereby they allocate to specific accounting periods certain portions of the original money outlay for capital goods. In this way, depreciation or capital consumption is accounted for during each production period. Various methods are used which base depreciation estimates on time, use, or a combination of both.

Suppose, for example, that a $100,000 machine is purchased by a firm in 1965. If its estimated life is ten years, then the portion used up during each year would have to be calculated and charged to income. If it is determined that an equal amount should be charged each year it would be $10,000. This amount is called a depreciation charge and allows for a more accurate estimate of profits over a specified period of time.

For purposes of analysis, the data summarized in an income statement can also be converted into percentages. It is customary to compare all amounts with net sales—that is, with sales less returns and allowances. Net sales are considered to be 100 per cent, and all other items are then reported as a percentage of net sales. The data in an income statement can also be used to develop ratios. For example, the ratio of inventory to sales can be an important indicator of how closely inventory costs are staying in line with business activity. In addition to comparing the items on a particular income statement, one may also compare individual items with the same items in previous statements, to form a *comparative income statement*. In addition, it is also very useful to reflect the *change* that occurs in an item from year to year, perferably as a percentage. For example, the cost of goods may be 20 per cent of net sales one year and 20 per cent of net sales the following year; however, an increase from $20,000 to $30,000 would be revealed as a 50 per cent change in the cost of goods.

Balance Sheet

Unlike the income statement, which reflects a flow of money receipts and outlays during a period, the *balance sheet* is a condition statement. It tells what is owned and what is owed, showing the stock of assets a firm has acquired as of a certain date as well as the liabilities resulting from short- and long-term borrowing. It also reflects the interest in or claim on the business enterprise by the owners.

A balance sheet is illustrated in Table 4–5. Close perusal will reveal that assets equal the total of liabilities and proprietorship (equity); this is why the statement is called a balance sheet. The balance sheet items are self-explanatory. Assets include cash, customer notes and accounts, inventories, and the valuation of buildings and equipment. Liabilities include short-term debt and the accounts the firm has with its suppliers as well as the long-term debt re-

TABLE 4–5

HYPOTHETICAL BALANCE SHEET

Items			Items as Per cent of Total
Assets			
Current assets			
Cash	$ 6,500		3.7
Notes receivable	2,000		1.2
Accounts receivable	28,200		16.1
Inventory	12,900		7.4
Total current assets		$ 49,600	28.4
Fixed assets			
Building	$90,000		51.5
Equipment	35,000		20.1
Total fixed assets		125,000	71.6
Total assets		$174,600	100.0
Liabilities			
Current liabilities			
Notes payable	$11,000		6.3
Accounts payable	15,500		8.9
Total current liabilities		$ 26,500	15.2
Fixed liabilities			
Bonds payable		46,000	26.3
Total liabilities		$ 72,500	41.5
Proprietorship			
Equity			
Common stock	$60,000		34.4
Surplus	42,100		24.1
Total equity		$102,100	58.5
Total liabilities and equity		174,600	100.0

flected by bonds outstanding. Finally, net worth or owners' claims include the amounts paid to purchase stock and the surplus that may have resulted from the earnings which have been retained by the firm and which partially support the asset items above.

Comparisons of the balance sheet items can also be expressed in percentage form; such comparisons with items on previous statements are useful for business analysis. In addition, certain other valuable comparisons are available from balance sheet items, from which several important ratios can be developed. For example, the *current ratio* expresses current assets in relation to current liabilities. In Table 4–5, the current ratio is 1.87 ($49,600/$26,500). The *acid test* is another ratio which reflects a firm's ability to meet its short-term commitments. Unlike the current ratio, it relates the more liquid assets[1] to current liabilities. Using the figures in Table 4–5 the acid-test ratio is 1.38 ($36,700/$26,500). Such ratios are particularly useful in determining the advisability of obtaining new credit extensions. One more ratio offered as an example is the ratio of accounts receivable to net sales. This ratio, which uses information from both the income statement and the balance sheet, reflects

[1] Liquidity refers to the extent and ease to which assets can be converted into cash.

the extent to which sales are being made on credit. Many ratios are used for business analysis, and each has a particular significance to business decisions. The significance of each ratio depends upon the size and nature of the enterprise as well as on its particular business classification. For example, a large manufacturer of furniture would depend upon ratios applicable to his industry and not on those relevant to a small men's clothing store.

In summary, financial statements such as income statements and balance sheets reflect the business establishment's economic activities in monetary terms. These statements are valuable sources of quantitative information which can be used for business analysis and decisions. The use of such data will be revealed more clearly in some of the remaining chapters of this book.

COMBINATIONS IN BUSINESS

Principal Methods

Many of today's large business enterprises have grown to their present size as a result of combining two or more firms rather than expanding a single firm. There are three principal methods by which combinations are accomplished: by *mergers*, by *amalgamations*, or by *holding companies.*

The principal distinguishing characteristic of a *merger* is that the identity of one of the firms remains intact. The smaller firm is absorbed, so to speak, by the larger, when the physical and financial assets of the two firms are consolidated. The owners of the smaller company are compensated with cash, stock in the surviving firm, or a combination of both. Of course, the merger depends upon the approval of the owners of both companies concerned. Mergers usually involve only two firms at a time, but multi-mergers do occur. Furthermore, two merged firms may merge later with another firm, and so on.

In the case of an *amalgamation*, the identities of the old firms are lost. A new company is formed which buys the assets and liabilities of the old firms, and the owners of the old companies are compensated for their claims on the assets of the old firms. Changes of management may be more pronounced with amalgamations than with mergers, where the dominant firm remains in control. As in the case of mergers, more than two firms can be involved in the proceedings.

A popular device for combining business enterprises is the *holding company*. The holding company is not as complete a form of combination as are mergers and amalgamations; the physical and financial assets of the companies remain separate. The holding company merely attempts to buy a sufficient amount of the voting stock in other companies to insure control.

Theoretically, this should be 51 per cent. In actual practice, however, holding companies can maintain effective control with less than this amount, sometimes as little as 10 or 20 per cent. This may not require much capital. Often the holding company will own all the stock of its subsidiary companies. The American Telephone and Telegraph Company, a well-known American corporation, is a holding company for several operating subsidiaries. The ability to maintain effective control over many operating subsidiaries allows a coordination of operations that may or may not be in the public's best interest.

Objectives of Combinations

Several important objectives are satisfied by combining business enterprises, including *diversification, efficiency, independence,* and *competition.* Among the reasons for *diversification* is the seasonal nature of some products; thus, a boat manufacturer may find it desirable to devote his efforts to the manufacture of toys during the off-season period for boats. A close relationship between products also may suggest diversification; a soft-drink bottler may find it feasible to complement his activities with a potato chip or cookie firm because the final distribution and consumption of the products are so closely related. Finally, geographical diversification may be desirable in order to widen a firm's markets. One hotel can only service a limited area, but a chain of hotels can serve an entire region or country, or even the world.

Efficiency or economy of operation may be improved as a result of combinations. Basic to this is the specialization of effort that can be achieved by large-scale operations. The centralization of such activities as financing, advertising, engineering, distribution, accounting, and research results in greater efficiency for the firm. Often duplication of already efficient operations may be all that is required to improve activities such as financing or advertising. In addition, the combination of several firms may eventually lead to combination with one that can process waste into a usable byproduct. If the revenue from the sale of the byproduct is applied to the other production costs, it will have the same effect as improved efficiency—lower costs.

Independence is a strong motivation for combination. Although firms often depend upon outside suppliers to support their activities, greater assurance of a continuous supply of materials can be achieved if they own their own sources. They can do this by combining with other firms. Manufacturers may combine with transportation companies and financial institutions to insure a continuous flow of money or goods, or they may extend beyond the manufacturing stage into sales so that their marketing effort is less dependent upon outside firms.

The fourth objective of combination is *competition.* In one sense, companies combine in order to meet competition, since cost advantages accrue when operations are conducted more efficiently. On the other hand, they also combine to restrict competition. The effect of the combination of two firms selling the same product in the same market is usually easier to appraise than the effect of the combination of two firms selling different products. For example, a paper company combines with an envelope manufacturer and refuses to sell paper to other envelope manufacturers; the extent to which this restricts competition in the envelope market is dependent upon the paper company's dominance in the paper market.

Nature of Combinations

A business combination can be described as being either *horizontal*, *vertical*, or *nondirectional*. When two or more competitors combine, the combination is *horizontal*. A chain of drugstores, restaurants, banks, chemical companies, or hotels illustrates this type. A combination of companies which are not competitors but which stand in a supplier-customer relationship (buyers and sellers) is *vertical* in nature. If a mining company owns vast acres of timberland, a lumber mill, a paper company, an envelope factory, a printing company, and a greeting card chain, the combination is vertical. All other forms of business combinations can be classified as *nondirectional*.

Many *nondirectional* combinations appear to be a conglomeration of firms which bear no relationship to each other. For example, a drug company may own a chemical company, a container or glass manufacturer, a chain of hotels, a textile mill, and an insurance company. Under such circumstances, centralization of financing, advertising, engineering, distribution, and accounting may be conducted on a more efficient scale. This type of non-directional combination is often referred to as a conglomerate. Another type of non-directional combination is represented when the diverse firms complement each other, such as the boat manufacturer that combines with a toy manufacturer to compensate for the seasonal nature of their respective markets. Another example would be the combination of a chain of motels with a national bus line for the purpose of complementing each other's business or perhaps for the purpose of developing a national touring and lodging service.

Consequences of Combinations

The consequences of business combinations can be seen by their impact on the structure, behavior, and performance of American industry. Market structure, firm behavior, and industry performance are related to each other. Structure determines behavior and behavior influences performance in terms of economic contribution.

Let us first look at what is meant by market structure, and then discuss several important conditions associated with it. Economic theory provides a description of four distinct market situations: *pure competition, pure monopoly, monopolistic competition*, and *oligopoly*.

A main feature of *pure competition* is the presence of a large number of sellers. Competitive firms produce products which are identical or perfect substitutes for each other. Conditions of entry and exit from the industry are unrestricted; virtually anyone is free to start a business in this type of market. Because there are so many sellers, they cannot determine their own prices. Instead, each adjusts his output to prices determined in the market.

At the opposite extreme is *pure monopoly*. The monopolist is the only producer or seller; there are no close substitutes or other alternatives available to buyers. In addition, no other producer can enter the market, since monopoly requires a dependence upon barriers to entry. Since the monopolist is the only seller, he can set his own price according to demand and costs. The monopolist usually charges higher prices than those set by competition and restricts sales.

Between these two extremes are *monopolistic competition* and *oligopoly*. While pure monopoly and pure competition never exist in reality, elements of each exist in different degrees in monopolistic competition and oligopoly. The essential difference between the latter two market structures can be reflected by the number of firms they contain, ranging from two to hundreds. Like pure competition, monopolistic competition depends on a large number of sellers in the market; oligopoly, on the other hand, has only a few. Another important difference depends upon the type of barriers to entry that may exist.

Monopolistic competition is very much like pure competition. Many firms exist, although the product of each firm is a little different from the others. Sometimes the difference is real; other times it is only imagined. In other words, the products of firms engaged in monopolistic competition are close, but not perfect, substitutes. Product differentiation appears in various forms—in packaging, surroundings, advertising, services, and credit arrangements. Because of this, entry into the market is a bit more difficult than it is with pure competition. A new firm must be willing to promote its product in order to break into the market. Also because of product differentiation, a monopolistic competitor has some, though very little, control over his prices. Competition is ordinarily not in terms of price but in terms of brand names, advertising, and trademarks. In summary, monopolistic competition resembles pure competition more than monopoly, even though each firm tries to act a little like a monopolist by controlling his market with product differentiation. Monopolistic competition usually exists in cities where there is a large number of grocery stores, clothing stores, drugstores, barber shops, restaurants, and gasoline stations, each of which provides a differentiated product or service.

A basic characteristic of oligopoly is the few number of firms. The products can be either identical, as within various grades of steel in the steel market or aluminum in the aluminum market, or differentiated, as with different brands of tires in the tire market or cigarettes in the cigarette market. Entry into the market is difficult but not impossible as it would be with a monopoly. Because there are so few firms, oligopolists usually must consider the action of their rivals in regard to prices. A price change can have a noticeable effect on sales, because there is not a large number of firms to absorb the change. For this reason, individual control over price in oligopoly is almost nonexistent, and prices will appear to be very stable. This mutual interdependence has often given rise to collusion and price fixing, where the oligopolists may get together in order to exert control over prices in much the same way as monopolists do; the type and degree of collusion varies greatly. Finally, oligopoly is not necessarily restricted to the giants of industry. It can also exist in local, isolated markets where there are only a few small firms.

One other point may be mentioned concerning market structure; that is, the elements of competition and monopoly are not limited to the seller side of of product markets. They also exist in different degrees in the buyer side of the markets. There can be one, a few, or many buyers of a product. These elements exist in resource markets as well. One firm, such as a lumber mill in a small town, can be the principal buyer of a resource, such as labor. When only one buyer exists in either a product or resource market economists refer to this situation as *monopsony*.

In summary, this brief review of the various types of market structures suggests that they have certain conditions in common,which can be the basis for analyzing the effect business combination may have on the behavior and performance of American industry. These conditions are *concentration of firms, product differentiation,* and *barriers to entry.* It is not the purpose of this chapter to provide extensive coverage of these conditions. Nevertheless, they play a vital role in the analysis of market structures; the degree to which each is present reflects the market structure and thus suggests market behavior.

The *market behavior* of American industry is reflected by pricing and product policies and by the coercive practices of existing firms. In the case of pure competition and pure monopoly, firms simply react to market forces. Competitive firms accept the market price and adjust their output to it. The monopolist's behavior is also a reaction to the market because he is the only firm in it. Consequently, pure competition and pure monopoly represent clearly defined and predictable but quite different behavior in terms of pricing and product policies. Coercive practices do not exist in either, since with competition there are too many firms to coerce and with monopoly no other firms exist.

In monopolistic competition, the market characteristics and market conduct do not deviate enough from pure competition to warrant a detailed discussion. Moreover, since there is an absence of high concentration, the consequences of combination are irrelevant. However, the consequences of product differentiation and other forms of nonprice competition do not go unheeded by economists.

In *most* oligopolistic industries, the small number of firms is testimony to the fact that business combinations have occurred. Oligopolistic market behavior is complex because unlike competition or monopoly, the firms react to one another. It is for this reason that oligopoly will not receive extensive coverage here that it deserves. However, general reflections of oligopolistic market behavior can be presented in terms of *pricing policies, product policies,* and *coercive practices.*

Because oligopolistic pricing policies depend a great deal upon the expected reactions of rivals, prices may remain stable over extended periods of time. It is safer to maintain established patterns than to take the chance of losing large numbers of customers with a price hike or by altering profits if rival firms follow a price reduction. Firms may employ sophisticated mathematical techniques, such as game theory, to suggest alternative price policies. Frequently, oligopolistic firms coordinate pricing decisions by outright price-fixing agreements, follow-the-leader practices, or informal arrangements worked out on the golf course or at a cocktail party. At other times, simple rule-of-thumb devices are used. Normal rate of return on investment and standard markup over costs are two such devices.

Product policies are more prominent when product differentiation exists. Changes of model and style are used by oligopolists in lieu of price changes. Product policies are not likely to start price wars. A firm that has instituted changes in its product has a good chance to hold the edge over its competitors, since they may take six months to put a similar change into effect.

Coercive practices attempt to change the market structure. A firm may try to drive out or weaken existing rivals by price cutting; a financially strong firm can weaken or eliminate its rivals if their prices become unprofitable. Coercive practices may alter the market structure with a predictable effect—a greater degree of monopoly.

Finally, the consequences of business combination are also revealed by the manner in which an industry contributes to overall economic effort and progress, and is referred to as *performance.* Pricing practices in concentrated industries may make it difficult for the economy to achieve full employment without inflation because of their tendency to maintain rigid prices. There is also a tendency for oligopolists to pass on higher resource prices to consumers in the form of higher prices for their product. Finally, excess profits by concentrated industries may represent an unequitable distribution of income.

On the other hand, concentrated industries can devote large amounts of effort to research and development with beneficial results. This is not to say, however, that innovation and technical achievements are associated only with large-scale concentrated industries. Small firms in unconcentrated industries often make significant contributions. As a matter of fact, evidence is available which indicates that at times both concentrated and unconcentrated industries may stimulate or retard progress. However, when demand is insufficient to support many firms, technical efficiency and therefore progress can only be achieved by large-scale enterprises. In these circumstances, concentration may be required in order for an industry to make a contribution.

Performance may also depend upon how well resources can shift among different markets. Normally, resources would be attracted from one use to another by higher profit rates. When monopoly is strong, or a high degree of concentration exists in a market, profit rates are usually higher compared to more competitive markets where these conditions are absent. Performance would be improved if a shift of resources would occur. The high profits signal the desire for such a change. Monopolists, however, would prefer not to expand output; barriers to entry may prevent more competitive markets from making the adjustment. Consequently, performance in a market is affected when resources are not properly allocated among different markets.

Finally, performance is affected by advertising and sales promotion activities. Certain types of advertising and sales promotion in concentrated industries may represent inefficient utilization of resources. This is especially true of the type of advertising and sales promotion which is not necessarily informative to the buyer but which attempts to get him to switch brands, although in reality the products are identical. Advertising of the various brands of aspirin is often cited as an example of this. These activities represent inefficient use of resources because they are not really necessary; the resources could be utilized better in other activities.

We have seen by now that although business enterprise is the chief agent of production, certain undesirable features may emerge when concentrated markets exist. It is for this reason that public policies such as the antitrust laws and the regulation of public utilities have developed over the years. These policies seek to promote competition and to control monopoly.

The antitrust laws have not always been easy to administer, especially since their intent has been interpreted differently by the courts from time to time. During the early part of the twentieth century, the attitude of the courts was based upon an analysis of the circumstances with primary concern directed toward the behavior or intent of the concentrated industries. By the middle of the century, the courts placed primary emphasis on the conditions of the market structure or market power. In recent years, more and more guidelines on antitrust policy have been developed by the government to prevent too much seller concentration. This policy has been increasingly applied to all types of local and national markets, to big firms and small firms alike. It seems that a close scrutiny of market structures can provide the best guidelines to the improvement of economic performance.

Public policy in regard to natural monopolies has been to regulate them directly. A natural monopoly refers to that market situation where there is insufficient market demand to support more than one firm and at the same time provide the opportunity to capture economies that are associated with large-scale operations. The cost advantages that can be achieved by a public utility justify support for this type of monopoly as long as price and output controls are administered by the government in the public interest. However, some industries under Federal regulation do not match the natural-monopoly prototype as closely as do those regulated by state agencies. The railroads and airlines, for example, usually operate in highly competitive national markets; several interstate railroads may serve a large metropolitan market, while only one may be available to a small rural community. Interindustry competition also exists. Railroads, for example, compete with trucking, airlines, barge lines, and automobiles. Since legislation may unintentionally restrict inter-industry competition, it requires careful analysis and alteration from time to time. While public policy toward business enterprise may not always be correct, it generally is administered in the public interest.

All this is not to imply that government is always right and business wrong or that business is always right and government wrong. Neither business nor government has a monopoly on virtue and wisdom. Both represent the actions of fallible people and both make valuable contributions to progressive democracy and economic survival. We cannot expect either one to provide all of the answers. Instead, what we should expect from them is mutual respect and responsibility. The future aspirations and problems of American society and the world as well will depend upon an expansion of the responsibilities and activities of both government and business. Government agencies and business enterprise can work together toward the common goal of a better life for all Americans.

PROBLEMS AND PROJECTS

1. Refer to *Moody's Stock Guide* in the library and obtain a description of the various products and services each of the following companies represents. Then indicate whether each company represents a horizontal, vertical, or nondirectional combination.

   Ford Motor Company   _____
   Rexall Drug and Chemical   _____
   Teledyne, Inc.   _____
   W. R. Grace   _____
   Transamerica   _____
   Kroger Grocery, Inc.   _____

2. Complete the table below with data obtained from the Business Enterprise section of the current *Statistical Abstract of the United States* (1966), p. 495, Table 694. Discover the relationship, if any, between the asset size of active corporations and economic activity. The table is divided into three sections which will allow you to rank your data as First, Second, and Last.

In other words, match the quantitative amount of each item suggested in the *Item* column of the table that is recorded in the *Abstract* according to asset size-class and rank each pair as suggested by column headings in the table. Briefly state the conclusions you have extracted from this information.

Item	First		Second		Last	
	Asset Size	*Amount*	*Asset Size*	*Amount*	*Asset Size*	*Amount*
Number of returns Total assets Total receipts Net income less deficit						

3. The income statement below is for the Williamson Supply Company. Find the percentage of net sales for each of the items.

Item	Amount (dollars)	Percentage
Net sales	$382,600	100
Cost of goods sold	210,040	
Gross profit on sales	$172,560	
Operating expenses	141,731	
Wages and salaries	$ 95,586	
Interest	9,358	
Depreciation	15,105	
Taxes	21,682	
Net profit	$ 30,829	

4. The balance sheet below is for the Williamson Supply Company. Calculate the following ratios:

Current ratio _____

Acid test _____

Accounts receivable to sales _____

(Hint: You may need to refer to Problem 3.)

Assets		Liabilities and Equity	
Current assets	$ 48,964	Current liabilities	$ 17,300
Cash	11,627	Fixed liabilities	15,000
Accounts receivable	9,005	Total liabilities	$ 33,300
Inventory	28,332	J. M. Williamson	100,664
Fixed assets	$ 85,000		
Total assets	$133,964	Total liabilities and equity	$133,964

5. An interesting article which describes the processes involved when two business firms combine is "How McDonnell Won Douglas," by T. A. Wise, *Fortune* (March, 1967), pp. 155 ff. Report on several of the incidences that you found particularly interesting.
6. An address by Henry Ford II, Chairman of the Board of Ford Motor Company, which was given in New York City on January 12, 1967, was reprinted in *U. S. News and World Report* (January 23, 1967), pp. 83–85. It presents the views of a leading businessman concerning the relationships between government and business. Read this article and outline briefly the two main conclusions.

SELECTED REFERENCES

Caves, Richard, *American Industry: Structure, Conduct, Performance.* Englewood Cliffs, N. J.: Prentice-Hall, Inc., 1964.

Jucius, Michael J., and George R. Terry, *Introduction to Business.* Homewood, Ill.: Richard D. Irwin, Inc., 1966.

McConnell, Campbell R., *Economics: Principles, Problems, and Policies*, Chap. 8. New York: McGraw-Hill Book Company, 1966.

Weiss, Leonard W., *Case Studies in American Industry*, New York: John Wiley & Sons, Inc., 1967.

5

MANAGEMENT

FUNCTIONS

A successful business depends on how businessmen make use of their available resources. This requires effective organization of the factors of production and good management of the firm's activities in the direction of sound objectives. In a business enterprise an individual or group of individuals is responsible for making the decisions necessary to direct the firm's activities.

The task of management, or the type of work managers do, involves several basic functions, commonly referred to as *management functions*. As fundamentals for business analysis, these management functions will be classified as: *planning, organizing, implementing,* and *controlling*. Although the specific requirements of these functions will vary from one firm to another and from one level of management to another, each function represents a distinct management activity. In practice, however, business managers find themselves carrying on all of these functions without any particular attention to order. Since the functions are all interdependent, the arrangement given here should not be considered as arbitrary.

The functions of management are universal and are relevant to all organized business activities. Compared to a large corporation, the organization and management of a one-man barber shop is relatively simple, but the same basic management functions are performed in each instance. This suggests that although activities may differ from one firm to another, there are still certain similarities. What is true for a business organization is also true for a governmental unit, a university, or a church. And since management is universally applicable, the president of one corporation could change jobs with the president of another corporation. This concept is often referred to as the principle of the *universality of management*. It is this characteristic that qualifies management functions as fundamentals for business analysis.

The purpose of this chapter is to explore the essential elements of each of the management functions. The characteristics and patterns of planning; the principles, practices, and patterns of organization; the characteristics and techniques of implementation; and the devices necessary for control represent the important elements that will be discussed.

PLANNING

Planning is the process of selecting and developing a course of action. In a sense, it is a blueprint for business action, the basis or foundation from which future actions emanate. The main purpose of planning is to facilitate an accomplishment—that is, to assist in getting things done properly.

Characteristics of Planning

The essential nature of planning can perhaps be best understood by pointing out several of its important characteristics. First of all, planning is a *conscious* effort. Courses of action are determined by an intellectual process. Without planning, business behavior would be random; things would just happen by chance.

Another characteristic of planning is that it is a *continuous* effort. Planning is very much a day-to-day activity. There should be a plan behind each business activity, but once the basic plans have been established, there still is a great amount of detailed or routine planning to do. For example, a basic plan to add to existing production facilities must be followed by detailed plans, which might be concerned with the actual construction of the additional facilities, the purchase of new equipment, the hiring of additional personnel, and the rearrangement of existing processes. Moreover, in a dynamic growing economic environment, changing conditions demand that business enterprises be alert and that they be prepared to appraise their plans, alter them if necessary, or even make new ones.

A third characteristic of planning is that it is a *common* effort; it is a function of every manager in an enterprise. Planning is accomplished by personnel at all levels of management, from the plant superintendent or president to the foreman or department head. It is true, however, that the nature and scope of planning will vary at these different levels. The foreman must plan his crew's efforts within a framework of predetermined guidelines and procedures; his freedom is limited compared to that of the plant superintendent. The superintendent's plans will affect more people and cut across wider areas of activity than, for example, the department head's. Because of his position in the organization structure, the superintendent may have more planning to do or may be involved in more important planning; it will usually take up a proportionately larger share of his time and effort than will the other management functions. The fact remains, however, that regardless of the level of management, planning is common to all managers.

Planning also has the characteristic of being the *primary* management function. This should not be misunderstood to mean that it is more important than organizing, implementing, or controlling. Neither does it mean that planning occurs initially and then disappears. However, planning does precede all other activities. The establishment of objectives, which is part of the planning function, must precede every worthwhile group activity. Plans are also necessary to indicate what kinds of organizational relationships are needed. In addition, the direction of people and projects depends upon predetermined arrangements. In essence, one must know *what* to do before deciding *how* to do it. Finally, planning is related to the control functions in a unique way. Control itself means correcting deviations from plans. Without an idea of what is to be accomplished, control would be meaningless. Plans provide the necessary standards.

A fifth characteristic of planning is that it is *decision oriented*. Planning is an intellectual process that involves the selection of a course of action. This selection should be made in light of the firm's objectives and expected outcomes, which themselves must be planned. A prerequisite of this process is the careful investigation of all possible alternatives. To develop alternatives, the manager must acquire a sense of discretion or a technique for limiting the vast range of choices. For example, a firm anticipating a purchase of new equipment may have several hundred models from which to choose. Half or more may be eliminated on the basis of some rigid requirement such as cost, capacity, or size. Selection from among the alternatives can then proceed according to several basic approaches. Properly used, experience provides a valuable basis for making a selection. In a marketing situation, an obvious approach is to experiment with several of the alternatives. For example, if various product designs are feasible, it may be worthwhile to test-market them before making a final selection. Finally, thorough research and analysis of each proposal can reveal important advantages and disadvantages which will provide a basis for the final selection.

The sixth characteristic of planning is that it contains an element of *risk*. Since plans involve an assessment of future conditions and events, they necessarily include a certain degree of uncertainty. The more that planning depends upon factors external to the firm such as population growth, business cycles, or the political environment, the greater the element of risk. If the factors are internal and thus more controllable, such as working conditions, morale, or levels of production, the element of risk is less. Sound planning can help reduce risk but it cannot eliminate it.

Patterns of Planning

In a business enterprise planning is accomplished in various ways. It is incorporated into business activities according to certain forms or patterns, which are classified as objectives, policies, procedures, programs, rules, and budgets.

Objectives constitute the basic purpose of the firm. An objective which is probably common to all business enterprises in the United States is profit making. However, a business firm also has other objectives. A firm may be interested in empire building and power, social prestige, public acceptance, maintaining a certain share of the market, maximizing sales revenues, being the dominant firm in the industry, developing new products and ideas, or keeping the business friendly and small.

Objectives are also established for the integral parts of a business enterprise. A department's specific objectives contribute to the overall objectives of the firm. If the objective of a mailbox manufacturer is to make a profit from the sale of mailboxes, the production department would complement this goal by establishing the objective of producing a certain number of mailboxes of a particular design at the lowest possible cost.

Planning also takes the form of *policies*, which are established by management. Policies provide broad guidelines for thought and action, while allowing subordinates to use a certain amount of discretion and judgment in resolving particular problems. The subordinates are given the authority to make decisions; policies merely confine their actions within certain limits. A policy can save time and effort especially when the same situation recurs frequently; once the policy has been established, it eliminates the need to evaluate and analyze the situation over and over again. Policies also add an element of consistency to business activities. For example, if credit policies are applied to all customers in the same manner, no one can suspect unfair treatment. Good employee relations can be promoted by policies particularly when they are written and understood; employees develop a sense of confidence because they know what is expected of them.

There are many categories or types of policies. A price policy for salesmen may state that the firm intends to meet competitive prices. It may be personnel policy to grant promotions from within the organization, while "the customer is always right" is a merchandise policy. An example of a product policy is the one which states that the quality of craftsmanship will not be sacrificed for production shortcuts. Policies like these and many more are used extensively by business enterprises.

Another pattern of planning frequently found in a business enterprise is the *procedure*. Procedures are truly guides to action because they give strict attention to the manner in which a certain activity must be performed. In this way, they facilitate, even insure, certain results. Common to most procedures is the step-by-step sequence of tasks. For example, the procedure for handling an incoming order for mailboxes may contain several steps; this insures that the order will be properly handled by the various departments involved. The sale must be recorded, payment acknowledged or credit established, instructions issued to obtain the mailboxes from stock, and finally shipping and billing arrangements completed. All these activities will be contained and described in the firm's procedure for handling incoming orders. Procedures of this kind are appropriate to many business activities, particularly those that are routine in nature.

The *program*, another pattern of planning, represents a major effort requiring a combination of policies and procedures. A program usually is associated with a massive undertaking, involving the major segments, if not the entire operations, of a company. For example, a firm may decide to engage in several mergers, expand operations, develop a new division, improve customer relations, or improve employee morale. In recent years, the J. C. Penney Company has followed a program to convert itself into a full-line department store and mail-order firm. In the process the firm's image has changed, new stores have been built, new policies have been developed concerning credit sales, and many procedures have been established to complement these changes.

The fifth pattern of planning, the *rule*, is similar to the procedure; it too is a guide to action. However, it is quite different in one respect. Unlike the procedure, the rule is not related to a series or sequence of acts. The rule also is more definite and specific. It does not allow for discretion or judgment as policies do, but rather it reflects a prior decision that requires a definite action for a specific situation. For example, "Waitresses will not smoke when serving" is a rule that is very definite, pertains to a specific situation, and allows for no discretion. This particular rule is designed to insure proper appearance and hygiene. Many such rules are common to business enterprises.

Finally *budgets*, which represent another form of planning, deserve brief mention. Budgets are quantitative statements of future expectations. They may be expressed in dollars and cents, units of output, units of resource, or units of time. Budgets provide the guidelines for the control function. Because the construction of budgets requires advanced thinking, they qualify as a planning device.

ORGANIZING

Organizing is the process of grouping and assigning the activities required to accomplish a firm's objectives. It is concerned with the delegation of authority and the span of control. The purpose of the entire organizing effort

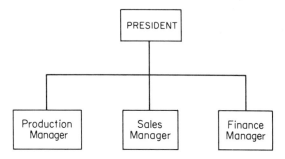

FIGURE 5-1.   Sample functional organizational structure.

or process is to bring together the individual parts of a firm and transform them into one working unit. The cooperation and coordination that are thus achieved can mean more efficient production. The essence of organization is that it makes possible even to small firms the achievements usually associated with large-scale, mass-production industries. It is our purpose here to investigate certain principles and practices of organization and some basic patterns of organization.

Grouping and Assignment of Activities

The grouping of activities in a business enterprise is very often accomplished along *functional* lines. The basic operating functions of a business enterprise consist of *production* (creating or making something useful), *marketing* (promoting, selling, and distributing goods), and *financing* (acquiring funds and paying for activities). Often different terms will be used for the same or similar activities. For example, a railroad may be departmentalized into operations, traffic, and finance divisions. The relative importance of each of these functions will also vary from firm to firm. A manufacturing firm whose significant area is production may de-emphasize its selling activities. Another firm may emphasize selling and have very little to do with actual production. A firm organized along functional lines would have an organizational structure similar to that illustrated in Fig. 5–1.

Another very common way to group a firm's activities is on a *product* basis. When certain production and sales activities are closely identified with a particular line of goods, it may become feasible to set up a separate division for these products. A chemical company, for example, may set up a division each for gases, liquids, and solids. An organizational structure illustrating departmentalization along product lines is depicted in Fig. 5–2.

Grouping by products, however, may be suitable only for very large firms. In a small firm, the specialization of finance, advertising, engineering, and transportation activities would usually be ruled out, although in large

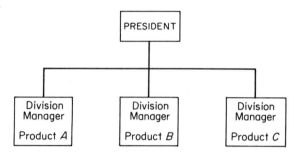

FIGURE 5-2. Organizational structure showing departmentalization according to product lines.

firms, specialization of these activities may even exist within each division. When a firm's activities are grouped upon product lines, the operating functions (production, sales, and finance) become an integral part of each division.

There are other bases upon which workloads can be divided. For example, a firm may group activities upon a *customer* basis. A large furniture and equipment manufacturer might departmentalize its selling activities according to its types of customers—industrial, commercial, medical, or household. Operations may also be grouped on a *geographical* basis. This is particularly relevant when a firm's operations are widely dispersed. A firm might typically divide its firm into Eastern, Western, and Foreign divisions.

Once the firm's activities have been grouped, the next consideration is to assign them to individuals according to their skills. When the activity and the skills are similar, the process of assignment is easily accomplished on a *logical* basis; when they are not, other means must be instituted. For example, engineering could be assigned either to sales or production, depending upon the particular emphasis of the firm. It would be assigned on the basis of where it would have the *most use*. Another guide to use when similarities do not exist is *interest*. If the production manager has the necessary mathematical background and an interest in market research and economic forecasting, he should be chosen to perform these activities instead of a sales manager who does not.

Span of Control

Grouping and assignment of activities are vital to the management process because of the limitations of human ability and time. It is humanly impossible to manage effectively an infinite number of subordinates. For example, it would be ridiculous for the president of General Mortors to be the sole manager with every employee being required to report to him. The scope of organization is such that in order for management to be effective, a certain *span of control* must be established. The span of control is the number of subordinates a manager can handle effectively.

Over the years, the general rule has developed that an effective span of control ranges from three to seven subordinates. While there is a limit to the number of subordinates a manager can effectively handle, the optimum number depends upon various circumstances. For one thing, the more routine the tasks are that must be accomplished, the larger is the number of subordinates that can be managed. Furthermore, the activities, training, and skills of both managers and subordinates vary significantly. A well-trained, able manager can command a large group of dependable, intelligent, well-trained workers. Just the opposite would be true if both the manager and his subordinates were incompetent.

Closely related to span of control is the *unity of command* principle, which states that each subordinate should report to only one superior. This principle is basic to effective management. In application, it works in two directions. Every subordinate in the organization should know *to whom* he is responsible, and every supervisor should know *for whom* he is responsible. While it is possible for a subordinate to be responsible to two or more masters, the practical difficulties are obvious. For one thing, the subordinate may develop a conflict of goals. In addition, buck-passing becomes more likely. Unity of command considers the proper number of superiors, in contrast to span of control, which considers the proper number of subordinates.

Delegation of Authority

Delegation of authority is the vital link in organization. Grouping and assignment of activities are meaningless unless subordinate managers are given the power to command. A subordinate must be given the right amount of authority to accomplish an assigned job. Too little authority may dampen his initiative or even frustrate him because he is not able to perform as he should. Too much authority, resulting in overlap among individuals and duplication of activities, may cause confusion in the organization.

There are several principles or practices associated with the delegation of authority. Generally, it is a good practice for authority to be written out and to be specific; this removes much uncertainty. However, at higher levels of management, it may be more desirable not to be specific. It is argued that at higher levels more flexibility is required for managers to acquire adequate experience and develop properly. In any event, clarity is important. Even if the delegation is not specific, it should be accompanied by a definite understanding between the parties involved as to its nature.

Under certain circumstances, it may be wise to share authority, particularly on decisions that will affect the entire organization. A decision on the quality, design, and price of a new product may require that the managers of the production, sales, and finance departments share authority by combining their efforts.

Authority and responsibility should be commensurate. A subordinate should not be expected to perform his duties without adequate authority. If he has not been given the authority, for example, to requisition materials and equipment, he should not be held responsible for not completing an assignment because of lack of supplies. The superior should first look at the task he expects his subordinates to do and then determine how much authority should be granted to accomplish the job.

When an occasion arises where a subordinate does not have the authority to make a certain decision, it should be made at a higher level. However, only those decisions that cannot be made at a given level should be referred upward in the organization. It would be a violation of the entire concept of delegation if a subordinate were given adequate authority for certain decisions and then continuously referred those decisions to a higher echelon. Another important characteristic of authority that may be mentioned here is that delegated authority can be recovered when the need arises. The superior does not permanently dispossess himself of his power by delegating it. He can take it back whenever he desires.

The degree to which authority in a business enterprise is delegated from the upper levels to the lower levels of management depends upon the attitude of top-level management. The president of one firm may keep almost all authority in his own hands, while another may delegate a substantial amount of authority to his subordinates. The true significance of any managerial position depends upon the extent to which authority is centralized or decentralized. A highly centralized organization reduces the number of subordinate managers and increases the span of control of top-level management. On the other hand, decentralized management makes use of more managers and limits the span of control of each. It also provides an opportunity to train managers who may someday be the leaders of the organization.

There is a difference between advocating delegation of authority and actually doing it. The latter requires a certain attitude on the part of the delegator. He must be willing to accept the idea that sometimes the subordinate will make a decision which may not be to his particular liking or preference. Furthermore, once he has delegated the authority, he must give it a chance to work and not continuously meddle in the decision-making process of his subordinates. That can only undermine their confidence. It is good practice to be somewhat removed physically from the subordinates' work areas. In addition, the superior should learn to trust his subordinates and to expect them to make some mistakes. Learning from one's mistakes is a valuable element in management development. Of course, the superior should have some effective means of controlling activities. This control should be general enough to allow discretion, but adequate to keep operations from getting out of hand.

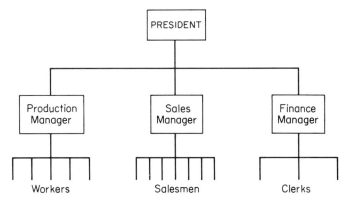

FIGURE 5-3.   Sample line organization structure.

Patterns of Organization

Authority relationships in a business enterprise are reflected by its organizational structure, which generally will vary with the firm's particular requirements. Firms engaged in different kinds of business and even firms that produce the same type of goods will have different organizational structures. Although there is no single structure that is suitable to all circumstances, it would be worthwhile to explore two basic patterns of organization: the *line* organization and the *line-and-staff* organization. In small organizations these two patterns may appear quite simple, while in larger organizations they are modified extensively.

The *line* organization refers to that kind of relationship in which a superior exercises direct command over a subordinate. It is the simplest pattern, signifying a direct flow of authority from top to bottom. The chain of command used in military organizations is such an arrangement. A line organization is shown in Fig. 5-3. Two levels of management are illustrated. These can be referred to as top management and middle management. Note that there is a direct relationship from the president to each manager and down to the workers. The president has three lines of authority, one through each manager.

The line organization can be expanded to cope with the growth of a firm by merely adding additional levels or additional units at each level. For example, if the firm expands to two plants, then two plant superintendents can be established directly under the production manager, with workers being responsible to their respective plant superintendents. Lines of authority can be established within each plant through foremen, and so on. Likewise, an existing organization can be expanded by adding workers to the present arrangements. The same kind of changes could be applied to the other operating functions. An expanded version of the line organization structure is illustrated in Fig. 5-4.

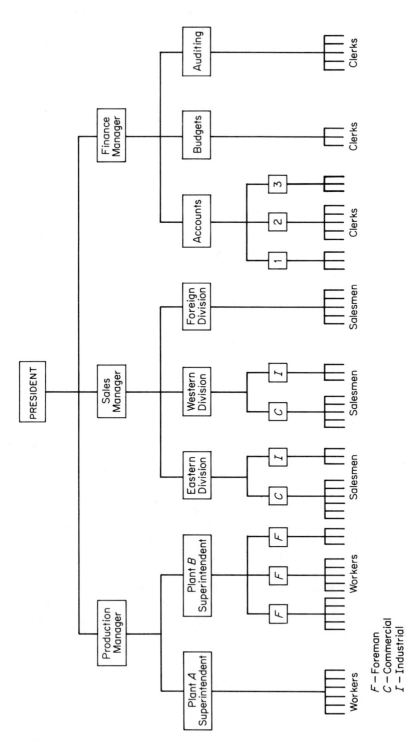

FIGURE 5-4. Sample line organization structure with workers.

F – Foreman
C – Commercial
I – Industrial

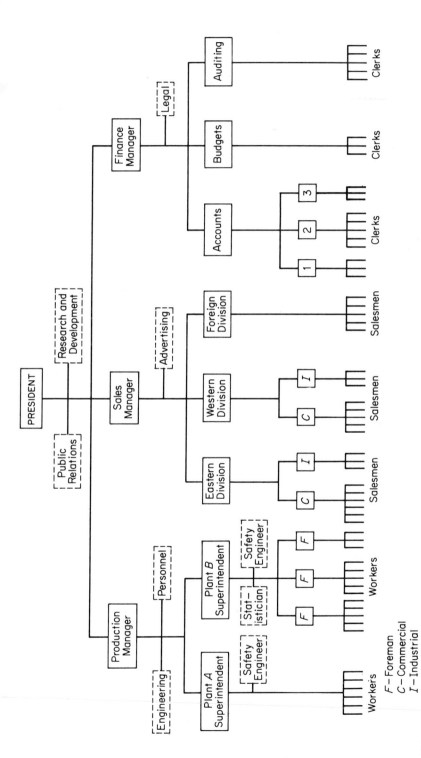

FIGURE 5-5. Sample "line-and-staff" organization structure.

F – Foreman
C – Commercial
I – Industrial

The *line-and-staff* organization is the other basic pattern of organization. It is the combination of two kinds of authority relationships: *line*, which is command, and *staff*, which is advisory. Staff personnel are usually specialists in a certain field who give counsel to their supervisor. Within their respective departments, they have line authority over their own subordinates. Line and staff designations do not refer to a type of departmentalization; activities are not grouped according to whether they are line or staff in nature. Rather, the terms characterize authority relationships. Research and development may be a staff function in one company and a line function in another. The nature of the business activity will usually determine what authority relationships it will have.

Staff positions can be created at all levels of management. For example, the president of a company might want to have a public-relations specialist and a department to perform overall research and development activities immediately below him but not in a direct line with other personnel. The sales manager can have staff personnel handle all the advertising for the firm. The finance manager might need a legal advisor, and the production manager may desire two staff members, one for engineering matters and one to handle personnel relations and union negotiations. A plant superintendent may require a safety engineer to maintain proper working conditions, or a statistician to supervise quality control. Thus line and staff relationships can be combined to produce a *line-and-staff* organization such as the one illustrated in Fig. 5–5.

The staff in a line-and-staff organization have advisory authority. The line managers hold the command authority which flows from top to bottom, and make the final decisions. The line-and-staff organization gives a firm the use of expert counsel while preserving the lines of authority necessary for business decisions.

A special type of authority relationship is *functional authority*, which is often superimposed upon a *line* or a *line-and-staff* pattern of organization. It often emerges when personnel with special skills, such as staff members, are delegated the authority to issue instructions directly to the line organization. At first, the staff man is given the authority to provide information and advice to line subordinates. Next, he may offer actual proposals and consult with the line subordinates. Finally, functional authority is firmly established when he is allowed to actually direct certain activities. For example, the personnel director who is a staff member responsible to the production manager (see Fig. 5–5) may be given functional authority over the plant superintendent concerning certain personnel practices. The personnel director may be responsible for conducting interviews and tests, administering wages and salaries, and handling grievances as well as for other matters concerning personnel relations. This functional authority is illustrated by the dashed lines in Fig. 5–6.

Notice in Fig. 5–6 that functional authority does not extend beyond the level immediately below that of the staff member's own superior. This is generally a good practice in order to preserve as much as possible the line executives' unity of command.

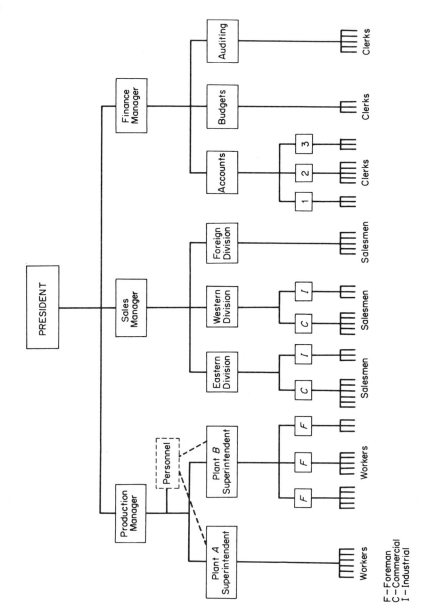

FIGURE 5-6. Functional authority in a "line-and-staff" organization structure: personnel director.

F — Foreman
C — Commercial
I — Industrial

103

Functional authority is also exercised by line managers. For example, a sales manager may have authority over the plant superintendent concerning packaging and certain design modifications. This type of functional authority is illustrated in Fig. 5–7.

Functional authority should be used with caution because it violates one of the basic principles of management, the principle of unity of command. Generally, functional authority should be limited to specific activities and should be completely understood by the personnel involved. However, strong justification for the use of functional authority should not be ignored. Functional authority can be expanded into a formal organizational structure in which specialists are responsible for specific phases of all operations. They consequently possess line authority over a portion of all employee activities, and each employee will therefore have more than one supervisor.

The discussion so far has revolved around what is generally known as *formal* organization. However, group behavior also involves *informal* organization. Informal organization is the result of the contact that occurs at coffee breaks, cocktail parties, Christmas parties, the car pool, and various other activities that bring personnel together. The type of informal relationship most commonly found in a formal organization is the so-called "grapevine." The grapevine thrives on information and is probably the most important way information is unofficially transmitted to all members of the organization. Being a trusted participant in the grapevine can be an invaluable aid to a manager who likes to receive information from lower echelons and from his own subordinates.

IMPLEMENTING

Implementing is simply the act of putting into use the plans and organizational relationships that have been established. As a management function, implementing involves the direction of people and procedures and the staffing of personnel. Specific matters such as discipline, morale, communication, and various directing techniques will be discussed in this section.

Directing

Directing involves guiding and supervising subordinates. It is through them that work assignments are achieved. The manager also directs procedures and methods as well as people. Although procedures and methods govern the specific duties of people, they also depend on people for their fulfillment; therefore, it is not necessary to separate one from the other when discussing implementation.

When authority is delegated to a subordinate, he receives the power to direct. However, directing is more than just ordering or commanding things

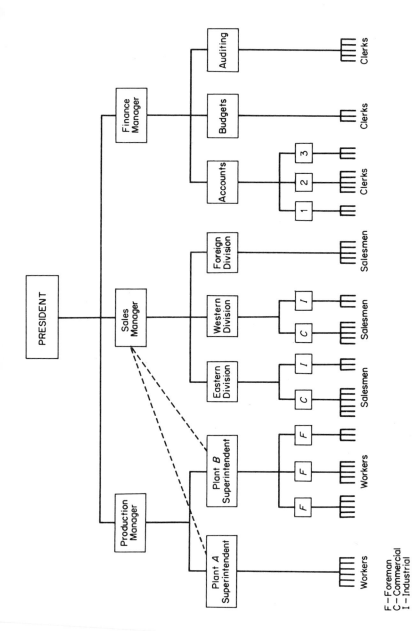

FIGURE 5-7. Functional authority in a "line-and-staff" organization structure: sales manager.

F – Foreman
C – Commercial
I – Industrial

105

to be done; it requires that people respond favorably to these orders. It is thus very important for a manager to also be a good leader. He must motivate his subordinates in such a way that both their needs and the goals of the enterprise are fulfilled. The manager also plays the role of a pseudo-teacher. He must explain, illustrate, describe, and correct his subordinates. It is not surprising, therefore, that an interest in human relations and a knowledge of individual and group psychology are fundamental requirements of a good business manager. By the same token, human-relations remedies can be dangerously exaggerated and improperly applied if they are assumed to be some sort of "cure-all" for all production and labor problems.

Discipline and Morale

Discipline and morale are two ingredients that are vital to the behavior of subordinates. It is important for subordinates to conform to rules, orders, procedures, and other acceptable practices. Discipline appears to be related in a special way to the respect a subordinate has for his superior; it is dependent upon the mutual understanding they share for some common purpose and upon the leadership qualities of the superior himself.

When disciplinary action is required, it should be administered with the purpose of improving the behavior of subordinates and not as punishment. Most disciplinary actions are negative in nature; they include such things as delays in promotion, transfer to a less desirable position, forfeiture of a wage increase, or even dismissal.

Morale is not nearly as specific as discipline and is therefore more difficult to explain. It can be thought of as a state of mind and is closely akin to attitude. Morale depends upon one's attitude, on a sense of well-being, recognition, belonging, doing something worthwhile, and so on. There have been conflicting results in research conducted on the effects that fatigue, monotony, illumination of work areas, rest periods, and human relations have on morale and productivity. Certain social and psychological factors such as association with a group, recognition, self-respect, and a feeling of participation seem to be very important in improving morale and in bringing about increased productivity. It appears, then, that the subordinate is interested not only in the higher income that may result from greater productivity but also with the social and psychological values associated with the working environment.

Communication

The guidance and supervision of subordinates requires communication. Information about objectives, selected courses of action, and procedures should be transmitted to all personnel in an organization before the organizational machinery is put into motion. The purpose of direction is to inform, to instruct, to oversee, and to improve the performance of subordinates. All of these goals require effective communication between superior and subordinate.

Information can be transmitted in two basic ways, orally or in writing. Oral transmission can be accomplished in person or by mechanical means such as telephones. Face-to-face communication has an advantage in that it allows for immediate "feedback." The participants can observe each others' reactions, including facial expressions, and correct or clarify the communication. Although written communications are more time-consuming than oral communications, there are several good reasons for using them. They are particularly appropriate for policies and procedures as well as for instructions which are lengthy or involved or which require frequent referral. They also are permanent, making it difficult for subordinates to deny their existence.

Patterns of communication are classified according to the direction of their flow: down, up, or across; each type has distinct features. A brief examination of these patterns will suffice. Obviously communication from superior to subordinate is in the downward direction. If it is an order or a directive, it is expected to be obeyed. Upward patterns are more informative in nature, and are vital to the manager's control over operations, through them, information about performance and results are transmitted from the lower echelons. Horizontal communication has no regard for lines of authority. The conference is widely used for this type of communication; it is particularly useful when many persons are required to coordinate operations and when it is important to assure common understanding. The conference provides an excellent opportunity to exchange ideas and viewpoints.

Directing Techniques

There are three general techniques commonly used by supervisors to direct activities: the *dictatorial, loose-rein*, and *participative* methods. The choice of methods depends upon the attitude of the supervisor, the type of subordinates, and the situation.

The *dictatorial* method develops naturally from a supervisor's belief that he must assume full control of the organization, usually because he has little confidence in his subordinates and feels that he cannot trust them to act for themselves. This attitude may stem from the superior's own personality or from the fact that his subordinates really are not capable. They may lack the intelligence, educational attributes, training, or experience necessary to perform without definite orders, minute and specific instructions, and close supervision.

As a matter of fact, the nature and personality of a subordinate may demand the use of the dictatorial method. Uneducated and timid persons may depend upon such a method and may become frustrated and emotionally upset without it. And often an overly aggressive subordinate requires the firm hand of a dictatorial manager. Dictatorial direction is also justified when the time element or the safety factor is important. Sometimes the occasion does not allow enough time to warrant the use of any other method; at other times, strict adherence to safety practices depends upon strong directives.

The *loose-rein* method implies that subordinates are given substantial freedom to act, although the superior usually provides broad guidelines for action. This method is particularly useful for developing the potentialities of subordinates. It stimulates their initiative and creative imagination, and allows them to respond with the maximum effort. However, the superior must be willing to delegate substantial authority; this method of direction allows very little supervision compared to the dictatorial method. The loose-rein method can be extremely successful when the subordinates are highly educated or well trained.

The third technique, *participative* direction, is just that. When the manager consults with his subordinates he automatically implicates them in departmental plans and decisions. The informal or formal conference is the device most often used to achieve participative direction. Subordinates usually respond to this technique because they gain a feeling of importance and a better understanding of why certain actions are taken. Since they themselves have had a hand in developing the directives, they are more likely to react favorably to them. Individual and group psychology play vital roles in determining the success of this method.

Staffing

No business can run without people. The individuals who operate a business enterprise can make or break it; its success depends upon the type of personnel hired at the subordinate level as well as at the management level. Staffing basically involves the recruitment, selection, training, promotion, retirement, and dismissal of all personnel in an organization. It must be remembered that these activities are not entirely controlled by business management. Decisions are influenced by Federal and state laws, social pressures, union demands, and workers' desires as well as by the goals of business management itself.

Although at first gance the goals of management and labor may seem quite opposed, they have a direct relationship to each other. Business firms need profits to survive, but the survival of the firm is also of vital interest to the worker, who desires a satisfactory income and good working conditions so that he can achieve his personal goals. And the business firm in turn depends upon the contributions of labor to achieve its goals.

Nevertheless, there are bound to be conflicts at times, because there is an inverse relationship between profits and labor costs. Profits may be sacrified for higher labor costs, or vice versa. The task of labor and management is to reach some workable solution. The public interest is also involved in this process particularly when prolonged disagreement results in unnecessarily long idleness of both workers and capital. The public may also be adversely affected when labor and management reach agreement without taking into account the public interest. Business may succeed in satisfying profit goals and labor demands at the cost of unwarranted higher prices for consumers.

The government has shown a keen interest in American workers since the 1930's. Social security laws, compensation laws, and other laws affecting the working environment have paved the way for improved social and economic conditions. Labor unions have also played an important role in improving the lot of the American worker. The union has become the workers' chief spokesman in labor-management disputes.

The work-force requirement of a business enterprise depends upon the type of product or service produced and the manufacturing method employed. One firm may require a highly skilled machine operator, while another may need large numbers of unskilled workers. The work-force requirement will also determine to what extent training programs will exist and what kind they will be.

At managerial levels, personnel requirements depend upon whether the firm is centralized or decentralized. A decentralized firm must take greater care in selecting its managers than would a centralized firm which can depend upon a few top-level men.

The number of personnel needed depends upon sales and production schedules. Overall requirements are broken down into the various departments: a certain number of machine operators, drivers, typists, and so on. Once the manufacturing process is determined, the number will still vary, since production and sales requirements will continue to change.

Generally speaking, selection of personnel consists of finding and hiring the people with the skills needed for a particular job. There are two steps involved in this process. First, the requirements of the job should be determined and described. The abilities of prospective employees should then be measured to see who best matches the job. Some recognition and consideration should be given to the employee's potential for future development and advancement within the organization.

Recruitment is a part of this selection process that precedes the actual hiring. When business enterprises actively seek out prospective employees and encourage them to apply for employment, they are engaged in recruitment. This is generally done to provide management with a wider range of selection. It is justified on the basis that a poor selection is costly to the firm.

After an individual has been selected and hired for a particular position, it is usually wise to provide some sort of *orientation* to acquaint him with the firm's operation and with his particular job. The employee's job and responsibilities should be clearly spelled out, and he should know what his relationship is to the other members of the department. Properly conducted, orientation can be beneficial to both the employee and the organization.

Training of personnel for particular jobs depends upon the job requirements and the employees' own skills. Business enterprises are vitally concerned with utilizing their work forces with maximum efficiency. High levels of productivity depend upon the use of modern equipment and trained personnel. This can justify higher salaries and greater job security. However, training must be a continuous process if it is to provide continuous job security. As new skills are demanded, old skills should be abandoned.

Promotion, transfer, and *dismissal* are other activities closely related to staffing. A clearly-defined promotion policy should be established by a business enterprise to reduce future friction within the organization. Two basic approaches can be developed. A firm may promote from within, relying on its own employees to fill positions, or it may fill them with personnel from outside the firm; the use of either method depends upon the circumstances. Transfers refer to changes in assignment that usually do not involve a change in the level of responsibility; otherwise it would be a promotion. Transfers can be requested by the employee or initiated by management in the interest of the firm. Dismissal is the termination of employment. Although it is sometimes necessary, justifying it is often difficult. It is not good practice for a firm to have a reputation for high dismissals. It affects morale, damages the firm's image, and increases costs associated with employee turnover.

CONTROLLING

Controlling is the management function which attempts to achieve conformity between goals and results. This necessarily requires management to determine precisely what is occurring and to alter operations if the organization is not achieving its goals. There are several distinct steps that should be followed if control is to be accomplished. First, there must be some norm or standard of performance established for each operation. Second, the actual performance should be compared with the standard. Third, the reason for any deviation, if one exists, must be uncovered. And fourth, corrective action must be applied.

We will not expound on standards other than to say that they are predetermined measures of achievement. Standards are established in production, sales, and finance. They may be considered in physical terms or monetary terms, and may be quantitative or qualitative. For example, man-hours per unit of output and barrels transported per unit of horsepower are quantitative measures; closeness of tolerance and durability levels are qualitative. Cost standards, revenue standards, and capital standards arise from the application of monetary measurements to physical items; machine costs per unit of output, sales per capita, and typical financial ratios are but a few examples.

Essentially, the procedure for comparing performance with standards consists of establishing a system of checks on certain key operations and procedures. In this way, mistakes or deviations are detected at critical points. Management by exception is a procedure commonly used: certain limits or standards are established, and if they are attained, no management action is taken.

The procedure for comparing performance with standards requires the use of a control device. Often budgets are used as control devices because they reflect anticipated performance. Other devices such as statistical techniques, special reports, charts, and personal observations may be used in the control process.

To test performance, vast amounts of data must be collected and analyzed. The application of statistical techniques and the use of electronic data processing systems are essential to this task. Sampling techniques, statistical measures of location and variation, tests of significance, and control charts are just a few procedures that can be used.

The statistical control chart is a device that is commonly used with production processes that require continuous attention. Consider the Hypothetical Mailbox Manufacturing Company, which prides itself on producing waterproof mailboxes. The company's cutting process must produce uniform pieces, since the waterproof feature depends upon tightly fitting parts. Hence, once the process has been designed and installed, it is of the utmost importance to maintain precision cutting of the mailbox parts. This requires continuous observation and periodic checking of the process to insure that the cuttings remain within tolerance levels. For example, the equipment used in the cutting process could deteriorate from use and reduce the quality level of the process. The task, therefore, is to set up a quality control procedure.

The quality control procedure requires a periodic sampling of the cuttings. A particular cutting may need to be 20 inches long, plus or minus a small tolerance, in order to fit properly with the other parts of the mailbox. The procedure may call for a sample of five cuttings to be measured every two hours. The mean or average measurement of the sample is then recorded on a control chart. A portion of a control chart, with the cuttings that were checked on one particular day, is illustrated in Fig. 5–8. The dashed lines are the upper and lower control levels, which reflect the acceptable amount of variation from sample to sample. These control limits depend upon the standard deviation of sample means. (The mean and the standard deviation are explained in Chapter 19.)

Since control limits are usually based upon 3 standard deviations, the area between the two control limits would represent the range in which 99 per cent of the sample means are expected to appear. A sample mean recorded outside either tolerance level could indicate that the process was out of control. This indication could occur merely by chance or it could be attributed to various identifiable causes, among which might be those caused by operator error, worn parts, a machine in need of adjustment, or electrical power variations. The control chart also will indicate that the process is going out of control if a definite pattern of points emerges within the tolerance levels. For example, an upward trend of points would indicate that the process is

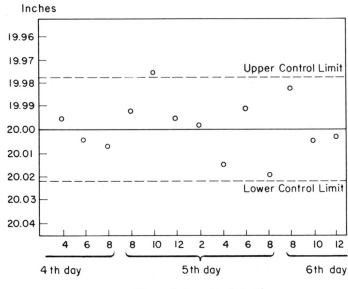

FIGURE 5–8.   Control chart.

gradually cutting longer and longer pieces. This might be due to a gradual voltage drop which is causing a slight time delay in the placement of the cutting apparatus. An established trend on a control chart can indicate corrective action before serious difficulties arise.

Determining the cause and taking corrective action are the third and fourth steps of the control function. If the deterioration in the output of a particular machine was caused by a worn part, the corrective action would be to replace the part. No further discussion of these two steps are offered because they usually depend upon very specific circumstances.

In conclusion, it can be stated that the manager of a business enterprise performs four distinct management functions: planning, organizing, implementing, and controlling. In addition to these functions, he performs one more essential task. He brings together all the separate elements, activities, and functions to form a cohesive unit. An organization that involves more than one person or product or .process requires *coordination*. This is not achieved by an order or directive; it requires understanding and appreciation of the efforts of others in relation to one's own tasks and the acceptance of joint action. It is more than cooperation because it implies a combination of efforts to achieve an objective. People can cooperate and still not achieve anything. Coordination binds together the functions of management and the efforts of everyone in the organization.

ANNEX: INVENTORY CONTROL MODEL

Modern approaches to the problem of inventory control are based on mathematical models, which range from simple mathematical ones to complicated probabilistic ones, depending upon the circumstances and the assumptions.

A simple model known as the economic-order-quantity or EOQ model is a basic step in treating the more sophisticated inventory models. This simple model is based on two considerations: the cost of holding goods and the cost of ordering and procuring goods or raw materials. The holding costs, sometimes referred to as carrying costs, can include such items as storage costs and interest costs on cash used to buy inventory. Reorder costs involve the placement and delivery of an order.

The usual plan is to hold carrying costs down by maintaining the smallest inventory possible to meet requirements. However, smaller inventories require more frequent orders and deliveries; therefore, reorder costs increase. Carrying costs and reorder costs change inversely to each other as different inventory levels are maintained. If small inventories are desired, reorder costs increase; if reorder costs are restricted, larger inventories are necessary and carrying costs increase. The objective is to find the optimal inventory level—that is, to select the quantities to order and intervals between orders that will minimize both carrying costs and reorder costs. If reduced inventories are preferred, savings in inventory costs must be balanced against increased reorder costs.

The solution to this model assumes that a certain quantity of materials is ordered and that it is depleted in the production process on a straight-line basis until all the materials are gone; that a replenishment consisting of the same quantity of materials is placed in the stockpile and then used up at the same rate as before, and so on. These assumptions can be portrayed as a sawtooth graph, as in Fig. 5–9.

Underlying the model are several other assumptions:

1. There is a constant cost of procuring each unit of material.
2. There is a constant cost of holding each unit per unit of time.
3. All necessary capital and storage space are available.

This model has proved useful when large numbers of low-cost units are involved which are used regularly; it can be illustrated by applying it to the Hypothetical Mailbox Manufacturing Company. First the necessary formulas and equations are developed in general terms; then the appropriate data pertaining to the production of mailboxes are inserted in the formulas. Let:

D = quantity of raw materials delivered per shipment

c = carrying costs involved in holding one unit of inventory
for one year

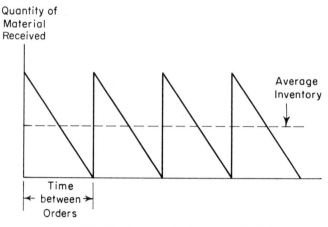

FIGURE 5-9.   Sawtooth graph of inventory depletion.

$\dfrac{D}{2}$ = average inventory, since $\dfrac{(D + 0)}{2}$ represents the inventory which lies halfway between the top and the bottom of the sawtooth graph

Therefore, the total carrying cost (TCC) is:

$$\text{TCC} = \frac{cD}{2}.$$

This is the annual carrying cost per unit times the average number of units in inventory. Now let

Q = total units of material needed per year

$\dfrac{Q}{D}$ = required number of deliveries each year

$a + bD$ = cost per delivery, where a is the administrative cost of processing an order and b is the shipping cost per item

The total annual reorder cost (TRC) is

$$\text{TRC} = (a + bD)\,\frac{Q}{D},$$

or

$$\text{TRC} = \frac{aQ}{D} + bQ.$$

Combining TCC and TRC results in a total cost (TC) as follows:

$$TC = TCC + TRC,$$

or

$$TC = \frac{cD}{2} + \frac{aQ}{D} + bQ.$$

This equation represents the total cost the manufacturer lays out on his inventory. Now suppose in the case of manufacturing mailboxes that $Q = 120$ units, $c = \$6$, $a = \$20$, and $b = \$8$. Then

$$TC = \frac{6D}{2} + \frac{20\ (120)}{D} + 8\ (120)$$

$$TC = 3D + \frac{2,400}{D} + 960.$$

The optimal value for D in order to minimize TC can be determined by solving the equation for TC with various values of D and then selecting the value of D that minimizes TC. When the arbitrary values of 10, 20, 30, 40, and 50 are used for D, the following table results:

D	10	20	30	40	50
TC	$1,230	$1,140	$1,130	$1,140	$1,158

When D is equal to 30 in the equation, TC is $1,130; this is the minimum TC for all of the D's used. The optimum reorder quantity is therefore approximately 30 units. Since 120 units are needed for the entire year, it is clear that four orders per year of 30 units each would be required.

This problem can also be solved by using calculus.[1] The procedure is

---

[1] The following details are given to expose students to the application of calculus to a business problem. The formula for D is derived as follows:

$$TC = \frac{cD}{2} + \frac{aQ}{D} + bQ$$

$$\frac{d(TC)}{d(D)} = \frac{c}{2} - \frac{aQ}{D^2}$$

$$0 = \frac{c}{2} - \frac{aQ}{D^2}$$

$$\frac{c}{2} = \frac{aQ}{D^2}$$

$$D^2 = \frac{2aQ}{c}$$

$$D = \sqrt{\frac{2aQ}{c}}.$$

Unless a student has knowledge of differential calculus, his understanding of this derivation will be limited.

to take the derivative of the expression for TC with respect to D, set this derivative equal to zero, and solve for D. This results in the following formula:

$$D = \sqrt{\frac{2aQ}{c}}.$$

This formula tells us that inventory should increase proportionately to the square root of the annual requirements Q. Substituting the figures for a, Q, and c used in the previous method, we have

$$D = \sqrt{\frac{2 \times 20 \times 120}{6}}$$
$$D = \sqrt{800}$$
$$D = 28.3.$$

Thus the exact answer to the problem is determined.

PROBLEMS AND PROJECTS

1. Construct an organizational chart for the Hypothetical Mailbox Manufacturing Company, which is a corporation. The company has two assembly plants; it markets its product through hardware wholesalers and by direct sales to department stores. In addition to a vice president for each of the operating functions, there is a legal counsel who advises the president. The vice president in charge of production has an engineering staff and a statistician who has functional authority over each plant manager in regard to quality control. Each plant manager has a director for personnel and labor relations. There are three departments in each plant—purchasing, operations, and storage. Direct sales to department stores are handled by one sales manager and several salesmen. Four sales managers and several salesmen are geographically located to service wholesalers. The department managers for accounting and development report directly to the vice president in charge of finance.

2. The following is a small case problem for you to study and solve, if you think a solution is necessary:

   Among his other duties, Dr. Stewart, the statistician of the Hypothetical Mailbox Manufacturing Company, is responsible to Mr. Vickery, vice president in charge of production, for quality control in all six departments in the operations division of each plant. At each of the two plants, Dr. Stewart has an assistant who periodically obtains and records production samples at various production points in each department. The assistant in the Eastern plant is Mr. Allison, a recent college graduate who graduated *cum laude* with a double major in mathematics and business administration. When Mr. Allison notices an undesirable trend developing on a control chart, he immediately tells the worker that he is out of line and had better be careful. Often Mr. Allison shows the worker how to improve his operating procedure.

After lunch one day, Mr. Willard, a relatively new employee in the cutting department of the Eastern plant, was severely reprimanded by the cutting department supervisor, Mr. Sumpter, who incidentally has been with the company for 30 years. Before Mr. Sumpter could continue, Mr. Willard explained that Mr. Allison had told him that the quality of his work was falling off and then had shown him how to deviate from the normal procedure, explaining that the existing procedures were out-of-date. Mr. Sumpter told Mr. Willard that he was not to deviate from the alleged "out-of-date" standard operating procedures; that he would receive a written directive from Mr. Sumpter's office when a deviation was authorized. The next day Mr. Willard called in and said that he was quitting.

The following day Mr. Sumpter received a phone call from Mr. Vickery, the vice president in charge of production. Mr. Vickery stated that he had heard from the personnel director at the Eastern plant that Mr. Willard, whom they had spent considerable time and effort in recruiting, had quit. After a polite exchange of words, Mr. Sumpter finally said, "Look here, Mr. Vickery, I am kind of fed up with the entire mess here myself." Mr. Vickery replied, "Just hold on, Pete. Haven't we always been close friends? You should have come directly to me long before this."

What do you think about the situation? Have any principles of management been violated? If so, explain. Present your suggestions concerning the problem and how you might correct the situation.
3. Solve the following problem, based upon the material in the Annex. Determine the economic order quantity *D* for an inventory problem where *a* (administrative cost) is $8, *Q* (total units demanded per year) is 300 units, and *c* (carrying cost to hold one unit of inventory for one year) is $3.

SELECTED REFERENCES

Koontz, Harold, and Cyril O'Donnell, *Principles of Management*, New York: McGraw-Hill Book Company, 1968.

Massie, Joseph L., *Essentials of Management*, Englewood Cliffs, N. J.: Prentice-Hall, Inc., 1964.

Newman, William H., *Administrative Action*, Englewood Cliffs, N. J.: Prentice-Hall, Inc., 1963.

Terry, George R., *Principles of Management*, Homewood, Ill.: Richard D. Irwin, Inc., 1964.

6

QUANTITATIVE

METHODS

The decision-making process is rapidly becoming less of an art and more of a science. Basing decisions on intuition has become unacceptable because problems are more complex and more interdependent than they were in the past. A more exact procedure or scientific approach is required. The basic scientific disciplines—mathematics, statistics, and economics—provide the basic tools needed by the present-day decision maker.

The science of decision making has had as great an impact on management as the industrial revolution has had on production. Decision making concerned itself first with problems of a technical nature. In 1940 a group of scientists met in England to provide decision-making information and analysis regarding the utilization of military resources. This was the first *operations research* group.

Today, operations research is firmly established as a professional staff activity in most large companies. Many universities in this country offer degrees with a major in operations research. The science of decision making is an outgrowth of operations research, mathematical economics, statistics, the behavioral sciences, and other fields; it is generally referred to as *management science*. This science has grown out of efforts to develop criteria for solving the complex problems of modern business operations.

The decision-making environment is a result of interactions among competitors, conflicts of objectives, the uncertainties of nature, fluctuations in the national economy, and many other interacting activities involving human and physical variables. The management scientist, perhaps even more than the physical scientist, must solve problems in the face of many unpredictables, interrelationships, and risks.

There is no standard approach to the decision-making process that is either clearcut or easy, and no standard procedure is available that will fit every situation. However, a few examples of popular methods that have been used are discussed in this chapter. These examples illustrate, respectively, a problem based on a deterministic solution, a problem that contains a degree of uncertainty and that is solved on probabilistic grounds, and a situation where game theory is applicable in a competitive situation.

THE DETERMINISTIC PROBLEM

Problems which are solved with a degree of certainty are classified as deterministic. The following example is given to illustrate this type of problem solving.

A manufacturer of electronic kitchen ranges assembles his product in three locations in the United States. The demand for his product, however, originates from many parts of the country. In order to satisfy these demands, the Electron-Range Company has placed warehouses in four other areas.

Let us suppose that the three assembly plants are located in central Texas, Cincinnati, and Kansas City. The four warehouses are located in northern California, Chicago, Jackson (Mississippi), and Philadelphia. The assembly plants are labeled "P" on the map of the United States shown in Fig. 6–1; the warehouses are marked "W."

The management must decide how many electronic ranges should be sent from the Texas plant to the Jackson warehouse, how many from the Cincinnati plant to the Jackson warehouse and the Chicago warehouse, and so forth. The decision depends to a great extent upon the production capacity and warehouse capacity of each location.

If each assembly plant were allowed to send the finished stoves to each warehouse, the 12 shipping routes would appear as marked by the arrows in Fig. 6–1. However, this pattern of shipping routes, in all likelihood, would be unnecessarily expensive. Depending on the various capacities of each plant and warehouse, it may be cheaper, say, for the plant located in Texas to send all of its output to the Chicago warehouse and for the Kansas City plant to supply part of the requirements of the California warehouse.

A criterion that is measured in quantitative terms is needed in order to make the proper decision. One relevant measure would be the shipping costs between the various points of origin and destinations. The decision will be strictly deterministic because all that is required is for the management to pick the least expensive combination of shipping routes.

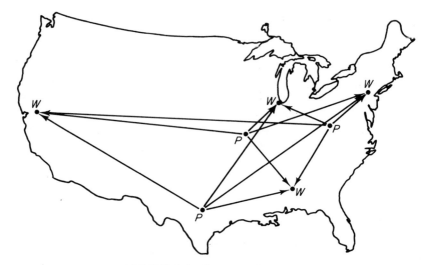

FIGURE 6-1.   Transportation routes.

Let us suppose that the costs of shipping one stove from the various assembly plants to the various warehouses are as follows:

From Texas	to Chicago	$10
	California	8
	Jackson	5
	Philadelphia	7
From Kansas City	to Chicago	6
	California	8
	Jackson	6
	Philadelphia	6
From Cincinnati	to Chicago	4
	California	12
	Jackson	4
	Philadelphia	3

These figures can be placed into a convenient form known as a matrix, shown in Table 6–1. The assembly plants are listed down the left-hand side and the warehouse locations are listed across the top. The total capacity of each assembly plant and warehouse at any one time is listed in the appropriate margin of each row and column.

The following solution was selected on a trial-and-error basis. First, the shipping routes with the lowest shipping costs per unit were selected; this is just good common sense. For example, it would seem sensible to ship to Philadelphia 80 of the 120 units assembled in Cincinnati to take advantage of the low shipping cost of $3 per unit. The remaining 40 units assembled in Cincinnati should be shipped to Chicago to take advantage of the $4 per-unit

TABLE 6-1

SHIPPING COSTS

Assembly Plant Locations	Warehouse Locations				Plant Capacity
	Chicago	California	Jackson	Philadelphia	
Texas	$10	$8	$5	$7	240
Kansas City	$6	$8	$6	$6	160
Cincinnati	$4	$12	$4	$3	120
Warehouse Capacity	140	200	100	80	520

shipping cost between those two locations. As an alternative, these 40 units could be shipped to Jackson because that also would cost only $4 per unit.

Since there now remains space for an additional 100 units at the Chicago warehouse, it would make sense to ship 100 units to Chicago from the Kansas City plant. Since the Kansas City plant has a capacity of 160 units, there would still be 60 units remaining to be shipped from Kansas City. These units are shipped to Jackson, Mississippi because the cost per unit is only $6 compared to $8 for shipping a unit to California. The remaining space for 40 units at Jackson is filled by a shipment from Texas. This leaves a total of 200 units to be shipped from the Texas plant to the California warehouse.

We now have all the warehouses filled to capacity and each of the assembly plants have been exhausted of their product. This is an unusual case because it is exhaustive: the total assembly capacity is equal to the total warehouse capacity. This situation does not generally occur, but it simplifies the working of the problem. Many textbooks on the subject treat nonexhaustive situations.

In summary, then, we have

> 80 units shipped from Cincinnati to Philadelphia
> 40 units shipped from Cincinnati to Chicago
> 100 units shipped from Kansas City to Chicago
> 60 units shipped from Kansas City to Jackson
> 40 units shipped from Texas to Jackson
> 200 units shipped from Texas to California
> 520 *total units shipped*

This solution utilizes only half of the 12 possible shipping routes which were previously indicated. Its total cost is computed as follows:

$$
\begin{aligned}
80 \times \$3 &= \$ \ \ 240 \\
40 \times \ \ 4 &= \ \ \ \ 160 \\
100 \times \ \ 6 &= \ \ \ \ 600 \\
60 \times \ \ 6 &= \ \ \ \ 360 \\
40 \times \ \ 5 &= \ \ \ \ 200 \\
200 \times \ \ 8 &= \ \ 1{,}600 \\
\textit{Total cost} &= \$3{,}160
\end{aligned}
$$

Another solution exists which is lower in cost. You may try your own luck by picking out a combination of routes and computing its total cost. The best or optimal solution turns out to be $3,100.

The trial-and-error approach, in this case, worked out rather well. However, this method does not indicate the optimal solution nor does it guarantee that making another trial will be worthwhile. Generally, if we were to try to improve on our first trial-and-error solution by testing other combinations, we would become confused and exhausted long before we found a solution that would render a lower total cost than the others.

A systematic method for solving this problem, consisting of a simple arithmetic algorithm, is contained in the Annex to this chapter. This mathematically based procedure enables you to obtain a minimum (optimal) cost by a method which indicates when an optimal solution has been reached. If one is not reached, the procedure will indicate the changes necessary in order to approach a final and optimal solution.

A PROBLEM WITH UNCERTAINTY

When the outcome or result of each action is known in advance or can be determined in advance, as in the case of the preceding problem, it is called "decision making under certainty." However, with other problems, a degree of uncertainty may exist. In many problems encountered in business, this uncertainty can be measured or predicted. For example, insurance companies provide protection against risks of many kinds because these risks can be calculated. Although a man operating a hot dog concession is faced with an uncertain demand, he may be able to estimate from past records the probable number of hot dogs he will need. Or we may take the example of an oil speculator who must decide whether to drill a well or sell his oil lease. If the chances of hitting a dry hole are known, he can make his decision on a probability basis. When the risk or uncertainty of this type of problem can be expressed in terms of probability, we say that the degree of uncertainty is measurable.

Still other problems may have to be approached on the basis of complete uncertainty. We cannot offer much help with these problems; they still must be solved by trial and error. However, we can offer approaches to those business problems where the degree of uncertainty is not complete—that is, where the risks of uncertainty are measurable and predictable. The example given here illustrates a technique for solving a problem under a degree of uncertainty. This example is similar to one that appears in *Finite Mathematics with Business Applications*.[1]

Mrs. Reed owns a floral shop near a large university. Each weekend that

[1] J. Kemeny, A. Schleifer Jr., J. Snell, and G. Thompson, *Finite Mathematics with Business Applications* (Englewood Cliffs, N. J.: Prentice-Hall, Inc., 1962), p. 306.

there is a football game on campus, she needs N number of corsages. Mrs. Reed makes a profit of $1.00 on each corsage sold; the unsold corsages, if any, result in a loss of $.80 each. Her estimates of the probabilities of selling various numbers of corsages are as follows:

d = number of corsages demanded: 30   40   50   60
p = probability of that demand: 0.2   0.4   0.3   0.1

The demand for various numbers of corsages depends upon how many people attend the games. Of course, this is unpredictable because of the weather, the number of dances scheduled for a particular weekend, the interest or rivalry associated with the opposing team, and many other factors. However, it is not entirely hopeless, since estimates of probability can be derived from past records of sales. The probabilities listed above simply show that 20 per cent of the time only 30 corsages were sold, 40 per cent of the time 40 corsages were sold, 30 per cent of the time 50 corsages were sold, and 10 per cent of the time 60 corsages were sold.

It is clear that Mrs. Reed's net profit is as follows:

$$\text{Net profit} = 1.00d - 180(N - d)$$
$$= 1.80d - 0.80N.$$

This is true because Mrs. Reed makes $1.00 on the corsages she sells and loses $.80 on those she does not sell (N is the number of corsages she can order). Now we must use this formula to compute her profit for each of the ways she can provide 30, 40, 50, and 60 corsages in combination with the various numbers of corsages demanded. These profit calculations can be placed in a matrix as in Table 6–2. It is suggested that the reader verify the elements in the profit matrix.

TABLE 6–2

PROFIT MATRIX

		Number of Corsages Demanded (d)			
		30	40	50	60
Number of Corsages Provided (N)	30	30	30	30	30
	40	22*	40	40	40
	50	14	32	50	50
	60	6	24	42	60

*Derived by using the formula for net profit: for example, $1.80(30) - 0.80(40) = 22.00$.

In order for Mrs. Reed to determine how many corsages she should order, she must calculate the *expected profit* for each size of order. This is accomplished by using the profit matrix.

The *expected profits* associated with each size of order are generally calculated by a method utilizing matrix algebra, for example, the profit matrix (M) is multiplied by the probability vector ($\mathbf{p}$). The matrix product of M and $\mathbf{p}$ gives another vector, $\mathbf{e}$, the expected profit vector for the corresponding number of corsages provided. The multiplication is demonstrated as follows:

$$M \times \mathbf{p} = \mathbf{e}.$$

In expanded form, we have

$$\begin{pmatrix} 30 & 30 & 30 & 30 \\ 22 & 40 & 40 & 40 \\ 14 & 32 & 50 & 50 \\ 6 & 24 & 42 & 60 \end{pmatrix} \times \begin{pmatrix} 0.2 \\ 0.4 \\ 0.3 \\ 0.1 \end{pmatrix} = \begin{pmatrix} 30.00 \\ 36.40 \\ 35.60 \\ 29.40 \end{pmatrix}$$

The corresponding values that appear in the column vector $\mathbf{e}$ are obtained by multiplying each row of M by the $\mathbf{p}$ vector and summing. For example,

$$(30 \times 0.2) + (30 \times 0.4) + (30 \times 0.3) + (30 \times 0.1) = 30.00.$$

The calculation of the second element of the $\mathbf{e}$ vector follows similarly:

$$(22 \times 0.3) + (40 \times 0.4) + (40 \times 0.3) + (40 \times 0.1) = 36.40.$$

For the third element, we have

$$(14 \times 0.3) + (32 \times 0.4) + (50 \times 0.3) + (50 \times 0.1) = 35.60.$$

Finally,

$$(6 \times 0.2) + (24 \times 0.4) + (42 \times 0.3) + (60 \times 0.1) = 29.40.$$

The foundation of matrix algebra is explained in most basic mathematics textbooks. However, an introduction to matrix algebra is also provided in the Annex to Chapter 14.

We now have the expected profit for each number of corsages Mrs. Reed may provide. For example, she can expect a profit of $30.00 if she orders 30 corsages, a profit of $36.40 on 40 corsages, and so forth. The various expected profits are as follows:

Corsages provided:	30	40	50	60
Expected profit:	$30.00	$36.40	$35.60	$29.40

It is obvious that Mrs. Reed should order 40 corsages, since she would then expect the maximum profit of $36.40.

THE COMPETITIVE PROBLEM AS
A GAME OF STRATEGIES

A highly competitive problem can be approached as a game of strategies. The decision-making aspect of this type of problem is treated as part of the *theory of games*. This approach is very difficult mathematically; however, the basic concepts that can be derived from simple models are important for establishing a framework or way of thinking for the decision maker.

The idea of game theory can be introduced with simplicity by describing a game that is often played by youngsters, the paper–rock–scissors game. This game requires that there be two players, each of whom has three choices. Each can indicate that he possesses either a piece of paper, a rock, or a pair of scissors.

Each player must indicate with his hand which one of the items he chooses to possess. For example, a clenched fist represents a rock, a hand opened in a flat manner indicates paper, and the movement of two fingers in a scissors-like manner designates a pair of scissors. Each player must reveal his choice independently of the other but both must act simultaneously. One round of play may result in player *A* having chosen scissors and player *B* paper. Player *A* is the winner since scissors can cut paper. Player *B* is then required to give *A* payment in the form of an object on which they have agreed previously. Children usually make payment in the form of marbles, picture cards, or even pennies. Adults play games of strategy for much higher stakes; businessmen may deal with millions of dollars.

The game is governed by the following rules or conditions:

Rock breaks scissors
Paper covers rock
Scissors cut paper

According to the first rule, the possessor of a rock wins. The second rule designates that paper is the winner. And by the third rule, scissors win.

The paper-rock-scissors game is played many times, with each player choosing a different strategy each time in order to outguess his opponent. It isn't wise to choose the same strategy repeatedly, because your opponent can act accordingly, taking advantage of your play to win every time.

This game can be structured into a simple matrix showing the various strategies and their relationships to the various payoffs. Player *A*'s strategies are listed along the left-hand side of the matrix, and player *B*'s across the top. Each player has three strategies. The payoffs are indicated by a $+1$, 0, or -1 in the body of the matrix. The zero indicates no payoff because each player has selected the same object. These outcomes are indicated by the payoffs on the right-to-left diagonal of the matrix. Thus -1 indicates a payment by player *A* to player *B*, and $+1$ is a payment by player *B* to player *A*. We then have the following game matrix:

		Player B		
		Rock	Scissors	Paper
Player A	Rock	0	+1	−1
	Scissors	−1	0	+1
	Paper	+1	−1	0

It is obvious that if this game is played a large number of times, both players should break even, especially if the players are choosing their strategies in a random manner so that each strategy is chosen a third of the time. This type of game is classified as a *zero-sum game* because one person's gain is equal to another's loss. The value of the game is zero; that is, neither player should win in the long run. Although the value of a game is usually difficult to determine without some mathematical training, in this particular case it can be done because the diagonal elements are equal to zero.

Now consider a case where there are two producers of stereo sets who operate in a competitive market. They each have three strategies they may employ, which may correspond to price changes, advertising campaigns, or other campaigns designed to counter competitive action. The following payoff table reflects the consequences when the various strategies are employed by the two competitors. The payoffs represent the change in sales in thousands of dollars.

		Producer B		
		Strategy B_1	Strategy B_2	Strategy B_3
	Strategy A_1	13	10	−14
Producer A	Strategy A_2	12	13	11
	Strategy A_3	−10	12	− 8

One competitor is identified as producer A; he has possible strategies A_1, A_2, and A_3. The payoff matrix is oriented to competitor A; that is, the positive payoffs will indicate increases in sales for A and decreases in sales for B. In other games the payoffs may be all positive, which simply indicates that there are no losses possible for player A.

Competitor A must first decide what strategy to choose. If he chooses A_1, the worst he can do is lose $14,000 (if competitor B chooses strategy B_3). If player A chooses strategy A_2 and B chooses B_3, the worst producer A can do is gain $11,000 in sales. And if producer A chooses strategy A_3 and B chooses B_1, then the most producer A can lose is $10,000. Note that these are the minimum values of each row, circled in the payoff matrix. In other words, the circled values indicate the greatest loss of sales producer A can experience when he chooses one of his strategies.

If competitor A assumes that competitor B is intelligent and has estimated the payoffs in the same way he has, then A's best choice is obviously strategy A_2. This strategy results in the largest minimum gain of each of producer A's strategies. This "conservative" criterion, which maximizes A's minimum gain, is called the *maxmin* criterion. It minimizes the player's risk.

Considering the game from the point of view of producer B, it is clear that his maximum losses for strategies B_1, B_2, and B_3 would be $13,000, $13,000, and $11,000, respectively. Remember that positive figures represent gains to A and losses to B. These maximum values in each column are boxed in the payoff matrix. If producer B uses a conservative criterion—that is, one which will minimize his maximum possible losses—he will select the strategy with the smallest of the maximum losses (the largest entries of each column). Competitor B will therefore select strategy B_3 as his best play. It is a *minmax* selection because B has minimized the maximum possible loss for himself. He also is maximizing his minimum gain.

By coincidence, the best strategies for both players are based on the same entry in the payoff matrix, the maxmin (or minmax) value. Both competitors, therefore, have chosen strategies which protect them from their worst possible outcome. In this "game," competitor B lost $11,000 in sales. If he had chosen any other strategy, he could have lost more than $11,000. And if producer A had used any strategy other than A_2, he could have gained less than $11,000, or even lost in sales.

This is a simple game. It has been solved by inspection because it has a so-called *saddle point*. That is, the maxmin (minmax) element is in the same place in the payoff table for either player. A pure strategy, where each player uses only one strategy rather than a mixture, is the optimal one for both players.

Games with *saddle points* are called *strictly determined* games. More sophisticated methods must be used to solve cases where there is no saddle point. In nonstrictly determined games, graphic methods and linear programming are employed. A single or pure strategy is generally not an optimal solution in nonstrictly determined games; a *mixed strategy* is required, as in the paper-rock-scissors game where each player uses each of his strategies one-third of the time.

SUMMARY

The decision-making process is complex, involving many conflicts. We have demonstrated several simple problems in this chapter. One problem was solved in a state of certainty, another was solved in a state of risk (or uncertainty), and the third was solved in a state of competition. An important step in the decision-making process is to identify all possible objectives and then to list all alternatives or strategies. The consequences of the strategies must be measurable and the proper strategy chosen on a rational basis.

Decision making is not easy, and reliance on intuition or hunches alone is inadvisable and out-of-date. In many situations, the application of quantitative techniques is most helpful in making the proper decision or choice.

ANNEX: AN ITERATIVE METHOD[2] FOR SOLVING THE TRANSPORTATION PROBLEM

The transportation costs between the assembly plants and warehouses of the Electron-Range Company are provided in Table 6–3. The trial-and-error solution given in the text of this chapter is also inserted in the table. The various quantities that were specified in the first solution are placed alongside their corresponding cost figures and circled to distinguish them from the cost figures. As you may recall, the trial-and-error solution rendered a total cost of $3,160, which was calculated as follows:

$$(80 \times 3) + (40 \times 4) + (100 \times 6) + (60 \times 6) + (40 \times 5) + (200 \times 8)$$
$$= \$3,160.$$

TABLE 6–3

TRANSPORTATION COSTS

Assembly Plant Locations	Warehouse Locations				Plant Capacity
	Chicago	California	Jackson	Philadelphia	
Texas	$10	$8 (200)	$5 (40)	$7	240
Kansas City	$6 (100)	$8	$6 (60)	$6	160
Cincinnati	$4 (40)	$12	$4	$3 (80)	120
Warehouse Capacity	140	200	100	80	520

[2] When the iterative method is employed instead of the trial-and-error approach, a few special techniques are used to determine if the solution is optimal (having the minimum cost). There will be no attempt to explain the basis for this iterative method; it must be accepted on faith. However, the mathematical basis for the procedure is explained in most college mathematics textbooks.

One requirement must be met in using the iterative method; that is, there must be only (and exactly) a specified number of activities in the solution. The correct number of activities can always be predetermined by adding the number of rows in the matrix to the number of columns and subtracting 1 (rows + columns − 1 = the number of active routes or activities in the solution). In this case we were lucky, because the trial-and-error beginning provided us with the correct number of activities, six in this case. There are only six routes over which the finished product is shipped to the four warehouses.

Our next step is to transform the cost figures associated with each of the activities in the solution to zeros. This is easily accomplished by subtracting from or adding to each element in a row or column whatever number is needed to change those cost figures to zero. The process can be started at any point; we have started with the first row.

Subtracting 8 from each element of the first row, we obtain

$$
\begin{array}{cccc}
2 & 0^{\,\textcircled{200}} & -3^{\,\textcircled{40}} & -1
\end{array}
$$

Adding 3 to each element of the third column, we have

$$
\begin{array}{cccc}
2 & 0^{\,\textcircled{200}} & 0^{\,\textcircled{40}} & -1 \\
 & & 9^{\,\textcircled{60}} & \\
 & & 7 &
\end{array}
$$

The matrix is partially altered, and we have obtained the desired zeros at two of the positions desired. We now subtract 9 from the second row, obtaining

$$
\begin{array}{cccc}
2 & 0^{\,\textcircled{200}} & 0^{\,\textcircled{40}} & -1 \\
-3^{\,\textcircled{100}} & -1 & 0^{\,\textcircled{60}} & -3 \\
 & & 7 &
\end{array}
$$

In order to change the -3 in the first column to a zero, we must add 3 to the elements of the first column. This is necessary because the 100 indicates that it is one of the activities in the solution. Therefore, we have

$$
\begin{array}{cccc}
5 & 0^{\,\textcircled{200}} & 0^{\,\textcircled{40}} & -1 \\
0^{\,\textcircled{100}} & -1 & 0^{\,\textcircled{60}} & -3 \\
7^{\,\textcircled{40}} & 7 & &
\end{array}
$$

Now 7 must be subtracted from the elements of the last row to change the 7 in the first column to a zero:

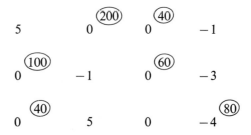

Finally, 4 must be added to the elements of the last column to change the -4 in the lower right-hand corner to a zero:

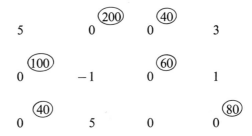

We now have zeros at all the positions in the matrix where activities of the solution are indicated. The zero appearing in the third row, third column is also permissible.

We are now able to determine if this solution is an optimal one. If all the transformed cost figures are zero or positive, the solution is optimal, but if a negative number appears anywhere in the matrix, it is not. In this example, only one negative number appears, the -1 in row 2, column 2; it indicates that this activity (a shipment from Kansas City to California) should be included in the solution instead of one of the other shipments in order to reduce the total cost. If more than one negative number appears, the one with the largest absolute value should be chosen as the activity to be inserted. Only one activity can be added during each iteration. However, even if there is more than one negative number, the others may disappear when the next solution is derived.

The next step is to decide which activity will be replaced by the activity associated with the negative cost figure. This is accomplished easily by a method called *looping*. The amount of the new activity for row 2, column 2 (shipment from Kansas City to California) is temporarily designated by the symbol α (alpha). This symbol is inserted in the table as the amount to be added and subtracted from rows and columns until a *loop* is completed. The levels of activities are adjusted, then, as follows:

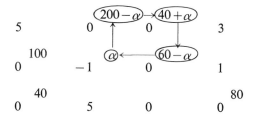

This shows that the amount of α to be added at row 2, column 2 is subtracted from the second column in row 1 (200 − α). It then must also be added to row 1, so it is added at column 3 of row 1 (40 + α). This requires α to be subtracted from column 3, which is done in row 2 (60 − α). This looping does not result in any change in the row totals (assembly capacities) or the column totals (warehouse capacities).

How large should α be? This question is easily answered by letting it be equal to the smallest activity where α is subtracted. Therefore, in our example, α is 60. If it were 200 (or more than 60), we would end up with a negative amount of shipment at the (60 − α) position, which would be ridiculous and is not allowed. All activities must be positive.

The new solution can now be obtained by substituting 60 for α in the cost table above. The results of adding and subtracting α give the following cost table and its associated levels of activity for the new solution. First the new total cost will be figured, and then we will test again to see if this new solution is optimal:

	5		0	$\overbrace{200-60=140}$	0	$\overbrace{40+60=100}$	3
0	⓾ⓞⓞ	0	⑥⓪	−1		⑥⓪−⑥⓪=⓪	1
0	④⓪	0		5	0	⑧⓪	0

Returning to the original cost table to get the appropriate cost figures, we find that the total cost for this solution is

$$
\begin{aligned}
(40 \times 4) &= \$ \ \ 160 \\
(100 \times 6) &= \ \ \ \ 600 \\
(60 \times 8) &= \ \ \ \ 480 \\
(140 \times 8) &= \ \ 1{,}120 \\
(100 \times 5) &= \ \ \ \ 500 \\
(80 \times 3) &= \ \ \ \ \underline{240} \\
\textit{Total cost of new solution} &= \$3{,}100
\end{aligned}
$$

We again must alter the relative cost figures in our new solution to determine whether it is optimal. As you recall, we must adjust the -1 located at the intersection of row 2 and column 2, which is the location of the new activity where 60 units are shipped from Kansas City to California. This is accomplished by adding 1 to each element in column 2. Therefore, we have

$$
\begin{array}{c|c|cc}
5 & 1 & 0 & 3 \\[2ex]
0 & 0 & 0 & 1 \\[2ex]
0 & 6 & 0 & 0
\end{array}
$$

We then subtract 1 from row 1 to transform the second element of row 1 to a zero:

$$
\begin{array}{cccc}
\hline
4 & 0 & -1 & 2 \\
\hline
\end{array}
$$
$$
\begin{array}{cccc}
0 & 0 & 0 & 1 \\[2ex]
0 & 6 & 0 & 0
\end{array}
$$

Next 1 must be added to column 3:

$$
\begin{array}{cc|c|c}
4 & 0 & 0 & 2 \\[2ex]
0 & 0 & 1 & 1 \\[2ex]
0 & 6 & 1 & 0
\end{array}
$$

We must now check to see if all activities of the new solution have zeros for their costs. This is accomplished by inserting the activity levels of the new solution in the cost table.

$$
\begin{array}{cccc}
4 & \overset{\textstyle (140)}{0} & \overset{\textstyle (100)}{0} & 2 \\[3ex]
\overset{\textstyle (100)}{0} & \overset{\textstyle (60)}{0} & 1 & 1 \\[3ex]
\overset{\textstyle (40)}{0} & 6 & 1 & \overset{\textstyle (80)}{0}
\end{array}
$$

Since we have no negative numbers in our relative cost table, we have an optimal solution. It is unusual to obtain an optimal solution after only one iteration.

This method does not find the only optimal solution; there may be many other combinations that render a total (minimum) cost equal to the one obtained here. However, the iterative method will at least provide one of the combinations that gives an optimal solution and will indicate optimality.

PROBLEMS AND PROJECTS

1. A company operates five warehouses and four manufacturing plants. How many different routes are possible for shipping the finished products from each plant to each warehouse?

2. Mr. Carter invests money in securities listed on the New York Stock Exchange. He estimates the capital gains of a $5,000 investment in several securities over a three-month period to be as follows:
   a. $600.
   b. $1,400.
   c. $200.
   d. $500.

   The probabilities associated with the actual occurrence of these estimates are
   a. 0.30.
   b. 0.10.
   c. 0.40.
   d. 0.20.

   What is Mr. Carter's expected gain if he invests the $5,000?

3. Does the following competitive game have a saddle point?

Player B Strategies

		1	2	3
Player A Strategies	1	7	3	16
	2	12	10	8
	3	6	16	10

4. (Problems 4 and 5 are based on the material contained in the Annex.) A solution to a transportation problem is shown in the following tableau. The warehouse capacities are shown along the bottom margin of the tableau, and the plant capacities are shown in the farthest left column. The

Tableau.

Warehouses

	1	2	3	4	Plant Capacities
Plant 1	(10) 7	(70) 3	(10) 5	(90) 10	180
Plant 2	(100) 4	10	2	9	100
Plant 3	8	7	(250) 6	16	250
Warehouse Capacities	110	70	260	90	530

*The data for this tableau originated from a problem in TEMAC.

internal portion of the tableau consists of the cost figures and the solution (the solution is comprised of those figures which are circled).

a. What is the total transportation cost for this solution?

b. Is this solution an optimal one? Why?

c. If this solution is not an optimal one, then derive another solution from this tableau.

5. You are scheduling the activities at a firm that manufactures a single product in three different factories. This firm also owns four warehouses in different locations; finished goods from the factories are sent to the warehouses to be sold. The table below shows the transportation costs for shipping one ton of the finished product from each of the factories to each of the warehouses.

Plant capacities:
   Factory 1—18 tons
   Factory 2—26 tons
   Factory 3—36 tons.

Warehouse capacities:
   Warehouse 1—16 tons
   Warehouse 2—30 tons
   Warehouse 3—14 tons
   Warehouse 4—20 tons.

Warehouse

	1	2	3	4
Factory 1	7	10	9	8
Factory 2	4	7	6	7
Factory 3	10	13	11	10

Determine the number of tons of the finished product you would schedule for shipment from each factory to each warehouse, so that

a. Warehouse requirements are met.
b. Factory capacities are not exceeded.
c. The lowest possible total cost is achieved.

SELECTED REFERENCES

Carlson, P. G., *Quantitative Methods for Managers.* New York: Harper & Row, Publishers, 1967.
Hein, L. W., *The Quantitative Approach to Managerial Decisions.* Englewood Cliffs, N. J.: Prentice-Hall, Inc., 1967.
Manne, A. S., *Economic Analysis for Business Decisions.* New York: McGraw-Hill Book Company, 1961.
Sisson, R. L., with H. F. Sieber and R. P. Nagin, *Management Science Selections.* Park Ridge, Ill.: Data Processing Digest, Inc., 1965.
Theil, H., John C. G. Boot, and T. Kloek, *Operations Research and Quantitative Economics—An Elementary Introduction.* New York: McGraw-Hill Book Company, 1965.

7

PRODUCTION

THEORY

One of the great success stories of the American economy is the high standard of living its citizens enjoy. A high standard of living requires a high level of production, and in the United States, the business enterprise is the chief agent of that production. Gross national product, described in an earlier chapter, reflects in total terms the results of this business effort. Expenditures by consumers, the purchase of goods and services by government, and the purchase of capital goods by other businesses provide tangible evidence of the vast supply of goods and services produced annually by businesses for the benefit of society.

The purpose of this chapter is to take a careful look at some important characteristics associated with production. In a broad sense, "production" applies to services such as transportation, financing, and wholesaling just as much as it refers to manufacturing. Two important aspects of production will be discussed. The first concerns the fact that production is a process that combines resources. Certain relationships exist between the physical inputs or resources and the physical outputs or products of a firm; in addition, there is a very close connection between these relationships and the costs of production, which are analyzed in Chapter 8. The second aspect to be discussed is the situation where there is more than one output or product. Many firms produce several products, some related, some not. Under such circumstances the firm must choose a combination of outputs from the range of production possibilities that is available. The more input and output alternatives there are available, the more complex the business decision becomes. Linear programming is introduced to provide an example of how more complex decisions may be resolved. The Annex to this chapter gives an application of the critical-path method to a scheduling problem typical in many production situations.

Production Functions

The *production function* is a relationship economists often use when they refer to the output of a firm. Regardless of its nature, all production combines inputs to obtain outputs. The production function is a convenient device that relates these two elements. There are many combinations of natural, human, and produced resources that will produce a given output; therefore, resources may often be substituted for each other. What this means to the businessman is that he may choose from many combinations of resources in order to produce a particular quantity of output.

The Hypothetical Mailbox Manufacturing Company, which produces mailboxes, may have available to it several combinations of resources. The mailboxes could be made from aluminum, plastic, steel, wood, or a combination of these materials. Likewise, the process can involve the use of simple hand tools or complicated automatic machinery. A building, a plot of land, supplies, men, and many other resources may be required. The combinations of all these resources can be conveniently expressed in the form of a production function.

In order to illustrate a production function and the substitution of inputs, it will be most convenient to divide all resources into two categories. One category will be known as "resource A" and the other as "resource B." A unit of resource A can be thought of as including a certain mixture of land, buildings, machines, and tools, and a unit of resource B as including a certain mixture of men, materials, and supplies.

Resource A and resource B can be substituted for each other to a certain degree. Instead of using ten men and two machines, it may be possible to use six men and three machines. However, there are limits to these replacements. For example, if resources A and B are used to produce mailboxes, some quantity of B would always have to be used since it includes the materials out of which the mailboxes are to be made. Therefore, resources A and B are not perfect substitutes for each other. A certain amount of each will usually have to be combined with the other.

Table 7–1 illustrates the possibilities of substituting and combining resources A and B to produce a certain number of mailboxes. The different combinations of A and B provided in the table will all produce the same number of mailboxes; in this case, 30.

TABLE 7–1

RESOURCE COMBINATIONS

Quantity of Output		Alternative Combinations of A and B							
30	A	47	38	30	23	17	13	10	8	7
	B	7	8	10	13	17	23	30	38	47

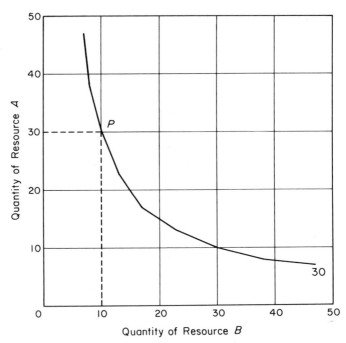

FIGURE 7–1.   Resource combinations.

The same information also can be shown in "snapshot" form—that is, graphically. The production information in Table 7–1 appears in Fig. 7–1 as a production function. The graph is read from the lower left-hand corner. The left-hand scale represents the units of resource A and the bottom scale the units of resource B. The resource combinations from Table 7–1 are illustrated in Fig. 7–1 as points; they are determined by projecting an imaginary perpendicular line (illustrated in Fig. 7–1 as dashes) from the left-hand scale and one from the bottom scale for each combination of A and B. For example, point P represents the combination of 30 units of resource A and 10 of resource B. When all the points are connected by a line, a production function emerges. All combinations of A and B on this production function will produce an equal quantity of output—30 mailboxes.

TABLE 7–2

PRODUCTION INFORMATION

Quantity of Output		Alternative Combinations of A and B								
30	A	47	38	30	23	17	13	10	8	7
	B	7	8	10	13	17	23	30	38	47
70	A	54	45	37	30	24	20	17	15	14
	B	14	15	17	20	24	30	37	45	54
130	A	60	51	43	36	30	26	23	21	20
	B	20	21	23	26	30	36	43	51	60
170	A	64	55	47	40	34	30	27	25	24
	B	24	25	27	30	34	40	47	55	64
200	A	67	58	50	43	37	33	30	28	27
	B	27	28	30	33	37	43	50	58	67
220	A	69	60	52	45	39	35	32	30	29
	B	29	30	32	35	39	45	52	60	69
230	A	70	61	53	46	40	36	33	31	30
	B	30	31	33	36	40	46	53	61	70
270	A	80	71	63	56	40	46	43	41	40
	B	40	41	43	46	40	56	63	71	80
290	A	90	81	73	66	60	56	53	51	50
	B	50	51	53	56	60	66	73	81	90

Similar production functions can be extracted from other production information. Table 7–2 includes such information; it uses various combinations of resource A and resource B to obtain other levels of production. Since this type of information is determined by the physical or technical requirements of production, the firm's engineering department should be able to provide it. Certain selected levels of production appear in Table 7–2. Intermediate levels, such as those between 30 and 70, for example, could have been included just as easily. However, the table would have become quite cluttered, which would have distracted from its real purpose.

The production functions illustrated in Table 7–2, representing the additional levels of output, can also be shown graphically. These functions appear in Fig. 7–2, conveniently displaying in graph form alternative resource combinations for these other levels of production. To produce 200 mailboxes, one selects the production function for that amount and then reads on the left-hand and bottom scales the required amounts of resources A and B, respectively. For example, at point P in Fig. 7–2, 200 mailboxes can be produced with 37 units of resource A and 37 units of resource B.

Other combinations of resources A and B can be used to produce 200 mailboxes. The combinations indicated by the production function can be determined by reading on the left-hand scale and the bottom scale of Fig. 7–2 the respective quantities of A and B. A perpendicular line from point T to the

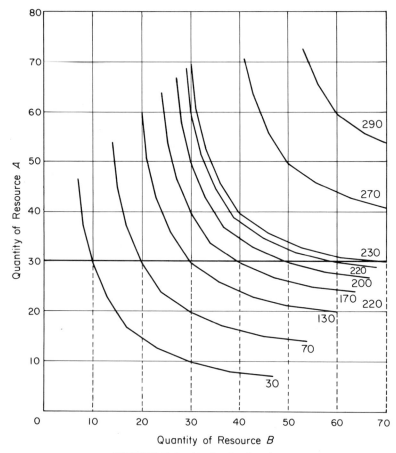

FIGURE 7–2. Production functions.

left-hand scale indicates a requirement of 30 units of resource A; a perpendicular line from point T to the bottom scale indicates a requirement of 50 units of resource B. Therefore, the 200 mailboxes can also be produced with 30 units of A and 50 units of B. The production function indicates many such combinations of A and B that can be used to produce a certain quantity of mailboxes. The same information is available in Table 7–2.

Least-Cost Combinations

The technical conditions of production described by a production function comprise one important determinant of the costs of production. Another is the price of the inputs. Knowledge about the price of inputs, combined with production information, make it possible for the businessman to select the combination of resources for a particular level of production

TABLE 7–3

LEAST-COST COMBINATION

Quantity of Output		Alternative Combinations of A and B							
30	A	47	38	30	23	17	13	10	8	7
	B	7	8	10	13	17	23	30	38	47
		$680	$620	$600	$620	$680	$820	$1,000	$1,220	$1,480

which can be provided at the lowest cost. This is known as the *least-cost* combination of resources.[1] Once it has been determined, for example, which level of output would provide the best profit, the least-cost combination of resources for that particular quantity of output must be selected. Any other combination would not maximize profits.

To choose the least-cost combination, the businessman must take into account the respective prices of the inputs. This decision can be illustrated by returning to the production of mailboxes as described by the production information in Table 7–2; the data for an output of 30 are extracted from Table 7–2 and duplicated in Table 7–3. The price of resource A is given as $10 per unit.[2] The price of resource B is given as $30 per unit. The total cost of each combination of resources A and B is indicated below that combination in the table. A brief investigation of the cost calculations immediately reveals that the least cost of $600 is achieved by combining 30 units of resource A with 10 units of resource B.

The least-cost combination of resources A and B to produce 30 mailboxes also can be shown graphically. This is accomplished by comparing the production function with the prices of the inputs. In order for this to be accomplished on the same graph, the prices of the inputs must be expressed as a ratio in terms of physical quantities of A and B (as depicted on each axis) rather than in dollars ($10 and $30). This is illustrated in Fig. 7–3 by what can be called a *cost-outlay line*.

One cost-outlay line in Fig. 7–3 represents an outlay of $600; it is constructed to show that resource A costs one-third as much as resource B. This can be explained by noting that on the left-hand scale, representing different quantities of A, the cost-outlay line intersects at 60 units; on the bottom scale, representing different quantities of B, it intersects at 20 units. This reflects the fact that at a price of $10 for resource A, 60 units of A can be acquired for $600 (60 × $10), while at a price of $30 for resource B, 20 units of B can be acquired for $600 (20 × $30). Since three times as many units of

[1] In like manner, he may also determine the maximum output that can be achieved with a given money outlay.
[2] Since capital goods do not come in small packages, it is appropriate to consider the $10 price of resource A as the price for that portion of the resource that is used up during the production period.

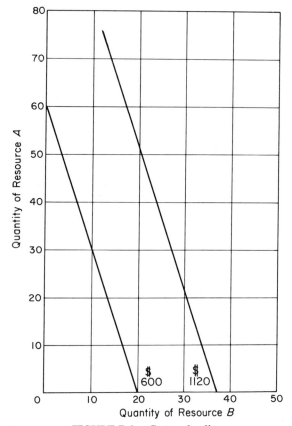

FIGURE 7–3.   Cost-outlay line.

A can be bought for the $600, each unit of resource *A* must cost one-third as much as a unit of *B* ($10 compared to $30). The other points on the cost-outlay line represent other combinations of *A* and *B* that can be acquired for $600 when the price of *A* is $10 and the price of *B* is $30. Similar cost-outlay lines can be shown which reflect the same price of *A* and *B* but a different total outlay. The other cost-outlay line illustrated in Fig. 7–3 is for an outlay of $1,120 when the price of resource *A* is $10 and resource *B* is $30. It is parallel to the first cost-outlay line. This will always hold true as long as the ratio of prices is 1 to 3. If the price ratio of resources *A* and *B* were other than 1 to 3, the cost-outlay line would have a different slope. In any event, the cost-outlay line compares the prices of resources *A* and *B* to each other in terms of the quantity of each resource, this is illustrated in Fig. 7–3.

Since the left-hand scale and the bottom scale in Fig. 7–3, illustrating cost-outlay lines, measure quantities of resources *A* and *B* respectively, production functions and cost-outlay lines can be displayed together. The cost-

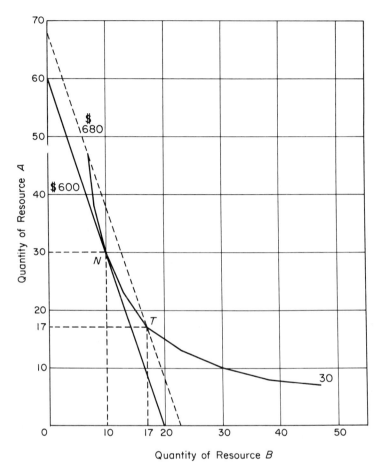

FIGURE 7–4.   Cost-outlay line and production function showing least-cost combination of resources A and B.

outlay line for $600 and the producion function for 30 mailboxes are combined into one graph in Fig. 7–4.

Fig. 7–4 shows the least-cost combination of resources A and B to produce 30 mailboxes. This combination occurs where the cost-outlay line is tangent to the production function. In Fig. 7–4, this takes place at point N on the production function. With a price of $10 for resource A and $30 for resource B, the least cost of $600 occurs when 30 units of resource A are combined with 10 units of resource B. Any other point on the production function would be intersected by a cost-outlay line farther to the right. Such a cost-outlay line would be greater than $600; therefore, the 30 mailboxes would be produced at a higher cost. The quantities of resources A and B represented by point T produce the same amount of output as do the quantities of resources A and B represented by point N. The cost-outlay line for point T—the dashed line—lies farther to the right and represents an outlay of $680 (17 units of A at $10 per unit and 17 units of B at $30 per unit). Therefore, tangency between a cost-outlay line and a production function means least cost. (A cost-outlay line to the left of the $600 line would not represent sufficient outlay to produce 30 mailboxes.)

Although production functions and cost-outlay lines may appear to be too abstract and somewhat remote from reality, an analysis of them provides a good foundation for business decisions. For example, if the price of one resource rises, it more than likely will be replaced by a substitute. Such a substitution would be indicated graphically by a change in the point of tangency between the production function and the cost-outlay line, which would be due to a change in the slope of the cost-outlay line. The slope of the cost-outlay line changes in a particular way when the price of only one resource changes. It must pivot at its intersection with the axis representing the resource which has not changed in price. If the price rises, the cost-outlay line will pivot toward the origin; if it falls, it will pivot away.

More specifically, if the price of resource A were to increase to $30 per unit, a least cost of 30 mailboxes would be achieved by using 17 units of resource A instead of 30, combined with 17 units of resource B instead of 10. It is obvious that at the higher price for resource A, it should be replaced by resource B. The least cost is obtained where the cost-outlay line in Fig. 7–5 is tangent to the production function at point T instead of at point N. This new cost-outlay line has a different slope from the original one. It also intersects each axis at equal quantities of A and B, reflecting the fact that their prices are the same. At a price of $30 for each unit of resource A or resource B, the total cost-outlay line will represent a larger money outlay. Point T, however, is still the least-cost combination for 30 mailboxes at these prices. The least cost at a price of $30 for each unit of A and B would be $1,020 ($30 × 17A plus $30 × 17$B$). Estimates of other least-cost combinations may provide a guide to businessmen in planning future plant and equipment expansion. Since future requirements are indicated by higher levels of production, least-cost combinations for these levels can provide a basis upon which to plan future growth. This is illustrated in Chapter 11.

The analysis so far has restricted itself to a problem with two inputs—resource A and resource B—and one output—mailboxes. Reality is certainly more complicated than this simple example. However, with the aid of mathematics and the use of computers, there is no great difficulty in extending the analysis to multiple inputs and multiple outputs. This is dealt with in the linear programming section of this chapter.

The least-cost demonstration just completed seems to imply that the businessman can always produce at least cost merely by changing the mixture of resources as different quantities of mailboxes are produced. This is true if

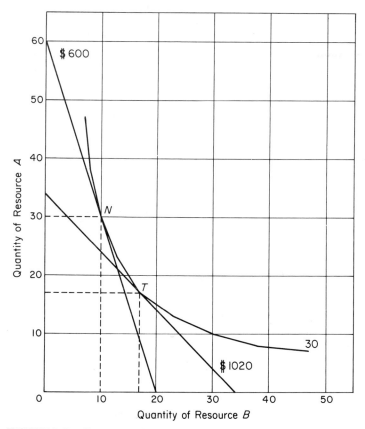

FIGURE 7–5. Cost-outlay line and production function showing least-cost combination of resources A and B.

there is enough time to acquire the necessary resources; however, in short periods of time, least-cost combinations may not always be feasible. For example, if for several months 30 mailboxes were produced each day, it could be assumed that the least-cost combination for 30 mailboxes had been attained. However, if demand either increased or decreased for a while, it might not be possible to produce the new number of mailboxes per day at least cost. It could take several months to acquire and set up additional units of resource A to produce, for example, 70 or 130 mailboxes at least cost. A unit of resource A was previously defined as a mixture of land, buildings, machines, and tools. Acquiring additional land or constructing an additional building would take considerable time. It might take several months to make these changes, perhaps a year or more depending upon the availability of the land or the nature of the building. Even if the land and buildings were available, more machines would have to be installed and more tools would have to be ordered. Additional units of resource B, on the other hand, would not be nearly as difficult to obtain. Such resources as men, materials, and supplies are usually more flexible. Additional manpower may be hired easily, and materials and supplies can be delivered from suppliers' inventories within hours.[3] Similarly, least cost will not be achieved if production is reduced to less than 30 mailboxes per day. In this case, idle units of resource A would exist; the smaller number of mailboxes produced would have to carry the cost represented by these idle resources. There are times, then, when least-cost combinations cannot be attained. This usually occurs when time is not sufficient to adjust production to the right mixture of resources.

Law of Diminishing Returns

Since business activity is constrained during short periods of time by certain limited or fixed resources, it would seem desirable to have a description of production under these conditions. Such a description will also play an important role in explaining the behavior of costs over short periods of time, which is described more fully in the next chapter.

Production activities in short-run periods experience what economists call the *law of diminishing returns*. This occurs when varying quantities of certain resources are utilized with a fixed quantity of another resource. The law of diminishing returns describes a certain characteristic associated with most production activities: the tendency for production to proceed to a certain point, after which it continues to increase its output, but at a decreasing rate. For example, if corn is being raised on an acre of land, the grower will experience more and more output each season if he applies more variable resources: men, machines, and tools. However, he will also discover that a point is reached where increases in corn output become less and less as he applies more units of the variable resource to the same plot of land.

The law of diminishing returns can be conveniently illustrated by returning to the production information for mailboxes in Table 7–2. This information, which also appeared in Fig. 7–2, is duplicated in Fig. 7–6, where the production functions for different levels of output are recognized.

The production of mailboxes can be constrained in day-to-day operation by resource A. Assume that the production of mailboxes has developed to the point where 30 units of resource A are used. This is illustrated in Fig. 7–6 by the line perpendicular to the left-hand scale at 30 units of resource A. In order to vary production of mailboxes, different quantities of resource B must be used. This is illustrated by the intersections of the perpendicular and the various production functions. These intersections indicate the various quantities of resource B that must be combined with the fixed amount of

[3] Of course, there are times when these more variable resources might not be so easily obtained. When the economy is fully employed, additional manpower may still be obtained, but at higher prices. Certain supplies may also be temporarily out of stock.

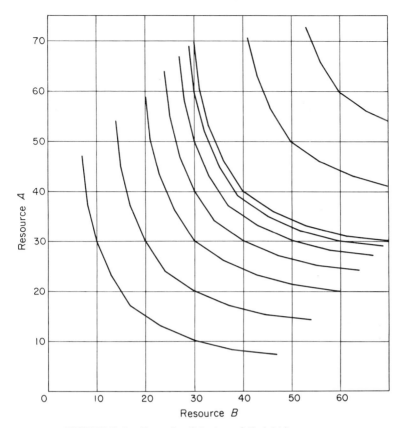

FIGURE 7–6. Example of the law of diminishing returns.

resource *A*. The combinations are also indicated in Table 7–4, which is a duplication of the original production information in Table 7–2. The shaded combinations correspond to the intersections in Fig. 7–6. The quantity of mailboxes produced can be found in the left-hand column of the table. These same combinations and levels of output are conveniently displayed in Table 7–5. The change in output (referred to by economists as *marginal product*) reflects the law of diminishing returns. While the output of mailboxes increases with additional equal applications of resource *B*, the amount of increase eventually becomes less and less.[4] This tendency for output to eventually increase at a decreasing rate is typical of production in the short-run period.

In summarizing, it can be said that the businessman has several important production decisions to make. For a particular quantity of output, he can achieve a least-cost combination of resources by considering the combinations available and the prices of the resources. Graphically, the least-cost combination occurs where a cost-outlay line is tangent to a production function. The cost-outlay line is a comparison of resource prices that represents a certain money outlay, and the production function represents alter-

[4] In order to obtain the *marginal product per unit* of resource *B*, simply divide by 10, getting 4, 6, 4, 3, 2, and 1.

TABLE 7–4

PRODUCTION INFORMATION

Quantity of Output		Alternative Combinations of A and B								
30	A	47	38	30	23	17	13	10	8	7
	B	8	8	10	13	17	23	30	38	47
70	A	54	45	37	30	24	20	17	15	14
	B	14	15	17	20	24	30	37	45	54
130	A	60	51	43	36	30	26	23	21	20
	B	20	21	23	26	30	36	43	51	60
170	A	64	55	47	40	34	30	27	25	24
	B	24	25	27	30	24	40	47	55	64
200	A	67	58	50	43	37	33	30	28	27
	B	27	28	30	33	37	43	50	58	67
220	A	69	60	52	45	39	35	32	30	29
	B	29	30	32	35	39	45	52	60	69
230	A	70	61	53	46	40	36	33	31	30
	B	30	31	33	36	40	46	53	61	70
270	A	80	71	63	56	50	46	43	41	40
	B	40	41	43	46	50	56	63	71	80

TABLE 7–5

DIMINISHING RETURNS

Resource A	Resource B	Mailboxes	Change in Output
30	10	30	
30	20	70	40
30	30	130	60
30	40	170	40
30	50	200	30
30	60	220	20
30	70	230	10

native combinations of resources for a particular output. Finally, the law of diminishing returns explains typical conditions of production when least-cost combinations are not achieved because certain resources are not sufficiently flexible or readily available.

MULTIPLE-OUTPUT PRODUCTION

Production Possibilities

The production functions of the previous sections relate two inputs to one output: resources A and B were combined to produce mailboxes. Sup-

TABLE 7–6

PRODUCTION POSSIBILITIES OF TYPES *R* AND *H* MAILBOXES

Type of Mailbox	Production Alternatives					
R	0	40	80	100	110	115
H	150	140	120	80	40	0

pose that the Hypothetical Mailbox Manufacturing Company produces two types of mailboxes: the standard rural mailbox and a smaller house mailbox, which can be attached to a flat surface or a door. We shall designate the rural mailbox as type *R* and the house mailbox as type *H*. The problem now becomes one of relating one input (or a package of inputs) to two outputs. Table 7–6 notes some of the alternative combinations of type *R* and type *H* mailboxes which the company can produce with a given package of inputs or resources.

A *production-possibilities* curve can be used to relate the quantity of the input to alternative quantities of the two different outputs. This relationship is illustrated in Fig. 7–7. The various quantities of the two outputs are shown along the axes of the graph, type *R* mailboxes along the left-hand scale and type *H* mailboxes along the bottom.

An examination of the production-possibilities curve illustrated in Fig. 7–7 indicates that a given package of inputs can be used to produce several different combinations of type *R* and type *H* mailboxes. For example, point *P* on the curve indicates that the given package of inputs can be used to produce 80 type *R* mailboxes and 120 type *H* mailboxes. Point *N* indicates that 40 type *R* mailboxes and 140 type *H* mailboxes can be produced. Note that 40 type *R* mailboxes are sacrificed to produce the additional 20 of type *H*.

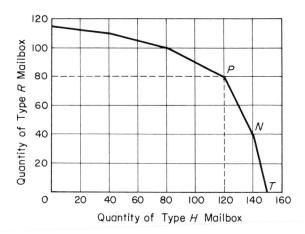

FIGURE 7–7. Production-possibilities curve.

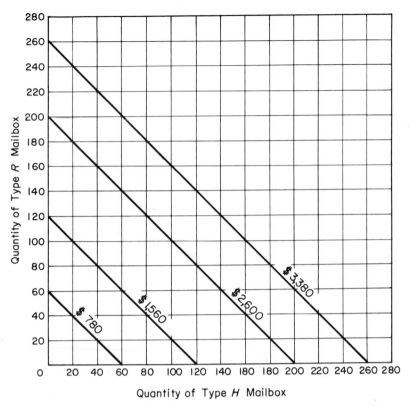

Quantity of Type R Mailbox

Quantity of Type H Mailbox

FIGURE 7–8. Sample price lines representing revenue from the sale of two types of mailboxes.

Moving from the combination at *P* to the combination at *N* reduces total production from 200 to 180. Likewise, moving from *N* to *T* sacrifices 40 type *R* mailboxes to produce only 10 more type *H* mailboxes. Thus, in moving from *P* to *N*, just two type *R* mailboxes are sacrificed for each type *H* mailbox, but going from *N* to *T* involves the sacrifice of four type *R* mailboxes for each type *H* mailbox. The sacrifice of type *R* mailboxes increases as more type *H* mailboxes are produced. The reason for this is that economic resources are not completely adaptable to alternative uses. This is one way of saying that some of the resources used to produce type *R* mailboxes are not as well suited for producing those of type *H*. For example, suppose that the type *H* mailbox (house mailbox) is more elaborate and requires more skilled hands to produce. As fewer of the simple rural mailboxes are produced, fewer additional house mailboxes can be produced with the same package of resources, since not all of the existing workers will be highly skilled.

The determination of the optimal output of type *R* and type *H* mailboxes depends on the relative prices of the outputs. This analysis is very similar to the one which determined the least-cost combination of resources to produce a particular quantity of output. There, the relative prices of resources *A* and *B* were needed to determine the right combination. In like manner, a price

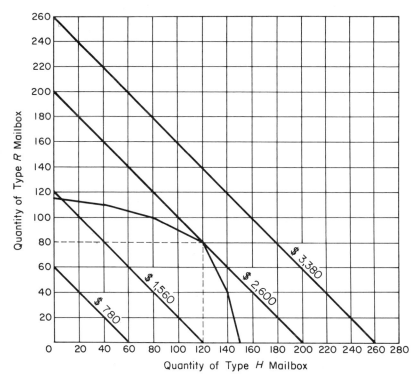

FIGURE 7-9. Optimal output.

line can be superimposed upon a pioduction-possibilities curve to illustrate the optimal output. If the selling prices of the type *R* and type *H* mailboxes were each $13, the several price lines reflecting the ratio of these prices would resemble those in Fig. 7–8. Each line represents a different amount of total revenue from the sale of both types of mailboxes.

When the production-possibilities curve in Fig. 7–7 and the price lines in Fig. 7–8 are brought together (by superimposing one graph on the other), the optimal output is indicated. The optimal output occurs when the price line is tangent to the production-possibilities curve. Any other combination indicated by the production-possibilities curve would not generate as much revenue. Figure 7–9 illustrates the optimal output, which would be 80 type *R* mailboxes and 120 type *H* mailboxes. Total revenue would be $2,600.

Linear Programming

When a firm produces one product with two inputs, economics provides the least-cost combination analysis; if two products are produced with one input or a package of inputs, economics provides the production-possibilities analysis. In reality, however, firms are faced with much more complicated decisions. They usually produce several products and may even manufacture similar products of different qualities. Firms also have many more than just two inputs available to them. For these reasons, other mathematical techniques are employed. However, the simple economic analyses of least cost and production possibilities provide the foundation for one modern technique—*linear programming*. The following discussion of linear programming is introductory and nontechnical; it is aimed at showing the relationship between this technique and economic analysis.

The term "linear programming" refers to the use of linear algebraic equations which express the various production relationships. (The reader may wish to refer to Chapter 12, which contains the algebra of linear equations.) The basic algebraic form is $Y = a + bX$; this equation will appear as a straight line on regular graph paper.[5] Linear programming is based on constant relationships and on several assumptions: for example, that output prices are not dependent on the particular firm's output, that unit costs will remain constant over a wide range of production levels, and that no diminishing returns are experienced when switching from one product to another. These assumptions are reasonable in many manufacturing situations if the level of production does not vary substantially.

The linear programming approach can be illustrated by the hypothetical production of mailboxes. Two resources, A and B, are employed to produce types H and R mailboxes. One unit of the type H mailbox requires one unit of resource A and one unit of resource B, while one unit of the type R mailbox requires $\frac{1}{2}$ unit of resource A and two units of resource B. The available supplies are limited to 160 units of resource A and 280 units of resource B. We assume that the firm can sell as many of each type of mailbox as it wishes at the going price of \$13 each. Each mailbox contributes \$13 per unit to revenue regardless of the quantity produced. The problem is to determine how many units of each type of mailbox should be produced to maximize revenue.

The available supply of each resource can be expressed in the form of an inequality. Each inequality indicates that the total usage of each resource must be less than or equal to the supply available. If each type H mailbox requires one unit of resource A, while each type R mailbox requires $\frac{1}{2}$ unit of resource A, it follows that one unit times the quantity of type H plus $\frac{1}{2}$ unit times the quantity of type R must not exceed the available supply of resource A. Since resource A is limited to 160 units, the inequation for resource A utilization would be

$$x + \tfrac{1}{2}y \le 160,$$

where x is the quantity of type H mailbox produced, and y is the quantity of type R mailbox produced. For resource B, the inequation would be

$$x + 2y \le 280.$$

[5] It would appear as a curve on logarithmic graph paper.

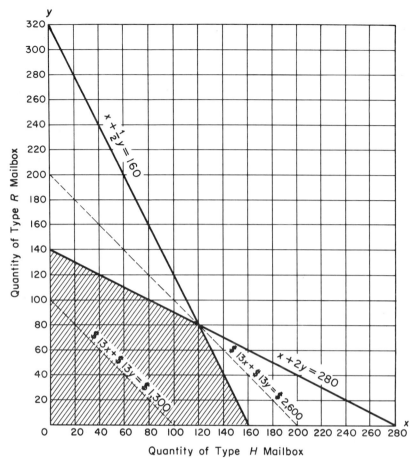

FIGURE 7-10. Determining the optimal feasible point.

We therefore have two unknowns, quantity x and quantity y, and two inequalities. In order to maximize revenues, we next construct what is known as the *objective function*, which gives the various quantities of type R and type H mailboxes that may contribute to revenues. The function is

$$\text{Revenue} = \$13x + \$13y.$$

We now have two inequalities and one equality:

$$x + \tfrac{1}{2}y \leq 160$$
$$x + 2y \leq 280$$
$$\text{Revenue} = 13x + 13y.$$

The techniques of linear programming determine the optimal quantity of type R and type H mailboxes—80 of type R and 120 of type H, with a maximum revenue of \$2,600. This solution can be arrived at algebraically or by use of a graph.

In Fig. 7-10, the function $x + \tfrac{1}{2}y = 160$ (rearranged as $y = 320 - 2x$

153

to provide the vertical intercept and slope) has been plotted and labeled. Any point on or below it is a *feasible point;* that is, the total mailbox output may be equal to or less than the available supply of resource *A*. The function $x + 2y = 280$ (rearranged as $y = 140 - \frac{1}{2}x$) has also been plotted and labeled. Any point on or below it is a feasible point in terms of the use of resource *B*. The shaded area represents the *area of feasible points*, which is subject to the supply limitations of both resources. Any point within this area represents a production-possibilities combination within the two given supply constraints.

The *optimal feasible point* within this region is the production possibility that maximizes revenues. In Fig. 7–10 the objective function $(R = \$13x + \$13y)$ is displayed as a broken line. The problem is to select the objective function which will yield the highest revenue while remaining within the range of production possibilities. Since each type of mailbox contributes $13 apiece to revenue, the objective function for a total revenue of $1,300 would intersect the left-hand scale at 100. That is to say, if 100 type *R* mailboxes and no type *H* mailboxes were sold, the total revenue would be $1,300. In the same manner, with 100 type *H* mailboxes and no type *R* mailboxes, the objective function would intercept the bottom scale at 100, which also wuold result in $1,300.

The next step is to shift to another objective function farther from the origin that represents a larger total revenue and the same $13 price for each type mailbox. The objective function labeled $2,600 is such an example which also contains the optimal feasible point, indicated at *P*, where 80 type *R* mailboxes and 120 type *H* mailboxes are produced. No other combination of mailbox output would produce this much revenue, given the constraints established by each resource supply.

This can be verified algebraically. Since $x + \frac{1}{2}y = 160$ and $x + 2y = 280$, we can solve for y after rearranging each expression and setting one equal to the other. The calculations are as follows:

$$x = 160 - \tfrac{1}{2}y$$
$$x = 280 - 2y$$
$$160 - \tfrac{1}{2}y = 280 - 2y$$
$$1\tfrac{1}{2}y = 120$$
$$y = 80.$$

Solving for x by substitution,

$$x = 160 - \tfrac{1}{2}(80)$$
$$x = 120.$$

Revenue is maximized at $2,600 ($13 × 120 + $13 × 80). This maximization can be verified by selecting any other combination of x and y and calculating the revenues.

Often manufacturing or production activities are divided into departments or processes. Before the final product is available for sale, several of
these departments or processes must be utilized to convert the raw materials
into a finished product. The Hypothetical Mailbox Manufacturing Company
uses five departments to manufacture mailboxes: the cutting, stamping, shaping, finishing, and assembling departments. First, parts of the mailbox are
cut from metal sheets. Several of the parts are then stamped with certain
indentations. Other cuttings are formed into either a rectangular or a rounded
shape. In the finishing department, various parts and accessories are plated,
painted, or polished. Finally, all parts are attached and assembled to make
the complete mailbox. Now that several departments are required to produce
mailboxes, a multi-input dimension has been added to production.

Different procedures are used in each department depending upon the
type and quality of mailbox to be produced. The flow of materials and partially completed mailboxes through these various departments should be accomplished as efficiently as possible. This efficient flow can be achieved by using
proper scheduling techniques. (New methods are being perfected for solving
scheduling problems in industry and in military logistic operations. One of
these, the *critical-path method*, is explained in the Annex to this chapter.)

The finished mailbox requires a certain amount of each department's
capacity. This may be expressed in such units as machine time, man-hours, or
heat intensity. Each department will also have certain capacity limits. Suppose
that one unit of a type *H* mailbox requires one unit of the cutting department's
capacity, one unit of the stamping department's capacity, one unit of the plating department's capacity, two units of the finishing department's capacity,
and four units of the assembling department's capacity. The similar requirements for one unit of a type *R* mailbox might be eight, four, two, one, and
one. These requirements and departmental capacities are summarized in
Table 7–7.

TABLE 7–7

CAPACITY REQUIREMENTS FOR TYPE *R* AND TYPE *H* MAILBOXES

Mailbox Type	Department	Capacity Requirement Per Unit of Mailbox
H	1 (cutting)	1
H	2 (stamping)	1
H	3 (shaping)	1
H	4 (finishing)	2
H	5 (assembling)	4
R	1 (cutting)	8
R	2 (stamping)	4
R	3 (shaping)	2
R	4 (finishing)	1
R	5 (assembling)	1

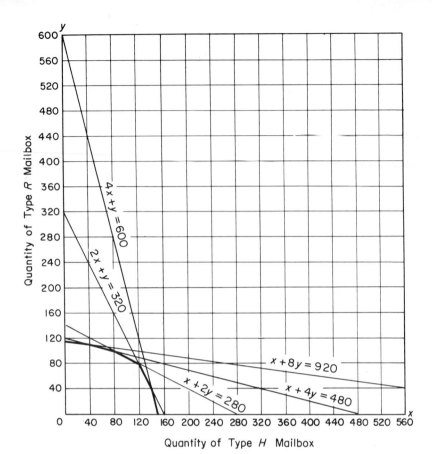

FIGURE 7–11. Area of feasible points.

The capacities of the five departments are: cutting department, 920 units; stamping department, 480 units; shaping department, 280 units; finishing department, 320 units; and assembling department, 600 units. With x standing for the quantity of type H mailboxes and y for the quantity of type R mailboxes, the departmental contributions may be expressed as follows:

Cutting department: $x + 8y \leq 920$
Stamping department: $x + 4y \leq 480$
Shaping department: $x + 2y \leq 280$
Finishing department: $2x + y \leq 320$
Assembling department: $4x + y \leq 600$.

These inequalities are presented graphically in Fig. 7–11. The area of feasible points is limited by the heavily shaded portion of each line, which also constitutes a production-possibilities curve (discussed previously); this reveals the relationship between economic analysis and linear programming.

Using the objective function, Revenue $= \$13x + \$13y$, the optimal quantities of type R and type H mailboxes are 80 and 120, respectively. This solution is conveniently determined graphically. The objective function

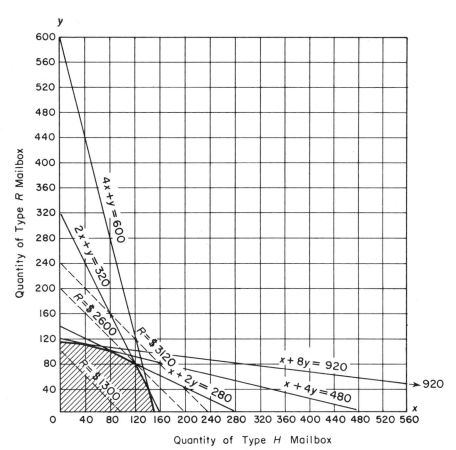

FIGURE 7-12. **Optimal feasible solution.**

can be graphed for different values of revenue as a series of parallel lines. Several of these parallel lines are shown as the dashed lines in Fig. 7-12. Two of the lines are the same ones that were shown in Fig. 7-10 when only two constraints were present. In each of the graphs, the lines representing objective functions have slopes of 1. The task is to locate the optimal quantities of type R and type H mailboxes on the highest of these parallel lines which makes contact with the shaded area. The dashed line labeled R(revenue) = \$2,600 in Fig. 7-12 is the highest line that does not fall outside this area. Therefore, the point $x = 120$, $y = 80$, which lies both on this line and within the shaded area, is the best solution; revenue is maximized and all the inequalities are satisfied. This graphic procedure is only practical when there are no more than two variables.

An algebraic procedure for solving this same problem requires solving the different sets of simultaneous equations over and over until all the possible solutions have been exhausted and the set of variables that has yielded the highest value of the objective function has been selected. This value is subject to the restriction that all the inequalities must also be satisfied. Therefore, the calculations can only solve those unique pairs of equations that represent the

157

inequality constraints which are corners of the feasible region. The solutions are represented by intersections of the inequalities which appear in Fig. 7–11. The algebraic method thus requires finding solutions to the following six pairs of equations:

1.	$x = 0$	4.	$x + 2y = 280$	
	$x + 8y = 920$		$2x + y = 320$	
2.	$x + 8y = 920$	5.	$4x + y = 600$	
	$x + 4y = 480$		$2x + y = 320$	
3.	$x + 4y = 480$	6.	$4x + y = 600$	
	$x + 2y = 280$		$y = 0.$	

These six solutions are illustrated in Fig. 7–11 as the intersections that form the corners of the shaded area.

Other pairs of equations that may have unique solutions represent intersections outside the shaded area. The shaded area is referred to as the *feasible* region; it contains all feasible solutions. The solutions on the edge of the feasible region represent *basic* feasible solutions. The best basic feasible solution is called the *optimal* feasible solution.

When they are solved, the six pairs of equations render the following values for x and y. These values are substituted into the objective function to determine the revenue in each case.

1.	$x = 0$	4.	$x = 120$	
	$y = 115$		$y = 80$	
	Revenue $= \$1,495$		Revenue $= \$2,600$	
2.	$x = 40$	5.	$x = 140$	
	$y = 110$		$y = 40$	
	Revenue $= \$1,950$		Revenue $= \$2,340$	
3.	$x = 80$	6.	$x = 150$	
	$y = 100$		$y = 0$	
	Revenue $= \$2,340$		Revenue $= \$1,950.$	

The fourth pair of equations results in the solution that renders the largest value of revenue. Therefore, $x = 120$, $y = 80$ is the *optimal* feasible solution.

As long as production involves only two outputs (or two algebraic unknowns), an analysis can proceed according to a two-dimensional graph. Even when there are more than two inputs, as when five departments are needed to produce mailboxes, if they are expressed in terms of no more than two products or unknowns, the analysis can proceed according to graphic procedures or·simple algebraic methods. However, more complex problems, especially those which involve several unknowns, require the use of *matrix algebra* or the *simplex method.* The simplex method is used to solve the mailbox problem in Chapter 14, where the problem is made more complex by considering the production of four, instead of two, types of mailboxes. In this way, it is expanded into a multi-product as well as multi-input problem, which is more typical of those found in modern business operations.

ANNEX: THE CRITICAL-PATH METHOD

Production managers must keep tight control over the timing and budgets of many complex, widely scattered production activities. Scheduling of activities actually consists of a multitude of interrelated decisions—e.g., when to promise delivery, how many painters or machinists to request for a given week and project, when to order materials, which subcontractors to employ, and when to employ them. The production manager is not the only manager faced with complex scheduling jobs, however. The organization and scheduling required for the building of a house, skyscraper, factory, ship, or aircraft are also quite complicated. These projects require very careful planning and timing to prevent bottlenecks or at least to anticipate where they might occur.

Interest in the quantitative methods of decision theory is now booming, due partly to the striking success of two new scheduling procedures: the critical-path method (CPM) and the program evaluation and review technique (PERT), which differ from each other in only a few details. Both of these procedures were developed in the United States more or less simultaneously. It is rumored that PERT speeded up by two years the construction of the Polaris submarine.

Much of the credit for CPM belongs to James E. Kelley, Jr. In 1957, while working for Remington Rand, Kelley joined with a group of operations research specialists from E. I. Du Pont de Nemours to design a procedure for scheduling chemical-plant construction. With the aid of the critical-path concept, Kelley introduced new ways to expedite a project more economically.

Critical-path scheduling is a technique with three phases: (1) planning and diagramming, (2) allocating resources and determining costs and job durations, and (3) analyzing. By its very nature, CPM is an example of the various management functions in action. Its purpose is to complete a project in the shortest possible time with the least waste of resources.

Briefly, CPM requires analyzing all the work that must be done, breaking the work down into individual tasks, and estimating how long each task will take and how much it will cost. The information is then diagrammed as a network that shows which activities must await the completion of other jobs as well as which tasks can be coordinated with other phases of the project.

The first phase of CPM is planning and diagramming, in which everything that must be done is listed in proper sequence. For instance, wooden forms must always be put into place before concrete can be poured. Next, the diagramming, which is the heart of the technique, pictures the entire project

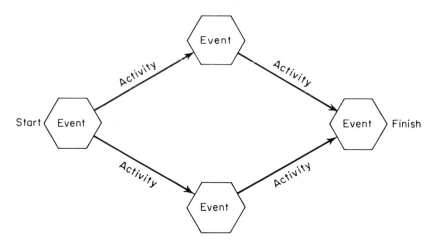

FIGURE 7–13.   CPM network.

as a network of events and shows the specific points in time when segments of the plan must be begun or finished. Each job is indicated by an arrow; although the length of the arrow is not important, its direction is because it indicates the sequence of jobs. The completion of a specific activity in the project, whether it is a decision point or a physical accomplishment, is defined as an *event*. Events and activities are illustrated in the network diagram of Fig. 7–13. The main advantage of a network diagram is that it allows the decision maker to see the interrelationships of the jobs at a glance.

Allocating resources and determining costs and job durations constitute the second phase of CPM. Each activity requires the allocation of manpower, materials, equipment, and facilities. This is important because the allocation of resources determines the elapsed time and the cost of each activity. Estimates are made of the time needed to complete an activity and the costs involved. No costs are involved in *events* because they represent the completion of activities.

A *path* may be defined as the chain of sequential events and activities required to move from the starting point of a project to its completion. Work may be carried out along any one path or concurrently along several. The various paths represent a network; the longest is the *critical path*. The determination of the critical path (or paths) is the core of the analyzing phase. Once this path has been determined, resources can be shifted from slack activities to critical ones. With CPM, managers have a tool by which this can be accomplished.

An uninformed manager may shorten the completion time of a project by simply increasing resources across the board for all activities. However, this shotgun approach will increase total costs more than is necessary. The manager who uses CPM applies a precision-rifle approach to achieve more

TABLE 7–8

TIME AND COST DATA FOR CPM

| Job | Normal | | Crash | | Additional Cost per |
	Hours	Cost	Hours	Cost	Hour for Expediting
A	4	$10	3	$15	$5
B	3	5	2	7	2
C	6	14	4	22	4
D	3	10	2	15	5
E	9	20	7	26	3
F	5	15	2	36	7
Total		$74		$121	

effective employment of resources, directing his attention to the critical areas.

The essential steps in CPM are demonstrated by the analysis of a scheduling problem involving the Hypothetical Mailbox Manufacturing Company; the data are given in Table 7–8. The problem is to determine the cheapest way to expedite the production of an order of mailboxes. The jobs signified by letters in the table are identified in the following list:

Job A—cutting the lids and accessories
Job B—cutting the boxes
Job C—stamping the lids
Job D—shaping the boxes
Job E—plating and finishing the accessories
Job F—painting the lids and boxes.

The *normal* time in hours for each job is listed in column 2 of Table 7–8; the total cost that normally results for each job is given in column 3. The minimum time and total cost for each job under *crash* conditions appear in columns 4 and 5, respectively, and the additional cost per hour for expediting each job is given in column 6. The total cost for each job under crash conditions reflects the normal costs plus the costs required to speed up the job. For example, the normal cost for job A, which takes four hours, is $10. The total cost for completing the job in only three hours (crash program) would be $15. Consequently, the additional cost for expediting job A is $5 ($15 − $10 = $5). This is indicated in column 6.

A glance at job C reveals a slightly different situation. You will notice that the cost, for completing the job in the normal time of six hours is $14 and the cost for completing the job in four hours is $22. Although this should reflect an additional cost of $8, column 6 indicates an additional cost of only $4. This can be clarified by pointing out that the $4, as well as each of the other costs in column 6, reflects the additional cost *per hour*. The reduction of job C by two hours requires additional costs of $8, which average out to $4 per hour.

The various network paths are demonstrated and labeled in Fig. 7–14.

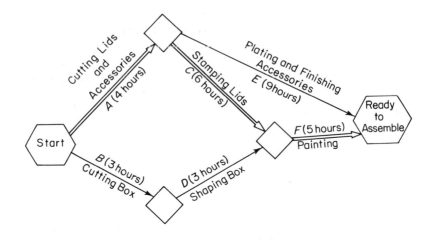

Job path A—C—F requires 15 hours
Job path A — E   requires 13 hours
Job path B—D—F requires 11 hours

FIGURE 7–14.   Network of job paths for the Hypothetical Mailbox Manufacturing Company.

The normal completion time for each job is also indicated. The critical path (the longest in time) is the combination of jobs *A*, *C*, and *F*, which requires a total of 15 hours; it is indicated by the heavier line. The other two job paths, *A–E* and *B–D–F*, require 13 hours and 11 hours, respectively. The jobs on the critical path determine the time needed to complete the whole project; the other two can be delayed if necessary.

As the totals in Table 7–8 show, the manager can get all the jobs done as quickly as possible by spending an extra \$47 (\$121 − \$74 = \$47). However, he may be able to shorten the completion time of the entire project without "crashing" every job by investigating the alternatives. The network of job paths in Fig. 7–14 and the data in Table 7–8 help to indicate these alternatives.

Investigating the jobs on the critical path is the key to selecting the proper alternative. The first step is to look at these jobs and select the one that has the lowest expediting cost per hour. The cost of expediting job *C* is only \$4 per hour as compared with job *A*, which is \$5 per hour, and job *F*, which is \$7 per hour (column 6, Table 7–8). When job *C* is reduced by one hour at an additional cost of \$4, job path *A–C–F* still remains the only critical path. It can be shortened to 13 hours by reducing job *C* another hour at an additional cost of \$4.

Next, *A* is reduced by one hour at a cost of \$5; this reduction shortens the critical paths *A–C–F* and *A–E* to 12 hours. This procedure could continue as long as there was leeway in the various jobs involved in the critical paths.

The remaining steps proceed as follows: Job F and job E are reduced by one hour each at an additional cost of $7 and $3, respectively, for a total cost of $10. This reduces A–C–F and A–E to 11 hours. Job path B–D–F, at 11 hours, now also is a critical path. If B, E, and F are reduced one hour each at a total cost of $12, the overall project will require ten hours, with some leeway or additional time available in job F and job D. This would not reduce overall time because job path A–E cannot be shortened any more.

The manager has now spent an additional $35 on the CPM program compared with the $47 he might have spent to crash all the jobs; this is a savings of $12. As one might expect, $12 is the total value of slack time available in job F and job D.

Other factors must be considered in using CPM. For instance, in a contracting job, there may be a penalty for failing to complete the project on schedule. However, in practice, contractors have found that they can make more profit by proceeding slowly and paying a penalty rather than by paying the heavy overtime costs associated with a crash program. In other instances, costs associated with time periods, such as depreciation on equipment, may make it possible to reduce the overall costs when the project time is reduced.

PROBLEMS AND PROJECTS

1. Calculate the cost to produce 200 mailboxes for each combination of resource A and resource B. Use the production data in Table 7–2. The price of resource A is $10; resource B costs $30. Indicate the least-cost combination. (The cost for each combination necessary to produce 30 mailboxes appears in Table 7–3.)
2. Plot the alternative combinations of resources A and B necessary to produce 200 mailboxes. The information appears in Table 7–2. Plot the combinations on a piece of graph paper, indicating the least-cost combination by a cost-outlay line. The price of resource A is $10 and resource B is $30. (The least-cost combination for 30 mailboxes at these same resource prices is illustrated in Fig. 7–5. Point N indicates the least-cost combination.) Verify your results with the calculations in Problem 1 above.
3. Using the graph and instructions in Problem 2, plot another cost-outlay line reflecting different resource prices. Resource A is now $30 and resource B is $10. Verify this new least-cost combination by calculating the cost for each combination of resources A and B available to produce 200 mailboxes. Summarize in a statement the effect of a change in resource prices on the allocation or use of resources.
4. This exercise represents the first part of a *continuous* problem involving a hypothetical firm that produces folding chairs. The first part of the problem deals with the production information of the Hypothetical Chair Manufacturing Company. The problem continues in the Problems and Projects section of the next chapter.

a. The Hypothetical Chair Manufacturing Company produces a high-quality folding chair. The following production information represents the alternative combinations of resources A and B required to produce various quantities of chairs. Each unit of resource A and each unit of resource B is a mixture of various factors of production as defined in the text material. Plot the various production functions on a piece of graph paper. On the left-hand scale graduate 0 to 140 units of resource A. On the bottom scale graduate 0 to 140 units of resource B. Each scale should be identical.

b. The price of resource A is $10 and the price of resource B is $30. Indicate on your graph the least-cost combination of resources A and B to produce 50 folding chairs. Construct a cost-outlay line and indicate the point of tangency. Verify this to be the least-cost combination by calculating and listing the total cost for each combination of resources A and B required to produce 50 folding chairs.

c. The law of diminishing returns is also applicable to the Hypothetical Chair Manufacturing Company. The firm is operating over a short-run period with a fixed quantity of resource A. Indicate on the graph constructed in part (b) above the various quantities of resource B that must be combined with 35 units of resource A to produce different outputs.

HYPOTHETICAL CHAIR MANUFACTURING COMPANY

Qunatity of Output		Alternative Combinations of A and B							
20	A	44	35	27	20	14	10	7	5	4
	B	4	5	7	10	14	20	27	35	44
50	A	52	43	35	28	22	18	15	13	12
	B	12	13	15	18	22	28	35	43	52
120	A	59	50	42	35	29	25	22	20	19
	B	19	20	22	25	29	35	42	50	59
180	A	65	56	48	41	35	31	28	26	25
	B	25	26	28	31	35	41	48	56	65
220	A	69	60	52	45	39	35	32	30	29
	B	29	30	32	35	39	45	52	60	69
240	A	72	63	55	48	42	38	35	33	32
	B	32	33	35	38	42	48	55	63	72
250	A	74	65	57	50	44	40	37	35	34
	B	34	35	37	40	44	50	57	65	74
280	A	84	76	68	61	55	51	48	46	45
	B	45	46	48	51	55	61	68	76	84
300	A	100	91	83	76	70	66	63	61	60
	B	60	61	63	66	70	76	83	91	100

First, draw a line parallel to the bottom scale that intercepts the left-hand scale at 35 units of resource A. At the intersection of this horizontal line with each production function, drop a dashed line to the bottom scale. Indicate the quantity of resource B each of these dashed lines suggests on the bottom axis. (This is illustrated for mailboxes in Fig. 7–6.) Verify these combinations of A and B with the production information for the Hypothetical Chair Manufacturing Company. Make a table similar to Table 7–5 and indicate in the respective columns the units of resources A and B and the output of chairs for each combination. Then calculate the change in output (what economists call "marginal product"). Summarize in a statement what the change in output reflects. This information will be used in the next part of the problem, which continues in the Problems and Projects section of the next chapter.

PRODUCTION LEVELS FOR HYPOTHETICAL CHAIR MANUFACTURING COMPANY

Resource A	Resource B	Chairs	Marginal Product

5. Use linear programming to solve the production problem of the Hypothetical Infratronic Manufacturing Company. The company produces two types of infrared broilers that can cook food in a matter of seconds. It sells the standard model for $10 and the deluxe model for $20. The following information describes the operating requirements and capacities of each department: department A has a daily capacity of 360 units; department B a daily capacity of 160 units; and department C a daily capacity of 280 units. The standard broiler (which can be designated as x) requires one unit of department A's capacity, two units of department B's

capacity, and four units of department C's capacity. The deluxe broiler (which can be designated as y) requires four units of department A's capacity, one unit of department B's capacity, and one unit of department C's capacity.

a. Illustrate graphically the three department capacities and utilization rates.

b. Determine algebraically the quantity of each model of broiler that should be produced in order to maximize the company's revenue each day. Be sure to solve the pairs of equations that represent feasible points, then select the optimal solution.

c. Plot the price line (objective function) on the graph in part (a) to verify your algebraic solution.

6. The Hypothetical Satellite Swimming Pool Company has been assigned the job of installing a Galaxy-model pool at the Moonmist apartment house. There is a scheduling problem associated with constructing the pool, because the various aspects of the job require that certain phases be completed before others. However, some tasks can be accomplished simultaneously. For example, the hole in the ground must be dug before cement and tile can be placed; on the other hand, the diving board and the filter system can be installed at the same time. The various tasks required to complete the job are shown in the critical-path diagram given below. The time for each task is also supplied.

a. List the paths in this network and designate which is the critical path.
b. What does the critical path indicate?
c. What can be done to alter the completion time?

The solution of this problem depends upon an understanding of the material in the Annex.

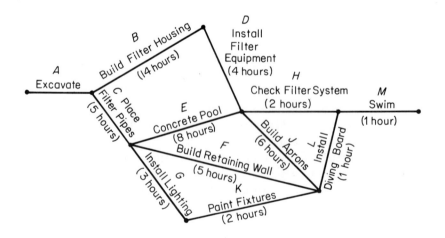

SELECTED REFERENCES

Allen, Clark Lee, *The Framework of Price Theory*, Chaps. 13, 14. Belmont, Calif.: Wadsworth Publishing Company, Inc., 1967.

Brennan, Michael J., *The Theory of Economic Statics*, Chap. 9. Englewood Cliffs, N. J.: Prentice-Hall, Inc., 1965.

Leftwich, Richard H., *The Price System and Resource Allocation*, Chap. 7, Appendix. New York: Holt, Rinehart & Winston, Inc., 1966.

McKenna, Joseph P., *Intermediate Economic Theory*, Chaps. 3, 4. New York: Dryden Press, 1958.

Stonier, Alfred W., and Douglas C. Hague, *A Textbook of Economic Theory*, Chap. 10. New York: John Wiley & Sons, Inc., 1964.

Watson, Donald S., *Price Theory and Its Uses*, Chaps. 9, 10, 12. Boston: Houghton Mifflin Company, 1963.

8

COST ANALYSIS

The cost of producing a good or service is vital information for making business decisions, since costs play an important role in determining a business firm's willingness to offer goods and services for sale. For example, as costs per unit of output rise, business firms may become reluctant to produce. In making such decisions, however, it is equally important to consider the demand and price of the product or service. We will see in a later chapter how prices and costs interact to provide a basis for business decisions.

The purpose of this chapter is threefold. First, the nature of costs will be examined, including some important cost classifications which require further attention. Second, the structure of costs in a business enterprise will be explored. This will be accomplished chiefly by studying a hypothetical business firm. Third, adjustments in the size of a firm will be considered. Business firms experience changes in cost conditions as they alter their scale of operation. Procedures for estimating costs are contained in the Annex to this chapter.

THE NATURE OF COSTS

Various Concepts of Costs

Costs reflect in money terms the amount of resources used to produce goods and services. The concept that costs represent actual *money outlays* is usually included in any analysis. According to this concept, costs reflect money expenditures for such things as labor and materials. The costs in this category represent the money outlay for the amount of each resource used to produce a certain quantity of output. For example, 200 mailboxes could be produced with a money outlay of $500 for men, materials, and supplies.

However, other resources must also be used to produce this quantity of mailboxes.

Depreciation is another reflection of cost that represents an actual money outlay, although the outlay usually does not occur during the same time period in which the 200 mailboxes are actually produced. Depreciation is a method of estimating the portion of a resource that is used up during a specific period of time: a week, month, or year. For example, the wear and tear on a machine during a given period of time would be reflected by depreciation estimates or charges. If the machine cost $2,400 and was expected to last for 24 months, a cost of $100 might be allocated to its depreciation each month. (Assume that the machine would not have any scrap value.) Other methods can be used in calculating depreciation; they are designed to reflect as accurately as possible the actual wear and tear that occurs.

Another important consideration is the concept of *opportunity costs*. This concept reflects the fact that almost anything we do means giving up the opportunity to do something else. The businessman who employs men and machines must always consider their alternative uses. In order to attract resources, he must pay at least what they are worth to someone else. Consequently, most costs recorded by business firms are a reflection of opportunity costs.

In some cases, however, these costs go unrecorded. Sometimes the owner of a small business overlooks his opportunity costs. He should consider as a cost to his business the higher salary he could earn managing a business for someone else. In like manner, when an owner obtains the services of his wife three afternoons a week to "ring up the cash register" or to "post the journals," the cost to the firm is what she could earn working for someone else. (In real terms the cost to the husband might be the sacrifice of a well-cooked meal that evening.) Moreover, investing money in a business means forgoing the opportunity to earn a return by lending the money to someone or investing it somewhere else.

The costs of the owner's or his wife's services are the costs of doing business. Money invested in one's own business need not go unpaid, or without return, sometimes it is included in profits. Nevertheless, the costs of operation are often understated. If some costs are not recorded, incorrect decisions may be made. Including all costs may make it apparent that the firm is not efficient and may even suggest that the business should close down. Or it may suggest that the prices of the products should be raised.

Another type of cost that usually is not reflected in a business firm's records is what economists call *social cost*. Business firms generally will not pay these costs unless they are forced to by law or taxation. For example, when industrial wastes pollute the rivers and streams from which communities obtain their water, society—in the form of either individuals or communities —bears the cost of softening and purifying the water before use. Other production activities may produce harmful byproducts, such as odors, fumes, and smoke, that affect the general populace.

Classification of Operating Costs

For purposes of business analysis, it is convenient to classify operating costs into two categories: those that do not vary with the amount of output, called *fixed costs*, and those that do, called *variable costs*. Fixed costs are associated with fixed resources and variable costs with variable resources.

Fixed costs typically include contracted rent for land, charges for depreciation, taxes on real estate, and interest on borrowed funds, to cite only a few. Variable costs typically include wages for labor, payments for materials and supplies, expenses for transportation, and remittances to utility companies.

The distinction between fixed and variable resources depends upon the period of time under consideration. In the short run, some resources such as land, buildings, and machines are not readily available; however, such resources as men, materials, and supplies can be acquired easily. In the long run, all resources are variable, assuming that the period is long enough. Therefore, when costs are separated into "fixed" and "variable" categories, it is automatically assumed that the analysis is concerned with the short run.

The time period of production will vary from industry to industry. In some, fixed resources can be added to or subtracted from other assets in a short period of time; in others, the addition of fixed resources may take several years. The short run is much shorter for a restaurant than for a basic steel firm. The capacity of the restaurant can be increased in a few months by adding chairs and tables or even floor space, while it may take several years to add a furnace to the capacity of the steel firm.

Some costs are difficult to classify. Wages for a watchman may be more fixed than variable because his services do not change with the level of production. Depreciation is another problem. Sometimes machines wear out faster with greater use. Although part of the depreciation charge can be allocated to fixed costs, that part associated with the rate of use should be allocated to variable costs. In many instances, costs are a mixture of fixed and variable characteristics.

COST STRUCTURE

There are two convenient methods of describing and calculating the costs of a business firm: as *totals* or as *averages*. The short-run cost structure of the Hypothetical Mailbox Manufacturing Company will be used to explain each method. This will be accomplished by expanding on the production information for the company that was presented in Chapter 7.

Total-Cost Approach

Total costs are merely the sum of total fixed costs and total variable costs. Total fixed costs are those allocated by the firm for the fixed resources that are used up during the production period. The firm cannot vary the quantities of the fixed resources it uses in each short-run period of time. Total fixed costs will remain the same or constant regardless of the amount of output produced during each time period. Total variable costs, however, are a different matter; they change as output changes. The total variable costs will depend upon the amount of variable resources used during the production period.

The total-cost schedule of the Hypothetical Mailbox Manufacturing Company is presented in Table 8–1. The data come from the production information presented in Chapter 7. By varying the quantity of variable resources, different quantities of mailboxes are produced. For 30 units of resource *A* at $10 a unit, the total fixed costs will be $300. The cost for each unit of the variable resource, resource *B*, is $30. While the total fixed cost will remain at $300, total variable costs will change as additional units of resource *B* are used to produce different quantities of mailboxes.

TABLE 8–1

TOTAL COSTS OF HYPOTHETICAL MAILBOX MANUFACTURING COMPANY

Units of Resource A	Units of Resource B	Quantity of Mailboxes	Total Fixed Costs	Total Variable Costs	Total Costs
30	10	30	$300	$ 300	$ 600
30	20	70	300	600	900
30	30	130	300	900	1,200
30	40	170	300	1,200	1,500
30	50	200	300	1,500	1,800
30	60	220	300	1,800	2,100
30	70	230	300	2,100	2,400

From the top row of figures in Table 8–1, we see that 30 units of resource *A* and 10 units of resource *B* will produce 30 mailboxes. These 30 mailboxes will require $300 of fixed costs and $300 of variable costs, a total of $600. If the production scheduled for one day required the production of 170 mailboxes, then total cost would be $1,500 (shaded row). To produce 170 mailboxes would require 30 units of the fixed resource *A*, totaling $300 (30 × $10), and 40 units of the variable resource *B*, totaling $1,200 (40 × $30). The other rows represent costs associated with other levels or rates of production. Since resource *A* is fixed in quantity, the costs in the table are necessarily short-run costs.

The corresponding total-cost curves for the Hypothetical Mailbox Manufacturing Company are plotted in Fig. 8–1. Note that the total-fixed-cost

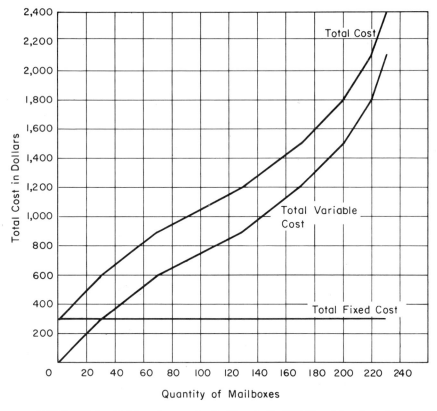

FIGURE 8–1.   **Total-cost curves for the Hypothetical Mailbox Manufacturing**
Company.

curve is parallel to the quantity axis and is above the axis by the amount of
total fixed costs; i.e., by $300. The total-variable-cost curve shows a charac-
teristic that usually is typical of a firm's total variable costs: that is, as output
increases by a constant amount, total variable costs at first increase at a decreasing rate, then increase at an increasing rate. This characteristic of the
total-variable-cost curve reflects the law of diminishing returns, explained
in Chapter 7. The total-cost curve is merely the summation of the total-
fixed-cost and total-variable-cost curves. Total-cost curves are useful in
breakeven analysis, which will be developed in Chapter 10.

Average-Cost Approach

Average-cost concepts are another way of analyzing the cost structure
of a business firm. Average cost reflects the cost per unit of output; it is obtained by dividing total costs by the quantity of output. Unit or average

costs are useful in price and output analysis. The unit-cost curves are the average-fixed-cost curve, the average-variable-cost curve, the average-cost curve, and the marginal-cost curve.

Average fixed costs, or fixed costs per unit of output for different levels of production, are obtained by dividing total fixed costs by each level of output. Average variable costs, or variable costs per unit of output for different levels of production, are obtained by dividing total variable costs by each level of output. Average costs, or the entire cost per unit of output for different levels of production, are obtained by adding together the unit fixed costs and unit variable costs for each particular level of output. And marginal costs, or the changes in cost per unit of output, are obtained by dividing the changes in total variable cost (or total cost) by the changes in output that occur from one level of production to the next. (The marginal-cost figures in Table 8–2 are placed at half-intervals because each represents the average change in cost between two levels of output.)

A few calculations will verify these cost relationships. The cost information for the Hypothetical Mailbox Manufacturing Company appears in Table 8–2. The total-cost data are extracted from Table 8–1. At an output of 130

TABLE 8–2

COSTS OF HYPOTHETICAL MAILBOX MANUFACTURING COMPANY

Quantity of Mailboxes	Total Fixed Costs	Total Variable Costs	Total Costs	Average Fixed Costs	Average Variable Costs	Average Costs	Marginal Costs
30	$300	$ 300	$ 600	$10.00	$10.00	$20.00	
70	300	600	900	4.29	8.57	12.86	$ 7.50
130	300	900	1,200	2.31	6.92	9.23	5.00
170	300	1,200	1,500	1.76	7.06	8.82	7.50
200	300	1,500	1,800	1.50	7.50	9.00	10.00
220	300	1,800	2,100	1.37	8.18	9.55	15.00
230	300	2,100	2,400	1.30	9.13	10.43	30.00

mailboxes (shaded area), the total fixed costs of $300 divided by 130 mailboxes provide an average fixed cost of $2.31. At this same output or level of production the total variable costs of $900 divided by 130 mailboxes produce an average variable cost of $6.92. When the average fixed cost and the average variable cost are added together, they yield an average cost of $9.23. This $9.23 is the cost per mailbox when 130 mailboxes are produced. It can also be arrived at by dividing the total cost of $1,200 by 130.

Marginal cost requires careful explanation. It is a reflection of the *change* in unit costs as the level of production changes. The $5.00 marginal-cost figure in the last column of Table 8–2 was derived by dividing the $300 change in total cost by 60 (the change from 70 to 130 units in the quantity of mailboxes produced). Therefore, the $5.00 marginal cost represents the average change in cost for this particular change in output of 60 mailboxes. The *total* marginal cost for the 60 mailboxes would be $300.

The marginal cost per unit of output reflects the extent to which the costs of production change from one level of output to another. For this reason, marginal cost is very useful in making price and output decisions. For example, in deciding whether or not to increase output, it would be helpful to know the effect this would have on costs. If the additional cost of producing one more mailbox exceeds the additional revenue from its sale, the effect will be to depress profits; and it therefore will not be desirable to increase production. It is very important to realize that the *additional* cost per unit is provided by marginal-cost data; it is not evident from the other average-cost data. Average cost, for example, divides the additional cost into the *total number* of mailboxes produced. For this reason it would not give the additional cost of producing one more unit.

There are certain interesting and very important characteristics of the cost structure of the Hypothetical Mailbox Manufacturing Company that are also applicable to business enterprise in general. These characteristics can be best explained when the average or unit-cost data are illustrated as *cost curves*. The average-cost data in Table 8–2 are plotted in Fig. 8–2. The bottom scale measures the quantity of mailboxes produced, and the left-hand scale, in contrast to Fig. 8–1, measures the average or unit cost in dollars.

The average-fixed-cost curve starts off at $10.00 and continues to fall as the level of output becomes greater. Since the total fixed cost remains the same regardless of the level of output, fixed costs per unit will fall because the total is spread over more and more units of output. This is where the common notion of "spreading fixed costs" comes from. It is particularly relevant to firms that have high fixed costs relative to other costs.

Next, it is obvious from the curves in Fig. 8–2 that the average-variable-cost and average-total-cost curves are *U-shaped*. This is explained by the law of diminishing returns. The *U*-shaped nature of the two cost curves verifies the production principle that output first increases at an increasing rate, then reaches a point where it starts to increase at a decreasing rate. This is reflected in the fact that average variable costs decrease with higher levels of output, then reach a point where they increase with higher levels of output. Furthermore, the average-variable-cost and average-cost curves are separated by the fixed costs per unit at each quantity of output. Since fixed costs per unit become smaller and smaller as the quantity of output increases, the average-variable-cost curve and the average-cost curve will approach each other.

Since the average-cost curve reflects all costs, its lowest point is important. The lowest point on this curve represents the most efficient rate of production for the firm with a given amount of the fixed resource. The marginal-cost curve will intersect the average-cost curve at this point.

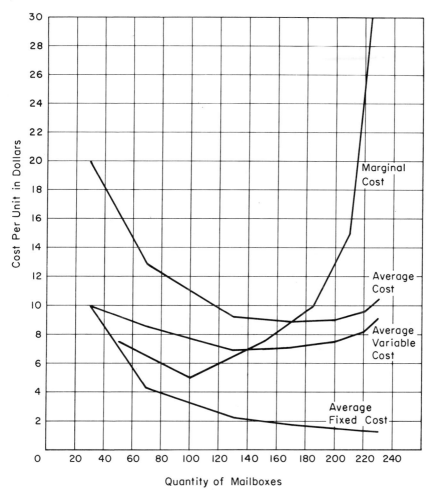

FIGURE 8–2. Average-cost data of the Hypothetical Mailbox Manufacturing Company.

The Hypothetical Mailbox Manufacturing Company reaches a minimum average cost of $8.82 at an output of 170 mailboxes. This is the most efficient rate of production for the firm when its scale of operations is limited by the use of 30 units of the fixed resource, resource *A*. However, if the company altered its capacity (that is, if it increased the use of resource *A*), it could achieve an even lower unit cost because a least-cost combination of resources *A* and *B* for 170 mailboxes could be achieved. The present use of 30 units of resource *A* and 40 units of resource *B* to produce 170 mailboxes is not a least-cost combination of the resources with their given prices of $10 and

$30, respectively. In other words, the firm should expand. It should build a larger building and acquire more machines. This is the next fundamental phase of business operations that will be analyzed.

It was stated earlier that if sufficient time were available, all resources used by business firms could become variable, and there would therefore be no need to distinguish between fixed and variable resources. In other words, the Hypothetical Mailbox Manufacturing Company could vary the use of resource A as well as resource B, allowing the firm to obtain a least-cost combination for any particular level of production. Thus, in the long-run period, business firms will usually plan to vary their size of operations in order to produce as efficiently as possible. This is the essence of capital planning and expansion programs.

Long-Run Cost

The preceding section suggested that the Hypothetical Mailbox Manufacturing Company should expand its plant and equipment to produce 170 mailboxes. In addition, if the output of 170 mailboxes appears to be a permanent level of production, the company should strive to produce these mailboxes at least cost.

The production information in Table 7–4 for the Hypothetical Mailbox Manufacturing Company contains the least-cost combination for 170 mailboxes, which is 47 units of resource A and 27 units of resource B instead of 30 and 40, respectively. This information is reproduced in Table 8–3. With the same price of $10 for resource A and $30 for resource B, total costs would be $1,280 instead of $1,500. The average cost would be $7.53 instead of $8.82 (compare the shaded areas). The use of 47 units of resource A instead of 30 simply means that the firm should expand its use of plant and equipment.

The least-cost combination for 170 mailboxes is illustrated in Fig. 8–3, and the least-cost combinations for the other levels of production are given in Fig. 8–4. The prices of resources A and B remain at $10 and $30, respectively. The least-cost combinations are indicated by X's where the production functions and cost-outlay lines are tangent. These least-cost combinations are verified in Table 8–4, which reproduces the information in Table 7–4, adding the total cost for each combination. The least-cost combinations that appear in Table 8–4 (shaded area) are identical to those indicated in Fig. 8–4.

The important implication of these least-cost combinations for business analysis is that they provide a guide for directing the growth and expansion of the firm. As markets expand, business management can make plans for future plant and equipment expansion based upon the least-cost combina-

TABLE 8–3

LEAST-COST COMBINATION

Quantity of Output		Alternative Combinations of A and B								
170	A	64	55	47	40	34	30	27	25	24
	B	24	25	27	30	34	40	47	55	64
Total Cost		$1,360	$1,300	$1,280	$1,300	$1,360	$1,500	$1,680	$1,900	$2,160
Average Cost		$8.00	$7.65	$7.53	$7.65	$8.00	$8.82	$9.88	$11.18	$12.71

TABLE 8–4

PRODUCTION AND COST

Quantity of Output		Alternative Combinations and Total Cost								
30	A	47	38	30	23	17	13	10	8	7
	B	8	8	10	13	17	23	30	38	47
		$680	$620	$600	$620	$680	$820	$1,000	$1,220	$1,480
70	A	54	45	37	30	24	20	17	15	14
	B	14	15	17	20	24	30	37	45	54
		$960	$900	$880	$900	$960	$1,100	$1,280	$1,500	$1,760
130	A	60	51	43	36	30	26	23	21	20
	B	20	21	24	26	30	36	43	51	60
		$1,200	$1,140	$1,120	$1,140	$1,200	$1,340	$1,520	$1,740	$2,000
170	A	64	55	47	40	34	30	27	25	24
	B	24	25	27	30	34	40	47	55	64
		$1,360	$1,300	$1,280	$1,300	$1,360	$1,500	$1,680	$1,900	$2,160
200	A	67	58	50	43	37	33	30	28	27
	B	27	28	30	33	37	43	50	58	67
		$1,480	$1,420	$1,400	$1,420	$1,480	$1,620	$1,800	$2,020	$2,280
220	A	69	60	52	45	39	35	32	30	29
	B	29	30	32	35	39	45	52	60	69
		$1,560	$1,500	$1,480	$1,500	$1,560	$1,570	$1,880	$2,100	$2,360
230	A	70	61	53	46	40	36	33	31	30
	B	30	31	33	36	40	46	53	61	70
		$1,600	$1,540	$1,520	$1,540	$1,600	$1,740	$1,920	$2,140	$2,400
270	A	80	71	63	56	50	46	43	41	40
	B	40	41	43	46	50	56	63	71	80
		$2,000	$1,940	$1,920	$1,940	$2,000	$2,140	$2,320	$2,540	$2,800
290	A	90	51	73	66	60	56	53	51	50
	B	50	51	53	56	60	66	73	81	90
		$2,400	$2,340	$2,320	$2,340	$2,400	$2,540	$2,720	$2,940	$3,200

tions. In this way, an effort can be made to obtain the lowest possible unit cost for any particular level of production. Even if output were to fluctuate within a satisfactory range of the least-cost output, other levels would approximate the lower unit cost.

Least-cost combinations of resources for all available levels of output (possible only in long-run periods) can be illustrated as long-run average or unit costs. These long-run average costs for particular levels of output of the Hypothetical Mailbox Manufacturing Company appear in Table 8–5 and

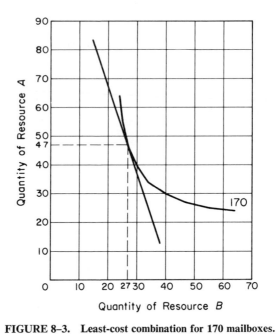

FIGURE 8–3.   Least-cost combination for 170 mailboxes.

TABLE 8–5

LONG-RUN COSTS OF HYPOTHETICAL MAILBOX MANUFACTURING COMPANY

Quantity of Output	Least-Cost Combinations	Total Cost	Average Cost
30	A 30	$ 600	$20.00
	B 10		
70	A 37	880	12.57
	B 17		
130	A 43	1,120	8.62
	B 23		
170	A 47	1,280	7.53
	B 27		
200	A 50	1,400	7.00
	B 30		
220	A 52	1,480	6.73
	B 32		
230	A 53	1,520	6.61
	B 33		
270	A 63	1,920	7.11
	B 43		
290	A 73	2,320	8.00
	B 53		
300	A 83	2,720	9.07
	B 63		
310	A103	3,520	11.35
	B 83		

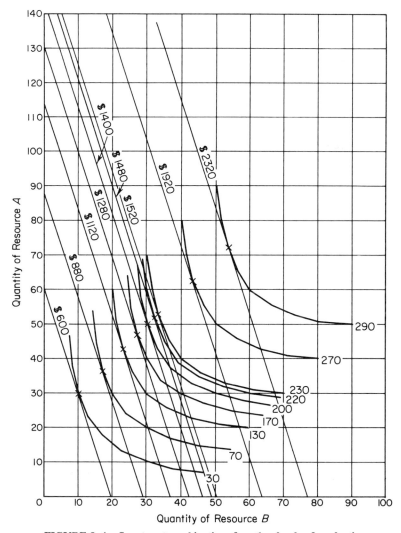

FIGURE 8–4.   Least-cost combinations for other levels of production.

Fig. 8–5. The curve in Fig. 8–5 is known as the long-run average-cost curve. Long-run average costs for the firm reflect the least-cost combinations of resources for every level of production.

The left-hand scale indicates the average or unit cost, and the bottom scale is a measure of the various levels of production. It is very noticeable from Fig. 8–5 that long-run average costs decline up to an output of 230 mailboxes, then begin to rise. The declining phase of this curve represents the economies of scale. When long-run average costs rise as they do after an output of 230, diseconomies of scale become predominant.

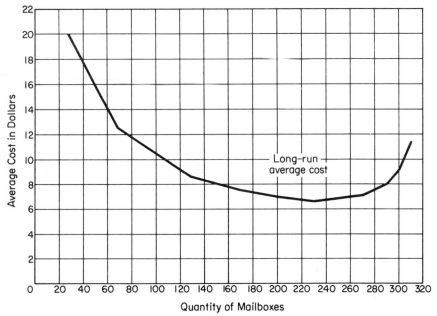

FIGURE 8–5.   Long-run average costs for selected levels of output of the Hypothetical Mailbox Manufacturing Company.

Economies and Diseconomies of Scale

There are several reasons why production activities experience economies and diseconomies of scale in long-run periods. Economies are the result of greater specialization of effort. When labor and management can concentrate their respective efforts on special areas, they can accomplish their tasks better and more efficiently. There are still other reasons for economies of scale. Certain production processes lend themselves to mass production and the use of specialized, large, or expensive equipment that would be out of the question for a small firm. Other advantages accrue to large-scale producers. For example, it sometimes becomes feasible to produce byproducts. When the firm is small, this is uneconomical because the waste materials are not sufficient to justify further processing. Large firms also may be able to buy resources in larger lots, take advantage of lower freight rates, and compete for more favorable financing costs.

Diseconomies, which eventually affect long-run average costs, primarily result from certain inefficiencies associated with the growth of the firm. As the firm grows larger, it becomes more and more difficult for management to oversee, coordinate, and control all operations.

Economies and diseconomies vary among different firms and industries. In some industries, economies are exhausted with relatively small firms. This is particularly true in many retailing and service-type establishments. In other industries, diseconomies do not appear until gigantic operations are attained. Such is the case in the so-called "heavy industries," such as steel and automobiles. Finally, in many industries there may exist a wide range over which there is no appreciable change in the long-run average cost. In this case, economies exist in small firms and larger firms alike with little noticeable effect on long-run costs. Diseconomies appear only when firms reach an extremely large size. Under these circumstances, a wide range of firm sizes may exist. This is the case in such industries as meat packing and household-appliance manufacturing. Economies of scale, in summary, are exhausted in each industry according to and consistent with its particular circumstances.[1]

ANNEX: COST ESTIMATION

Cost Systems

Adequate records of a business firm's activities provide the information from which accounting statements are derived. The balance sheet and the income statement are two of the accounting statements that summarize a firm's activities. The balance sheet reflects the financial condition of the firm at a specific point in time. It compares the things owned with the things owed (including the claims of the owners). The income statement, on the other hand, summarizes the expenses and incomes of the firm over a specified period of time.

Wholesalers, retailers, and service organizations rely on this type of accounting information to make decisions. However, manufacturing firms must, in addition, rely on a cost-accounting system. Wholesalers, retailers, and service organizations have little need for a cost-accounting system because costs are determined by the price of the wares purchased for resale. More detailed records are required in manufacturing to determine the actual unit cost of a product.

There are three basic cost-accounting systems. The *job-order system* records all costs associated with each particular order, on the premise that each order is different from all others; for example, a firm that makes paper containers will receive a different order from each customer to meet his specific requirements. The *process-cost system* attempts to measure the unit cost of a process. To illustrate, assume that a firm makes hubcaps for automobiles. There are two basic processes, stamping and plating. During the accounting period the costs of each process are determined separately; then, as the hubcaps pass from stamping to plating, the plating costs are added to

[1] McConnell, C. R., *Economics: Principles, Problems, and Policies*, 3rd ed. (New York: McGraw-Hill Book Company, 1966), pp. 451–455.

the stamping costs. In this manner the unit cost of the hubcaps can be determined along with the costs associated with each process. The *standard-cost system* merely assigns predetermined costs to a product based upon efficient conditions of production. Deviations from such standards provide management with information by which to judge the efficiency of the enterprise. These standard costs must be revised periodically to reflect more accurately the effect of changed circumstances.

Any cost system involves the process of allocating material, labor, and overhead (fixed) costs. This is the tedious task the cost accountant performs for the enterprise. The allocation of certain elements of cost will merely be an estimate; for example, an accountant can only guess as accurately as possible what overhead costs will be for a given period.

Cost Determination

The Hypothetical Mailbox Manufacturing Company can accurately allocate all costs based on the prices and productivity of its resources; the costs of alternative levels of production also are available. The cost curves for this company illustrate how costs depend upon the level of production. Actually, only one level of production occurs at any one time. When another level of production is reached, the price of resources or the technique of producing the product may have changed. Thus, costs of production will vary because of factors other than the rate of production. In the case of the Hypothetical Mailbox Manufacturing Company, these other factors are considered to remain unchanged. In reality, however, they are changing constantly. Consequently, an enterprise does not have available at any instant of time the actual costs of alternative levels of production.

Many firms have estimated their costs of production to be constant over a wide range. This means that their average-cost curve would be shaped like a flat *U*. Such a curve is illustrated in Fig. 8–6. This would seem to indicate a great deal of flexibility in the firm's operations over a wide range of production. It could also reflect the use of a standard-cost system in estimating unit costs for different levels of production. This use of standard costs in itself would mean constant unit costs over a wide range of output.

There are three basic approaches in estimating the cost structure of a firm. The *accounting approach* merely classifies expenses as fixed, variable, or semivariable. It requires constancy in wage rates, material prices, size, technology, and many other factors. The *engineering approach* uses physical data such as the rated capacity of machines, man-hours, and pounds of material to project future costs, using price estimates. The *statistical approach* attempts to isolate from raw data the influence of all cost determinants other than the output rate. All these approaches require a wide range of fluctuations in the output rate, since the purpose of cost-output analysis is to determine how costs vary with output. A narrow range of output may not reveal significant cost differences.

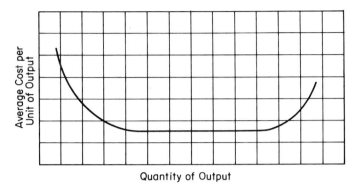

FIGURE 8–6.   Average-cost curve remaining constant over a wide range.

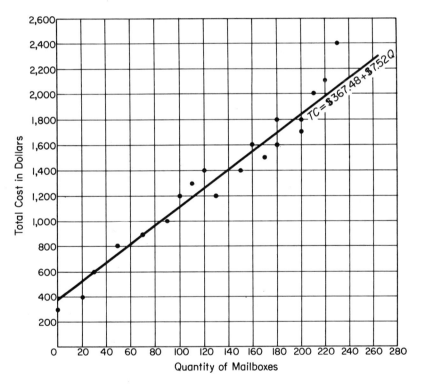

FIGURE 8–7.   Sample cost observations illustrating a statistical cost function.

The typical situation is to analyze cost-output data for one firm or plant over an extended period of time. Frequently, however, cross-sectional data may be useful. That is, cost-output data for different firms or plants for the same period of time may reveal meaningful information. Under these circumstances, such things as managerial efficiencies, firm size, and accounting methods may vary widely.

For purposes of illustration, a statistical cost function can be derived from the total-cost data of the Hypothetical Mailbox Manufacturing Company (Table 8–1). In addition to these data, costs for other levels of production have been arbitrarily selected. These arbitrary cost-output observations may be considered the actual costs the company would incur if it operated in reality; they therefore would reflect factors other than the output rate that might affect costs. All of these cost observations appear in Fig. 8–7. The *method of least squares* (see Chapter 13) can be employed to produce a linear cost curve to fit these cost observations. Calculations reveal the algebraic expression of the cost-output data to be

$$TC = \$367.48 + \$7.52Q.$$

This expression states that total cost (TC) is equal to $367.48 when output is zero and that total cost increases by $7.52 for each unit of output (Q). Since the cost function is linear, the $7.52 is also the marginal cost. This cost function is displayed graphically in Fig. 8–7.

A linear curve, however, would not be a true reflection of the firm's cost structure in this case. It should be curvilinear, as was illustrated in Fig. 8–1. The arbitrary cost observations that were added reflect variations in costs due to factors other than the rate of production. More refined statistical techniques are required to isolate and identify these other factors. The curve's true curvilinear nature would then be revealed. In any event, the mathematical determination of a firm's cost structure, whether linear or curvilinear, is a valuable fundamental for business analysis.

PROBLEMS AND PROJECTS

1. This is the second part of the continuous problem introduced in Problem 4 of Chapter 7. The purpose of this exercise is to develop the short-run cost structure for the Hypothetical Chair Manufacturing Company. Since various quantities of resource *B* are to be utilized with 35 units of resource *A*, different levels of production will produce different unit costs.

   a. Using the information developed in Problem 4 of Chapter 7, develop a table of costs similar to Table 8–2. The price of resource *A* is $10 per unit and the price of resource *B* is $30 per unit. Calculate the total fixed cost, total variable cost, total cost, average fixed cost, average variable cost, average total cost, and marginal cost. Use the following quantities of output: 20, 50, 120, 180, 220, 240, and 250.

   b. Plot on a piece of graph paper the total fixed cost, total variable cost, and total cost for the various quantities of chairs. The curves should look similar to those that appear in Fig. 8–1.

   c. Plot on a piece of graph paper the average fixed cost, average variable cost, average cost, and marginal cost for the various quantities of chairs. The curves should look similar to those that appear in Fig. 8–2. When plotting the *marginal cost*, be sure to locate each marginal cost at the quantity of output that is halfway between the two outputs for which the marginal cost is relevant. Since marginal cost reflects the average change in cost per unit of output as production proceeds from one level of production to another, the marginal cost for the change between the output of 20 chairs on the graph and the output of 50 chairs would be the cost per unit of an output of 35 chairs; an output of 35 would be halfway between 20 and 50.

d. Since this is part of a continuous problem, the calculations for this exercise will be used again in the Problems and Projects section of the next chapter.

SELECTED REFERENCES

Allen, Clark Lee, *The Framework of Price Theory*, Chap. 8. Belmont, Calif.: Wadsworth Publishing Company, Inc., 1967.

Brennan, Michael J., *The Theory of Economic Statics*, Chaps. 10, 11, 14. Englewood Cliffs, N. J.: Prentice-Hall, Inc., 1965.

Leftwich, Richard H., *The Price System and Resource Allocation*, Chaps. 8, 9. New York: Holt, Rinehart & Winston, Inc., 1966.

Watson, Donald S., *Price Theory and Its Uses*, Chap. 11. Boston: Houghton Mifflin Company, 1963.

9

PRICE AND OUTPUT

DETERMINATION

A business enterprise would indeed be difficult to run without some knowledge of production and costs. Equally important, however, is information about revenue. The business firm should have a good idea about such things as demand and price and the effect they may have on sales. A business firm that produces a product which has no market will soon discover that without revenue it cannot survive. In this way, there is a close connection between revenue and cost. Revenue is necessary to stimulate production, and costs are necessary to achieve production.

One purpose of this chapter is to explore the concept of demand and supply. From this investigation, a basic framework will emerge which will explain how price can be determined by the interaction of these two elements. The concept of elasticity will also be explored before proceeding to the determination of output. Since price is the same thing as revenue per unit of output (referred to by economists as *average revenue*), it plays a vital role in determining the level of production; for example, by matching or comparing revenue and cost in a certain way, the best-profit level of output can be revealed. This technique will be explained in terms of the Hypothetical Mailbox Manufacturing Company. The Annex to this chapter discusses various techniques of forecasting demand and explains the procedures of estimating demand.

FUNDAMENTAL DETERMINANTS OF PRICE

Prices often rise when a product becomes scarce and go down when it becomes oversupplied. They also may rise when a product suddenly becomes attractive and go down when it becomes less appealing. Although there are many reasons why prices fluctuate, the price of a commodity at any particular instant in time depends to some extent on the interaction of two very fundamental relationships—demand and supply. A close look at demand, supply, and the process of interaction is necessary to understand the mechanics of price.

Demand

Demand reflects a set of price and quantity relationships during a specific period of time. Quantities of a good or service are based upon desire, plus the ability and the willingness to pay. Demand does not exist merely because someone desires a commodity. No matter how many people may want Buick Rivieras, unless they are both willing and able to pay for them, a demand does not really exist.

The various quantities of a good or service demanded at different prices actually represent a set of alternatives during a specific period of time. The time period may be an instant, an hour, a week, or several months, but it becomes significant when changes in demand are considered. Thus demand can be described as a schedule of various quantities of a product demanded at certain prices for a specific period of time.

The concept of demand can be illustrated by a hypothetical example. Suppose that a housewife goes shopping one afternoon to pick up an Excello "Teflon" skillet which she has seen advertised by a department store for $3.00. On her way to the department store she drives by a hardware store that is conducting a special sale, and she decides to stop there first. In the hardware store she notices the same Excello "Teflon" skillet priced at $2.00. She immediately picks out two skillets and proceeds to the cashier, since at that price she can easily make use of two skillets. Upon arriving at the cashier's counter, she is informed that the Excello "Teflon" skillets have been further reduced to $1.50 each; she then goes back and selects another one. The third skillet (she thinks) will make an excellent gift for a next-door neighbor to whom she owes a favor. After all, $1.50 per skillet is a bargain. Within a relatively short span of time, then, the housewife's demand schedule for the skillets is revealed. At $3.00 she demanded one skillet, at $2.00 she demanded two, and at $1.50 she demanded three. Table 9-1 is a demand schedule showing the various quantities of skillets demanded at certain prices for a specific period of time by the housewife.

Table 9-1 is illustrated graphically in Fig. 9-1. Although it is obvious that the housewife cannot buy half a skillet, the price and quantity relationships are connected to project the continuous nature of a demand curve.

An important relationship exists between price and quantity demanded. As price falls, quantity demanded increases; this is known as the *law of demand*. This inverse relationship is revealed in Fig. 9-1.

TABLE 9–1

DEMAND SCHEDULE

Price	Quantity of Skillets Demanded
$3.00	1
2.00	2
1.50	3

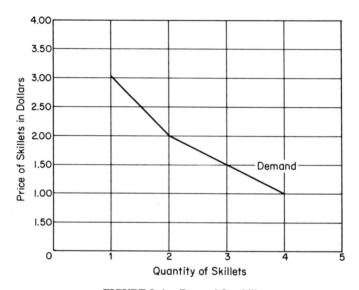

FIGURE 9–1.   Demand for skillets.

There are three main reasons why more units are demanded at lower prices. First, as we acquire more units of a product at any one time, additional units are worth less; that is, they diminish in usefulness. While the first skillet is very desirable, the second is merely convenient to have, and the third may be used only occasionally. The purchase of additional units consequently requires lower prices. A second reason more units are demanded at lower prices is the greater ability to purchase at those prices; this is known as the *income effect*. The same amount of money will now go farther. The housewife could buy only one skillet with $3.00. At a price of $1.50 she can buy two with the same $3.00. The $3.00 therefore represents a greater purchasing power or income when prices are lower. However, since the housewife bought three skillets instead of two at a price of $1.50, she evidently had more than $3.00 to spend in the first place. This begins to explain the third reason why quantity demanded usually increases with a fall in price. Apparently the housewife was willing to substitute a skillet for something else for which she could just as easily have spent the other $1.50. For instance, she may have been willing

TABLE 9–2

REVISED DEMAND SCHEDULE

Price	Quantity of Skillets Demanded
$3.00	2
2.00	3
1.50	4

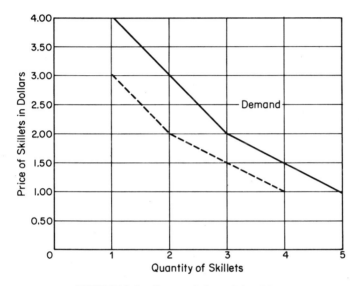

FIGURE 9–2.   Increased demand for skillets.

to substitute the skillet for a pair of nylons she originally intended to buy as a gift for her neighbor. This third reason is known as the *substitution effect*.

Since a demand curve represents various alternatives at a given point in time, a change in price will cause a movement along the curve. For example, when the price of the "Teflon" skillet changed from $2.00 to $1.50, the housewife *demanded* a larger quantity. This is not the same thing as a change in demand. The housewife's demand curve or various alternatives were still the same. In order for a change in demand to occur, there must be a shift or movement of the entire curve. Such a movement would be reflected in the schedule by an entirely new group of quantities demanded at the same range of prices. A new demand schedule for skillets might resemble the alternatives in Table 9–2.

Now instead of one skillet being demanded at $3.00, two are demanded. Instead of two at $2.00 and three at $1.50, three are demanded at $2.00 and four at $1.50. At each of the original prices, one more skillet is demanded. Such a change in demand is illustrated in Fig. 9–2, where the curve to the left

TABLE 9–3

MARKET DEMAND

Price	Quantity for Skillets Demanded
$3.50	10,000
3.00	20,000
2.50	30,000
2.00	40,000
1.50	50,000
1.00	60,000

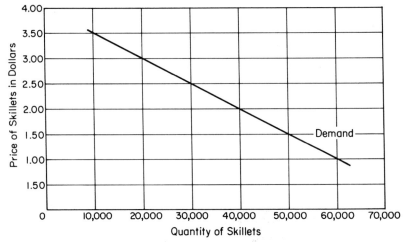

FIGURE 9–3.   Market demand for skillets.

represents the original demand as it appears in Fig. 9–1 and the curve to the right is the new demand. Since larger quantities of skillets are demanded at the same respective prices, the demand for skillets has increased. A movement to the left of the original curve would reflect a decrease in demand.

A change in demand may occur for several reasons. An increase, for example, can be traced to such things as: (1) a greater desire or preference, possibly prompted by advertising; (2) larger income, which permits the purchase of more of the commodity; (3) higher prices of other goods, particularly substitutes, which will appear less attractive by comparison; and (4) expectations of higher future prices or incomes, which may encourage immediate purchases. One other factor that may increase demand is an increase in the number of buyers, which may be due to growth in the population. However, this reason is related to a change in *market demand* rather than *individual demand*.

So far, we have been dealing principally with the demand of one individual, the housewife buying skillets. The concept of *equilibrium price*, which will be discussed later, depends upon the utilization of market demand. The transition from individual to market demands can be accomplished by simply adding or summing up the quantities demanded by each individual at the various possible prices. Market demand then would reflect the amounts of a good all buyers will buy at each of the possible prices. In the case of skillets, the market demand might be represented by the quantities and price relationships that appear in Table 9–3 and Fig. 9–3.

Supply

There is a *law of supply* as well as one for demand. As prices rise, correspondingly larger quantities for a good or service will be offered or supplied. This direct relationship is noted in Table 9–4, which illustrates a hypothetical supply schedule for skillets.

At a price of $.50 the quantity offered by all producers would be 10,000 skillets; at a price of $1.00 the quantity offered would be 20,000; at $1.50 it would be 30,000; etc. This supply schedule is also illustrated in Fig. 9–4, appearing as an upward-sloping curve[1]. The law of supply simply says that producers are willing to produce and offer for sale more of their wares at higher prices than at lower prices. Price is an inducement or incentive to produce and sell a product. At higher prices producers can afford to pay more to attract workers from other activities or induce them to work overtime; in fact, it may be necessary to incur higher costs when output expands beyond a certain point. In the discussion of production and cost, it was stated that average-cost curves are usually *U*-shaped in nature. Marginal cost also swings up as the rate of production proceeds to greater levels. Since marginal cost reflects the additions to cost as additional quantities are produced, it expresses what the producer would be willing to offer at various levels of prices. In this sense, the marginal-cost curve is a producer's supply curve.

As in the case of demand, the market supply curve is obtained by adding or summing up the quantities offered (or supplied) by each individual producer at the various possible prices. Since the supply curve illustrated in Fig. 9–4 is a market supply curve, it expresses the possible actions of all the producers in the market.

The distinction between a change in *supply* and a change in *quantity supplied* also is similar to the difference between a change in demand and a change in quantity demanded. The change in the quantity supplied refers to the movement from one point to another on a given supply curve; the supply curve itself shows what the quantity supplied would be at different prices.

---

[1] The supply curve in Fig. 9–4 expresses the general nature of supply. Under certain circumstances the curve may represent a fixed quantity, as in the case of a rare work of art, an antique, or perishable goods that are available for a very short period of time. Under such circumstances the supply curve may go straight up instead of merely sloping upward.

TABLE 9–4

SUPPLY SCHEDULE

Price	Quantity of Skillets Supplied
$ .50	10,000
1.00	20,000
1.50	30,000
2.00	40,000
2.50	50,000
3.00	60,000

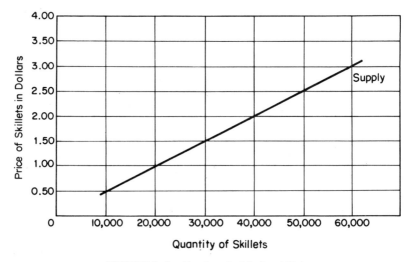

FIGURE 9–4. **Supply schedule for skillets.**

A change in supply, on the other hand, refers to a shift in the supply curve and indicates that the entire schedule has changed; at the various possible prices, greater (or lesser) quantities would be supplied in the market by producers. Greater quantities supplied at the same prices would mean an increase in supply; lesser quantities would mean a decrease in supply. An increase would shift the curve to the right, a decrease to the left.

As already mentioned, supply is a reflection of cost. For our purposes, it is sufficient to note that anything that causes lower production costs, i.e., improved techniques or a decline in resource prices, will increase supply. Besides technology and resource prices, there are several other factors that may explain a shift in supply. For example, changes in the prices of other goods can cause supply to shift. A decline in the price of coffeepots may encourage manufacturers to produce skillets instead. Expectations about future prices can affect producers' willingness to produce skillets now; this will increase or decrease supply. Finally, a growth or reduction in the number of producers may make the market supply curve shift, since this curve is the summation of the individual supply curves. A shift in supply may also result when producers change the scale of their operations.

Equilibrium Price

We are now in a position to put together the concepts of demand and supply to see how the behavior of buyers and sellers interact to determine price. The price at which quantity demanded and quantity supplied are identical is referred to as the *equilibrium price* and can be shown graphically by the

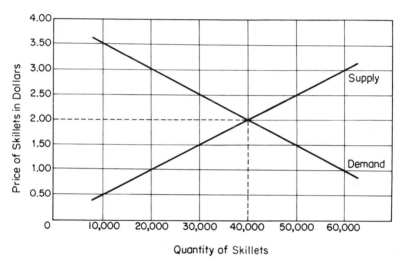

Quantity of Skillets

FIGURE 9–5.   Market demand and supply for skillets.

intersection of the demand and supply curve. In Fig. 9–5 the market demand and supply for skillets are illustrated. The price indicated by their interaction is $2.00; at this price, the quantities demanded and supplied are equal.

The $2.00 equilibrium price is the price that is likely to exist in a given market for a particular period of time under given conditions.[2] At another price—$2.50, for example—the quantity of skillets demanded would be less than the quantity supplied. This situation would not last long. The suppliers experiencing a surplus would lower their prices and reduce production. At a lower price the quantity demanded would tend to increase; quantity demanded and supplied would again be equal at $2.00. Equilibrium price can also be thought of as a target price that provides the direction in which the price will move.

---

[2] These conditions include desire, income, other prices, technology, costs, and expectations, all of which have been discussed previously.

FIGURE 9–6.   Surplus and movement toward an equilibrium price for skillets.

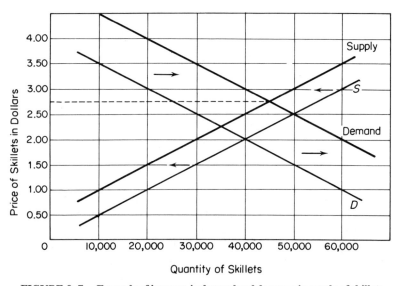

FIGURE 9–7.   Example of increase in demand and decrease in supply of skillets.

The surplus and movement toward an equilibrium price for skillets is illustrated in Fig. 9–6. The 20,000 skillets represented by the difference between 30,000 and 50,000 on the quantity axis is the amount of surplus that would temporarily exist at a price of $2.50. The tendency of producers to cut back production and the tendency of buyers to demand more at a lower price are indicated by the arrows showing the movement along each curve.

Changes in equilibrium price and quantity will really occur only when there are changes in either demand or supply. In graphic terms, either the demand curve or the supply curve must shift to cause a change in price. There are many combinations of demand and supply changes that will affect price. It is even possible for price to remain the same if the changes in demand and supply offset each other. In Fig. 9–7, an increase in demand and a decrease in supply are illustrated; in this case, demand increases more than supply decreases. The heavy lines indicate the new curves. The equilibrium price has increased from $2.00 to $2.75.

Prices and quantities are influenced by factors other than demand and supply, such as noncompetitive market structures and the policies of individual firms. While such factors may provide a basis upon which to depart from the demand and supply determination of price, pricing decisions by business establishments nevertheless can never completely disregard these forces. An examination of pricing in business establishments, large and small alike, will reveal serious consideration of demand and supply.[3]

ELASTICITY OF DEMAND

It has been shown that because of the nature of demand, a reduction in price can cause an increase in the quantity demanded. For example, according to the market demand for "Teflon" skillets (Table 9–3), a drop in price from $2.50 to $2.00 would cause quantity demanded to increase from 30,000 to 40,000. The important aspect of this change in quantity demanded is the extent of the change compared to the change in price. In other words, how *responsive* is quantity demanded to price changes? This concept, known as the *price elasticity of demand*, is an important fundamental for business analysis that requires special attention.

It is not adequate to consider merely the fact that quantity demanded changes with a given change in price. The important relationship to consider is the *percentage* change in quantity demanded compared to the percentage change in price; this emphasizes the *relative* nature of elasticity. Price elasticity of demand can be measured numerically by comparing the percentage changes in quantity demanded and price, or it can be reflected by the impact these changes have on the dollar sales or total revenue of a firm.

First, to illustrate how price elasticity works, we will return to the example of "Teflon" skillets. A hypothetical demand schedule for a firm selling skillets is illustrated in Table 9–5. The first column indicates different possible prices of skillets and the second gives the physical volume of sales that would occur at each price. The third column is obtained by multiplying

[3] See W. W. Haynes, *Pricing Decisions in Small Business* (Lexington, Ky.: University of Kentucky Press, 1962); and A. D. H. Kaplan, *et al.*, *Pricing in Big Business* (Washington, D. C.: The Brookings Institution, 1958).

FUNDAMENTALS OF BUSINESS ANALYSIS

TABLE 9–5

DEMAND SCHEDULE

		Price of Skillets	Quantity of Skillets Demanded at Each Price	Total Revenue at Each Price
Relatively elastic demand	{	$3.00	200	$600
		2.50	300	750
		2.00	400	800
Relatively inelastic demand	{	1.50	500	750
		1.00	600	600

each price by the quantity of skillets that would be sold at that price; this provides dollar sales.

Consider first a price change from $3.00 to $2.50. This represents a $16\frac{2}{3}$ per cent change in terms of the $3.00 price. The quantity of skillets demanded changes from 200 to 300, representing a 50 per cent change in terms of the quantity of 200. It can be seen that the 50 per cent change in quantity is greater than the $16\frac{2}{3}$ per cent change in price. When the percentage change in quantity is greater than the percentage change in price, it is said that demand is *relatively elastic* for that change in price or there is an *elastic response*. This may be made clear by arranging the definition of elasticity into a simple formula:

$$\text{Elasticity} = \frac{\text{percentage change in quantity}}{\text{percentage change in price.}}$$

Elasticity can now be expressed in numerical form:

$$\text{Elasticity} = \frac{50}{16\frac{2}{3}} = 3.[4]$$

[4] Elasticity can be numerically determined in other ways. For example, the percentage change can be expressed in terms of the new quantity or price, or it can be calculated as an average change by measuring the change in terms of an average of the original and new quantities. The price change can also be expressed as an average change by measuring the change in terms of an average of the original and new prices. For example, taking the above skillet example, the average percentage change in quantity demanded would be 100 divided by 250[(200 + 300)/2]; the average percentage change in price would be $.50 divided by $2.75[($3.00 + $2.50)/2]. This would result in a value for elasticity of 2.2. It is sometimes more convenient to work in fractions than in percentages. The 2.2 can be derived as follows:

$$\text{Elasticity} = \frac{\dfrac{100}{500}}{\dfrac{0.50}{5.50}}.$$

$$\text{Elasticity} = \frac{\dfrac{1}{5}}{\dfrac{1}{11}} = \frac{1}{5} \times \frac{11}{1} = \frac{11}{5} = 2.2.$$

Note that a different value for elasticity is derived—2.2 instead of 3. This is due to the different method of calculation. Since elasticity is measured by changes, accuracy will vary depending upon the type of calculation used. The precise measure of elasticity at a given price, known as *point elasticity*, can be determined by the use of calculus.

Since demand curves usually slope downward, a decrease in price will mean a negative change in price. Consequently, the numerical value of elasticity in this example is really -3. However, the sign of the number has no economic relevance to elasticity; it merely indicates the downward-sloping nature of the demand curve. The significance of the number is whether it is less than 1 or greater than 1.

Since the numerical value of 3 is larger than 1, demand is relatively elastic. As long as the numerator of the elasticity formula is greater than the denominator, the numerical result will be greater than 1. This is another way of saying that the percentage change in quantity is greater than the percentage change in price. Thus, elasticity of demand is a comparison of the extent to which quantity responds to a price change. When the response in quantity is greater, it is *elastic;* when it is smaller, it is *inelastic.*

Returning to Table 9–5, elasticity of demand can be calculated for a change in price from \$1.50 to \$1.00; its numerical value will be $\frac{3}{5}$. Since this is less than 1, demand is relatively inelastic for this price change. In other words, at this level, quantity demanded is not very responsive to a change in price. Its percentage change will be smaller than that of price.

Elasticity of demand has practical significance when the effect of a price change on total revenue is understood. In Table 9–5, total revenue at each price is reflected in the last column on the right. Note that when demand is relatively elastic, total revenue (dollar sales) will increase with a drop in price. On the other hand, when demand is relatively inelastic, a drop in price will cause a decrease in total revenue. In the latter case, the owner of a business will sell more of his goods for a smaller total amount of money. By the same token, when demand is relatively inelastic, a rise in price will generate a larger total amount of money. Whether or not prices should be raised or lowered will depend on the elasticity of demand.

However, this is not all that matters. As more or less is produced and sold, the costs of production may vary. This is an equally important consideration in calculating profits. For example, if demand is relatively elastic, a drop in price to stimulate sales will generate a larger amount of total revenue. However, if the increase in total costs to achieve the higher amount of production exceeds the additional amount of revenue, the firm will be decreasing its profits. Even with a relatively elastic demand, a reduction of price may or may not be profitable. This is illustrated in Table 9–6. If the unit cost of skillets is \$1.00 each, a decrease in price from \$3.00 to \$2.50 will *increase* profits by \$50. If the unit cost of skillets is \$2.00 each, a decrease in price from \$3.00 to \$2.50 will *decrease* profits by \$50. In summary, even though total revenue may increase \$150 because demand is elastic, profits nevertheless will rise or fall depending on the change in costs.

There are many applications of elasticity of demand to business situations. For example, suppose that a retail store owner is interested in attracting

TABLE 9–6

COMPARISON OF PROFITS (ELASTIC DEMAND—DIFFERENT UNIT COSTS)

Unit Cost	Price of Skillet	Quantity Sold	Total Sales Revenue	Total Cost	Profit (Revenue Less Cost)
$1.00	⌠$3.00	200	$600	$200	$400
	⌡ 2.50	300	750	300	450
2.00	⌠ 3.00	200	600	400	200
	⌡ 2.50	300	750	600	150

new customers to his store. He decides to have a special sale over a three-day period and selects one product to advertise—a high-quality stereo radio. He chooses the stereo radio because of the relatively elastic demand at its $100 price. Since quantity demanded is very responsive in this price range, an advertised price of $80 will attract many potential buyers to the store and increase his total revenue substantially. In order to prevent any one buyer from taking advantage of the sale, particularly if large sales at the lower price would reduce profits, the store owner might impose a limit of one radio to a customer. The purpose of the sale, after all, is to attract new customers into the store in the hopes that they will also buy other items and that after becoming acquainted with the store, they will return.

On the other hand, if the store owner had chosen a relatively inelastic product, he would not have attracted very many new customers. Quantity demanded would not have been as responsive to a price reduction. Suppose that the item had been salt. The demand for salt tends to be highly inelastic; therefore, a reduction from $.10 a box to $.08 would not attract many customers. Note that the reduction of $.02 from $.10 represents the same percentage change as does the reduction of $20 from $100 for stereo radios. The resultant change in quantity demanded, however, would be relatively less for salt and would actually cause a decrease in total revenue.

Measuring elasticity of demand is a tricky and difficult task. However, there are several general conditions upon which elasticity depends. One important condition is the urgency of need. If there is no urgency of need, as with stereo radios, demand will be relatively elastic. Another important condition is the availability of substitutes. There are many substitutes for stereo radios: phonographs, television sets, regular radios, and even other household appliances. A third condition of elasticity is the proportion the money outlay represents of a person's total budget or income. The price of a stereo radio is a substantial sum to most consumers.

The demand for an item may appear to be either elastic or inelastic when judged on the basis of only one of these conditions. For this reason, it is best to consider them all, in order to determine their combined effects, before making a final judgment. The demand for salt, for example, tends to be inelastic for all the reasons just cited. Salt is considered a necessity for most cooking; there are no good substitutes for it; and the expenditure of $.10 for a box of salt, which will last a long time, is a small fraction of most family incomes.

In summary, then, it is apparent that elasticity is a fundamental concept for business analysis. Some idea about the degree of elasticity of demand is useful for business decisions, particularly for certain pricing and output decisions. Even though price elasticity of demand is difficult to measure, many studies have been undertaken to estimate its numerical value. But regardless of this numerical estimation, the conditions of elasticity just described can provide guides to one's judgments about the elasticity of demand for a particular good or service. These judgments can have an important bearing on the decision to raise or lower price.

OUTPUT DETERMINATION

The price and output decisions of a business enterprise depend upon a number of important factors. The costs of production and the nature of demand, already discussed, are vital considerations. However, such things as the market structure, operating goals, the nature of the product, promotion activities, the distribution function, and other special conditions also influence the pricing and output decisions of firms.

Product pricing and promotion will be discussed in the next chapter. For now, however, attention will be briefly directed to one type of pricing policy in order to determine the output of the Hypothetical Mailbox Manufacturing Company.

Between pure competition and pure monopoly, there exists the market structure of *imperfect competition.* This structure reflects the range of market reality in which the elements of both monopoly and competition exist in varying degrees and in which sellers must decide on a price policy of some sort.

Some firms within this range follow a passive attitude or policy toward pricing. These firms usually accept the prevailing price or follow the already established price pattern. In some cases, the price may represent a competitive price set in the market by the interaction of all firms. In the case of oligopoly, however, firms may merely follow the leader. Small firms, which make only a small contribution to the overall volume of goods offered for sale, may have little choice but to follow the larger firms. Even in the case of monopolistic competition, firms usually compete on other than a price basis. Many firms, then, are "price-takers." They sell their product at the going price regardless of whether competition is among many or few. For purposes of demonstrating output determination, the Hypothetical Mailbox Manufacturing Company will be assumed to be a price-taker.

It is common in economic analysis to assume the objective of profit maximization, however, this alone cannot adequately describe firm behavior. First, there are other important motivations to consider. Second, the profit decision itself is complicated by uncertainty. And third, there are other ways of affecting profits than by pricing prescriptions. Nonprice competitive methods such as advertising, selling efforts, and product policies can improve profits as can attention to costs and production techniques. It is therefore impossible to apply a single, simple theory of price and output determination to all firms. The one important value of assuming the profit maximization objective, however, is that it is operational for broad segments of the economy. Because it can lead to useful predictions, it is one of the fundamentals of output determination. Therefore, the Hypothetical Mailbox Manufacturing Company will be assumed to be seeking its best-profit output.

A third assumption concerning output determination for this company is that we are dealing with the short-run period. In its attempt to maximize profits, the company tries to adjust its output through changes in the amounts of variable resources (men, materials, and supplies) it employs.

There are two complementary approaches to determining the level of output at which a firm will realize maximum profit (minimum loss) when it is a price taker. One involves a comparison of total revenue to total costs, and the other a comparison of marginal revenue to marginal cost. Both approaches can be used to reflect a firm's behavior. Revenue and cost data for the Hypothetical Mailbox Manufacturing Company, as well as graphical analysis, will be used to demonstrate these two approaches.

Total-Revenue—Total-Cost Approach

Assume that the price set in the market (or by a price leader) for mailboxes is $13. The total revenue for each level of output can be calculated by simply multiplying price times output. These results are illustrated in the third column of Table 9–7. Column 1 represents alternative levels of output that can be obtained during a production period. The various levels of output depend upon the quantity of resource B utilized with the fixed amount of resource A (see Table 8–1). The total fixed cost, total variable cost, and total cost in Table 9–7 are the same as those illustrated in Table 8–1 and Fig. 8–1 and discussed in Chapter 8. The profit or loss at each level of production is indicated in the last column of Table 9–7; each figure is obtained by calculating the difference between total revenue and total cost for that particular output. For example, at an output of 200 (shaded row) the difference between the total revenue ($2,600) and the total cost ($1,800) is $800. This $800 profit also represents the maximum profits the company can achieve. Thus the company should produce an output of 200 mailboxes, because it is at this output that profits will be at a maximum. This is the best-profit output for the company.

Fig. 9-8 compares total revenue and total cost graphically. Total revenue is a straight line because the Hypothetical Mailbox Manufacturing Company can sell any quantity of mailboxes it can produce at a price of $13 each; under these circumstances, total revenue will change by the same amount each time that one more mailbox is sold. If the company had to lower the price of mailboxes to sell larger quantities, as is typical when a firm is not a price taker, the total-revenue line would not be straight. Because the Hypothetical Mailbox Manufacturing Company is a price taker, its demand curve will not slope downward like a typical market demand curve. The curve for a price taker is a line parallel to the bottom axis that intercepts the price or left-hand axis at the given price.

Total costs of the Hypothetical Mailbox Manufacturing Company are also illustrated in Fig. 9-8. Total costs increase with output. At first the company will experience efficiencies associated with the utilization of resources, and costs will increase at a slower and slower rate; when the point of diminishing returns is reached, total costs will begin to increase at an increasing rate. The curvature of the total-cost curve therefore reflects the law of diminishing returns and the fact that total costs do not change by a constant amount, as depicted by the Total Cost column in Table 9-7. This is reconciled by the fact that costs were recorded in Table 9-7 according to unequal changes in total output, whereas the output scale in Fig. 9-8 reflects equal increments in output changes.

The best-profit output for the company is obviously achieved where the vertical difference between total revenue and total cost is greatest. For the Hypothetical Mailbox Manufacturing Company, this occurs at an output of 200 mailboxes.

A *break-even point*, where total revenue equals total cost, occurs just beyond an output of 70. If data were available for levels of output beyond 230, another brea-keven point would occur. Such a point has been projected from the given data; it occurs at an output of 240 mailboxes. Any output within these breakeven points will represent output at a profit.

Assuming no change in this cost pattern, the company may occasionally have to operate at a loss. Suppose that the price of mailboxes were only $8 each. The last column in Table 9-8 indicates that at this price all levels of output will result in a loss. The table also indicates that the least loss will occur at an output of 170 mailboxes (shaded row). Under such circumstances the company should produce 170 mailboxes. This is also illustrated in Fig. 9-9. The least loss of 140 occurs at an output of 170 mailboxes; this is indicated as the smallest difference between the total-cost line and the total-revenue line. The total-variable-cost line is also illustrated in Fig. 9-9, to show that the total-revenue line lies between it and the total-cost line. When the total-revenue line falls below the total-variable-cost line, the firm should shut down. This will be explained next.

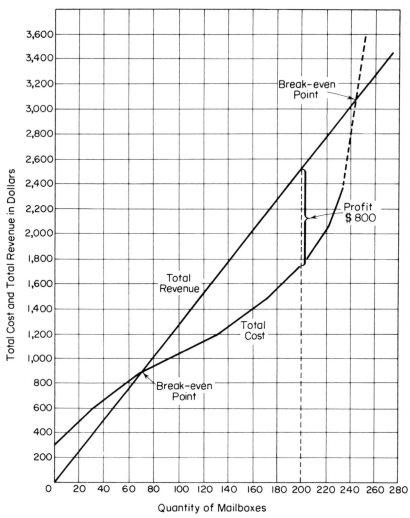

FIGURE 9-8. Comparison of total revenue and total cost for mailboxes.

TABLE 9-7

BEST-PROFIT OUTPUT FOR HYPOTHETICAL MAILBOX MANUFACTURING COMPANY

Total Output	Price	Total Revenue	Total Fixed Cost	Total Variable Cost	Total Cost	Profit (+) or Loss (−)
30	$13	$ 390	$300	$ 300	600	$−210
70	13	910	300	600	900	− 10
130	13	1,690	300	900	1,200	+490
170	13	2,210	300	1,200	1,500	+710
200	13	2,600	300	1,500	1,800	+800
220	13	2,860	300	1,800	2,100	+760
230	13	2,990	300	2,100	2,400	+590

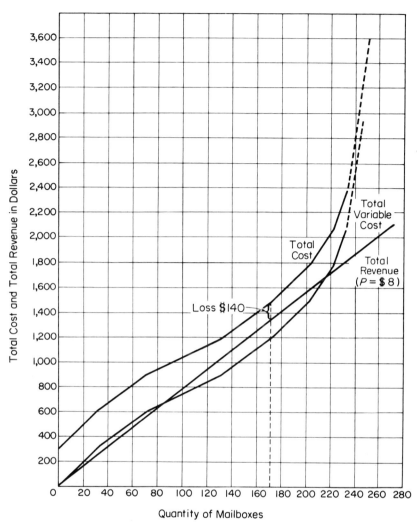

FIGURE 9–9. Example of least loss in output of mailboxes.

TABLE 9–8

LEAST-LOSS OUTPUT FOR HYPOTHETICAL MAILBOX MANUFACTURING COMPANY

Total Output	Price	Total Revenue	Total Fixed Cost	Total Variable Cost	Total Cost	Profit (+) or Loss (−)
30	$8	$ 240	$300	$ 300	$ 600	$ − 360
70	8	560	300	600	900	− 340
130	8	1,040	300	900	1,200	− 160
170	8	1,360	300	1,200	1,500	− 140
200	8	1,600	300	1,500	1,800	− 200
220	8	1,760	300	1,800	2,100	− 340
230	8	1,840	300	2,100	2,400	− 560

203

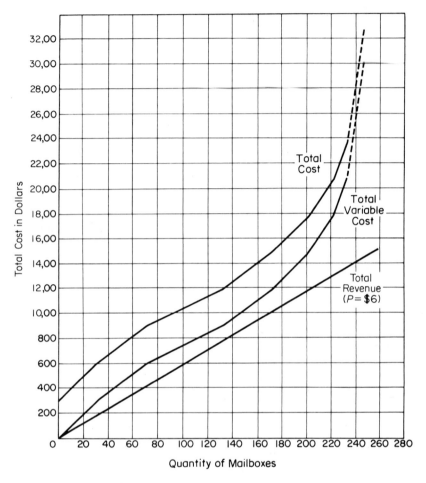

FIGURE 9–10. Shut-down point for Hypothetical Mailbox Manufacturing Company.

TABLE 9–9

**SHUTDOWN POINT FOR HYPOTHETICAL MAILBOX
MANUFACTURING COMPANY**

Total Output	Price	Total Revenue	Total Fixed Cost	Total Variable Cost	Total Cost	Profit (+) or Loss (−)
30	$6	$ 180	$300	$ 300	$ 600	$−420
70	6	420	300	600	900	−480
130	6	780	300	900	1,200	−420
170	6	1,020	300	1,200	1,500	−480
200	6	1,200	300	1,500	1,800	−600
220	6	1,320	300	1,800	2,100	−780
230	6	1,380	300	2,100	2,400	−1,020

If the price of mailboxes is only $6 and this appears to be a permanent situation, the company should probably shut down or stop producing mailboxes. Under these circumstances, the company will be unable to cover its variable costs at any level of output. When the price was $8, it was desirable to operate even at a loss, because the variable costs were being met and some of the fixed costs, which had already been paid, were also being recovered. At a price of $6, however, not even all the variable costs are being covered. One alternative to shutting down would be to try to lower costs. Under such circumstances business firms usually instigate cost-cutting programs.

In Table 9–9, the necessity of shutting down is illustrated in the last column by the fact that each loss is greater than the total fixed cost of $300, which means that some of the variable costs are not being met. This situation is also illustrated in Fig. 9–10 by the fact that the total-revenue line lies below the total-variable-cost curve at all levels of output.

Marginal-Revenue—Marginal-Cost Approach

Another method for determining the output of the Hypothetical Mailbox Manufacturing Company is to compare the change in revenue with the change in cost at each level of output. By comparing the extra revenue and cost that each additional unit of output will add to total revenue and total cost, one can determine the effect on profits. If production is cut back, the reductions in revenue and cost will provide a similar indication about profits. In this way the firm will be comparing the *marginal revenue* (MR) and *marginal cost* (MC) pertaining to each unit of output or each level of production.

Since most business firms are continuously engaged in production activities, it would seem worthwhile to have some idea about the effect a change in production and sales would have on profits. For example, any unit of output whose marginal revenue exceeds its marginal cost obviously should be produced because the unit would add to profits (or reduce losses). If marginal cost exceeds marginal revenue, the unit should not be produced; it would then reduce profits (or add to losses). While this is relevant to all producers, it is probably most obvious to job-lot producers, because each order represents a specific change in the level of production.

Marginal revenue and marginal cost can help to determine the effect on profits of variations in production levels; they also are key elements of the fundamental of output determination, particularly if profits are to be maximized. This fundamental for business analysis can be stated as follows: *Profits will be maximized (losses will be minimized) when the firm produces at the point where marginal revenue equals marginal cost.* This profit-maximizing fundamental can be expressed as the MR = MC rule. In most instances, output levels cannot be broken down into enough detail to reveal the exact output where MR equals MC. Under such circumstances, production should

TABLE 9-10

BEST-PROFIT OUTPUT FOR HYPOTHETICAL MAILBOX MANUFACTURING COMPANY

Quantity of Mailboxes	Average Fixed Cost	Average Variable Cost	Average Cost	Marginal Cost (MC)	Price (=MR)	Profit (+) or Loss (−)
30	$10.00	$10.00	$20.00		$13.00	$−210
				$ 7.50		
70	4.29	8.57	12.86		13.00	− 10
				5.00		
130	2.31	6.92	9.23		13.00	+490
				7.50		
170	1.76	7.06	8.82		13.00	+710
				10.00		
200	1.50	7.50	9.00		13.00	+800
				15.00		
220	1.37	8.18	9.55		13.00	+760
				30.00		
230	1.30	9.13	10.43		13.00	+590

be as close to this point as possible. That is, the firm should produce the next unit of output as long as MR exceeds MC. At the point where MC exceeds MR, production has gone beyond the best-profit output.

The MR = MC rule can now be applied to the Hypothetical Mailbox Manufacturing Company to determine its best-profit output. Since the company is a price taker, it can sell all the mailboxes it produces at $13 each. This means that the price of $13 represents the extra revenue the company would receive for each additional unit of output. Since marginal revenue is defined as the extra revenue for each additional unit of output, price and marginal revenue are identical for the Hypothetical Mailbox Manufacturing Company. This would be true for all firms that are price-takers.

Under other circumstances, price cannot equal marginal revenue because the firm's demand curve will slope downward. If it wants to sell more, it must lower price. When demand slopes downward, marginal revenue will be less than price at each level of output. As a matter of fact, marginal revenue is equal to price minus the ratio of price to elasticity of demand: i.e., MR = price − price/elasticity. For example if price were $8 and elasticity of demand were 4, then MR would be 6 (MR = 8 − 8/4). In plain language, increasing the physical volume of sales by lowering price will change revenue by some amount less than the new price because some revenue will be forgone on all other units at this new, lower price. Whether or not total revenue will increase or decrease depends upon the elasticity of demand.[5]

Marginal cost for the Hypothetical Mailbox Manufacturing Company is displayed in Table 9–10. The unit- and marginal-cost data are reproduced

[5] For a thorough explanation, See R. H. Leftwich, *The Price System and Resource Allocation*, 3rd ed. (New York: Holt, Rinehart & Winston, Inc., 1966), p. 186.

from Table 8–2. The best-profit output for the company can be located by comparing MR with MC for each level of output. Each and every level of production up to and including 200 mailboxes adds more to total revenue than to total cost and therefore adds to the company's profits. In other words, MR exceeds MC at each level of production up to and including 200 mailboxes. The best-profit level is obtained when 200 mailboxes are produced. At any output less than 200 mailboxes, MR exceeds MC, indicating that output should be increased. At any output greater than 200, MC exceeds MR, indicating that output should be reduced. Since intermediate levels of production are not available, 200 appears to be the best output. This best-profit output is verified in the last column of Table 9–10 as a profit of $800.

The comparison of MR and MC for the Hypothetical Mailbox Manufacturing Company appears graphically in Fig. 9–11. The best-profit output of 200 mailboxes takes place where MR and MC intersect. By using continu-

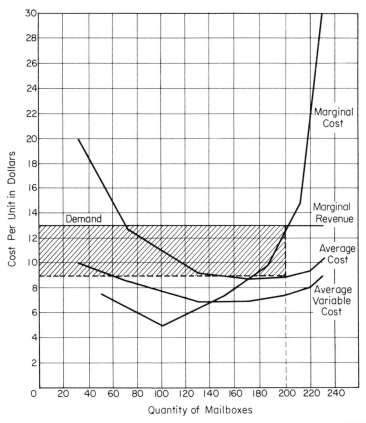

FIGURE 9–11. Comparison of marginal revenue and marginal cost for the Hypothetical Mailbox Manufacturing Company.

ous lines and plotting MC halfway between each level of output to reflect the fact that it is an average change in cost per unit, equality between MR and MC can be achieved graphically. The other cost curves are plotted from the data in Table 9–10. The difference between the price of $13 and the average cost of $9 at an output of 200 represents unit profit. This unit profit of $4 multiplied by 200 mailboxes gives a total profit of $800, shown by the shaded area in Fig. 9–11.

The MR curve that intersects the left-hand scale at a price of $13 is also the average-revenue or demand curve for the firm. Since the Hypothetical Mailbox Manufacturing Company is a price-taker, it can sell any quantity of mailboxes it wishes at $13. Thus 30 mailboxes, 70 mailboxes, or 130 mailboxes may be demanded. The demand curve will be a straight line parallel to the bottom quantity scale. Price, marginal revenue, and demand are all one and the same for a price taker. The company then simply satisfies that quantity demanded which coincides with its best-profit output.

TABLE 9–11

LEAST-LOSS OUTPUT FOR HYPOTHETICAL MAILBOX MANUFACTURING COMPANY

Quantity of Mailboxes	Average Fixed Cost	Average Variable Cost	Average Cost	Marginal Cost (MC)	Price (MR)	Profit (+) or Loss (−)
30	$10.00	$10.00	$20.00		$8.00	$− 360
				$ 7.50		
70	4.29	8.57	12.86		8.00	− 340
				5.00		
130	2.31	6.92	9.23		8.00	− 160
				7.50		
170	1.76	7.06	8.82		8.00	− 140
				10.00		
200	1.50	7.50	9.00		8.00	− 200
				15.00		
220	1.37	8.18	9.55		8.00	− 340
				30.00		
230	1.30	9.13	10.43		8.00	− 560

The MR = MC rule can also indicate the least-loss level of output. Assuming a price of $8 for mailboxes, the company will experience a loss at all levels of production. This is indicated in Table 9–11. To minimize the loss, the company's best available production alternative is to produce 170 mailboxes. Marginal cost between 130 and 170 is $7.50; marginal revenue (price) is $8.00. Since MR exceeds MC, production should be stepped up to 170. Pushing production beyond 170—to 200, for example—means that a marginal cost of $10 will be experienced while marginal revenue is still $8. Since MC would exceed MR, greater losses would be incurred at an output of 200 than at 170.

The company should not shut down, however, as long as the variable costs are being covered. At an output of 170, the price of $8 per mailbox covers the average variable cost of $7.06. If the price of mailboxes were $6, it would be impossible to cover the variable costs and a shutdown should be considered. These are the same conclusions determined by the total-revenue—total-cost approach.

In order to maximize profit (minimize loss) in the short run, a firm must pay strict attention to both cost and revenue. The firm's output decision depends upon this important fundamental for business analysis. In the long run, however, the output decision involves the adjustment of all resources to achieve a least-cost combination of resources. Consequently, the long-run decision takes on the characteristics of an investment decision—i.e., one must determine the future plant and equipment requirements and arrange for these capital expenditures. However, the long-run decision must also pay strict attention to the additional revenue and additional cost of a prospective investment project.

To summarize, this chapter has demonstrated several fundamentals for business analysis. First, the general nature of demand and supply were explained. The interaction between them provides the general framework upon which pricing and output decisions can be based. Second, the nature of demand and its elasticity were investigated, since elasticity is also an important concept for business decisions. (Additional material concerning the estimation of demand is presented in the Annex to this chapter.) Third, the output determination of the Hypothetical Mailbox Manufacturing Company was illustrated. This hypothetical situation was a convenient vehicle to show how quantitative information such as revenue and cost must be brought together to make correct decisions concerning business operations.

ANNEX: DEMAND IDENTIFICATION

The demand and supply determination of price, like the theory of the atom, is intended to explain behavior. Before physical scientists could harness the energy of the atom, they had to know what to expect. Likewise, before decisions about price, production, and sales can be made, the business manager must be aware of the nature of demand. Even though the concept of demand as it was presented in this chapter appears at first glance to be an abstraction, it is still very useful because it provides the business manager with a basis for prediction. Identification of demand curves from everyday experience would be valuable for two reasons: to verify the theory of demand and to provide more accurate information for business decisions. Verification itself depends upon theory, for without the theory of demand, the observer would not know what to look for. The purpose, then, of this Annex is to expose the student to some techniques that can be used to identify demand.

The measurement of demand may proceed along two quite different paths. *Forecasting* is the attempt to measure and predict the sales of particular industries or individual firms. This usually depends first upon the measurement and estimation of general business conditions. *Estimating*, on the other hand, is the attempt to derive a demand schedule or curve for a particular product or service from price and quantity observations. Both methods are widely used and represent the application of important fundamentals for business analysis.

Forecasting Demand

For purposes of forecasting, gross national product may be considered a measure of aggregate demand. Projecting GNP itself would be one way to predict future demand. This can be achieved by the statistical method of least squares, an explanation of which is contained in Chapter 13. By fitting figures of past performance to a mathematical function, future results can be predicted.

The components of GNP, however, provide a more detailed breakdown of the various sectors in the economy. Each of the various components can be broken down even further. For example, personal consumption expenditures can be broken down into durable goods, nondurable goods, and services. Each of these can be divided into more specific categories, such as automobiles and refrigerators.

Forecasting each component or subcomponent separately may provide more accurate results, since each segment is subject to a different set of circumstances. Separation of the various segments allows the forecaster to focus attention on these different influences. For example, present holdings of durables make up a very important determinant of the demand for consumer durables; therefore, saturation of the automobile market would indicate depressed sales for the near future. In forecasting residential construction, the availability of credit and the level of interest rates are probably more important than for any other sector.

Forecasting GNP and its components in this manner makes use of both quantitative and qualitative information. Past historical data are used as a basis for the forecast, which is also subject to the consideration of present circumstances. The forecaster should adjust his predictions according to his own subjective judgment of the impact of certain factors, such as interest rates and market saturation.

Since GNP and its components are so interrelated, it may appear impossible to achieve a satisfactory forecast. The level of consumption, for example, depends upon the level of GNP, and the level of GNP depends upon the level of consumption. Investment expenditures depend to some extent on present and future patterns of spending. To resolve such a situation properly requires the simultaneous solution of all parts; therefore, a series of simultaneous equations must be constructed to reflect this interdependence.

Forecasts of GNP are continuously being made by various government, financial, business, and research organizations. The forecasts of these different organizations achieve various levels of sophistication. Of course, the accuracy of a GNP forecast depends a great deal on how well the past, present, and future conditions have been analyzed. Even sophisticated econometric models, which will be explained next, vary in accuracy.

Econometrics combines economic theory, mathematics, and statistics to build economic models. These models express the statistical measurement of economic behavior in mathematical language. A system of simultaneous equations is used to forecast general business conditions; such equations describe the specific relationships of economic variables such as income, consumption, savings, investment, prices, and output. Some of these equations define specific characteristics. For example, the three major components of GNP are consumption expenditures (C), gross private domestic investment (I) (net foreign investment may be included), and government expenditures (G). These three components represent a definition of GNP, expressed as

$$GNP = C + I + G.$$

Other equations express the behavior of activities that depend on other variables. One such equation is the expression of consumption for the entire economy (in billions of dollars) as a function of disposable personal income (Y); it may appear as

$$C = 150 + 0.7Y.$$

Statistical methods, such as the method of least squares, are used to determine the coefficients or constants from past data. In the above consumption function the constants are 150 and 0.7. The number 150 indicates that consumption would be $150 billion when income is zero. The 0.7 states that consumption (C) changes by $7 billion for every $10 billion change in income (Y). The equation also expresses the absolute level of consumption at any instant in time. If Y were $600 billion, then consumption would be $150 billion plus 0.7 of $600 billion, which would equal $570 billion. Other equations could be devised to describe other components of GNP. Even subcomponents can be expressed in the form of an equation. For example, expenditures on automobiles or other durables, or on residential construction, would include variables relevant to each sector.[6]

---

[6] An actual model for the U. S. economy is described briefly by W. W. Haynes in *Managerial Economics: Analysis and Cases* (Homewood, Ill.: Dorsey Press, 1963), p. 143.

A widely-accepted method for making a short-run forecast of business conditions is based upon the observation of a series of economic data, which may change direction before, during, or after a change in business conditions. The three types are known as *leading series, coincident series,* and *lagging series;* they can be useful in forecasting because they signal changes in business activity. One popular leading indicator is average hours in manufacturing worked per week. If the average increases, one can expect an increase in general business conditions, while a decrease may signal a reduction in business conditions. No one indicator, however, is sufficient to make such a forecast. The National Bureau of Economic Research has released a list of these series, all of which should be analyzed before making a prediction. The best source of leading and lagging series is in *Business Cycle Developments,* the monthly publication of the Bureau of the Census.

Economic forecasts can be used to predict the sales of particular industries or individual firms. Most large companies know what percentage of a GNP component their sales constitute. The annual report of Sears Roebuck and Co. for fiscal 1965 showed sales of $5.74 billion in the year ended January 31; this volume constituted 1.42 per cent of 1964 personal consumer expenditures. This type of information can be useful in forecasting sales. For example, if it is estimated that personal consumer expenditures will be $600 billion in a few years, then Sears can expect a sales volume of approximately $7.5 billion. Other important future planning can be based upon such an estimate of sales. In contrast to Sears, which is one of the nation's leading retailers, an auto manufacturer may base its forecast on the durable goods component of personal consumer expenditures.

Economic forecasts can also be utilized to make predictions of the sales of a particular product. For example, if a general business forecast indicates a 4 per cent increase in personal disposable income, the income elasticity of demand for a given product can be applied to that increase to forecast the increase in sales of the product. Income elasticity of demand expresses numerically the responsiveness of quantity demanded to changes in income. It is derived in the same manner as is price elasticity of demand, except that the percentage change in quantity is compared to the percentage change in income rather than to the percentage change in price. If the income elasticity of demand for a product is 1.5, then a 4 per cent increase in personal disposable income would be the basis for forecasting a 6 per cent increase in sales of the product.

Some products and services may not be this responsive to income changes. For example, food is considered to have an income elasticity of less than 1. That is, the percentage change in quantity of food demanded is less than the percentage change in income. If only $.50 is spent on food for every dollar that income is increased, the income elasticity of food would be 0.5. Furthermore, in the case of food, income elasticity tends to decrease as income increases. For some other goods and services, income elasticity will increase as income rises.

It should be apparent by now that some of the aggregate economic concepts introduced in an earlier chapter have an important bearing on business decisions. It is of primary importance to be able to interpret the available information which describes the economy. Using this information to forecast demand starts a chain reaction for all kinds of decisions concerning such things as price, output, personnel, inventories, supplies, equipment, and plant expansion, just to mention a few.

Estimating Demand

In contrast to the development of a forecast of demand or sales from general business conditions, an estimate of demand depends upon actual observations of price and quantity; it is an attempt to discover or expose an actual demand curve for a particular product or service.

The equilibrium price and equilibrium quantity for a product or service are determined by the interaction of demand and supply. This price and quantity represent a point on a particular demand curve and a particular supply curve; in the next interval of time, they may represent another point on a demand and supply curve. Observations over an extended period of time would show these different prices and quantities. A group of equilibrium observations is needed to estimate a demand curve, which then is derived by statistical methods.

There are two kinds of data that can be used to make up a sample of price and quantity observations. One type is called *time-series* data. Such data represent a collection of the price and quantity relationships that have occurred in the same place at different times. The data in Table 9–12 represent a hypothetical series of prices and a hypothetical series of quantities sold or traded over an extended period of time.

The other kind of price and quantity data is called *cross-sectional* data. Table 9–13 displays an imaginary cross-sectional sample. Such a sample represents a collection of the price and quantity relationships that have occurred in different places at the same time.

When the time-series sample and the cross-sectional sample are displayed on a graph, they each produce a pattern that roughly resembles the shape of a demand curve. The scatter of points for each sample is shown in Fig. 9–12 and Fig. 9–13, respectively. Both diagrams indicate that the demand curve was relatively stable and that price and quantity equilibrium points resulted from shifts in supply.

In Fig. 9–14, a fixed demand curve is intersected by several supply curves; this illustrates how shifts in supply can produce a scatter of points that resembles a demand curve. However, the scatter using cross-sectional

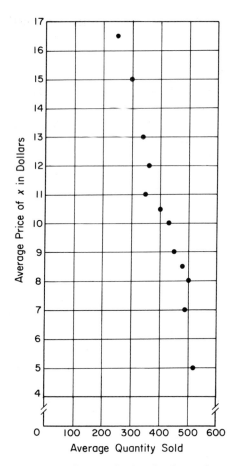

FIGURE 9–12. Scatter of points for time-series sample.

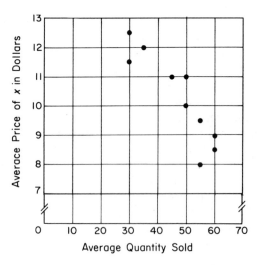

FIGURE 9–13. Scatter of points for cross-sectional sample.

TABLE 9–12

HYPOTHETICAL TIME-SERIES SAMPLE FOR PRODUCT X

Period	Average Price of X	Average Quantity Sold
January	$11.00	350
February	10.00	430
March	8.00	500
April	5.00	520
May	7.00	490
June	15.00	300
July	16.50	250
August	10.50	400
September	12.00	360
October	13.00	340
November	9.00	450
December	8.50	480

TABLE 9–13

HYPOTHETICAL CROSS-SECTIONAL SAMPLE FOR PRODUCT X

Market	Average Price of X	Average Quantity Sold
A	$11.00	50
B	9.50	55
C	8.50	60
D	10.00	50
E	11.00	45
F	9.00	60
G	12.00	35
H	11.50	30
I	12.50	30
J	8.00	55

data (Fig. 9–13) does not produce a linear demand curve that intersects all the points. The statistical method of least squares must be used to fit a demand curve to the sample scatter. In essence, what has happened is that both demand and supply have been shifting, although the shifts in demand have been relatively small.

Another sample of data might produce a scatter of points such as that displayed in Fig. 9–15. This would represent a supply curve because the various equilibrium points result from shifts in demand. If a sample of data produces a scatter much like a shot-gun blast would produce, it is apparent that both demand and supply have been changing considerably. Such a situation would require further identification of the data by additional mathematical methods in order to isolate each influence.

The first step in the estimation procedure is to construct a scatter diagram of price and quantity observations. Such scatters are depicted in Fig. 9–12 and Fig. 9–13. The general form of the scatter diagram in each case will suggest whether a straight line or a curved line will give the best fit to the points.

Using the cross-sectional data from Table 9–13, a linear demand equation can be obtained by the method of least squares, which is explained in

Chapter 13.[7] The estimate of the demand equation for product X is
$$q = 117.05 - 6.8p.$$
The $-$ 6.8 denotes the slope of the demand curve in terms of the change in quantity (q) for a change in price (p). The straight line corresponding to this equation is shown in Fig. 9–16, where the points represent the hypothetical price and quantity observations.

Since the demand equation for product X has been estimated, the price elasticity of demand can be computed by the formula for elasticity:

$$\text{Elasticity} = \frac{\dfrac{\text{change in } q}{q}}{\dfrac{\text{change in } p}{p}}$$

which can be rearranged to

$$\text{Elasticity} = \frac{\text{change in } q}{\text{change in } p} \times \frac{p}{q}.$$

[7] The calculations for the linear demand equation are as follows:

DEMAND ESTIMATION USING HYPOTHETICAL CROSS-SECTIONAL DATA

Market	Quantity (q)	Price (p)	p^2	qp	q^2
A	50	$11.00	$121.00	550.00	2,500
B	55	9.50	90.25	522.50	3,025
C	60	8.50	72.25	510.00	3,600
D	50	10.00	100.00	500.00	2,500
E	45	11.00	121.00	495.00	2,025
F	60	9.00	81.00	540.00	3,600
G	35	12.00	144.00	420.00	1,225
H	30	11.50	132.25	345.00	900
I	30	12.50	156.25	375.00	900
J	55	8.00	64.00	440.00	3,025
Totals	$\Sigma q = 470$	$\Sigma p = \$103.00$	$\Sigma p^2 = \$1,082.00$	$\Sigma qp = 4,697.50$	$\Sigma q^2 = 23,300$

*$n = 10$, average $q = \dfrac{\Sigma q}{n} = 47$, average $p = \dfrac{\Sigma p}{n} = 10.3$.

Using the least-squares method,

$$\text{Intercept} = \frac{(\Sigma p^2)(\Sigma q) - (\Sigma p)(\Sigma qp)}{n(\Sigma p^2) - (\Sigma p)^2}$$
$$= \frac{(1,082)(470) - (103)(4,697.50)}{10(1,082) - (10,609)}$$
$$= 117.05.$$

$$\text{Slope} = \frac{n(\Sigma qp) - (\Sigma p)(\Sigma q)}{n(\Sigma p^2) - (\Sigma p)^2}$$
$$= \frac{10(4,697.50) - (103)(470)}{10(1,082) - (10,609)}$$
$$= -6.80.$$

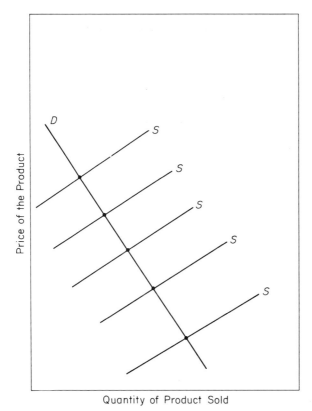

FIGURE 9–14.   **Fixed demand curve intersected by several supply curves.**

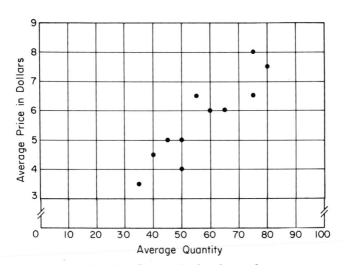

FIGURE 9–15.   **Scatter of points for supply curve.**

Since the slope is − 6.8, for every dollar change in price there will be a 6.8-unit change in quantity demanded. Consequently, when demand is expressed as above, the slope will be equal to change in q divided by change in p in the elasticity formula. Using the − 6.8 slope and the average p and q from the data in Table 9–13, the price elasticity of demand is

$$\text{Slope} \times \frac{p}{q} = (-6.8)\left(\frac{10.3}{47}\right) = -1.49.$$

The demand for product X is therefore relatively elastic.

Information about price and quantity can be obtained in various ways. Private institutions and government agencies regularly publish data on many products that can be used to estimate demand curves. The absence of readily available information means that other ways will have to be devised to obtain the necessary data.

One method of obtaining adequate data is experimenting with the market. To do this, the business firm selects several different markets and establishes different prices in each. The quantities sold in the various markets provide cross-sectional data. In order to obtain time-series data, prices are

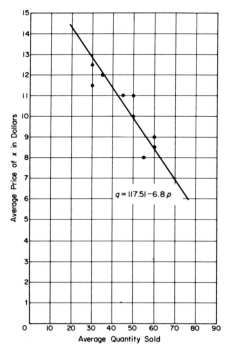

FIGURE 9–16.   Slope of demand curve with scatter of points for hypothetical price and quantity observations.

periodically changed in a given market over an extended period of time; an accurate record will reveal the necessary information.

Another method of obtaining demand information is sending out questionnaires or conducting personal interviews. This method requires that the questionnaires and interviews be carefully designed. Sometimes an indirect method is used, in which later analysis of an interview reveals demand information. Other interviews are designed in such a manner that the respondents are not aware of their purpose. The real demand information is obtained after a general interview when the person is offered several gifts and then asked why he or she picked a particular one. The respondent's comments provide the demand information being sought.

Finally, demand information can be collected from the firm's salesmen or from other personnel who have close contact with the market. However, this is not quantitative information; it is merely a composite opinion.

The information on price and quantity collected from real market experiences rarely conforms to the assumptions of theoretical economics. Such things as consumer tastes, consumer income, the price of other goods, and future expectations are continuously influencing demand. Although the price and quantity relationships obtained by research are not likely to imitate true demand relationships, the mathematical demand function may include these other variables. Therefore, instead of a simple relationship such as

$$q = a + bp,$$

the formula might be extended to take the form

$$q = a_0 + a_1 p + a_2 y + a_3 p' + a_4 p''.$$

In this formula, the quantity demanded (q) depends upon price (p), consumer income (y), the price of a close substitute (p'), and the price of a complementry good (p''). Other variables can also be added. A mathematical equation representing the demand function for food was obtained by Girshick and Haavelmo and is described briefly by Cohen and Cyert. The demand appeared as

$$F = 97.677 - 0.246\frac{p_f}{p} + 0.247\,Y + 0.051\,Y_1 - 0.104t;$$

it included the influences of prices, present income, past income, and a time trend.[8]

    [8] See Cohen, Kalman J., and Richard M. Cyert, *Theory of the Firm* (Englewood Cliffs, N. J.: Prentice-Hall, Inc., 1965), p. 86.

The measurement of demand is quite difficult and involved, and the brief presentation in this Annex has been provided merely to expose the student to some of the problems and techniques that must be considered. However, an understanding of economic theory, mathematical maturity, and familiarity with statistical methods are vital if one is to become a competent business manager.

PROBLEMS AND PROJECTS

1. This is the third part of the continuous problem introduced in Chapter 7 and continued in Chapter 8. The purpose of this exercise is to bring revenue and cost together in order to determine the best-profit output for the Hypothetical Chair Manufacturing Company.
   a. Calculate the total revenue and profit (loss) for each level of output. Assume that the company is a price taker and that the price for chairs is $12.50. Display these calculations in the table below, which also contains the cost data from Problem 1 of Chapter 8. Indicate the best-profit output for the company.
   b. Plot the total-revenue curve on the same piece of graph paper on which the total-cost curves were plotted in Problem 1 of Chapter 8, and label it "TR" ($12.50). Indicate the best-profit output and the amount of profit on the graph.

BEST-PROFIT OUTPUT FOR HYPOTHETICAL CHAIR
MANUFACTURING COMPANY

Quantity of Chairs	Price	Total Revenue	Total Cost	Profit (+) or Loss (−)
20			$ 500	
50			800	
120			1,100	
180			1,400	
220			1,700	
240			2,000	
250			2,300	

   c. Assuming a price of $6.50 for the chairs, calculate the total revenue for each level of output and compare it to the total cost used in part (a) above. Display these data in the table on page 221. Should the company shut down? If not, what would be the best output? Does this output provide a profit or a loss? How much? Plot this total-revenue curve on the same graph used in part (b) above and label it "TR" ($6.50).
   d. Calculate the average revenue for each level of output by dividing the total revenue by the quantity of chairs at each level of output. You

BEST-PROFIT OUTPUT FOR HYPOTHETICAL CHAIR MANUFACTURING COMPANY

Quantity of Chairs	Price	Total Revenue	Total Cost	Profit (+) or Loss (−)
20	$6.50		$ 500	
50	6.50		800	
120	6.50		1,100	
180	6.50		1,400	
220	6.50		1,700	
240	6.50		2,000	
250	6.50		2,300	

should notice a peculiar relationship between average revenue and the price of $12.50. Now calculate marginal revenue for each level of output. It also should be the same as price. Display these data in the table below, which includes the average- and marginal-cost data from Problem 1 of Chapter 8. Applying the MR = MC rule, what is the best-profit output for the Hypothetical Chair Manufacturing Company? Does this reconcile with the answer in part (a) above when the total approach was used?

BEST-PROFIT OUTPUT FOR HYPOTHETICAL CHAIR MANUFACTURING COMPANY

Quantity of Chairs	Average Fixed Cost	Average Variable Cost	Average Cost	Marignal Cost (MC)	Price (MR)	Profit (+) or Loss (−)
20						
50						
120						
180						
220						
240						
250						

2. The purpose of this exercise is to consider the relevance of some demand information to business decisions. Below is the fare structure of the Hypothetical Transit Company and its effect on passenger travel.

Fare (cents)	Passengers (millions per year)	Revenues (millions per year)
5	950	$ 47.5
10	820	82.0
15	710	106.5
20	600	120.0
25	520	130.0
30	450	135.0
35	380	133.0
40	320	128.0

    a. Is the demand for the company elastic or inelastic? Why?

    b. Over the past years the fares have been steadily increased from $.10 to the present $.30. From the standpoint of revenue, has this been a wise policy? Why or why not?

    c. The management of the company is presently seeking a fare hike to $.35 from the local public service commission. For the last two years costs have exceeded revenues, resulting in operating losses. Should the company try to raise its fares? Why or why not? In what way should costs be considered? What alternative actions do you think the company might consider?

3. As mentioned in the Annex, econometric models of the economy are valuable aids for business decisions. Familiarize yourself with a model of the economy by reading "A Quarterly Econometric Model of the United States: A Progress Report," in the May, 1966, issue of the *Survey of Current Business*, pp. 13ff, and by perusing the Appendix of that issue to get an idea of the application of mathematics and statistics to economic analysis.

4. As mentioned in the Annex, *Business Cycle Developments* is a good source of economic and business indicators. Obtain the latest issue of *Business Cycle Developments* and prepare a brief report of its contents. You might include a brief description of a diffusion index.

SELECTED REFERENCES

Dean, Joel, *Managerial Economics*. Englewood Cliffs, N. J.: Prentice-Hall, Inc., 1951.

Haynes, W. Warren, *Managerial Economics: Analysis and Cases*, Chaps. 4–6. Homewood, Ill.: Dorsey Press, 1963.

——*Pricing Decisions in Small Business*. Lexington, Ky.: University of Kentucky Press, 1962.

Kaplan, Abraham D. H., Joel B. Dirlam, and Robert F. Lanzillotti, *Pricing in Big Business*. Washington, D. C.: The Brookings Institution, 1958.

Leftwich, Richard H., *The Price System and Resource Allocation*, 3rd ed., Chaps. 3, 4. New York: Holt, Rinehart & Winston, Inc., 1966.

McConnell, Campbell R., *Economics: Principles, Problems, and Policies*, 3rd ed., Chaps. 4, 23, 26. New York: McGraw-Hill Book Company, 1966.

10

SALES STIMULATION

In addition to production, business firms are concerned with the process of getting goods and services from the point of production to the point of consumption. This process is commonly referred to as marketing. Broadly defined, marketing accounts for many of today's business activities. The physical distribution of goods and services encompasses such routine activities as transportation, storage, warehousing, wholesaling, and retailing. Those activities that are intended to stimulate sales include pricing, product variation, packaging, advertising, publicity, and personal selling. All of the latter activities require a certain amount of marketing research to obtain information about market conditions and potentials, consumer attitudes and behavior, and product acceptance and improvement. It is not our intention to describe all of these marketing activities, only the activities pertaining to sales stimulation that qualify as fundamentals for business analysis.

Sales stimulation plays a vital role in determining a firm's rate of production and level of profits. Therefore, this chapter will be devoted to price promotion and to some types of nonprice promotion. More specifically, the chapter will deal with certain general pricing considerations, specific pricing methods, and discount pricing. It also will discuss the effect of product variation and illustrate the impact of advertising. Although personal selling is another form of nonprice promotion, its description does not fall within the scope or purpose of this text and will not be treated here.

PRICE PROMOTION

A business establishment can manipulate its sales volume by changing its prices. A change in price causes a movement along a given or existing demand curve, even though it does not alter the demand. Product pricing provides the basis from which many fundamentals for business analysis emerge.

Pricing Considerations

A major pricing consideration of business enterprises is the establishment of a *pricing objective*. One basic pricing objective of all business enterprises is profit. Profits are necessary in order for a business enterprise to survive. Owners must hope for a profit to justify taking risks and struggling with the uncertainties and changes inherent in a market economy. Thus one pricing objective may be that of maximizing profits. However, long-run objectives, competition, public attitudes, and government policies may limit the extent to which a business enterprise may pursue such an objective. Considering these influences, maximum profits in the long run may mean only reasonable profits in the short run.

Another pricing objective is the achievement of a target return on investment or on net sales. The price is established in such a manner that the sales revenue will yield a predetermined average return on the capital invested in the company. Such a target return considers the overall return in the industry and recognizes the need to expand or replace present capital.

In some companies the major pricing objective is the maintenance or growth of its share of the market. In this way the firm measures its success in relation to the entire market. Having attained a comfortable position in terms of profit and sales, the firm merely tries to duplicate its past performance. Although it may also attempt to improve upon past performance, obtaining a larger share of the market by holding down prices could result in lower profits. On the other hand, a firm may increase sales but lose its share of a rapidly expanding market, which may indicate the need for an adjustment in price.

Another major pricing objective of some business enterprises is the stabilization of prices. "Live and let live" is a common attitude among oligopolists who wish to avert price wars. A price war in an oligopoly could have disastrous results on profits, since each firm might end up with approximately the same share of the market it had before, but at lower prices and lower profits.

The second pricing consideration of a business enterprise that will be discussed is recognition of *the changing nature of the product*. Many products are believed to experience what is known as a life cycle, during which the product is introduced, achieves maturity, and eventually experiences degeneration. The life cylce recognizes such things as the development of a better design, the growth of competition, and changes in consumer tastes. For example, the ball-point pen has experienced the first two phases; buggy whips

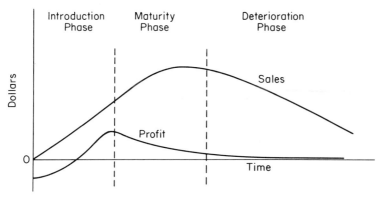

Introduction | Maturity | Deterioration
Phase | Phase | Phase

Dollars

Sales

Profit

O

Time

FIGURE 10–1. Product life cycle.

have experienced all three. Often a product may experience a prolonged maturity phase because of continuous product alteration and improvement. According to E. Jerome McCarthy, "In the United States, the markets for most automobiles, boats, many household appliances, most groceries, television sets, and tobacco products are in the market maturity stage."[1]

The sales and profit patterns during the life cycle of a typical product are illustrated in Fig. 10–1. During the early part of the first phase, losses are sustained because of product promotion and development expenses. Eventually, however, profits emerge and grow as more and more customers enter the market. Sales rise throughout the introductory phase; finally, profits reach a peak, which marks the end of the phase.

During the maturity phase, sales continue to rise; they eventually reach a maximum and finally begin to decline. Profits decline throughout the maturity phase. As more and more competing products emerge, advertising and promotional costs rise. Price cuts also may be instituted, causing profits and sales to decline.

The last phase witnesses a further decline of sales and profits due to the introduction of substitute products and the use of even more vigorous price competition to combat falling sales.

The concept of the life cycle is an important fundamental of business analysis. The general pattern of profits and sales during the various phases clearly indicates the need to keep a constant eye on the changing nature of the product. A well-defined marketing strategy is required as well as continuous supervision of the firm's product mix. Innovation and improvement must be a never-ending process.

Different pricing policies are related to the phases or stages in the product's life cycle. When a product is first introduced, it may be unique or at least have a high degree of distinctiveness. Under such circumstances, a firm may choose to charge a high price. This is sometimes referred to as "skimming

---

[1] McCarthy, E. Jerome, *Basic Marketing* (Homewood, Ill.: Richard D. Irwin, Inc., 1964), p. 334.

the cream off the market"; its purpose is to maximize profits as quickly as possible. This approach is often used with fad items, since they usually die out quickly. Products that can be associated with popular movies or television shows, such as "Daniel Boone" caps, "Batman" masks, and "007" after-shave lotion, are a few examples.

At other times a new product may be priced low to discourage competition or new entrants into the market; a high price, by producing large initial profits, may serve as a signal to others to enter the field. Certain food products are priced low because they can be easily duplicated by other producers. Sometimes a new product may face stiff competition from identical or similar products already in existence. Thus a low price may be necessary to penetrate the market.

Other considerations exist in pricing new products. For example, the management may want the product to yield a regular rate of return despite new competition or changes. In addition, speedy acceptance and recovery of development costs are always critical considerations.

During the final phase of the product's life cycle, when it experiences a declining market, two clear choices emerge: to lower prices or to eventually discontinue operations. The choice will depend upon the extent of the decline and the extent to which other firms leave the industry. Some products, such as fad items, may experience very rapid market deterioration. Price falls below cost, and the only solution is to recover all possible costs until the supply is exhausted.

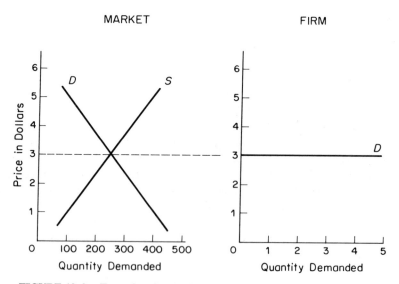

FIGURE 10–2. Example of a horizontal demand curve facing the purely competitive seller.

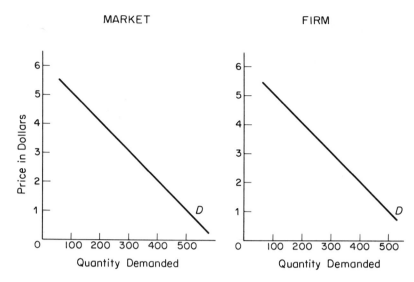

MARKET   FIRM

FIGURE 10–3.   Example of a demand curve for a pure monopoly.

The third pricing consideration of a business enterprise is the influence of *market structures*. In the case of pure competition, the seller or firm has no choice of price; it must sell at a price set in the market by demand and supply. The market sets the price according to demand and supply pressures. The demand curve facing the purely competitive seller is horizontal and is equal to the market price, as illustrated in Fig. 10–2. In pure competition the seller is a price taker.

In pure monopoly, the demand curve (illustrated in Fig. 10–3) slopes downward to the right; this is the industry or total-market demand curve. For pure monopoly to exist, there must be only one seller and no close substitutes. The pure monopolist can determine price: at high prices he will sell a small quantity, and at low prices a larger quantity. The monopolist charges the price, indicated by demand, that will maximize profit, using the MR = MC rule.

The real world is unlike either one of the extremes, pure competition or pure monopoly, but rather is a mixture of both. In the real world of imperfect competition, sellers decide on price. The demand curve is not horizontal as in pure competition, nor does it slope downward as much as in pure monopoly, since sellers in the real world have many close substitutes with which to compete. The demand curve for imperfect competition is illustrated in Fig. 10–4. The very fact that the demand curve slopes downward means that the seller has discretion over price in order to promote sales. In addition, sellers in the real world can manipulate the position of the demand curve through other promotional activities.

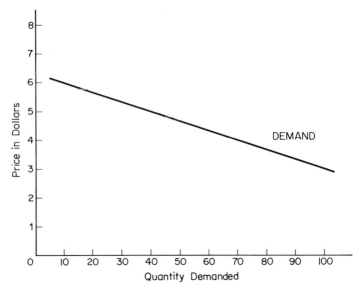

FIGURE 10–4. Normal demand curve.

Finally, the number of sellers in any one market may vary from a few to many. Consequently, many forms of pricing behavior exist. Where there are many sellers, a seller can ignore any impact his price policy may have on others. When there are only a few, a change in price on the part of one will be noticed by the others and may set off a chain reaction. As a result, many different price policies emerge in oligopoly, including price wars, price leadership, collusion, and secret price concessions. In both cases (few sellers or many sellers), nonprice promotion is prevalent. Firms constantly compete in such things as advertising, style, sales activity, and brand names.

Pricing Methods

There are many methods by which firms can determine price when they are operating under conditions of imperfect competition. Although sometimes the price method used appears to be quite different from another method, usually the difference is only a variation on a basic technique. Several pricing methods will be presented here to serve as fundamentals for business analysis.

The *going-rate* method is probably the simplest and the easiest of all methods to administer. The seller merely accepts the price already set by the market or by some other seller. There are no calculations to perform. The seller produces and markets his product according to the prevailing price. The Hypothetical Mailbox Manufacturing Company followed such a policy. In many cases prices are stabilized or maintained by legislative action. In some states, milk prices are established by state milk boards. "Fair-trade" laws have also been used to fix prices.

The *cost-plus* method is probably the most common pricing method in use today. It requires the addition of some predetermined markup to a base cost to allow for profit. When the markup is added to average cost, it is called *average-cost pricing*. The United States Steel Corporation employs a "stable-margin" price policy in conjunction with standard costs, which are a form of average cost determined by a specific cost-accounting technique.[2]

Cost-plus pricing is widely used by wholesalers and retailers when they take the purchase price of their goods and add a percentage to cover operating expenses and a profit. For example, a retailer may buy a mailbox from a manufacturer for $13, add 40 per cent for his expenses and profit, and sell the mailbox for $18.20. The $18.20 selling price is found as follows:

$$\$13 \times 40\% = \$5.20 \text{ markup}$$
$$\$13 + \$5.20 = \$18.20 \text{ selling price.}$$

Often the markup is based on the selling price. This method is still considered cost-plus pricing, because the seller wishes to maintain a certain ratio of sales—for example, 60 per cent to cover the cost of the goods and 40 per cent for expenses and profit. Assume that a mailbox costing $13 must have a markup of 40 per cent based on the selling price. The selling price is determined in the following way:

$$\$13 \text{ cost of mailbox} = 60\% \text{ of selling price}$$
$$\$13/60\% = \text{selling price}$$
$$\$13/0.60 = \$21.67 \text{ selling price.}$$

This yields a higher selling price than the 40 per cent markup based on cost, because the selling price on which the markup is based is greater than cost. When cost-plus pricing is used by manufacturers, the markup is based on the cost of producing the goods; in any event, it is used to recover expenses not associated with the production of the goods and to yield a certain profit.

Cost-plus pricing makes use of a flexible markup when factors other than cost are to be considered. The markup may be changed, for instance, because of the state of demand. A producer or seller who is experiencing a strong demand may easily raise his markup because the elasticity of demand allows him to get away with it. He may raise markup because he begins to experience rapidly rising marginal costs as capacity limits are reached or because he prefers to ration his product rather than to lower its quality just to satisfy a larger demand. The latter would be particularly true for an item that has been developed as a prestige product. At other times a lower markup may be imposed when new firms enter the market or if a new model is imminent. In any event, markup variations resulting from such factors clearly indicate that cost-plus pricing recognizes demand and supply conditions.

Another approach to cost-plus pricing bases price on marginal cost instead of total cost. Assume that the Hypothetical Mailbox Manufacturing

[2] Kaplan, A. D., Joel B. Dirlam, and R. F. Lanzillotti, *Pricing in Big Business* (Washington, D. C.: The Brookings Institution, 1958), p. 14.

Company's rate of production is presently 130 mailboxes per period. When output is boosted to 170 mailboxes, instead of selling the additional 40 mailboxes at a price based on their average cost of $8.82, they are sold at a price based on their marginal cost of $7.50 each (see Table 9–10). In this way, the company tries to cover only the additional out-of-pocket (variable) costs for the 40 mailboxes. The fixed costs, which represent money already sunk in plant and equipment, can be temporarily disregarded. A firm may consider it desirable to quote a price based on marginal cost because it wants to keep its labor force employed during a slack season and prefers to keep the plant running rather than face costly shutdowns and startups. Sometimes such an arrangement is used to acquaint a new customer with the product, since the marginal-cost price may be lower than the normal price.

In the third pricing method known as *target-return* pricing, the firm establishes its price according to a target rate of return on its investment. General Motors, for example, seeks to achieve a certain overall rate of return on its investment when it prices its automobiles.[3] Alcoa bases the price of each product it manufactures on full cost and a margin with the intention of earning a general target return.[4] If a company seeks a 20 per cent return after taxes each year on a $1-million investment, it must price its products to yield $200,000 net profits.

The Hypothetical Mailbox Manufacturing Company can be used to illustrate the target-return pricing method. Assume that the company feels it can sell 50,000 mailboxes per year at any reasonable price it selects. If there are 250 working days per year, the company could produce the 50,000 mailboxes at a rate of 200 per day. According to the average-cost information in Table 8–2, a mailbox can be produced at $9 per unit if the output rate of 200 per day is maintained throughout the year. If the firm has an investment of $750,000 and a target rate of return of 20 per cent, it will seek to make a profit of $150,000 per year. Dividing the $150,000 desired total profit by 50,000 units, we get $3 per mailbox. Thus the price the company seeks is $12 per mailbox: the $3 profit added to the $9 cost per unit. If the company can sell 50,000 mailboxes for $12 each, it will earn $150,000 or 20 per cent of its $750,000 investment.

The target-rate-of-return method of pricing is used more by large-scale, multiproduct businesses than by small firms. Companies that have millions and even billions of dollars invested in plant and equipment can use this method across product lines and can even break it down into product divisions. This device also becomes valuable in measuring the overall performance of different departments or divisions of the firm.

Another method of determining price is *breakeven* analysis. This method can be particularly useful for pricing a relatively new product, because it

[3] Kaplan, *op. cit.*, p. 50.
[4] *Ibid.*, p. 28.

indicates the breakeven points for various prices, revealing the one that will yield the best profit. Breakeven analysis makes use of both revenue and cost information, as was explained in Chapter 9. The total-cost data of the Hypothetical Mailbox Manufacturing Company and additional hypothetical demand information will be used to illustrate how breakeven analysis can be used in pricing.

Assume that the Hypothetical Mailbox Manufacturing Company is no longer a price taker (as was the case in Chapter 9), but must sell its product in a market of imperfect competition. The company has collected demand information from consumers, dealers, and other sellers, which is displayed in Table 10–1. Five prices and the corresponding quantities demanded are arrayed in the first two columns. Total revenues were obtained by multiplying price times quantity, total costs were extracted from Table 8–1, and profit is simply total revenue minus total cost. The best profit for the company occurs at an output of 130 and a price of $18.

TABLE 10–1

PRICING AND BREAKEVEN ANALYSIS FOR HYPOTHETICAL MAILBOX
MANUFACTURING COMPANY

Unit Price	Quantity Demanded	Total Revenue	Total Cost	Profit	Breakeven Output
$20	70	$1,400	$ 900	$ 500	30
18	130	2,340	1,200	1,140	36
15	170	2,550	1,500	1,050	50
12	200	2,400	1,800	600	80
10	220	2,200	2,100	100	110

The price line for each level is superimposed on the total-cost curve in Fig. 10–5 to reveal the breakeven points, which occur at the outputs where the price lines for each level intersect the total-cost curve. This reflects the general fact that higher prices mean lower breakeven points. The quantity demanded at each price (from Table 10–1) is indicated in Fig. 10–5 by the point on each price line. The total-revenue curve for the company under the given demand conditions would emerge as a line connecting the points on each price line. The best profit is indicated by the dashed line between the $18 price line and the total-cost curve. According to the demand and cost data, the company would incur the best profit by producing 130 mailboxes per period and selling them at a price of $18 each.

Finally, two other pricing methods deserve brief mention. One is the "intuitive" method of pricing, which is based upon feelings and hunches. This method is usually used for fad items. The other method depends upon experimentation or trial-and-error techniques: the price that seems best after several trials is charged in all markets. Neither method is very scientific.

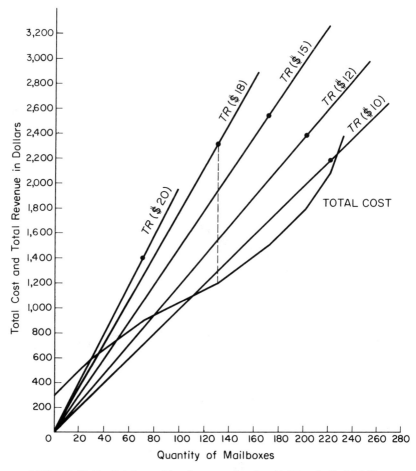

FIGURE 10–5.   Pricing and break-even points for the Hypothetical Mailbox Manufacturing Company.

Discounting

Many business establishments have fixed price lists for merchandise. In order to be more competitive, a seller may offer discounts on these prices. Discounting is often referred to as an indirect pricing method because it represents an alteration of the fixed list price. Discounts might be particularly desirable in an oligopoly because they can reduce the risk of price wars. They also are quite prevalent among manufacturers and distributors.

Several types of discounts are offered as modifications of the list price. Quantity discounts, trade discounts, and cash discounts will be given full treatment here. However, two other types, seasonal and promotional discounts, deserve brief mention. Seasonal discounts are offered to customers of seasonal products to allow the producers to level out production or to reduce the possibility of later bottlenecks. Promotional discounts are used to introduce new products. For example, coupons worth a certain amount of money toward the purchase of soap products are frequently mailed to households. This represents a reduction of the list price at which the product is offered.

Quantity Discounts. These are usually offered by a seller in order to encourage a customer to buy in large amounts. There are two methods of determining the size of the purchase. One method bases the discount on the number of items purchased of one particular product. The expression "cheaper by the dozen" is appropriate here. The other method measures the purchase in dollar terms. A full-line grocery wholesaler would use the latter method to encourage his customers to buy all their items from him.

When the quantity discount is based upon one order, it is known as a *noncumulative discount.* Thus, a wholesaler may sell canned peas at $3.60 per case or six cases for $18.00 ($3.00 per case). The retailer may sell the same peas at $.20 per can or two cans for $.35. As you can see, quantity discounts are available to consumers as well as to businesses.

When the quantity discount is based upon the total volume of several orders over a period of time, it is known as a *cumulative discount.* The cumulative discount encourages regular patronage as opposed to large single orders. In any event, quantity discounts offer a competitive price advantage to buyers, allowing them to buy at lower unit costs and offer lower selling prices to their customers.

Trade Discounts. These are sometimes called "functional" discounts and are another important type of discount. Trade discounts offer wholesalers and distributors a reduction from the list price for performing certain marketing functions. For example, the net price of a mailbox, listed at $20 less a trade discount of 40 per cent, is calculated as follows:

$$\$20 \times 40\% = \$8 \text{ discount}$$
$$\$20 - \$8 \quad = \$12 \text{ net price.}$$

A manufacturer may quote a retail list price and a series of discounts. To illustrate, assume that mailboxes are typically distributed first through regional distributors, then through local wholesalers, and finally through retailers to the consumer. The list price might appear as "$20 less 25–10–5." (When two or more discounts are expressed in a series, they are calculated on a decreasing basis.) The first discount is 25 per cent of the original list price. The second discount of 10 per cent is figured on the $15 that remains after the first discount has been subtracted from the list price. The third discount of 5 per cent is figured on the $13.50 that remains after the second discount has been subtracted. Thus the net price for mailboxes listed as "$20 less 25–10–5" is calculated as follows:

$$\$20 \times 25\% = \$5 \text{ first discount}$$
$$\$20 - \$5 = \$15 \text{ retailer's price}$$
$$\$15 \times 10\% = \$1.50 \text{ second discount}$$
$$\$15 - \$1.50 = \$13.50 \text{ wholesaler's price}$$
$$\$13.50 \times 5\% = \$0.68 \text{ third discount}$$
$$\$13.50 - 0.68 = \$12.82 \text{ distributor's price.}$$

It should be noted that the 25, 10, and 5 do not constitute a total discount of 40 per cent off the list price. The previous 40 per cent calculation will verify this: it produced a net price of $12, while the series discounts produce a net price of $12.82.

A series of discounts can also be used by manufacturers who sell to different classes of customers. If mailboxes are sold to both regional distributors and wholesalers, the series discount calculations can reveal the price to each type of customer; that is, $12.82 to distributors and $13.50 to wholesalers. Wholesalers are charged a higher price than distributors because the latter may be expected to perform some of the marketing and promotional activities. Often a "discount sheet" showing the allowance to the trade accompanies the seller's catalog.

Cash Discounts. These comprise another important type of discount, which is granted to encourage prompt payment. The main purpose of providing this inducement is to reduce collection expenses and credit risks. Probably the most typical cash discount terms call for 2 per cent off if paid in 10 days, and the full invoice price due in 30 days. Such terms are written as "$\frac{2}{10}$ net 30" (read as "two ten, net thirty"). Assume that an invoice for $1,200, with terms of $\frac{2}{10}$ net 30, is paid within 10 days. The discount and the amount to be paid are calculated as follows:

$$\$1,200 \text{ net amount}$$
$$\times 0.02 \text{ rate of cash discount}$$
$$\overline{\$24.00} \text{ amount of cash discount}$$
$$\$1,200 - \$24.00 = \$1,176.00 \text{ amount paid.}$$

If the bill is not paid within the 10-day period, the total amount, $1,200, must be paid within 30 days after the date of the invoice. Other terms of payment such as "$\frac{1}{15}$ net 60" and "$\frac{2}{20}$ net 45" are common.

Since payment is not due for several days, depending on the terms, and since the use of the money is free for that period, it would not be wise to make payment early. However, it would be wise to take advantage of the cash discount rather than pay the full amount when due, even if a bank loan is necessary. This situation can be illustrated by an example. Assume that a hardware store has purchased $1,200 worth of mailboxes on account, the terms being "$\frac{2}{10}$ net 30." Assume also that the hardware store owner can borrow from a bank at 5 per cent and that he expects to sell all the mailboxes in 30 days. On the tenth day, he should pay $1,176, the invoice price less the cash discount, and borrow that amount from the bank for 20 days. At 5 per cent, his interest will be $3.27. (Interest calculations are discussed in Chapter. 15 However, the calculations are as follows: Interest $= \$1,176 \times 0.05 \times \frac{20}{360} = \$3.27$.) As you can see, by borrowing the $1,176 at $3.27 interest, the hardware store owner saved his firm $20.73 ($24.00 less $3.27 interest). Taking advantage of cash discounts is an important fundamental for business analysis.

NONPRICE PROMOTION

A business establishment can stimulate its sales volume by means other than price. For instance, a seller can avoid price competition through product differentiation—that is, by making his product different or by making it seem different. Product differentiation is accomplished in two ways: by advertising and by product variation. Product variation refers to the quality (real or alleged) and the design aspects of a product (or service). Advertising is a means by which product variation as well as prices and product information may be communicated to the consumer.

Unlike pricing promotion, product variation and advertising affect sales volume by causing a change or shift in demand; pricing promotion merely causes a change in the quantity demanded and is reflected by a movement along a given demand. Product differentiation provides the basis for many business activities.

Advertising

Advertising performs several important functions. It informs prospective customers of the availability and price of a product and educates them to use new products or find new uses for existing products, thereby stimulating demand. Advertising media such as newspapers, magazines, billboards, radio, television, and direct mail are familiar to most consumers.

Most advertising is directed toward stimulating demand for specific products, rather than for entire industries. This type of advertising usually emphasizes brand names. The rival advertising campaigns that result may succeed only in increasing the cost to the individual seller, since the overall market for the product may not be expanded at all. As a result, prices will be higher or profit margins will decrease, depending on the nature of the market.

If, on the contrary, advertising activity is directed toward the products of an entire industry, the industry may be able to expand its markets. Under such circumstances, advertising can have very desirable effects, particularly if the industry experiences lower costs of production. That is, as output expands, all of the firms experience certain benefits that provide them with lower unit costs. These lower costs can mean lower prices to consumers or greater profits to producers.

Two illustrations will provide a clearer understanding of these two advertising appeals. An advertising campaign which emphasizes a particular brand of automobile oil filter represents an attempt to capture a larger share of a given market and may lead to similar campaigns by rival producers. The end result may be that each firm will experience higher costs but little change in sales volume. On the other hand, if the filter manufacturer appeals to the motorist's desire to protect his car's engine for longer mileage and suggests a particular brand, the entire industry and consumers as a whole may benefit. Consumers may change their oil filters more frequently, regardless of the brand, now that they have been informed of the benefits. Thus the entire industry may experience an expansion in sales and a reduction of costs without the high advertising costs associated with rival campaigns.

The economic effects of advertising on the demand for a product are illustrated in Fig. 10–6. The demand curve D_1 is shifted to a new position, D_2, as a result of advertising. At price P', the quantity demanded is increased from Q_1 to Q_2; this indicates that more of the quantity is demanded at the same price. At Q_2, the same quantity is demanded at a higher price, P', which means that the buyer is willing to pay more for the same quantity.

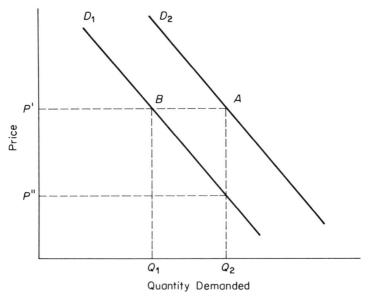

FIGURE 10–6.   Economic effects of advertising on the demand for a product.

An increase in demand caused by advertising, may also make the demand less elastic at each price. Point A on D_2 is less elastic than point B on D_1, even though the price, P', is the same for both. This means that demand D_2 is less elastic than demand D_1 at price P'. The less elastic the product demand is, the less it competes with close substitutes.

The increase in demand from D_1 to D_2 increases the firm's revenue by the amount represented by the area BAQ_1Q_2 in Fig. 10–6. This increase also requires advertising expenditures. As long as the advertising cost is less than the increase in revenue, profits will be increased. When the marginal cost of advertising exceeds the marginal revenue, profits will decrease.

In conclusion, advertising is often used to gain publicity. It not only can be directed to a specific product but also can be used to improve or maintain a firm's image with its customers. Institutional advertising, as this is often called, appeals to the patronage motive. The announcement of changes in key personnel or plant expansion are examples of this type of advertising.

Product Variation

Variation in quality and design is a device used by sellers along with advertising to differentiate their products. Like advertising, product variation attempts to increase customer preference for a product. And like advertising, it accomplishes this by shifting the demand curve to the right and making it less elastic.

The development of different quality lines for different groups of buyers is a worthwhile form of product differentiation. There are often real differences among standard, deluxe, and super-deluxe models, which allows the consumer a wide range of choice. This also means that a business firm can extend the market for its basic product, increase its sales volume, or even lower overall unit costs.

Variations in design do not necessarily add to the quality of the product. For example, some automobile manufacturers depend upon year-to-year style changes to maintain their share of the market. Such variations may include horsepower ratings, mechanical improvements, new accessories, new interiors, and different exterior trim and overall body lines. Some of these changes are worthwhile, particularly those that improve the automobile's safety or represent real innovation or improvement. Differently shaped fenders and new grille assemblies, however, would not seem to represent any real, worthwhile improvement, any more than the large tailfins and abundant chrome trim that were so common during the late 1950's.

Packaging, another form of product variation, is often designed to gain consumer attention. Attractive packaging is important to sales volume. A newly designed, brightly colored package may make the difference between the initial success or failure of a product. However, continued sales will depend upon satisfied users regardless of the package. Packaging can be deceiving. Making a package thinner while giving it a larger face to attract attention may mislead consumers as to the actual volume of its contents. This type of packaging may be subjected to eventual consumer rejection or government regulation.

Convenience-oriented marketing places a great deal of emphasis upon utility. A package, for example, should be designed to be conveniently handled and easily opened. Plastic milk cartons and throwaway beer bottles are convenient because they do not need to be returned; plastic shampoo tubes will not shatter when dropped from slippery fingers. The tab-top beer can, the reclosable cereal box, and the twist-close bread wrapper are other examples of convenience-oriented packaging.

Other forms of nonprice promotion not directly related to the product include services, location, and trading stamps. Some firms offer a variety of services, such as liberal credit terms, free delivery, return privileges, free installations, and product warranties. Other firms stress the nearness or convenience of their establishments as an important factor; these include suburban shopping centers, branches, factory outlets, and sales offices. Trading stamps, another type of nonprice promotion, have become very popular in recent years. Many customers are attracted to stores that give trading stamps, where they apparently feel they are getting something for nothing. These forms of nonprice promotion can have a noticeable effect upon a firm's sales volume.

After considering all of these attributes of products, one is led to the conclusion that a consumer buys more than just some physical object. He is also buying his image of the product and many additional benefits. Thus an important fundamental for business analysis is to remember that a business firm does not sell just a product, it also sells product benefits and consumer satisfaction.

ANNEX: SIMULATION OF CONSUMER BEHAVIOR

Special probabilistic methods can be used to predict or describe consumer behavior. Generally, these methods are referred to as *stochastic models*. Let us illustrate two such methods by applying them to the problem of predicting consumers' buying habits with television sets.[5] The problem concerns those people who turn in their television sets for new ones every year. We will consider only three makes of television sets, which we will call Telex, Video, and TVN. The tendency to switch brands can be expressed in terms of prob-

[5] This example was developed from one given by J. Kemeny, A. Scheifer, Jr., J. Snell, and G. Thompson, in *Finite Mathematics with Business Applications* (Englewood Cliffs, N. J.: Prentice-Hall, Inc., 1962), p. 201.

ability figures; these figures can be thought of as representing the relative number of times that consumers will make the various changes. For example, a probability of 0.2 means that a particular activity will occur two-tenths (or 20 per cent) of the time.

People who own the Telex brand in any given year tend to switch to the Video brand with a probability of 0.2 and to TVN with a probability of 0.4; the probability that they will purchase a Telex set again also is 0.4. Owners of Video sets change to Telex sets with a probability of 0.6 and to TVN sets with a probability of 0.2; they keep their Video sets with a probability of 0.2. Finally, owners of TVN sets have a tendency to change to Telex sets with a probability of 0.4 and to Video sets with a probability of 0.4; they will purchase another TVN model with a probability of 0.2.

These probability figures can be placed in a matrix as follows:

Currently Own:	Switching to:		
	Telex	Video	TVN
Telex	0.4	0.2	0.4
Video	0.6	0.2	0.2
TVN	0.4	0.4	0.2

According to the Markov chain process, this matrix is called a transition matrix of transition probabilities. The sum of each row must equal 1.00; this is a simple requirement, since we assume that each consumer will purchase one of the three brands again.

This transition matrix provides a convenient summary of the probabilities of switching brands as stated in the problem. By reading across the top row we can readily observe the probabilities of keeping a Telex set or switching to a Video or TVN model. The second row gives us the transition probabilities of keeping a Video set or switching to Telex or TVN; the third row provides the same information for the TVN set.

The next task is to use these transition probabilities to simulate the buying behavior of the consumers. This part of the process is known as *Monte Carlo simulation*. The first step is to use a table of random numbers as a device to simulate the nine possible outcomes associated with the consumers' choices. (If the student is not familiar with the table of random numbers, he should first read the portion of Chapter 17 that deals with this concept.) A scheme based on the ten numbers of our decimal numbering system is used in conjunction with the table of random numbers to produce the various outcomes according to the transition probabilities that were given.

Our procedure is based on the following scheme: If event *A* has a probability of 0.3, event *B* has a probability of 0.5, and event *C* has a probability of 0.2, then the occurrence of any given numbers—say, 0, 1, or 2—can be designated to represent the probability of event *A* happening; the occurrence of the numbers 3, 4, 5, 6, or 7 can then be used to represent the probability of event *B*; and the occurrence of the numbers 8 or 9 necessarily represents the probability of event *C*. A similar technique is used to solve the problem that deals with the purchase of television sets.

The simulation process is first started by assuming that the consumer currently owns a TVN set. We assign the numbers 0, 1, 2, and 3 to reflect the probability that he will choose a Telex set for his next purchase, since the probability of purchasing Telex when TVN is the currently owned set is 0.4, as shown in the lower left-hand corner of the transition matrix. The numbers 4, 5, 6, and 7 are assigned to reflect the 0.4 probability that he will switch to the Video brand, and the numbers 8 and 9 are assigned to correspond to the 0.2 probability of purchasing a TVN set.

When Video is the current brand, the numbers are assigned as follows to correspond to the various probabilities indicated in the second row of the transition matrix:

0, 1, 2, 3, 4, 5 = 0.6 probability of switching to Telex
6,7   = 0.2 probability of keeping Video
8, 9   = 0.2 probability of switching to TVN.

For Telex, we have

0, 1, 2, 3   = 0.4 probability of keeping Telex
4, 5   = 0.2 probability of switching to Video
6, 7, 8, 9   = 0.4 probability of switching to TVN.

Shown below are the random digits chosen from the table of random numbers that appears in Chapter 17. The numbers were selected from right to left starting with the first column and first row of the table.

Random Number	Brand Chosen
0	Telex
6	TVN
2	Telex
5	Video
1	Telex
2	Telex
6	TVN
4	Video
2	Telex
2	Telex

The first random number chosen was zero; therefore, according to our scheme, we assume that the consumer will shift from a TVN set to a Telex set.

As you will notice, the zero is one of those numbers contained in the group that reflects the probability of switching to a Telex set if a TVN set is currently owned.

We must look at the first row of the matrix to see what the next purchase will be, because the first row shows the transition probabilities when Telex is the currently owned brand. The next number chosen was 6; since the consumer now owns a Telex, he will shift back to a TVN set. We now return to the third row of the matrix and to the third number selected from the table of random numbers, which was 2. This tells us that the consumer will shift back to Telex. The next number, 5, indicates that the consumer will shift to a Video set, and so forth. The reader should check the rest of the results shown above.

The results of this simulation show the pattern of purchases that is likely to occur over the years. The buying habit of a consumer was simulated over a span of ten purchases. This simulation shows that the consumer will purchase a Telex model six out of the ten times, a TVN set twice, and a Video set twice. Of course, many more simulations should be completed to establish a more general pattern or distribution of purchases. A mathematical technique is also available that is used in Markovian models such as this one to determine the long-run distribution of purchases; however, discussion of this technique is beyond the scope of this book.

PROBLEMS AND PROJECTS

1. Calculate the 30 per cent retail markup on a surfboard that was acquired from a manufacturer at a price of $21. What is the retail price of the surfboard?
2. Calculate the retail price of a surfboard that was acquired from a manufacturer at a price of $21, and that is to yield a markup equal to 30 per cent of the selling price.
3. Calculate the manufacturer's selling price of surfboards that cost $19 per unit to produce. The operation must yield a 10 per cent return on an investment of $500,000 in plant and equipment that is capable of producing 25,000 surfboards in a year.
4. Solve the following problem[6] using the material in the Annex: A person buys brand X coffee according to a Markov chain process, with the following matrix of transition probabilities:

	X	$Not\ X$
X	0.6	0.4
$Not\ X$	0.2	0.8

[6] Kemeny, *et al.*, *op. cit.*, pp. 204–205 (Exercise 6). Reprinted by permission of Prentice-Hall, Inc.

Simulate ten consecutive purchases given that:
(a) The last purchase was X.
(b) The last purchase was not X.
(c) The last purchase was X with a probability of $\frac{1}{3}$ and not X with a probability of $\frac{2}{3}$.

5. Solve the following problem[7] using the material in the Annex: A model for the behavior of a stock traded on the New York Stock Exchange is that its price goes up, stays the same, or goes down from day to day according to a Markov chain process, with the following matrix of transition probabilities:

	Up	Unchanged	Down
Up	0.7	0.2	0.1
Unchanged	0.3	0.4	0.3
Down	0.1	0.3	0.6

Suppose, in addition, that *if* the price goes up or down, the *amount* by which it changes is given by the following probabilities:

Amount of Change	Probability
$\frac{1}{2}$	0.30
1	0.40
$1\frac{1}{2}$	0.20
2	0.05
$2\frac{1}{2}$	0.05

Simulate the next 20 days' trading on the assumption that the stock closed yesterday unchanged at 100.

[7] *Ibid.*, p. 205 (Exercise 7). Reprinted by permission of Prentice-Hall, Inc.

SELECTED REFERENCES

Dean, Joel, *Managerial Economics*. Englewood Cliffs, N. J.: Prentice-Hall, Inc., 1951.

Leftwich, Richard H., *The Price System and Resource Allocation*, 3rd ed., Chaps. 11, 12. New York: Holt, Rinehart & Winston, Inc., 1966.

McCarthy, E. Jerome, *Basic Marketing: A Managerial Approach*, rev. ed., Chaps. 11, 16, 22, 25. Homewood, Ill.: Richard D. Irwin, Inc., 1964.

Oxenfeldt, Alfred R., *Pricing For Marketing Executives*. Belmont, Calif.: Wadsworth Publishing Company, Inc., 1961.

11

FINANCE

A business enterprise combines natural, human, and produced resources to achieve production. It also devotes a great deal of effort to the marketing function, and particularly to the stimulation of sales. However, this is not enough. Besides producing and distributing goods and services, a business enterprise must also make arrangements to finance these activities. Payments generally fall into two categories: immediate and deferred. Cash transactions represent immediate payment, and noncash transactions represent deferred or delayed payment. In other words, the acquisition of resources can be financed by either cash or credit.

Financial activity is the management and analysis of the various capital or asset needs of business enterprises. The management of capital is important because it has a direct bearing on a firm's profits. Too much cash may mean that profits are being sacrificed for liquidity; likewise, insufficient plant and equipment may mean reduced profits because the least-cost combination of resources is not being employed. It is the responsibility of management to analyze the firm's financial situation and to apply sound principles to the use of capital in the interest of the firm's creditors and owners.

The capital requirements of an enterprise can be divided into two main categories: working capital and fixed capital. The employment of this capital is reflected by the assets listed in the firm's balance sheet. Working capital refers to the funds invested in the firm's current assets; these typically consist of cash, accounts and notes receivable, and inventory. Fixed capital refers to the funds invested in the firm's more permanent or fixed assets; that is, in the physical plant and facilities.

Financial activity also concerns itself with the nature and source of the funds required to meet the capital needs of the business enterprise; this includes the acquisition of funds from owners and outsiders, and the use of

243

funds from internal sources. Short-term credit combined with some long-term arrangements provide the funds necessary to take care of a firm's current or more immediate capital needs, while long-term debt and equity capital (ownership claims) provide the funds typically used to establish and maintain the physical plant and facilities. Short-term funds are available from various financial institutions and from other business establishments; long-term funds are usually available initially from the investment of the owners and subsequently from retained earnings. Long-term funds also can be obtained from financial institutions, individuals, and other business enterprises.

This chapter is divided into two parts. The first part covers the *working-capital* requirements of a firm and the various sources of funds available to meet these requirements. The second part is devoted to the *fixed-capital* requirements of a firm and the sources of funds available for these requirements. Financial analysis also requires an understanding of the concepts of interest, present value, and annuities, all of which are available for study or review, whichever is applicable, in Chapter 15.

WORKING CAPITAL

The primary purpose of working capital is to provide a business enterprise with adequate liquidity, so that it has cash to pay its current bills. When a firm experiences difficulty in meeting short-term credit liabilities, it impairs its credit standing and its ability to utilize such sources again. This reflects poor planning on the part of management. By the same token, too much cash, receivables, and inventory may represent excess capital, which results in higher capital costs as well as lower profits and smaller returns to the owners. Correcting the situation by resorting to inventory reductions or restrictions of credit to customers may lose sales. The task of financial management, therefore, is to see that there is neither too much nor too little working capital on hand, and that a balance is maintained between liquidity and profit. Thus one very important fundamental for business analysis is constant supervision and direction of the flow of working capital, in order to keep receivables and inventory moving toward cash.

Working-Capital Concepts

There are several important aspects of working capital that can be explored. When working capital is defined as current assets minus current liabilities, it is referred to as *net* working capital; when identified as total current assets, it is referred to as *gross* working capital. Current assets are represented by cash and government securities, accounts receivable, and inventories. Since increases in receivables and inventories use up cash during the production process, careful attention must be directed to working-capital requirements. Net working capital is significant for two reasons: it indicates to short-term creditors their primary source of repayment and thus determines their willingness to make a commitment of funds, and it reflects the extent to which current assets are financed from long-term sources. Gross working capital, on the other hand, emphasizes the total working-capital requirements of a firm.

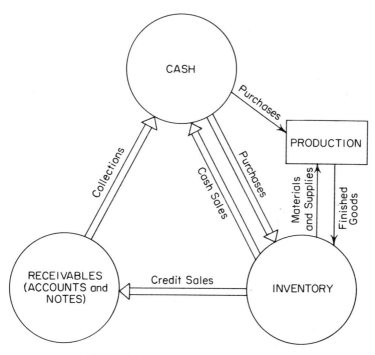

FIGURE 11-1.   The working-capital cycle.

Working capital is often referred to as *circulating capital*; it represents those assets that are converted into cash within a year of normal business operations. In this sense, working capital circulates or flows into cash over a short period of time. Fixed capital also circulates into cash but over a much longer period. A firm's working capital usually flows or circulates over a definite path. As illustrated in Fig. 11-1, the circular flow of working capital involves cash, inventory, and receivables. Cash is used to purchase materials and supplies that are placed either in inventory or in production. Finished goods flow from production into inventory, where they are sold for either cash or credit. If they are sold for cash, the cycle has been completed. If they are sold on credit, the sale usually will be recorded as an account receivable; the cycle is then completed when the account receivable is collected and thus converted into cash. Working-capital requirements depend heavily upon how effectively receivables and inventory move toward cash.

Working capital can also be classified as either *permanent* or *temporary*; this concept is useful in managing a firm's capital needs. Permanent working capital consists of those funds invested in current assets that are needed to meet the firm's minimum requirements over its normal cycle of business activity. This portion of the current assets should be financed by long-term funds; otherwise, it may periodically become difficult for the firm to meet its current obligations. Unlike fixed assets, which remain static, permanent working capital continues to circulate among the various current assets in short-run periods. Temporary working capital also changes its form from cash to inventory to receivables and back to cash. However, it may become idle at times; it varies with the seasonal or cyclical nature of the firm's production or sales. For example, a canning campany will have a large working-capital requirement during the canning season. Likewise, a department store may have a large requirement during the Christmas season. During slack business periods, working-capital requirements will be less, and excess working capital will exist unless short-term credit is used to meet the temporary seasonal needs.

Determination of Working Capital

The amount of working capital required by a firm depends upon a variety of factors, of which the most important are those that influence the amount of cash, receivables, and inventory required to support a given volume of output. Several of these factors will be considered. But first, two general observations require attention. Since working capital is an aggregate or total concept, it is natural to assume that a large firm will have a greater working-capital requirement than a small firm. The working capital of General Motors would have to be larger than that of a local auto dealer. The extent to which a firm uses variable resources (materials, supplies, and labor) relative to fixed resources (plant and equipment) also influences the absolute level of its working-capital requirements. A firm that is extensively automated will require less working capital than one of equal size that is not automated.

Determining the amount of working capital to satisfy cash needs depends upon several factors, which include the need to distinguish between normal and abnormal cash requirements, the credit position of the firm, the nature of demand, and management's attitude toward risk.

Most cash requirements can be anticipated with a reasonable degree of accuracy. These normal requirements can be determined by an analysis of the firm's cash inflow and cash outflow over a period of time. Unpredictable events that interrupt these flows give rise to abnormal cash requirements. In addition to these emergency or precautionary considerations, a business enterprise may want to earmark cash for speculative purposes. On occasion, firms will hold excess cash to take advantage of a decline in the price of materials and supplies. Sound cash management requires enough cash to be on hand at all times to meet normal requirements, with a small amount for any abnormal needs.

A sound credit position reduces a firm's cash requirements, allowing it to borrow funds without difficulty. In this way it becomes unnecessary to hold large cash reserves for an emergency or an unpredictable event. The ability of a firm to acquire borrowed funds will also enhance its ability to more closely synchronize its cash inflow and cash outflow. By matching and timing the credit it extends to its customers with the credit it obtains from its own suppliers (trade credit), the firm may substantially reduce its cash requirements.

The nature of demand also affects cash requirements. The more stable a firm's demand, the lower its need for cash will be. A grocery store would need less cash than a dress shop that sells fashion items or seasonal clothes. Although the grocery store has a steady conversion of inventory to cash, abrupt delays in conversion may occur for the dress shop if a preseason judgment on styles was miscalculated or if styles changed in the meantime.

Finally, management's attitude and outlook affect cash requirements. A conservative management usually desires more liquidity than a less conservative one. Proper planning and analysis of a firm's cash needs reduces the uncertainties upon which conservative managements base the need for large cash reserves.

The *cash budget* is a device based upon anticipated receipts and disbursements that is very useful in predicting a firm's cash requirements. A six-month budget and worksheet is shown in Table 11–1; it will be used to illustrate the mechanics of determining short-run cash requirements. Receipts and expenditures for capital items, such as the sale of stocks and bonds or the purchase of new equipment, are indicated as zero in the table. Fixed-capital requirements, such as sinking-fund payments, other debt retirements, acquisitions, and receipts from the sale of stocks and bonds, must be paid regardless of the time period under analysis. However, the maintenance of long-run liquidity, which is the flow of liquid assets needed to meet long-run cash commitments, requires a more comprehensive analysis. The purpose of illustrating a cash budget here is to emphasize the importance of cash as part of the working capital necessary to maintain short-run liquidity.

The cash budget depends first of all on a sales forecast by months. Combining this information with inventory requirements allows the firm to plan its production rate and to calculate expected cash outlays for materials and labor. Table 11–1 indicates the predicted sales volume by months. Sales for the month just ending (January) amounted to $12,000. Materials and supplies are ordered a month in advance and are paid for at the beginning of the month following production. It is also assumed that all accounts are collected

TABLE 11–1

HYPOTHETICAL CASH BUDGET

	Jan.	Feb.	Mar.	Apr.	May	June
Sales	$12,000	$12,000	$15,000	$10,000	$8,000	$10,000
Cash balance	3,000	5,400	6,800	5,500	7,200	7,000
Cash receipts:	12,000	12,000	13,000	13,500	9,500	8,500
Cash sales	$ 2,000	$ 2,000	$ 3,000	$ 1,500	$1,000	$1,500
Accounts receivable	10,000	10,000	10,000	12,000	8,500	7,000
Borrowing	0	0	0	0	0	0
Sale of stock	0	0	0	0	0	0
Sale of assets	0	0	0	0	0	0
Cash disbursements:	9,600	10,600	14,300	11,800	9,700	12,600
Purchases	3,000	4,000	4,000	5,000	3,500	3,000
Wages and salaries	3,000	3,000	3,200	3,000	2,500	2,800
Administrative Expense	2,500	2,500	2,600	2,500	2,400	2,500
Selling expense	600	600	1,000	800	800	800
Interest payment	500	500	1,500	500	500	1,500
Payment for fixed assets	0	0	0	0	0	0
Dividend payment	0	0	2,000	0	0	2,000
Cash from operations	2,400	1,400	(1,300)	1,700	(200)	(4,100)
Beginning cash balance	3,000	5,400	6,800	5,500	7,200	7,000
Cumulative cash balance	5,400	6,800	5,500	7,200	7,000	2,900
Minimum cash requirement	4,800	4,800	6,000	4,000	3,200	4,000
Excess (shortage)	600	2,000	(500)	3,200	3,800	(1,100)

in the first month following sale and that no bad debts occur. Accounts receivable outstanding on January 1 are $10,000. A minimum cash balance to take care of intramonth transactions has been estimated on the basis of 40 per cent of the month's sales (second last line in Table 11–1). Other assumptions are self-evident in the data. Some data have been included on a purely arbitrary basis.

Careful investigation of Table 11–1 will reveal an interesting story about this hypothetical cash flow. Sales are indicated for each month. Total receipts minus disbursements for each month allow for calculation of the cash that is generated from operations or used up. Combining the cash generated (or used up) with the beginning-of-the-month cash balance provides the cumulative cash balance. This end-of-the-month cash balance can be compared with the minimum requirements to reveal the excess or shortage of cash for that period. Note that a shortage of cash is indicated in March and June; in April and May substantial excesses emerge. Following through each month will reveal how each particular cash requirement resulted from a fluctuating sales volume and from periodic interest and dividend payments.

The cash budget is an important tool that indicates when cash on hand is insufficient or excessive. When the budget indicates a temporary shortage, the firm should plan to borrow funds; when an excess occurs, the firm should consider alternative uses of its funds. Idle cash funds reduce profits because of the opportunity cost they represent.

An additional indication of a firm's liquidity can be obtained by making a comparison of current assets and current liabilities. Assuming that current assets are of a high enough quality and that they can be converted to cash, an excess of current assets over current liabilities will indicate liquidity. The extent of liquidity is indicated by the ratio between current assets and current liabilities, known as the *current ratio*; it is calculated by dividing current assets by current liabilities. Another closely related ratio is the *acid-test* or *quick ratio*, which compares cash and some other "near"-cash items with current liabilities. The ratio of 2 to 1 for the current ratio and 1 to 1 for the acid-test ratio have come to be regarded as bench marks of liquidity in financial circles. However, the most significant test of liquidity is probably the cash budget combined with an investigation of the quality and nature of the current assets, because this represents a more complete analysis of the firm's condition.

Let us now turn our attention to the variety of factors that determine the amount of working capital required by a firm to carry *receivables*. The extent to which a firm sells on credit is one such factor. Some firms follow a liberal attitude toward credit sales, while others are very strict and may allow only cash payments. In addition, large firms generally are able to extend more credit than small firms because of their greater opportunities to borrow funds in the capital markets to carry accounts receivable. Products or services that have a high unit price, such as furniture, may have to be sold on credit terms. Products with a low unit price, such as magazines, have little need for credit. It is difficult to imagine the operator of a newspaper and magazine stand on a street corner in a large city selling on credit to the man on the street.

Another important factor that affects the amount of receivables is the level of business activity. In prosperous times, when more goods and services are sold to customers, the total amount of receivables will necessarily rise. This would also be true for a long-run secular increase in sales.

Other factors that influence the amount of working capital required to carry receivables are related in some way to the turnover of these receivables. First, the turnover of receivables is affected by the credit terms normally extended to a customer. The longer customers are given to pay, the slower the turnover will be and the greater the working-capital requirement will be. However, when cash discounts are included in the credit terms, they encourage prompt payment and may cause a higher turnover.

The second category of factors that affects turnover deals with the selection of credit accounts. The criteria for accepting credit sales can have an important influence on the amount of receivables and on their turnover. Lenient credit standards will automatically generate more sales and larger amounts of receivables than would strict terms. But low standards also may mean a greater number of delinquents, which will reduce turnover. Low standards may even mean bad debts and eventual losses. Selection of credit customers depends upon the firm's past credit experience and upon information from such sources as credit-rating bureaus, Dun & Bradstreet's *Reference Manual*, the customer's own financial statements, and a credit interview.

Finally, turnover is affected by the firm's collection procedures. Collection procedures that reduce working-capital requirements include prompt billing; arrangements with banks to allow for regional payments, thereby reducing the time it takes to clear checks; regional sales offices, which facilitate collections; and, finally, the use of a post office box to collect payments, which are then serviced by the firm's regional bank.

Techniques that measure the turnover of receivables can be helpful in controlling the use of working capital. Turnover ratios can indicate a deviation from the norms established by management. An investigation of this deviation may reveal the need for correction or a change in policy. Measurement of turnover reflects the speed with which working capital moves through receivables; it therefore is a direct measurement of the effectiveness of a firm's working capital. More specifically, it measures the effectiveness of the firm's credit and collection policies.

One method of measuring the turnover of receivables can be illustrated by an example using the Hypothetical Mailbox Manufacturing Company. Assume that the company has annual credit sales of $600,000 and that its receivables average $75,000. The $75,000 was determined by adding the beginning-of-the-year balance of $90,000 to the end-of-the-year balance of $60,000 and dividing by 2. The receivable turnover is then calculated as follows:

$$\text{Turnover} = \frac{\text{annual sales on account}}{\text{average receivables}}$$
$$= \frac{\$600,000}{\$75,000}$$
$$= 8.$$

According to the calculations, the receivables turnover is 8. This means that the average amount of $75,000 is collected each $1\frac{1}{2}$ months or every 45 days (12 months divided by the turnover of 8, or 360 days divided by 8).

The next step is for management to compare its turnover calculations with the norms set by top management to detect deviations. Past-period turnover rates provide an excellent base with which to compare the present rate in order to determine whether or not a noticeable trend has been established in either direction. For example, suppose that the turnover rate for the company in previous years has been around 10 (a collection period of 36 days). The slower turnover rate of 8 suggests the need of an investigation and an explanation; the slower rate definitely indicates a larger working-capital requirement.

Industry averages also offer an opportunity to compare a firm's turnover experience with that of other similar firms. Industry associations and credit-rating agencies can make these industry turnover rates available.

An analysis of the turnover of receivables may suggest corrections or changes in credit and collection policies or procedures. The ultimate purpose of such an analysis and possible corrective action is to keep the receivables moving toward cash. The efficient use of working capital is therefore an important fundamental for business analysis.

Inventory is the other major category of current assets that influences a firm's working-capital requirements. The management of inventory involves both *physical* and *financial* considerations. The production department of a manufacturing firm and the buying department in a merchandising concern are vitally interested in the physical management of inventory. Inventory is the lifeblood of production and sales activities; if it were improperly managed, production processes would collapse. Sales personnel also want inventory to be properly managed so that goods will be available for delivery when sales are made.

Inventory also influences the working-capital needs of the firm from the financial standpoint. Funds tied up in inventory are one step farther removed from cash in the working-capital cycle. Since inventory is farther removed from cash than receivables are, it needs financial attention if the firm's liquidity is to be maintained.

The amount of inventory needed in relation to sales is affected by a number of factors. For instance, if the inventory is of a perishable nature, an effort will usually be made to keep it at a minimum. Another factor is the firm's attitude concerning the effect that a large assortment of goods will have on sales. A greater variety or larger assortment of goods usually means a larger inventory. The third factor involves uncertainties that are associated with inventory levels. Firms stockpile materials when future deliveries are uncertain. Distant sources are more risky than local ones. In addition, labor strikes, political instability, and acts of God often interrupt deliveries. Uncertainty also increases as the length of time required to produce or grow a product increases. Oil companies hold control over a vast inventory of oil reserves because the discovery and development of new sources is time-consuming and difficult.

Working-capital requirements associated with inventory can be tested by the use of the turnover test. To firms that maintain a large inventory, turnover is of vital concern because it is one way of measuring the effectiveness with which working capital is being utilized; thus it is an important fundamental of business analysis. Inventory turnover is found by dividing the total cost of goods sold during a year by the average inventory. Inventory for the Hypothetical Mailbox Manufacturing Company is calculated as follows:

$$\text{Inventory turnover} = \frac{\text{total annual cost of goods sold}}{\text{average inventory}}$$

$$= \frac{\$450,000}{\$50,000}$$

$$= 9.$$

A high inventory turnover is usually a favorable indication, although the average turnover varies from industry to industry. The inventory ratio allows a firm to compare its recent operations with previous periods or with other firms in the industry. If the ratio is unfavorable, an investigation of inventory management and an improvement in control are in order.

There may be many reasons for an unfavorable turnover ratio. If the cause is determined to be improper inventory control, various mathematical models can be used to correct the situation. One such model was illustrated in the Annex to Chapter 5.

Meeting Working-Capital Needs

As stated previously, working-capital needs should be provided for by both short-term and long-term funds. Long-term funds should be used to take care of the more permanent portion of working-capital needs. They can come from either owners or lenders. However, these long-term sources are also a principal means of meeting the fixed-capital requirements of a firm;

for this reason, they will not be discussed here, but will be reserved for the next part of the chapter, which deals with fixed capital.

Short-term financing is obtained from both financial and nonfinancial institutions. The first group includes commercial banks, finance companies, and a special type of financial institution known as a factor. In addition, business enterprises that are suppliers for other business firms provide short-term credit to their customers; this is called *trade credit* or *commercial credit*. Trade credit can be considered a substitute for borrowing because the business enterprise is merely delaying payment; this will be discussed first.

Trade credit represents a substantial portion of total short-term financing; it, therefore, is probably more important to small firms than to large firms. However, the use of trade credit varies among industry groups. Firms operating in industries that typically carry an inventory that is a large percentage of total assets will usually rely on relatively more trade credit.

Trade credit is reflected on the buyer's balance sheet as an account payable and on the seller's balance sheet as an account receivable. (Loans from financial institutions will show up as notes payable.) The account receivable is usually the only evidence that credit has been extended by the seller. These open or book accounts are extremely flexible and relatively simple and inexpensive to maintain. The account payable on the buyer's balance sheet represents part of the firm's current liabilities and reflects the extent to which working capital is financed by trade credit.

There is no discernible cost involved when a business firm takes advantage of trade credit; in essence, the credit is free. However, many firms offer a discount to their customers if they pay cash within a certain period of time. If the buyer does *not* take advantage of this discount, he will incur a high cost for the period of time between the end of the discount period and the end of the net period. An example of a cash discount was presented in the previous chapter. It was stated then that the discount period represented a free finance period. However, if the buyer failed to take advantage of the discount, the amount of the discount would become the cost of financing the purchase until the end of the net period. For example, if the hardware store owner who bought $1,200 worth of mailboxes on terms of "$\frac{2}{10}$ net 30" failed to pay his bill on the tenth day, he would have lost his $24 discount. Thus he would have paid 2 per cent for the use of $1,200 for 20 days. Translated to an annual rate of interest, the cost of *not* taking the discount would be 36 per cent, calculated as follows:

$$I = P \times i \times T$$
$$\$24 = \$1,200 \times i \times \frac{20}{360}$$
$$0.02i = \frac{\$24}{\$1,200}$$
$$i = 0.36 = 36\%.$$

Commercial banks are a major source of short-term funds for business firms. Although they also supply funds for longer periods of time, they are traditionally considered short-term lenders.

A convenient arrangement used by business firms to obtain working capital on short notice is the *line of credit*. In essence, this amounts to prearranged financial support. The officers of the firm discuss with the bank their current financial condition and expected needs. The balance sheet, income statement, and cash budget provide the information for this discussion. Once the line of credit has been established, the business firm simply draws against it. Promissory notes are signed and the money is advanced by the bank. There is not always a charge for the line of credit, and interest is charged on the amount of funds actually borrowed.

Banks usually collect interest in advance. The interest collected in this manner is called *bank discount*; it is calculated by the same method as simple interest. For example, if the Hypothetical Mailbox Manufacturing Company were to borrow $1,000 from a bank for 60 days at 6 per cent, the discount would be $10. After signing the note, the company official would receive $990. If the same amount were borrowed at simple interest, the proceeds would be $1,000 and $1,010 would be paid at maturity. As you can see, the discount rate will be slightly higher than the interest rate because the borrower is really only getting the use of $990.

Often a business establishment in need of immediate funds may discount some of its own customers' notes or I.O.U.'s when borrowing from a bank. Determining the proceeds from a loan of this sort requires several calculations. First, the number of days the bank holds the note must be calculated. Next, the amount of the discount must be determined. And finally, the discount must be subtracted from the maturity value of the loan in order to find the proceeds. If the instrument is a noninterest-bearing note, the face value and the maturity value will be identical. If it is an interest-bearing note, the maturity value will have to be determined beforehand, by adding the dollar amount of interest to the face value. For example, suppose that an official of the Hypothetical Mailbox Manufacturing Company decides to discount a 90-day, 4 per cent note for $1,000 at its bank. The note has 60 days remaining to maturity, and the bank's discount rate is 6 per cent. The proceeds are calculated as follows:

$$\text{Maturity value} = \$1,000 + (\$1,000 \times 0.04 \times \tfrac{1}{4}) = \$1,010$$
$$\text{Amount of discount} = \$1,010 \times 0.06 \times \tfrac{1}{6} = \$10.10$$
$$\text{Proceeds} = \$1,010 - \$10.10 = \$999.90.$$

Bank borrowers often are required to maintain a minimum deposit balance when a loan is outstanding. This has the effect of increasing the rate of interest and causing the firm to borrow more than it needs. For example, suppose that a firm borrows $100,000 at 5 per cent and must maintain a 20 per cent *compensating balance*. The borrower actually has the use of $80,000 instead of $100,000, and the effective rate of interest is $6\frac{1}{4}$ per cent ($5,000/80,000) instead of 5 per cent ($5,000/100,000). The total cost of borrowing $80,000 for 6 months at 5 per cent would have been $2,000, but since the firm was required to borrow $100,000 to obtain that $80,000, the dollar cost will be $2,500.

A firm has other alternatives to bank financing. The task of financial management is to compare all alternatives and select the source that best suits its requirements. The firm even has the choice of obtaining long-term funds and then investing temporary excesses of cash in short-term government securities or lending money to other firms through the money markets. However, these other alternatives may very well be too expensive or unsuitable to the firm's needs. Banks are very popular with the business community as a source of short-term funds, especially with small- and medium-sized firms, which may have no other alternative but to use their bank connections.

Business firms can also obtain funds to meet their working-capital needs by borrowing from *finance companies*. Loans obtained from commercial finance companies are usually secured by receivables, inventory, or short-term securities. These companies also occasionally supply funds to finance fixed assets. Manufacturing and wholesaling firms typically can secure credit from commercial finance companies more easily than retailers, because their receivables and inventory are more acceptable as security. Retailers can obtain funds by selling their installment sales contracts on consumer durables, such as automobiles and appliances, to sales finance companies, which supply capital primarily for consumer purchases.

Another method a firm can use to obtain cash is that of *factoring* its accounts receivable by actually selling these accounts to a firm called a factor. Commercial finance companies also can purchase outright (factor) accounts receivable. In addition to providing funds in return for these purchases, the factor may also perform the necessary credit and collection functions. For this reason the cost of factoring is expensive. However, when comparing factoring to other finance alternatives, the cost of credit and collections should not be overlooked.

There are several advantages to factoring which will be briefly mentioned. Cash is received quickly, credit and collection costs are saved, no liability is created as in the case of a loan, other borrowing may become feasible, and the uncertainties regarding credit and collection costs and debt losses are eliminated. Certain disadvantages also can be cited. The firm is separated somewhat from its credit customers, the factor may restrict credit sales, and it charges a commission fee in addition to the interest charge.

The factor arrangement may be particularly desirable for small- and middle-sized companies. The credit and collection activities can be performed more efficiently because the factor is a specialist in his field. Factors also make secured and unsecured loans to their customers, including inventory loans and loans on fixed assets.

In summary, working capital refers to the funds that support current assets: cash, receivables, and inventory. Working capital is constantly on the move, following a cyclical path from cash to inventory to receivables and back to cash. Many factors determine working-capital requirements; since the major components of working capital are cash, receivables, and inventory, efficient use of these assets can indicate the effectiveness of working-capital management. The cash budget, turnover of receivables, and the inventory-turnover test are used to measure the efficient use of these assets. Working-capital funds need not be obtained from long-term equity and debt sources; the principal sources of short-term funds are trade credit, commercial banks, certain types of finance companies, and factors.

FIXED CAPITAL

Managing fixed capital is probably one of the most important and most difficult tasks that faces the management of a business enterprise. One reason for this is the nature of the assets to which fixed capital is committed. The physical plant and facilities of a business enterprise represent a commitment of funds for a long period of time; that is why they are called "fixed assets." Funds so committed are also recovered over a long period of time; the longer the life of the asset is, the longer the recovery time will be. Another characteristic of fixed capital is the high cost or size of the commitment compared with current assets. The more fixed capital contributes to cost, the greater its influence will be on profits. Consequently, the amount of the funds as well as the length of time they are committed can increase the element of risk associated with fixed-capital decisions. An error in the acquisition of a fixed asset can have very serious effects upon a firm's profits.

The amount of fixed capital required to do business depends upon several factors. For example, a large firm generally requires more fixed capital than a small one. The type of activity performed by the business enterprise also influences the fixed-capital requirement; the so-called heavy industries, such as aluminum, steel, automobiles, chemicals, and petroleum, usually require large capital commitments. As a matter of fact, technical requirements may demand large commitments just to establish production. Service and merchandising firms generally can be established with relatively limited amounts of fixed capital.

Fixed capital is not only committed to establishing business enterprises. Funds are also used to make replacements and improvements. As old facilities wear out or become obsolete, fixed capital is needed to acquire new buildings and equipment. Additions to fixed assets in order to expand existing capacity also require fixed capital. These additions generally are the result of much forethought and planning. However, research and development efforts and unexpected growth often demand unusual and substantial fixed-capital expenditures.

Generally speaking, the fixed-capital needs of a firm are planned five to ten years in advance. Long-run objectives concerning profits, firm size, market shares, and sales volume are established and the fixed capital necessary to accomplish these goals is estimated. Since business enterprises do not operate in a vacuum, the task of determining fixed-capital requirements is not easy; such things as population trends, changes in consumer preferences, entry of new firms in the market, competition from other products, new technology, and overall economic trends continually demand attention.

Having established the importance of fixed-capital management, we can now proceed according to the following sequence. First, the reader will be exposed to several devices that can be used to determine fixed-capital requirements. Next, certain techniques for evaluating various investment proposals will be explained. This will be followed by a discussion of the various sources of funds that can be used to meet the fixed-capital requirements of a firm.

Determining Fixed-Capital Needs

Estimating the fixed-capital requirements of an enterprise is quite involved. One major approach is to prepare a *long-run budget* of the firm's needs. This process necessarily requires a forecast of sales, because most of the asset items in the balance sheet vary with sales. Thus an estimate of the various balance sheet items can be based upon the sales forecast. Two principal methods are available to forecast financial requirements by basing them on sales. The first method applies the relation between sales and the other asset components indicated in the current balance sheet, in order to construct an estimated balance sheet. If fixed assets are presently a certain percentage of sales, they will probably maintain the same relationship in the future. Another technique is to compare average daily sales to a particular fixed asset. For example, suppose that a given asset presently accounts for 60 days of sales. If the sales forecast indicates daily sales of twice the present rate, the fixed-asset requirement will probably double too, in order to support the larger sales.

Another method based upon a sales forecast uses past information to predict future needs. A close correlation between sales and GNP provides the basis for projecting sales from GNP forecasts. Future requirements can be revealed by projecting the pattern, which is obtained from data that represent a correlation between sales and a particular asset. This method is superior to the first, particularly for long-term forecasts, because the ratio between sales and an asset item does not always remain constant. For example, if there is a tendency for the ratio of sales to fixed assets to decline as sales increase, the first method may result in large errors. The regression technique compensates for such built-in tendencies because it is based upon a series of past data.

A projection of all asset items can also be used to construct an estimated balance sheet. The projection of each item will reveal the additional fixed capital as well as the permanent working capital needed to support future operations.

Breakeven analysis, which was introduced in Chapter 9 as the TR-TC approach for determining the best-profit output, is another useful device for indicating fixed-capital requirements. If sales tend to persist at some point considerably beyond the breakeven point, the firm's profits can be increased by an addition to the firm's fixed assets. This will increase the firm's *operating leverage*, which is the effect on profits of the ratio of fixed costs to variable costs. If fixed costs are increased relative to variable costs, the breakeven point will increase as will the opportunity for profits at the higher levels of production. An example is offered to illustrate how operating leverage is affected by an increase in fixed capital.

Two hypothetical situations with different degrees of operating leverage are compared, one *before* and one *after* fixed capital has been increased. In both examples, the selling price of the product is $10.00. Unit costs are assumed to vary by a constant or fixed amount as output varies (marginal costs are constant). Therefore, the total cost line in a graph will be a straight line. The data for both situations appear in Table 11–2.

TABLE 11–2

OPERATING LEVERAGE

Units Sold	Sales	Before Costs	Before Profit (Loss)	After Costs	After Profit (Loss)
20,000	$ 200,000	$ 250,000	$ (50,000)	$400,000	$(200,000)
40,000	400,000	400,000	0	500,000	(100,000)
60,000	600,000	550,000	50,000	600,000	0
80,000	800,000	700,000	100,000	700,000	100,000
100,000	1,000,000	850,000	150,000	800,000	200,000
120,000	1,200,000	1,000,000	200,000	900,000	300,000

Fixed costs allocated to the production period in the *before* situation are $100,000; variable costs are $7.50 per unit. Fixed costs in the *after* situation are $300,000, due to the greater fixed capital invested in plant and facilities, and variable costs are $5.00 per unit. Note that the breakeven point before is 40,000 units; after, it is 60,000 units. Operating leverage is reflected by the larger increments of profit that are added as production levels increase. For example, at an assumed output level of 100,000 units, profits are $150,000. With greater operating leverage, profits at the 100,000-unit output level are $200,000, an increase of $100,000 instead of $50,000 over the 80,000-unit

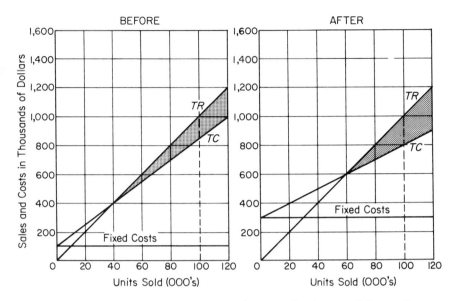

FIGURE 11-2. Break-even charts showing operating leverage before and after fixed capital has been increased.

output level. The effect of this operating leverage is also illustrated by the shaded areas in the two break-even charts in Fig. 11–2.

A third important indication of a firm's fixed-capital requirements is the use of *least-cost information* similar to that developed in Chapter 7 for the Hypothetical Mailbox Manufacturing Company. The fixed-capital requirements for that company can be determined from the least-cost combinations of resource data. At present the company is producing 200 mailboxes per day and selling them at $13.00 each. This is the best-profit output for the firm, as was indicated in Table 9–7. However, these 200 mailboxes are not being produced at a least-cost combination of all resources. As indicated in Table 8–4, it can be achieved with 50 units of resource A and 30 units of resource B. This means that a greater amount of fixed resources should be combined with fewer variable resources. The least-cost combination would yield a total cost of $1,400 instead of the present $1,800 (as indicated in Table 8–4).

Since the least-cost combination requires 50 units of resource A instead of 30 for each production period, additional fixed assets must be acquired. This increase can be based upon the relationship between the 30 units of resource A used per period and the 50 units proposed to attain least cost. The increase from 30 to 50 represents a $66\frac{2}{3}$ per cent increase; therefore, a $66\frac{2}{3}$ per cent increase in fixed capital is required. If the present plant and facilities of the Hypothetical Mailbox Manufacturing Company are valued

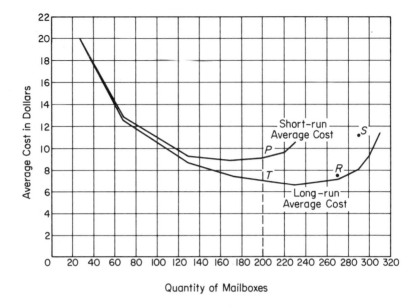

FIGURE 11–3. Effect of increase in fixed capital on average cost curve of the Hypothetical Mailbox Manufacturing Company.

at $150,000, then an increase of $100,000 in fixed capital is needed to bring the amount up to $250,000.

Such an increase in the company's fixed assets would require the firm to be larger. Consequently the firm's average-cost curve would drop to a lower curve. In effect, the lower costs are achieved by a better combination of fixed and variable resources, using more of the former and less of the latter.

The transition from a small firm to a larger one is illustrated in Fig. 11–3. The short-run, average-cost curve for the Hypothetical Mailbox Manufacturing Company (from Fig. 8–2) is superimposed on the company's long-run, average-cost curve (from Fig. 8–5). The jump from point *P* on the short-run curve to point *T* on the long-run curve occurs along the dotted line that indicates the level of production at 200 mailboxes. On the long-run average-cost curve, the point represents the least-cost combination of resources *A* and *B* for an output of 200 mailboxes.

Another short-run average-cost curve representing this larger-sized firm would be tangent at this point. It could be obtained from data similar to the data given in Table 8–4 and illustrated in Fig. 8–4. The various amounts of resource *B* that would be combined with 50 units of resource *A* to produce the different levels of output could then be used to calculate the firm's new cost structure, and these new average costs could be plotted on Fig. 11–3. Two such combinations are indicated in Table 8–4. At an output of 270, 50 units of *A* and 50 units of *B* would cost $2,000. At an output of 290, 50 units of *A* and 90 units of *B* would cost $3,200. The average costs for these two points are $7.41 and $11.03, respectively. These points (*R* and *S*) plus the least-cost combination (point *T*) for an output of 200 mailboxes indicate that the new size of the firm and the new short-run cost curve will lie somewhere between the two curves in Fig. 11–3.

In effect, the least-cost data (when obtainable) can be a valuable aid in planning future fixed-capital requirements. Projection of future sales and production levels can be the basis for selecting the correct least-cost combination. In this way, fixed-capital planning will automatically include planning for efficient production costs as well.

Measuring the Merit of Fixed-Capital Usage

In a market-directed economy, profits perform the vital role of directing the use of capital. For this reason the merit or attractiveness of various investment opportunities must constantly be measured. As a general rule, fixed capital should not be committed to acquiring an asset whose *return* will not equal or exceed the *cost* required to finance the asset. This rule may be violated if the cost of *not* acquiring the asset (to meet competition) would be greater. When several alternatives are available, the decision merely requires selection of the one that will yield the best results.

Two types of information are needed to make a fixed-capital decision: the *cost of capital* and a measure of each project's worth, such as its *rate of return*. Both of these will be explained at length.

The cost of capital is the cost of obtaining the funds used by a firm regardless of their source. The dollar amount of this cost is expressed as a rate or percentage of the funds obtained. The firm's overall cost of capital is usually calculated as a weighted average of the capital costs of each type of financing used by the firm to meet its capital requirements. The financing alternatives or sources of long-term funds available to a business enterprise are discussed in the next section of the chapter; because the method for determining the cost of capital varies with each financing alternative, its discussion will be reserved until then. Thus the source and the cost of funds can be discussed together.

Our attention now will be directed to the various methods of measuring the worth or merit of fixed-capital commitments in order to more easily select the best alternative. The most commonly used methods are *payback*, *average rate of return*, and *discounted cash flow*.

The *payback* method is the most convenient to use. It stresses the length of time required to recover funds from profits and depreciation charges. Therefore, it permits a firm to compare various alternatives on the basis of the time required to recapture its original investment. (In the following discus-

TABLE 11–3

MONEY FLOW COMPARISON

Year	Project A	Project B
1	$ 500	$500
2	900	500
3	1,200	500
4		500
5		500
6		500

sion, this has been arbitrarily selected to be $1,800.) This reflects the relative degree of risk for each proposal. The payback period can be calculated by determining the number of years required to recover the original commitment or cost of the asset. The appropriate money flows (before depreciation and after taxes) from two projects, requiring an investment of $1,800 each, are given in Table 11–3. It takes two years and four months for project A to recover the original $1,800 and almost four years for project B. Based upon these calculations, the payback method indicates selection of project A.

The payback method has particular merit for a firm that is short of cash and must therefore rely on a quick return of funds. However, it has two important drawbacks. For one thing, it ignores income beyond the payback period. In the example, project B would yield a total money flow of $3,000, while project A, which was selected, would yield only $2,600. The other drawback is that the payback method does not take into account the time value of the money flows.[1] Compare the money flows of project A and another project, project C. (In order to make the payback periods identical for each project, assume a total investment of $2,600.) Each project generates an equal money flow over a three-year period, as illustrated in Table 11–4. In this case, the present value of the stream of money flows is greater for project C than for project A. Even though both projects return the same total amounts and have equal payback periods, project C is more desirable because more of its money flow is represented by an earlier return. This can be verified by calculating the

TABLE 11–4

MONEY FLOW COMPARISON

Year	Project A	Project C
1	$ 500	$1,200
2	900	900
3	1,200	500

[1] The time value of money is an expression of present value that will be explained in Chapter 15. However, it will be calculated for this example.

present value of each flow. Assuming a given value of 10 per cent for the interest rate (i), the present values of projects A and C are calculated as follows:

$$\text{Present value} = \frac{A}{(1+i)} + \frac{A}{(1+i)^2} + \frac{A}{(1+i)^3}$$

$$\text{Present value of project } A = \frac{\$500}{(1.10)} + \frac{\$900}{(1.10)^2} + \frac{\$1,200}{(1.10)^3}$$
$$= \$454.54 + \$743.40 + \$901.20$$
$$= \$2,099.14$$

$$\text{Present value of project } C = \frac{\$1,200}{(1.10)} + \frac{\$900}{(1.10)^2} + \frac{\$500}{(1.10)^3}$$
$$= \$1,090.91 + \$743.40 + \$375.50$$
$$= \$2,209.81.$$

Therefore, the present value of the flow from project C is larger.

Another method used to determine the worth of an investment project is the *average-rate-of-return* method, which is calculated by dividing average earnings by average investment. The money flows for project A and project B will be used to illustrate this method. Since the money flows include depreciation, this must be subtracted to obtain the earnings for each project. Depreciation for both circumstances is figured on a straight-line basis; that is, as equal increments over the life of the asset. The average earnings are calculated in Table 11–5.

TABLE 11–5

AVERAGE RATE OF RETURN COMPARISON

	Project A				Project B		
Year	Flow	Depr.	Earnings	Year	Flow	Depr.	Earnings
1	$ 500	$600	$(100)	1	$500	$300	$ 200
2	900	600	300	2	500	300	200
3	1,200	600	600	3	500	300	200
4				4	500	300	200
5				5	500	300	200
6				6	500	300	200
			Total = $800				Total = $1,200

Average earnings, $800/3 = $267   Average earnings, $1,200/6 = $200

Since straight-line depreciation is assumed for the table, the average investment in each project is the ending and beginning amount divided by 2. Since the ending amount is zero, average investment in each project is one-half the original investment ($1,800/2). The calculation of average rate of return for each project then proceeds as follows:

$$\text{Average rate of return} = \frac{\text{average earnings}}{\text{average investment}}$$

$$\text{Average rate of return for project } A = \frac{\$267}{\$900} = 29\%$$

$$\text{Average rate of return for project } B = \frac{\$200}{\$900} = 22\%.$$

Calculations for project C, had they been illustrated, would have yielded the same average rate of return as project A above. Thus the average-rate-of-return method reflects the relative profitability of each project. However, it ignores the time value of money, since the present value of project C's money flow was greater than project A's, and yet they both yield the same average rate of return.

The third method of determining the worth of an investment project is the *discounted-cash-flow* method. This method takes into consideration the time value of funds; that is, the fact that current income is more valuable than income received at a later date. The cash flow of each project is discounted at a rate that yields a present value equal to the original cost. In other words, this is the same as solving for the rate of interest (i) in the present-value formula, but referred to as the rate of discount, for a series of amounts when the original investment is substituted for present value. For example, the cash flow for project A amounted to $500, $900, and $1,200. The rate of discount i, which almost equates the present value of the flow ($1,779) to the original commitment or investment of $1,800, is 20 per cent. (The exact rate would be slightly less.) This expresses the rate of return on an investment that the flow of receipts represents. Obviously the project with the greatest return will be the most desirable, provided it exceeds the firm's cost of capital.

The results of calculating the rate of return by using the discounted-cash-flow method for projects A, B, and C are illustrated in Table 11–6. In each case the rate of interest (i) was obtained by a process of elimination until one yielded a present value amount as close as possible to the $1,800 original investment. Obviously, project C is most desirable because it yields the highest rate of return when the flows are equated (approximately) to the $1,800 commitment.

This discussion of fixed-capital needs will be concluded with a brief look at several overall measures of performance. The rate of return on total investment is one device that measures the overall efficiency of a firm and is calculated by dividing earnings by total capital invested in the firm. If the results are unsatisfactory, changes should be made. Another device that measures a firm's profitability is the so-called margin of profit. This is calculated by dividing net profit by net sales and converting the answer to a percentage. The earning capacity of all capital invested in a firm can be determined by dividing net profit by invested capital to obtain a ratio of net profit

TABLE 11-6

DISCOUNTED-CASH-FLOW COMPARISON

Year	Project A Flow	Project A Present Value	Project B Flow	Project B Present Value	Project C Flow	Project C Present Value
1	$ 500	$417	$500	$ 427	$1,200	$ 968
2	900	625	500	365	900	570
3	1,200	737	500	312	500	257
4			500	267		
5			500	228		
6			500	195		
	Total = $1,779		Total = $1,794		Total = $1,795	
	i = 20%		i = 17%		i = 24%	

to total investment. There also are many other ratios and techniques with which to inspect a firm's overall performance.

Meeting Fixed-Capital Needs

Various types of funds can be obtained to meet the fixed-capital needs of a business enterprise. Funds can be divided into three main categories: *debt funds*, *equity funds*, and *internal funds*. As stated previously, the permanent portion of working capital can also be satisfied by these types of funds; both needs are usually thought of as being satisfied by long-term financing. For our purposes, short-term financing is defined as financing that requires a duration of less than one year. All other forms of financing will fall into the long-term category.

The *term loan* is a type of debt financing (borrowing) that has become popular with business enterprises in recent years. It is basically an installment loan available to business firms and requiring repayment over a relatively short period of time. The maturity of such loans is usually less than five years. Small- and medium-sized firms find such arrangements attractive because their access to capital markets is not as extensive as it is for large firms. The funds are used primarily to finance durable goods, such as machines and equipment. Term loans are available from life insurance companies, commercial finance companies, and commercial banks, although banks are the principal source for this type of credit.

Long-term funds can be obtained from the public by the use of *long-term-debt* instruments. These instruments range from long-term notes to formal types of bonds. While the former are usually privately placed, the latter are generally handled by middlemen. The two major types of middlemen are investment bankers and mortgage bankers; each offers various arrangements to assist in the financing of a business firm. Even though middlemen may serve in an advisory capacity, their principal function is to place the firm's securities with lenders in order to obtain funds. They also can act as agents and sell the securities on a commission basis, or they can *underwrite* an issue by outright purchase and then offer the securities for sale to the public.

The bondholder is not an owner but a creditor, who has loaned money to the firm and therefore has a claim on it. The lender agrees to pay the bondholder a definite rate of interest at fixed intervals and to repay the principal when the bond matures. Maturities generally range between 10 and 30 years; bonds can mature either all at once or at regular intervals. The latter type are called *serial bonds*, because the serial numbers on the bonds are used to construct a schedule of redemptions.

Bonds are generally issued with a *trust indenture*, which is a covenant or contract between the lender and the borrower. The trust indenture indicates all the provisions of the bond issue, ranging from a description of the issue to a list of the responsibilities required of the borrower. It includes the restrictive and limiting clauses and stipulates the privileges that are available to the borrower. Finally, it requires the appointment of a third party, the *trustee* (usually a bank), to look after the interests of the bondholders, who are usually widely scattered about the country.

In many cases, bonds are secured by a mortgage on the physical property of the firm. In the case of *mortgage bonds* and *equipment bonds*, the creditor (bondholder) is given a lien (claim) against certain assets so that he can seize the pledged property if there is a default on the bonds. *Collateral-trust bonds* are secured by stocks, bonds, and personal property. An *equipment-trust certificate* is issued with a claim upon a specific piece of equipment, such as a diesel locomotive or a jet airliner. Although *debenture bonds* are considered unsecured bonds, they are actually secured by the general credit of the firm.

Equity funds are obtained from the owners of a firm. The single proprietor and the partners in a partnership contribute equity funds when they commit funds to the firm (unless the funds are borrowed). In corporations, equity funds are obtained by the sale of stocks.

Several characteristics distinguish equity capital from debt capital. First, even though dividends are usually expected to be paid on stocks, the firm is not required to pay them (except in the case of preferred stocks). Second, equity claimants are the owners of the firm and thus control it; stockholders exercise their control rights by voting or by delegating their votes to a proxy. Third, there is no stipulation that equity funds are to be returned by the firm at a particular time. Stockholders can obtain their funds at any time by selling their claims to someone else. This can be accomplished with little difficulty through stockbrokers and various securities exchanges.

There are two principal types of stock: *common* and *preferred*. Preferred stock is so named because preferred stockholders have certain priorities in the distribution of company profits and in the distribution of assets if the firm is liquidated. In contrast to common stockholders, their dividend payments are stipulated to be a certain amount and never fluctuate. For this reason, common stock carries with it both greater risk and greater opportunity. If earnings fall, common stockholders may forfeit their dividends, but if earnings rise, they may reap extra benefits that preferred stockholders may not be able to share. Common stockholders also can participate more in the rewards associated with the growth of a firm, because the value of their stock is more likely to increase.

Additional stocks can be sold to either present stockholders or new owners. If the present stockholders have a *preemptive right*, new stock must be offered to them first. In this way they can maintain their proportionate interest in assets, earnings, and control of the firm. Investment bankers are also available to assist in offering new stocks. They act in various capacities to help place the securities and obtain funds for the firm.

Equity funds are also obtained *internally* when a firm retains part of its profits; this is called retained earnings and accounts for a substantial source of funds. An increase in stockholders' claims is usually reflected by a higher stock price. Stockholders generally approve of this retention because it contributes to the growth and development of the firm. However, some firms do not retain as many earnings as others. Retained earnings offer stockholders the opportunity of reducing their income tax liability, since income tax is not usually paid on retained earnings. Even though high stock prices that reflect the larger equity claims carry a capital gains tax liability when the stock is sold, the capital gains tax is considerably lower than the income tax rate, usually half. Firms that retain large amounts of earnings frequently issue stock dividends or split the stock in order to recognize stockholders' claims on retained earnings. Retained earnings also allow a firm to save flotation costs; if cash dividends were paid instead, new funds would have to be sought in capital markets, which would incur certain fees and distribution costs.

Two other important devices that are a part of the financing process merit attention. The first device, *depreciation*, is an accounting technique that can be used to indicate the availability of funds for a firm's use. Depreciation charges are estimated portions of revenue that result from product sales and are intended to account for that portion of fixed assets which were used up to produce the product. While no mention has been made of the outright sale of assets it should be evident that if a firm sells a building or a piece of equipment, the proceeds also become available to the firm. Like the funds indicated as depreciation, they can be used by management for any valid purpose.

There are several ways to estimate depreciation. Some methods are quite rigid; others are more flexible. An estimate can be based on many factors and may reflect such things as the rate of production, the declining value of an asset, its average value, and its replacement cost. In any case, the method that best represents an estimate of the particular firm's requirements should be used. Each year, depreciation accounts for 40 to 50 per cent of all funds available to corporations. It is the largest single classification of funds, although its percentage may vary from time to time depending upon the tax rates and capital markets.

The other important device included in the financing process is *leasing*. National retail chains have used this device for years, by leasing buildings in popular trading areas. Today firms can lease almost any type of asset, including trucks, automobiles, machines, and office equipment. A lease is merely an arrangement to use an asset rather than to buy it. In this sense it is not a source of capital but rather a means whereby funds can be released from fixed assets to be used for other purposes. Various techniques may be employed to arrange for a lease. One common technique is the sale-leaseback arrangement, where the firm sells an asset to another party from whom it is leased back on a long-term basis. Financial institutions find these arrangements very desirable.

It was mentioned previously that the financing decision requires the rate of return to be matched to the firm's cost of capital. As long as the rate of return exceeds the cost of capital, the project is worthwile. Several methods have been presented that can be used to reflect a project's merit. Methods of calculating the cost of capital from various sources of funds will now be considered.

The cost of long-term debt is basically the investor's (lender's) yield to maturity. However, the calculations must be adjusted for flotation or distribution costs and for the firm's income tax rate. If the bond is sold at face value (par value), the yield to maturity will be the same as the stated rate. For example, a $1,000, 10-year, 5 per cent bond that was initially sold at $1,000 would have a yield to maturity of 5 per cent. If a firm's tax rate is 50 per cent, its cost of debt capital will be expressed as one half its stated rate, or $2\frac{1}{2}$ per cent in this case. This can be explained by comparing the capital cost of a firm that is financed entirely by equity capital with one that is financed entirely by debt capital, and by assuming that both offer the same rate of return to investors. A $100,000 profit for a company that is financed entirely by equity capital represents a capital cost of $200,000, because one half of the $200,000 must be paid out as income tax (assuming a 50 per cent tax rate), leaving $100,000 to be paid as dividends. By contrast, a company financed entirely by debt capital has a capital cost of only $100,000, because interest cost is not taxable as income. The interest of $100,000 in this case represents the same return to investors (bondholders) as the $100,000 dividend does to the investors (stockholders) in the first case. As a result, the interest cost on debt capital is adjusted by an amount equal to the income tax rate, so that the capital cost of debt capital is comparable to the capital cost of equity capital, which is subject to income tax. The cost of short-term capital can be computed in a similar manner.

When the debt instrument is not sold at face value, the yield to maturity must take into account the premium or discount. A premium results if the bond is sold above its par value, and a discount results if it is sold below its par value. The discount represents a lower cost to the investor (lender) for the income from the security. He also will experience a capital gain equal to the discount when the security matures. If the exact yield to maturity is obtained from bond tables, the time value of the premium or discount can be included. However, when the time to maturity is 10 years or less and the premium or discount is small, only an approximate yield to maturity is necessary.

The yield to maturity can be approximated by dividing the annual amount of income received by the average amount invested. For example, assume that a $1,000, 10-year, 5 per cent bond was sold at a price of $900. The current yield is 5.55 per cent ($50/$900), but the yield to maturity is calculated as follows:

$$\text{Yield to maturity} = \frac{\text{average annual income}}{\text{average amount invested}}$$
$$= \frac{\$50 + \$100/10}{(\$1,000 + \$900)/2}$$
$$= \frac{\$60}{\$950}$$
$$= 6.32\%.$$

The average annual income includes the interest income ($50) plus one year's portion of the difference between the maturity value (par value) and the sale price of the bond [($1,000 − $900)/10]. The average amount of investment is simply an average of the maturity value and the sale price of the bond. When the 6.32 per cent rate is adjusted by the firm's income tax rate (50 per cent), the actual cost of capital is found to equal 3.16 per cent.

The cost of equity capital is somewhat simpler to calculate than the cost of debt capital. Stocks are issued in perpetuity; that is, they do not mature. For this reason there is no need to account for premiums and discounts as was the case with bonds. The cost of equity capital is equal to the ratio of the annual dividend income per share to the current market price of the stock. Since common stocks often experience increased dividends and capital gains, the annual dividend income per share should include an estimate of these future expectations. The rate of return on preferred stock is fixed; therefore no such estimate of expectations is included. The cost of equity capital for a stock that can be issued at $100 with expected annual earnings of $5 per share is calculated as follows:

$$\text{Cost of equity capital} = \frac{\text{expected annual income}}{\text{market price of stock}}$$
$$= \frac{\$5}{\$100}$$
$$= 5\%.$$

The cost of retained earnings can be calculated in a similar manner. However, since the stockholder foregoes some tax payment, the cost of retained earnings may be less if this fact is included in the calculations.

Since a firm's financial structure is made up of several types of capital, it would be useful to have some idea of its overall cost of capital. This can be accomplished by calculating a *weighted-average cost of capital*. The cost of each component in the firm's financial structure is weighted according to the relative proportion of the total structure it represents. This technique is shown in Table 11–7. (Assume a 50 per cent income tax rate and assume that suppliers are paid during the discount period.)

Financial requirements obviously will vary from one business enterprise to another. A particular firm's finance mix usually is the result of its past arrangements and attitudes. However, three important factors ought to be kept in mind in determining future arrangements; *adaptability, burden*, and *control* are the ABC's of a finance mix.

Adaptability is the power to alter an existing financial structure. A substantial decrease in interest rates is of no use to a firm if it cannot replace its high-interest debts. For example, a firm should insist upon premature redemption and call features in its bond indentures. Likewise, the principal and interest payments that can be considered a financial *burden* on the firm should be kept within manageable proportions; costs of financing vary with the different sources of funds. Third, *control* of the corporation may be diluted by additional sales of common stock. Bondholders and creditors are not owners and have no voting privileges. However, they will have a say in business operations if the firm does not meet its obligations to them. These ABC's of

TABLE 11–7

WEIGHTED-AVERAGE COST OF CAPITAL

Type of Security	Percentage of Structure		After-tax Cost (%)		Weighted Cost (%)
5%, 10-year bond (sold at $900)	20	×	3.16	=	0.632
Short-term bank debt (6%)	20	×	3.00	=	0.600
Trade credit	10	×	0.00	=	0.000
Stock	20	×	8.00	=	1.600
Retained earnings	30	×	6.00	=	1.800
Weighted-average cost of capital				=	4.632

TABLE 11-8

TRADING-ON-THE-EQUITY

Item	Year 1	Year 2	Year 3
Earnings After Taxes	$10,000	$20,000	$ 6,000
Firm A: $ 50,000 debt, $150,000 equity			
Interest on debt ($50,000 × 5%)	$2,500	$2,500	$2,500
Profit to stockholders	$7,500	$17,500	$3,500
Total equity capital invested	$150,000	$150,000	$150,000
Percentage earned on equity capital	5%	$11\frac{2}{3}$%	$2\frac{1}{3}$%
Firm B: $100,000 debt, $100,000 equity			
Interest on debt ($100,000 × 5%)	$5,000	$5,000	$5,000
Profit to stockholders	$5,000	$15,000	$1,000
Total equity capital invested	$100,000	$100,000	$100,000
Percentage earned on equity capital	5%	15%	1%

a finance mix are presented here merely to point out that there are many considerations involved in the financing decision.

One basic decision about the finance mix is whether to use long-term debt funds or equity funds. While there are many factors involved in such a decision, one fundamental of business analysis can be presented here. This fundamental, known as *trading-on-the-equity*, generally expresses the extent to which long-term-debt capital is used in relation to equity capital. The use of long-term-debt capital depends on, and is even limited by, the extent to which equity capital is employed; hence the term "trading-on-the-equity." The effect of trading-on-the-equity is called *leverage* (financial leverage as opposed to operating leverage, which was introduced earlier in the chapter). As the following example indicates, the rate of return to the owners can be affected substantially by the use of lower-cost debt financing. The more that capital requirements are financed by lower-cost debt funds, the greater will be the earnings and the rate of return available to the owners. An example of the effects of trading on the equity is provided in Table 11-8.

In the table, both firm A and firm B have total capital structures of $200,000. Firm A is financed with $50,000 debt capital and $150,000 equity capital, which is a debt-to-total-capital ratio of $\frac{1}{4}$. Firm B is financed with $100,000 debt capital and $100,000 equity capital, a debt-to-total-capital ratio of $\frac{1}{2}$. Firm B therefore is trading on the equity to a greater extent than firm A. The earnings after taxes for each of three years are also indicated in the table. The effect on each firm of trading on the equity is reflected by the percentage earned on equity capital invested. When firm A's earnings doubled to $20,000 in the second year, the rate of return on equity capital jumped from 5 per cent to $11\frac{2}{3}$ per cent. The following year, when earnings fell, the rate also fell. Bondholders received $2,500 each year. The leverage is even greater for firm *B*. The debt capital equals half the total capital invested, or $100,000 instead of the $50,000 for firm *A*. The rate of return on equity capital fluctuates even more. When earnings doubled from $10,000 to $20,000, the rate of return jumped from 5 per cent to 15 per cent. Note that when income was $10,000, the debt and equity capital in both firms earned 5 per cent. At any other income, however, the effect of trading on the equity was evident; this leverage effect is even greater when the debt-to-total-capital ratio is higher.

There is no such thing as an ideal capital structure; they vary with each business enterprise depending upon the circumstances. Since these circumstances are always changing, the firm must continuously seek out its best finance mix. What might be ideal for one firm would not necessarily be ideal for another. Managements usually select a structure that will balance yield and safety within a range that provides a satisfactory cost of capital. However, the overall cost of capital may still rise if there is too much equity or too much debt in the firm's financial structure, because of security prices and the interest rates required for the various financial structures. For example, since lenders generally consider a higher ratio of debt to equity as more risky, they usually demand a higher rate of interest.

In summarizing this section, fixed capital refers to the funds that support fixed assets and the permanent portion of working capital. Because the fixed-capital decision represents a long-run commitment, it requires careful consideration. Several techniques can be used to determine the merit of the various investment projects. In any event, the rate of return and the cost of capital provide guidelines for fixed-capital decisions. Fixed-capital funds are usually obtained from long-term sources, both debt and equity. The long-term funds are accounted for primarily by depreciation, retained earnings, term loans, notes, bonds, and stocks (or owners' equity).

PROBLEMS AND PROJECTS

1. Translate into an annual rate of interest the cost of not taking the discount on a $1,200 invoice with terms "$^1/_{15}$ net 30."
2. Calculate the proceeds that result from discounting a customer's 60-day, 5 per cent note for $3,600 at a bank. The note has 45 days remaining to maturity and the bank's discount rate is 6 per cent.
3. Report on the sources and uses of corporate funds as described in the *Survey of Current Business* (May, 1964), p. 11, or from a more current issue.
4. Determine which of the following $900 investment projects is most desirable. The firm's cost of capital is 5 per cent. Use all three methods described in the chapter to determine which flow of income would be most profitable; indicate the results of your calculations.

Year	Project A	Project B	Deprec.	Earnings A	Earnings B
1	$600	$300			
2	200	300			
3	100	300			
4	100	100			
		Totals			
		Average earnings			
		Average investment			
		Average rate of return			

Fill in the blanks with the appropriate word(s):

a. According to the payback method, project *A* is _____ project *B* because _____ .

b. According to the average-rate-of-return method, project *A* is _____ ____ project *B* because _____ .

c. According to the discounted-cash-flow method, project *A* is _____ __ project *B* because the present value of *A*'s cash flow is equal to _____ _____ , and the present value of *B*'s cash flow is equal to _____ .

SELECTED REFERENCES

Archer, Stephen H., and Charles A. D'Ambrosio, *Business Finance: Theory and Management.* New York: The Macmillan Company, 1966.

Foulke, Roy A., *Practical Financial Statement Analysis.* New York: McGraw-Hill Book Company. 1968.

Johnson, Robert W., *Financial Management*, 3rd ed. Boston: Allyn & Bacon, Inc., 1966.

Walker, Ernest W., *Essentials of Financial Management.* Englewood Cliffs, N. J.: Prentice-Hall, Inc., 1965.

12

ALGEBRA OF

LINEAR EQUATIONS

The title of this chapter may be misleading to students with training in mathematics because the term "algebra of linear equations" often is interpreted to encompass the algebra of vectors and matrices as well. In this book, we will limit the expression to include only the very basic and elementary rules used in the algebraic manipulation of simple linear equations. The main purpose of this chapter is to provide the reader with a review of the basic mathematical rules for solving equations and systems of equations. Most of these rules may seem elementary, but many students may find that some of the material in other chapters will be mastered more easily if this one is reviewed.

The chapter is divided into three parts that cover the following main topics: (1) principles for solving equations and inequalities, (2) graphs of linear equations and inequalities, and (3) methods for solving systems of linear equations. The Annex will provide some basic rules for operating with signed numbers.

PRINCIPLES FOR SOLVING EQUATIONS AND INEQUALITIES

The area of a circle is defined by the formula $A = \pi r^2$. The volume of a rectangular solid equals the length times the width times the height, or, symbolically, $V = lwh$. The interest on a sum of money equals the principal times the rate times the time; its formula is $I = pit$. These formulas are equations, each of which has several independent variables.

An equation is simply a statement about two sets of expressions that are equal to each other. Every equation has two parts separated by an equal sign. The part to the left of the sign should be equal to the part on the right. The values of the unknowns that satisfy the equality are called *roots*. Let us illustrate this with a simple one-variable equation. What value of X satisfies the equality $4X = 24$? It is 6, because 6 times 4 equals 24. The equality is satisfied when the root 6 is substituted in the equation:

$$4 \times 6 = 24$$
$$24 = 24.$$

Note that finding the root of an equation that has only one unknown means solving the equation.

One or more of four basic principles can be used to solve equations. Among the many forms in which equations may appear are the following:

$$4X = 24$$
$$\frac{1}{3}X = 33$$
$$X + 5 = 21$$
$$X - 17 = 13.$$

Solving each of these equations requires the application of a different principle.

The first equation, $4X = 24$, can be solved by the *principle of solving equations by division*, which can be stated as follows: *Both sides of an equation can be divided by the same constant without changing the root of the equation or disturbing the equality between both members.* (However, dividing by zero is not permissible.)

Let us illustrate this principle by solving $4X = 24$. Dividing both sides by 4, we obtain

$$\frac{4}{4}X = \frac{24}{4};$$

consequently,

$$X = 6.$$

The second equation, $\frac{1}{3}X = 33$, requires a different principle, known as the *principle of solving equations by multiplication*. It is stated as follows: *Both sides of an equation can be multiplied by a constant without changing its root or altering its equality.*

If the second equation is altered by this principle, its root can be directly obtained. Multiplying both sides of $\frac{1}{3}X = 33$ by 3, we obtain

276 FUNDAMENTALS OF BUSINESS ANALYSIS

$$\frac{3}{3}X = 99$$

$$X = 99.$$

The third principle is needed for the equation $X + 5 = 21$. This principle is called the *principle of solving equations by subtraction*. It is stated as follows: *A constant can be subtracted from both sides of an equation without changing its root or altering its equality*.

When the number 5 is subtracted from both sides of the equation $X + 5 = 21$, the root of the equation is obtained:

$$X + 5 - 5 = 21 - 5$$
$$X = 16.$$

The fourth principle is called the *principle of solving equations by addition*. It states: *A constant can be added to both sides of an equation without changing its root or altering its equality*. We will use $X - 17 = 13$ to illustrate this principle. Adding 17 to both sides of the equation, we get

$$X - 17 + 17 = 13 + 17$$
$$X = 30.$$

In each of these cases demonstrating the principles of equations, we derived the root of the equation. You should have noticed that in each case an inverse operation was the key to solving the equation. In the first case, the equation $4X = 24$ was divided by 4, which is the inverse of 4 times X. In the second case, the equation $\frac{1}{3}X = 33$ was multiplied by 3, which is the inverse of X divided by 3. In the third case, 5 was subtracted from both sides of the equation $X + 5 = 21$ to form the inverse of X plus 5. And finally, 17 was added to the equation $X - 17 = 13$, which is the inverse of X minus 17.

Now let us combine all four operations to find the root of one equation, using the practice of inverse operations. The equation is

$$\frac{3X + 4}{2} - 5 = 10.$$

Multiplying by 2,

$$(2)\frac{3X + 4}{2} - (2)5 = (2)10$$
$$3X + 4 - 10 = 20.$$

Adding 10, we get

$$3X + 4 - 10 + 10 = 20 + 10$$
$$3X + 4 = 30.$$

We next subtract 4, obtaining

$$3X + 4 - 4 = 30 - 4$$
$$3X = 26.$$

Dividing by 3,

$$\frac{3X}{3} = \frac{26}{3}$$
$$X = 8\frac{2}{3}.$$

Now let us apply these principles to solve an equation with two unknown values: $2X + 3Y = 12$. To solve for Y, we first subtract $2X$ from the equation:

$$2X - 2X + 3Y = 12 - 2X$$
$$3Y = 12 - 2X.$$

Dividing by 3, we obtain

$$\frac{3Y}{3} = \frac{12}{3} - \frac{2X}{3}$$

or

$$Y = 4 - \frac{2}{3}X.$$

This can also be written as

$$Y = 4 - \frac{2X}{3}.$$

The value of Y can then be determined if a value for X is given.

Many important and useful problems are stated as inequalities rather than as equations. We will first illustrate the uses of inequalities, then the rules for their operation.

Suppose that we are engaged in manufacturing electric golf carts and electric go-carts. Each golf cart requires four man-hours of work in the assembly department and each go-cart requires two man-hours. If the capacity of the department is limited to 470 man-hours, the relationships must be expressed in the form of an inequation, because the department does not have to use all of its 470 man-hours. The inequation appears as

$$4X + 2Y \leq 470,$$

where X denotes the number of golf carts manufactured and Y is the number of go-carts manufactured. The familiar equality sign is replaced by an inequality sign, which in this case is the symbol $\leq$, translated as "less than or equal to." The inequation is interpreted to mean that 4 times the X number of golf carts plus 2 times the Y number of go-carts must be less than or equal to the total number of man-hours available (470).

Let us first display and define the various symbols that express an inequality:

$<$ stands for "less than"
$>$ stands for "greater than"
$\leq$ stands for "less than or equal to"
$\geq$ stands for "greater than or equal to."

For example, "cost $<$ revenue" means that the costs of a business must be less than its revenue. Another example, "TM $\geq X + Y + Z$," indicates that total money on hand must be greater than or equal to the costs related to projects X, Y, and Z.

There are six principles or rules for solving inequations, two more than there are for equations. The two extra rules are needed for multiplication and division problems involving negative numbers. All six rules will be stated, then two illustrations will be given to substantiate rules 5 and 6.

Rule 1: Equal numbers may be added to both sides of an inequation without changing the inequality.

Rule 2: Equal numbers may be subtracted from both sides of an inequation without changing the inequality.

Rule 3: Both sides of an inequation may be multiplied by equal *positive* numbers without changing the inequality.

Rule 4: Both sides of an inequation may be divided by equal *positive* numbers without changing the inequality.

Rule 5: Both sides of an inequation may be multiplied by equal *negative* numbers provided that the sign of the inequality is *reversed*.

Rule 6: Both sides of an inequation may be divided by equal *negative* numbers provided that the sign of the inequality is *reversed*.

Let us demonstrate the basis for these last two rules. Suppose that we multiply both sides of the inequality $10 > 8$ by a minus 1. We have

$$(-1)10 > (-1)8$$
$$-10 > -8.$$

Since this is not true, the sign must be reversed, which results in

$$-10 < -8.$$

As an alternative, the members of the inequality can be exchanged to give

$$-8 > -10.$$

Now if the inequality $10 > 8$ were divided by, say, a minus 2, we would have

$$\frac{10}{-2} > \frac{8}{-2}$$
$$-5 > -4,$$

which is not true. Reversing the inequality symbol will provide the correct relationship,

$$-5 < -4,$$

or alternatively,

$$-4 > -5.$$

Many problems in linear programming are expressed in the form of inequations. In the next section, both equations and inequations are presented in graphic form.

GRAPHIC REPRESENTATIONS OF LINEAR RELATIONSHIPS

An advantage of equations with one, two, or three unknowns is that they can be represented by lines on a graph. To form a graph of an equation or inequation with one unknown, we need only one axis. You may recall that the equation $4X = 24$ was reduced to its root as $X = 6$. Graphed in one dimension, this equation would appear as the single point circled in Fig. 12–1.

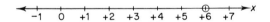

FIGURE 12–1.   Graph of equation with one unknown ($4X = 24$).

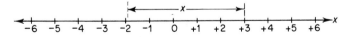

FIGURE 12–2.   Graph of inequation with one unknown ($X \leq 3,\ X > -2$).

On the other hand, an inequation in which $X \leq 3$ and $X > -2$, could be represented in Fig. 12–2.

The Two-Dimensional Graph

Relationships with one unknown are usually represented on the two-dimensional graph called the *rectangular system of coordinates.*The 2 one-variable relationships given above will be shown on such a graph.

To form a rectangular system of coordinates, we place a vertical number scale so that its zero point intersects a horizontal number scale perpendicularly at its zero point. The intersection of these two lines is called the *origin*; each line is referred to as an *axis*. The horizontal axis is usually designated as the X axis and the vertical axis as the Y axis. The X axis is usually assigned to the independent variable and the Y axis to the dependent variable.

A rectangular system of coordinates appears in Fig. 12–3. Any point in this two-dimensional space has a directed distance from the Y axis and a directed distance from the X axis. The directed distance from the Y axis is called the *abscissa* or X coordinate of a point P, and the directed distance from the X axis is called the *ordinate or Y* coordinate of P. The point P then has the coordinates (X, Y).

In writing the coordinates of a point, we must pay proper attention to their algebraic signs as well as to their numerical values, because the signs indicate the directions in which the distances are measured from the axes. We must also follow the notation carefully, writing first the X and then the Y, with the parentheses and comma. For example, the point in Fig. 12–3 at which $X = 4$ and $Y = 3$ is written as (4, 3).

The rectangular system of coordinates can be used to give a picture of the relationship between one and two variables. The two cases of one-variable relationships that were represented in the one-dimensional graphs appear in two dimensions in Fig. 12–4.

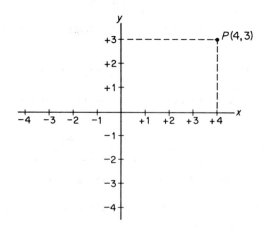

FIGURE 12–3.   Rectangular system of coordinates.

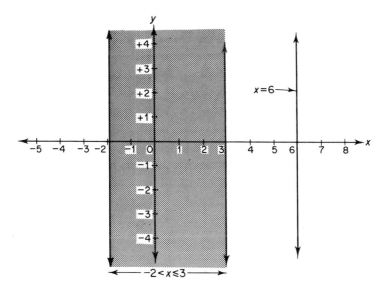

FIGURE 12–4.   Rectangular system of coordinates with one variable.

The simplest two-variable relationship is a *linear equation* of the first degree (that is, variables are of the first power) in X and in Y. The equation is called "linear" because it is plotted as a straight line on the coordinate system. For example, the equation $2X - Y = -3$ would appear as a straight line in the two-dimensional graph of rectangular coordinates. To plot the graph of this equation, we first construct a table of coordinates like the one in Table 12–1, substituting various values for X and calculating the Y values (or vice versa). These values are plotted for X and Y in Fig. 12–5.

TABLE 12–1

TABLE OF COORDINATES

X	X Substituted in $2X - Y = -3$	Y
-4	$-8 - Y = -3$	-5
-2	$-4 - Y = -3$	-1
0	$0 - Y = -3$	3
$+2$	$4 - Y = -3$	7
$+4$	$8 - Y = -3$	11

Actually, only two points are required to draw a straight line; therefore, we only must solve the equation $2X - Y = -3$ twice. The most convenient thing to do is to let $X = 0$ and solve for Y, then let $Y = 0$ and solve for X. This gives us the so-called Y intercept and X intercept for the linear equation.

Calculating and plotting the intercepts results in the following two values:

$$\text{When } X = 0, \; Y = 3$$
$$\text{When } Y = 0, \; X = -1\tfrac{1}{2}.$$

This can be shown graphically in Fig. 12–6.

The equation $2X - Y = -3$ can be changed into an inequation of the form $2X - Y \geq -3$. If this inequation is plotted, it will be represented by the line plotted in Fig. 12–6 and the entire area below it. This can be shown more easily if the terms in the inequation are rearranged (according to the principles of equations and the rules for inequations) into the form $Y \leq 2X + 3$. This inequation represents the points on the line $Y = 2X + 3$ and the shaded area below the line, as shown in Fig. 12–7. If we make the restriction that the X and Y values cannot be negative, the shaded area will be limited to the area below the line that appears in the first quadrant of the system of rectangular coordinates. The first quadrant is the portion to the right of the Y axis and above the X axis. The other three quadrants are numbered in a counterclockwise direction around the origin.

The standard form of a linear equation in X and Y is

$$Y = a + bX,$$

where Y is the dependent variable, a is a constant called the Y intercept,

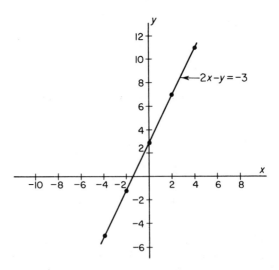

FIGURE 12–5.   Rectangular system of coordinates with two variables showing
a linear equation.

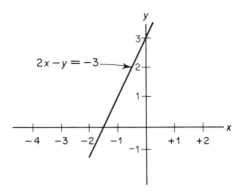

FIGURE 12–6.   Plotting the linear equation $(2X- Y= -3)$ showing the
Y-intercept and the X-intercept.

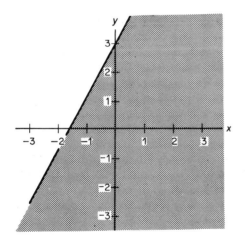

FIGURE 12–7.   Plotting the inequation $(2X- Y\geq -3)$.

b is a constant called the slope, and X is the independent variable. When
$X = 0$, $Y = a$ (the Y intercept). Therefore, when this line is plotted, the
value of the Y intercept gives the point where the line crosses the Y axis, or
the ordinate. The intercept may be positive or negative.

When X is given a value, a value can be determined for Y. The amount
by which Y changes for each unit change in X is called the *slope* of the equation; it is usually designated by the letter b. The value of b determines how
much a line on graph paper will slant or slope. It may be positive or negative.
The following equations and Fig. 12–8 describe a line with a negative slope
and one with a positive slope (the symbol $\triangle$ is read as "change in").

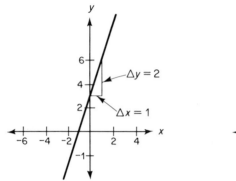
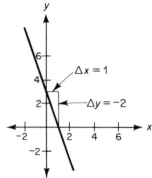

$$\text{Slope} = \frac{\triangle Y}{\triangle X} = \frac{+2}{+1} = 2 \qquad\qquad \text{Slope} = \frac{\triangle Y}{\triangle X} = \frac{-2}{+1} = -2$$

FIGURE 12–8. Plotting linear equations with a positive slope $\left(\dfrac{\triangle Y}{\triangle X} = \dfrac{+2}{+1} = 2\right)$ **and a negative slope** $\left(\dfrac{\triangle Y}{\triangle X} = \dfrac{-2}{+1} = -2\right).$

The Three-Dimensional Graph

Suppose that we have a fixed amount of money and that we spend it on three items: refreshments (R), clothes (C), and food (F). The prices of these commodities average \$1, \$2, and \$1, respectively, and the amount of money we have to spend is \$200. Thus the various ways in which we may spend the entire \$200 must satisfy the relationship

$$1R + 2C + 1F = \$200,$$

where R is the number of units of refreshment; C is the number of units of clothing; F is the number of units of food; and R, F, and C must be equal to or greater than zero.

We can plot this relationship in three dimensions by constructing a graph with three axes. This is done by finding the intercepts of each axis and connecting these points by a straight line to form a plane. The intercepts are found by setting two variables equal to zero and solving the equation for the remaining variable. For example, if C and F each equal zero,

$$R + 2(0) + 1(0) = \$200.$$

Therefore, R = \$200. If both R and F equal zero, C = \$100; and if R and C each equal zero, F = \$200. This procedure is summarized in Table 12–2.

TABLE 12–2

SOLVING THREE VARIABLES

R	C	F
\$200	0	0
0	\$100	0
0	0	\$200

The equation $1R + 2C + 1F$ = \$200 appears as a plane in the three-dimensional graph in Fig. 12–9. Any position on this plane represents a combination of units of the three items that can be purchased for \$200. The point P on the plane is one such example.

The corresponding *inequation*, $1R + 2C + 1F \leq$ \$200, would be represented in Fig. 12–9 by the solid area shaped like a pyramid. All points included within this solid area represent combinations of which \$200 or less can be spent.

Graphic displays of relationships are limited to three dimensions. Relationships with four or more variables must be solved by algebraic methods using vectors and matrices.

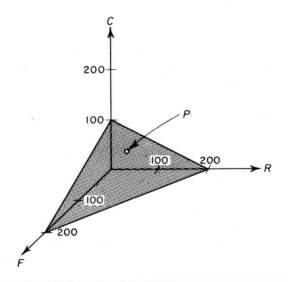

FIGURE 12–9. Plotting the three-dimensional graph $(1R + 2C + 1F =$ \$200).

SYSTEMS OF LINEAR EQUATIONS

We have learned how to solve problems using one variable. Many problems are easier to solve if we use more than one variable. These problems must be solved by being stated in the form of more than one equation; that is, in a *system of equations*. Let us illustrate with an example.

Mrs. Reed owns a floral shop located near a large university. One weekend she sold a total of 40 corsages, collecting $64.00. The chrysanthemums sold for $2.50 each and the carnations for $1.00 each. Mrs. Reed would like to determine how many flowers of each kind were sold without bothering to take an inventory of what was left. The problem can be stated in the form of two equations with two unknowns:

$$\$2.50M + \$1.00C = \$64.00$$
$$M + C = 40,$$

where M is the number of chrysanthemums sold and C is the number of carnations sold.

Given two equations with two unknowns, it is possible to find the values of X and Y that will satisfy both equations simultaneously. Before solving Mrs. Reed's problem, we will illustrate graphically three basic systems that each consist of two equations. In addition, various algebraic methods for solving a system of two or more equations will be explained.

Graphic Displays of Systems of Linear Equations

It is probably obvious that two straight lines, if extended, might have any one of three relations to each other: (1) they might intersect, (2) they might be parallel, or (3) they might coincide (that is, they might overlap). These three relations are illustrated separately by graphing pairs of equations on the two-dimensional graph.

Example 1 : Intersecting Lines

$$Y = 6 - 2X \qquad Y = -4 + 3X$$

The two lines intersect at $(+2, +2)$ in Fig. 12–10. If the values for X and Y are substituted in each equation, the equations are satisfied. Hence, $X = 2$, $Y = 2$ is the common solution of the two equations $Y = 6 - 2X$ and $Y = -4 + 3X$. A system of equations that has only one common solution—that is, where the solutions intersect at only one point—is called *consistent*. Equations in a consistent system are sometimes referred to as *independent equations*.

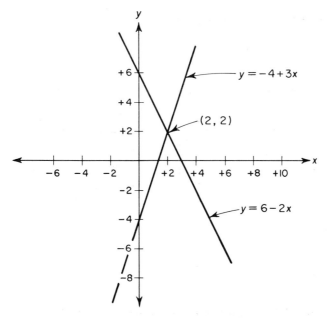

FIGURE 12-10. Plotting a pair of equations with intersecting lines on a two-dimensional graph ($Y = 6 - 2X$ and $Y = -4 + 3X$).

Example 2 : *Parallel Lines*

$$X + 2Y = 4 \qquad 2X + 4Y = 12$$

X	Y		X	Y
0	2		0	3
4	0		6	0

The two lines in Fig. 12-11 are parallel. There is no pair of values for X and Y that satisfies both equations and therefore there is no common solution. Such a system of equations is called *inconsistent*.

If these two equations were transformed into the familar standard form, $Y = a + bX$, we would see that they would be plotted as parallel lines. For example, $X + 2Y = 4$ can be changed to $Y = 2 - \frac{1}{2}X$, and $2X + 4Y = 12$ corresponds to $Y = 3 - \frac{1}{2}X$. They have equal slopes; only their Y intercepts are different. This implies that the two equations represent parallel lines.

Example 3 : *Coinciding Lines*

$$X + 2Y = 6 \qquad 2X + 4Y = 12$$

These two equations can be transformed into the standard form:

$$Y = 3 - \frac{1}{2}X \qquad Y = 3 - \frac{1}{2}X.$$

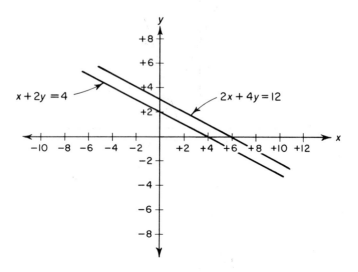

FIGURE 12–11. Plotting a pair of equations with parallel lines on a two-dimensional graph ($X + 2Y = 4$ and $2X + 4Y = 12$).

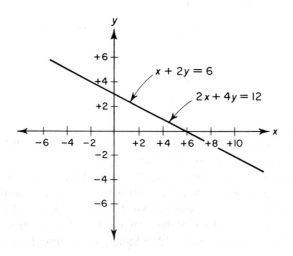

FIGURE 12–12. Plotting a pair of equations with coinciding lines on a two-dimensional graph ($X + 2Y = 6$ and $2X + 4Y = 12$).

They are obviously equivalent equations because they form the same line. If both sides of the equation $2X + 4Y = 12$ are divided by 2, we obtain $X + 2Y = 6$, which is the same as the other equation. These two equations, therefore, plot as the same straight line in Fig. 12–12.

The two lines coincide, or overlap; every point on one is a point on the other. Each pair of numbers that satisfies one of the equations also satisfies the other. We say that a system of equations whose graphs coincide is *indeterminate*. Equations in an indeterminate system are sometimes referred to as *dependent equations*.

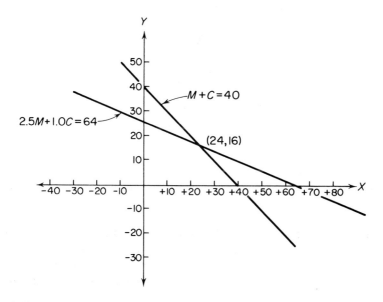

FIGURE 12–13.   Plotting the linear equations (2.5M + 1.0C = 64 and M + C = 40).

Let us now return to our original problem concerning Mrs. Reed's floral shop. The problem was formulated in the following two equations:

$$\$2.50M + \$1.00C = \$64.00$$
$$M + C = 40.$$

Is this a consistent system of equations? Are the equations independent? Is there a solution? We will plot the two equations on the same set of axes in Fig. 12–13 and see if there is a solution; if so, we will determine it graphically. Thus,

$$2.5M + 1.0C = 64 \qquad M + C = 40.$$

M	C
0	64
25.6	0

M	C
0	40
40	0

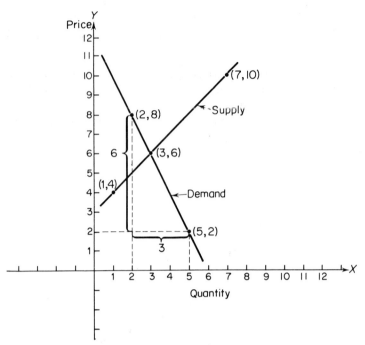

FIGURE 12–14. Plotting the points represented by the linear schedules in Table 12–3.

The two lines intersect at the point that has the coordinates (24, 16). Therefore, the two equations are independent and the system of linear equations is consistent. The solution to the problem is indicated by the point of intersection, which shows that 24 carnations and 16 chrysanthemums were sold.

There is one final topic that should be discussed because it is related to the graphic display of linear relationships. Suppose that we are given demand and supply schedules for a certain commodity and that these schedules must be transformed into algebraic expressions.

One way to make this transformation is to plot the points represented by the schedules and then read the Y intercept and this will determine the slope for each schedule. Let us assume that we have the demand and supply schedules given in Table 12–3. If it is evident that the relationships are linear, only two points from each schedule must be plotted. In this case, investigation of the schedules indicates that they are both linear. Therefore, in Fig. 12–14, we will plot only the two points checked in each schedule.

The equation for the demand curve is

$$Y = 12 - \frac{6}{3}X$$
$$Y = 12 - 2X,$$

because the demand curve intercepts the Y axis at 12. The change in Y from

290

the first point plotted to the second point plotted is 6 (shown in Fig. 12–14), while the change in X is 3. Therefore, the slope is $\frac{6}{3}$ or 2. Verify that the equation for the supply schedule is

$$Y = +3 + X.$$

What does the intersection of the two schedules represent in the economic sense? That is, what does the fact that three units are demanded at the price of $6 mean?

TABLE 12–3

DEMAND AND SUPPLY SCHEDULES

Demand Schedule		Supply Schedule	
Price (Y)	Quantity (X)	Price (Y)	Quantity (X)
$12	0	$12	9
10	1	10 ✓	7
8 ✓	2	8	5
6	3	6	3
4	4	4 ✓	1
2 ✓	5	2	−1
0	6	0	−3

Solving Systems of Linear Equations

The demand–supply problem introduced in the previous section will be used to demonstrate three different methods for determining a solution to a system of linear equations. The three methods are *the substitution method*, *the comparison method*, and *the addition–subtraction method*.

The Substitution Method:
Solve the following system of equations:

$$Y = 12 - 2X \qquad \text{(demand equation)}$$
$$Y = \ \ 3 + X. \qquad \text{(supply equation)}$$

Solving the supply equation for X, we have

$$X = Y - 3.$$

Substituting this value of X in the demand equation results in

$$Y = 12 - 2X$$
$$Y = 12 - 2(Y - 3).$$

Solving for Y,

$$Y = 12 - 2Y + 6.$$

Collecting terms,

$$3Y = 18$$
$$Y = 6.$$

Substitute $+6$ for Y in the supply equation; this results in

$$Y = 3 + X$$

and, since

$$X = Y - 3,$$

we get

$$X = 6 - 3$$
$$X = 3.$$

Therefore, $X = 3$, $Y = 6$ is the solution to this system.

The Comparison Method:
Solve the same system of equations:

$$Y = 12 - 2X \qquad \text{(demand equation)}$$
$$Y = 3 + X. \qquad \text{(supply equation)}$$

These equations can be set equal to each other, since they both are equal to Y. We therefore are comparing two values of Y in terms of their X values, and

$$12 - 2X = 3 + X.$$

We solve for X by collecting terms:

$$-3X = -12 + 3$$
$$-3X = -9$$
$$X = \frac{-9}{-3}$$
$$X = +3.$$

(A minus number divided by a minus number gives a positive quotient; see the Annex to this chapter.) Substitute $+3$ for X in either equation. Substituting it in the first equation (the demand equation), we obtain

$$Y = 12 - 2(3)$$
$$Y = 12 - 6$$
$$Y = 6.$$

These are the same two values that were obtained by the substitution method.

The Addition–Subtraction Method:
We again use the same two equations:

$$Y = 12 - 2X \qquad \text{(demand equation)}$$
$$Y = 3 + X. \qquad \text{(supply equation)}$$

We subtract the second equation from the first equation to eliminate Y:

$$Y = 12 - 2X$$
$$\underline{Y = 3 + X}$$
$$Y - Y = 12 - 3 - 2X - X$$

Collecting terms,

$$0 = 9 - 3X.$$

Transposing,

$$3X = 9$$
$$X = 3.$$

Substituting $+3$ for X in the first equation,

$$Y = 12 - 2(3)$$
$$Y = 12 - 6$$
$$Y = 6.$$

It can be shown that these values satisfy both equations. In other instances, it may be appropriate to add the two equations rather than subtracting them. If one of the Y's had been negative, the equation could have been added to eliminate the Y variable.

The addition–subtraction method can be used conveniently to solve linear equations in three unknowns. To solve a system of three linear equations in three unknowns, one of the unknowns must be eliminated between each of two pairs of the equations. This results in two linear equations in the other two unknowns. These two equations may then be solved for the remaining unknown quantities, and the unknown that was eliminated first may be found by substitution.

Example

Solve the following equations for X, Y, and Z:

$$(1) \quad 4X + 5Y + 3Z = 26$$
$$(2) \quad X + 6Y + 4Z = 19$$
$$(3) \quad 2X - 3Y + 5Z = -16.$$

We will eliminate Y between equations (1) and (2) by multiplying equation (1) by $+6$ and equation (2) by $+5$. This results in

$$
\begin{aligned}
\text{(1a)} \quad 24X + 30Y + 18Z &= 156 \\
\text{(2a)} \quad 5X + 30Y + 20Z &= 95.
\end{aligned}
$$

Subtracting equation (2a) from equation (1a), we have

$$\text{(4)} \quad 19X - 2Z = 61.$$

We also must eliminate Y between equations (2) and (3). Multiplying equation (3) by $+2$ results in

$$\text{(3a)} \quad 4X - 6Y + 10Z = -32.$$

Adding equation (3a) to equation (2), we get

$$\text{(5)} \quad 5X + 14Z = -13.$$

We now solve equations (4) and (5) for X and Z. Multiply equation (4) by $+7$ and add the resulting equation to equation (5):

$$
\begin{aligned}
\text{(4a)} \quad 133X - 14Z &= 427 \\
\text{(5)} \quad \underline{5X + 14Z = -13} \\
138X + 0Z &= 414
\end{aligned}
$$

Collecting terms,

$$
X = \frac{414}{138}
$$
$$
X = 3.
$$

Substitute 3 for X in equation (5):

$$
\begin{aligned}
5(3) + 14Z &= -13 \\
15 + 14Z &= -13 \\
14Z &= -13 - 15 \\
Z &= \frac{-28}{14} \\
Z &= -2.
\end{aligned}
$$

This solution for equations (4) and (5), $X = 3$ and $Z = -2$, can be substituted in any of the three original equations to obtain a value for Y. For example,

$$\text{(2)} \quad X + 6Y + 4Z = 19.$$

Substituting the values for X and Z in this equation,

$$3 + 6Y + 4(-2) = 19$$
$$6Y = 19 + 8 - 3$$
$$6Y = 24$$
$$Y = 4.$$

The solution is therefore $X = 3$, $Y = 4$, and $Z = -2$. Substitution of these values in equations (1), (2), and (3) will satisfy them. This solution graphically represents a point in three-dimensional space where the three planes represented by each equation intersect.

Solving Systems of Three or More Linear Equations

Two methods are available for solving systems of three or more linear equations. The method illustrated in this section relies on a knowledge of determinants and the employment of Cramer's rule. The other method requires a knowledge of matrix algebra, which is briefly introduced in the Annex to Chapter 14. Even though the method of determinants is illustrated here with a system of only two equations, it must be reemphasized that Cramer's rule also holds true for systems of three or more linear equations with an equal number of unknowns.

Determinants of the Second Order
The symbol

$$\begin{vmatrix} a & b \\ c & d \end{vmatrix}$$

is called a *determinant of the second order;* it is a 2-by-2 array of numbers in which a, b, c, and d, representing any numbers, are the elements. A determinant of the third order is a 3-by-3 array of numbers, and so forth. A determinant of the second order is defined as follows:

$$\begin{vmatrix} a & b \\ c & d \end{vmatrix} = a \times d - b \times c.$$

For example,

$$\begin{vmatrix} 2 & 1 \\ -3 & 1 \end{vmatrix} = (2)(1) - (-3)(1) = 5.$$

Therefore, a determinant is a special numerical evaluation of a square array of numbers.

Cramer's rule for solving a system of equations by determinants is used as follows for two equations:

Write a system of two linear equations in X and Y in the form

$$a_1 X + b_1 Y = c_1$$
$$a_2 X + b_2 Y = c_2.$$

The values of X and Y are determined as follows:

$$X = \frac{\begin{vmatrix} c_1 & b_1 \\ c_2 & b_2 \end{vmatrix}}{\begin{vmatrix} a_1 & b_1 \\ a_2 & b_2 \end{vmatrix}} \qquad Y = \frac{\begin{vmatrix} a_1 & c_1 \\ a_2 & c_2 \end{vmatrix}}{\begin{vmatrix} a_1 & b_1 \\ a_2 & b_2 \end{vmatrix}},$$

if the denominators do not equal zero. If the determinants that are the denominators equal zero, the equations are either inconsistent or dependent.

In summary, the value of any unknown is equal to a fraction whose denominator is the determinant of the system and whose numerator is the same determinant but with the column of coefficients of the unknown in question replaced by the column of constant terms.

The basis for Cramer's rule is illustrated with a system of two linear equations in X and Y. Given

$$(6) \quad a_1 X + b_1 Y = c_1$$
$$(7) \quad a_2 X + b_2 Y = c_2,$$

we can solve for X by using the addition–subtraction rule. That is, multiply equation (6) by b_1 and equation (7) by b_2, and subtract the resulting equation (7a) from equation (6a):

$$
\begin{aligned}
(6a) \quad & a_1 b_2 X + b_1 b_2 Y = c_1 b_2 \\
(7a) \quad & \underline{a_2 b_1 X + b_1 b_2 Y = c_2 b_1} \\
& a_1 b_2 X - b_2 b_1 X = c_1 b_2 - c_2 b_1
\end{aligned}
$$

This reduces to

$$(a_1 b_2 - a_2 b_1)X = c_1 b_2 - c_2 b_1.$$

Solving for X, we get

$$X = \frac{c_1 b_2 - c_2 b_1}{a_1 b_2 - a_2 b_1}.$$

Similarly,

$$Y = \frac{a_1 c_2 - a_2 c_1}{a_1 b_2 - a_2 b_1}.$$

Note that when a determinant such as

$$\begin{vmatrix} c_1 & b_1 \\ c_2 & b_2 \end{vmatrix}$$

was defined, it was equal to $c_1b_2 - c_2b_1$;

$$\begin{vmatrix} a_1 & c_1 \\ a_2 & c_2 \end{vmatrix}$$

was equal to $a_1c_2 - a_2c_1$; and

$$\begin{vmatrix} a_1 & b_1 \\ a_2 & b_2 \end{vmatrix}$$

was equal to $a_1b_2 - a_2b_1$. By substituting these determinants in the above equations for X and Y, we get the arrangement of determinants needed to solve the equations according to Cramer's rule:

$$X = \frac{c_1b_2 - c_2b_1}{a_1b_2 - a_2b_1} = \frac{\begin{vmatrix} c_1 & b_1 \\ c_2 & b_2 \end{vmatrix}}{\begin{vmatrix} a_1 & b_1 \\ a_2 & b_2 \end{vmatrix}}$$

$$Y = \frac{a_1c_2 - a_2c_1}{a_1b_2 - a_2b_1} = \frac{\begin{vmatrix} a_1 & c_1 \\ a_2 & c_2 \end{vmatrix}}{\begin{vmatrix} a_1 & b_1 \\ a_2 & b_2 \end{vmatrix}}.$$

We will now solve two equations by determinants using Cramer's rule:

$$2X + Y = 6$$
$$-3X + Y = -4.$$

The system is in the proper form. The determinant of the system is

$$\begin{vmatrix} 2 & 1 \\ -3 & 1 \end{vmatrix} = 5.$$

The solution is obtained as follows:

$$X = \frac{\begin{vmatrix} 6 & 1 \\ -4 & 1 \end{vmatrix}}{5} = \frac{6 - (-4)}{5} = \frac{10}{5} = 2$$

$$Y = \frac{\begin{vmatrix} 2 & 6 \\ -3 & -4 \end{vmatrix}}{5} = \frac{(-8) - (-18)}{5} = \frac{10}{5} = 2.$$

This is the solution that was determined graphically for the system in its standard form for a straight line; that is,

$$Y = 6 - 2X$$
$$Y = -4 + 3X.$$

In order to solve a system of three or more equations, it is necessary to use a method for finding higher-order determinants. These methods rely on the technique known as *expansion by minors*, which is discussed in standard mathematics textbooks. However, as an example, the third-order determinant appears as follows:

$$\begin{vmatrix} a_1 & b_1 & c_1 \\ a_2 & b_2 & c_2 \\ a_3 & b_3 & c_3 \end{vmatrix}.$$

If three equations in three unknowns appear as

$$2X + 4Y - 3Z = -9$$
$$3X + Y - 2Z = 4$$
$$5X + 2Y + 4Z = 28,$$

the coefficients of the unknowns in the equations form a third-order determinant:

$$\begin{vmatrix} 2 & 4 & -3 \\ 3 & 1 & -2 \\ 5 & 2 & -4 \end{vmatrix}.$$

Cramer's rule is then used to solve this system of equations.

ANNEX: RULES FOR OPERATING WITH SIGNED NUMBERS

The four rules for operating algebraically with positive and negative numbers are stated here briefly for the purpose of review. The rules are as follows:

Addition Rule

1.   To add numbers with *like* signs, find the *sum* of their unsigned values and affix their common sign.

Examples:
$$(+6) + (+7) = +13$$
$$(-9) + (-8) = -17.$$

2.   To add two numbers with *unlike* signs, find the *difference* of their unsigned values and affix to the difference the sign of the number that has the larger unsigned value.

Examples:
$$(+13) + (-2) = +11$$
$$(+9) + (-12) = -3.$$

Subtraction Rule

To subtract one signed number from another, change the sign of the subtrahend and add according to the two rules given above for adding signed numbers.

Examples:
$$(+7) - (+3) = (+7) + (-3) = +4$$
$$(+5) - (-3) = (+5) + (+3) = +8$$
$$(-3) - (-5) = (-3) + (+5) = +2$$
$$(+2) - (+4) = (+2) + (-4) = -2$$
$$(+2) - (-5) = (+2) + (+5) = +7.$$

Multiplication Rule

If two numbers have *like* signs, the product has a *positive* sign. If they have *unlike* signs, the product has a *negative sign.*

Examples:
$$(+7) \times (-3) = -21$$
$$(-3) \times (+7) = -21$$
$$(-3) \times (-7) = +21$$
$$(+3) \times (+7) = +21.$$

Division Rule

The quotient of two numbers having like signs is a positive number. The quotient of two numbers having unlike signs is a negative number.

Examples:
$$(+8)/(-2) = -4$$
$$(-8)/(+2) = -4$$
$$(+8)/(+2) = +4$$
$$(-8)/(-2) = +4.$$

PROBLEMS AND PROJECTS

1. Solve the following equations for A, B, x, or y:

a. $3A = 9$.
b. $x - 4 = 8$.
c. $B - 3 = C$.
d. $\dfrac{x}{4} = 2$.
e. $\dfrac{3}{x} = 5$.
f. $y + 10 = 4$.

g. $B^2 = 2$.
h. $\sqrt{x} = 5$.
i. $\sqrt{y} + 3 = 8$.
j. $B^2 = M$.
k. $\dfrac{x^2}{2} = D$.
l. $\dfrac{6}{\sqrt{x}} = 3$.

2. Plot the following limitations:

a. $4 > x > -3$.
b. $x > 0$.
c. $x < -3$.

d. $0 \le x \le 1$.
e. $x > 2$.
f. $-\infty \le x \le +\infty$.

3. Plot the following inequalities:

a. $x \ge y$.
b. $x + y < 0$.

c. $x - y > 2$.
d. $x - y < 1$.

4. Plot the following systems of equations by the intercept method:

a. $4x + 2y = 6$
   $2x + y = 8$.

b. $x - y = 1$
   $5x + y = 1$.

5. Plot the following systems of equations by the slope–intercept method:

a. $y - 3x = 0$
   $y = 2x + 4$.

b. $2x + y = 8$
   $4x + 2y = 16$.

6. Solve the following systems of equations by the addition–subtraction method, the substitution method, or the comparison method:

a. $4x + 5y = 13$
   $2x - 3y = -21$.
b. $x - y = 1$
   $5x + y = 1$.

c. $3x - 2y = 5$
   $x - y = 2$.
d. $y = 12 - 2x$
   $y = 3 + x$.

7. Mr. Spencer borrowed money from two loan companies. At one he pays 6 per cent annual interest and at the other, 8 per cent. The total amount

he borrowed was \$1,200, and the total interest he will pay is \$86 a year. How much did he borrow at each rate?

8. Solve the following system of three equations by the method of parallel addition–subtraction:

$$2x + 4y - 3Z = -9$$
$$3x + y - 2Z = 4$$
$$5x + 2y + 4Z = 28.$$

9. Compute the following determinants:

a. $\begin{vmatrix} 7 & 3 \\ 2 & 1 \end{vmatrix}.$
b. $\begin{vmatrix} 6 & 0 \\ 4 & 1 \end{vmatrix}.$

10. Solve the following system of equations by using Cramer's rule.

$$4x - y = 7$$
$$-2x + 3y = -1.$$

SELECTED REFERENCES

Adams, L. J., *Modern Business Mathematics.* New York: Holt, Rinehart & Winston, Inc., 1963.

Fehr, H. F., W. H. Carnahan, and M. Beberman, *Algebra: Its Key Concepts and Fundamental Principles.* Boston: D. C. Heath & Company, 1955.

Flexer, R. J., and A. S. Flexer, *Programmed Reviews of Mathematics.* New York: Harper & Row, Publishers, 1967. (A series of six topics: Fractions, Linear and Literal Equations, Quadratic Equations, Exponents and Square Roots, Logarithms, and Introduction to Statistics.)

Huffman, H., *Programmed Business Mathematics.* New York: McGraw-Hill Book Company, 1963. (In four parts: Fundamentals of Business Mathematics; Interest, Negotiable Instruments, and Payroll Mathematics; Business Mathematics in Management Decisions; and Mathematics of Accounting and Finance.)

Kleppner, D., and N. Ramsey, *Quick Calculus.* New York: John Wiley & Sons, Inc., 1965.

Meier, R. C., and S. H. Archer, *An Introduction to Mathematics for Business Analysis.* New York: McGraw-Hill Book Company, 1960.

Meyer, H., and R. V. Mendenhall, *Techniques of Differentiation and Integration, A Program for Self-Instruction.* New York: McGraw-Hill Book Company, 1966.

Rutledge, W. A., and T. W. Cairns, *Mathematics for Business Analysis.* New York: Holt, Rinehart & Winston, Inc., 1963.

13

CURVE FITTING

In the previous chapter the mathematical function was expressed graphically as a line, with each equation representing a dependent relationship between two variables. In the functional sense, there was a one-to-one correspondence between the two variables; in mathematical terms this simply means that for every value of X there is a single corresponding value of Y. In this chapter, however, we are interested in fitting a particular line to a set of X and Y values where one-to-one correspondence is not the rule. Therefore, in the statistical sense, curve fitting applies to a problem that may have many observed values for each value of the independent variable. Although several methods will be illustrated, the method of least squares has the greatest significance because it provides a way to extrapolate (or extend), forecast, and predict.

The first portion of the chapter will deal with some instructions concerning summation notation. The remaining sections require the reader to have some knowledge of this notation, which is a convenient way of abbreviating the techniques used in curve fitting and in other statistical calculations that will appear in later chapters.

SUMMATION NOTATION

It is often necessary to reduce large quantities of data to a meaningful form. The ordinary average, which is based on a total or summation of values, is an attempt to give a meaningful description of the data—that is, a summary of the data from one viewpoint. It depends upon the simple operation of summing many values and dividing the total by the number of items included. When there are relatively few items—three, for example—the operation can be expressed as follows:

$$\text{Average} = \frac{X_1 + X_2 + X_3}{3}.$$

However, with many items—say 25 or more—a different type of notation is convenient. In addition, the special symbol that indicates summation is Σ, the upper-case Greek letter sigma.

Now the average, for example, can be written in an abbreviated form using the summation notation:

$$\text{Average} = \frac{\sum_{i=1}^{3} X_i}{3}.$$

The subscript i that appears next to the variable X identifies a particular value of X. The first or initial value of i is defined below the summation symbol. Its maximum value appears above the symbol. To summarize (by using only the numerator), we have

$$\sum_{i=1}^{3} X_i = X_1 + X_2 + X_3.$$

The three values of X are now divided by 3 to obtain the average.

A few expressions will be expanded and abbreviated next to illustrate various ways in which the summation symbol is used.

Examples of Abbreviations and Expansions

First, several examples of expansion will be given to familiarize the reader with the notation. This will be followed by some examples where expressions are abbreviated using the summation notation. The following examples show the expansion of the abbreviated expressions that appear to the left of the equal signs:

$$\sum_{i=1}^{4} Y_i = Y_1 + Y_2 + Y_3 + Y_4$$

$$\sum_{i=1}^{4} X_i = X_1 + X_2 + X_3 + X_4$$

$$\sum_{i=1}^{4} X_i Y_i = X_1 Y_1 + X_2 Y_2 + X_3 Y_3 + X_4 Y_4$$

$$\sum_{j=1}^{4} X_j^2 = X_1^2 + X_2^2 + X_3^2 + X_4^2$$

$$\sum_{i=1}^{n} (X_i + Y_i) = (X_1 + Y_1) + (X_2 + Y_2) + \cdots + (X_n + Y_n)$$

$$\sum_{j=2}^{5} k^j X_j = k^2 X_2 + k^3 X_3 + k^4 X_4 + k^5 X_5,$$

where k is a constant.

If the process is reversed, we can derive the equivalent abbreviations for each expression; for example,

$$(X_1^2 - Y_1) + (X_2^2 - Y_2) + (X_3^2 - Y_3) = \sum_{i=1}^{3}(X_i^2 - Y_i)$$

$$X_1Y_1^2 + X_2Y_2^3 + \cdots + X_nY^{(n+1)} = \sum_{i=1}^{n} X_iY_i^{(i+1)}.$$

Rules of Operation

Suppose that we wish to evaluate the expression

$$\sum_{i=1}^{3}(X_i - a)$$

and that the corresponding numeric values of each of the X_i's and the constant a are

$$X_1 = 4$$
$$X_2 = 7$$
$$X_3 = 5$$
$$a = 2.$$

One way to accomplish this evaluation is by expanding the expression and substituting the appropriate numeric values, as follows:

$$\sum_{i=1}^{3}(X_i - a) = (X_1 - a) + (X_2 - a) + (X_3 - a)$$
$$= (4 - 2) + (7 - 2) + (5 - 2)$$
$$= 2 + 5 + 3$$
$$= 10.$$

Another way would be to alter the expression $\sum_{i=1}^{3}(X_i - a)$ into another form, such as $\sum_{i=1}^{3} X_i - 3a$. The evaluation would then require only one subtraction; for example,

$$\sum_{i=1}^{3} X_i - 3a = 4 + 7 + 5 - 3(2)$$
$$= 16 - 6$$
$$= 10.$$

These manipulations are based upon two of the three rules for transforming or altering expressions which appear in the form of summation notation. These three rules of operation, which follow, are helpful in minimizing calculations.

Rule 1 :

$$\sum_{i=1}^{n} (X_i + Y_i + Z_i) = \sum_{i=1}^{n} X_i + \sum_{i=1}^{n} Y_i + \sum_{i=1}^{n} Z_i.$$

This rule simply says that the total of the rows in a rectangular array of numbers is equal to the total of the columns. This is demonstrated with the example given in Table 13–1.

TABLE 13–1

RECTANGULAR ARRAY

	X_i	Y_i	Z_i	*Totals*
Row 1	$X_1 = 4$	$Y_1 = 6$	$Z_1 = 5$	$X_1 + Y_1 + Z_1 = 15$
Row 2	$X_2 = 8$	$Y_2 = 3$	$Z_2 = 7$	$X_2 + Y_2 + Z_2 = 18$
Row 3	$X_3 = 2$	$Y_3 = 2$	$Z_3 = 1$	$X_3 + Y_3 + Z_3 = \ 5$
Totals	$\sum_{i=1}^{3} X_i = 14$	$\sum_{i=1}^{3} Y_i = 11$	$\sum_{i=1}^{3} Z_i = 13$	$\longrightarrow \quad \boxed{38}$

Algebrically, the calculations are as follows:

$$\sum_{i=1}^{3} X_i + \sum_{i=1}^{3} Y_i + \sum_{i=1}^{3} Z_i = \sum_{i=1}^{3} (X_i + Y_i + Z_i)$$
$$14 + 11 + 13 = (X_1 + Y_1 + Z_1) + (X_2 + Y_2 + Z_2) + (X_3 + Y_3 + Z_3)$$
$$38 = 15 + 18 + 5$$
$$38 = 38.$$

Rule 1 demonstrates the manner in which the summation symbol is multiplied through an algebraic expression in much the same way that a variable or constant is used to eliminate a set of parentheses in ordinary algebraic expressions. For example, it is true that

$$a(X + Y) = aX + aY;$$

similarly,

$$\sum_{i=1}^{n} (X_i + Y_i) = \sum_{i=1}^{n} X_i + \sum_{i=1}^{n} Y_i.$$

Rule 2 :

$$\sum_{i=1}^{n} kX_i = k \sum_{i=1}^{n} X_i,$$

where k is a constant. This rule states that a constant can be factored so that it will appear outside the summation operation. An example will demonstrate this conversion:

$$\sum_{i=1}^{2} kX_i = kX_1 + kX_2$$

$$\sum_{i=1}^{2} kX_i = k(X_1 + X_2)$$

$$\sum_{i=1}^{2} kX_i = k \sum_{i=1}^{2} X_i.$$

Rule 3 :

$$\sum_{i=1}^{n} k = nk.$$

This rule stipulates that the sum of n constants can be written as n times the constant. For example, the addition of four 3's is the same as multiplying 4 times 3.

Rules in Action

We will now employ these three rules to show that

$$\sum_{i=1}^{n} (X_i - k)^2 = \sum_{i=1}^{n} X_i^2 - 2k \sum_{i=1}^{n} X_i + nk^2.$$

The term on the left contains the familiar square of a binomial. When a binomial is squared it appears as follows:

$$(a + b)^2 = a^2 + 2ab + b^2;$$

that is,

$$
\begin{array}{r}
a + b \\
\times\, a + b \\
\hline
ab + b^2 \\
a^2 + \ ab \\
\hline
a^2 + 2ab + b^2.
\end{array}
$$

This operation can also be applied to an expression that contains the summation symbol:

$$\sum_{i=1}^{n} (X_i - k)^2 = \sum_{i=1}^{n} (X_i^2 - 2kX_i + k^2).$$

The expression on the right-hand side of the equation can now be altered by employing rule 1. The result is

$$\sum_{i=1}^{n}(X_i^2 - 2kX_i + k^2) = \sum_{i=1}^{n} X_i^2 - \sum_{i=1}^{n} 2kX_i + \sum_{i=1}^{n} k^2.$$

This result can be changed slightly by using rule 2, since the $2k$ in the second term is a constant:

$$\sum_{i=1}^{n} X_i^2 - \sum_{i=1}^{n} 2kX_i + \sum_{i=1}^{n} k^2 = \sum_{i=1}^{n} X_i^2 - 2k\sum_{i=1}^{n} X_i + \sum_{i=1}^{n} k^2.$$

Finally, the third rule stipulates that $\sum k^2$ is equal to nk^2; hence,

$$\sum_{i=1}^{n} X_i^2 - 2k\sum_{i=1}^{n} X_i + \sum_{i=1}^{n} k^2 = \sum_{i=1}^{n} X_i^2 - 2k\sum_{i=1}^{n} X_i + nk^2.$$

Thus we have shown that

$$\sum_{i=1}^{n}(X_i - k)^2 = \sum_{i=1}^{n} X_i^2 - 2k\sum_{i=1}^{n} X_i + nk^2.$$

Let us now demonstrate the procedure for evaluating various expressions when the numeric values of the variables are given. If we have

$X_1 = 4$	$X_4 = 5$	$Y_3 = 1$
$X_2 = 2$	$Y_1 = 9$	$Y_4 = 6$
$X_3 = 6$	$Y_2 = 3$	$k = 10,$

the expression

$$\sum_{i=1}^{3} X_i^2 Y_i$$

can be evaluated without using the rules, as follows:

$$\begin{aligned}\sum_{i=1}^{3} X_i^2 Y_i &= X_1^2 Y_1 + X_2^2 Y_2 + X_3^2 Y_3 \\ &= (4^2)(9) + (2^2)(3) + (6^2)(1) \\ &= (16)(9) + (4)(3) + (36)(1) \\ &= 144 + 12 + 36 \\ &= 192.\end{aligned}$$

Another expression can be evaluated in which the initializing index i

begins with a 2 rather than a 1. In this case the subscript also starts with a 2. This is illustrated as follows:

$$\sum_{i=2}^{4} (X_i - k) = (X_2 - k) + (X_3 - k) + (X_4 - k)$$
$$= (2 - 10) + (6 - 10) + (5 - 10)$$
$$= (-8) + (-4) + (-5)$$
$$= -17.$$

Using rules 1 and 3, this expression is evaluated as follows:

$$\sum_{i=2}^{4} (X_i - k) = \sum_{i=2}^{4} X_i - 3k$$
$$\sum_{i=2}^{4} (X_i - k) = (2 + 6 + 5) - (3)(10)$$
$$= 13 - 30$$
$$= -17.$$

This is the same answer as obtained above; however, the collection of terms is allowed in order to reduce the algebraic operations. It should be noted that when i does not equal 1, $\sum k = (n - i + 1)k$.

Precautions

Certain basic expressions are mistakenly assumed to be equal. Frequently, the expression $\sum_{i=1}^{n} X_i^2$ is assumed to be the same as $(\sum_{i=1}^{n} X_i)^2$. In addition, the term $\sum_{i=1}^{n} X_i \sum_{i=1}^{n} Y_i$ is sometimes interpreted as being the same as $\sum_{i=1}^{n} X_i Y_i$. The relationship between each pair of expressions is shown, using the same numeric values for the X_i's and Y_i's that were assigned previously:

$$\sum_{i=1}^{3} X_i^2 = (4)^2 + (2)^2 + (6)^2 = 56$$
$$(\sum_{i=1}^{3} X_i)^2 = (4 + 2 + 6)^2 = 144.$$

In the first example, the numbers are squared and then totaled. In the second example, the numbers are added, then the total is squared. It should be obvious that $\sum_{i=1}^{n} X_i^2$ does not equal $(\sum_{i=1}^{n} X_i)^2$. The two terms $\sum_{i=1}^{n} X_i Y_i$ and $\sum_{i=1}^{n} X_i \sum_{i=1}^{n} Y_i$ are also unequal. The reader may verify this fact with an example of his own.

METHODS OF CURVE FITTING

Relationships between two or more variables are summarized by establishing lines of best fit. Fitting lines to data is often referred to as *curve fitting*. The four methods of curve fitting that are explained in this chapter are the *freehand method*, the *semi-average method*, the *moving-average method*, and the *least-squares method*. The last method requires the use of summation notation.

The first two techniques are rather crude; they are used when only a rough idea of the data is needed. These two methods are also used when timeliness rather than accuracy is important. The first three methods are generally used with data that represent a series of time periods. The least-squares method is used widely in regression and correlation problems, as well as with time-series problems. Regression and correlation problems are those which determine the relationships between two or more variables.

We will restrict the application of the least-squares method to the linear case. However, students should be informed that this method is also used to fit nonlinear lines to data.

Freehand Method

This method is sometimes called the "eyeball" method, because a line is simply drawn through the data on the basis of sight. Table 13–2 gives data on the sales of the Hypothetical Mailbox Manufacturing Company. These figures can be put into graphic form by having the horizontal axis show years and the vertical axis show sales for each year. The graph appears in Fig. 13–1.

TABLE 13–2

FREEHAND METHOD

Year	Sales (Thousands of dollars)
1960	17
1961	12
1962	20
1963	25
1964	21
1965	32
1966	30

The dashes on the graph represent a freehand straight line. The line should be drawn so that it passes through the data in a representative manner. The dotted line is the result of the semi-average method, which is described next.

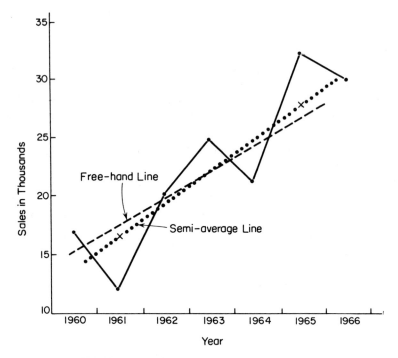

FIGURE 13–1.   Free-hand method of curve fitting.

TABLE 13–3
SEMI-AVERAGE METHOD

Year	Sales (Thousands of dollars)	
1960	17	
1961	12	$\dfrac{49}{3} = 16\dfrac{1}{3}$
1962	20	
1963	25	
1964	21	
1965	32	$\dfrac{83}{3} = 27\dfrac{2}{3}$
1966	30	

Semi-Average Method

This method is based on a crude method of dividing data into two parts and then simply averaging the values that correspond to the vertical axis. The data given for the mailbox company are divided and averaged in Table 13–3. The middle item (25) is disregarded when there is an odd number of items. The two figures shown at the right are the two averages that are used to plot a straight line representing the semi-average fit. These two figures are plotted in Fig. 13–1 above 1961 and 1965 respectively (the two X's), because these two years represent the middle of the time periods that were averaged.

Moving-Average Method

Another method that relies on a special averaging process is used extensively in isolating the various components of data that change over time. The moving-average method tends to smooth data changes; this clarifies the general relationships. The sales data already given for mailboxes will be used to illustrate the method for computing a four-year moving average. The selection of a four-period average is arbitrary; a five-, six-, or seven-year period may be applicable in other cases.

In this case, the moving average is derived by computing averages of the data that correspond to consecutive four-year periods. This is demonstrated in Table 13–4. The figures 21, 19½, 22½, and 27 represent an averaged summary of the data; each figure is plotted at an appropriate position on the time scale. For example, the number 21 is plotted on the graph between the years 1961 and 1962; this would indicate December 31, 1961. The other three figures are aligned respectively at December 31, 1962, December 31, 1963, and December 31, 1964. These results are shown in Fig. 13–2. The four figures are marked with an X and are joined by a dashed line.

TABLE 13–4

MOVING-AVERAGE METHOD

Year	Sales (Thousands of dollars)			
1960	17			
1961	12	$84/4 = 21$		
1962	20		$78/4 = 19.5$	
1963	25			$98/4 = 22.5$
1964	21			$108/4 = 27$
1965	32			
1966	30			

In these problems, the time period of the moving average usually must be selected; this selection depends to some degree on the amount of data available and on the reason for fitting the moving average. For example, if monthly data are available and the computation of a seasonal index is desired, a 12-month moving average is used. In many instances, a 24-month moving average may be preferred, and a 7- or 8-year period may be appropriate to follow cyclical movements.

Up to this point, the reader may have the feeling that the science of fitting curves is not very exact. The three methods just described illustrate

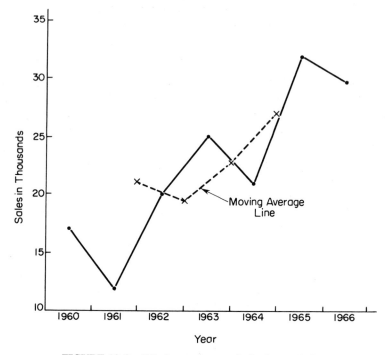

FIGURE 13–2.   Moving-average method of curve fitting.

some aspects of this science. The fourth technique, known as the least-squares method, is more exact because it is based on mathematical principles.

Least-Squares Method

The least-squares method of curve fitting is widely used by analysts to make predictions. The relationship between two or more variables must be determined in order to predict results associated with the various stages of the phenomena involved. For example, the growth rate of a certain vegetable may vary according to the amount of fertilizer applied. The scientist is interested in establishing a way to predict the growth rate when a certain amount of fertilizer is used. A technique he might use is *regression analysis*, where a line is fitted to the data by the method of least squares.

Business analysts are often involved in forecasting future events such as sales levels, fuel consumption, the level of expenditures for new plant and equipment, and levels of GNP. The method of forecasting usually is based on a least-squares line, which is commonly referred to as a *trend line*.

In the method of least squares, the line of fit is obtained mathematically, using summation notation. On the following pages, a least-squares line is defined, then a regression line and a trend line are calculated. Prediction with a regression line and a trend line is also illustrated.

The Least-Squares Line.   A least-squares line is a line that is fitted to data so that the total sum of the squares of the deviations will be at a minimum. The deviations are the vertical differences between the data and the fitted line as measured on the vertical axis. The idea of a least-squares straight line is illustrated in Fig. 13–3, where Y is a variable measured on the vertical axis. Only straight-line fits will be discussed in this book; however, the procedure for fitting a curvilinear line by the method of least squares is available in standard statistics textbooks. The line of least squares shown in Fig. 13–3 represents the only straight line that will fit the five data points (the dots in the figure) so that the total of their squared differences (the distances represented by the dashed lines) is a minimum. This minimum or least-square line is sometimes referred to as the *best* fit.

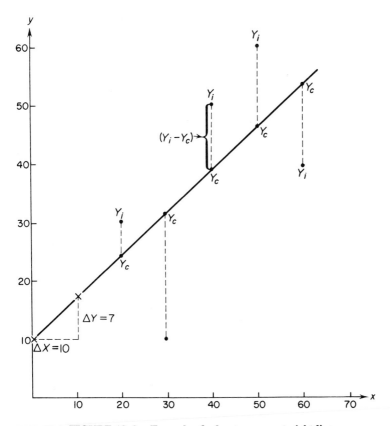

FIGURE 13–3.   Example of a least-squares straight line.

A straight line is represented mathematically as
$$Y = a + bX,$$
where Y is the dependent variable (measured on the vertical axis) and X is the independent variable (measured on the horizontal axis). The symbols a and b are *parameters*; they represent, respectively, the Y intercept and the slope of the line. The Y intercept is the value of Y where the line crosses the Y axis, or where X is equal to zero. The slope of the line (b) measures the change in Y with respect to a change in X.

For any particular set of data, a and b can be calculated by using the following formulas:

$$a = \frac{\sum Y}{n} - b\frac{\sum X}{n}$$

$$b = \frac{n\sum XY - \sum X \sum Y}{n\sum X^2 - \sum X \sum X}.$$

The subscripts are omitted in these formulas because the summation of the X_i's is understood to be from 1 to n. The two formulas are derived by differential calculus. Their derivation is provided in the Annex to this chapter for those who are familiar with calculus.

The Regression Problem.   Let us use the two preceding formulas and the method of least squares to determine the values for the regression line shown in Fig. 13–3. The corresponding X and Y values for the points plotted in Fig. 13–3 are listed in Table 13–5, which calculates the values used in the formulas.

When the appropriate totals are inserted in the formulas for a and b, we have

$$a = \frac{190}{5} - (0.7)\frac{200}{5}$$
$$a = 38 - 0.7(40)$$
$$a = 10$$

and

$$b = \frac{5(8,300) - (200)(190)}{5(9,000) - (200)(200)}$$
$$b = \frac{3,500}{5,000} = 0.7.$$

These two values are now inserted in the algebraic form of a straight line:

$$Y = a + bX$$
$$Y = 10 + 0.7X.$$

TABLE 13–5

WORKSHEET FOR X AND Y VALUES

X	Y	XY	X^2
50	60	3,000	2,500
40	50	2,000	1,600
60	40	2,400	3,600
20	30	600	400
30	10	300	900
$\sum X = 200$	$\sum Y = 190$	$\sum XY = 8,300$	$\sum X^2 = 9,000$

This equation tells us that the line intercepts the Y axis at 10 and that the slope of the line is 0.7—that is, for one unit change in X, Y changes by 0.7 unit. This can be verified by Fig. 13–3.

We will now assume that these five pairs of values represent the scores that five students earned on pop quizzes in a statistics course and an accounting course. Once the score of a pop quiz is known, the line of regression provides a means of predicting the score a student is likely to obtain in a related quiz. However, it must be emphasized that this procedure assumes a cause-and-effect relationship between the two variables—that is, between grades in accounting and grades in statistics. Generally, a large set of observations is needed for the results to have reliability. In addition, more than one Y value can occur for each X value.

If we assume that the variable X stands for the accounting grades, then Y represents scores students are likely to receive in statistics. If a student received 30 points on an accounting quiz, his expected score on the statistics quiz would be obtained by substituting 30 into the equation as follows:

$$Y = 10 + 0.7(30)$$
$$Y = 10 + 21$$
$$Y = 31.$$

A grade of 31 is therefore predicted for the student on a statistics quiz. However, the range of prediction should be restricted to the range of the X variable. In this case, any extension or extrapolation of the regression line to a value of X greater than 60 is invalid.

The method of least squares can also be used to fit a line to cross-sectional data. This type of problem was illustrated in the Annex to Chapter 8. The problem dealt with the total cost of the Hypothetical Mailbox Manufacturing Company; the data were illustrated in Fig. 8–7. The line of least squares in that particular case was simply a regression line that showed the nature of the relationship between total cost and the various levels of production measured by the quantity of mailboxes produced. The calculations rendered a least-squares line of the form

$$TC = \$367.48 + \$7.52Q.$$

The calculations were not shown in Chapter 8 but are provided here. The worksheet and calculations appear in Table 13–6.

TABLE 13–6

WORKSHEET FOR PROBLEM USING CROSS-SECTIONAL TOTAL

Q	TC	Q^2	$Q(TC)$
0	300	0	0
20	400	400	8,000
30	600	900	18,000
50	800	2,500	40,000
70	900	4,900	63,000
90	1,000	8,100	90,000
100	1,200	10,000	120,000
110	1,300	12,100	143,000
120	1,400	14,400	168,000
130	1,200	16,900	156,000
150	1,400	22,500	210,000
160	1,600	25,600	256,000
170	1,500	28,900	255,000
180	1,600	32,400	288,000
180	1,800	32,400	324,000
200	1,700	40,000	340,000
200	1,800	40,000	360,000
210	2,000	44,100	420,000
220	2,100	48,400	462,000
230	2,400	52,900	552,000
2,620	27,000	437,000	4,243,000
ΣQ	$\Sigma(TC)$	ΣQ^2	$\Sigma Q(TC)$

The mean of the Q's ($\bar{Q}$) is $\dfrac{2,620}{20} = 131$ and the mean of the TC's

($\overline{TC}$) is $\dfrac{27,000}{20} = 1,350.$ Thus

$$a = (\overline{TC}) - b\bar{Q} = 1,350 - 7.5(131)$$
$$= 1,350 - 982.50 = 367.48$$

and

$$b = \frac{n\Sigma Q(TC) - \Sigma Q \Sigma(TC)}{n\Sigma Q^2 - (\Sigma Q)^2} = \frac{(20)(4,243,000) - (2,620)(27,000)}{(20)(437,100) - (2,620)^2}$$

$$= \frac{84,860,000 - 70,740,000}{8,732,000 - 6,864,400} = \frac{14,120,000}{1,877,600} = 7.52.$$

Therefore, the equation is

$$TC = \$367.48 + 7.52Q.$$

Forecasting with a Trend Line. The method of least squares is also useful for problems of forecasting. The independent variable X becomes the element of time; its units are time periods such as a year or a month. Although the procedure for calculating the least-squares line is basically the same as in the case of the regression problem, several shortcuts are available because the X values are of equal intervals. The fitted line is called a trend line; it is extended beyond the range of the X values in order to make forecasts of Y values for future time periods.

The information on mailbox sales that was given previously is now fitted with a least-squares line. The data are shown in Table 13–7; however, an adjustment has been made on the X values because yearly designations would have resulted in unusually large numbers. The center of the time period is selected to represent the value corresponding to the Y intercept; for example, X is set equal to zero for the year 1963.

TABLE 13–7

WORKSHEET FOR MAILBOX SALES DATA

Year	X	(Sales in Thousands of dollars) Y	XY	X^2
1960	-3	17	-51	9
1961	-2	12	-24	4
1962	-1	20	-20	1
1963	0	25	0	0
1964	$+1$	21	21	1
1965	$+2$	32	64	4
1966	$+3$	30	90	9
	$\sum X = 0$	$\sum Y = 157$	$\sum XY = 80$	$\sum X^2 = 28$

The value for b is calculated as follows:

$$b = \frac{n\sum XY - \sum X \sum Y}{n\sum X^2 - \sum X \sum X}$$

$$= \frac{7(80) - (0)(157)}{7(28) - (0)(0)}$$

$$= \frac{80}{28} = 2.8.$$

The formula can now be reduced to

$$b = \frac{\Sigma XY}{\Sigma X^2}$$

because $\Sigma X = 0$. This will always be true when the middle of the time period is set equal to zero. The calculation of a is also shortened. Previously, a was defined as

$$a = \frac{\Sigma Y}{n} - b\frac{\Sigma X}{n}$$

$$= \frac{157}{7} - 2.8\frac{0}{7}$$

$$= \frac{157}{7} = 22.4.$$

The reduced form of the formula for a appears as

$$a = \frac{\Sigma Y}{n}.$$

The least-squares trend line is

$$Y = 22.4 + 2.8X.$$

This trend line is fitted to the mailbox sales data and is shown in Fig. 13–4.

There are two ways of plotting the trend line. In the first method, the a value is plotted at the middle of the time period. This point is the origin of the trend equation. The next point needed for drawing the straight line is obtained by increasing the Y value by the value of the slope. For example, one point is plotted at 22.4 (the value of Y where $X = 0$) above the point corresponding to 1963, and the other point, 25.2 (22.4 + 2.8), is plotted above the year 1964. A straight line is then drawn by extending the line that connects these two points. In the second method, two X values are selected and solved for their corresponding Y values. The straight line drawn through the two points represents the trend line.

The first of the two methods was used in Fig. 13–4, with the two points designated by a circled X.

The shortcut formula for a and b works well when there is an odd number of years (and, of course, when the X values are evenly spaced as they are in time-series data). A minor alteration is employed when the data cover an even number of years; it is indicated in Table 13–8, where the same data are used with the year 1959 added. It is desirable to force ΣX to equal zero so

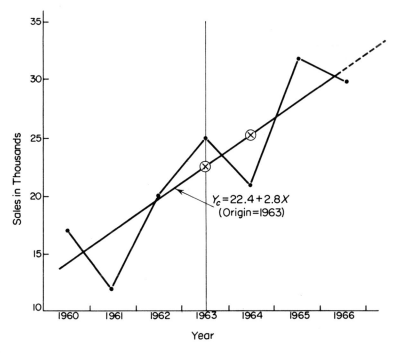

FIGURE 13–4. **Forecasting with a trend line for the Hypothetical Mailbox Manufacturing Company.**

TABLE 13–8

SHORTCUT FORMULA WITH EVEN NUMBER OF YEARS

Year	X	Sales (Thousands of dollars)
1959	$-3\frac{1}{2}$	15
1960	$-2\frac{1}{2}$	17
1961	$-1\frac{1}{2}$	12
1962	$-\frac{1}{2}$	20
1963	$+\frac{1}{2}$	25
1964	$+1\frac{1}{2}$	21
1965	$+2\frac{1}{2}$	32
1966	$+3\frac{1}{2}$	30

that the shortcut formula can be used. This can be done easily by designating the center of the time period to be between 1962 and 1963. Therefore, the center of 1962 (that is, June 30) is half of an X unit ($\frac{1}{2}$ year) from the selected center of December 31, 1962. The calculations are performed the same way, except that the origin of the trend equation will be December 31, 1962. Note that $\sum X$ is equal to zero again.

If the manager of the mailbox firm is interested in forcasting sales for a particular year—say, 1968—he may use the trend equation. The forecast can be obtained graphically by extending the trend line through 1968. It also can be obtained algebraically by simply solving the trend equation for the year 1968. The trend equation is

$$Y = 22.4 + 2.8X,$$

where the origin is 1963. Since the number 5 corresponds to the X value for the year 1968, it is substituted in the trend equation, and we have

$$Y = 22.4 + 2.8(5)$$
$$Y = 36.4.$$

Translated, this tells the manager that if the trend continues in which sales increase by \$2,800 each year, then sales of \$36,400 should occur in 1968. This type of algebraic forecasting is only possible with the least-squares method. The other three methods of curve fitting introduced in this chapter must rely on graphs.

ANNEX : A MATHEMATICAL NOTE ON LEAST SQUARES

The formulas for the intercept and slope of a straight line are derived by differentiating the expression $\sum(Y - Y_c)^2$ and then finding the values for a and b that minimize this expression. The expression is a representation of the sum of the squared deviation between observed Y values and the corresponding values on the regression line (Y_c). A formal derivation follows.

Minimize $\sum(Y - Y_c)^2$, where $Y_c = a + bX$. By substitution, we have $\sum(Y - a - bX)^2$; differentiating this expression with respect to a and then b, we have

$$\frac{df}{da} = 2\sum(Y - a - bX)(-1)$$

$$= -2(\sum Y - \sum a - b\sum X).$$

Setting this equation equal to zero,

$$\sum Y - na - b\sum X = 0$$
$$na = \sum Y - b\sum X$$
$$a = \frac{\sum Y}{n} - b\frac{\sum X}{n}.$$

Similarly,

$$\frac{df}{db} = 2\sum(Y-a-bX)(-X)$$

$$= 2\sum(XY - aX - bX^2)$$

$$= -2(\sum XY - a\sum X - -b\sum X^2).$$

Set equal to zero,

$$\sum XY - a\sum X - b\sum X^2 = 0$$

$$b\sum X^2 = \sum XY - a\sum X.$$

Solving for a in order to make substitutions,

$$a = \frac{-b\sum X^2 + \sum XY}{\sum X}.$$

Then, since

$$a = \frac{\sum Y}{n} - b\frac{\sum X}{n}$$

as derived above, we can set these two expressions equal to each other and solve for b:

$$\frac{\sum Y}{n} - b\frac{\sum X}{n} = \frac{\sum XY - b\sum X^2}{\sum X}$$

$$\sum X\sum Y - b(\sum X)^2 = n\sum XY - nb\sum X^2$$

$$nb\sum X^2 - b(\sum X)^2 = n\sum XY - \sum X\sum Y$$

$$b[n\sum X^2 - (\sum X)^2] = n\sum XY - \sum X\sum Y$$

$$b = \frac{n\sum XY - \sum X\sum Y}{n\sum X^2 - (\sum X)^2}.$$

The formula for a (in terms of b) was derived as

$$a = \frac{\sum Y}{n} - b\frac{\sum X}{n}.$$

PROBLEMS AND PROJECTS

1. Expand the following expressions—that is, write their equivalents without the summation symbol:

   a. $\sum_{i=1}^{4} X_i$.

   b. $\sum_{i=3}^{6} Y_i$.

   c. $\sum_{i=2}^{5} X_i^2$.

   d. $\sum_{i=1}^{4} X_i Y_i - 14$.

2. Show that $\sum_{i=1}^{n}(X - \bar{X})^2$ is equal to $\sum_{i=1}^{n} X^2 - (\sum_{i=1}^{n} X)^2/n$, where $\bar{X}$ is defined as $\sum_{i=1}^{n} X_i/n$. Is $\sum_{i=1}^{n} X_i^2 - (\sum_{i=1}^{n} X)^2/n$ equal to $\sum_{i=1}^{n} X_i^2 - n\bar{X}^2$?

3. Write the following expressions in the form that uses the summation symbol:

   a. $(X_1 - 3) + (X_2 - 3) + (X_3 - 3)$.

   b. $(X_3 - Y_3) + (X_4 - Y_4) + (X_5 - Y_5)$.

   c. $X_1 Y_1 + X_2 Y_2^2 + X_3 Y_3^3 + X_4 Y_4^4$.

   d. $X_1^2 + X_2^2 + X_3^2 + X_4^2$.

   e. $(Y_1^2 - 1) + (Y_2^2 - 2) + (Y_3^2 - 3) + (Y_4^2 - 4)$.

4. Given the following values for the variables X and Y, evaluate the expressions in Problems 1 and 3.

$$X_1 = 4 \qquad\qquad Y_1 = 7$$
$$X_2 = 1 \qquad\qquad Y_2 = 2$$
$$X_3 = 3 \qquad\qquad Y_3 = 4$$
$$X_4 = 2 \qquad\qquad Y_4 = 3$$
$$X_5 = 5 \qquad\qquad Y_5 = 1$$
$$X_6 = 3 \qquad\qquad Y_6 = 2.$$

5. Use the values given in Problem 4 to show that $\sum_{i=1}^{3} X_i Y_i$ does not equal

$$\sum_{i=1}^{3} X_i \sum_{i=1}^{3} Y_i.$$

6. Use the values given in Problem 4 to show that

$$\sum_{i=1}^{4}(X_i + Y_i) = \sum_{i=1}^{4}X_i + \sum_{i=1}^{4}Y_i.$$

7. Given the following array of numbers, write the summation expression that designates the total of all four numbers:

$$\begin{bmatrix} 4 & 7 \\ 6 & 3 \end{bmatrix}.$$

8. Expand the expression you obtained in Problem 7 and evaluate it by substituting numerical values. Does the expression equal the total of the four numbers—that is, does it total 20?

9. Fit a line to the following data by (a) the semi-average method and (b) the moving-average method. Use a five-period moving average.

Year	Sales (Thousands of Dollars)
1958	14
1959	18
1960	17
1961	15
1962	19
1963	20
1964	24
1965	22
1966	19
1967	18
1968	22

10. Compute a regression line for the data below by using the method of least squares. These are hypothetical cross-sectional data similar to that given in Table 9–13.

Market	p (Dollars)	q
A	10	40
B	8	50
C	7	60
D	10	50
E	9	40
F	8	55
G	11	30
H	10	25
I	12	25
J	8	50

11. a. Fit a trend line to the following data by the method of least squares.

Year	Sales (Thousands of Dollars)
1960	130
1961	145
1962	150
1963	165
1964	170

b. Plot the data and the trend line.

c. Compute a sales forecast for 1968.

12. The trend equation for sales of the Electron-Range Company is

$$\text{Sales} = 10 + 0.8X,$$

where the origin is 1964. Change the equation so that the origin will be 1967.

SELECTED REFERENCES

Dubois, E. N., *Essential Methods in Business Statistics*. New York: McGraw-Hill Book Company, 1964.

Freund, J. E., and F. J. Williams, *Elementary Business Statistics, The Modern Approach*. Englewood Cliffs, N. J.: Prentice-Hall, Inc., 1964.

Hoel, P. G., *Elementary Statistics*. New York: John Wiley & Sons, Inc., 1966.

Kleppner, D., and N. Ramsey, *Quick Calculus*. New York: John Wiley & Sons, Inc., 1965.

Meyer, H., and R. V. Mendenhall, *Techniques of Differentiation and Integration, A Program for Self-Instruction*. New York: McGraw-Hill Book Company, 1966.

Meyers, C., *Elementary Business and Economic Statistics*. Belmont, Calif.: Wadsworth Publishing Company, Inc., 1966.

14

THE SIMPLEX
METHOD

The simplex technique is an abbreviated procedure for solving complex linear programming problems and is capable of determining an optimal solution with minimum calculations. In the simplex method, all pairs of unique solutions are not necessarily computed; the method begins with the feasible solution where $X = 0$ and $Y = 0$, and proceeds to find the optimal solution by moving from one corner of the feasible region to the next. This is in contrast to the algebraic method, which requires the solution of many sets of simultaneous equations.

Basically, the mailbox problem consisted of only two products and relatively few input constraints or bottlenecks; therefore, it was easily solved by graphic and algebraic methods. When such a problem is expanded to include more than three products and constraints, its solution cannot be derived easily (if at all) by these approaches. Thus the advantages of the simplex technique become apparent when it is applied to the many complex and practical problems that are encountered in business and industry.

Much of the computational technique for the simplex method is based on advanced mathematical methods such as numerical analysis, vector analysis, and matrix algebra. Because these mathematical methods will not be explained in detail here, you will have to accept some of the procedures on faith. However, an extensive understanding of the procedure employed with the simplex method can be obtained intuitively.

In order to demonstrate the essential calculating procedures employed in the simplex method, the basic mailbox problem will be used; the solution to an expanded version of this problem will then be illustrated. The expanded version will entail the production of two deluxe models of mailboxes in addition to the two standard models (R and H). This will show the limitations of the graphic method while demonstrating the convenience of the simplex technique.

The original (or simple) mailbox problem was formalized as follows: Maximize the function $13X_1 + 13X_2$, where X_1 and X_2 represent the quantities of each type of mailbox. (Previously X_2 was denoted as Y.) The number 13 represents the revenue derived from each mailbox produced. The total quantity of mailboxes that can be produced is restricted by the production processes rendered by the various departments. These restrictions or constraints appear algebraically as follows:

$$X_1 + 8X_2 \leq 920 \qquad \text{(cutting department)}$$
$$X_1 + 4X_2 \leq 480 \qquad \text{(stamping department)}$$
$$X_1 + 2X_2 \leq 280 \qquad \text{(shaping department)}$$
$$2X_1 + X_2 \leq 320 \qquad \text{(finishing department)}$$
$$4X_1 + X_2 \leq 600. \qquad \text{(assembling department)}$$

The first step toward obtaining a solution is to change the inequality signs in these constraint inequations to equality signs. This is accomplished by adding slack variables to the inequations. Each slack variable represents the unused capacity when X_1 and X_2 requirements do not absorb a department's total capacity; it "takes up the slack," and changes each inequation into an equation. The constraints are now represented by equations, which appear as follows:

$$X_1 + 8X_2 + X_3 = 920$$
$$X_1 + 4X_2 + X_4 = 480$$
$$X_1 + 2X_2 + X_5 = 280$$
$$2X_1 + X_2 + X_6 = 320$$
$$4X_1 + X_2 + X_7 = 600.$$

When X_1 and X_2 equal zero, the slack variables represent a basic feasible solution—that is, $X_3 = 920$, $X_4 = 480$, $X_5 = 280$, $X_6 = 320$, and $X_7 = 600$. However, since this is a "do-nothing" solution, the slack variables can be considered artificial. The introduction of slack–artificial variables also alters the revenue function; therefore, these variables must be added to this function. Zero coefficients are assigned to each of the slack–artificial variables in the revenue function because the unused capacity of any department adds nothing to revenue. Hence, the maximizing function is changed as follows:

$$\text{Revenue} = 13X_1 + 13X_2 + 0X_3 + 0X_4 + 0X_5 + 0X_6 + 0X_7.$$

In solving a linear programming problem, it is necessary to introduce a convenient worksheet to facilitate the orderly manipulation of the equations. These worksheets are normally called *tableaus*. We will only partially fill in the following tableaus in order to explain in detail the step-by-step numerical manipulations necessary to complete each tableau for each iteration. The first tableau contains the basic information given in the problem and the relevant slack–artificial variables. The completed first stage of this tableau appears in Fig. 14–1.

The first stage is accomplished according to the following steps:

1.   The revenue coefficients for the relevant and slack variables are inserted across the top of the tableau below their respective subscripted variable notations—that is, X_1, X_2, X_3, X_4, X_5, X_6, and X_7.

2.   The quantities of resources available in each department are inserted in the column labeled Q_i; these are the figures that appeared on the right-hand side of the constraint equations.

3.   The coefficients to the X_j's on the left-hand side of each constraint equation are inserted in one of the rows marked I, II, III, IV, and V. Therefore they also appear in the appropriate columns labeled with the various X_j's.

4.   The revenue coefficients of the variables pertaining to the basic feasible solution being investigated are inserted in the column labeled P_j.

		P_j	Q_i	X_1 13	X_2 13	X_3 0	X_4 0	X_5 0	X_6 0	X_7 0	
											Ratio
I	$j=3$	0	920	1	8	1	0	0	0	0	
II	$j=4$	0	480	1	4	0	1	0	0	0	
III	$j=5$	0	280	1	2	0	0	1	0	0	
IV	$j=6$	0	320	2	1	0	0	0	1	0	
V	$j=7$	0	600	4	1	0	0	0	0	1	
		Z_j									
		P_j-Z_j									

FIGURE 14–1.   Initial tableau for mailbox problem.

In this case, the initial solution involves X_3, X_4, X_5, X_6, and X_7, all of which have zero coefficients. The j subscripts corresponding to the P_j's that were previously inserted are placed in the column immediately to the left of the column labeled P_j. In this case, the numbers 3, 4, 5, 6, and 7 are used.

This tableau is sufficient to indicate a solution to the problem. The entries in the Q_i column give the levels of each variable in any particular solution. The X_j that corresponds to each Q_i is indicated by the number 1 appearing in a column with zeros in all the remaining positions. These 1's are shaded in the first tableau. In this instance, $X_3 = 920$, $X_4 = 480$, $X_5 = 280$, $X_6 = 320$, and $X_7 = 600$.

This first solution, as mentioned previously, is a do-nothing solution, because it involves only the slack–artificial variables. The total revenue for this solution can be calculated by multiplying the entries in the P_j column by their corresponding values in the Q_i column and summing the resulting products. In this instance, total revenue is zero. [Total revenue $= (920 \times 0) + (480 \times 0) + (280 \times 0) + (320 \times 0) + (600 \times 0)$.] In general, total revenue is determined by multiplying the Q_i's by the P_j's.

The next step is to test the solution inserted in Fig. 14–1 to determine if it can be improved. This involves two procedures. First, the Z_j's must be calculated, and second, they must be compared to the corresponding P_j's to determine if an optimal has been achieved. If not, a new solution must be sought by the generation of another tableau.

The Z_j's are derived algebraically by multiplying each entry in each X_j column by the corresponding value in the P_j column. The cross products are then added for each column. For example, $Z_1 = (0 \times 1) + (0 \times 1) + (0 \times 1) + (0 \times 2) + (0 \times 4) = 0$. (In this instance, the other Z_j's are also zero because all the P_j's are zero.) The Z_j's for this solution appear in Fig. 14–2, which further completes the first tableau.

In the figure, the Z_j's appear as zeros because it is obvious that unused capacity in each activity is worth \$0 per unit. The Z_j's represent the op-

		P_j	Q_i	X_1 13	X_2 13	X_3 0	X_4 0	X_5 0	X_6 0	X_7 0	Ratio
I	$j=3$	0	920	1	8	1	0	0	0	0	
II	$j=4$	0	480	1	4	0	1	0	0	0	
III	$j=5$	0	280	1	2	0	0	1	0	0	
IV	$j=6$	0	320	2	1	0	0	0	1	0	
V	$j=7$	0	600	4	1	0	0	0	0	1	
		Z_j		0	0	0	0	0	0	0	
		$P_j - Z_j$		13	13	0	0	0	0	0	

FIGURE 14–2.   Initial tableau with Pj–Zj row.

portunity cost of the resources that are needed to produce the revenue from one unit of product. In other words, they indicate the amount by which revenue would be reduced if one unit of a particular product (X_1, X_2, X_3, etc.) were added to the output mix.

The Z_j's are compared to the P_j's by simply subtracting each Z_j from a P_j; the results are shown in the $P_j - Z_j$ row. These values represent the *net* revenue that will result from introducing one unit of product to the product mix or solution. For example, if one unit of X_1 adds $13 of revenue to the solution *and* if its introduction causes no loss, then $P_j - Z_j$ for $X_1 = \$13$.

The optimal solution is reached when there are no positive numbers in the $P_j - Z_j$ row—that is, when revenue cannot be increased. By examining the numbers in the $P_j - Z_j$ row of Fig. 14–2, we can see, for example, that total revenue can be increased by $13 for each unit of X_1 (type *H*) or X_2 (type *R*) added to the mix. Thus a positive number in the $P_j - Z_j$ row indicates that revenue can be improved by that amount for each unit of X_1 or X_2 added. On the other hand, a negative number in the $P_j - Z_j$ row would indicate the amount by which revenue would *decrease* if one unit of the variable heading that column were added to the solution.

When no optimal solution is indicated, an additional stage is attached to the first tableau. Information contained in the completed tableau is used to determine which new product or variable should be added and which old one should be deleted. It is obvious that the variable which will add the most to revenue per unit is the one which should be included in the next solution. The largest positive number in the $P_j - Z_j$ row indicates how the greatest improvement can be made. In this case, either X_1 or X_2 should be selected to replace one of the variables (an artificial variable in this instance) in the present solution. The column that gives the variable selected for the new solution is called the *replacing column*.

The next step is to determine which variable will be replaced (or deleted). This is done by computing a ratio for each row. Ratios are computed for each row by dividing the Q_i's by their corresponding elements in the replacing column. (The replacing column is the one indicated with an arrow in Fig. 14–3.) For instance, since X_1 was selected as the replacing variable, the ratio for row I would be $\frac{920}{1} = 920$. The number 920 is the Q_i in row I; the number 1 in the denominator is the same one that appears in row I of the replacing column. (These two numbers are circled in Fig. 14–3.) The remaining ratios appear in the figure under the column labeled "Ratio." (This column is shaded in the figure.)

The ratios will now be used to determine which row to replace. Since the *replaced row* will be the one with the smallest ratio (negative ratios are ignored), it will be row V (variable X_7) in this case. The ratio also indicates the number of units of the replacing variable to substitute; here, 150 units of X_1 replace the 600 units of X_7 in the initial solution.

		P_j	Q_i	X_1 13	X_2 13	X_3 0	X_4 0	X_5 0	X_6 0	X_7 0	Ratio
I	$j=3$	0	⑨②⓪	①	8	1	0	0	0	0	920/1=920
II	$j=4$	0	480	1	4	0	1	0	0	0	480/1=480
III	$j=5$	0	280	1	2	0	0	1	0	0	280/1=280
IV	$j=6$	0	320	2	1	0	0	0	1	0	320/2=160
V	$j=7$	0	600	4	1	0	0	0	0	1	600/4=150
		Z_j		0	0	0	0	0	0	0	
		P_j-Z_j		13	13	0	0	0	0	0	

↑
Replacing
Column

FIGURE 14–3.   Tableau showing calculation of ratios.

Having selected the replacing column and the replaced row, we can develop the second tableau and the second simplex solution, which is an improved solution. The generation of the second tableau for the simplex method is based on matrix algebra. Instead of solving each set of relationship equations by simultaneous equations (the algebraic method), the simplex method relies on matrix algebra. In the simplex method we are actually computing a form of an inverse to solve a set of simultaneous equations. Although the inverse is not derived in the straightforward manner of matrix algebra, it will still be an inverse.

The objective of the second tableau is to transform the replacing column into a column that has zeros in every position except where the replacing column and replaced row intersect; the number 1 must be produced at this intersection. The various mathematical operations that are performed on the rows of Fig. 14–3 produce Fig. 14–4, the second tableau. These operations are referred to as *row operations*.

Row operations on a tableau give the same results that multiplying by the inverse does in matrix algebra; both operations provide a unique solution

		P_j	Q_i	X_1 13	X_2 13	X_3 0	X_4 0	X_5 0	X_6 0	X_7 0	Ratio
I	$j=3$	0	770	0	31/4	1	0	0	0	-1/4	
II	$j=4$	0	330	0	15/4	0	1	0	0	-1/4	
III	$j=5$	0	130	0	7/4	0	0	1	0	-1/4	
IV	$j=6$	0	20	0	1/2	0	0	0	1	-1/2	
V	$j=1$	13	150	1	1/4	0	0	0	0	+1/4	
		Z_j									
		P_j-Z_j									

FIGURE 14–4.   Tableau showing intersection of replacing column and replaced row.

to a system of equations. In row operations, the replacing column and replaced row are transformed (the shaded area in Fig. 14-4). The desired zeros are produced in the replacing column and the number 1 appears at the intersection of the replacing column and the replaced row. We now have a new solution that indicates the production of 150 units of X_1 (mailbox H); this yields a revenue of $1,950. We do not as yet know if this is an optimal solution, because the $P_j - Z_j$'s have not been evaluated.

Let us now backtrack and investigate in detail how Fig. 14-4 was produced. Although an understanding of the technique used depends somewhat on a knowledge of matrix algebra, the technique can be learned if it is kept in mind that the method is simply a fancy numerical process with a mathematical foundation.

		P_j	Q_i	X_1	X_2	X_3	X_4	X_5	X_6	X_7	Ratio
I	$j=$										
II	$j=$										
III	$j=$										
IV	$j=$										
V	$j=1$	13	600/4	4/4	1/4	0	0	0	0	+1/4	
		Z_j									
		P_j-Z_j									

FIGURE 14-5.   Partial tableau showing manipulation on replaced row.

The first step in transforming Fig. 14-3 into Fig. 14-4 is to convert the element located at the intersection of the replaced row and replacing column in Fig. 14-3 into the number 1. In this tableau, the number is 4. The simplest way to change this 4 into the number 1 is to divide it by 4. In order to do this, however, we must also divide each other element in the row by 4, because this is one of the requirements of the row operation procedure. The division of each element of row V in Fig. 14-3 by 4 is shown in Fig. 14-5 (in the shaded portion).

The first two numbers in row V do not receive algebraic treatment; they are simply replaced by appropriate numbers that are associated with the new variable. The subscript of the X_j that heads the replacing column (in this instance, the number 1) is inserted opposite the "$j =$" of row V. The number 1 replaces the 7 that appeared in Fig. 14-3. In addition, the P_j (revenue coefficient) associated with the replacing variable (the variable of the replacing column) is substituted for the revenue coefficient of the replaced row. Since the payoff coefficient (P_j) for X_1 is 13, this number is inserted in row V in the column headed P_j.

The next step is to convert each of the other elements in the replacing column X_1 of Fig. 14–3 into zeros. This step is probably the most difficult of all; however, the newly created row V makes this step easy because it serves as a pivotal point for transforming row IV and all the other rows.

The simplest way to change the number 2 in the X_1 column of Fig. 14–3 to zero is to subtract the 2 from itself. However, a manipulation on any element of a particular row must be performed on all other elements of that row. Hence, the number subtracted from elements of a particular row of Fig. 14–3 must be derived from an appropriate multiple of the elements in row V of Fig. 14–5. Therefore, each element in row IV of Fig. 14–3 is changed in the following manner: Each element in row V of Fig. 14–5 is multiplied by 2 and this product is subtracted from the corresponding elements of row IV of Fig. 14–3. This results in the new elements for row IV of Fig. 14–4. The P_j column is not subjected to alteration in this step.

The calculations for deriving the new row IV for Fig. 14–4 are shown in Table 14–1. The figures in column 6 of this table appear in row IV of Fig. 14–4.

This method of calculation is repeated to generate the elements for other rows of Fig. 14–4. However, note that the multiplication factor is different and that it depends on the elements in the X_1 column. In the case of row III, the multiplication factor is 1. The calculations for the elements in row III of Fig. 14–4 are shown in Table 14–2. The figures in column 6 of this table appear in row III of Fig. 14–4.

The calculations for the elements in row II of Fig. 14–4 are shown in Table 14–3. The figures in column 6 of this table appear in row II of Fig. 14–4.

The calculations for the elements in row I of Fig. 14–4 are shown in Table 14–4. The figures in column 6 of this table appear in row I of Fig. 14–4.

TABLE 14–1

CALCULATIONS FOR ROW IV OF FIGURE 14–4

Column Heading (1)	Elements in Row IV of Figure 14-3 (2)	Elements in Row V of Figure 14-5 (3)	Multiply Factor (4)	= (Product) (5)	Elements for Row I of Figure 14-4 (Col. 2 − Col. 5) (6)
Q_i	320	150 ×	2	= 300	20
X_1	2	1 ×	2	= 2	0
X_2	1	$\frac{1}{4}$ ×	2	= $\frac{1}{2}$	$\frac{1}{2}$
X_3	0	0 ×	2	= 0	0
X_4	0	0 ×	2	= 0	0
X_5	0	0 ×	2	= 0	0
X_6	1	0 ×	2	= 0	1
X_7	0	$\frac{1}{4}$ ×	2	= $\frac{1}{2}$	$-\frac{1}{2}$

TABLE 14–2

CALCULATIONS FOR ROW III OF FIGURE 14-4

Column Heading (1)	Elements in Row III of Figure 14-3 (2)	$\begin{bmatrix}\text{Elements in}\\ \text{Row V of}\\ \text{Figure 14-5}\end{bmatrix} \times \begin{bmatrix}\text{Multiply}\\ \text{Factor}\end{bmatrix} = (Product)$ (3)			Elements for Row III of Figure 14-4 (Col. 2 − Col. 5) (6)
		(3)	(4)	(5)	
Q_i	280	150 ×	1 =	150	130
X_1	1	1 ×	1 =	1	0
X_2	2	$\frac{1}{4}$ ×	1 =	$\frac{1}{4}$	$\frac{7}{4}$
X_3	0	0 ×	1 =	0	0
X_4	0	0 ×	1 =	0	0
X_5	1	0 ×	1 =	0	1
X_6	0	0 ×	1 =	0	0
X_7	0	$\frac{1}{4}$ ×	1 =	$\frac{1}{4}$	$-\frac{1}{4}$

TABLE 14–3

CALCULATIONS FOR ROW II OF FIGURE 14-4

Column Heading (1)	Elements in Row II of Figure 14-3 (2)	$\begin{bmatrix}\text{Elements in}\\ \text{Row V of}\\ \text{Figure 14-5}\end{bmatrix} \times \begin{bmatrix}\text{Multiply}\\ \text{Factor}\end{bmatrix} = (Product)$ (3)			Elements for Row II of Figure 14-4 (Col. 2 − Col. 5) (6)
		(3)	(4)	(5)	
Q_i	480	150 ×	1 =	150	330
X_1	1	1 ×	1 =	1	0
X_2	4	$\frac{1}{4}$ ×	1 =	$\frac{1}{4}$	$\frac{15}{4}$
X_3	0	0 ×	1 =	0	0
X_4	1	0 ×	1 =	0	1
X_5	0	0 ×	1 =	0	0
X_6	0	0 ×	1 =	0	0
X_7	0	$\frac{1}{4}$ ×	1 =	$\frac{1}{4}$	$-\frac{1}{4}$

TABLE 14–4

CALCULATIONS FOR ROW I OF FIGURE 14-4

Column Heading (1)	Elements in Row I of Figure 14-3 (2)	$\begin{bmatrix}\text{Elements in}\\ \text{Row V of}\\ \text{Figure 15-4}\end{bmatrix} \times \begin{bmatrix}\text{Multiply}\\ \text{Factor}\end{bmatrix} = (Product)$ (3)			Elements for Row I of Figure 14-4 (Col. 2 − Col. 5) (6)
		(3)	(4)	(5)	
Q_i	920	150 ×	1 =	150	770
X_1	1	1 ×	1 =	1	0
X_2	8	$\frac{1}{4}$ ×	1 =	$\frac{1}{4}$	$\frac{31}{4}$
X_3	1	0 ×	1 =	0	1
X_4	0	0 ×	1 =	0	0
X_5	0	0 ×	1 =	0	0
X_6	0	0 ×	1 =	0	0
X_7	0	$\frac{1}{4}$ ×	1 =	$\frac{1}{4}$	$-\frac{1}{4}$

One more step is needed to complete Fig. 14–4. The remaining elements (zeros) in the column headed P_j are the same as those which appeared in Fig. 14–3. They were not changed because they were not a part of a replaced row. However, the P_j element of row V, was changed because row V was the replaced row.

The new solution that appears in Fig. 14–4 is located in the columns labeled P_j and Q_i.[1] This solution is $X_3 = 770$, $X_4 = 330$, $X_5 = 130$, $X_6 = 20$, and $X_1 = 150$. The original solution that appeared in Fig. 14–1 was $X_3 = 920$, $X_4 = 480$, $X_5 = 280$, $X_6 = 320$, and $X_7 = 600$; this was a do-nothing solution because no units of X_1 (mailbox H) or X_2 (mailbox R) were produced. The new solution specifies that 150 units of type-H mailboxes should be produced. The revenue calculated for the first solution shown in Fig. 14–1 was $0. The revenue for the second solution is derived from Fig. 14–4. Represented algebraically, the calculations are as follows:

$$\text{Revenue} = P_3X_3 + P_4X_4 + P_5X_5 + P_6X_6 + P_1X_1$$
$$\text{Revenue} = (0 \times 770) + (0 \times 330) + (0 \times 130) + (0 \times 20) + (13 \times 150)$$
$$\text{Revenue} = 13 \times 150 = \$1,950.$$

This solution is obviously an improvement over the first one because revenue has increased. The next step is to test the new solution to determine whether it is optimal.

The process of checking for an optimal solution is again put in motion. First, the Z_j's and the $P_j - Z_j$'s are calculated; if any $P_j - Z_j$ is positive, an optimal solution has not been reached. The $P_j - Z_j$'s for the second iteration are shown in Fig. 14–6.

If no optimal solution is present, the ratios necessary to determine the replaced row are recalculated and the largest $P_j - Z_j$ value is used to select the replacing column.

Since one of the $P_j - Z_j$'s is positive, we do not yet have an optimal solution. Consequently, another tableau is required; in fact, two more tableaus will be required before the optimal solution is obtained. Note that in Fig. 14–7 a positive value remains in the $P_j - Z_j$ row. However, Fig. 14–8 has either negative values or zeros in the $P_j - Z_j$ row; this signals that an optimal solution has been reached.

The results of the four tableaus are summarized and listed in Table 14–5 to show the total revenue and products of each. If these results are compared

---

[1] This new solution is also reflected in the tableau in another way. As in the case of Fig. 14–1, the arrangement of the columns with zeros and a single 1 signifies the variables in the current solution. In Fig. 14–4, the columns headed X_1, X_3, X_4, X_5, and X_6 have zeros and a single 1 in the appropriate rows. The location of the number 1 in each column is another means of identifying the Q_i associated with the X_j in the current solution. The number 1 is simply located in an X_j column and the Q_i located in the row in which the 1 appears; of course, these same results are also conveniently provided in the first three columns of the tableau.

		P_j	Q_i	X_1 13	X_2 13	X_3 0	X_4 0	X_5 0	X_6 0	X_7 0	Ratio	
I	$j=3$	0	770	0	31/4	1	0	0	0	-1/4	$\frac{770}{31/4}=99\frac{11}{31}$	
II	$j=4$	0	330	0	15/4	0	1	0	0	-1/4	$\frac{330}{15/4}=88$	
III	$j=5$	0	130	0	7/4	0	0	1	0	-1/4	$\frac{130}{7/4}=74\frac{2}{7}$	
IV	$j=6$	0	20	0	1/2	0	0	0	1	-1/2	$\frac{20}{1/2}=40$	Smallest
V	$j=1$	13	150	1	1/4	0	0	0	0	1/4	$\frac{150}{1/4}=600$	
		Z_j		13	13/4	0	0	0	0	13/4		
		P_j-Z_j		0	39/4	0	0	0	0	-13/4		

Largest

FIGURE 14-6. Complete tableau showing second solution.

to those of the algebraic and graphic approaches, it will be apparent that the simplex technique started at the origin and moved around the feasible area, with the solution for each tableau representing a corner on the feasible region. In this example, the iterative process moved around in a counterclockwise direction.

The simplex method has thus far provided a solution to the problem of how to allocate the available resources to produce an optimal product mix. The various elements in the tableaus had mathematical significance in the problem of finding an optimal solution, and the main body of the original tableau consisted of the coefficients of technical production for each product. The slack-artificial variables formed an identity matrix (number 1's in the diagonal) that was used to produce an easy initial (do-nothing) solution. They also served as a partial basis for deriving the inverse matrix.

		P_j	Q_i	X_1 13	X_2 13	X_3 0	X_4 0	X_5 0	X_6 0	X_7 0	Ratio	
I	$j=3$	0	460	0	0	1	0	0	-31/2	30/4	$\frac{460}{15/2}=61\frac{1}{3}$	
II	$j=4$	0	180	0	0	0	1	0	-15/2	14/4	$\frac{180}{14/4}=51\frac{3}{7}$	
III	$j=5$	0	60	0	0	0	0	1	-7/2	3/2	$\frac{120}{3}=40$	Smallest
IV	$j=2$	13	40	0	1	0	0	0	2	-1	$\frac{40}{-1}=-40$	
V	$j=1$	13	140	1	0	0	0	0	-1/2	1/2	$\frac{140}{1/2}=280$	
		Z_j		13	13	0	0	0	39/2	-13/2		
		P_j-Z_j		0	0	0	0	0	-39/2	13/2		

Largest

FIGURE 14-7. Complete tableau showing third solution.

TABLE 14–5

RESULTS OF TABLEAUS

Tableau	Total Revenue	Type H X_1	Type R X_2
1	$ 0	0	0
2	1,950	150	0
3	2,340	140	40
4	2,600	120	80

	P_j	Q_i	X_1 13	X_2 13	X_3 0	X_4 0	X_5 0	X_6 0	X_7 0	Ratio
I $j=3$	0	160	0	0	1	0	-5	2	0	
II $j=4$	0	40	0	0	0	1	-7/3	2/3	0	
III $j=7$	0	40	0	0	0	0	2/3	-7/3	1	
IV $j=2$	13	80	0	1	0	0	2/3	-1/3	0	
V $j=1$	13	120	1	0	0	0	-1/3	2/3	0	
		Z_j	13	13	0	0	13/3	13/3	0	
		P_j-Z_j	0	0	0	0	-13/3	-13/3	0	

Optimal

FIGURE 14–8.   Final tableau showing optimal solution.

ECONOMIC IMPLICATIONS OF VARIOUS TABLEAU ELEMENTS

Various elements in the simplex tableaus have economic interpretations as well as mathematical significance. Some reflect the extent to which the production activity of certain departments would have to be altered when various *substitutions* are made due to a change in the output mix. Others, particularly in the last tableau, contain *implicit values* that can tell the decision maker how he should allocate additional funds if expansion or improvement is desired.

Substitution

The technical coefficients, which are the coefficients in the original constraint inequations, are transformed into values that represent substitution rates between the various products. In essence, they indicate how production is altered if one product is substituted for another.

Fig. 14–1 shows that one unit of X_1 requires four units' absorption of resources in the assembling department (row V). If only X_1 is to be produced, it must use up the 600 units of resources available in the assembling department. The production of X_1 (as shown in Fig. 14–4) uses up all 600 units of the resources of the assembling department to produce 150 units of X_1 (the solution in Fig. 14–4). Therefore, the production of anything else in this department would require some of the units of X_1 to be given up. For example, if one unit of X_7 (which is one unit of the resources in the assembling department, since X_7 represents the unused capacity of this department) is made available for producing X_2 (mailbox type R), $\frac{1}{4}$ unit of X_1 (mailbox type H) would have to be given up. Stated in another way, every unit of idle resources in the assembling department that is added to the solution reduces the production of X_1 by $\frac{1}{4}$ unit. Substitutions between products and between the variables that represent unused capacities are necessary to obtain an optimal solution.

It can be seen that in order to produce some units of X_2 (mailbox type R) as shown in Fig. 14–7 trading off of resource units in the various departments must occur. The unused capacity of the finishing department (20 units of X_6) as shown in Fig. 14–6 indicates that some X_2 (type R) can be produced when enough resources of the assembly department (X_7) are released by reducing the production of X_1 (type H). For example, the reduction of 10 units of X_1 would make available 40 units of the resources of the assembling department for the production of 40 units of X_2 because the technical coefficient for X_2 is 1. The original constraint inequation for the assembling department is $4X_1 + 1X_2 \leq 600$.

At the same time, 20 units of the resources of the finishing department are released because the technical coefficients indicate that two units of the resources of the finishing department are absorbed for every unit of X_1 produced. (The original constraint inequation for the finishing department is $2X_1 + 1X_2 \leq 320$.) Therefore, the 20 units of unused capacity of the finishing department, reflected by X_6 (see Fig. 14–6), and the 20 units released by reducing the production of X_1 by 10 units make available a total of 40 units of the resources in the finishing department for the production of X_2-type mailboxes. Since the technical coefficient of X_2 in the finishing department inequation is 1, 40 units of X_2 can be produced.

It can be seen, therefore, that trading of resource units must occur among the various departments in order to alter production results. However, the mathematical process employed in the simplex technique accomplishes the appropriate trades with relative ease.

Implicit Values

We now turn to an economic interpretation of the elements in the Z_j row, especially those that appear in the final tableau. The Z_j values represent the incremental worth of each constraint; in our example, they measure implicitly the economic value of each department's resources. These implicit or incremental values for each department can be used to indicate where the most significant changes will occur if alterations in the constraints are possible. For instance, the manager can determine which department has the biggest bottleneck, and hence which should be modernized or have its capacity increased.

Modernization of a department would result in a change in the technical coefficients that appear in its corresponding constraint inequation. These coefficients would in all likelihood reflect a reduction in the required absorption of the department's resources to produce one unit of a product. For instance, the shaping department could be modernized to the extent that only one unit of its resources would be absorbed in the production of X_2. Therefore, the original constraint inequation would change from $X_1 + 2X_2 \leq 280$ to $X_1 + X_2 \leq 280$. An expansion of a department's capacity would be reflected simply by an increase in the figure appearing on the right-hand side of the inequation.

In the final tableau (Fig. 14–8), the implicit values (Z_j's) for each of the departments are located under the X_j's of the original identity matrix (that is, in the columns headed X_3, X_4, X_5, X_6, and X_7). The identity matrix is a result of the slack–artificial variables and the Z_j's, because the X_j's of the identity matrix correspond to the constraint equations in the order in which they appear in the worksheet. In this case, the implicit values for each department are Z_3, Z_4, Z_5, Z_6, and Z_7; numerically, they are 0, 0, $4\frac{1}{3}$, $4\frac{1}{3}$, and 0, respectively. The units of measurement of the Z_j's are the same as the corresponding payoff coefficients of the objective function. In this case, because revenue is expressed in terms of dollars, the Z_j's are also.

The fact that Z_5 is \$4.33 per unit of resource in the shaping department gives us a measure of the revenue-producing value of each unit of resource in that department. The same is true for Z_6, which is the implicit value for the finishing department. Z_5 and Z_6 measure the incremental worth of these two departments. In this case, the firm could gain more by expanding or modernizing the shaping and finishing departments than any of the other three, because these two represent the significant bottlenecks—that is, revenue could be increased most if these two departments were altered.

However, it is important to remember that the implicit values actually measure the loss of revenue that results from the addition of one unit of a particular slack–artificial variable. In essence, these values were calculated on the basis of the amount of revenue that would be lost with an increase in unused capacity. But their significance results from extending their application to the possibility that production will be increased beyond its existing utilization.

The importance of implicit values is clearly expressed by Alan S. Manne in his book, *Economic Analysis for Business Decisions*. He concludes his discussion of implicit values as follows:

In all likelihood, the most important thing to be derived from the linear programming calculation is not the optimal product mix itself, but rather the implicit values of problems of economic choice. We are interested in finding optimal solutions to a problem under carefully defined given conditions—precisely so that we can find out what it would be worth to us if those conditions could themselves be altered.[2]

The implicit prices that we have been calculating resemble break-even points. They are yardsticks by which we may measure restrictions initially stipulated for our economic model. The more arbitrary these stipulations, the more important it is for us to be able to explore the implications of changing them. If linear programming provided nothing but a more reliable framework for estimating incremental costs and values, this alone would justify its importance to management.[3]

It is clear that the shaping and/or finishing departments should be modernized or their capacity increased if greater revenue per dollar invested is desired. One of the exercises at the end of this chapter requires altering the capacity of the shaping department to determine the effect of a change in the capacity of a bottleneck department.

EXPANDED VERSION OF THE MAILBOX PROBLEM

A two-product problem has been used to simplify the illustration of the calculating procedure for the simplex technique. However, the merits of the simplex technique do not become apparent until an expanded or complex problem is encountered. The solution to an expanded version of the two-product mailbox problem is illustrated in this section.

The problem deals with four products instead of just two; this makes the straightforward or naïve algebraic method impractical. In the expanded version, it may be assumed that the Hypothetical Mailbox Manufacturing Company has decided to alter its plans to include the offering of two deluxe models of each of the simple mailboxes. The problem is formulated as follows: Maximize the equation

$$\text{Revenue} = 13X_1 + 13X_2 + 20X_3 + 15X_4$$

subject to the following departmental capacities:

$$X_1 + 8X_2 + 2X_3 + 10X_4 \le 920$$
$$X_1 + 4X_2 + X_3 + 4X_4 \le 480$$
$$X_1 + 2X_2 + 2X_3 + 2X_4 \le 280$$
$$2X_1 + X_2 + 2X_3 + X_4 \le 320$$
$$4X_1 + X_2 + 4X_3 + X_4 \le 600,$$

[2] A. S. Manne, *Economic Analysis for Business Decisions* (New York: McGraw-Hill Book Company, 1961), p. 19.

[3] *Ibid.*, p. 42.

where X_1 is a type-H mailbox (house), X_2 is a type-R mailbox (rural), X_3 is a type-DH mailbox (deluxe house model), and X_4 is a type-DR mailbox (deluxe rural model); in addition, $X_1 \geq 0$, $X_2 \geq 0$, $X_3 \geq 0$, and $X_4 \geq 0$.

The payoff or revenue per unit of each type of mailbox is indicated in the revenue equation. The revenues for the original two types of mailboxes remain at $13 each; for type DH they are $20, and for type DR, $15.

The constraint inequations are extended to include the production co-efficients for the deluxe models. However, the departmental capacities are not expanded; therefore, the manufacturing facilities have been altered only enough to perform the additional tasks required to produce the two new models. Additional resources are not provided in this case.

The relevant data for this problem are inserted in the first tableau (Fig. 14–9). Since this do-nothing solution is not an optimal one, the replacing column and the replaced row are selected and are indicated by arrows, and the variable X_3 replaces the variable X_7 in the next solution. The revenue for this first solution is obviously zero.

The second tableau (Fig. 14–10) provides a solution where 140 units of X_3 are produced and the total revenue is $2,800; this is an improvement. Nevertheless, a positive number appears in the $P_j - Z_j$ row, which indicates that this solution is not an optimal one. Therefore, the ratios are computed and the replacing column and replaced row are again determined. The completion of these steps signals that X_9 should be replaced by X_1 in the next tableau.

After the appropriate row operations are completed to produce the third tableau (Fig. 14–11), the $P_j - Z_j$'s are tested to determine if an optimal solution has been obtained. This tableau is the final one because it has no positive $P_j - Z_j$'s. The solution specifies that 20 units of X_1 and 130 units of X_3 should be produced. This solution renders a total revenue of $2,860, an

		P_j	Q_i	X_1	X_2	X_3	X_4	X_5	X_6	X_7	X_8	X_9	Ratio
				13	13	20	15	0	0	0	0	0	
I	$j=5$	0	920	1	8	2	10	1	0	0	0	0	$\frac{920}{2} = 460$
II	$j=6$	0	480	1	4	1	4	0	1	0	0	0	$\frac{480}{1} = 480$
III	$j=7$	0	280	1	2	2	2	0	0	1	0	0	$\frac{280}{2} = 140$ ←
IV	$j=8$	0	320	2	1	2	1	0	0	0	1	0	$\frac{320}{2} = 160$
V	$j=9$	0	600	4	1	4	1	0	0	0	0	1	$\frac{600}{4} = 150$
			Z_j	0	0	0	0	0	0	0	0	0	
			$P_j - Z_j$	13	13	20	15	0	0	0	0	0	

FIGURE 14–9.   Initial tableau showing first solution for expanded mailbox problem.

		P_j	Q_i	X_1 13	X_2 13	X_3 20	X_4 15	X_5 0	X_6 0	X_7 0	X_8 0	X_9 0	Ratio
I	$j=5$	0	640	0	6	0	8	1	0	-1	0	0	$\frac{640}{0}=\infty$
II	$j=6$	0	340	1/2	3	0	3	0	1	-1/2	0	0	$\frac{340}{1/2}=680$
III	$j=3$	20	140	1/2	1	1	1	0	0	1/2	0	0	$\frac{140}{1/2}=280$
IV	$j=8$	0	40	1	-1	0	-1	0	0	-1	1	0	$\frac{40}{1}=40$
V	$j=9$	0	40	2	-3	0	-3	0	0	-2	0	1	$\frac{40}{2}=20$ ←
			Z_j	10	20	20	20	0	0	10	0	0	
			P_j-Z_j	3	-7	0	-5	0	0	-10	0	0	

↑

FIGURE 14–10. Tableau showing second solution to expanded mailbox problem.

		P_j	Q_i	X_1 13	X_2 13	X_3 20	X_4 15	X_5 0	X_6 0	X_7 0	X_8 0	X_9 0	Ratio
I	$j=5$	0	640	0	6	0	8	1	0	-1	0	0	
II	$j=6$	0	330	0	15/4	0	15/4	0	1	0	0	-1/4	
III	$j=3$	20	130	0	7/4	1	7/4	0	0	1	0	-1/4	
IV	$j=8$	0	20	0	1/2	0	1/2	0	0	0	1	-1/2	
V	$j=1$	13	20	1	-3/2	0	-3/2	0	0	-1	0	1/2	
			Z_j	13	31/2	20	31/2	0	0	7	0	3/2	
			P_j-Z_j	0	-5/2	0	-1/2	0	0	-7	0	-3/2	

Optimal

FIGURE 14–11. Final tableau showing optional solution to expanded mailbox problem.

increase of $60 over the previous solution. Total revenue is determined as follows:

$$\begin{aligned}
\text{Revenue} &= 13X_1 + 13X_2 + 20X_3 + 15X_4 \\
&= (13 \times 20) + (13 \times 0) + (20 \times 130) + (15 \times 0) \\
&= \$2,860.
\end{aligned}$$

The implicit values associated with each of the five departments are read from the final tableau. For the cutting department, the implicit value is Z_5, or $0; for the stamping department it is Z_6, or $0; for the shaping department it is Z_7, or $7; for the finishing department it is Z_8, or $0; and for the assembling department it is Z_9, or $1.50. These implicit values measure the incremental worth of the bottleneck factors. Since the figure of $7 per hour for the shaping department is the largest, it tells the industrial manager that he should start thinking of ways to break the shaping department's bottleneck—by modernization, overtime, or some other means. The largest implicit value alerts the manager to the largest bottleneck.

ANNEX: A NOTE ON MATRIX ALGEBRA

Some definitions and illustrations are given here to prepare the reader for an awareness of the algebra of matrices. Many problems that consist of equations or relationships typical of management science require the techniques of matrix algebra.

A *matrix* is a rectangular array of numbers. Some examples are

$$\begin{bmatrix} 8 & 3 & 2 \\ 1 & 2 & 5 \end{bmatrix}, \quad \begin{bmatrix} 4 & 6 \\ 2 & 1 \end{bmatrix}, \quad [4 \quad 5 \quad 3], \quad \begin{bmatrix} 5 \\ 6 \\ 3 \end{bmatrix}.$$

An $m \times n$ (m-by-n) matrix has m rows and n columns. The second matrix shown above is commonly referred to as a *square matrix*; these matrices have special significance in solving systems of equations. The last two matrices are *row* and *column vectors*, respectively. A vector is simply an m-by-1 or 1-by-n matrix.

Usually capital letters are used to designate a matrix; for example,

$$A = \begin{bmatrix} 4 & 5 & 3 \\ 1 & 6 & 4 \\ 2 & 3 & 5 \end{bmatrix}.$$

If the rows and columns of a matrix are interchanged, the result is called the *transpose* of the given matrix. The transpose of the matrix A is

$$A^T = \begin{bmatrix} 4 & 1 & 2 \\ 5 & 6 & 3 \\ 3 & 4 & 5 \end{bmatrix}.$$

One should not confuse a matrix with the *determinant* of a matrix. A determinant is a numerical value of a matrix that is calculated in a precise and prescribed manner; it is indicated symbolically by a set of vertical bars on either side of the matrix. For example, the determinant for a 2-by-2 matrix is

$$\begin{vmatrix} a_{11} & a_{12} \\ a_{21} & a_{22} \end{vmatrix} = a_{11}a_{22} - a_{21}a_{12}.$$

The technique for solving a system of equations by the use of determinants is given in Chapter 12; therefore, it will be avoided here.

There are various rules to follow in adding and multiplying vectors and matrices. These are explained in detail in textbooks. All that will be illustrated here is the way in which a system of linear equations can be solved by utilizing the inverse of a matrix. The term "inverse" will be defined and illustrated. The main purpose of this Annex is to familiarize the reader with some of the rudiments of matrices to provide some idea of the algebraic basis of the simplex method.

The inverse of a number is the reciprocal of that number. For example, the number 6 has the inverse $\frac{1}{6}$; this can also be written with the negative exponent -1 as 6^{-1}. This number 6 raised to the negative power of 1 is called the inverse because when it is multiplied by 6 the result will be 1; that is, $6 \times \frac{1}{6} = 1$. The product of a number and its inverse is *unity* (1). There is a similar but not identical situation in square matrices that possess inverses.

The inverse of the square matrix,

$$A = \begin{bmatrix} 4 & 6 \\ 2 & 1 \end{bmatrix},$$

is defined to be another matrix,

$$A^{-1} = \begin{bmatrix} -\frac{1}{8} & \frac{6}{8} \\ \frac{2}{8} & -\frac{4}{8} \end{bmatrix}.$$

From this matrix, $AA^{-1} = I$, where I is a square matrix with ones in the primary diagonal as follows:

$$I = \begin{bmatrix} 1 & 0 \\ 0 & 1 \end{bmatrix}.$$

Since the multiplication of A times A^{-1} is equal to I (the identity matrix),

$$AA^{-1} = \begin{bmatrix} 4 & 6 \\ 2 & 1 \end{bmatrix} \begin{bmatrix} -\frac{1}{8} & \frac{6}{8} \\ \frac{2}{8} & -\frac{4}{8} \end{bmatrix} = I.$$

The multiplication of A and A^{-1} is accomplished as follows:

$$4(-\tfrac{1}{8}) + 6(\tfrac{2}{8}) = 1 \qquad \text{(first element in first row of } I \text{ matrix)}$$
$$4(\tfrac{6}{8}) + 6(-\tfrac{4}{8}) = 0 \qquad \text{(second element in first row of } I \text{ matrix)}$$
$$2(-\tfrac{1}{8}) + 1(\tfrac{2}{8}) = 0 \qquad \text{(first element in second row of } I \text{ matrix)}$$
$$2(\tfrac{6}{8}) + 1(-\tfrac{4}{8}) = 1. \qquad \text{(second element in second row of } I \text{ matrix)}$$

Therefore,

$$AA^{-1} = \begin{bmatrix} 1 & 0 \\ 0 & 1 \end{bmatrix};$$

furthermore,

$$A^{-1}A = \begin{bmatrix} 1 & 0 \\ 0 & 1 \end{bmatrix}.$$

The method for multiplying matrices and the method for obtaining the inverse of a square matrix are explained in most basic mathematics textbooks. However, we will further define and illustrate the latter approach because it is the basis for the simplex method.

Let us apply the method of matrix inversion to the problem of solving a system of linear equations. Suppose that we have the following system of equations:

$$4X + 6Y = 16$$
$$2X + 1Y = 4.$$

This can be written in matrix form as

$$\begin{bmatrix} 4 & 6 \\ 2 & 1 \end{bmatrix} \begin{bmatrix} X \\ Y \end{bmatrix} = \begin{bmatrix} 16 \\ 4 \end{bmatrix}$$

or

$$A \times \begin{bmatrix} X \\ Y \end{bmatrix} = \begin{bmatrix} 16 \\ 4 \end{bmatrix}.$$

Now if both sides are multiplied by the inverse of A—that is, A^{-1}—which is a familiar operation in basic algebra, we have

$$A^{-1}A \times \begin{bmatrix} X \\ Y \end{bmatrix} = A^{-1} \times \begin{bmatrix} 16 \\ 4 \end{bmatrix}.$$

Consequently, we have

$$\begin{bmatrix} -\frac{1}{8} & \frac{6}{8} \\ \frac{2}{8} & -\frac{4}{8} \end{bmatrix} \begin{bmatrix} 4 & 6 \\ 2 & 1 \end{bmatrix} \begin{bmatrix} X \\ Y \end{bmatrix} = \begin{bmatrix} -\frac{1}{8} & \frac{6}{8} \\ \frac{2}{8} & -\frac{4}{8} \end{bmatrix} \begin{bmatrix} 16 \\ 4 \end{bmatrix},$$

which reduces to

$$\begin{bmatrix} 1 & 0 \\ 0 & 1 \end{bmatrix} \begin{bmatrix} X \\ Y \end{bmatrix} = \begin{bmatrix} 1 \\ 2 \end{bmatrix}$$

or

$$\begin{bmatrix} X \\ Y \end{bmatrix} = \begin{bmatrix} 1 \\ 2 \end{bmatrix}.$$

In familiar form, we have

$$X = 1$$
$$Y = 2.$$

This same operation is inherent in the simplex solution to the simple mailbox problem that was presented in the chapter. If the figures that appear in Fig. 14–8 are placed in the matrix form

$$A^{-1}AX = A^{-1}q,$$

where X is a set of X_i's, the equation reduces to

$$X = A^{-1}q.$$

The symbols q and X are column vectors. The system of tableaus appears as

$$\begin{bmatrix} X_3 \\ X_4 \\ X_7 \\ X_2 \\ X_1 \end{bmatrix} = \begin{bmatrix} 1 & 0 & -5 & 2 & 0 \\ 0 & 1 & -\frac{7}{3} & \frac{2}{3} & 0 \\ 0 & 0 & \frac{2}{3} & -\frac{7}{3} & 1 \\ 0 & 0 & \frac{2}{3} & -\frac{1}{3} & 0 \\ 0 & 0 & -\frac{1}{3} & \frac{2}{3} & 0 \end{bmatrix} \begin{bmatrix} 920 \\ 480 \\ 280 \\ 320 \\ 600 \end{bmatrix};$$

after multiplication of the right-hand side, we have

$$
\begin{aligned}
X_3 &= 160 && \text{(slack variable)} \\
X_4 &= 40 && \text{(slack variable)} \\
X_7 &= 40 && \text{(slack variable)} \\
X_2 &= 80 && \text{(mailbox type } R\text{)} \\
X_1 &= 120. && \text{(mailbox type } H\text{)}
\end{aligned}
$$

This is the same optimal solution that was obtained by the simplex method.

This Annex should not be considered to be a thorough explanation of matrix algebra. It was primarily intended to give the student an introductory exposure to this field in order to stimulate him to study it more rigorously.

PROBLEMS AND PROJECTS

1. The simple mailbox problem that was demonstrated in the text was solved by selecting X_1 as the replacing variable in the first tableau (see Fig. 14–3). Solve the same problem by the simplex method but select X_2 as the replacing variable in the first tableau instead of X_1.
2. Increase the shaping department's limits in the *expanded* mailbox problem from 280 hours to 320 hours, and solve this new problem.
3. Using the simplex method, solve the following problem:

Maximize:

$$100X_1 + 100X_2 + 100X_3 + 100X_4$$

$$\text{Subject to: } 4X_1 + 2X_2 + X_3 + 2X_4 \leq 140$$
$$X_1 + 2X_2 + 2X_3 + 4X_4 \leq 260.$$

4. Solve the following problem by the simplex method:

$$\text{Maximize: Profit} = 210X_1 + 480X_2 + 600X_3$$

Maximize subject to:

$$\text{Subject to: } 10X_1 + 23X_2 + 26X_3 \leq 700$$
$$5X_1 + 13X_2 + 22X_3 \leq 550$$
$$7X_1 + 9X_2 + 11X_3 \leq 450.$$

SELECTED REFERENCES

Adams, J. J., *Modern Business Mathematics.* New York: Holt, Rinehart & Winston, Inc., 1963.

Carlson, P. G., *Quantitative Methods for Managers.* New York: Harper & Row, Publishers, 1967.

Horowitz, I., *An Introduction to Quantitative Business Analysis.* New York: McGraw-Hill Book Company, 1965.

Levin, R. I., and C. A. Kirkpatrick, *Quantitative Approaches to Management.* New York: McGraw-Hill Book Company, 1965.

Spivey, W. A., *Linear Programming, An Introduction.* New York: The Macmillan Company, 1963.

Wasson, C. R., *The Economics of Managerial Decision: Profit Opportunity Analysis.* New York: Appleton-Century-Crofts, 1965.

15

INTEREST

Interest and finance are inseparable concepts; one cannot become involved with finance without understanding the concept of interest and its various computations. It is not the intent of this chapter to provide an economic explanation of how interest rates are determined. Rather it will be our purpose to explain interest calculations and to relate interest to financial analysis and business decisions.

THE CONCEPT OF INTEREST

Put simply, interest is a method of paying for the privilege of deferring payment. A great deal of business activity is conducted on a deferred-payment basis. A customer may acquire some goods for immediate use and arrange to make payment for all or part of the purchase at some later date. To do this, he is usually required to pay interest, especially if payment is deferred for an extended period of time. Often he may be able to defer payment for a brief period without incurring an interest charge; such is the case with purchases made through an open account or on a charge account. However, in most instances, interest is either an explicit payment required of a customer or an implicit expense absorbed by the supplier.

Arrangements for deferring payment can be made *orally* or *in writing*. A written promise to pay represents evidence of debt and may therefore be more desirable, particularly for new customers or customers who do not have a good credit reputation. In the event of default or liquidation, a claim can be easily established. Written evidence may be in the form of a letter or a specially designed document. In either case the rate of interest will usually be stipulated in writing.

Deferred payments are usually classified as *short-term* or *long-term*. Short-term credit covers transactions of less than one year's duration, usually 30 to 120 days. Promissory notes (written promises to pay) are very common in short-term credit. Such things as merchandise, materials, and supplies can be acquired easily with this type of credit. Long-term credit covers transactions involving a period of more than one year; the credit instrument commonly used is the bond. This credit is used to make plant improvements, to acquire new equipment, and to construct additional buildings. The rate at which interest is charged depends upon the duration of the deferred period. Long-term rates are usually higher than short-term rates, all other things being equal.

Interest is charged on the basis of a percentage of the principal for a specified period of time. In this sense, it is much like the rate of speed that registers on the speedometer of a moving automobile; both are stated in terms of a certain time standard. The speedometer registers the rate of speed as the number of miles traveled in a given period of time, usually an hour—that is, in miles per hour. Interest is a rate that reflects the amount of money charged on a given principal in a standard period of time, usually a year.

The rate of interest is not stated in dollars and cents. Instead, it is expressed as a percentage of the principal. The use of percentages is very convenient because it reduces all interest charges to a common denominator regardless of the amount of principal or the period of time. It thus makes it possible to compare large and small, short- and long-term financial arrangements. This is much like being able to add up oranges and apples. For example, a $60 interest charge on a $1,000 loan for one year is comparable to a $24 interest charge on a $200 loan for two years because both represent a 6 per cent rate of interest. This identity can be proved by using the simple-interest formula described in the next section.

Simple Interest

There are two basic methods for determining simple interest. The 360-day method is called the *ordinary-interest* method; it is the one most often used. Sometimes 365 days are used to determine the exact fraction of a year that a given number of days represents. This is known as the *exact-interest* method. For purposes of illustration only the *ordinary-interest* method will be depicted here.

If the rate of interest is 6 per cent, the interest on a loan of $1,000 for one year would be $60. The amount of interest (I) is determined by multiplying the principal (P) by the rate of interest (i) and the time (T). This is expressed in formula form as follows:

$$I = P \times i \times T$$
$$= \$1,000 \times 6\% \times 1 \; year$$
$$= \$1,000 \times 0.06 \times 1$$
$$= \$60.$$

If the duration of the loan is for two or more years, T would reflect the number of years. If the duration is less than one year, such as 6 months or 90 days, T would be expressed as a fraction of a year. For example, 6 months would be $\frac{6}{12}$ or $\frac{1}{2}$; 90 days would be $\frac{90}{360}$ or $\frac{1}{4}$. The amount of interest on a \$500 loan at 4 per cent for 90 days would be determined by substituting these numbers in the formula and solving for I as follows:

$$I = P \times i \times T$$
$$= \$500 \times 0.04 \times \frac{90}{360}$$
$$= \$500 \times 0.04 \times \frac{1}{4}$$
$$= \$500 \times 0.01$$
$$= \$5.$$

Sometimes it may be necessary to determine one of the other variables in the formula $I = P \times i \times T$. As long as three variables are given, the fourth may be calculated by merely rearranging the formula. For example, if the other variables are given, principal (P) can be determined by dividing both sides of the original equation by i and T:

$$I = P \times i \times T$$
$$\frac{I}{i \times T} = \frac{P \times i \times T}{i \times T}$$
$$\frac{I}{i \times T} = P.$$

In like manner, the formula for finding i would be $i = I/PT$, and the formula for finding T would be $T = I/iP$. The formula for finding i can be used to prove the identity mentioned on page 348 as follows:

$$i = \frac{I}{P \times T} \qquad\qquad i = \frac{I}{P \times T}$$
$$= \frac{\$60}{\$1,000 \times 1} \qquad\qquad = \frac{\$24}{\$200 \times 2}$$
$$= \frac{\$60}{\$1,000} \qquad\qquad = \frac{\$24}{\$400}$$
$$= 0.06 = 6\% \qquad\qquad = 0.06 = 6\%.$$

Compound Interest

Interest and principal are calculated for most savings accounts on a compounded basis. Under these circumstances, the amount due at the end of the period is an accumulation of the interest and principal. Compound interest is the result of adding the interest to the principal in each period before calculating the interest on this new principal for the next period. The amount A that will result at the end of one year, for example, can be derived by incorporating this accumulation process into the simple-interest formula. The compound-interest formula is determined by the process of substitution as follows:

$$A = P + I$$
$$I = P \times i \times T$$
$$A = P + (P \times i \times T).$$

Since interest rates are usually calculated in terms of an annual rate, T is equal to 1 and can be dropped from the formula, which now becomes

$$A = P + (P \times i).$$

It can be seen that at the end of one year, the amount A is equal to the original principal P times the interest i for the period, added to the original principal. For example, if the principal P were $1,000 and the interest i were 6 per cent, then A would be $1,060 [$1,000 + ($1,000 × 0.06)].

A more convenient form of this formula results when the common factor, P, is removed from each term in the expression. The formula then becomes

$$A = P(1 + i).$$

Now suppose that A is to be determined for two years. The formula then becomes

$$A = [P + (P \times i)] + i[P + (P \times i)].$$

The expression in the first bracket is identical to the one in the formula for one year. The second year is taken into account by the rest of the expression, $i[P + (P \times i)]$. According to this formula, the amount for the first year $[P + (P \times i)]$ is added to the amount for the second year $i[P + (P \times i)]$, which is merely the result of multiplying the amount at the end of the first period by i, the rate of interest. The formula can be rewritten in a more convenient form by factoring P as follows:

$$A = [P(1 + i)] + i[P(1 + i)].$$

After further factoring,

$$A = P(1 + i)(1 + i)$$
$$A = P(1 + i)^2.$$

Using this formula, the amount due on $1,000 compounded annually for two years at 6 per cent would be calculated as follows:

$$A = \$1,000(1 + 0.06)^2$$
$$= \$1,000(1.1236)$$
$$= \$1,123.60.$$

Note that the difference between the expression for one year and the expression for two years is the addition of an exponent. The basic formula is $A = P(1 + i)^n$, where the exponent n stands for the number of periods. Hence the formula for 20 years would appear as $A = P(1 + i)^{20}$.

The longhand method of calculating the amount A for $1,000 compounded at 6 percent for two years would proceed as follows:

principal first year	$1,000
rate of interest	× 0.06
interest first year	$60.00
principal at beginning of first year	+ $1,000.00
amount at end of first year	$1,060.00
rate of interest	× 0.06
interest second year	$63.6000
principal at beginning of second year	+ $1,060.00
amount at end of second year	$1,123.6000

This calculation yields the same amount, $1,123.60, that was obtained by using the formula. For longer periods of time, such as 20 years, calculations by the longhand method would become quite cumbersome.

Interest may also be compounded on a semiannual, quarterly, or monthly basis. If it is compounded semiannually, each six months represent one period, and the rate of interest is one-half the annual rate; if it is compounded monthly, there would be 12 periods in each year, and the rate of interest would be $\frac{1}{12}$ of the annual rate. For example, $1,000 compounded semiannually for two years at an annual rate of 6 per cent (semiannual rate of 3 per cent) would be calculated as follows:

$$A = \$1,000(1 + 0.03)^4$$
$$= \$1,000(1.125508)$$
$$= \$1,125.51.$$

This yields a larger amount ($1,125.51) than the $1,000 compounded annually at an annual rate of 6 per cent ($1,123.60). If it were compounded quarterly at an annual rate of 6 per cent (quarterly rate of $1\frac{1}{2}$ per cent), the $1,000 would yield an even larger amount.

Present Value

Present value is another concept of interest that has particular significance to financial analysis and business decision. Receiving a certain sum of money 5, 10, or 20 years from now is not as desirable as receiving the same money now. Receiving it now allows the recipient to invest it and earn interest on it for 5, 10, or 20 years. Consequently the present value of a given amount of money that will be received in the future is less than its value would be if it were received now. For example, the present value of $1,123.60 to be received two years from now, using a 6 per cent annual rate of interest, is $1,000. This shows that present value is just the reverse of compounding. The formula is derived from the compound-interest formula as follows:

$$A = P(1 + i)^n$$
$$\frac{A}{(1 + i)^n} = P.$$

Although P now stands for present value, in essence it is the same as principal in the compound-interest formula; it will be designated as present value in order to distinguish one calculation from the other.

The process of deriving the present value of an amount of money is known as *discounting*. (This is not to be confused with *price discounting*, which was explained in a previous chapter.) In this process, the future value of the money is divided by one plus the available rate of interest. In the formula, A is divided by $(1 + i)$; the number of periods is indicated by the exponent n.

Since the calculations for compounding and for determining present value are time-consuming, convenient compound-interest tables and present-value tables have been constructed for the sum of $1. The foregoing explanation purposely avoided their use so that the reader may grasp basic understanding of the processes of compounding and present value.

THE CONCEPT OF ANNUITY

When a series of payments or amounts is involved rather than one lump sum of money, the term *annuity* is applicable. The amounts are usually equal and occur at regular intervals. However, unequal amounts and irregular intervals need not be excluded. This concept is vital to certain fundamentals for business analysis. It provides a framework for capitalizing (*i. e.*, calculating total value of) future incomes, sales receipts, and payments of any kind over a period of time; this makes possible certain financial desicions concerning the future commitment of funds. For example, the present value of an expected stream of income can be compared to the cost of acquiring that income in order to determine whether or not it would be worthwhile. This is explained and illustrated in Chapter 11.

Two Types of Annuities

The mathematics of annuities rests squarely upon the principles of compound interest. There are two types of annuities. The *annuity due* involves a series of amounts associated with the *beginning* of each period (year), and the *ordinary annuity* involves a series of amounts associated with the *end* of each period (year).

Let us consider an annuity due that consists of five amounts. At the end of the five periods, the first amount will have earned interest for the full five periods; the second amount, for four periods; the third amount, for three periods; the fourth amount, for two periods; and the final amount, for one period. Suppose now that the Hypothetical Mailbox Manufacturing Company places $1,000 in a depreciation fund at the *beginning* of each year for five years. If the amounts earn interest at the rate of 4 per cent per annum, the $1,000 set aside at the beginning of each year will accumulate to $5,632.97. By the compound-interest formula, the first $1,000 at 4 per cent would accumulate in five years to $P(1 + i)^5$; the second $1,000 would accumulate in four years to $P(1 + i)^4$; the third $1,000 would accumulate in three years to $P(1 + i)^3$; and so on. The formula and the calculations for the entire series of amounts would be as follows:

$$A = P(1 + i)^5 + P(1 + i)^4 + P(1 + i)^3 + P(1 + i)^2 + P(1 + i)^1$$
$$A = \$1,000(1.04)^5 + \$1,000(1.04)^4 + \$1,000(1.04)^3 + \$1,000(1.04)^2$$
$$+ \$1,000(1.04)^1$$
$$A = \$1,216.65 + \$1,169.86 + \$1,124.86 + \$1,081.60 + \$1,040.00$$
$$A = \$5,632.97.$$

When the principal amounts (P) are applied at the *end* of each period, the value or amount (A) of the annuity will be different. If an ordinary annuity consists of five amounts, the first amount will earn interest for only *four* periods; the amount is not entitled to interest for the first time period because it occurs at the end of the period. In the same way, the second amount will earn interest for three periods, and so on. The final amount will earn no interest. Suppose that the Hypothetical Mailbox Manufacturing Company is required to pay $1,000 into a sinking fund at the end of each year for five years; this fund will ultimately be used to pay off a bond issue. By the compound-interest formula, the $1,000 deposited in the fund at the end of each year at 4 per cent per annum accumulates as follows:

$$A = P(1 + i)^4 + P(1 + i)^3 + P(1 + i)^2 + P(1 + i)^1 + P$$
$$A = \$1,000(1.04)^4 + \$1,000(1.04)^3 + \$1,000(1.04)^2 + 1,000(1.04)^1 + \$1,000$$
$$A = \$1,169.86 + \$1,124.86 + \$1,081.60 + \$1,040.00 + \$1,000$$
$$A = \$5,416.32.$$

Looking at the calculations, the first amount of $1,000 accumulates in four years to $1,169.86; the second amount accumulates in three years to $1,124.86; and so on. All five amounts accumulate to $5,416.32.

Present Value of an Annuity

It is also valuable in business to know how to work with the present value of an annuity (or series of amounts). Suppose that the Hypothetical Mailbox Manufacturing Company leases a building for five years. The lease agreement states that the company is to pay the landlord $1,000 at the beginning of each year. The present value of the lease (an annuity due, in this case) is determined by adding together the present values of the separate amounts for the different periods. Since the first amount is payable immediately, it need not be discounted. Its present value, therefore, is $1,000. The second amount is due after only one period (the first year) has elapsed; thus it is discounted for one period. The present value of the second amount would be expressed as $\dfrac{A}{(1 + i)^1}$; the present value of the third amount is $\dfrac{A}{(1 + i)^2}$; and so on. If money in the capital markets is generally worth 4 per cent, the total of the present values of the five lease payments would be calculated as follows:

$$P = A + \frac{A}{(1 + i)^1} + \frac{A}{(1 + i)^2} + \frac{A}{(1 + i)^3} + \frac{A}{(1 + i)^4}$$

$$P = \$1,000 + \frac{\$1,000}{(1.04)^1} + \frac{\$1,000}{(1.04)^2} + \frac{\$1,000}{(1.04)^3} + \frac{\$1,000}{(1.04)^4}$$

$$P = \$1,000 + \$961.54 + \$924.56 + \$889.00 + \$854.80$$

$$P = \$4,629.90.$$

The $4,629.90, which is the present value of the five lease payments, is the actual worth or value of the lease when it is initiated.

The present value of an ordinary annuity also has business applications. The value of an earning asset such as a machine that has a limited life can be determined by calculating the present value of the expected stream of income or net receipts associated with the machine. Since the expected earnings from a machine result from its operation during a given time period, it is customary to assume that the income or net receipts will become available at the end of that period. For this reason, the capitalization of periodic income from the operation of a machine that has a limited life involves the same process as finding the present value of an ordinary annuity. The total of the individual present values (the income for each period), which equals the present value of the ordinary annuity, in this case will be the capitalized value of the machine. If the machine is expected to produce $1,000 per period for five periods, the present value of this stream of income (payments) can be calculated as follows, assuming a 4 per cent rate of interest:

$$P = \frac{A}{(1 + i)^1} + \frac{A}{(1 + i)^2} + \frac{A}{(1 + i)^3} + \frac{A}{(1 + i)^4} + \frac{A}{(1 + i)^5}$$

$$P = \frac{\$1,000}{(1.04)^1} + \frac{\$1,000}{(1.04)^2} + \frac{\$1,000}{(1.04)^3} + \frac{\$1,000}{(1.04)^4} + \frac{\$1,000}{(1.04)^5}$$

$$P = \$961.54 + \$924.56 + \$889.00 + \$854.80 + \$821.93$$

$$P = \$4,451.83.$$

The present value of the $1,000 available at the end of the first period is equal to the discounted value of that amount. The $1,000 in this case is discounted at 4 per cent, which could be the market rate of interest. The discounted value of the $1,000 available at the end of the second period is equal to $\frac{\$1,000}{(1 + i)^2}$. The exponent was explained earlier; in this case, it represents the number of time periods in the future for each calculation.

By comparing the present value of this stream of income to the present cost of the machine, the firm can determine whether or not the machine is worth buying. If the present value of the income (capitalized value) is less than the machine's cost, it would not be advisable to make the purchase; it would be better to take the money that would purchase the machine and invest it at 4 per cent.

Another very common business problem involves finding the periodic payment needed to produce a predetermined amount. This type of problem requires a rearrangement of the annuity formula. Suppose that the Hypothetical Mailbox Manufacturing Company estimates that in five years it will need additional equipment costing approximately $5,633. The company must know how much it should invest at the beginning of each year for five years in order to accumulate this amount. At a prevailing interest rate of 4 per cent, the amount is calculated as follows:

$$A = P(1 + i)^5 + P(1 + i)^4 + P(1 + i)^3 + P(1 + i)^2 + P(1 + i)^1.$$

Since P is to be determined, it must be factored from the expression as follows:

$$A = P[(1 + i)^5 + (1 + i)^4 + (1 + i)^3 + (1 + i)^2 + (1 + i)^1].$$

The equation is now rearranged to solve for P, the amount that must be set aside each year for five years:

$$P = \frac{A}{(1 + i)^5 + (1 + i)^4 + (1 + i)^3 + (1 + i)^2 + (1 + i)^1}$$

$$P = \frac{\$5,633}{(1.04)^5 + (1.04)^4 + (1.04)^3 + (1.04)^2 + (1.04)^1}$$

$$P = \frac{\$5,633}{1.216 + 1.170 + 1.125 + 1.082 + 1.040}$$

$$P = \frac{\$5,633}{5.633}$$

$$P = \$1,000.$$

This is really a variation of the calculations used earlier to illustrate an annuity due. In this case, P is solved for instead of A; the formula shows that $1,000 should be invested at the beginning of each year.

EFFECTIVE RATE OF INTEREST

Consumers and business establishments may borrow money on either a lump-sum basis or an installment basis. An important fundamental for business analysis when purchases or loans are arranged on an installment basis is what is known as the *effective rate of interest*.

The effective rate of interest is substantially higher than the stated rate of interest. The general rule is that the effective rate will be approximately twice the stated rate, although the larger the number of installment periods, the more closely the effective rate will approach twice the stated rate. The effective rate is higher because the loan is being paid back on an installment basis, while the actual interest charge was calculated on the total amount of the loan for the total length of the installment period, and not on the unpaid balances.

Several examples are presented to illustrate the difference between the effective rate and the stated rate. Suppose that the Hypothetical Mailbox

Manufacturing Company decides to borrow $6,000 for five years to purchase some new equipment. The company arranges to borrow the $6,000 at a total interest charge of $1,500 for the five years to be paid back in a lump sum at maturity. Using the simple-interest formula, the interest rate is calculated as follows:

$$I = P \times i \times T$$

$$\$1,500 = \$6,000 \times i \times 5$$

$$\$300 = \$6,000i$$

$$i = \frac{\$300}{\$6,000}$$

$$i = 0.05 = 5\%.$$

This 5 per cent is the effective rate as well as the stated rate because this is a lump-sum loan.

Compare this 5 per cent interest rate with an arrangement where the company is to pay back the $6,000 in five equal annual installments. The interest charge of $1,500 is the same as that used for the lump-sum loan; the stated rate is therefore 5 per cent $[i = I/PT = \$1,500/(\$6,000 \times 5)]$. In calculating the effective rate of interest, the *average principal outstanding* of $3,600 is used instead of the principal of $6,000. Since the first installment of $1,200 was paid at the end of the first year, the $6,000 was really loaned for only one year. The payment of the second installment of $1,200 at the end of the second year means that only $4,800 was loaned for two years; $3,600 was loaned for three years; and so on. The calculation of the average principal of $3,600 is as follows:

Amount borrowed for one year	$ 6,000
Amount borrowed for two years	4,800
Amount borrowed for three years	3,600
Amount borrowed for four years	2,400
Amount borrowed for five years	1,200
	$18,000

The average principal outstanding is $18,000/5 = \$3,600$. The effective rate of interest is calculated by using the simple-interest formula:

$$I = P \times i \times T$$

$$\$1,500 = \$3,600 \times i \times 5$$

$$i = \frac{\$1,500}{\$18,000}$$

$$i = 8\tfrac{1}{3}\%.$$

The effective rate of interest of $8\frac{1}{3}$ per cent is not double the stated rate of 5 per cent because the number of periods is too small. If the payments had been arranged on a monthly installment basis, there would have been 60 payments in the five-year period, and the average principal outstanding would have been $3,050 (the $6,000 borrowed for the first month plus $100 borrowed for the last month, divided by 2). The effective rate of interest would be almost twice the 5 per cent stated rate; it can be calculated as follows:

$$I = P \times i \times T$$

$$\$1,500 = \$3,050 \times i \times 5 \text{ years}$$

$$i = \frac{\$1,500}{\$18,000}$$

$$i = 0.09836 = 9.8\%.$$

Consumers are often confronted with this type of situation because the effective rate of interest is applicable to consumer installment purchases and personal loans. The schedule of repayments in Table 15–1 is typical of financial institutions that advertise their services to prospective borrowers.

TABLE 15–1

EXAMPLES OF REPAYMENTS*

Cash Received	Monthly Payments
$ 284.60	$17.00
522.90	33.00
997.74	49.00
1,358.48	68.00
1,507.48	74.00
1,752.32	86.00

*The first two examples are based on 24 months, the others on 36 months. Payments include all charges and insurance.

The effective rate of interest can be easily determined for the items in the table, even though the advertisement did not mention the interest rate. The total amount of the payments in the first example is $408.00 ($17.00 × 24 months). The difference between the cash received and the total amount of payments is $123.40 ($408.00 − $284.60). This $123.40 is often referred to as the *carrying charge*, because it includes the cost of such items as bookkeeping and credit investigation. In this example, insurance is also included. It is customary to consider the entire carrying charge as an interest charge. The average balance outstanding for the first example is $150.80 ($284.60, the amount borrowed for the first month, plus $17.00, the amount borrowed during the last month, divided by 2). The effective rate of interest for the first example is calculated as follows:

$$I = P \times i \times T$$

$$\$123.40 = \$150.80 \times i \times 2 \text{ years}$$

$$i = \frac{\$123.40}{\$301.60}$$

$$i = 0.4091 = 40.9\%.$$

Consumers rarely are aware of the interest rate charged on installment purchases and on personal loans of the type just illustrated.

In conclusion, our analysis of the effective rate of interest clearly indicates that the real rate of interest on installment loans is much higher than the stated rate. This is primarily due to the fact that calculation of the effective rate of interest is based upon the average principal outstanding rather than on the total loan amount. This should be taken into consideration when making business decisions.

PROBLEMS AND PROJECTS

1. Calculate to what amount $1,000 would accumulate at the end of three years, compounded at an annual rate of 3 per cent.
2. Calculate $1,000 compounded every four months for two years at an annual rate of 6 per cent; compare the results with the example illustrating $1,000 compounded semiannually for two years at 6 per cent that appears on page 351 of the text.
3. Calculate the present value of a stream of income from a machine which is estimated to be $10,000 for the first year, $800 for the second year, and $300 for the third year. Assume the rate of interest to be 4 per cent.
4. Assume that you are an insurance company executive representing the Hypothetical Mutual Insurance Company, which is in court to settle a legitimate liability claim. One of the company's policyholders permanently disabled a nurse in a recent automobile-pedestrian accident. The nurse, who is 40 years of age and quite competent as a surgeon's assistant, claims a loss of income per year of $3,000 until the retirement age of 60. Since she is permanently disabled, she will not be eligible to assist in surgery. She is requesting payment of $60,000 from the company to be deposited to her 5 per cent savings account at the bank.

   As the executive handling this case, what suggestion would you make to the court in determining the amount of the settlement? Would it be more or less than $60,000? On what basis would you justify this amount as a final settlement at this time? What alternative might you suggest in lieu of a lump-sum settlement?

5. Calculate the effective rate of interest on the first 12-month plan illustrated in the advertisement and on the 48-month plan. What would you estimate the stated or nominal rate to be in the two plans?

LOANS ARRANGED UP TO $3,000 OR MORE

Miss   1–66

TYPICAL PAYMENT PLANS

CASH YOU GET	MONTHLY PAYMENT	CASH YOU GET	MONTHLY PAYMENT
12 Months		18 Months	
$ 109.28	$ 11.00	$ 275.53	$ 20.00
198.68	20.00	482.17	35.00
496.68	50.00	694.03	50.00
1,004.87	100.00	1,192.18	85.00
1,564.51	155.00	1,619.15	115.00
25 Months		48 Months	
$ 141.18	$ 8.00	$3,037.98	$100.00
494.13	28.00		
675.77	38.00		
1,080.06	60.00		
2,274.56	125.00		

Reprinted by permission of the State Loan and Finance Management Corporation, Silver Spring, Maryland.

SELECTED REFERENCE

Bowen, Earl K., *Mathematics: With Application in Management and Economics.* Homewood, Ill.: Richard D. Irwin, Inc., 1967.

16

PROBABILITY

Most individuals associate probability with card games and games of chance. Gamblers are indeed interested in the possibilities of obtaining certain combinations of cards or of selecting alternatives in other games of chance. However, probability and its terminology also appear in many of our everyday experiences and business operations.

Weathermen give their weather forecasts in terms borrowed from probability experts; it is common to have the chances of rain on a particular day expressed as a percentage. Businessmen are willing to accept material from their suppliers on the basis of spot checks, or *acceptance samples*. They understand what their acceptance inspections mean. Accounting firms conduct audits of their clients' books and records with faith in the probabilities associated with the sampling procedures that are employed.

The space program works toward maximum *reliability* in the operation of its various space systems. Reliability is another form of probability. The success of any space system depends on the successful operation of hundreds of components and subsystems. Each subsystem is built with the objective of almost perfect performance; that is, it should perform successfully nearly every time. The association of reliability and probability is cleverly illustrated by the problem of successfully driving a nail with a hammer, given by Carl O. Holmquist in his article, "Reliability of Reliability,"[1] A reprint of the article is provided in the student workbook to this text, *Study Props*. Holmquist concludes that the probability of successfully completing the hammer-nail operation is only 0.058. That is, there is roughly a 1-in-20 chance that the nail will be driven successfully. There are eight different elements necessary to the successful completion of the act—for example, finding a hammer, finding

[1] Carl O. Holmquist, "Reliability of Reliability," *Ground Support Equipment* (August-September 1961), 42–43.

a nail, hitting the nail, preventing the hammer head from flying off the handle, and so forth.

One of the classical exercises in probability that is used in the classroom is discovering if any two persons in the class have the same birthday. The results are surprising, in half of the classes with only 23 students, two persons will have the same birthday. With classes of 30 students, there will be individuals with the same birthday better than two out of three times. In a class of 50 students, it is almost certain that two persons will have the same birthday. The formulation of the birthday problem for 30 students appears as follows:

$$\text{Probability} = 1 - \frac{365}{365} \times \frac{364}{365} \times \frac{363}{365} \times \ldots \times \frac{336}{365};$$

the last term, $\frac{336}{365}$, accounts for the thirtieth student.

Let us be sure that it is clear what "two out of three times" means in this case. If all classes have 30 students, an instructor can expect that two persons will have the same birthday in two-thirds of all his classes over the years. This equation does not provide the odds that a given person will have the same birthday as any one of the other 29 persons. It merely gives the odds that any two persons in the class will have the same birthday.

PROPERTIES OF PROBABILITY MEASURES

The symbol we will use for designating the probability of an event—say A—is $P(A)$. Thus the probability of the event of two persons having the same birthday in a class of 30 students can be written as

$$P(A) = \frac{2}{3}.$$

It is assumed here (and throughout this chapter) that the events we are studying belong to a finite set of possible outcomes.

Probability measures have several properties; one of these properties, which reflects the fact that probability is measured by a real number, can be stated as follows:

$$0 \leq P(A) \leq 1.$$

The probability of event A must be 0, 1, or any real number between 0 and 1. The fact that an event has a probability of 1 simply means that it is certain to occur. For example, the probability of a head occurring is certain if a coin has heads on both sides (unless the coin lands on its edge or rolls away where it cannot be recovered). A probability of zero would refer to an impossible situation—for example, obtaining tails on a two-headed coin. Of course, the closer the measure of probability of an event is to 1, the greater its chance is of occurring.

Another property reflects the fact that the sum of the probabilities of all possible events adds up to 1. This rule is expressed as follows:

$$\sum P(A)_i = 1.$$

In addition some definitions will now be given to familiarize the student with the terms associated with the calculus of probability. An experiment is comprised of a set of *outcomes*. The set of all possible outcomes of an experiment is called the *sample space* or *probability space* of the experiment, and each possible outcome is called a *point* of the sample space. The tossing of a die constitutes an experiment with six possible outcomes—the points of the probability space. The probability space of the die experiment is the set of points {1, 2, 3, 4, 5, 6}. If we are only interested in the subset of points that consists of even numbers, we are specifying an *event*. Therefore, an event is defined as a subset of a sample space.

The probability of each of the points in the die experiment, assuming a fair die, is $\frac{1}{6}$; therefore, the sum of all the points of the sample space is also 1. The probability of the event of an even number is

$$P(A) = \sum p_i$$

where p_1 is the probability of obtaining a 2, p_2 is the probability of obtaining a 4, and p_3 is the probability of obtaining a 6. The event A is comprised of the sample points whose result is even; thus

$$P(A) = \frac{1}{6} + \frac{1}{6} + \frac{1}{6}$$
$$P(A) = \frac{1}{2}.$$

When two or more events cannot occur at the same time, they are called *mutually exclusive*. For example, the occurrence of an even number on a die (event A) is mutually exclusive with the occurrence of an odd number (event B), since both events cannot occur at the same time.

TWO WAYS OF DETERMINING PROBABILITIES

The probability of an outcome can be measured in the classical sense by one of two methods. For the sake of simplicity, one method will be referred to as the *empirical* approach; the other as the *mathematical* approach. The empirical method relies on the *frequency* of an outcome—that is, the observed number of times it occurs—to predict future outcomes. The mathematical method relies on the theoretical occurrence of an outcome, determined by the specifications of the sample space. The results of these two methods are frequently called *a priori* probabilities. A method for calculating *a posteriori* probabilities (probabilities based on hindsight) is illustrated in the Annex to this chapter; these probabilities are commonly referred to as *Bayesian probabilities*.

Empirical Probabilities

If a coin is flipped over and over again, the number of times heads appears should be approximately the same as the number of times tails appears. The observation and recording of these outcomes constitutes the empirical approach to determining the probability of obtaining a head. The empirical approach is used by those who try to outsmart the gambling tables by observing and recording the frequency of occurrence of a certain outcome in order to predict possible future outcomes.

Suppose that we wish to determine the probability that a thumbtack will land on its head. An experiment in which 10 tacks are tossed is repeated 20 times to obtain the number of times the tacks land point up. This experiment could have been conducted just as well by tossing 200 tacks once; for all practical purposes, the results would be the same. The 20 tosses of 10 tacks might result in 120 of the tacks landing point up; the probability of a tack landing point up would then be approximately $\frac{120}{200}$ or 0.60. The shape of the tacks makes the empirical method more desirable than the mathematical method in this case.

In many instances, either the empirical or the mathematical method can be used. The choice of one method over the other will usually be made because of circumstances; more time and effort may be required to conduct an experiment than to make the necessary calculations, or vice versa. For example, the probability that one particular side of a perfectly shaped, six-sided die will land facing up can be determined by either method. However, the probability of a specified event occurring when two dice are involved is found more easily by the mathematical method.

Mathematical Probabilities

It is useful to enumerate the various outcomes of tossing two dice (ordinary six-sided dice with the numbers 1, 2, 3, 4, 5, or 6 each appearing on one side) in order to determine the probabilities of the events defined as the total of the two numbers appearing face up; the 36 outcomes appear in Table 16–1.

TABLE 16–1

OUTCOMES OF 36 TOSSES OF TWO DICE

Outcome	Die No. 1	Die No. 2	Total	Outcome	Die No. 1	Die No. 2	Total
1	1	1	2	19	4	1	5
2	1	2	3	20	4	2	6
3	1	3	4	21	4	3	7
4	1	4	5	22	4	4	8
5	1	5	6	23	4	5	9
6	1	6	7	24	4	6	10
7	2	1	3	25	5	1	6
8	2	2	4	26	5	2	7
9	2	3	5	27	5	3	8
10	2	4	6	28	5	4	9
11	2	5	7	29	5	5	10
12	2	6	8	30	5	6	11
13	3	1	4	31	6	1	7
14	3	2	5	32	6	2	8
15	3	3	6	33	6	3	9
16	3	4	7	34	6	4	10
17	3	5	8	35	6	5	11
18	3	6	9	36	6	6	12

TABLE 16–2

FREQUENCY OF OCCURRENCE OF OUTCOMES OF TWO DICE

Total	Frequencies	Probabilities
2	1	$\frac{1}{36}$
3	2	$\frac{2}{36}$
4	3	$\frac{3}{36}$
5	4	$\frac{4}{36}$
6	5	$\frac{5}{36}$
7	6	$\frac{6}{36}$
8	5	$\frac{5}{36}$
9	4	$\frac{4}{36}$
10	3	$\frac{3}{36}$
11	2	$\frac{2}{36}$
12	1	$\frac{1}{36}$
	Total $= 36$	Total $= \frac{36}{36}$

The total is computed for the pair of numbers appearing on each die. The outcomes occur with the frequencies given in Table 16–2. Determining these probabilities empirically would have taken a great deal more time than was devoted here, since the tossing of the dice would have to have been repeated a very large number of times.

Another example emphasizes the importance of the mathematical approach and illustrates the need for using special counting techniques to compute probabilities in more complex problems. The problem illustrates an approach for determining the probabilities that the baseball World Series will last either four, five, six, or seven games. Several realistic assumptions are made to simplify the presentation. The first assumption is that the two teams engaged in the World Series are evenly matched. Specifically, we assume that the probability of either club winning any particular game is $\frac{1}{2}$. This also implies that neither team will experience an unusual winning streak.

The problem can now be divided into four parts, which are the probabilities that the series will last (1) four games, (2) five games, (3) six games, or (4) seven games. These solutions appear as follows:

(1) P(series $= 4$ games) $= P$(National League wins in 4 games) $+ P$(American League wins in 4 games)

This can be simplified by calculating the probability of one team winning and multiplying by two, since the two events above are equally likely. Therefore,

$$P(S = 4) = 2 \times P(\text{National League wins in 4})$$
$$= 2 \times P(NNNN)$$
$$= 2 \times \left(\frac{1}{2}\right)\left(\frac{1}{2}\right)\left(\frac{1}{2}\right)\left(\frac{1}{2}\right)$$
$$= 2 \times \left(\frac{1}{2}\right)^4 = \frac{1}{8} = 0.125.$$

This says that since the probability of one of the teams winning any game is $\frac{1}{2}$ and since there are four games, we simply multiply together the chances of winning each game. The outcome of any one game has no effect on the other games.

For the five-game series, the probability is as follows:

(2) $P(S = 5) = 2 \times P$(National League wins in 5)
$= 2 \times [P(ANNNN) + P(NANNN) + P(NNANN) + P(NNNAN)]$.

The National League team can win the series in five games in four different ways, which are represented in the above equation. The first way shown is for the American League team to win the first game and the National League team to win the next four. The second way is for the American League team to win only the second game, and so forth. The equation is solved by inserting the probability of winning any particular game, which is $\frac{1}{2}$; we then have,

$$P(S = 5) = 2 \times \left[\left(\frac{1}{2}\right)^5 + \left(\frac{1}{2}\right)^5 + \left(\frac{1}{2}\right)^5 + \left(\frac{1}{2}\right)^5\right]$$
$$= 2 \times 4 \times \left(\frac{1}{2}\right)^5$$
$$= \frac{8}{32} = 0.250.$$

The probability of the series continuing for six games requires the American League team to win two games:

(3) $P(S = 6) = 2 \times P(\text{National League wins in 6})$
$= 2 \times [P(AANNNN) + P(NAANNN) + P(NNAANN) +$
$P(NNNAAN) + P(ANANNN) + P(ANNANN) + P(ANNN\text{-}$
$AN) + P(NANANN) + P(NANNAN) + P(NNANAN)]$
$= 2 \times 10 \times \left(\dfrac{1}{2}\right)^6$
$= \dfrac{20}{64} = 0.3125.$

There are 20 different ways for the series to last seven games, which will be reserved for the reader to determine. The calculations reduce to the following series of expressions:

(4) $P(S = 7) = 2 \times P(\text{National League wins in 7})$
$= 2 \times [P(AAANNNN) + \cdots + P(NANANAN)]$
$= 2 \times 20 \times \left(\dfrac{1}{2}\right)^7 = \dfrac{40}{128} = 0.3125.$

It should not seem surprising that the probability of the World Series lasting six or seven games is the most likely one. The historical data on the World Series outcomes are surprisingly close to these mathematically determined probabilities.

The calculation of the seven-game series (and even the six-game series) can be simplified by some special counting rules which act as shortcuts for determining the number of ways an event can occur. These rules will be introduced next.

COUNTING FOR PROBABILITY

Counting techniques are useful with problems that require a collection of items to accomplish a specific event or outcome. A few basic techniques and rules are available for determining the number of ways an outcome can occur instead of having to enumerate them. The basic approaches illustrated in this text are divided into two categories: The first applies to cases in which repetition or replacement of objects or items in a collection is allowed; the second, to cases in which replacement is not allowed or is not possible. The reader is reminded at this point that the illustrations of the counting techniques are provided mainly to explain the formulas that are used in conjunction with the mathematical method of probability.

Counting with Replacement

We will illustrate the first method of counting by an example. A disk from a set of three disks marked with the letters *A*, *B*, or *C* is selected and tabulated, then replaced in the set. This process is repeated twice more. One outcome might appear as *A–B–A*, another as *C–B–A*, and so forth. All the possible outcomes are illustrated by the tree diagram in Table 16–3, which systematically enumerates these possibilities. The table shows that there are 27 outcomes that can be obtained.

TABLE 16–3

TREE DIAGRAM

First Disk Selected	Second Disk Selected	Third Disk Selected	Sets or Configurations
A	A	A	AAA
		B	AAB
		C	AAC
	B	A	ABA
		B	ABB
		C	ABC
	C	A	ACA
		B	ACB
		C	ACC
B	A	A	BAA
		B	BAB
		C	BAC
	B	A	BBA
		B	BBB
		C	BBC
	C	A	BCA
		B	BCB
		C	BCC
C	A	A	CAA
		B	CAB
		C	CAC
	B	A	CBA
		B	CBB
		C	CBC
	C	A	CCA
		B	CCB
		C	CCC

It is not really necessary to use the tree diagram to determine that there are 27 ways in which the three disks can be arranged. The results of the pattern that was developed can be obtained by the formula

$$N = n^r,$$

where *N* represents the number of ways that an *n* number of distinct items can be arranged when an *r* number of items is selected for each arrangement or configuration. In the example in Table 16–3 there were three items (A, B, and C) arranged in groups of exactly r items (also three). Therefore, N is directly obtained by

$$N = 3^3$$
$$N = 27.$$

This example is the special case where r was equal to n. If only two of the three disks were selected and arranged each time, r would only be 2 and n would remain equal to 3. We then would obtain only the nine configurations that result when two disks are selected. These also appear in the tree diagram; they can be seen in the column labeled "Second Disk Selected." In this case,

$$N = 3^2$$
$$N = 9.$$

Another way to illustrate this case is to place the configurations in a rectangular display as shown in Table 16–4.

TABLE 16–4

RECTANGULAR DISPLAY WITH REPLACEMENT

		Second Disk Selected		
		A	B	C
First	A	AA	AB	AC
Disk	B	BA	BB	BC
Selected	C	CA	CB	CC

The same nine configurations that appeared in Table 16–3 (under the heading "Second Disk Selected") are shown in Table 16–4. In the later case, again,

$$N = n^r$$
$$N = 3^2$$
$$N = 9.$$

This formula also applies if r is greater than n. The important thing to keep in mind is that regardless of the number of items in each collection, the formula $N = n^r$ can only be applied to cases where one item is replaced before another one is selected. Other rules are used when replacement is not intended.

Counting without Replacement

The rules provided in the previous section are applicable to those counting situations where an item can be counted more than once. Specifically, the configuration consisting of three A's represents an instance where an item is repeated. In contrast, the rules in this section are applicable to those cases where repetition is *not* allowed; the occurrence of an item in a configuration more than once is not considered. The discussion of these procedures is divided into two categories. The first applies to cases where the order of the selected items is relevant, and the second to those in which it is not—for example, those where *AB* is the same as *BA*. The first category deals with what are called *permutations*; the latter group is concerned with *combinations*.

Permutations. The selection of three disks marked *A*, *B*, or *C* will be used to illustrate the conditions related to permutations. A permutation is defined as an ordered arrangement of objects. If the three disks are selected one at a time, there will be six *ordered* arrangements possible in each trial: *ABC*, *ACB*, *BAC*, *BCA*, *CAB*, and *CBA*.

The reader can verify this by constructing a tree diagram. The number of ordered ways that exist in any situation can be determined by solving the following formula for permutations ($_nP_r$), given *n* items selected in groups of size *r*:

$$_nP_r = n(n - 1)(n - 2) \cdots (n - r + 1)$$
$$_3P_3 = 3(3 - 1) \cdots (3 - 3 + 1)$$
$$_3P_3 = 3 \times 2 \times 1$$
$$_3P_3 = 6.$$

If *n* and *r* are both 5, we have

$$_nP_r = 5(5 - 1)(5 - 2)(5 - 3)(5 - 5 + 1)$$
$$_5P_5 = 5 \times 4 \times 3 \times 2 \times 1$$
$$_5P_5 = 120.$$

The reader must be reminded that the situation where *r* is equal to *n* is also a special case. For example, if only *r* were 3, then

$$_5P_3 = 5(5 - 1)(5 - 3 + 1)$$
$$_5P_3 = 5 \times 4 \times 3$$
$$_5P_3 = 60.$$

The case where *r* = *n* is sometimes determined by using the formula for a factorial (written as *n*!):

$$n! = n(n - 1)(n - 2) \cdots 3 \times 2 \times 1.$$

For *n* = 5,

$$5! = 5(5 - 1)(5 - 2) \times 2 \times 1$$
$$5! = 5 \times 4 \times 3 \times 2 \times 1$$
$$5! = 120.$$

This is the same result as the one for $_nP_r$ when $r = n$ (or simply for $_nP_n$).

When working with factorials, one should remember that 0! is equal to 1. This is proven as follows: Since $n! = n(n - 1)!$ [note the $(n - 1)!$ term], then let $n = 1$; therefore,

$$1! = 1(1 - 1)!$$
$$1! = 1(0)!$$
$$1 = 0!$$

Let us now return to the case where r is less than n and we have the same three disks marked A, B, and C. If only two disks are selected at a time, we will have six ordered arrangements, since

$$_nP_r = n(n - 1)(n - 2) \cdots (n - r + 1)$$
$$_3P_2 = 3(3 - 2 + 1)$$
$$_3P_2 = 3 \times 2$$
$$_3P_2 = 6.$$

The six arrangements appear in the same matrix as the one in Table 16–4 which was used to illustrate the nine configurations or arrangements when replacement was permitted. Table 16–5 shows this matrix with the diagonal elements crossed out; they do not represent an *ordered* way—that is, a permutation—because repetition is not allowed. The remaining elements consist of the six *ordered* ways that three disks marked A, B, or C can be selected one at a time for a collection of two.

TABLE 16–5

RECTANGULAR DISPLAY WITHOUT REPLACEMENT

		Second Disk Selected		
		A	*B*	*C*
First	*A*	~~AA~~	AB	AC
Disk	*B*	BA	~~BB~~	BC
Selected	*C*	CA	CB	~~CC~~

Combinations. There are other situations where one might want to consider that BA and AB are the same arrangement and, therefore, that CA is the same as AC and CB is the same as BC. When the items in one collection are identical to the items in another collection but different in order, the collections are identified as *combinations*; none of these are counted more than once.

The six ordered ways previously illustrated can be divided into two groups (or subsets): AB, AC, and BC make up one group and BA, CA, and CB the other. Therefore, we must divide $_nP_r$ by 2 to arrive at the correct number of combinations. The formula for determining the number of combinations is

$$_nC_r = \frac{n(n-1)(n-2)\cdots(n-r+1)}{r!}.$$

The numerator is the same expression as that for permutations; however, the denominator is r!, which represents the number of subsets associated with the permutation of n items selected r at a time that is necessary to reduce $_nP_r$ to $_nC_r$. In our example, $n = 3$ and $r = 2$; therefore,

$$_nC_r = \frac{(3)(2)}{2!}$$

$$_3C_2 = \frac{3 \times 2}{2 \times 1} = 3.$$

These three arrangements appear in Table 16–5. They include either the three items above the diagonal elements that were crossed out or the three below them; that is, AB, AC, BC, or BA, CB, and CA.

The number of combinations into which the three disks marked A, B, and C can be arranged when three are taken one at a time is calculated as follows:

$$_3C_3 = \frac{3(3-1)(3-3+1)}{3!}$$

$$_3C_3 = \frac{3 \times 2 \times 1}{3 \times 2 \times 1} = 1.$$

The configuration ABC is the same as BCA, CBA, or any others.

Before these two rules of combinations and permutations are applied to a problem, we will provide the reader with a computational formula for calculating $_nP_r$ and $_nC_r$. Since $_nP_r$ is defined as $n(n-1)(n-2)\cdots(n-r+1)$, we can alter it slightly by multiplying it by the term $\frac{(n-r)!}{(n-r)!}$. This does not change its value, but it does result in the following form:

$$_nP_r = n(n-1)(n-2)\cdots(n-r+1)\frac{(n-r)!}{(n-r)!}$$

$$_nP_r = \frac{n!}{(n-r)!},$$

because

$$n(n-1)(n-2)\cdots(n-r+1)(n-r)! = n!.$$

Similarly, $_nC_r$ can be changed to

$$_nC_r = \frac{n!}{r!(n - r)!}$$

by multiplying by the same factor. Both of these formulas are much easier to use than the definitional ones given previously. One must also keep in mind that in these two cases, r should not be greater than n.

Three examples are given to illustrate the calculation of permutations and combinations. The first example shows that there are 720 ordered ways in which a six-volume set of books can be arranged on a shelf. The calculation uses the formula for permutations when $r = n$; for instance,

$$_6P_6 = \frac{n!}{(n - r)!}$$

$$_6P_6 = \frac{6!}{(6 - 6)!} = 6! \qquad \text{(or simply } n!\text{)}$$

$$_6P_6 = 6 \times 5 \times 4 \times 3 \times 2 \times 1 = 720.$$

The second example provides the answer to the number of ways in which a president, vice-president, secretary, and treasurer can be elected from a slate of seven candidates. The answer is obtained by finding $_7P_4$:

$$_7P_4 = \frac{7!}{(7 - 4)!} = 7 \times 6 \times 5 \times 4 = 840.$$

Although the third example may seem similar to the second, it clearly calls for the determination of combinations rather than of permutations. Suppose that it is desirable to determine how many different committees of four can be selected from the same group of seven persons. It should be apparent that positions on a committee are not distinct (or identifiable) as they are with the organizational positions associated with the previous problem. Since the combinational approach is appropriate,

$$_7C_4 = \frac{n!}{r!(n - r)!} = \frac{7!}{4!3!} = 35.$$

(Note that $r! = 4 \times 3 \times 2 \times 1$ and, since $_nC_r = \frac{_nP_r}{r!}$ we also have $\frac{840}{r!}$

$= \frac{840}{24} = 35.$)

The counting rules for determining probabilities are most essential in determining the probabilities of events. The number of ways in which a particular event can occur, as related to the total ways in which all possible events can occur, is the basis for determining the probability of a simple event. The rules for determining the probabilities of combined events are also given in the next section.

DETERMINING THE PROBABILITY OF AN EVENT

The first step in determining the probabilities of simple or single events is to establish the number of ways in which a given event can occur; this figure serves as the numerator in the probability ratio. The second step is to determine the denominator, which consists of the total number of ways in which all events that are associated with the experiment can occur.

Often complex events are simply identifiable as combinations of simple events. However, the procedure for determining the probabilities of combined events depends upon certain relationships among these events. Mutually exclusive events must be identified; independent events must be treated differently from those that are not independent. Each of these situations is illustrated in this section.

Simple Events

The toss of a die can result in six different events: the numbers 1, 2, 3, 4, 5, or 6. There is only one way that the number 1 can occur, one way that the number 2 can occur, and so forth; thus, each number represents a simple event with a probability of $\frac{1}{6}$. Let us take another example related to the tossing of a die. This time we are interested in the probability that a given die will have an even number. It is obvious that there are three ways in which an even number can result (2, 4, or 6). Since the experiment can end up in a total of six ways, the probability of an even number occurring is 3 divided by 6. In summary, the probability of an event (A) is

$$P(A) = \frac{\text{number of ways } A \text{ can occur}}{\text{number of ways all events in experiment can occur}}.$$

If we go one step further and calculate the probability of obtaining an even number or the number 1, we are combining two simple events. The probability of A (obtaining an even number) or B (obtaining a 1) is simply

$$P(A \text{ or } B) = P(A) + P(B)$$
$$P(A \text{ or } B) = \frac{3}{6} + \frac{1}{6} = \frac{4}{6}.$$

However, if we ask for the probability of obtaining an even number and/or a 2, we must use another approach. We will now define and illustrate the basic rules for calculating the probabilities of combined events.

Combined Events[2]

There are four basic rules that apply to combined events: two for addition and two for multiplication. In the case of addition, there are two rules because the events being combined may or may not be mutually exclusive; in the case of multiplication, they may or may not be independent. The two rules for addition are stated first with several examples, then the two rules for multiplication are given.

Addition Rules. The first rule applies to mutually exclusive events—that is, to events which cannot occur simultaneously. This is illustrated with what are known as *Venn diagrams*, as shown in Fig. 16–1. The circle labeled *A* includes all the points or outcomes that result in event *A*. The other circle contains all the points that result in event *B*. The rule for addition, when the events are mutually exclusive, is as follows:

Rule 1: If *A* and *B* are mutually exclusive, the probability that *A* or *B* will occur is the sum of both probabilities. Symbolically, this is

$$P(A \text{ or } B) = P(A) + P(B).$$

Example: The probability that a single card drawn from an ordinary deck of cards will be a king (*K*) or a queen (*Q*) is

$$P(K \text{ or } Q) = P(K) + P(Q)$$
$$P(K \text{ or } Q) = \frac{4}{52} + \frac{4}{52} = \frac{2}{13}.$$

The rule to use when events are *not* mutually exclusive—that is, when they may occur at the same time—is diagrammed in Fig. 16–2. The overlapped area represents the simultaneous occurrence of *A* and *B*. This is generally referred to as the *intersection* of *A* and *B*, written as *AB*.

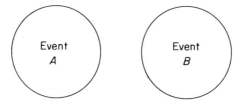

Event
A

Event
B

FIGURE 16–1.   Venn diagram of events that are mutually exclusive.

[2] These four rules were adapted from D. V. Huntsberger, *Elements of Statistical Inference* (Boston: Allyn & Bacon, Inc., 1961), pp. 75–78.

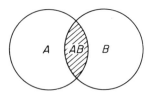

FIGURE 16–2.   Venn diagram of events that are not mutually exclusive.

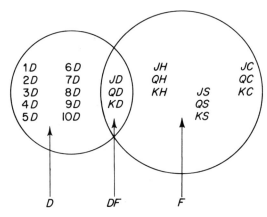

FIGURE 16–3.   Venn diagram showing points associated with events.

Rule 2: If *A* and *B* are not mutually exclusive, the probability of *A* and/or *B* is the sum of the probabilities of *A* and *B* minus the probability of their joint occurrence—that is, *AB*. In symbol form,

$$P(A \text{ and/or } B) = P(A) + P(B) - P(AB).$$

Example: The probability that a card drawn from a deck will be a diamond (*D*) or a face card (*F*) (where aces are not counted as face cards) is

$$P(D \text{ and/or } F) = P(D) + P(F) - P(DF)$$
$$P(D \text{ and/or } F) = \frac{13}{52} + \frac{12}{52} - \frac{3}{52} = \frac{22}{52}.$$

Let us illustrate this example in more detail by inserting the various points associated with each event into a Venn diagram as in Fig. 16–3. The *DF* area contains those three instances where the diamonds are face cards or, if you like, where the face cards are diamonds. In any event, *DF* represents the points that are common to both *D* and *F*; it shows the joint occurrence of a diamond and a face card—that is, a diamond which is a face card. Note that if we simply added $P(A)$ and $P(B)$, we would be adding the three points in DF twice; therefore, $P(DF)$ must be subtracted once. Determining the probability of a joint occurrence such as (DF) requires the information in the next section.

Multiplication Rules. The multiplication rules are applicable to some of the calculations that are required to determine the probabilities of events which are not mutually exclusive. In particular, calculating the probabilities of joint events—for instance, (DF) in the previous example—follows the rules of multiplication. Joint events may be either independent or dependent. Rule 3 gives the procedure for determining the probabilities of joint events that are independent; in other words, the occurrence or nonoccurrence of one event does not affect the probability of occurrence of the other.

Rule 3: If A and B are independent, the probability of their joint occurrence is the product of their individual probabilities; for instance,

$$P(AB) = P(A)P(B).$$

Example: If we have a bowl containing five white and two red disks and a second bowl with four white and three red disks, and if we draw one disk from each bowl, the probability that both disks will be white is

$$P(W_1 W_2) = P(W_1)P(W_2)$$
$$P(W_1 W_2) = \left(\frac{5}{7}\right)\left(\frac{4}{7}\right) = \frac{20}{49}.$$

The subscripts simply identify the first and second bowls. You must keep in mind that there are two different bowls, as shown in Fig. 16–4. The case of nonindependent events can be demonstrated by using only one bowl.

5 white
2 red

4 white
3 red

FIGURE 16–4. Calculating the probability of events that are not mutually exclusive (illustration of Rule 3 Example).

The second multiplication rule applies to events that are not independent (that is, *dependent* events).

Rule 4: If A and B are not independent, the probability of their joint occurrence is the product of the probability of A and the probability of B given that A has occurred. This is written as follows, with the slash mark standing for "given":

$$P(AB) = P(A)P(B/A).$$

Example: Suppose that we have only the first bowl, which contains five white and two red disks; that we draw two disks without replacing either one; and that we want to find the probability that both will be white. The solution is formulated as

$$P(W_1W_2) = P(W_1)P(W_2/W_1).$$

The probability of the first disk being white is simply $\frac{5}{7}$, because there are a total of seven disks of which five are white. Therefore, $P(W_1)$ is $\frac{5}{7}$. The probability of the second disk being white depends upon whether a white disk or a red one was drawn first. If the first disk was white, the probability of the second being white is $\frac{4}{6}$, because there are only four white disks remaining. If a red disk was drawn on the first draw, the probability of a white one on the second draw would be $\frac{5}{6}$. The solution is

$$P(W_1W_2) = \left(\frac{5}{7}\right)\left(\frac{4}{6}\right) = \frac{20}{42}.$$

Let us now list the probabilities for this joint event as well as for the other three possible joint events. Since each of the joint events is mutually exclusive, the total probabilities must add up to the number 1. The four events are as follows:

$$P(W_1W_2) = P(W_1)P(W_2/W_1) = \left(\frac{5}{7}\right)\left(\frac{4}{6}\right) = \frac{20}{42}$$

$$P(W_1R_2) = P(W_1)P(R_2/W_1) = \left(\frac{5}{7}\right)\left(\frac{2}{6}\right) = \frac{10}{42}$$

$$P(R_1W_2) = P(R_1)P(W_2/R_1) = \left(\frac{2}{7}\right)\left(\frac{5}{6}\right) = \frac{10}{42}$$

$$P(R_1R_2) = P(R_1)P(R_2/R_1) = \left(\frac{2}{7}\right)\left(\frac{1}{6}\right) = \frac{2}{42}$$

$$Total = \frac{42}{42}.$$

By simple algebraic manipulation, we can also find the probability of obtaining a white disk on the second draw if one was obtained on the first. We are now asking for the conditional probability $P(W_2/W_1)$. (This is not the same formula as for two white disks because we know the first disk is white.) We must now return to our original rule, which was

$$P(W_1W_2) = P(W_1)P(W_2/W_1).$$

Dividing each side of the equation by $P(W_1)$, we have

$$\frac{P(W_1W_2)}{P(W_1)} = \frac{P(W_1)P(W_2/W_1)}{P(W_1)}.$$

By cancellation and rearrangement,

$$P(W_2/W_1) = \frac{P(W_1W_2)}{P(W_1)}$$

$$P(W_2/W_1) = \frac{20/42}{5/7} = \frac{20}{42} \times \frac{7}{5} = \frac{20}{30} = \frac{2}{3}.$$

If we allow the disks to be replaced before each draw, we obtain a problem of independent events; that is,

$$P(W_1W_2) = P(W_1)P(W_2/W_1)$$

becomes

$$P(W_1W_2) = P(W_1)P(W_2)$$

because

$$P(W_2/W_1) = P(W_2)$$

if replacement is allowed.

SELECTED TOPICS

Two topics are briefly introduced in this section. The calculation of binomial probabilities and the definition of expected value are useful in applying probabilities to the decision-making process.

Binomial Probabilities

Often the number of events in a problem can be limited to two situations, which may take such forms as "failure or success" or "acceptable or rejectable." The binomial formula is appropriate in many situations where only two events are defined. We will illustrate this formula by enumerating, first, the results that are possible with the toss of a coin. Such a toss has only two outcomes; it can be repeated endlessly with the same probability that a head, say, will occur. The basic requirement for the binomial application is that there be only two outcomes, which result in a series of independent repeated trials. We will illustrate the probabilities associated with the toss of a coin when it is tossed once, twice, or three times.

The probability of a head occurring when a coin is tossed once is simply

$$P(H_1) = \frac{1}{2}.$$

The probability of heads occurring when the toss is repeated is

$$P(H_0) = \frac{1}{4}$$

$$P(H_1) = \frac{2}{4}$$

$$P(H_2) = \frac{1}{4}.$$

These results are substantiated by observing the number of ways in which they can occur; that is, HH, TH, HT, and TT. There are two ways to get two heads and one way to get no heads; therefore, these probabilities are $\frac{1}{4}$, $\frac{1}{2}$, and $\frac{1}{4}$, respectively.

If the coin is tossed three times, we have

$$P(H_0) = \frac{1}{8}$$

$$P(H_1) = \frac{3}{8}$$

$$P(H_2) = \frac{3}{8}$$

$$P(H_3) = \frac{1}{8}$$

The reader should enumerate the eight results to verify these probabilities.

We will now employ the binomial formula to obtain the same results as those for the above enumeration. The formula

$$P(r; n) = \binom{n}{r} p^r (1 - p)^{n-r},$$

where the semicolon is translated as "on", $\binom{n}{r}$ is another way to designate $_nC_r$, p is the probability of the success of the particular event and n is the number of tosses. Therefore, the probability of obtaining one head on one toss is as follows:

$$P(1 \text{ head}; 1 \text{ toss}) = \frac{1!}{1!0!}\left(\frac{1}{2}\right)^1\left(\frac{1}{2}\right)^0$$

$$P(1; 1) = \frac{1}{2}.$$

For two tosses of the coin, we have

$$P(H_0; 2) = \frac{2!}{0!2!}\left(\frac{1}{2}\right)^0\left(1 - \frac{1}{2}\right)^{2-0}$$

$$P(0; 2) = 1 \times 1 \times \left(\frac{1}{2}\right)^2 = \frac{1}{4}$$

$$P(1; 2) = \binom{2}{1}\left(\frac{1}{2}\right)^1\left(\frac{1}{2}\right)^1 = \frac{2}{4}$$

$$P(2; 2) = \binom{2}{2}\left(\frac{1}{2}\right)^2\left(\frac{1}{2}\right)^0 = \frac{1}{4}.$$

For three tosses of the coin, we have

$$P(0; 3) = \binom{3}{0}\left(\frac{1}{2}\right)^0\left(\frac{1}{2}\right)^3 = \frac{1}{8}$$

$$P(1; 3) = \binom{3}{1}\left(\frac{1}{2}\right)^1\left(\frac{1}{2}\right)^2 = \frac{3}{8}$$

$$P(2; 3) = \binom{3}{2}\left(\frac{1}{2}\right)^2\left(\frac{1}{2}\right)^1 = \frac{3}{8}$$

$$P(3; 3) = \binom{3}{3}\left(\frac{1}{2}\right)^3\left(\frac{1}{2}\right)^0 = \frac{1}{8}.$$

The binomial formula allows us to determine the probability that a certain number of heads will occur when a coin is tossed n times. The binomial can also be used to determine the probability of, for example, obtaining three sixes when an ordinary six-sided die is tossed four times:

$$P(3; 4) = \binom{4}{3}\left(\frac{1}{6}\right)^3\left(\frac{5}{6}\right)^1 = 4\left(\frac{1}{216}\right)\left(\frac{5}{6}\right) = \frac{20}{1,296}.$$

The probability of two sixes is

$$P(2; 4) = \binom{4}{2}\left(\frac{91}{6}\right)^2\left(\frac{5}{6}\right)^2 = 6\left(\frac{1}{36}\right)\left(\frac{25}{36}\right) = \frac{155}{1,296}.$$

Binomial probabilities are used to make decisions in many business operations. The inspection of manufactured articles represents a sequence of independent trials, where each trial is an inspection of an article that results in one of two outcomes, acceptance or rejection. For instance, suppose that 4 per cent of all items coming off a production line are defective. If 15 such items are chosen and inspected, what is the probability that at most two defectives will be found? Suppose that an integrated circuit produced by an electronics firm is used in a particular space satellite. If the probability of its functioning in a certain prescribed manner is known, then we can determine the probability that any particular number of circuits—say 20—will function properly. The probability that a machine operator will make a series of errors can also be found; this may be used to explain the production of a series of inferior products.

Expected Value

The expected value is simply an average computed on the basis of the probability of each event; it gives a theoretical figure that indicates what can be expected in the long run. The expected value for a single die is calculated as follows:

$$\text{Expected value} = \left(\frac{1}{6} \times 1\right) + \left(\frac{1}{6} \times 2\right) + \left(\frac{1}{6} \times 3\right) +$$
$$\left(\frac{1}{6} \times 4\right) + \left(\frac{1}{6} \times 5\right) + \left(\frac{1}{6} \times 6\right)$$
$$\text{Expected value} = 3\frac{1}{2}.$$

This result may seem peculiar since the number $3\frac{1}{2}$ is not possible with the toss of an ordinary die. However, it emphasizes the fact that the expected value is an average of the actual values of events, which depends upon the probability of each event occurring.

Originally, the concept of mathematical expectation was used in games of chance and lotteries. But the approach is also applicable to such problems as the number of children that can be expected in certain families, the average number of years families are expected to stay in one house, the expected number of responses from mail questionnaires, the expected profits on construction jobs where bids are let, and the expected profit from the sale of a house. Generally, the concept of expected value is meaningful when probabilities of consequences—that is, probabilities associated with losses and gains—are involved.

The probabilities that the World Series would end in four, five, six, or seven games were calculated, respectively, as $\frac{1}{8}$, $\frac{1}{4}$, $\frac{5}{16}$, and $\frac{5}{16}$. The expected number of games the World Series will last is calculated as follows:

$$\text{Expected length of World Series} = \left(\frac{1}{8} \times 4\right) + \left(\frac{1}{4} \times 5\right) + \left(\frac{5}{16} \times 6\right) +$$
$$\left(\frac{5}{16} \times 7\right)$$
$$\text{Expected value} = 5\frac{13}{16}.$$

This represents the number of games the World Series is expected to average in the long run. Actual data on the World Series show that since it began in 1903, it has lasted an average of 5.01 games.

ANNEX : BAYESIAN PROBABILITY

An approach to probability that supplements the classical approach is called *Bayesian probability*. The Bayesian approach appears to be more subjective than the classical approach; however, it has gained a great deal of popularity and its uses are widespread. For example, it can be used to determine the probability that a postdated check will not be covered, or which member of a large mail-order house is most likely to be responsible for a mistake found in a particular order. If a company makes machine parts in three different plants and a part selected at random is found to be defective, the Bayesian method can provide the probability that the defective part comes from one or the other of the plants.

The calculation of Bayesian probability is shown with an example, which will enable the reader to identify the differences and similarities of the Bayesian and classical calculations.

The bowl with five white and two red disks mentioned previously will be used to illustrate the calculation of Bayesian probabilities. A tree diagram is also provided to show the various outcomes and their probabilities. The Bayesian approach relies on the fact that the series of events are related; therefore, non-independence and conditional probabilities are applicable. The tree diagram appears in Fig. 16–5.

The probabilities associated with the results of the four branches of the tree diagram are calculated according to the multiplication rule of non-independent events. They are as follows:

$$P(W_1W_2) = P(W_1)P(W_2/W_1) = \left(\frac{5}{7}\right)\left(\frac{4}{6}\right) = \frac{20}{42}$$

$$P(W_1R_2) = P(W_1)P(R_2/W_1) = \left(\frac{5}{7}\right)\left(\frac{2}{6}\right) = \frac{10}{42}$$

$$P(R_1W_2) = P(R_1)P(W_2/R_1) = \left(\frac{2}{7}\right)\left(\frac{5}{6}\right) = \frac{10}{42}$$

$$P(R_1R_2) = P(R_1)P(R_2/R_1) = \left(\frac{2}{7}\right)\left(\frac{1}{6}\right) = \frac{2}{42}.$$

The classical approach to conditional probability described in the previous section showed, for instance, that

$$P(W_2/W_1) = \frac{P(W_1W_2)}{P(W_1)} = \frac{(5/7)(4/6)}{(5/7)} = \frac{(20/42)}{(5/7)} = \frac{2}{3}.$$

This is the probability that a white disk will be drawn on the second draw, given that a white disk was selected on the first draw. The other three results can be shown similarly as

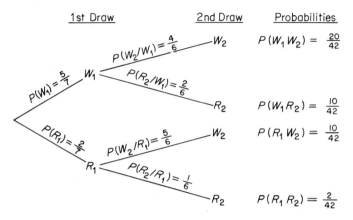

FIGURE 16–5. Calculating Bayesian probability with a tree diagram.

$$P(R_2/W_1) = \frac{P(W_1R_2)}{P(W_1)} = \frac{10/42}{5/7} = \frac{1}{3}$$

$$P(W_2/R_1) = \frac{P(R_1W_2)}{P(R_1)} = \frac{10/42}{2/7} = \frac{5}{6}$$

$$P(R_2/R_1) = \frac{P(R_1R_2)}{P(R_1)} = \frac{2/42}{2/7} = \frac{1}{6}.$$

The probabilities shown on the four branches of the tree diagram correspond to the outcomes of the second draw (they are circled). These are only the classical conditional probabilities. There is a definite cause-and-effect relationship in each instance, and each case or result is treated and observed separately. The calculation of the classical probabilities results in a movement through the tree diagram in a left-to-right direction.

Now let us introduce the Bayesian way of thinking. Suppose that we would like to know the probability that a white disk was selected on the first draw, given that a white disk was selected on the second draw. This is not simply the probability of obtaining two white disks, which is

$$P(W_1W_2) = \frac{20}{42},$$

nor is it the conditional case of

$$P(W_2/W_1) = \frac{2}{3};$$

rather it is

$$P(W_1/W_2).$$

Note that the role of W_1 and W_2 are reversed. The Bayesian question is asking for the probability of the first event occurring after knowing the results of the second event. This is a complete reversal of the classical approach of conditional probability. In order to find $P(W_1/W_2)$, we must select those cases in the tree diagram which resulted in a white disk on the second draw; these cases then represent a new and reduced sample space. In Figure 16–5, the first and third branches of the tree diagram are the relevant events. The answer to the Bayesian problem can now be obtained by dividing the joint probability of having two white disks by the sum of the probabilities that constitute the new sample space—that is, we must divide by the sum of the probabilities of all events in which one white disk appears on the second draw. This is expressed as follows:

$$P(W_1/W_2) = \frac{P(W_1W_2)}{P(W_1W_2) + P(R_1W_2)}$$
$$= \frac{20/42}{20/42 + 10/42}$$
$$= \frac{2}{3}.$$

It is merely an accident that $P(W_1/W_2) = P(W_2/W_1)$ in this example. In essence the $P(W_1/W_2)$ is used as a revision of the $P(W_1)$ which was equal to $\frac{5}{7}$. The related information of observing the outcome on the second draw allows for a revision of the probability of the prior event–that is, the $P(W_1/W_2)$ serves as a revision of $P(W_1)$.

The Bayesian approach represents the probability of hindsight, a sort of backward or inverse reasoning. The method uses the information on the right-hand side of the tree diagram to establish the probability of an event that may be represented on the left-hand side of the diagram.

The Bayesian formula generally appears in a form that contains conditional probabilities as follows:

$$P(W_1/W_2) = \frac{P(W_1)P(W_2/W_1)}{P(W_1)P(W_2/W_1) + P(R_1)P(W_2/R_1)}$$

The example that follows is more typical of the problems that are solved by the Bayesian formula.

A department store found that customers who pay cash return merchandise very infrequently—say, five times in a hundred—while customers who have charge accounts return merchandise more frequently, perhaps 60 per cent of the time. The group with charge accounts is three-quarters of the total. If a clerk at the return desk receives returned merchandise, what is the probability that the customer has a charge account? The problem is solved by defining the various events as follows:

B_1 is the event that identifies the group of customers who pay cash, therefore, $P(B_1) = 0.25$.

B_2 is the event in which the customer has a charge account; therefore, $P(B_2) = 0.75$.

A/B_1 are those customers who return merchandise after paying cash; therefore, $P(A/B_1) = 0.05$.

A/B_2 are those customers who return merchandise that they have charged; therefore, $P(A/B_2) = 0.60$.

These values are substituted in the Bayesian formula for this problem; it appears as

$$P(B_2/A) = \frac{P(B_2)P(A/B_2)}{P(B_2)P(A/B_2) + P(B_1)P(A/B_1)}$$
$$= \frac{(0.75)(0.60)}{(0.75)(0.60) + (0.25)(0.05)}$$
$$= \frac{36}{37}.$$

This answer tells us with a better measure of probability that the customer who returned the merchandise has a charge account, because additional information was used in establishing the result.

PROBLEMS AND PROJECTS

1. Enumerate the 20 ways in which the World Series can last seven games.
2. Conduct an experiment using the ordinary thumbtack by tossing one tack 20 times and determining the percentage of times that it lands point up. Repeat the experiment using 10 thumbtacks. How many tacks land point up when the group of 10 tacks is tossed 10 times?
3. Construct a tree diagram to assist in determining the probability of selecting four differently colored disks so that you have at least three different colors; that is, what is the probability of selecting three or four differently colored disks with replacement when four disks are selected from a set of four differently colored disks?
4. Construct a tree diagram to show the permutations of $_3P_3$ and $_3P_2$. Construct a tree diagram of the combinations $_3C_2$.
5. Calculate $_nC_r$ when $r = n$. Let $r = 3$ and enumerate the ways in which A, B, and C can be arranged.
6. Explain the following expressions:

$$P(A \text{ or } B \text{ or } C) = P(A) + P(B) + P(C)$$
$$P(A \text{ or } B \text{ or } C) = P(A) + P(B) + P(C) - P(AB) - P(AC)$$
$$- P(BC) + P(ABC).$$

7. Enumerate the number of ways in which the events W_1R_2, R_1W_2, R_1R_2, and W_1W_2 may occur with an urn containing five white and two red disks.

The selection is accomplished without replacement. This is the same problem illustrated in the text; however, there the probabilities were not determined by the enumeration process. Establish the probabilities of these four events on the basis of the enumerations. Calculate the probability of W_2/W_1.

8. Repeat Problem 7 allowing replacement.
9. Calculate $P(W_1/W_2)$ for the urn described in Problem 7 when replacement is allowed. This problem is similar to the example in the Annex that demonstrated Bayesian probabilities, except that in that case replacement was not allowed.
10. Use the binomial formula to determine the probability of obtaining four heads in six tosses of an ordinary coin. What is the probability of getting four sixes in one toss of four dice?
11. Given a product that is 4 per cent defective, what is the probability that a sample of four items will contain no defective ones? (Use the binomial formula.)
12. Calculate the expected value of the total numbers appearing face up when two dice are tossed.
13. This problem pertains to material in the Annex. Jim prefers to play golf in good weather. When it is windy, he has a 50–50 chance of scoring under 90, but in good weather the probability that he will shoot under 90 is $\frac{3}{4}$. On Noriss Willy golf course, where he plays, it is known that in March one-third of the days are windy and the rest are calm. If you read in the *Golf Club Bulletin* that Jim shot an 88 on March 16, what is the probability that it was windy on that day?
14. This problem pertains to material in the Annex. Given that 40 per cent of families have no children, 30 per cent have one child, 15 per cent have two children, 10 per cent have three children, and 5 per cent have four children, what is the probability that a family will have three children, given that they have no girls.

SELECTED REFERENCES

Alder, H. L., and E. B. Roessler, *Introduction to Probability and Statistics.* San Francisco: W. H. Freeman & Co., 1964.

Bates, G. E., *Probability.* Reading, Mass.: Addison-Wesley Publishing Co., Inc., 1965.

Burford, R., *Introduction to Finite Probability.* Columbus, O.: Charles E. Merrill Books, Inc., 1967.

Freund, J. E., and F. J. Williams, *Elementary Business Statistics: The Modern Approach.* Englewood Cliffs, N. J.: Prentice-Hall, Inc., 1964.

Goetz, B. E., *Quantitative Methods: A Survey and Guide for Managers.* New York: McGraw-Hill Book Company, 1965.

Guenther, W. C., *Concepts of Statistical Inference.* New York: McGraw-Hill Book Company, 1965.

Levin, R. I., and C. A. Kirkpatrick, *Quantitative Approaches to Management.* New York: McGraw-Hill Book Company, 1965.

Lipschutz, S., *Theory and Problems of Finite Mathematics.* New York: Schaum Publishing Co., 1966.

Meier, R. C., and S. H. Archer, *An Introduction to Mathematics for Business Analysis.* New York: McGraw-Hill Book Company, 1960.

Rutledge, W. A., and T. W. Cairns, *Mathematics for Business Analysis.* New York: Holt, Rinehart & Winston, Inc., 1963.

PART FIVE: Statistical Methods for Decision Making

17

DATA COLLECTION

The availability of adequate and valid information is usually essential to the decision-making process, since decisions cannot be any better than the information or data upon which they are based. The objective of data collection and statistical methodology is to enable rational decisions to be made under conditions of uncertainty.

Information and data are often referred to as *statistics* (or, in the singular form, as a *statistic*.) In this case, the word "statistics" refers to items such as prices, wages, the number of residential buildings under construction, or the number of accidents occurring in a year. The word "statistics" also can have a very broad interpretation; it can be used to refer to the methodology and theory that normally comprise the study of statistics. Therefore, it is possible to look at this term from two viewpoints: that of information or data and that of methodology and theory.

This chapter concentrates on statistics used as data and on the classification of data. The collection of primary data and sampling designs will also be introduced in an elementary fashion.

CLASSIFICATION OF DATA

Data can be divided into two major categories: *primary* and *secondary* data. The basic difference between these two classifications is that secondary data are generally available in published form, in periodicals, almanacs, and abstracts, while primary data are not readily available; they are generated from research and experiments or are collected directly by questionnaires and other survey methods. Summaries and analyses of primary data can also appear in published form. Once this occurs, the primary data are reclassified as secondary data.[1]

Sometimes primary and secondary data are classified as either *internal* or *external*. The distinction is based upon the origin and availability of the data.

A firm's internal records arise from its day-to-day operations and can be used to provide pertinent information for making decisions, such as information on production or selling activities that may be available as secondary data. However, if an internal study (or self-study) is desired, it may be necessary to generate or collect some primary data—that is, internal data that are not readily available.

External secondary data are important in decision making. Management must make decisions not only on the basis of the firm's internal operations but also, on the basis of many highly interdependent activities in the market and in the economy, foreign as well as domestic. Thus the businessman needs information that reflects the state of the national economy or a

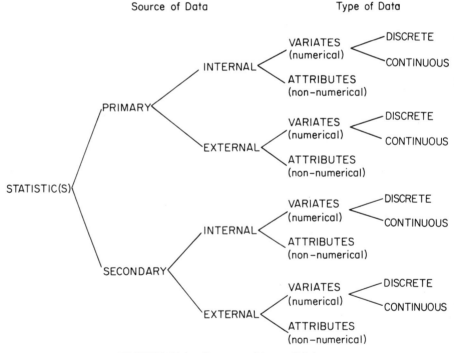

FIGURE 17–1.   Sources and types of data.

[1] There may be some disagreement among researchers in classifying primary data that are published in their original form. For our purposes, we will define such published primary data as secondary data because they have been published or made generally available to other users.

particular industry, in addition to other macroeconomic data. This type of secondary data is provided by governmental agencies, trade associations, and private research organizations.

External primary data must be collected by individuals by means of questionnaires or other data collection devices. The familiar television polls and popularity polls are examples of direct-data acquisition.

The terms *variate* and *attribute* distinguish between numerical and nonnumerical data. If data are numerical—that is, if they are expressed in units of measurement such as inches or pounds or if they consist of an enumeration of items—the information is referred to as a *variate*. If the data are not expressed numerically but are referred to by qualitative characteristics such as red or white, good or bad, accept or reject, large or small, then the data is called an *attribute*.

Variates can be divided into two groups, *discrete* and *continuous*. Basically, discrete variates are expressed in integer form (that is, in whole numbers), and continuous variates include a fractional or decimal part. For example, there may be a class of 35 students with an average height of 5.78 feet. The count of 35 students is a discrete variate, while the height of 5.78 feet is a continuous variate. The terms are summarized in Fig. 17–1.

COLLECTION OF PRIMARY DATA

Two approaches may be followed in collecting data, particularly primary data. One can use either an exhaustive, complete enumeration or a partial enumeration based on a valid selection procedure. Complete enumeration is often referred to as a *census;* the U. S. Census of population is a familiar example. A partial enumeration is commonly referred to as a *sample.* Political polls and toothpaste tests are techniques based on samples.

The body of information that is being investigated or enumerated is called the *population* or *universe.* A population is composed of the units (referred to as *elementary units*) that possess the characteristic being studied. For example, the students enrolled in a particular course are the elementary units of that population. The population is therefore defined as the students enrolled in the course. The list of elementary units is referred to as the *frame* of the population. In this example, the class roll serves as the frame.

If the characteristic being studied is the students' weights, then these weights comprise the variate to be analyzed. A census would consist of the weights (variates) of all the students enrolled in the course. A sample would be the weights for a portion of the students, since the sample is simply a subset of the population.

It must be pointed out that a population is a definable group of elementary units. If the previous example involved the weights of all students enrolled in the institution rather than just those in one course, we would have had a different population. The frame then would have been the list of students' names appearing in the student directory rather than a particular class roll.

In either event, a sample is selected or a census completed for the purpose of securing information to make an objective decision. Information is usually secured by means of a sample for several reasons, which will be outlined next.

Reasons for Sampling

There are five important reasons for using a sampling procedure rather than a census: (1) economy, (2) timeliness, (3) destructiveness, (4) accuracy, and (5) infinite populations.

Economy. It is obvious that a partial enumeration will cost less than an exhaustive one, since fewer people and less time will be needed to collect the data. In addition, relatively fewer people are required for sample collection, and therefore training is cheaper than it is for a larger number of census takers.

Timeliness. When a person talks about timeliness as a reason for sampling, he is not referring to time in an economic sense. Timeliness refers to the urgent need for immediate information with which the decision maker is often faced. If he must make production or marketing decisions in a few days or weeks, he cannot wait for the results of a complete count or census.

Destructiveness. Certain types of data may measure the results of a test or an experiment that destroys the unit being observed or renders it useless. A simple example will illustrate how sampling counteracts this destructive process. Let us assume that a certain manufacturer of light bulbs wishes to compete in the market on the basis of the quality of his product and offers a guarantee with the purchase of each light bulb. First of all, the company must determine the quality of its product. The most important characteristic is the length of time the light bulbs will burn. In this case, the average burning time of all the bulbs produced must be known. It is obvious that testing all bulbs would be disastrous to the company because there would be none left to place on the market. The company must therefore resort to a sampling procedure to estimate the average burning time of its product. A manufacturer of electric fuses would be faced with a similar problem.

As another example, certain diagnostic procedures require blood tests. However, it would be impracticable for a doctor to take more than a small sample of blood from his patients for analysis. Thus it can be seen that the destructive nature of various tests or means of obtaining data makes it almost mandatory that sampling techniques be employed.

Accuracy. In some cases, it is difficult to argue convincingly that a census is more accurate than sampling. An experience related to the Battle of

Britain during World War II amusingly illustrates the accuracy of partial information. At that time the Allies were interested in estimating the production of Nazi V-2 bombs. After the war was over, it was revealed that their estimates were more accurate than the Germans' own knowledge of V-2 production. This discrepancy can be partially explained by the delays resulting from the red type and massive paperwork that were characteristic of the German military government.

In data collection, some facts based on common sense tend to support the contention that sampling may be more accurate than a census. It is obvious that when there is a limited amount of funds available for collecting data, a small number of people can be trained more thoroughly than a large number. When sampling is used, only a few people are needed to collect the necessary data, and the results therefore may be more accurate. When too few people collect data for a census, they may become careless and prone to make mistakes because of fatigue and monotony. Thus a sample can be more accurate than a complete count, especially if time and money are critical.

Infinite Populations. The fifth reason for sampling has to do with the nature of the population; it is the only method to use when the population is infinite. Because many manufacturing firms are engaged in a continuous process of production, their entire population of items (elementary units) is never available at any particular time. Since part of the population has yet to be produced, periodic sampling is the only accurate means of measurement.

Methods of Collection

The four basic methods used to collect data are the personal interview, the mailed questionnaire, the telephone interview, and the automatic device.

The Personal Interview. The personal-interview technique is typified by door-to-door and man-on-the-street interviews. Basically, this method is the most personal type of approach. The respondent is face-to-face with the individual who is asking the questions. One of the main reasons this technique is popular is that it results in a very high rate of usable returns; that is, a high percentage of returns is obtained from the respondents who are selected. This is understandable because most people will be cooperative when approached properly.

This technique has built-in opportunities for checking the validity of the answers given by a respondent. For example, let us assume that an interviewer has asked a housewife a question about the brand of coffee she uses and she responds by saying that she uses brand A. By coincidence, the interviewer is able to see a can of brand B on the dining room table. Naturally, the interviewer is curious about the answer the respondent has given because of the conflict between the answer and his observations. The interviewer is instructed to investigate any discrepancies in the answers he receives. He can ask for an explanation directly or ask a supplementary question to clarify the discrepancy. Often the questionnaire itself may be designed to check the validity of the answers, although this is more commonly done with the mailed questionnaire where there is no interviewer who can check on the spot. The personal interview also affords an opportunity for respondents to ask for clarifications of questions.

In the door-to-door survey, a situation often occurs that can seriously affect the validity of the information collected. A common problem is the situation where the member of a particular household to be interviewed is not at home. If the proper procedure is not employed to handle the not-at-home cases, a serious bias of nonresponse will be inherent in the data. Families that are not usually at home during the day are different from those that are. A childless couple is more apt to be away from home than a family with several preschool children. When a crosssection of responses from all types of families is desirable, a call-back procedure should be used.

Call-back procedures used to eliminate nonresponse bias must be followed strictly. When an individual is not at home, the inteviewer should call back at a different time of day and never seek the easy way out by going next door merely because someone seems to be at home there. Failure to employ the call-back procedure can prevent a certain type of family from having the opportunity to make a response; this will affect the results since it is likely that responses to certain questions will vary widely depending on the family structure.

Nonresponse bias results from different causes, and sometimes its presence is not easily recognizable. For instance, when an experiment or new method is being tested, some people will avoid the entire area where the experiment is being conducted. This can be illustrated with an actual case. A certain community was considering converting a downtown street into a mall and was therefore interested in the responses of the inhabitants. However, many people stayed away from the downtown area during the trial week to avoid the congestion and crowds, and no responses were collected from these people.

Another form of bias that appears to be similar to nonresponse bias may occur if the selection procedure is not carefully designed. A sampling plan that directs an interviewer to select the first house in each block, which usually would be located on a corner lot, could result in a serious bias in the data collected. In this case, there may be upward bias in certain answers; since corner lots are usually more expensive, the families interviewed may have higher incomes than other residents of the area.

One of the most serious biases that should be considered in conducting a personal interview is interviewer bias, which may take various forms. The most obvious bias results from the interviewer's tone of voice or facial expression; another type occurs when the interviewer fails to follow specific instructions in conducting the survey.

The interviewer's facial expression or tone of voice can affect a respondent's answers in several ways. If the question is asked in a manner that reflects the interviewer's feelings, the respondent may try to answer in a way that will avoid any embarrassment or further discussion; he also may be made to feel that he is not knowledgeable enough to answer the question intelligently and may shorten his answers accordingly.

Interviewers may induce bias into the results of a survey by misinterpreting their instructions or by failing to read or follow these instructions. A national survey company once instructed its interviewers to conduct a special type of survey. A list of instructions was mailed to the interviewers to prepare them for certain peculiarities of the survey. The last instruction on the list directed them to return a postcard immediately upon receipt of the instruction package to receive a $10 bonus. Practically no postcards were sent back. Such a poor response would lead any survey firm or agency to be doubtful about the accuracy of the data collected by their interviewers.

Another type of interviewer bias that is rarely mentioned in textbooks has to do with the sex of the interviewer. Experience has shown that when the interviewer is left free to select his respondents on the spot and in a random fashion, a male interviewer will tend to seek out female respondents and a female interviewer to pick male respondents. Therefore, unless a team of interviewers is balanced with an equal numbers of males and females, some bias is bound to result.

The Mailed Questionnaire.   The mailed questionnaire is the most widely used data collection procedure. This method avoids interviewer bias and eliminates the extensive training of a staff of interviewers. The elimination of interviewers alone makes this method cheaper to conduct, since the costs of training interviewers and of paying them for their time are avoided.

Even though the mailed questionnaire is much less expensive to use than the personal interview, it has one serious drawback: a high level of nonresponse. In the personal interview, nonresponse can occur because the respondent is not at home; in the telephone interview (to be discussed next), a call may result in a busy signal. However, both these types of nonresponses can be reduced by a call-back procedure. It is much easier for prospective respondents to ignore a mailed questionnaire and to simply deposit it in the nearest wastebasket. Some firms have tried to prevent nonresponse in mailed questionnaires by including a pencil in the envelope. One company even encouraged respondents by rewarding them with a dollar bill that was enclosed with each questionnaire.

The mailed questionnaire may be structured to include more questions as well as more extensive questions than the personal interview. The questionnaire also allows more lengthy and detailed answers than are possible with a personal interview. The length of the questions and the number of questions that can be asked are even more limited with the telephone interview. An example of a questionnaire is shown in the Annex (Fig. 17 3).

The Telephone Interview. The third basic method of collecting data is the telephone interview. It is evident that this method of collecting data is less expensive than the personal interview because less time is needed to contact respondents by telephone than by ringing doorbells. However, the telephone interview is not as inexpensive as the mailed questionnaire.

In addition, a lower refusal rate can be expected with the telephone interview than with the personal interview. People are more apt to talk over the telephone than at the front door, especially if they feel that they are not presentable enough for company.

There are also some shortcomings associated with the telephone interview. For example, nonresponse bias is present because the frame is restricted to those individuals who are listed in the telephone directory. Whenever a list of respondents does not include the entire population, the procedure is subject to nonresponse bias.

It should be reemphasized that when the telephone interview is used, the number of questions should be kept as small as possible and the questions should allow for short answers. Individuals will generally answer their telephones and will be glad to answer some questions, but after a while, they are apt to become abrupt and conclude the interview.[2]

The Automatic Device. Automatic devices used to collect data can be seen every day. Highway counters are used to obtain information about the flow of traffic; "electric eyes" count the number of individuals entering and leaving a building; automatic turnstiles are used to control and register pedestrian movement.

Several types of automatic devices have been used as a substitute for mailed questionnaires to collect information about television viewing. These devices are usually attached to television sets to record the channel being viewed at any given time. However, this technique is not completely satisfactory; because a television set is turned on does not necessarily mean that anyone is watching it. To overcome the dilemmas of recording television viewing time when there are no viewers, a professor at Oklahoma State University developed a Dyna-Scope—a camera that takes a clear picture of an entire room and its contents every 15 seconds and records the exact time.

The Dyna-Scope was used to test the television viewing habits of some families living in Stillwater, Oklahoma. The Stillwater experiment showed

[2] "Helpful Consumers," a very interesting article that appeared on the front page of the *Wall Street Journal* on Wednesday, June 2, 1965, and is reprinted in the *Study Props* to this text, summarizes some experiences of firms that went directly to the consumer for aid in product development. A variety of techniques was employed to obtain consumer attitudes; telephone interviews, personal interviews, and mailed questionnaires were widely used.

that approximately 25 per cent of the viewing time was lost time. In other words, one-quarter of the time that television sets were turned on, there was no audience. One case was cited in which a woman had the television set on for three hours, while she did everything *but* watch the set. She ironed, wrote a letter, talked on the telephone, and even read a book. Even though the Dyna-Scope was successful in recording lost time as well as viewing time, it still has some minor limitations connected with its installation.

Special Types of Biases

In addition to the biases already mentioned, there are two special types that require careful attention. The first type is called *bias of auspices;* the other is referred to as *prestige bias.*

Bias of auspices occurs when knowledge of the nature of the agency conducting the survery has a significant effect on the respondent. Respondents may react differently to one agency than to another. Government agencies tend to have greater success in the number of returns and the care given to the responses than do private agencies, because many citizens feel that they have a greater responsibility in giving information to government agencies.

Prestige bias appears in various forms. Figures related to income will often reflect an upward bias as people pad their income figures to make a better impression. A downward bias often results when women are asked their ages; the ages are usually higher than they report them to be in surveys.

Sampling Designs

Various methods of collecting data have been discussed. Even though the techniques discussed are also applicable to censuses, the discussion was directed toward samples of respondents. We must now turn to the various plans or designs used to select the sample required for data collection, whether it is collected from respondents or from direct observations.

By sampling design, we specifically mean the techniques or procedures used to select the particular respondents or elementary units that will constitute the sample. There are two major groups of sampling designs. The naïve group includes nonprobability procedures; the most important group is composed of probability procedures. The various types of plans are listed in outline form as follows:

Types of Sampling Plans

I. Nonprobability sampling
   A. Judgment sampling
   B. Convenience sampling

II. Probability sampling
   A. Simple random sampling
   B. Systematic sampling
   C. Stratified sampling
   D. Cluster sampling
   E. Multiple and sequential sampling

   The size of a sample can be determined either before the sample is actually selected or while the results are being evaluated. In the latter situation, the ultimate size of the sample is not predetermined; the sample size increases until certain criteria are fulfilled. For instance, a sample of 25 units may be selected and evaluated. If no statistically significant results are apparent, another 25 elements will be selected. The process terminates only after the predetermined criteria are clearly fulfilled or violated. These plans, which are commonly referred to as sequential and multiple sampling plans, are only used in special circumstances and will not be discussed any further in this text. Any standard textbook on sampling will provide a detailed account of these plans.

   Nonprobability Samples.   One of the nonprobability sampling designs is based on a judgment sample; the other employs a convenience sample. Both of these plans allow the sample to be selected in a more or less arbitrary fashion. Since a truly random procedure is not employed, objective evaluation of the results cannot be based on the laws of chance.

   In the case of the judgment sample, the units are selected by an expert, a person whose knowledge about a particular study qualifies him to select those elementary units which are believed to be typical of the population. The sample is essentially chosen on the basis of the expert's judgment.

   The convenience sample does not require the services of an expert; the sample is selected strictly on a convenience basis. For example, if a sample of responses from ten people is desired, the interviewer can proceed to the nearest street corner and select the first ten people who happen to pass by. Although this may appear to be a random process, it lacks the true properties of randomness, since the people who do not pass that corner never have a chance of being selected.

   It is obvious that neither of these two procedures affords much opportunity for making a valid inference about the population. However, the two plans are useful as pilot studies for more extensive plans. They allow immediate information to serve as a guideline for a more detailed plan.

   Probability Samples.   In probability sampling designs, some sort of random process must be used to select the items to be included in the sample. Unlike nonprobability samples, the probability that any particular sample will be selected can be calculated. Calculation of the probabilities of sample selection provides a way to measure the accuracy of the sampling plan with varying degrees of competence.

Four popular types of samples used in statistical work are the simple random sample, the systematic sample, the stratified sample, and the cluster sample. These four plans will be explained by demonstrating each procedure as it applies to a hypothetical sampling problem.[3]

Let us suppose that we have a box containing grapefruit, oranges, and lemons. There are a total of 18 pieces of fruit: 9 lemons, 6 oranges, and 3 grapefruit. The problem is to estimate the total weight of all 18 pieces of fruit by selecting a sample of only 6 pieces. It ordinarily would be absurd to use a sampling procedure when so few items are involved, but it is done here to illustrate the various sampling procedures. For convenience, the 18 pieces of fruit have been tagged with numbers from 1 through 18 as follows: numbers 1–9 are lemons, 10–15 are oranges, and 16–18 are grapefruit. However, before the four types of samples are illustrated, we must first discuss randomness and the process of random selection.

Some sort of random device or random process must be used to select only six of the eighteen numbers. The numbers 1–18 could be written on pieces of paper and dropped in a hat; dice could be tossed; a coin could be flipped; or a special spinner or a deck of cards could be used. All of these methods are inconvenient and are usually avoided by using a table of random numbers. However, these procedures could be used to generate a set or table of random numbers. The numbers shown in Table 17–1 were generated by an arithmetic procedure programmed and produced by a CDC 6600 computer.

In our particular case, we need six numbers from 1 through 18 to indicate the six pieces of fruit to be selected from the box. A very simple and crude technique would be to shut one's eyes, drop a pointer on the page of random numbers, and read across the page to obtain the required pairs of two-digit numbers that are in the range of 1 through 18. Other schemes might be to read from right to left, to read down the page, or to skip digits or lines.

In this case, a pencil was dropped on the page to determine the starting point. It left a mark on the number 3 where column 7 and row 16 intersect. Numbers were then read across the page in pairs. The first pair was 36, the second was 27, the third was 96, etc. The numbers 1–18 were circled whenever they appeared, and no number was selected more than once. The six pairs of numbers selected from the table were 13, 07, 06, 12, 08, and 03. Thus the six pieces of fruit tagged with these numbers constituted the random sample. This sample, called a *simple random sample*, is defined as one in which every possible sample of a certain size has the same chance of being selected.

---

[3] This explanation was developed from an example in M. R. Slonim, *Sampling in a Nutshell* (New York: Simon and Schuster, Inc., 1960), pp. 43–59.

TABLE 17–1

TABLE OF RANDOM NUMBERS

Column	1	2	3	4	5	6	7	8	9	10	11	12	13	14	15	16	17	18	19	20
Row																				
1	0	6	2	5	1	2	6	4	2	2	8	4	2	1	6	6	0	7	4	2
2	1	4	4	5	8	8	0	1	5	0	8	0	9	3	1	1	1	1	6	8
3	0	2	3	5	0	5	5	2	0	7	6	9	0	9	5	5	1	7	4	4
4	0	4	1	5	1	7	2	2	1	6	1	1	2	0	1	9	0	7	6	3
5	1	4	5	5	1	1	7	0	1	5	6	1	0	7	0	6	2	3	6	0
6	0	8	5	1	1	1	4	8	1	0	6	0	1	2	3	6	1	3	7	9
7	2	4	8	9	1	9	5	1	0	2	8	0	0	7	8	3	1	6	8	1
8	1	7	8	0	1	6	8	4	2	4	1	5	1	6	0	0	1	6	6	1
9	1	5	3	0	0	5	5	1	2	1	7	2	0	9	7	6	1	8	5	0
10	0	7	3	3	1	2	1	0	0	4	7	6	2	2	6	5	1	3	0	2
11	4	2	5	0	3	9	0	6	2	5	6	8	3	5	4	9	4	5	0	1
12	2	5	9	0	3	0	5	0	3	0	2	4	4	7	9	1	4	5	9	9
13	2	7	4	0	3	6	4	2	2	6	4	1	3	0	4	7	2	8	4	2
14	4	2	2	2	4	3	8	2	3	6	8	8	4	3	6	7	4	9	8	4
15	4	3	3	0	4	4	6	5	3	1	7	9	2	8	8	2	3	0	5	9
16	3	5	7	4	3	7	3	6	2	7	9	6	4	0	3	1	2	8	1	3
17	3	3	8	6	4	6	4	9	2	9	0	7	4	5	0	6	3	0	4	0
18	2	5	5	6	4	1	9	5	3	7	0	2	4	9	9	6	3	4	8	8
19	3	4	0	8	3	0	3	6	4	8	0	6	4	2	2	4	3	9	3	4
20	4	7	6	3	4	7	3	9	4	5	8	1	4	6	4	0	3	3	0	3
21	3	9	1	5	3	2	7	2	5	9	4	6	5	9	5	4	7	0	8	0
22	5	9	7	6	7	1	2	5	6	1	4	3	7	3	6	4	6	9	1	5
23	5	5	0	5	6	0	4	9	5	9	0	4	5	0	7	5	5	9	1	3
24	5	9	5	3	5	8	2	1	6	0	1	3	5	9	3	6	5	6	9	5
25	7	4	8	9	7	2	4	2	6	4	7	0	5	2	7	6	6	9	9	7
26	7	2	3	9	6	1	3	0	5	7	6	9	6	1	3	2	6	0	1	4
27	5	3	3	1	5	9	8	0	6	6	8	5	6	8	9	2	5	5	9	9
28	5	9	2	9	6	1	4	4	7	4	8	7	7	1	7	5	7	2	5	6
29	6	4	9	5	6	8	6	1	5	3	7	2	6	6	7	8	5	9	5	6
30	5	2	9	6	6	9	5	2	5	0	3	9	7	0	5	9	8	9	6	8
31	7	6	5	6	8	1	7	2	7	8	1	5	7	7	4	4	9	6	9	5
32	9	9	3	0	8	5	7	2	9	5	3	6	9	3	5	2	7	5	5	6
33	8	6	6	7	9	7	4	8	9	6	3	5	8	3	3	2	8	2	5	2
34	9	1	2	0	9	6	5	2	8	8	4	0	8	4	0	2	9	3	6	2
35	8	6	0	9	8	3	6	1	9	0	6	3	9	0	1	6	7	7	3	4
36	8	1	4	7	9	5	7	6	9	5	8	0	7	7	6	4	8	1	7	6
37	8	4	6	9	8	0	6	4	9	1	2	9	8	2	5	7	8	3	5	8
38	8	5	6	1	8	3	2	2	7	6	0	4	8	2	0	8	7	7	8	9
39	9	6	0	0	7	5	8	9	9	5	2	5	8	4	2	1	9	1	3	2
40	8	5	8	3	9	8	5	5	9	0	9	8	7	7	3	6	8	4	5	6

The weights of these six pieces of fruit and other pieces in the population are listed in table 17–2. The sample (indicated by arrows in the table) consists of four lemons and two oranges. The absence of any grapefruit in this sample is simply due to chance. Another sample could contain as many as three grapefruit.

The four lemons and two oranges, in this case, weighed a total of 30½ ounces. This is determined in Table 17–3. The total figure of 30½ ounces

TABLE 17–2

WEIGHTS OF FRUIT IN POPULATION

Item Number	Type of Fruit	Weight, Ounces
1	lemon	$4\frac{1}{4}$
2	lemon	4
→ 3	lemon	$4\frac{1}{2}$
4	lemon	$3\frac{3}{4}$
5	lemon	$4\frac{1}{4}$
→ 6	lemon	4
→ 7	lemon	$4\frac{1}{2}$
→ 8	lemon	$4\frac{1}{4}$
9	lemon	4
10	orange	$7\frac{1}{2}$
11	orange	8
→12	orange	$6\frac{3}{4}$
→13	orange	$6\frac{1}{2}$
14	orange	7
15	orange	$7\frac{1}{4}$
16	grapefruit	$16\frac{1}{2}$
17	grapefruit	18
18	grapefruit	$15\frac{3}{4}$
	Total =	$130\frac{3}{4}$

TABLE 17–3

WEIGHTS OF FRUIT IN RANDOM SAMPLE

Item Number	Weight, Ounces
3	$4\frac{1}{2}$
6	4
7	$4\frac{1}{2}$
8	$4\frac{1}{4}$
12	$6\frac{3}{4}$
13	$6\frac{1}{2}$
Total =	$30\frac{1}{2}$

must be multiplied by 3 if it is to be used to estimate the total weight of all 18 pieces of fruit. The factor 3 is used simply because the population is three times larger than the sample. Therefore, $30\frac{1}{2} \times 3 = 91\frac{1}{2}$ ounces, which underestimates the actual total weight of $130\frac{3}{4}$ ounces.

It also would have been possible to select a sample that contained six lemons, with a total weight as small as $24\frac{1}{4}$ ounces (the weight of the six smallest lemons). The estimate of the total then would have been 3 times $24\frac{1}{4}$ or only $72\frac{3}{4}$ ounces. On the other hand, the heaviest sample could consist of the three grapefruit and the three largest oranges, which would have weighed 73 ounces, making the estimate of the total 3 times 73, or 219 ounces; this far exceeds the actual total weight of $130\frac{3}{4}$ ounces.

This procedure renders a simple random sample. However, it would be advantageous to eliminate the possibility of selecting the two extreme samples illustrated above. The next two types of samples defined in this chapter give some assurance of preventing the selection of such "bad" samples. For example, a sample that contained three lemons, two oranges, and one grapefruit would be ideal, because it would consist of one-third of each type of fruit. Such a sample would be more representative of the population than a simple random sample and would reduce variation in the sampling results.

Generally, any additional information about the elementary units can be helpful in specifying which sampling plan to use. In the case of the box of fruit, the fact that three types of fruit are involved can be used to great advantage. It makes sense to group the fruit according to type (grapefruit, oranges, and lemons) and then to select them proportionately from each group in such a way as to guarantee a representative sample; that is, the sample will be composed of a certain number of each type of fruit. This type of grouping is commonly referred to as stratified and the resulting sample is called a *stratified sample*.

In certain special cases, a simpler technique known as *systematic sampling* can be used to give similar results. This is partly due to the fact that the population of 18 items in our example can be arranged in an ordered fashion.

The systematic sample is sometimes referred to as a *chain* or *serial sample*. Once the first item is selected randomly, the remaining items for the sample are chosen "systematically" by selecting every nth item until the list is exhausted. The selection of a systematic sample will be illustrated by again using the example of the box of fruit.

Since a sample of six items is desired, we must divide the size of the population (18) by the sample size (6) to determine how many items will be skipped as we proceed down the list of items. In this case, since $18/6 = 3$, we must select every third (nth) item. The starting point for the systematic selection is determined by selecting either a 1, a 2, or a 3 from a table of random numbers. The numbers 1–3 are used because every third item is to be selected. If every fourth item were to be selected, a number from 1 through 4 would be chosen.

Suppose that the number 2 was randomly selected from the table. The systematic sample would then consist of the second, fifth, eighth, eleventh, fourteenth, and seventeenth items in the list of fruit. This would result in three lemons, two oranges, and one grapefruit, weighing a total of $45\frac{1}{2}$ ounces. Consequently, the estimate of the total weight of all 18 pieces of fruit would be $136\frac{1}{2}$ ounces ($45\frac{1}{2} \times 3$). This estimate is reasonably close to the actual value of $130\frac{3}{4}$ ounces.

The systematic grouping results in a sample that is proportionate to the number of each type of fruit; that is, one-third of the lemons, one-third of the oranges, and one-third of the grapefruit are included in the sample. This proportionality did not occur by accident but resulted from the relationship between the sample size, the population size, and the number of types of fruit. For instance, if only three items were to be selected for the sample, every sixth item would have to be chosen. In addition, the first item would be selected randomly from one of the first six items rather than from one of the first three. It should be clear that any sample of three could not result in proportionality; some of the samples would not even contain all types of fruit.

Nevertheless, the systematic sample is a simple and direct technique that can be employed whenever the list of population items is available. It is considered a probability sample because the selection of the first item is accomplished in a random manner.

Frequently, systematic sampling is used when the sample selection can be based on identification numbers, such as selective service numbers, social security numbers, registration numbers, or serial numbers. The military services often select systematic samples of servicemen on the basis of their service numbers.

We will now illustrate the technique employed in selecting a *stratified sample* by demonstrating a *proportionate stratified sample*. In order to choose a stratified sample, it is necessary to divide the elements of the population into various groups with common characteristics. Each of these groups is referred to as a *stratum*. In our example, it is possible to divide the 18 pieces of fruit into three groups, or *strata*, according to type. The nine lemons constitute one stratum, the six oranges another, and the three grapefruit a third. This grouping appears as follows:

$$
\begin{aligned}
&\text{Stratum 1 (lemons)} &= \text{items} \ \ 1–9 \\
&\text{Stratum 2 (oranges)} &= \text{items} \ \ 10–15 \\
&\text{Stratum 3 (grapefruit)} &= \text{items} \ \ 16–18.
\end{aligned}
$$

In order to sample proportionately from each stratum—that is, in order to select one-third of each fruit—it is necessary to choose three of the nine lemons, two of the six oranges, and one of the three grapefruit—that is, one-third of each stratum.[4] Consequently, the size of the sample will be 6.

The selection of the required items from each stratum is accomplished by using a table of random numbers or some other random process. In this case, the random selection of three numbers resulted in the selection of items

[4] If the stratified sample is not selected on a proportionate basis—for example, if two lemons, two oranges, and two grapefruit are selected—it will become necessary to weight these observations in proportion to the number in each stratum. In this case, the weight of the two lemons selected would be multiplied by a factor of $4\frac{1}{2}$ (9 divided by 2); the weight of the two oranges would be multiplied by a factor of 3 (6 divided by 2); and the two grapefruit would be multiplied by a factor of $1\frac{1}{2}$ (3 divided by 2). It is important for the basis of sample selection in a stratified method to be logically related to the calculation of the estimate.

4, 5, and 8 from stratum 1, items 10 and 14 from stratum 2, and item 16 from stratum 3. The total weight of the sample is shown in Table 17–4. The estimate of the total weight of the population is 3 times $43\frac{1}{4}$, or $129\frac{3}{4}$ ounces, which is reasonably close to the actual weight of $130\frac{3}{4}$ ounces.

It is possible for the stratified sample to weigh as little as $40\frac{3}{4}$ ounces and to give an estimate of $122\frac{1}{4}$ ounces, or it could weigh as much as $46\frac{3}{4}$ ounces and render an estimate of $140\frac{1}{4}$ ounces. These two extremes are much closer to the actual total than the two extremes of $72\frac{3}{4}$ ounces and 219 ounces that were possible with simple random sampling.

This difference in the spreads of the estimates under these two plans is very important in sampling. We wish to have as small a spread as possible because the estimates will then be closer, on the average, to the actual value. When the spread is small, the procedure is said to be efficient in a statistical sense. The greater a method's efficiency, the more precise the estimates will be.

The fourth and final type of probability sample to be discussed is *cluster sampling*. This technique requires that clusters be formed, each containing some of each different type of item. In this case, each cluster of fruit should be similar in proportion to the number of lemons, oranges, and grapefruit. Specifically, each cluster should contain three lemons, two oranges, and one grapefruit. The composition of the three clusters of fruit may appear as shown in Table 17–5. Each cluster contains the same amount of each type of fruit.

A sample is selected in this case by randomly choosing a number from 1 through 3, because there are three clusters; thus an entire cluster that is randomly chosen becomes the sample. Realistically, however, clusters are much larger than the sample size. Since each cluster contains six items, the sample size will again be six in number. The three clusters listed in the table weigh $43\frac{1}{4}$ ounces, 45 ounces, and $42\frac{1}{2}$ ounces, respectively, and the estimates of the total weight are $129\frac{3}{4}$ ounces, 135 ounces, and $127\frac{1}{2}$ ounces, respectively. It should be realized that a different arrangement of the clusters would render different estimates. Theoretically, cluster sampling

TABLE 17–4

WEIGHTS OF FRUIT IN A STRATIFIED SAMPLE

Item Number	Weight, Ounces
4	$3\frac{3}{4}$
5	$4\frac{1}{4}$
8	$4\frac{1}{4}$
10	$7\frac{1}{2}$
14	7
16	$16\frac{1}{2}$
Total =	$43\frac{1}{4}$

TABLE 17–5

CLUSTERS OF FRUIT

Cluster 1	Cluster 2	Cluster 3
Item 1—lemon	Item 4—lemon	Item 7—lemon
Item 2—lemon	Item 5—lemon	Item 8—lemon
Item 3—lemon	Item 6—lemon	Item 9—lemon
Item 10—orange	Item 11—orange	Item 12—orange
Item 13—orange	Item 14—orange	Item 15—orange
Item 16—grapefruit	Item 17—grapefruit	Item 18—grapefruit

results in greater sampling variation than either simple random sampling or stratified sampling.

To summarize, in the stratified sample, the items were selected from strata that each contained only one type of fruit; each stratum was completely different from the others. On the other hand, in cluster sampling, the clusters were grouped by mixing different types of items so that each cluster was similar in composition to the others; in the illustration given, the entire cluster was the sample.

The main disadvantage of the cluster sample is that generally the clusters must be accepted as they are. On the other hand, cluster sampling has an advantage in that the cost of gathering items is less than in stratified sampling. This can be clarified by an example.

Suppose that a state has three widely separated areas in each of which lemons, oranges, and grapefruit grow together. The travel expenses incurred in collecting a stratified sample would be greater than the cost of collecting a cluster sample because only one site must be visited to obtain the cluster sample. Therefore, cluster sampling may be more efficient on a per-unit cost basis than stratified sampling.

Another example of this advantage occurs in the collection of income data. Suppose that a state contains two cities that have similar classifications of wage earners. If a stratified or simple random sample were used, it would be necessary to travel to both cities to collect the sample data. However, if a cluster sample is used, the data can be collected without incurring unnecessary traveling costs.

PUBLISHED SOURCES OF SECONDARY DATA

A brief list of data sources published by private organizations and governmental agencies is given in this section. In both cases, data published on a more or less annual basis are listed first, followed by more frequently published sources. Additional sources are provided in the Selected References.

1. GENERAL COORDINATION

The statistical organization of the Federal Government has developed in a decentralized pattern, with different agencies having responsibilities for the collection, compilation or analysis of statistical data in specified areas. A central statistical office is therefore required to achieve an integrated and accurate system of governmental statistics and to prevent duplication.

OFFICE OF STATISTICAL STANDARDS BUREAU OF THE BUDGET
Develops a single coordinated statistical system in the Federal Government. Prevents duplication of statistics and reduces reporting burdens. Develops and enforces standards for the quality and comparability data.

2. GENERAL–PURPOSE STATISTICAL AGENCIES

The primary function of these agencies is collection, compilation and publication of statistics for general use. Each of these agencies is responsible for the regular collection, analysis and publication of data in specified fields. As a group, they account for a large proportion of Federal statistical activities.

STATISTICAL REPORTING SERVICE (Dept. of Agriculture)	BUREAU OF LABOR STATISTICS (Dept. of Labor)	BUREAU OF THE CENSUS (Dept. of Commerce)	NATIONAL CENTER FOR HEALTH STATISTICS (Dept. of Health, Education and Welfare)
Statistics on crop and livestock production; prices received and paid by farmers; farm employment and wage rates. Special surveys.	Statistics on labor force, employment and unemployment; earnings, man-hours and wage rates; productivity; industrial injuries; industrial relations; wholesale and retail prices; urban consumer price indexes; foreign labor conditions.	Censuses of population, housing, agriculture, manufactures, mineral industries, business, governments. Current statistics in these areas, and in foreign trade, shipping, construction.	Statistics on morbidity, health care, and demographic, social and economic factors related to health; and on births, deaths, marriages and divorces.

3. ANALYTIC AND RESEARCH AGENCIES

These agencies are major users of data collected by the public–purpose agencies, the administrative and regulatory agencies, and private sources. They are particularly important in the compilation, analysis and interpretation of statistics, though some direct collection of statistics for general use is involved in their activities.

COUNCIL OF ECONOMIC ADVISERS (Executive Office of the President)	ECONOMIC RESEARCH SERVICE (Dept. of Agriculture)	OFFICE OF BUSINESS ECONOMICS (Dept. of Commerce)	BOARD OF GOVERNORS OF THE FEDERAL RESERVE SYSTEM
Analyses of economic data on the general economic situation, and appraisal of related Federal activities. Assists the President in preparation of his economic reports to the congress.	Analyses of economic situation and outlook for farm products. Research and statistical studies on farm population, prices and income; food consumption and marketing margins; agriculture finance, farm costs and returns, and agricultural productivity.	Estimates of national income, gross national product, inter-industry sales and purchases, and related data on business developments; analyses of business trends; estimates of the balance of international payments and of foreign investments.	Analyzes economic and credit conditions. Prepares and publishes statistics on money, banking, international finance, industrial production, consumer credit, and department store activities for general public use.

HOUSEHOLD ECONOMICS RESEARCH DIVISION (ARS, Dept. of Agriculture)	BUSINESS AND DEFENSE SERVICES ADMIN. (Dept. of Commerce)	BUREAU OF INTERNATIONAL COMMERCE (Dept. of Commerce)	BUREAU OF MINES (Dept. of the Interior)
Statistics of household food consumption, dietary adequacy and rural family living.	Analyzes and disseminates information on the condition and levels of business activity in specific industries and trades.	Analyses of data compiled by the Census Bureau on U.S. foreign trade, and of data on trade of other countries.	Current statistics on production, consumption and stocks of metals, mineral fuels and other nonmetallic minerals; employment and injuries in mineral industries. Studies and analyses in these areas.

4. ADMINISTRATIVE, REGULATORY AND DEFENSE AGENCIES

These agencies provide many important and valuable statistical series used by the public and other agencies of the Government. They collect statistical information primarily as part of their administrative and operating responsibilities, such as the collection of taxes or regulation of public utilities, though a few of them have specialized statistical responsibilities.

OTHER AGENCIES AND UNITS LOCATED IN EXECUTIVE DEPARTMENTS

AGRICULTURE
a. AMS (Marketing Services Division)
b. Agricultural Research Service (various branches)
c. Commodity Exchange Authority
d. Farmers Home Administration
e. Forest Service
f. Rural Electrification Administration

COMMERCE
a. Area Redevelopment Administration
b. Bureau of Public Roads
c. Bureau of Standards
d. Maritime Administration
e. Weather Bureau

TREASURY
a. Bureau of Customs
b. Bureau of the Mint
c. Comptroller of the Currency
d. Fiscal Service
e. Internal Revenue Service
f. Office of International Finance

LABOR
a. Bureau of Apprenticeship and Training
b. Bureau of Employees' Compensation
c. Bureau of Employment Security
d. Bureau of Labor Standards
e. Wage, Hour and Public Contracts Division
f. Women's Bureau

HEALTH, EDUCATION AND WELFARE
a. Office of Education
b. Office of Vocational Rehabilitation
c. Public Health Service
d. Social Security Administration
e. Welfare Administration

JUSTICE
a. Antitrust Division
b. Bureau of Prisons
c. Federal Bur. of Investigation
d. Immigration and Nuturalization Service

DEFENSE
a. Army, Navy and Air Force produce economic statistics on: expenditures, contracts and purchases
b. Board of Engineers for Rivers and Harbors
c. Office of Civil Defense

INTERIOR
a. Bureau of Indian Affairs
b. Bureau of Land Management
c. Bureau of Reclamation
d. Fish and Wildlife Service
e. Nat'l Park Service

STATE
a. Agency for International Development
b. Foreign Service Reporting
c. Passport Office

INDEPENDENT OFFICES

CIVIL AERONAUTICS BOARD	FEDERAL POWER COMMISSION	RAILROAD RETIREMENT BOARD
FARM CREDIT ADMINISTRATION	FEDERAL TRADE COMMISSION	SECURITIES AND EXCHANGE COMMISSION
FEDERAL AVIATION AGENCY	HOUSING AND HOME FINANCE AGENCY	SELECTIVE SERVICE SYSTEM
FEDERAL COMMUNICATIONS COMMISSION	INTERSTATE COMMERCE COMMISSION	U.S. CIVIL SERVICE COMMISSION
FEDERAL DEPOSIT INSURANCE CORPORATION	NATIONAL SCIENCE FOUNDATION	U.S. TARIFF COMMISSION
FEDERAL HOME LOAN BANK BOARD	OFFICE OF EMERGENCY PLANNING	VETERANS ADMINISTRATION

EXPLANATORY NOTE

The various agencies and units are arranged on this chart to indicate the essential structure of the statistical activities of the Federal Government. Only those agencies and units whose statistical functions are readily identified are included. Some of the agencies might well be listed under several of the major categories, but to prevent excessive detail, they are classified under a single category. While all agencies have some performance or operational data, this chart considers such statistics only when they have also been adapted for general analytic use. A more detailed description of the system is presented in "Statistical Services of the United States Government."

FIGURE 17–2. The Federal statistical system.

407

Private Sources

1. *The Standard and Poor's Trade and Security Statistics*
2. *Moody's Manuals of Investment*
3. *The Economic Almanac*
4. Newspaper Almanacs
5. *Commodity Yearbook*
6. Various publications of trade associations, such as *Annual Statistical Report of the American Iron and Steel Institute, Iron Age, Gas Facts, Automobile Facts and Figures,* and *Life Insurance Factbook*
7. *Barron's Weekly*
8. *Business Week*
9. *Dun's Review*
10. *National City Bank Newsletter*

Government Sources

1. *Historical Abstract of the United States*
2. *Statistical Abstract of the United States*
3. *Agricultural Statistics*
4. *Banking and Monetary Statistics*
5. *Handbook of Labor Statistics*
6. *Economic Report of the President*
7. *Survey of Current Business*
8. *Federal Reserve Bulletin*
9. *Monthly Labor Review*
10. *Economic Indicators*

A description of the activities of the various statistical agencies of the Federal government is given in Fig. 17–2. The agencies are divided into four main groups: the General Coordination Agency; the General Purpose Statistical Agencies; the Analytic and Research Agencies; and the Administrative, Regulatory, and Defense Agencies. Fig. 17–2 summarizes clearly the functions of many of the government agencies in our Federal statistical system.

ANNEX: EXAMPLE OF A MAILED QUESTIONNAIRE

The following two-page questionnaire is accompanied by a brief covering letter of introduction.

The Metropolitan Research Organization

SUITE 1303 10 EAST 40th STREET, NEW YORK 16, N.Y. MU 3-6847

To Whom It May Concern:

Your name was selected at random as a young adult between the ages of 18-26. You represent the generation of American males who set the styles, trends and tempos of the world.

This research is non-political and admittedly commercial. It is sponsored by an advertising and marketing company whose objective is to sample the tastes and opinions of this most important segment of our population.

May we request a few moments of your time in filling out and returning the attached questionnaire. When this survey is completed and tabulated, we would be happy to forward to you the final results. You may be interested in the results from the point of curiosity or information. You are free to use the results for any commercial or personal purpose.

Your cooperation will be appreciated.

Sincerely yours,

Leonard E. Janklow

FIGURE 17–3(a). Sample letter of introduction to mailed questionnaire.

1. Your age?_____   What state do you live in?_____

2. If in school, what level? ____H.S.   ____Frosh   ____Junior
                             ____College   ____Soph.   ____Senior

3. Did you graduate from high school?   ____yes   ____no
                            College?   ____yes   ____no

4. Are you employed?   ____yes   ____no   Are you married?   ____yes   ____no

5. If you are employed, are you a ____blue collar worker   ____white collar worker
   What is your weekly salary bracket?   ____under $50   ____75-100   ____125-150
                                          ____50-75   ____100-125   ____over 150

6. If you are married, does your wife work?   ____yes   ____no
                        Do you have children? ____yes   ____no

7. What is your current draft classification?_____

8. Do you own your own car?_____

9. What make car would you like to own?_____

10. Do you participate in any of the following sports?
    _____Golf   _____Skin Diving   _____Billiards
    _____Tennis   _____Surfing   _____Snow Ski-ing
    _____Sailing   _____Horseback Riding   _____Other
    _____Water Ski-ing   _____Bowling

11. How much do you generally spend for the following items?
    _____Dress Shirt   _____Sport (Jacket) Coat _____Over Coat
    _____Sport Shirt   _____Suit   _____Outer Jacket
    _____Dress Slacks   _____Raincoat   _____Benchwarmer or Carcoat
    _____Sport Slacks   _____Topcoat   _____1 Pr. of Shoes
    _____Sweater

12. About how many of the following items do you own?
    _____Dress Shirts   _____Sport (Jacket) Coats _____Over Coats
    _____Sport Shirts   _____Suits   _____Outer Jackets
    _____Dress Slacks   _____Raincoats   _____Benchwarmers or Carcoats
    _____Sport Slacks   _____Topcoats   _____Prs. of Shoes
    _____Sweaters

FIGURE 17-3(b).   Sample mailed questionnaire.

13. Where do you prefer to shop for clothing. Check one.
    ____Dept. Store   ____Chain Store   ____Small Men's Shop
    ____Discount Store   ____Large Men's Shop   ____Other

14. Do any of the following people have influence on your choice of clothing purchases?
    ____Wife   ____Girl Friend   ____Male Companion
    ____Mother   ____Father   ____Store Clerk

15. Do any of the following items have influence on your choice of clothing purchases?
    ____Brand Names   ____Fiber Content   ____Fabric
    ____Durable Press   ____Shrinkage Control   ____Water Resistance
    ____Stain Resistance

16. Do any of the following advertising methods have influence on your choice of
    clothing purchases?
    ____T.V.   ____Radio   ____Newspapers
    ____Magazines   ____Catalogues   ____Outdoor Posters
    ____Direct Mail   ____Subway or Bus Cards

17. In purchasing clothing, in which order are these items most important to you
    (number 1,2,3,4,5)?
    ____Durability   ____Comfort   ____Style   ____Price   ____Brand Name

18. Which of these fashion concepts do you subscribe to and in what order?
    (1st, 2nd, 3rd choice only)

19. Are you concerned about the opinions your boss or older people have regarding
    your appearance?   ____yes   ____no   Your personality?   ____yes   ____no

20. Of your total wardrobe (excepting uniforms and work clothes) approximately what
    percentage is   ____dress clothes   ____casual clothes

           Your name and address is not necessary to the effectiveness
           of this questionnaire.

Are you interested in the results of this research?   ____yes   ____no

NAME_____ ADDRESS_____

CITY_____ STATE_____ ZIP_____

FIGURE 17–3(b) (*cont.*).

PROBLEMS AND PROJECTS

1. The questionnaire shown below has been used to collect data on students. It could either be sent through the mail or used in personal interviews.

STUDENT QUESTIONNAIRE

Directions: Please record your answers to the following questions in the boxes to the right of the question. Enter leading zeros; that is, if there are two boxes and your answer is, say, 5, please enter 05.
Answers to this questionnaire will remain anonymous.
1. Sex: 1–male; 2–female...☐
2. Age: age at last birthday ....☐☐☐
3. Marital status:
      1–single; 2–married; 3–other.....................................☐
4. Grade point average ....☐☐☐☐
5. Classification:
      1–freshman; 2–sophomore; 3–junior; 4–senior ....☐
6. Size of high school graduating class...............................☐☐☐☐

Use your school directory and select a sample of 25 students at random (use a table of random numbers). Send a copy of the above questionnaire to each of the 25 students. You may refer to two popular collections of random numbers: M. G. Kendall and B. Babington Smith, "Tables of Random Sampling Numbers," *Tracts for Computers No. XXIV* (London: Cambridge University Press, 1939), p. vii; and The RAND Corporation, *A Million Random Digits* (New York: The Free Press of Glencoe, Inc., 1955).

2. Design a questionnaire similar to the one shown above to collect information about faculty members at your school. Structure the questionnaire to seek information pertaining to sex, age, marital status, years of teaching, and highest degree earned.

3. In the section on systematic sampling, a sample was selected on the basis of the random number 2. The sample consisted of the second, fifth, eighth, eleventh, fourteenth, and seventeenth items of the population of 18 pieces of fruit. List the items that would be contained in the samples when 1 and 3 are the random numbers selected. Also, estimate the total weight of the fruit from these two samples.

4. Select a systematic sample of only three items from the total population of 18 pieces of fruit; what is the estimate of the total weight of the 18 pieces?

5. Merchants in Houston are interested in determining what the average volume of sales was in 1969 for their five major department stores. The following data are available:

Store	Sales in 1968
A	$4,000
B	3,000
C	6,000
D	4,000
E	2,000

Two stores were sampled in 1969 and the results were as follows:

Store	Sales in 1969
B	$4,000
C	8,000

What is your estimate of total sales for 1969?

SELECTED REFERENCES

Andreano, R. R., E. I. Farber, and S. Reynolds, *The Student Economist's Handbook*. Cambridge, Mass.: Schenkman Publishing Co., Inc., 1967.

Backstrom, C. H., and G. D. Hursh, *Survey Research*. Evanston, Ill.: Northwestern University Press, 1963.

Cox, E. B., ed., *Basic Tables in Business and Economics*. New York: McGraw-Hill Book Company, 1967.

Johnson, H. W., *How To Use the Business Library*, 3rd ed. Cincinnati, O.: South-Western Publishing Co., 1964.

Office of Statistical Standards, *Statistical Services of the United States Government*, rev. ed. Washington, D. C.: U. S. Government Printing Office, 1959.

Slonim, M. R., *Sampling in a Nutshell*. New York: Simon and Schuster, Inc., 1960.

18

DATA PRESENTATION

It is only logical that after data have been collected they should be arranged in a manner useful to the analyst. Basically, data presentation consists of two distinct processes: classifying and displaying data. When data are classified, they are simply grouped into an appropriate number of meaningful classes; they also can be displayed in various types of tables, figures, and charts.

Data are classified and displayed for a basic purpose that is common to both procedures: that of summarizing the information reflected by the data. First, classification of the data by the frequency distribution will be demonstrated, and second, the frequency distribution will be charted or displayed. Finally, examples of various types of data displays will be illustrated.

CLASSIFYING DATA

The Frequency Distribution

It is usually desirable to arrange data into groups that will summarize them appropriately. Generally, the count or occurrence of data by various classes or magnitudes is an appropriate measure. Basically, the question to be answered is how often the various types or sizes occur.

A very simple frequency distribution could be constructed to show the number of students who attend a college from within the state, from other states, or from foreign countries. If the college has an enrollment of 8,000 students, the distribution may appear as shown in Table 18–1. On the other hand, a simple frequency distribution could be constructed to show the distribution of students according to family income, as in Table 18–2. Both of these examples are frequency distributions.

414

TABLE 18–1

DISTRIBUTION OF STUDENTS

Student Origin	Frequency of Students
Home state	6,000
Out of state	1,800
Foreign country	200

TABLE 18–2

DISTRIBUTION OF STUDENTS BY INCOME

Family Income	Frequency of Students
Below $5,000	2,800
$5,000–$9,999	4,000
$10,000 or over	1,200

We will now turn to another hypothetical study and construct a frequency distribution from the data. The problems of over- and undersummarization will be introduced and the determination of the appropriate number of classes, which is related to the summarizing problem, will be outlined. Various parts of the frequency distribution will be defined, and a distinction will be made between absolute and relative frequencies.

Suppose that a sample is taken from the students enrolled in a college. The students provide the following information pertaining to their family incomes where the figures are rounded to hundreds of dollars:[1]

$8,000	$9,300	$9,000	$8,100
8,400	9,100	9,700	9,100
7,100	7,400	8,000	5,600
7,200	6,000	6,000	6,500
4,100	6,300	6,600	7,400
7,900	9,200	7,200	9,800
8,000	8,000	9,100	9,300
7,000	7,000	5,900	8,100
6,800	6,300	6,700	9,300
9,000	7,600	8,800	4,300
4,800	7,600	6,700	8,700
9,000	6,100	8,800	8,200
8,500	9,900	7,100	7,400
9,200	8,300	8,900	8,300
8,300	8,800	7,900	8,600
7,400	7,100	7,500	8,000
7,000	7,200	8,100	7,800
6,500	9,500	7,700	7,300
5,100	8,200	6,300	8,600
7,300	7,000	7,500	6,800

[1] See Annex II for the rules for rounding numbers.

TABLE 18–3

OVERSUMMARIZED FREQUENCY TABLE

Income	Frequency
$4,100–$6,000	8
6,100– 8,000	40
8,100–10,000	32

TABLE 18–4

UNDERSUMMARIZED FREQUENCY TABLE

Income	Frequency
$4,100–$4,400	2
4,500– 4,800	1
4,900– 5,200	1
5,300– 5,600	1
5,700– 6,000	3
6,100– 6,400	4
6,500– 6,800	7
6,900– 7,200	10
7,300– 7,600	10
7,700– 8,000	9
8,100– 8,400	9
8,500– 8,800	7
8,900– 9,200	9
9,300– 9,600	4
9,700–10,000	3

These data could be classified into as few as three classes to give the frequency distribution shown in Table 18–3. However, this frequency distribution tends to oversummarize the data; it does not provide much more information than the smallest and largest figures. On the other hand, the data could be grouped into 15 classes as shown in Table 18–4. This number of classes tends to under-summarize the data; it provides little improvement over the original items.

The decision of how many classes to establish is somewhat arbitrary. However, a special formula is often used to assist in determining a satisfactory number of classes. The formula appears as

$$k = 1 + 3.3 \log n,$$

where k is the number of classes to be constructed and n is the total number of items. In this case, since we have 80 items, the formula is solved as follows:

$$k = 1 + 3.3 \log 80$$
$$k = 1 + 3.3\,(1.9)$$
$$k = 1 + 6.3$$
$$k = 7. \qquad \text{(rounded)}$$

Now that the number of classes (7) has been established, we must deter-mine the boundaries of each class. This is accomplished by subtracting the smallest item in the group of numbers from the largest number in the group and adding 100. (The number 100 was chosen because the figures were rounded to hundreds of dollars.) The addition of the smallest significant digit, 100 in this case, is necessary so that the boundaries will be inclusive of all figures. This can be illustrated with a small set of numbers. Suppose that we have the numbers 4, 5, 6, and 7. The difference between the largest and smallest figures is 3 $(7-4)$. Since the figure 3 does not represent a large enough spread to include all four numbers, the number 1 must be added to the difference to make 4.

Returning to the example of the 80 income figures, we find that the difference between the largest and smallest figures is 5,800 ($9,900 − $4,100). The inclusive spread is therefore 5,900 ($5,800 + $100). We must now divide this spread into equal intervals. In our case, seven equal intervals must be established since we previously derived the number 7 from the formula for k. Equally spaced intervals are more desirable for computational reasons.

The number $5,900 is not evenly divisible by 7; the closest divisible number is $6,300. Therefore, if we add or extend both ends of our distribution by $200, we can establish seven equally spaced classes of $900 each as follows:

$3,900–$	4,700
4,800–	5,600
5,700–	6,500
6,600–	7,400
7,500–	8,300
8,400–	9,200
9,300–	10,100.

Of course, there is no value as small as $3,900 or as large as $10,100. This distortion of the class limits is of minor importance.

Major consideration should be given to the boundaries of the classes established for a frequency distribution. To avoid ambiguity, the limits of each class must not overlap. For instance, the class limits of a frequency distri-bution should not appear as follows:

$3,900–$	4,800
4,800–	5,700
5,700–	6,600
6,600–	7,500
6,500–	8,400
8,400–	9,300
9,300–	10,200.

The dilemma of overlapping classes is apparent; it would be impossible to determine whether the figure $5,700 should be placed in the second or third class. Thus the classes must be established carefully.

The next task is to determine the number (or frequency) of the items appearing in each of the seven classes. This is easily accomplished by reading the original figures as they occur and placing a tally mark beside the appropriate class. The final tallying for this problem appears in Table 18–5. This distribution summarizes the data appropriately. There are neither too few nor too many classes and the data are now in a more manageable form. The fact that the classes do not overlap and are equally spaced must be emphasized.

TABLE 18–5

DETERMINATION OF FREQUENCIES

Income Classes	Tally	Frequencies
$3,900–$ 4,700	//	2
4,800– 5,600	///	3
5,700– 6,500	﷼﷼ ////	9
6,600– 7,400	﷼﷼ ﷼﷼ ﷼﷼ ﷼﷼ /	21
7,500– 8,300	﷼﷼ ﷼﷼ ﷼﷼ ﷼﷼ /	21
8,400– 9,200	﷼﷼ ﷼﷼ ﷼﷼ //	17
9,300– 10,100	﷼﷼ //	7
Total		= 80

The frequencies obtained for each class are referred to as *absolute frequencies*. Sometimes it is desirable to convert these absolute frequencies into *relative frequencies*. This is easily accomplished by dividing each class frequency by the total of all the frequencies (the total number of items). These calculations are illustrated in Table 18–6.

TABLE 18–6

CALCULATION OF RELATIVE FREQUENCIES

Income Classes	Absolute Frequencies	Division	Relative Frequencies
$3,900–$ 4,700	2	2/80	= 0.0250
4,800– 5,600	3	3/80	= 0.0375
5,700– 6,500	9	9/80	= 0.1125
6,600– 7,400	21	21/80	= 0.2625
7,500– 8,300	21	21/80	= 0.2625
8,400– 9,200	17	17/80	= 0.2125
9,300– 10,100	7	7/80	= 0.0875
Total			= 1.0000

The relative frequencies can be multiplied by 100 and the results expressed as percentages. Consequently, the first class would contain 2.5 per cent of the total items, the second class 3.75 per cent, the third class 11.25 per cent, and so forth.

TABLE 18–7

CLASS LIMITS AND REAL CLASS LIMITS

Lower Real Class Limit	Lower Class Limit	Upper Class Limit	Upper Real Class Limit
($3,850)	$3,900	$ 4,700	($ 4,750)
(4,750)	4,800	5,600	(5,650)
(5,650)	5,700	6,500	(6,550)
(6,550)	6,600	7,400	(7,450)
(7,450)	7,500	8,300	(8,350)
(8,350)	8,400	9,200	(9,250)
(9,250)	9,300	10,100	(10,150)

There are three parts of the frequency distribution that must be identified, defined, and/or calculated. First, class limits and real class limits must be identified and defined; second, class intervals must be calculated; and third, class midvalues must be defined and calculated. The selection of appropriate class limits is related to the class midvalues.

The class limits appear in the frequency distribution as the smallest and largest values for each class. For example, the class limits for the first class are $3,900 and $4,700. The smaller figure is the lower limit and the larger figure the upper limit. Associated with class limits are real class limits. Basically, real class limits are determined by splitting the difference between the upper and lower class limits of adjacent classes. The upper real limit of the first class is $4,750; it is simply the value that appears halfway between the upper class limit of the first class ($4,700) and the lower class limit of the second class ($4,800). This is an imaginary value because $4,750 does not actually exist among the set of original numbers.

The upper real limit of the first class ($4,750) is also the lower real limit of the second class. The respective class limits and real class limits are shown in Table 18–7. The importance of the real class limit is mainly associated with charting frequency distributions. This will be discussed later.

Class intervals are defined as the width or spread of each class. Generally, it is desirable for the intervals of each class to be equal. The class interval is the count of the number of values that can appear in any class. Concentrating on the first class, it can be seen that there are nine numbers (rounded to hundreds) that can be included in the class: $3,900, $4,000, $4,100, $4,200, $4,300, $4,400, $4,500, $4,600, and $4,700. The class interval is really 900, since the values represent numbers rounded to the nearest hundred.

The class interval of any class is easily calculated by subtracting the lower limit of the class from the lower limit of the next class. Thus, for the first class, by subtraction, we have

Lower limit of second class = $4,800
Lower limit of first class =   3,900
Class interval = $ 900.

Exercise 1 in the Problems and Projects section at the end of this chapter demonstrates alternatively the determination of class intervals using real class limits.

Midvalues are simply the midpoints of each class; they represent an average of the values contained in the classes. The midvalue of any class can be calculated easily by computing an average of the upper and lower class limits. It also can be obtained by computing an average of the upper and lower real class limits.

TABLE 18–8

MIDVALUES OF INCOME CLASSES

Lower Class Limit	Midvalues	Upper Class Limit
$3,900	($4,300)	$ 4,700
4,800	(5,200)	5,600
5,700	(6,100)	6,500
6,600	(7,000)	7,400
7,500	(7,900)	8,300
8,400	(8,800)	9,200
9,300	(9,700)	10,100

The midvalues of each class are displayed in Table 18–8. Even though midvalues are calculated after the various classes are established, it is important that the class limits be chosen on the basis of some knowledge of the data and their concentration about class midvalues. This point justifies further explanation.

When class limits are established, consideration should be given to the pattern of concentration within the class intervals. The importance of midvalues is illustrated with a classic example. In previous years, commodities sold in "dime stores" were traditionally priced as multiples of a nickel—a dime, a quarter, etc. If the prices of the commodities were classified into a frequency distribution, it would make sense for the class limits to be set at $ .03–$ .07, $ .08–$ .12, $ .13–$ .17, and so forth, so that the midvalues would reflect the concentration of items in each class. The midvalues would be $ .05, $ .10, $ .15, and so forth.

Another point should be mentioned before we proceed to the charting of frequency distributions. When a class limit is not defined but is literally left "open," the midvalue of the class cannot be defined either. This is important to remember because it prohibits the calculation of some of the important descriptive measures defined in Chapter 19. An open-ended class would appear as follows:

Under 100

. . .

900 and over.

This procedure is sometimes used to avoid revealing a specific figure that may be extreme or may identify a specific individual. The procedure might be used by a church, for instance, to provide a frequency distribution of its members' giving records. If the church had one or two individuals whose financial support was known to be very generous, it would be appropriate to use an open-ended class to camouflage the amount they gave. The open-ended class thus would provide some protection for the generous supporters.

In other instances, the open-ended class may be used to reduce the number of classes in a frequency distribution to a manageable level, particularly if extremely high and low figures would require the establishment of many unnecessary classes between the bulk of the data and the extreme values.

Charting a Frequency Distribution

It has been said that a picture is worth a thousand words. Even though this expression is trite, it does convey the usefulness of constructing a picture or figure of a frequency distribution. The most commonly used chart to display a frequency distribution is the *histogram*. Although it resembles the familiar bar chart (or bar graph), there are certain differences. Both the histogram and the bar graph will be illustrated in this section. The *frequency polygon* will also be illustrated and cumulative frequency charts (known as *ogives*) will be constructed. Additional types of graphic presentations of statistical data will be shown in the last part of this chapter.

Frequency distributions are constructed primarily to reduce a large set of data into a manageable form so that its basic characteristics can be conveyed. A more vivid display of data can be provided in a histogram, an example of which is shown in Fig. 18-1. The histogram is constructed by representing the classified or grouped observations (family income) on the horizontal scale (abscissa) and the class frequencies on the vertical scale (ordinate). Both axes are labeled appropriately. Rectangular bars are drawn with the base of each rectangle equal to the class interval (900); the heights reflect the frequencies of the corresponding classes as measured along the vertical axis. The markings on the horizontal scale can be the real class limits as in Fig. 18-1, the class limits, or the class midvalues. It is preferable to use real class limits; otherwise spaces will appear between the rectangles, since they will not have a common side, and the data will form a bar chart, as shown in Fig. 18-2. Real class limits should be used when constructing histograms to keep them from looking like bar charts.

The bar chart is mainly used to display graphically data which represent attributes rather then variates. Data reflecting the geographic origin of college students can be appropriately displayed in a bar chart, as in Fig. 18-3. Note that the variables shown along the horizontal axis are attributes rather than variates.

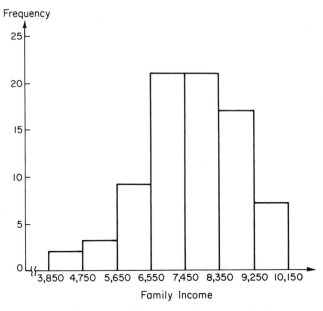

FIGURE 18–1.   Histogram with real class limits.

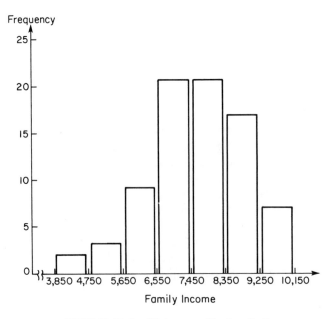

FIGURE 18–2.   Histogram with class limits.

Histograms and bar charts are different in two aspects. First, bar charts are constructed with spaces between the vertical rectangles while this is avoided in histograms. Furthermore, histograms are used to display variates (basically, continuous variates), while bar charts are used to display attributes. Histograms cannot be used in connection with frequency distributions having open-ended classes, and they must be used with extreme care if the classes are not all equal. Extreme care must also be used when bar charts are drawn in three dimensions.[2] Both the histogram and the bar chart can be constructed using relative frequencies instead of absolute frequencies.

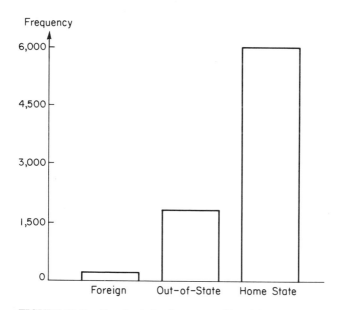

FIGURE 18–3.   Bar chart showing geographic origin of students.

The upper corners of a histogram are occasionally eliminated to produce a "smooth" curve known as a *frequency polygon.* In this type of chart, the midvalues of successive classes are connected by means of straight lines. The histogram shown in Fig. 18–1 can be converted to the frequency polygon shown in Fig. 18–4. The class midvalues and not the real class limits appear on the horizontal axis because the class frequencies appear directly above the midvalues.

This same technique of smoothing is applied to cumulative distributions, which are then used to obtain the so-called *ogive.* For example, the frequency

[2] For more information on this word of caution, see J. E. Fruend and F. J. Williams, *Elementary Business Statistics: A Modern Approach* (Englewood Cliffs, N. J.: Prentice-Hall, Inc., 1964), pp. 26–29.

TABLE 18–9

DERIVATION OF CUMULATIVE FREQUENCIES

Income Classes	Frequencies	Cumulative Frequencies
$3,850– $4,750	2	2
4,750– 5,650	3	5
5,650– 6,550	9	14
6,550– 7,450	21	35
7,450– 8,350	21	56
8,350– 9,250	17	73
9,250– 10,150	7	80

distribution of family income can be used to show the derivation of cumulative frequencies, and the results used to construct an ogive. Real class limits are used to plot the ogive. The frequency distribution of family income and the development of cumulative frequencies are shown in Table 18–9. These cumulative frequencies apply to a "less than" distribution of income data. The upper real limits of the corresponding classes are the reference points for the "less than" frequencies. For example, two items are "less than" $4,750, five items are "less than" $5,650, and so forth. Fig. 18–5 shows an ogive corresponding to the "less than" distribution.

When a "more than" distribution or ogive is desired, the lower real limits serve as the reference points and the accumulation of class frequencies begins with the seventh class. The accumulation process is accomplished in a reverse fashion.

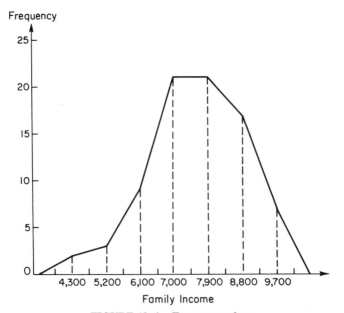

FIGURE 18–4.   Frequency polygon.

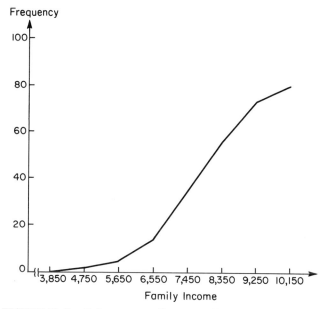

FIGURE 18–5. Ogive corresponding to the "less than" distribution.

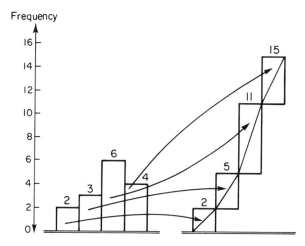

FIGURE 18–6. Ogive constructed directly from a histogram.

An ogive can be constructed directly from a histogram. This process is illustrated in Fig. 18–6.

Ogives are used to give the appropriate values of various percentiles when a percentage scale is placed on the right vertical axis. The general shape of a histogram or frequency polygon can be derived directly from its ogive.

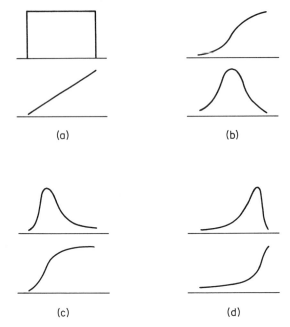

(a)   (b)

(c)   (d)

FIGURE 18–7.   Frequency polygons and corresponding ogives.

Fig. 18–7 depicts differently shaped frequency polygons and their corresponding ogives.

OTHER METHODS OF DISPLAYING DATA

Histograms, frequency polygons, and ogives have greater visual appeal
than frequency tables because they provide a simple interpretation of the data.
There are other ways in which distributions can be presented. Close to a
dozen examples of such pictorial presentations are given in the figures included in this section. The reader should be familiar with some of these
presentations because they appear frequently in newspapers and magazines.

Although books could be written on the subject of graphic presentations
of statistical data, we will not pursue this subject in great detail. Generally
speaking, it is a matter of artistic ingenuity; however, several rules will be
emphasized for the sake of consistency. A simple table will be illustrated first
to point out some important rules that are applicable to both tables and
figures.

Simple Tables

Data can sometimes be conveniently summarized in the form of a table
that resembles a frequency distribution. All tables and figures should have a

title and a number. Generally, various classifications of data are identified in a table by what are known as *stubs*. The data may also be cross-classified with another variable, which often is just a unit of time. The cross-classifications in a table are called the *captions*. Both stubs and captions are labeled in Table 18–10. Furthermore, any part of the table can be clarified by notes which are placed just below the body of the table. The source of the data for the table immediately follows the notes. If the data were obtained from a secondary source, this document is listed or identified; if the data are the result of independent or primary research, the appropriate indication should be given. The source of data should always appear with any table or figure.

Horizontal Bar Charts

The bar chart was introduced in a previous section of this chapter. Generally, the data in a bar chart are represented by vertical bars (or rectangles). Occasionally, if the label for each bar is relatively long and more categories are present, the rectangles are placed horizontally. Even if there are only a few categories, it is appropriate to make a horizontal bar chart if the magnitude of each category is represented according to time. In all charts and figures, it is customary to place time along the horizontal axis if at all possible.

In Fig. 18–8, two categories are presented for each region of the country and a legend is provided to identify the two time periods selected. The title of

TABLE 18–10

GROSS NATIONAL PRODUCT BY SECTOR*

	Sector	1963	1964	1965 Captions
	↗ Private	532.4	568.7	613.4
	Business	513.0	547.4	590.8
	Household	16.0	17.3	18.3
Stubs	→Rest of world	3.4	4.0	4.3
	General government	58.1	63.0	67.8
	↘ Total GNP	590.5	631.7	681.2

*In billions of current dollars.
Source: *Survey of Current Business* (December 1966).

Fig. 18–8 is styled in an acceptable form. Note that the title also tells what, where, and when. This should be the primary purpose of titles for all figures and tables.

Absolute Subdivided Bar Charts

The bar chart that appears in Fig. 18–9 is much like the one introduced in the first section of this chapter except that Fig. 18–9 has three variables

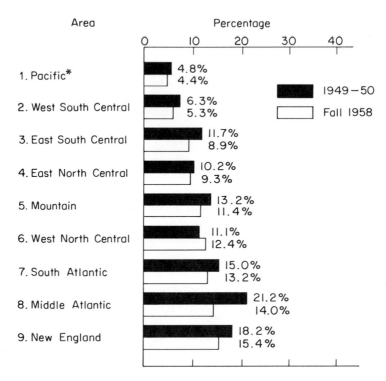

FIGURE 18–8. Percentage of College Undergraduates Migrating from Home-State Areas to Public Institutions in the U. S., 1949–1950 and Fall, 1958.

*Breakdown used by Bureau of Census, *Statistical Abstract of the United States, 1959.*
Sources: *Home State and Migration of American College Students, Fall, 1958;* and *Residence and Migration of College Students, 1949–1950.*

that represent the three periods of time selected. These variables are defined and identified by the legend appearing below the chart. Generally, legends should be avoided because their use causes the reader to glance back and forth from the chart to the legend. However, it cannot always be eliminated easily.

The purpose of the subdivided bar chart is to show the parts that make up the whole. The absolute subdivided chart reflects the data in terms of the absolute units of measurement.

In Fig. 18–9, the value of shares and the capital gains distribution are shown in absolute terms, dollar amounts, for each time period. A comparison of the magnitudes in absolute terms seems at a first glance to indicate that the value of the shares increases more than the capital gains distribution.

Relative Subdivided Bar Charts

The relative comparison of the three categories shown in Fig. 18–9 are given in Fig. 18–10. A relative subdivided bar chart such as the one that appears in Fig. 18–10 also shows the parts that make up the whole. In this case, however, the magnitude of the data is reflected in percentages.

The relative chart is easily derived from the same data that appear in the absolute subdivided chart. The data that appeared in Fig. 18–9 for the

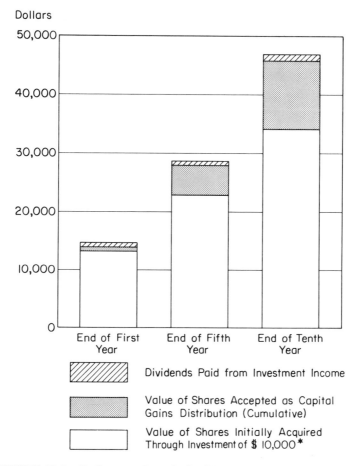

FIGURE 18–9.   Performance Record of a $10,000 Investment in a Mutual Fund.

*The initial Net Asset Value is $9,200 due to an 8% sales charge.
Source: Annual Report of the Fund (December 31, 1963).

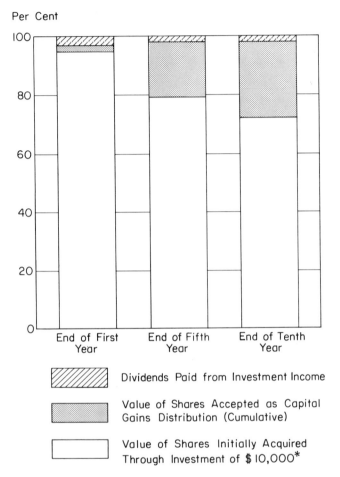

Per Cent

FIGURE 18–10.   Performance Record of a $10,000 Investment in a Mutual Fund.

*The initial Net Asset Value is $9,200 due to an 8% sales charge.
Source: Annual Report of the Fund (December 31, 1963).

"End of Tenth Year" are as follows:

Values of shares	$34,100
Capital gains distributions	12,044
Dividends	894
Total =	$47,038.

The percentage figures used to construct the relative chart (specifically, the bar farthest to the right) are derived from the above figures by dividing the three figures by the total:

Value of shares	(34,100/47,038) × 100 =	72%
Capital gains distributions	(12,044/47,038) × 100 =	26%
Dividends	(894/47,038) × 100 =	2%.

These percentages are plotted in Fig. 18–10. The relative bar chart shows that the value of the shares has decreased on a relative basis.

Multiple-Component Bar Charts

Unlike the subdivided bar chart, the multiple-component bar chart does not show a total of all categories. When a total of the various components is not desired, it is appropriate to place the rectangular bars side by side. A distribution of various types of hospital protection plans is shown in Fig. 18–11 as it appeared in *Health Insurance Facts, 1963*.

Pie Charts

One of the most widely used charts is the pie chart, so named because the various components or categories are segmented in a manner that gives the appearance of a pie, sliced and ready for serving. The pie chart is used to emphasize the proportionality of the various parts that make up the whole. An example is shown in Fig. 18–12.

Several rules should be followed when constructing a pie chart. First, the largest segment should begin at the 12 o'clock position and should include the area corresponding to a clockwise movement. Second, the arrangement

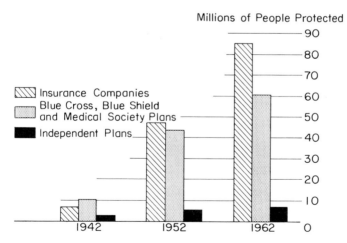

FIGURE 18–11.   Distribution of hospital expense protection in the United States by type of insurer, 1942, 1952, 1962 (totals not adjusted for duplication).

Source: Source Book of Health Insurance Data, 1963.

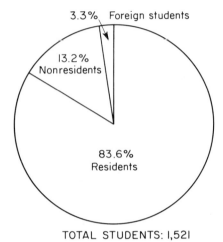

TOTAL STUDENTS: 1,521

FIGURE 18–12. **Geographic origin of students who received degrees in May 1963 from Oklahoma State University.**
Source: Registrar's office.

of the various categories should be such that their size diminishes in the same clockwise direction. (There is one exception to this rule. The miscellaneous group should always be placed last, no matter what its size is relative to the other categories. The miscellaneous class thus appears to the left of the 12 o'clock position.) And finally, all the printing or labeling should be placed horizontally on the chart.

In the procedure for constructing a pie chart, a protractor (a ruler used for measuring degrees of a circle) must be available. One simply converts the data, by categories, into percentages, which are then multiplied by 360 (the number of degrees in a circle); the results are the numbers of degrees that are to be measured with the protractor.

Statistical Maps

An example of a statistical map is shown in Fig. 18–13. The statistical map should be used mainly when the data are directly related to the geographic regions involved. Great care must be exercised when using geographic areas to depict data.

Occasionally, charts of this nature distort the data in order to emphasize a particular point of view. For example, all the states west of the Mississippi River could be shaded to represent, say, certain levels of government spending which are equal to the total incomes of the individuals living in those states. This would give the impression that Federal spending is large. On the other hand, a few populous states on the Atlantic seaboard, including

New York and Pennsylvania, could also represent the same amount of government spending; this Eastern version would make Federal spending appear small. Both presentations give a distorted version of the data. When constructing a map for this purpose, the states chosen should be those whose total area bears the same relation to the area of the United States that their total income does to national income.[3]

Pictograms

Basically, the pictogram does not differ significantly from the bar chart or statistical map. Instead of using rectangles to represent the data as was done with bar charts, images of the actual items are used. Automobile production could be represented in a chart by displaying a picture of an automobile or a number of automobiles. Drawings of coins could be used to reflect various monetary levels, as shown in Fig. 18–14. The pictogram is helpful to the reader because it provides a vivid picture of the data.

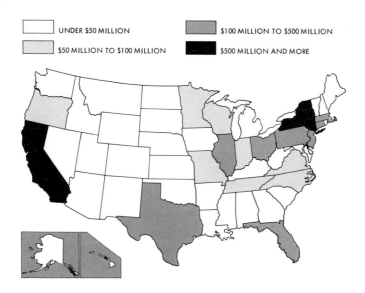

FIGURE 18–13.   Real estate owned by U. S. life insurance companies, by state, 1964.

Source: Life Insurance Factbook, 1964.

[3] This classic example of distortion is illustrated and discussed in detail by Darrel Huff in *How to Lie with Statistics* (New York: W. W. Norton Company, Inc., 1954), pp. 102–103.

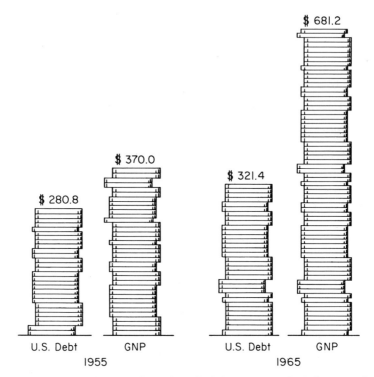

FIGURE 18–14.   A comparison of U. S. Federal debt to GNP for selected years, 1955 and 1965 (in current dollars).

Source: Federal Reserve Bulletin.

Line Charts

The line chart is a popular way to display data that change with time. Generally, data of this nature are plotted with the time variable assigned to the horizontal axis. It is customary to plot the data so that the points for each time period are placed in the middle of each respective interval labeled on the horizontal axis (each interval is separated by vertical guidelines). The line representing sales in Fig. 18–15 is plotted in the middle of each interval. In contrast, data that reflect a level of activity "as of" a particular date are plotted on a chart at the point that represents that particular date.

It is important to indicate whether the vertical scale is broken or not. In Fig. 18–15, it is unbroken; the entire range of values of the vertical axis is shown. However, if for some reason it is not necessary to have the vertical scale start at zero, or if some values between the relevant value and zero are omitted, then the scale must indicate that fact. Usually this is accomplished by showing the scale as follows:

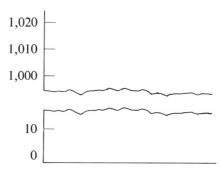

If this is not done, distortion may pass unnoticed.

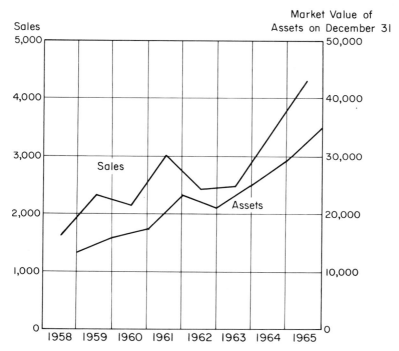

FIGURE 18–15.   **Sales and assets of open-end investment companies for the years 1958–1965 (in millions of dollars).**

Source: Federal Reserve Bulletin.

Multiple-Line Charts

The line chart shown in Fig. 18–16 is a basic line chart with more than one series of data represented. Its important characteristics are that no legends

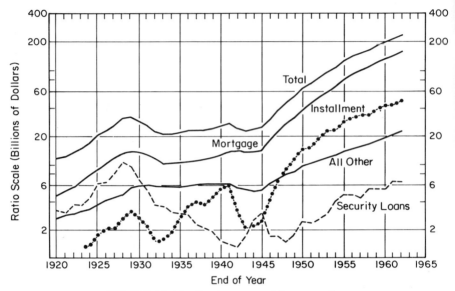

FIGURE 18–16.   Total consumer debt outstanding.

Source: Federal Reserve Historical Chart Book, 1963.

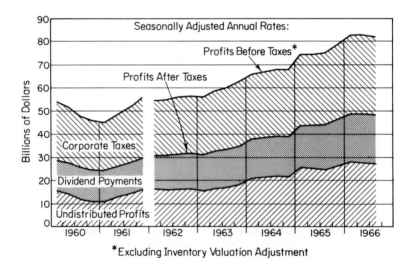

*Excluding Inventory Valuation Adjustment

FIGURE 18–17.   Corporate profits.

*Data beginning 1962 adjusted for effects of new depreciation guidelines and
therefore not comparable with preceding data.

Source: Economic Indicators (Washington, D. C.: U.S. Government Printing
Office, December 1966), p. 7.

are needed and that it displays the relationships among the variables. The vertical scale is a *ratio scale*, which is simply one in which equal relative changes are represented by equal distances on the scale. For instance, the change from 2 to 4 is a 100 per cent increase, as is the change from 4 to 8. The differences between 2 and 4 and between 4 and 8 are shown as equal on the vertical scale. This type of scale is conveniently provided on graph paper known as semilogarithmic paper. The semilogarithmic chart is explained in detail in Annex I to this chapter. It is good practice to use a ratio scale when several sets of data are shown on the same chart.

Absolute Subdivided Line Charts

The subdivided line chart is similar to the subdivided bar chart (Fig. 18–9) that was shown previously. An example of the line chart is shown in Fig. 18–17. This figure reveals the relationships among undistributed profits, dividends, and taxes. It shows separately changes in three variables, while at at the same time it displays profits before and after taxes.

The absolute subdivided line chart can be converted to a relative subdivided line chart in much the same manner as the absolute subdivided bar chart was changed to a relative bar chart (Fig. 18–10). The necessary data for converting Fig. 18–17 into a relative chart can be obtained from the December 1966 issue of *Economic Indicators*.

ANNEX I: THE SEMILOGARITHMIC CHART

Often it is not appropriate to compare two series of data on the familiar graph paper with arithmetic scales on both axes. If the magnitudes of the two series differ appreciably, relative changes provide a much better comparison. A multiple comparison of several series was provided in Fig. 18–16. The vertical scale was a ratio scale, basically the same as the vertical scale on a semilogarithmic chart, which is in terms of logarithms.

The data presented in Table 18–11 can be used to illustrate the importance and usefulness of semilogarithmic charts. The data are plotted on arithmetic graph paper in Fig. 18–18. As reflected by the data in the table, the absolute changes in free highway disbursements and toll facilities are approximately the same. The same data are plotted on semilogarithmic paper in Fig. 18–19. Note that the two lines are no longer parallel as they were in Fig. 18–18. The change in toll facilities is greater than the change in free highway disbursements. This is true because the vertical scale of Fig. 18–19 transforms the data graphically and directly into their corresponding logarithms. The lines in Fig. 18–19 now show the relative or percentage changes in the two series.

TABLE 18–11

MAJOR HIGHWAY CAPITAL DISBURSEMENTS

	Cost (Billions of Dollars)	
Year	Facilities	Highways
1952	0.2	2.7
1953	0.4	2.9
1954	0.8	3.2
1955	0.9	3.4
1956	1.1	3.8

Source: Survey of Current Business (Washington, D. C.: U. S. Dept. of Commerce, December 1956), p. 20.

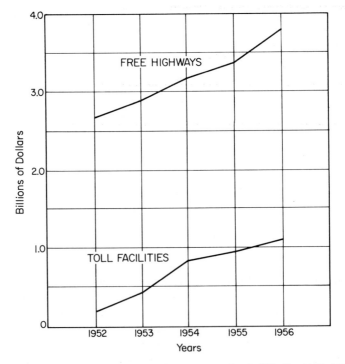

FIGURE 18–18.   Major highway disbursements in the U. S., 1952–1956.

Source: Survey of Current Business.

An alternative to using the semilogarithmic chart to show relative changes in two series is to find the logarithms of the original data and plot them on the customary arithmetic graph paper. This has been done and the results

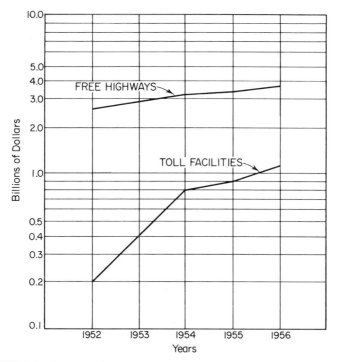

FIGURE 18–19.   Major highway disbursements in the U. S., 1952–1956.

Source: Survey of Current Business.

plotted in Fig. 18–20. If Figs. 18–19 and 18–20 could be superimposed on one another, the lines of both figures would be identical. However, the use of the semilogarithmic chart eliminated the need to know logarithms while giving the same desired relative comparisons.

Some general rules can be provided for setting up the scales for the *Y* axis of the semilogarithmic chart. The chart in Fig. 18–19, constructed on semilogarithmic paper which contains repeated sets of guidelines called cycles, is on two-cycle paper; the paper is available in one or more cycles. The first line can be arbitrarily assigned any value that is not zero. The next cycle begins with a value that is ten times the beginning value of the previous cycle. For example, the first cycle of Fig. 18–19 begins with 0.1 and the second cycle begins with 1.0 (1.0 is ten times 0.1). The second line in a cycle is double the value of the first; for example, 0.2 is twice 0.1 and 2.0 is twice 1.0.

Each additional line in a particular cycle is obtained by adding the amount of the difference between the first and second lines. For example, the third line is 0.3, which is 0.2 plus 0.1 (the difference between 0.2 and 0.1 is 0.1). Now check these rules to discover how the vertical scale of Fig. 18–16 was constructed.

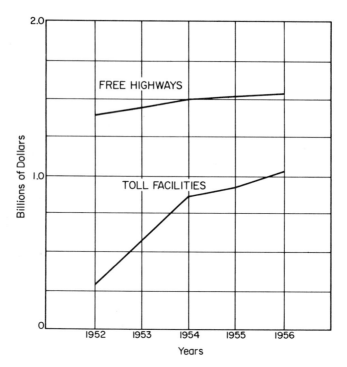

FIGURE 18–20. Major highway disbursements in the U. S., 1952–1956 (in logarithms).

Source: Survey of Current Business.

ANNEX II: SIGNIFICANCE OF ROUNDED NUMBERS

In working with data, one is generally faced with the need to round numbers. The problem of rounding will first be identified; then the rules of rounding will be defined.

It is a common practice to round quantities to, say, the nearest dollar, the nearest pound, the nearest thousand units of production, or the nearest million people. The figure $143.68, rounded to the nearest dollar, would be $144. Similarly, 8,674,341 automobiles, rounded to the nearest thousand, would be 8,674,000. These two examples illustrate the general rule to follow, which is that a number is rounded up or down according to the nearest unit. This rule leads to difficulties if a number lies exactly halfway between the two possible rounded units. For example, $143.50 and 8,674,500 automobiles can be rounded to $144.00 and 8,674,000 automobiles, respectively, if the first figure is rounded up and the second figure rounded down.

When the numbers to be rounded lie exactly midway between two units, a special *rule of exception* is followed. The rule of exception states that numbers should be rounded off in such a way that the last digit remaining on the right is an even number—that is, 0, 2, 4, 6, or 8. This means that half of the time these figures will be rounded up and half of the time they will be rounded down.

If this rule is not followed and numbers are consistently rounded up or rounded down, a systematic rounding bias will be introduced; for example, if numbers ending in 5 are consistently rounded up, there will be an upward bias in any presentation or calculation in which they are used. The rule of exception provides a means to eliminate the systematic error of rounding; in the long run the rounding bias will average out. In everyday encounters at the grocery store and the drug store, you may find that this rule is ignored. The grocer always rounds up.

One precaution in rounding deals with the danger of rounding too much or too little. For instance, if the number 143 is rounded to 100 and then multiplied by 1,000,000, the result will be 100,000,000. However, this understates the true result by 43,000,000 (43 times 1,000,000). This may be a significant amount.

Two rules for calculating with rounded numbers will be stated; one pertains to addition and subtraction, and the other to multiplication and division.

Rule 1:

In the addition and subtraction of rounded numbers, the answer should be rounded to the same number of digits as the number that was rounded off the most among the numbers that were added or subtracted. For example, when adding the rounded numbers 140.0, 68.32, and 251.437, the result is not 459.757 but 459.8 or even 460, since we cannot even be sure that the 0.8 is correct.

Rule 2:

In the multiplication and division of rounded numbers, the result should not have more *significant digits* than any one of the numbers that were multiplied or divided.

The term "significant digit" must be defined before the application of this rule can be demonstrated. Basically, significant digits include all the nonzero digits; however, zeros also can be counted as significant digits depending upon their location in a number. All zeros that appear to the left of the first nonzero digit are *not* significant. For example, the zeros in the number 00647 are not significant digits, but the zeros in the number 100647 are. The number 0.0034 has two significant digits; the zeros are not significant. In the case of a rounded number, the rounded digit is never significant.

Zeros that appear to the right of the last nonzero digit may sometimes be significant. For example, the number 140,268 rounded to tens of thousands is 140,000 and the zeros are not significant. However, if we round the number to thousand, the first zero appearing to the right of the 4 will be significant.

Now, we can return to the rule for multiplying and dividing rounded numbers and present an example. If the rounded numbers 24.8 and 1.3 are multiplied, the result is not 32.24 but 32, since there are only two significant digits in the number. The above rule does not apply if neither of the numbers is rounded.

PROBLEMS AND PROJECTS

1. In a toothpaste test, the number of cavities occurred with the following frequencies:

Total Number of Cavities	Number of Persons
1– 5	5
6–10	9
11–15	12
16–20	7
21–25	2

a. What are the class limits?
b. Compute the midvalues of each class.
c. Calculate the class interval using class limits and real class limits.
d. Construct a histogram, a frequency polygon, and a "more than" ogive.

2. Construct a relative subdivided line chart corresponding to the absolute subdivided line chart presented in the text that showed corporate profits before and after taxes. The absolute chart in the chapter was based on quarterly figures; however, yearly figures are provided here. It is suggested that you obtain data for 1965 and 1966 from the current issue of *Economic Indicators*.

CORPORATE PROFITS IN BILLIONS OF DOLLARS

Period	Corporate Tax Liability	Dividend Payments	Undistributed Profits
1960	23.0	13.4	13.2
1961	23.1	13.8	13.5
1962	24.2	15.2	16.0
1963	26.3	16.5	16.6
1964	28.4	17.3	21.3
1965	—	—	—
1966	—	—	—

3. Use the following data to construct a horizontal bar chart:

EXPECTATION OF LIFE AT BIRTH IN THE U. S. A. IN YEARS

Period	Male	Female
1900	48	53
1930	59	61
1955	65	68

4. Round each of the following numbers to one decimal place.
   a. 32.750
   b. 13.650
   c. 77.299
   d. 27.991
   e. 21.851
   f. 1.295

SELECTED REFERENCES

Croxton, F. E., and D. J. Cowden, *Practical Business Statistics*, 3rd ed. Englewood Cliffs, N. J.: Prentice-Hall, Inc., 1960.

Freund, J. E., and F. J. Williams, *Elementary Business Statistics: A Modern Approach*. Englewood Cliffs, N. J.: Prentice-Hall, Inc., 1964.

Huff, D., *How to Lie with Statistics*. New York: W.W. Norton & Company, Inc., 1954.

Stockton, J. R., *Introduction to Business and Economic Statistics*, 3rd ed. Cincinnati, O.: South-Western Publishing Company, 1966.

19

DESCRIPTIVE
MEASURES

After data have been collected or assembled, they must be analyzed by the investigator or scientist. Various measures can be computed that summarize or describe certain characteristics of the data. Descriptive measures are computed and used by the investigator to assist in various comparisons, descriptions, and analyses.

Two characteristics are important in describing a set of data. One indicates the position or location of the data; the other deals with the spread of the data. These characteristics are applicable to samples and populations.

Generally, the position or location of data is described by various *measures of central tendency*. These measures are the *arithmetic mean* (the most familiar average), the *median*, and the *mode*. All three measures are types of averages. It is at least equally important to determine the *spread* or *variation* of the data. The *range* and *standard deviation* are among the measures of variation that are discussed.

Measures of central tendency merely locate the data or distributions. The frequency polygons shown in Fig. 19–1 illustrate the difference between location and variation. Distribution *A* is centered or located at 30, while distribution *B* is located at 50. However, the two distributions have an equal spread or variation of 20 units. The two distributions in Fig. 19–2 are located at the same position, but distribution *A* has approximately twice as much variation as distribution *B*.

The ideas of location and variation are analogous to the blast patterns that result from firing a shotgun. Suppose that two shotguns are fired at a

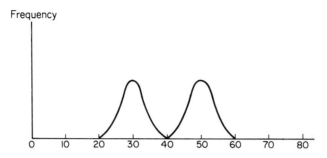

FIGURE 19–1.   Location and variation illustrated.

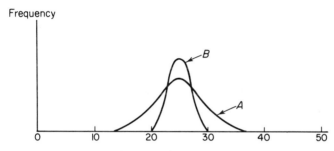

FIGURE 19–2.   Variation illustrated.

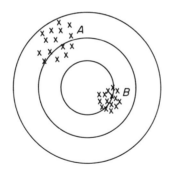

FIGURE 19–3.   Gun blast pattern.

target. The blast pattern of gun *A* is off-target; that is, it is not located as close to the bull's-eye as the blast pattern of shotgun *B*. This is illustrated in Fig. 19–3. In addition, there is relatively less variation in the blast pattern of gun *B* as compared with gun *A*. Location and spread are important not only in shotgun patterns but also in describing the distribution of observations or data.

In the first part of this chapter, various measures of location will be defined and compared and their calculating procedures demonstrated. The second part of the chapter will concentrate on measures of variation, and the third part will demonstrate procedures that are relevant to grouped data. The remainder of the chapter will be devoted to a few other useful descriptive measures.

MEASURES OF CENTRAL TENDENCY

Secondary data usually are summarized by being classified or grouped into appropriate frequency distributions. The calculating techniques required to compute the descriptive measures for classified data are different from the techniques used for unclassified data. Usually, when data are summarized into a frequency distribution, inexact descriptive measures have been used. When primary data are available that are not classified into a frequency distribution, calculating methods can be used that will produce exact results, although the methods are more time-consuming. However, the use of electronic computers has minimized the calculating time required to analyze ungrouped data.

Definitions

Abbreviated computational procedures for ungrouped data will be introduced in this section to assist in defining the arithmetic mean, median, and mode.

The Arithmetic Mean.   This measure is usually referred to as the "average." One merely divides the total of all the numbers by the number of items involved.

The Median.   This measure is the number that represents the middle value in an array of numbers. It can be thought of as the fiftieth percentile. There are an equal number of values above and below the median.

The Mode.   This measure is simply defined as the value or item that occurs most frequently.

These three measures can be illustrated by relating them to the frequency distribution. The mean is to a frequency distribution what the fulcrum is to a seesaw or teeter-totter. It is the point or location in the distribution that balances the weighted frequencies of all values. This is illustrated in Fig. 19–4. The greater distances of the small numbers to the left of the fulcrum are counterbalanced by the shorter distances of the relatively less frequent large items on the right.

The median is the measure that locates the middle of the distribution. As illustrated in Fig. 19–5, the median divides the area under the curve into two equal parts. The term "median" is often used in a special way to refer to

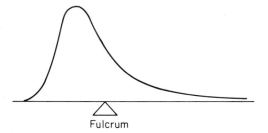

FIGURE 19–4.   The mean illustrated.

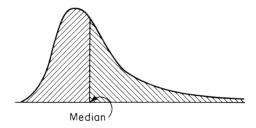

FIGURE 19–5.   The median illustrated.

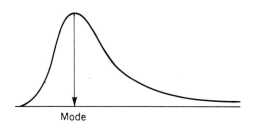

FIGURE 19–6.   The mode illustrated.

the middle part of an interstate highway (the space which separates the highway into two parts). Motorists are warned against "crossing over the median."

The mode simply locates the value that occurs most frequently. Since frequency is measured on the vertical axis, the peak of the curve will represent the point where the greatest number of any single value occurs. The value measured on the horizontal axis below this peak represents the mode. The mode is demonstrated in Fig. 19–6.

In most symmetrical distributions, these three measures are equal. In distributions that are not symmetrical they tend to maintain a stable relationship to each other; their order of size reverses when the direction of distortion changes. This type of distortion is called skewness; it means that the frequency

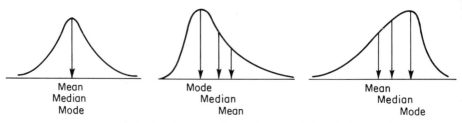

Mean	Mode	Mean
Median	Median	Median
Mode	Mean	Mode

FIGURE 19–7.   **Mean, median and mode relationship illustrated.**

distribution is bunched together on one side of the center and a few items are strung out on the other side. These relationships are described in Fig. 19–7.

Computing Procedures

The Mean.   The computation of the mean and the resultant formula are as follows, where the number of items N is 5:

$$X_1 = 8$$
$$X_2 = 7$$
$$X_3 = 6$$
$$X_4 = 15$$
$$X_5 = 4.$$

The total of the five items is 40. The arithmetic mean is $\dfrac{40}{5} = 8$; therefore, the formula for the arithmetic mean is

$$\mu = \frac{\Sigma X}{N}.$$

(The symbol μ, which is the Greek letter mu, is customarily used to designate the arithmetic mean.)

The Median.   In calculating the median, the data must first be *arrayed*— that is, rearranged into an ascending or descending order. It is then easy to pick out the median. This can be shown, using the same set of numbers, in Fig. 19–8. The middle item in the array is the median; in this case it is 7. The median can be systematically located by picking the $[(N + 1)/2]$th item in the array. In this example there are five items; therefore, $(5 + 1)/2 = 3$, indicating that the third item is the median. If there is an even number of items, one simply splits the difference between the two middle items (or computes their arithmetic mean). For example, if we have the six numbers 4, 6,

7, 8, 15, and 18, the median will be halfway between 7 and 8, or $7\frac{1}{2}$. In this case, the $[(N + 1)/2]$th expression still aids in locating the median. The median is $(6 + 1)/2$, which equals $3\frac{1}{2}$; thus it is the $3\frac{1}{2}$th item.

An investigation into the behavior of the mean and the median reveals two important characteristics. First, the arithmetic mean is distorted significantly when extreme items are included in the set of data; and second, the mean can be manipulated algebraically, while the median cannot.

Suppose that in the set of five numbers used previously the fifth item had been erroneously recorded as 115 instead of 15. The obvious outcome would be as follows:

$$
\begin{array}{c}
4 \\
6 \\
7 \\
8 \\
\underline{115} \\
140
\end{array}
$$

$$\mu = \frac{140}{5} = 28$$

$$\text{Median} = \left(\frac{N + 1}{2}\right)$$

$$\text{Median} = \left(\frac{5 + 1}{2}\right) = \text{third item.}$$

Thus the mean changed from 8 to 28, but the median, 7, remained the same. This illustration emphasizes how an extreme item can affect the mean and cause a distorted average, while having no effect on the median. The value of the median, 7, also seems more representative of the array than does the mean of 28.

For this reason, precaution should be exercised when using the arithmetic mean. It is wise to use the median if investigation of the data results in the discovery of the presence of either extremely high or extremely low values. Income distributions are typically skewed in the direction of the extremely high incomes of a few individuals. The practice of using the median as a

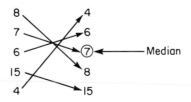

FIGURE 19–8.   Calculating the median.

measure of average income is becoming popular because of this characteristic of the mean.

There is a classic example of the salesman who visited a town of 20 families that appeared to have low incomes. In reply to the salesman's question, a citizen stated that the community's average income was about $100,000. The salesman was astounded, and requested an explanation. The citizen explained by pointing out that "19 of us earn about $2,000 a year, and the fellow on the hill pulls down about $2 million a year."

The arithmetic mean has one advantage over the median. The mean can be computed using only the number of items and the total of the values; the list of numbers is not needed. An enumeration of the values is needed to find the median. It is obvious that by simple algebraic manipulations

$$N\mu = \sum X$$

can be derived from

$$\mu = \frac{\sum X}{N}.$$

Therefore, with N and μ, $\sum X$ (the total) can be determined.

Suppose that the average sales figures of ten stores are available, but not the individual figures. To calculate the total sales of all ten stores, the number of stores N must simply be multiplied by the arithmetic mean μ of the average sales figures.

The Mode.   The mode is simply determined by counting the number of times each value occurs and then selecting the value that occurs the greatest number of times. In the following array, it is clear that the mode is 6, since no other number occurs three times:

$$
\begin{array}{c}
4 \\
6 \\
8 \\
15 \\
7 \\
6 \\
5 \\
6.
\end{array}
$$

The story of the three window contractors who wanted to mass-produce just one size window frame illustrates the usefulness of the mode. In measuring the window size, one contractor used the mean width of all window frames, another used the median width of all window frames, and the third used the modal width of all window frames. It is clear that the window frames of the first two contractors would not be acceptable, while the third contractor provided a popular-sized frame.

A recent issue of *The Wall Street Journal* stated: "Average annual income of more than 800 graduates of MIT's class of 1940 is $25,324 according to a 25th reunion survey; incomes range from $5,000 to $125,000."[1] This average income is most impressive; the indication of the variation as measured by the range is also informative. We will study measures of variation in the next section.

MEASURES OF VARIATION

A comparison of the two sets of numbers in Table 19–1 illustrates the fallacy of relying on just an average to describe an array of numbers. The

TABLE 19–1

COMPARISON OF AVERAGES AND RANGES WITH TWO SETS OF DATA

Group A	Group B
33	12
34	16
34	25
35	32
35	35
35	35
35	35
36	40
36	50
37	70
350	350

mean, median, and mode equal 35 in both groups. However, measures of variation will reveal the spread of the items to be different in each distribution.

Range

A simple measure of variation is the *range*, which is defined as the highest value minus the lowest value. The range is equal to 4 in the first group and 58 in the second group. This measure of variation reveals that the two distributions in the table are not alike. However, it is evident that such a measure is relatively crude because it is established on the basis of only two items of the array, the two extremes.

[1] *The Wall Street Journal* (June 15, 1965), p. 1.

Further behavior of the range can be demonstrated with the two sets of data in Table 19–2. The arithmetic mean of both sets is 19 and the range of both sets is 10. If the two extremes in both series are eliminated, the range is $20 - 18 = 2$ for group C and $23 - 15 = 8$ for group D. The major drawback of the range, therefore, is that it does not take into account the variation among all items.

Average Deviation

Another measure, the *average deviation*, utilizes the variations of all items in the array by measuring the variation of each item with respect to either the median or the mean. When the absolute deviations of a set of numbers are totaled, we obtain the results in Table 19–3. Note that the sum of the absolute deviations from the median (9) is less than the sum of the absolute deviations from the mean (10).

When the sums of the deviations are averaged, we obtain the average deviations:

$$\text{Average deviation (using median)} = \frac{9}{5} = 1.8$$

$$\text{Average deviation (using mean)} = \frac{10}{5} = 2.0.$$

(Note that if the algebraic sum is computed, the sum of the deviations from the mean is always zero.)

The average of the absolute deviations from the median is preferred to the average of the deviations from the mean for two reasons. First, the mean can be distorted by extreme items, and second, the sum of the absolute deviations from the median is less than the sum of the absolute deviations from the mean. (This second reason, the *property of minimization*, allows for better statistical testing.) Since it is preferable to use the median in the formula for the average deviation, we have

$$\text{Average deviation} = \frac{\sum |X - \text{median}|}{N},$$

where the vertical bars indicate absolute values.

Standard Deviation

The most popular and widely used measure of variation is the *standard deviation*, which is based on the *squared* deviations from the mean. The total of the squared deviations from the mean is smaller than it is for the median. This is illustrated in Table 19–4.

The property of minimization is one of the reasons for the popularity

TABLE 19–2

COMPARISON OF RANGES WITH TWO SETS OF DATA

Group C	Group D
	14
14	15
18	16
18	17
19	18
19	19
19	20
19	21
20	22
20	23
24	24
190	209

TABLE 19–3

COMPUTATION OF ABSOLUTE DEVIATIONS

Items	Deviations from Median (Median = 6)	Deviations from Mean ($\mu = 7$)
4	$4 - 6 = -2$	$4 - 7 = -3$
6	$6 - 6 = 0$	$6 - 7 = -1$
6	$6 - 6 = 0$	$6 - 7 = -1$
8	$8 - 6 = +2$	$8 - 7 = +1$
11	$11 - 6 = +5$	$11 - 7 = +4$
Total = 35	Sum of absolute values = 9	Sum of absolute values = 10

TABLE 19–4

COMPUTATION OF SQUARED DEVIATIONS

Items	Deviations from Median	Deviations from Median Squared	Deviations from Mean	Deviations from Mean Squared
4	$4 - 6 = -2$	4	$4 - 7 = -3$	9
6	$6 - 6 = 0$	0	$6 - 7 = -1$	1
6	$6 - 6 = 0$	0	$6 - 7 = -1$	1
8	$8 - 6 = +2$	4	$8 - 7 = +1$	1
11	$11 - 6 = +5$	25	$11 - 7 = +4$	16
		$\sum(X - \text{median})^2 = 34$		$\sum(X - \mu)^2 - 28$

of the standard deviation. We will first define the standard deviation and then demonstrate the reasons for using it. The definitional formula is

$$\sigma = \sqrt{\frac{\sum(X - \mu)^2}{N}},$$

where the Greek letter sigma (σ) designates the standard deviation. The numerator represents the sum of the squared deviations of all items from the mean. This is divided by the number of items, and the square root is extracted. Since the sum of the squared deviations in Table 19–4 was 28,

$$\sigma = \sqrt{\frac{28}{5}} = 2.3.$$

The standard deviation, like most measures of variation, measures the extent to which the elements of a set of numbers are unequal. Clearly a set of identical numbers, such as 4, 4, 4, and 4, would have a standard deviation of zero. The more unlike numbers are, the greater the variation will be.

The standard deviation behaves in a stable manner. A series of numbers that has a range twice as large as another series and a gap twice as large between each number will also have a standard deviation that is twice as large. This stable behavior is demonstrated in the two series of numbers given in Table 19–5. The standard deviation for series A is $2\sqrt{2}$ or twice the standard deviation for series B, which is $\sqrt{2}$. The standard deviation is consistent in reflecting the fact that the range and gaps of data of one set were twice the size of those in the other set.

The main reason that the standard deviation is one of the most widely used measures of variation is that it is relevant to the *normal distribution*. This is important because many statistical sampling theories are based on the random behavior of variables according to the normal distribution. The standard deviation has particular meaning in relation to the normal distribution. First, it determines the *point of inflection* in the curve. The point of inflection is

TABLE 19–5

STABLE BEHAVIOR OF STANDARD DEVIATION

	Series A			Series B	
X	$X - \mu$	$(X - \mu)^2$	X	$X - \mu$	$(X - \mu)^2$
2	$2 - 6 = -4$	16	4	$4 - 6 = -2$	4
4	$4 - 6 = -2$	4	5	$5 - 6 = -1$	1
6	$6 - 6 = \ 0$	0	6	$6 - 6 = \ 0$	0
8	$8 - 6 = +2$	4	7	$7 - 6 = +1$	1
10	$10 - 6 = +4$	16	8	$8 - 6 = +2$	4
$\overline{30}$	$\Sigma(X - \mu)^2 =$	$\overline{40}$	$\overline{30}$	$\Sigma(X - \mu)^2 =$	$\overline{10}$

$$\mu = \frac{30}{5} = 6 \qquad\qquad \mu = \sqrt{\frac{30}{5}} = 6$$

$$\sigma = \sqrt{\frac{40}{5}} \qquad\qquad \sigma = \sqrt{\frac{10}{5}}$$

$$\sigma = \sqrt{8} \qquad\qquad\qquad \sigma = \sqrt{2}$$

$$\sigma = 2\sqrt{2} \qquad\qquad\qquad \sigma = \sqrt{2}$$

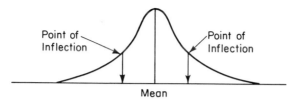

FIGURE 19–9.   Points of inflection in the normal curve.

that point where the curve bends in the opposite direction. The distances on either side of the center of the normal or bell-shaped curve, which are each precisely one standard deviation in length, are, by coincidence, also the spots where the curve changes direction. This is shown in Fig. 19–9.

The standard deviation is a device for measuring variation in much the same way that the yardstick is a device for measuring distance. If, in Fig. 19–9, the distance from the mean to the point of inflection had been three feet, it would be one yardstick's distance from the mean. But since the standard deviation would also be three units measured in feet, the point of inflection could be said to be one standard deviation from the center of the distribution.

The normal curve has a basic functional relationship that can be expressed in formula much like the one for the straight line that was discussed in a previous chapter. It was revealed that the general format for a straight line is

$$Y = a + bX,$$

where Y is the variable measured on the vertical axis and X is the variable measured on the horizontal axis. The symbols a and b were defined as the Y intercept and the slope of the line, respectively. These two terms are also referred to as *parameters;* they distinguish the line from other straight lines. In Fig. 19–10, two lines are drawn. One has a Y intercept of 4 and a slope of 2; the other has a Y intercept of 3 and a slope of $\frac{1}{2}$. These values or parameters define or distinguish the two straight lines. The Y values are determined in each equation for various values of X, and the results are shown in Fig. 19–10.

The following formula renders a bell-shaped or normal curve when various values are selected for X and the corresponding values for Y are determined and plotted. The equation for the normal curve is

$$Y = \frac{1}{\sigma\sqrt{2\pi}}e^{-\frac{1}{2}\left(\frac{X-\mu}{\sigma}\right)^2}.$$

In this case, the shape and location of the function are also determined by two parameters; the parameters here are the standard deviation (σ) and the mean (μ). The symbols π and e represent constants that have approximate values of 3.1416 and 2.7182, respectively.

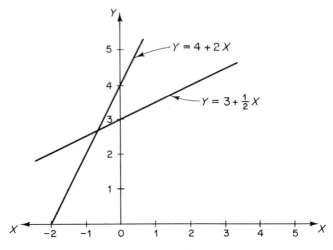

FIGURE 19–10. Straight lines demonstrated.

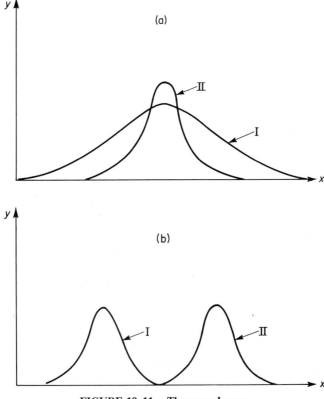

FIGURE 19–11. The normal curve.

In Fig. 19–11, the means are equal for both distributions, but the standard deviation is greater in distribution I than in distribution II; in addition, the standard deviations in drawing B are equal and the means unequal. The standard deviation's role as a parameter of the normal curve emphasizes its importance in studying variation, particularly since normal curve distributions are applicable to sample procedures.

The formula used to define the standard deviation has some serious limitations from the standpoint of computational techniques; for instance, it can introduce a rounding error if the mean is a rounded number. If the mean is equal to 5.66666... and is rounded to 5.667, this will cause a rounding error. This rounding error can be illustrated by simply comparing the results of two computations using three numbers.

TABLE 19–6

USE OF THE DEFINITIONAL FORMULA

X	$(X - \mu)$	$(X - \mu)^2$
4	$4 - 5.667 = -1.667$	2.77889
7	$7 - 5.667 = +1.333$	1.77689
6	$6 - 5.667 = +0.333$	1.10889
17		5.66467

$$\mu = \frac{17}{3} = 5.6666...$$

$$\sigma = \sqrt{\frac{5.66467}{3}} = \sqrt{1.88822}$$

In the first instance, as shown in Table 19–6, σ is derived using the definitional formula. However, a computational formula also can be derived from the definitional form; this derivation is shown in the Annex. The two formulas appear as follows:

$$\sigma = \sqrt{\frac{\Sigma(X - \mu)^2}{N}} = \sqrt{\frac{N\Sigma X^2 - (\Sigma X)^2}{N^2}}.$$

We will now demonstrate how simple it is to use the computational formula. Basically, the formula requires the use of totals, and since the mean is not used, there is no rounding error. The use of the formula is shown in Table 19–7. Note that the difference between 1.88822, using the definitional formula, and 1.55555, using the computational formula, represents the rounding error. This error resulted from the fact that the mean was rounded to three decimal places. In addition, the computation of squared deviations using the definitional formula is unnecessarily tedious. Of course, the use of a computer would shorten the work. However, the rounding error would still occur.

TABLE 19–7

USE OF THE COMPUTATIONAL FORMULA

X	X^2
4	16
7	49
6	36
$\Sigma X = 17$	$\Sigma X^2 = 101$

$$\sigma = \sqrt{\frac{N\Sigma X^2 - (\Sigma X)^2}{N^2}}$$

$$\sigma = \sqrt{\frac{3(101) - (17)^2}{3^2}}$$

$$\sigma = \sqrt{\frac{303 - 289}{9}}$$

$$\sigma = \sqrt{\frac{14}{9}}$$

$$\sigma = \sqrt{1.555\ldots}$$

If the mean is not rounded, the two formulas will render identical values. Tables 19–8 and 19–9 demonstrate the equality of the two formulas in finding the standard deviation. Both formulas are used with the same data, where the mean is a whole number.

A shortcut can be demonstrated for computing the standard deviation when large values are involved. For example, the squaring of the five values in the previous example required the manipulation of relatively large numbers. However, a constant could be subtracted from each number and the standard deviation would remain the same. Table 19–10 shows what happens when 20 is subtracted from the same five numbers. This technique can reduce the computation time considerably.

TABLE 19–8

DEFINITIONAL FORMULA

X	$(X - \mu)$	$(X - \mu)^2$
17	$17 - 22 = -5$	25
19	$19 - 22 = -3$	9
21	$21 - 22 = -1$	1
25	$25 - 22 = +3$	9
28	$28 - 22 = +6$	36
$\Sigma X = 110$		$\Sigma(X - \mu)^2 = 80$

$$\mu = \frac{110}{5} = 22$$

$$\sigma = \sqrt{\frac{\Sigma(X - \mu)^2}{N}} = \sqrt{\frac{80}{5}} = \sqrt{16} = 4$$

TABLE 19–9

COMPUTATIONAL FORMULA

X	X^2
17	289
19	361
21	441
25	625
28	784
$\sum X = 110$	$\sum X^2 = 2{,}500$

$$\sigma = \sqrt{\frac{N\sum X^2 - (\sum X)^2}{N^2}}$$

$$\sigma = \sqrt{\frac{5(2{,}500) - (110)^2}{5^2}}$$

$$\sigma = \sqrt{\frac{12{,}500 - 12{,}100}{25}}$$

$$\sigma = \sqrt{\frac{400}{25}}$$

$$\sigma = \sqrt{16}$$

$$\sigma = 4$$

TABLE 19–10

SHORT METHOD FOR COMPUTING STANDARD DEVIATIONS

X	$X - 20$	$(X - 20)^2$
17	-3	9
19	-1	1
21	$+1$	1
25	$+5$	25
28	$+8$	64
$\sum X = 10$		$\sum X^2 = 100$

$$\sigma = \sqrt{\frac{5(100) - (10)^2}{5^2}}$$

$$\sigma = \sqrt{\frac{400}{5}}$$

$$\sigma = \sqrt{16}$$

$$\sigma = 4$$

Variance

Another way to measure variation is to use the standard deviation in its squared form, σ^2, which is called *variance.*. The formula for variance is identical to the formula for the standard deviation except that the radical is absent:

$$\sigma^2 = \frac{N\sum X^2 - (\sum X)^2}{N^2}.$$

In this problem, the variance is determined as follows:

$$\sigma^2 = \frac{5(100) - (10)^2}{5^2}$$

$$\sigma^2 = \frac{500 - 100}{25}$$

$$\sigma^2 = \frac{400}{25} = 16.$$

(Note that $\sigma = 4$ and $4^2 = 16$.) When calculating standard deviation or variance, the results of the calculations in the numerator should never be negative; if they are, a mistake in arithmetic has been made.

The Coefficient of Variation

It is sometimes necessary to compare the variations of two sets of data. When both sets are measured in the same units, the standard deviation may be sufficient. However, it would be meaningless to compare a standard deviation expressed in inches, for example, to another one that is measured in pounds. The *coefficient of variation* can be used to compare these different sets of data. Usually designated as V, it has the following formula:

$$V = \frac{\sigma}{\mu} \times 100.$$

The coefficient of variation is simply the ratio of the standard deviation to the arithmetic mean expressed as a percentage. Since the units of measurement cancel out, we have a measure that gives the amount of variation with respect to the mean.

The coefficient of variation is important even when the various sets of data are measured in the same units. Table 19–11 shows an example where the

TABLE 19–11

COEFFICIENTS OF VARIATION

	Set 1	Set 2
	7	117
	9	119
	11	121
	15	125
	18	128
	$\mu = 12$	$\mu = 122$
	$\sigma = 4$	$\sigma = 4$
	$V = \frac{4}{12} \times 100 = 33.33\%$	$V = \frac{4}{122} \times 100 = 3.28\%$

variation of five numbers is the same although the means are different, and the data are measured in the same units. The results reveal that the variation is greater for set 1 than for set 2 when the standard deviation is compared to each respective mean.

Investigation of two sets of data with different standard deviations can lead to erroneous results when relative variation is not taken into account. Suppose that in set 1, the standard deviation is 5, while for set 2 it is 25. If the means are relatively equal, the standard deviation will be a relevant measure for comparison, since set 2 has greater variation than set 1. However, if there is a significant difference in the means, the conclusions can be wrong. For instance, assume that the mean in set 1 is 10 and the mean in set 2 is 100. When the coefficient of variation is used, the conclusion will be reversed. Thus for set 1 we will have

$$V = \frac{5}{10} \times 100 = 50\%,$$

and for set 2,

$$V = \frac{25}{100} \times 100 = 25\%.$$

The relative variation in set 1 is greater than that in set 2.

Now that we have looked at the computation of some measures of variation, it would be helpful if we could generalize about them. It can be said that all measures of variation measure the extent to which data or numbers are unequal. This is true for the range and the average deviation as well as for the standard deviation. If numbers in a set are all the same, the range, average deviation, and standard deviation will be equal to zero. If just one value in the set is different, the variation will be greater than zero.

Relevance of Formulas to Sampled Data

One final comment should be made pertaining to the general nature of the formulas that have been discussed. It should be pointed out that these formulas refer to situations where the data being investigated and described are not obtained from samples. If the data being described represent sampled data, then certain changes must be made in the notation and formulas for some of the measures mentioned. For example, in the case of the arithmetic mean, the symbol changes from μ to $\overline{X}$ in order to distinguish between a sample of data and the entire set or population. The term "population" is used by statisticians to refer to the complete set of data, which in many cases may be unwieldy or impossible to obtain. Therefore, statisticians must resort to sampling procedures.

In the case of the mean, only the symbol changes; the formula remains the same. (In all cases, the capital letter N is replaced by a lower case n.) With the standard deviation, both the symbol and the formula are changed. Usually the letter S is used and the formula is adjusted slightly to give

$$S = \sqrt{\frac{\Sigma(X - \bar{X})^2}{n - 1}}.$$

Note that $\bar{X}$ replaces μ and the denominator is adjusted by subtracting 1 from n. Since the population mean is unknown, it is replaced by the sample mean. This adjustment of the denominator is recommended by statisticians to prevent the bias that would result from the fact that the sample mean was utilized in the numerator.

In conclusion, we must emphasize that slightly different techniques are used when the data being described are obtained from a sample. These techniques appear in textbooks that deal with statistical inference.

APPLICATIONS TO GROUPED DATA

Often secondary data are only available in the form of a frequency distribution, since the individual items may no longer be available once they have been grouped into relevant classes. However, classification of data for the purpose of summarizing them does not eliminate the need to determine various descriptive measures.

The techniques for calculating the mode, median, mean, and standard deviation for grouped data can be illustrated in compact form by the example shown in Table 19–12, where the weights of 240 students enrolled in an elementary economics course are given.

The Mode

The *crude mode* is defined as the midvalue of the class that has the largest frequency—that is, the modal class. In Table 19–12, the crude mode

TABLE 19–12

FREQUENCIES OF WEIGHTS OF STUDENTS

Weights of Students (pounds)	Frequencies (f)
90–119	8
120–149	51
150–179	77
180–209	48
210–239	44
240–279	12
Total = $N = \Sigma f =$	240

is 164.5. The mode can be calculated by using the following formula:

$$\text{Mode} = L + \frac{d_1}{d_1 + d_2}(\text{c.i.}),$$

where L stands for the lower real limit of the modal class, d_1 is the difference between the frequencies of the modal class and the class one level lower, d_2 is the difference between the frequencies of the modal class and the class one level higher, and c.i. is the class interval. The computations are

$$L = 149.5$$
$$d_1 = 77 - 51 = 26$$
$$d_2 = 77 - 48 = 29$$
$$\text{c.i.} = 30.$$

Therefore,

$$\text{Mode} = 149.5 + \frac{26}{29 + 26}\ (30)$$
$$= 149.5 + 0.48\ (30)$$
$$= 149.5 + 14.4$$
$$= 163.9.$$

The Median

The technique for determining the median can be explained more easily without a formula. First, the class frequencies are accumulated until one-half of the items are counted. The results are

First class	=	8 items
Second class	=	51 items
Third class	=	61 items
		120 items.

In the third class, only 61 of the 77 items are needed to account for the first 120 of the 240 items in the distribution. Therefore, the median can be extrapolated from the third class by taking 61/77th of the third class interval of 30 and adding it to the lower real limit of the third class. Arithmetically,

$$\text{Median} = 149.5 + \frac{61}{77}\ (30)$$
$$= 149.5 + 23.8$$
$$= 173.3.$$

The Mean and the Standard Deviation

The computational formulas for the arithmetic mean and the standard deviation are presented together because part of the technique for calculating the standard deviation is identical to the approach used in computing the arithmetic mean. The formulas are

$$\mu = MV_a + \frac{\sum fd}{N}(\text{c.i.})$$

$$\sigma = \text{c.i.}\sqrt{\frac{N\sum fd^2 - (\sum fd)^2}{N^2}},$$

where MV_a stands for the midvalue of an arbitrary class, and fd stands for frequency of items in a class times the deviation of that class from the arbitrary class.

The same data of student weights are used to illustrate the computation of the arithmetic mean and the standard deviation for grouped data. The variables to be used in the above formulas are derived and indicated in Table 19–13. The third class (150–179) has been selected as the arbitrary class. Any class can be selected as the class with the arbitrary reference point MV_a. In effect, this technique involves making an educated guess, then correcting that guess. Each class has a deviation d from this arbitrary class.

TABLE 19–13

COMPUTATION OF THE MEAN AND STANDARD DEVIATION FOR GROUPED DATA

Weights of Students	Frequency (f)	Deviation by Class (d)	fd	fd^2
90–119	8	-2	-16	32
120–149	51	-1	-51	51
150–179	77	0	0	0
180–209	48	$+1$	$+48$	48
210–239	44	$+2$	$+88$	176
240–269	12	$+3$	$+36$	108
	$N = 240$		$\sum fd = 105$	$\sum fd^2 = 415$

$$\mu = MV_a + \frac{\sum fd}{N}(\text{c.i.})$$

$$\mu = 164.5 + \frac{105}{240}(30)$$

$$\mu = 177.6$$

$$\sigma = (\text{c.i.})\sqrt{\frac{N\sum fd^2 - (\sum fd)^2}{N^2}}$$

$$\sigma = (30)\sqrt{\frac{240(415) - (105)^2}{(240)(240)}}$$

$$\sigma = (30)\sqrt{\frac{99,600 - 11,025}{57,600}}$$

$$\sigma = (30)\sqrt{\frac{88,575}{57,600}}$$

$$\sigma = (30)\sqrt{1.5378}$$

$$\sigma = 37.2$$

If the midvalue of the first class was selected as the arbitrary reference point, the d values would all be positive. The selection of a midvalue of one of the center classes or a class with one of the largest frequencies will reduce the arithmetic computations; the same answer will result no matter which starting point is selected. However, it should be stated that the values obtained from data that have been summarized by being grouped generally are not the same as those determined from ungrouped or individual items. The answers derived from grouped data do not accurately measure their true values.

OTHER DESCRIPTIVE MEASURES

Certain measures used to describe the shape of the distribution of data will be discussed, as well as other measures that are used to partition data. In addition, two special-purpose averages will be introduced.

Measures of Shape

Two descriptive measures of distribution become useful when the data are not displayed graphically. One measures the concentration or peakedness of a distribution; the other measures the degree of nonsymmetry or skewness.

Peakedness and skewness are displayed in Fig. 19–12. In curves A and B, the two extremes of peakedness are demonstrated. The more familiar normal curve would appear in-between these two extremes. The amount of peakedness is revealed by the *measure of kurtosis*, whose formula is presented

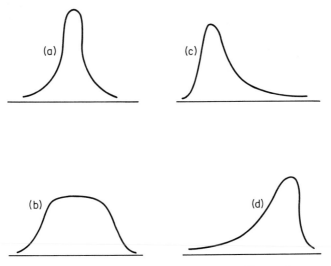

FIGURE 19–12.   Peakedness and skewness illustrated.

below; it is designated as alpha-4 or α_4:

$$\alpha_4 = \frac{(1/N)\sum(X - \mu)^4}{\sigma^4}.$$

Kurtosis is a property of frequency distributions that reflects the extent to which the items bunch together around the center. In the normal curve the value of α_4 is close to 3. In the case of the highly peaked curve with the long tails, the measure of kurtosis is greater than 3, and with example B, its value is less than 3.

The skewness illustrated by curves C and D can also be calculated. Usually skewness is represented by the presence of a long tail in one direction or the other. The formula for skewness is

$$\alpha_3 = \frac{(1/N)\sum(X - \mu)^3}{\sigma^3}.$$

In the case of a normal curve or any symmetrical curve, this measure is equal to zero. In most other cases the measure will be a positive or a negative value. In curve C of Fig. 19–12, the measure of skewness would be a positive value. This type of curve, where the longer tail of the distribution is to the right, is referred to as being *skewed right*. In curve D, the measure of skewness α_3 is negative and the longer tail appears on the left side of the distribution. This curve is *skewed left*.

Partitioning Measures

The median was discussed previously as the measure of central tendency that divided the distribution into two equal parts or halves. If a distribution is to be divided into four equal parts, then three *quartiles* can be determined to partition the data. The locations of the first, second, and third quartiles for a symmetrical curve are illustrated in Fig. 19–13.

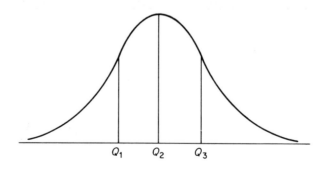

FIGURE 19–13.   Quartiles illustrated.

It is obvious that the second quartile is the same as the median. The technique for computing the first and third quartiles is basically the same as that for computing the median; the only difference is that the $[(N + 1)/4]$th and $[3(N + 1)/4]$th items are found in much the same way as the median is found when the $[(N + 1)/2]$nd item is located. It is obvious that a distribution can be divided into any number of partitions desired—five, six, ten, and so on. The familiar percentile corresponds to *deciles*, which divide the data into ten equal parts.

Special-Purpose Averages

Two other useful averages may be mentioned here. The *geometric mean* is used extensively in averaging the percentage of change, while the *harmonic mean* is useful to weight data that are given in different units—miles traveled per hour, units purchased per dollar and so forth. The geometric mean will be discussed first, then the harmonic mean.

The geometric mean is defined as the Nth root of the product of N number of items. This is formulated as

$$\sqrt[N]{X_1 \times X_2 \times X_3 \times \cdots \times X_N}$$

or

$$\sqrt[N]{\prod_{i=1}^{N} X_i}.$$

The symbol $\prod_{i=1}^{N}$ is used to designate multiplication as follows: $X_1 \times X_2 \times X_3 \times X_4 \cdots \times X_N$.

Let us demonstrate the geometric mean by an example. Suppose that we are interested in determining or predicting the enrollment at a certain college or university. First we will look at the change of enrollment over past years. This may appear as follows:

$$1930: \quad 500 \text{ students}$$
$$1945: 1{,}000 \text{ students}$$
$$1960: 8{,}000 \text{ students.}$$

From 1930 to 1945, the enrollment doubled. From 1945 to 1960, it increased eight times. The arithmetic mean of these two rates of change is

$$\mu = \frac{2 + 8}{2} = 5.$$

Thus enrollment increased an average of five times over an interval of 15 years. Applying this average percentage of change to the enrollment figure of

1930, we would have predicted a total of 2,500 students in 1945 and a total of 12,500 students in 1960. Obviously, this would have resulted in too high a prediction for 1960, when the enrollment was only 8,000.

However, if the geometric mean of the percentage of change in enrollment were calculated for the two periods of change, the results would be different and closer to the mark. For instance, the geometric mean would be

$$GM = \sqrt[2]{2 \times 8}$$
$$= 4.$$

The number 4 in the calculation indicates a quadrupling of enrollment on an average of every 15 years instead of the quintupling previously derived. Using the geometric mean would have rendered estimates of 2,000 and 8,000 for 1945 and 1960, respectively. This time the 1960 prediction would have been exactly right. Therefore, the geometric mean tends to give a more accurate and satisfactory average percentage of change. Using the geometric mean instead of the arithmetic mean as the basis for predicting enrollment for 1975 would render an accurate estimate of 32,000 students.

When more than two items are to be averaged using the geometric mean, it is almost impossible to use the definitional formula given above; however, logarithms will simplify the computation. The procedure appears as follows:

$$\log GM = \frac{\Sigma \log X}{N}.$$

The antilogarithm of this expression renders the geometric mean:

$$\log 2 = 0.30103$$
$$\log 8 = \underline{0.90309}$$
$$\Sigma \log X = 1.20412$$
$$\log GM = \frac{1.20412}{2} = 0.60206$$
$$\text{antilog } 0.60206 = 4.$$

This result is the same as the one above:

$$GM = \sqrt{2 \times 8} = 4.$$

Another special-purpose average, the *harmonic mean*, is defined algebraically as

$$HM = \frac{N}{\Sigma(1/X)}.$$

An example can be useful to illustrate this average and its calculating procedure. Let us assume that we have expended various amounts of money to buy some shares of common stock of company ABC on the following dates:

Jan. 15:   5 shares at $10 per share
June 15: 10 shares at $ 5 per share.

In each case, the total expenditure was $50; thus an average price per share (a weighted mean) would be $100/15 or $6.67 per share. However, if just the prices of both purchases are averaged, the arithmetic mean will be $7.50, which is misleading.

If the harmonic mean is calculated, the results will be as follows:

$$HM = \frac{2}{\dfrac{1}{10} + \dfrac{1}{5}}$$

$$= \frac{2}{3/10}$$

$$= \frac{2}{1} \times \frac{10}{3} = \frac{20}{3}$$

$$= \$6.67 \text{ per share.}$$

Therefore, the harmonic mean is the appropriate method in this instance, since it is consistent with the weighted mean when the total expenditure and total number of shares are known.

When many stock transactions are involved, the harmonic mean is not only more accurate than the arithmetic mean but more convenient to use. There is no need to total up the dollar amounts and calculate the number of shares purchased in each transaction; all that is needed are the prices per share.

Several notes of caution should be mentioned when utilizing the harmonic mean. In the example of the stock purchases, the two ratios $\dfrac{\$50}{5}$ and $\dfrac{\$50}{10}$ have the same numerators. When all the ratios have equal numerators, the harmonic mean is the appropriate measure to use. When the numerators are not equal but the denominators are, the arithmetic mean should be used. Finally, a weighted mean is the appropriate method to use when both the numerators and denominators are available.

In conclusion, it should be mentioned that the harmonic mean gives less weight (importance) to extremely large values than does the geometric mean or the arithmetic mean. The geometric mean should give equal weight to equal percentages of change.[1]

ANNEX :   MATHEMATICAL RECONCILIATION

The computational formula for the standard deviation is derived from the definitional formula. The definitional formula is as follows:

$$\sigma = \sqrt{\frac{\sum(X - \mu)^2}{N}}.$$

Therefore,

$$\sigma = \sqrt{\frac{\sum(X^2 - 2\mu X + \mu^2)}{N}}$$

$$= \sqrt{\frac{\sum(X^2) - 2\mu\sum X + N\mu^2}{N}}.$$

Since

$$\mu = \frac{\sum X}{N}$$

and

$$N\mu = \sum X,$$

substitution results in

$$\sigma = \sqrt{\frac{\sum(X^2) - 2\mu(N\mu) + N\mu^2}{N}}$$

$$= \sqrt{\frac{\sum X^2 - 2N\mu^2 + N\mu^2}{N}}$$

$$= \sqrt{\frac{\sum X^2 - N\mu^2}{N}}$$

$$= \sqrt{\frac{\sum X^2 - (N/1)(\sum X/N)^2}{N}}$$

$$= \sqrt{\frac{\sum X^2}{N} - \frac{N}{N}\left(\frac{\sum X}{N}\right)^2}$$

$$= \sqrt{\frac{N\sum X^2}{N^2} - \frac{(\sum X)^2}{N^2}}$$

$$= \sqrt{\frac{N\sum X^2 - (\sum X)^2}{N^2}}.$$

This is the computational formula.

[1] Further information can be obtained from basic statistics textbooks. For example, see Frederick Croxton, Dudley Cowden, and Sidney Klein, *Applied General Statistics* (Englewood Cliffs, N. J.: Prentice-Hall, Inc., 1967), pp. 177–188.

PROBLEMS AND PROJECTS

1. In a recent toothpaste test, records were kept for ten years of the number of cavities each participant had. Two different brands of toothpaste were used: brand *A* and brand *B*. The total number of cavities each participant had over the ten-year span is given in the table below. The table shows the number of persons in each group having various rates of cavity formation. In the case of brand *B* users, the data were not grouped or classified, since there were only five participants.

BRAND A USERS

Total Number of Cavities	Number of Persons
1– 5	5
6–10	9
11–15	12
16–20	9
21–25	5

BRAND B USERS

Total Number of Cavities
17
19
21
25
28

a. Compute the median number of cavities for users of brand *A*.
b. Compute the mean number of cavities for users of brand *A*.
c. Compute the standard deviation of the number of cavities for users of brand *A*.
d. Compute the arithmetic mean number of cavities for users of brand *B*.
e. Compute the standard deviation of the number of cavities for users of brand *B*.
f. Is there greater relative variability in the number of cavities for brand *A* or brand *B*? Show your computations.
g. What is the average number of cavities for all participants in the toothpaste test? Calculate the arithmetic mean.
2. From the following data for 1960 on the percentage of life insurance policies held by various income groups, find the appropriate average income of life insurance holders.

Income of Insured	Policies Held (Per Cent)
Under $3,000	11
$3,000 –$4,999	36
$5,000 –$7,499	34
$7,500 –$9,999	8
$10,000 and over	11

3. In Chapter 18, a distribution of the family income of students was constructed. The distribution appeared as follows:

Family Income of Students	Frequencies
$3,900–$ 4,700	2
4,800– 5,600	3
5,700– 6,500	9
6,600– 7,400	21
7,500– 8,300	21
8,400– 9,200	17
9,300– 10,100	7

Compute the arithmetic mean, median, mode, and standard deviation.
4. Using the following frequency distribution, calculate the arithmetic mean, the variance, and the mode.

Classes	Frequencies
23–25	2
20–22	3
17–19	0
14–16	8
11–13	6
8–10	3

SELECTED REFERENCES

Elzey, F. F., *A Programmed Introduction to Statistics*. Belmont, Calif.: Wadsworth Publishing Company, Inc., 1966.

Enrick, N. L., *Cases in Management Statistics*. New York: Holt, Rinehart & Winston, Inc., 1962.

Flexar, R. J., and A. S. Flexar, *Programmed Reviews of Mathematics: Introduction to Statistics*. New York: Harper & Row, Publishers, 1967.

Freund, J. E., and F. J. Williams, *Elementary Business Statistics: A Modern Approach*. Englewood Cliffs, N. J.: Prentice-Hall, Inc., 1964.

Sielaff, T. J., *Statistics in Action: Readings in Business and Economic Statistics*. San Jose, Calif.: The Lansford Press, 1963.

20

INDEX NUMBERS

Changes and fluctuations can help the decision maker choose among various alternative courses of action. In fact, data that reflect no change or that are predictable are of little use to the decision maker because of the lack of information they render. Data of this nature are said to have *low information content*. For example, a report that reflects no change in earnings by a corporation may warrant no action by investors; however, they would probably be interested in analyzing a company that reported a change in its profits. Data that reflect changes in a particular activity are said to have *high information content*. One of the most useful and basic devices for measuring change is the index number.

We will proceed in this chapter by providing a brief exposure to index numbers and the ways in which they can be used. Next, the general construction of index numbers will be explained. And finally, a brief classification of index numbers will be followed by illustrations of basic computational methods.

INDICATORS OF CHANGE

The index or index number is statistical in nature; it is used by the economist and the statistician as a tool in time-series analysis. Perhaps the crudest and simplest examples of index numbers are the price of a commodity as compared with the price of the same commodity at a different period of time or sales figures for one month expressed as a percentage of those for another month. Specifically, a sales figure of $437,500 for the *ABC* Corporation in a given month can be compared with a sales figure of $431,200 for the preceding month and the comparison presented in the form of a percentage—101.5 per cent. Such a comparison would be called a *simple quasi-index number.*[1]

In the majority of cases, we are interested in measuring change over a period of time and establishing a comparison between a group of items, whether of their prices, quantities, values, or qualitative characteristics. Usually the data employed in the construction of index numbers are chronological. However, geographical or categorical comparisons are also made. In any event, an index can be simply defined as an indicator of change.

EARLY DEVELOPMENTS AND USES

Price changes have been a main concern for many years. In 1764 an "inquiry into the causes of high prices" was mentioned in Adam Smith's famous book, *The Wealth of Nations*. The earliest attempt on record to make a true index was performed by Dutot in 1783.[2] Dutot compared the average of various prices in one period to the average of various prices in another period. Closely following this was the work done by Professor Willard Dicker, who established a standard that could be used to measure the depreciation of paper money. In Italy in the year 1761, Carli constructed simple averages of the prices of wine, grain, and oil for the year 1500 and compared them with the averages for the same products in 1750 in order to ascertain the effect the discovery of America had on the purchasing power of money.

Perhaps the first regularly published series of index numbers was the one adopted by an annual commercial review, the *Economist*. According to its method, the average prices of a number of selected articles were determined for a period of six years, 1845–1850.[3] The next contribution was made in 1863 by William Jevons, who has been called the "father of index numbers." Jevon's work on the reduction in the value of gold stimulated interest in the field of index numbers. In 1864, Laspeyres did some work on index numbers in Germany and in 1874 another German, Paasche, contributed to this science. However, it wasn't until 1886 that another famous index series was published. In that year, Sauerbeck presented a paper to the Royal Statistical Society and began a series in the *Statist* that is still continued. In this well-

---

[1] Statistically speaking, it would be more accurate to call it a form of a *simple price relative*. A series of index numbers or a "simple index" would consist of a series of these index numbers or simple relatives.

[2] A discussion of the method used by Dutot is given in C. M. Walsh, *The Measurement of General Exchange Value* (New York: The Macmillan Company, 1901), pp. 534–553 as cited in I. Fisher, *The Purchasing Power of Money* (New York: The Macmillan Company, 1911), p. 393.

[3] See G. Shuckburgh-Evelyn, "An Account of Some Endeavors to Ascertain a Standard of Wealth and Measure," *Philosophical Transactions of the Royal Society of London*, LXXXVIII (1798), pp. 133–182, as cited in I. Fisher, *ibid.*, p. 208.

known series, Sauerbeck took the prices of 45 commodities, using the 11 years of 1866–1877 as a standard basis. In 1878, the aggregate index number was 87 and in 1895 it was 62, as compared with the standard of 100.[4] In the year 1886, Soetbeer began a German series.

Several index numbers of wholesale prices appeared in America in the last decade of the nineteenth century. The Aldrich Senate Report of 1893 contained an index covering the period from 1840 to 1891; beginning with 1860, this index reflected the prices of 223 commodities. The U. S. Bureau of Labor constructed an index of 251 to 261 commodities beginning with the year 1890 that has been continued since 1908 on a biennial basis. The Dun index of prices from 1860 to 1906 is still being published. Bradstreet index numbers appeared in 1895, when they included the prices of 96 commodities. On the whole, these index numbers included many commodities and employed a fixed-base system.

CURRENT USES OF INDEX NUMBERS

Among the most important indexes are the *Consumer Price Index* and *Wholesale Price Index* of the U. S. Bureau of Labor Statistics, the *Index of Prices Paid by Farmers* and *Index of Prices Received by Farmers* of the U. S. Department of Agriculture, and the Federal Reserve System's *Monthly Index of Industrial Production.*

The *Consumer Price Index* (referred to as the *CPI*) measures changes in the prices of goods and services purchased by wage earners' and clerical workers' families in 46 cities. These goods and services constitute a close approximation of the "market basket" of nearly 40 per cent of the families in the United States.

The CPI is often used in wage negotiations. During World War II it was used by the National Labor Relations Board as a criterion in allowing wage increases. In recent years it has been designated as a basis for automatic wage-rate increases in labor contracts. It is also used to determine the purchasing power of current dollars.

There are some conditions and purposes for which the CPI should *not* be used: (1) it should not be used to measure changes in the standard of living; and (2) it should not be used for regional comparisons. However, such misuses of the CPI in the past can be easily explained. From 1913 until 1946, the CPI was known as the "cost-of-living index." Because of this nomenclature, the index was widely used to compare the costs of living in different localities. In a strict sense, a cost-of-living index should measure the variations in the total expenditures required in different price situations to maintain a

---

[4] See J. S. Nicholson, *A Treatise on Money and Essays on Monetary Problems* (London: A. and C. Black, 1903), p. 31.

given level of welfare or standard of living. The CPI does not measure costs of living nor does it allow for comparisons to be made on regional bases.

The *Wholesale Price Index* has been linked to other comparable data to provide a continuous series back to 1749. In spite of its name, this index does not measure changes in the prices charged by wholesalers; instead it measures changes in the prices at which commodities were sold by or to manufacturers or producers. In fact, it reflects transactions on organized commodity exchanges. This index is used widely in contracts that also contain price-increase clauses. The index today includes over 2,000 items and is divided into 15 major groups.

The *Index of Prices Paid by Farmers* and the *Index of Prices Received by Farmers* are used to establish the *parity ratio*, which in turn is used to determine government subsidies to farmers. The Federal Reserve System's *Monthly Index of Industrial Production* is an important barometer of economic weather; it tells whether production is moving up or down. Among other important indexes are the many indexes of security prices. The most familiar of these is the *Dow–Jones Index of Industrial Stock Prices*, which measures the price changes of 30 leading stocks.

Other indexes measure machine utilization, price changes of imports and exports, and the efficiency of employees in production and shipping departments. An index of department store sales is published in the *Federal Reserve Bulletin* every month.

Several indexes that measure qualitative changes have been constructed by Robert T. McMillan. His indexes do not compare changes over time, but rather differences in geographic areas; more precisely, they compare and rank the counties of a state as to the conditions of rural farm housing. Indexes have also been constructed to measure the adequacy of state care of mental patients, to compare religious work between dioceses, and to rate the agricultural values of soils.

CONSTRUCTION CONSIDERATIONS

The first problem in constructing an index is to define clearly the purpose for which it is to be used. Only after the specific purpose of the index has been determined is it possible to decide what data will be used and where they will be obtained. If we are interested in measuring changes in the prices of food products, we first need to gather data on the prices of food commodities, then to carefully define the types of food commodities and the group whose purchases they are to reflect. In other words, data should be selected for their representative quality rather than for their availability.

Consistency in collecting data is important. They should be collected according to a definite pattern and with caution. For example, in collecting consumer prices, one should not obtain prices for one period on a normal day and for another period on a nontypical day (such as the day of a sale). It is usually recommended that data be collected at a specific hour on the same day of the week.

All data should be adequately explained, and their characteristics should be known and understood. Any unusual or autonomous factor that may affect the data adversely should be revealed and noted, and proper adjustments should be made. In addition, all data should be adjusted for seasonal factors.

The *base period* is an arbitrarily established reference point. It should not take place so far in the past that a relevant comparison cannot be made; in addition, it should be a normal or typical period. An average of several years is often the best base period. As time goes on, it usually becomes necessary to shift the base period to more recent periods because consumption patterns change, requiring a change in the proportion of goods selected.

In his book, *The Making of Index Numbers*,[5] Irving Fisher gives over 150 different formulas for the construction of index numbers. These are based on a few simple principles of averaging. Most are arithmetic, harmonic, or geometric averages or their combinations. Needless to say, numerous other more complicated forms might be constructed. However, they would still be variations on the limited number of main types. On occasion, the mode and median have been used although they have certain limitations. The arithmetic mean is more advantageous because it is more easily computed; it also is more easily understood because of its common usage.

A few simple illustrations will be presented here to indicate some of the problems in constructing index numbers. The first two examples demonstrate the importance of weighting the various components. The third example indicates the problem of distortion that may be associated with the technique.

Example 1:

Suppose that a student earned the grades shown in Table 20–1 in one of his courses and wishes to find his final percentage grade. An average of his percentage grades will result in a grade of 64.25 per cent ($\frac{265}{4}$). This percentage probably would be either a grade of D or a failing grade. On the other hand, if the student totals his earned points and divides them by the total possible points, he will find that he has a grade of 78.8 per cent ($\frac{268}{340}$). This is somewhat better and would be at least a grade of C. This example emphasizes the importance of weighting elements properly. It is clear that the four percentage grades should not be given equal weight.

Example 2:

Suppose that we wish to determine the average price of all the bread sold in a town. Furthermore, suppose that the price of bread is $ .12 a loaf in the chain stores and $ .16 in the independent stores. If the chain stores and

[5] *The Making of Index Numbers* (N. Y.: Houghton Mifflin Company, 1922) is perhaps the oldest "handbook" of index numbers and one of the most inclusive.

TABLE 20–1

HYPOTHETICAL STUDENT'S GRADES

Type of Quiz	Earned Points	Possible Points	Grade (Per Cent)
Pop Quizzes	18	30	60
First Hour Exam	30	60	50
Second Hour Exam	30	50	60
Final Exam	190	200	95
Total	268	340	265

TABLE 20–2

BREAD PRICES

Bread	Price per Loaf	Quantity of Loaves Sold	Price Times Quantity
Chain stores	$ .12	10,000	1,200
Independents	$ .16	1,000	160
Total		11,000	1,360

independent stores sold the same quantity of bread, a simple average of $ .12 and $ .16 would result in a price of $ .14 for a loaf of bread. However, if the chain stores sold ten times as much bread as the independent stores, the prices would have to be weighted correspondingly.

The calculations are summarized in Table 20–2, where the average price of bread is determined by dividing 1,360 by 11,000; this renders a figure of $ .123, which is more realistic than $ .14.

Examples 1 and 2 have demonstrated the problem of weighting, which should be of prime importance when constructing index numbers. It has been briefly mentioned that consideration should also be given to the averaging process employed so that any distortion resulting from the arithmetic process will be minimized. This can be illustrated by an example.

Example 3:

The ratio of one number to another is called a *relative*. Suppose that there are two commodities A and B whose prices in 1964 were $1 and $2, respectively. In 1965 their prices changed to $2 and $1, respectively. The price of A in 1965 compared to the price of A in 1964 gives a relative of $\frac{2}{1}$, while the relative for B is $\frac{1}{2}$. The average of the two relatives in 1965, converted to a percentage, would be 125 per cent. The calculations are shown in Table 20–3.

TABLE 20–3

CALCULATION OF PRICE RELATIVES

Commodity	Prices in 1964	Prices in 1965	Price Relatives (1965)
A	$1	$2	$(^2/_1) \times 100 = 200\%$
B	$2	$1	$(^1/_2) \times 100 = 50\%$
			Total $= \overline{250\%}$

Average of price relatives for 1965 $= \frac{250}{2} = 125\%$
Average of price relatives for 1964 $= 100\%$

The 125 per cent is interpreted as an index number of the prices of commodities *A* and *B* that reflects an average increase in their prices of 25 per cent. However, the total prices for both years add up to $3; therefore, no increase in prices should have been reflected. A solution to this problem of distortion can be found by utilizing a different average.

If the geometric mean is substituted for the arithmetic mean, the results will be appropriate. In this case, the geometric mean is computed as follows:

$$GM = \sqrt{200\% \times 50\%}$$
$$= \sqrt{10{,}000\%}$$
$$= 100\%.$$

The index number for 1965 is now 100 per cent and is equal to the index number of 100 per cent for 1964; this reflects no change.

CLASSIFICATION OF INDEX NUMBERS

There are two basic procedures for classifying index numbers. The first procedure distinguishes among the three basic types of characteristics that can be measured: changes in price, changes in quantity, and changes in value. The *price index* is intended to measure price changes over a period of time; the *quantity index* measures changes in economic activity, usually over a period of time (for instance, changes in business activity, industrial production, or inventory); and the *value index* may indicate changes in the price and quantity of a particular segment of the economy, such as national income.

The second procedure for classifying index numbers emphasizes the basic computational techniques that may be employed; this procedure will be presented in detail. Fig. 20–1 may serve as a brief outline of this method of classification.

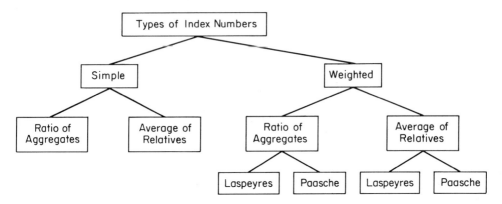

FIGURE 20–1.   Classification of index numbers by means of basic computational techniques.

The major separation is made by weighting the various items either explicitly or implicitly. The simple index number is sometimes called unweighted because the weighting process is implicit and usually unintentional. The use of simple index numbers is somewhat limited because of the absence of explicit weighting.

BASIC METHODS OF COMPUTATION

The computation of the basic types of index numbers will be illustrated with hypothetical data.

Simple or Unweighted Index Numbers

The *ratio of aggregates* and the *average of relatives* are the only two types of index numbers that will be discussed in this category.

The Ratio of Aggregates.   This method simply involves dividing the sum or aggregate of prices for any year by the sum or aggregate of prices for

TABLE 20–4

PRICE INDEX FOR TEXTBOOKS

Type of Textbook	Prices in 1964	Prices in 1965
Grammar	$ 6.40	$ 6.60
Mathematics	6.00	6.06
Economics	5.40	5.90
Totals	$17.80	$18.56

Index number for 1964 = (17.80/17.80) × 100 = 100
Index number for 1965 = (18.56/17.80) × 100 = 104.3

the base year. The method of computation is illustrated in Table 20–4. These results have a simple interpretation. The index number of 104.3 for 1965 means that prices have increased 4.3 per cent since 1964.

This computational procedure can be summarized by the formula

$$\text{Index number of prices} = \frac{\text{sum of prices of textbooks in 1965}}{\text{sum of prices of textbooks in 1964}} \times 100$$

or

$$\text{Index number of prices} = \frac{\sum P_n}{\sum P_o} \times 100,$$

where $\sum$ stands for "the sum of"; P stands for price; the subscript o denotes the prices in the base year (in this example, prices in 1964); and the subscript n designates the prices of the items in any given year (in this case, 1965).

The Average of Relatives. In this procedure one first calculates an individual relative of prices P_n/P_o for each of the three textbooks and then averages the relatives. The relatives of the three textbooks are made into percentages by multiplying by 100. The calculations are shown in Table 20–5.

TABLE 20–5

PRICE INDEX FOR TEXTBOOKS

Type of Textbook	Prices in 1964	Relatives in 1964	Prices in 1965	Relatives in 1965
Grammar	$6.40	$\frac{6.40}{6.40} = 100$	$6.60	$\frac{6.60}{6.40} = 103$
Mathematics	6.00	$\frac{6.00}{6.00} = 100$	6.06	$\frac{6.06}{6.00} = 101$
Economics	5.40	$\frac{5.40}{5.40} = 100$	5.90	$\frac{5.90}{5.40} = 109$
Totals		300		313

Index number for 1964 = $\frac{300}{3}$ = 100

Index number for 1965 = $\frac{313}{3}$ = 104.3

This procedure can be abbreviated by the formula

$$\text{Index number of prices} = \frac{\text{sum of price relatives} \times 100}{\text{number of items}}$$

or

$$\text{Index number of prices} = \frac{\sum (P_n/P_o) \times 100}{k},$$

where k is the number of items.

The index numbers for 1965 in these two examples are the same even though the computational methods are different. However, if the prices of the three textbooks had differed considerably, the two methods would have produced markedly different results, as illustrated in Table 20–6. In this table, the ratio of aggregates implicitly gives more weight to the price change of the mathematics textbook than to the changes for the other two textbooks, because of the significantly higher price of the mathematics book.

TABLE 20–6

COMPARISON OF PRICE INDEXES FOR TEXTBOOKS

Type of Textbook	Prices in 1964	Prices in 1965	Relatives
Grammar	$ 1.50	$ 1.80	120
Mathematics	20.00	21.00	105
Economics	2.00	2.50	125
Totals	$23.50	$25.30	350

$$\text{Ratio of aggregates} = \frac{\sum P_n}{\sum P_o} \times 100 = \frac{25.30}{23.50} = 107.6$$

$$\text{Average of relatives} = \frac{\sum(P_n/P_o) \times 100}{k} = \frac{350}{3} = 116.7$$

The average of relatives has an advantage over the ratio of aggregates in that it permits a comparison of the values of each commodity involved. Both methods have some disadvantages since the items are not weighted intentionally according to their importance. This is one reason why simple indexes are not used extensively.

Even though these two simple methods are called "unweighted," we must be cognizant of the fact that they may be weighted implicitly. If the prices of the items do not differ significantly, both methods will give an equal implicit weight. If the prices differ somewhat, the two methods will provide different results, since the ratio of aggregates no longer gives equal consideration to each item.

Weighted Index Numbers

A system of weights can be used to make index numbers more accurate. Generally, weights are values of the base year, a given year, or a typical period. The two most familiar weighting techniques are the Laspeyres and Paasche procedures, named after the individuals who developed them. These two procedures are easily distinguishable. The Laspeyres method uses the quantities of the items that correspond to the base year, while the Paasche type uses the quantities for the given year. The Laspeyres method is more suitable than the Paasche method and is more widely used.

TABLE 20–7

COLLEGE STUDENTS' PRICE INDEX

Commodity	Unit	Quantity in 1964 (Q_o)	Prices in 1964 (P_o)	$P_o \times Q_o$	Quantity in 1965 (Q_n)	Prices in 1965 (P_n)	$P_n \times Q_o$
Hamburgers	pound	20	$ .35	$ 7.00	25	$ .40	$ 8.00
Gasoline	gallon	100	$ .30	30.00	120	.32	32.00
No-Doze pills	bottle	2	$ .50	1.00	3	.60	1.20
Totals				$38.00			$41.20

Index number for base year $= \dfrac{38.00}{38.00} \times 100 = 100$

Index number for 1965 $= \dfrac{41.20}{38.00} \times 100 = 108.4$

The Laspeyres technique is illustrated in the next two sections. The first illustration is the weighted version of the ratio of aggregates, and the second is the weighted version of the average of relatives.

The Ratio of Weighted Aggregates. In calculating an index number of the Laspeyres type, the first step is to multiply each commodity price by its corresponding quantity for the base year. The quantity consumed in 1964 is the weighting factor used for both years. The next step is to add the weighted prices of the given year and divide them by the total of the weighted prices of the base year. The results are shown in Table 20–7. This procedure can be summarized and expressed by a simple formula as follows:

$$\text{Index number of prices} = \frac{\sum P_n Q_o}{\sum P_o Q_o} \times 100,$$

where Q stands for quantity. The use of base-year weights designates this as a Laspeyres index number.

The Paasche type of index number uses weights corresponding to the given year rather than weights for the base year. The difference between the Paasche and Laspeyres index numbers can be clearly indicated by comparing the Laspeyres formula to the formula for the Paasche method, which can be expressed simply as follows:

$$\text{Index number of prices} = \frac{\sum P_n Q_n}{\sum P_o Q_n} \times 100.$$

The basic difference is evident; in the Paasche method the weights Q_n are given-year quantities, rather than quantities for the base year.

Another commonly used weighting procedure is to choose the quantities for some typical year or to use an average of the quantities over a period of time. This would be abbreviated as follows:

$$\text{Index number of prices} = \frac{\sum P_n Q_t}{\sum P_o Q_t} \times 100,$$

where Q_t is the quantity for a typical year or an extended period of time.

The important thing to remember is that we are attempting to measure the change in prices; therefore, the weighting factor should be held constant. This is not as easy as it may appear. A thorough study of index numbers will enable the student to recognize and cope with the problems that will arise.

The Average of Weighted Relatives. An index number may be constructed by securing a weighted average of the price relatives for the period under consideration. However, quantities consumed cannot be used as weights, since each quantity is expressed in a different unit (tons, pounds, bushels, gallons, etc.); the column of figures resulting from the multiplication of the price relatives would be expressed in different units and could not be totaled. It therefore becomes necessary to express the weights in a common unit such as the dollar. Money values rather than just quantities consumed can now be used as weights.[6]

As mentioned before, variations on index numbers can be obtained by using different methods of averaging. In the following cases, the arithmetic mean is used. The calculation of a Laspeyres type of index number can be illustrated in Table 20–8. It should not be surprising that this method and the weighted aggregate, which was illustrated previously, will give equal answers. (See the Annex to this chapter.) If we derive the formula for this method, it will appear as follows:

$$\text{Index number of prices} = \frac{\sum [(P_n/P_o)(P_o Q_o)]}{\sum P_o Q_o} \times 100.$$

[6] In the case of the weighted aggregate, the units of measurement cancel out. For example, the $ .40 per pound for hamburger in 1965 times the quantity weight of 20 pounds would appear algebraically as

$$P_n Q_o = \frac{\$.40}{\text{pound}} \times \frac{20 \text{ pounds}}{1}.$$

The units of measurement are eliminated, allowing for simple totaling of each weighted result. However, in the case of the average of weighted relatives, the units of measurement will not cancel out conveniently when the quantity weights of the various units are used. This difficulty is demonstrated as follows:

$$\frac{P_n}{P_o} Q_o = \frac{\$.40/\text{pound}}{\$.35/\text{pound}} \times 20 \text{ pounds}.$$

We are left with a weighted relative expressed in pounds, which cannot be totaled with gallons and bottles; it is clear that this will not be satisfactory. However, measuring the weights in a common unit such as dollars affords a solution to this problem. Now the weighted relative will appear as

$$\frac{P_n}{P_o}(P_o Q_o) = \frac{\$.40/\text{pound}}{\$.35/\text{pound}} \times \frac{\$.35}{\text{pound}} \times \frac{20 \text{ pounds}}{1}.$$

All the units of measurement cancel out, leaving only a common unit expressed in dollars and cents. This would occur for each of the commodities.

Table 20–8

COLLEGE STUDENTS' PRICE INDEX

Commodity	Unit	1964 Quantity Consumed	Prices	Value Weights	Relatives	1965 Prices	Relatives	Weighted Relatives
Hamburgers	pound	20	$ .35	$ 7.00	100	$ .40	114.2	799.4
Gasoline	gallon	100	$ .30	30.00	100	$ .32	106.7	3,201.0
No-Doze pills	bottle	2	$ .50	1.00	100	$ .60	120.0	120.0
Totals				$38.00				4,120.4

$$\text{Index number for base year} = \frac{3,800}{3,800} = 100$$

$$\text{Index number for 1965} = \frac{4,120.4}{38.00} = 108.4$$

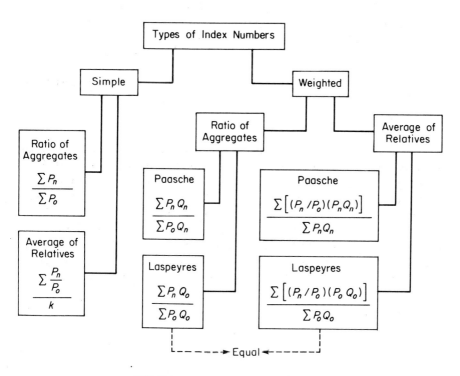

FIGURE 20–2. Types of index numbers.

Unlike the equivalent Laspeyres types, the weighted aggregate and the average of weighted relatives for the Paasche method are unequal. The computations to find the average of weighted relatives are not illustrated for the Paasche method, but the procedure can be abbreviated by the following formula:

$$\text{Index number of prices} = \frac{\sum[(P_n/P_o)(P_nQ_n)]}{\sum P_nQ_n} \times 100.$$

The student with some mathematical maturity can satisfy himself that this formula does not reduce to the Paasche version of the weighted aggregate.

The various types of index number calculations have now all been abbreviated to formulas. At the beginning of this section, index numbers were classified according to computational techniques. An outline of these techniques was given in Fig. 20–1; it is repeated in Fig. 20–2 with the formulas inserted for each of the computational methods.

Quantity index numbers are similar to price indexes except that quantity replaces price in the formulas. For instance, in a weighted-aggregate type of quantity index number, the quantities consumed are multiplied by price weights. The study of the computational methods used to calculate other index numbers should be reserved for advanced statistics.

USEFUL PRACTICES

The Chain Index

One may ask why index numbers are constructed by indirectly comparing given years to a fixed base. Why not make the comparison directly? It is possible to compare each year with the next, or, in other words, to make each year the base year for the next. In this way, a chain of index numbers is obtained where each number is related only to the preceding year. The main advantages of a chain index are that commodities may be more readily dropped and added and that weights can be changed more easily. However, even though they give accurate period-to-period changes, chain indexes are not commonly used because long-range comparisons may not be valid.

Deflating

A situation may arise where a quantity index is needed but neither the the index nor the data to construct one is available. On the other hand, a series of the total values of the commodities in question may be available, along with an index based on their prices. If we divide each successive money item (value) expressed as a relative by the corresponding value of the price index and multiply by 100, we will remove from the money or value figures most of the influence of the changing prices, leaving a quantity index. This procedure is called "deflating a monetary series." It may be noted that, strictly speaking, this quantity index will not be quite the same as the one that would be obtained by direct calculation of a quantity index.

As an example, suppose that you have a bond that was purchased 20 years ago at a purchase price of $100. Furthermore, assume that the CPI for 1945 was 100 and that in 1965 it was 240. The real money value of the $100 bond can be determined by deflating its original cost. This is accomplished simply by dividing the $100 by 240, the price index for 1965. As a result, the $100 bond is found to be worth a little over $41 in 1945 dollars.[7]

Splicing

Index series can be "spliced" when we have two homogeneous indexes that represent different successive periods of time and/or have different or unknown base periods. These two series can be spliced together as long as there is at least one period in which they overlap. The technique merely establishes the same relationship for the new index numbers that existed between the two overlapping numbers.[8]

Shifting

"Shifting" can be used to transfer the base period of a series of index numbers to another year. This can be accomplished merely by making the selected new base year equal to 100 (by dividing it by its own index number), then dividing the index numbers for all other periods by the "old" index number of the new base year.[9]

ANNEX: EQUALITY OF THE LASPEYRES METHOD FOR WEIGHTED AGGREGATES AND AVERAGE OF WEIGHTED RELATIVES

By simple cancellation, the formula for the average of weighted relatives can be reduced to the formula for the weighted aggregate:

[7] For a discussion of deflating, see J. E. Freund and F. J. Williams, *Modern Business Statistics* (Englewood Cliffs, N. J.: Prentice-Hall, Inc., 1958), pp. 373–375; and J. Neter and W. Wasserman, *Fundamental Statistics for Business and Economics*, 2nd ed. (New York: Allyn & Bacon, Inc., 1961), pp. 626–637.

[8] For a discussion of splicing, see W. Z. Hirsch, *Introduction to Modern Statistics* (New York: The Macmillan Company, 1957), pp. 231–232; E. E. Lewis, *Methods of Statistical Analysis in Economics and Business*, 2nd ed. (Boston: Houghton Mifflin Company, 1963), pp. 378–380; and Neter and Wasserman, *ibid.*, pp. 651–652.

[9] For a discussion of shifting, see Freund and Williams, *op. cit.*, pp. 372–373; and Neter and Wasserman, *ibid.*, pp. 649–651.

$$\frac{\sum[(P_n/P_o)(P_oQ_o)]}{\sum P_oQ_o} = \frac{\sum P_nQ_o}{\sum P_oQ_o}.$$

The figures from Table 20–8 can be inserted to simplify the formula for the average of weighted relatives:

$$
\begin{aligned}
\frac{\sum[(P_n/P_o)(P_oQ_o)]}{\sum P_oQ_o} &= \frac{(0.40/0.35)\,(0.35 \times 20) + (0.32/0.30)\,(0.30 \times 100) + {} + (0.60/0.50)\,(0.50 \times 2)}{(0.35 \times 20) + (0.30 \times 100) + (0.50 \times 2)} \\[2mm]
&= \frac{1.142(7.00) + 1.067(30.00) + 1.200(1.00)}{(7.00) + (30.00) + (1.00)} \\[2mm]
&= \frac{7.994 + 32.010 + 1.200}{38.00} \\[2mm]
&= \frac{41.204}{38.00} = 1.084 \text{ (or } 108.4).
\end{aligned}
$$

If some simple algebraic cancellations are performed in the first step of this equation, the result is as follows:

$$
\begin{aligned}
\frac{\sum[(P_n/P_o)(P_oQ_o)]}{\sum P_oQ_o} &= \frac{(0.40/0.35)\,(0.35 \times 20) + (0.32/0.30)\,(0.30 \times 100) + {} + (0.60/0.50)\,(0.50 \times 2)}{(0.35 \times 20) + (0.30 \times 100) + (0.50 \times 2)} \\[2mm]
&= \frac{(0.40 \times 20) + (0.32 \times 100) + (0.60 \times 2)}{(0.35 \times 20) + (0.30 \times 100) + (0.50 \times 2)} = \frac{\sum(P_nQ_o)}{\sum(P_oQ_n)} \\[2mm]
&= 1.084 = \frac{\sum(P_nQ_o)}{\sum(P_oQ_o)}.
\end{aligned}
$$

It should be clear that the weighted aggregate and the average of weighted relatives, which both use base-year weights, are equivalent.

PROBLEMS AND PROJECTS

1. Using the data in the table (page 489) and 1960 as the base year, compute the price index for 1965 by the method of:
   a. Simple ratio of aggregates.
   b. Simple average of relatives.
   c. Weighted aggregate (Laspeyres).
   d. Average of weighted relatives (Laspeyres).
2. A sales manager for a large firm is interested in predicting his sales for 1965 and instructs you to base a prediction on the gross national product.

CHILDREN'S PRICE INDEX

Item	Prices in 1960	Weekly Quantities in 1960	Prices in 1965	Weekly Quantities in 1965
Beatle records	$1.50	1	$2.00	2
Tom Swift books	$ .90	2	$1.00	2
Popsicles	$ .10	5	$ .08	6
Soda pop	$ .10	12	$ .15	10

Obtain the latest GNP figures and deflate them to give him a figure he can use to estimate his sales forecast.

3. What is meant by bias in index numbers? Explain in detail.[10]

SELECTED REFERENCES

Neiswanger, W. A., *Elementary Statistical Methods*. New York: The Macmillan Company, 1956. Chapters 13 and 14 list some requirements of a good index and discuss the uses of some current index numbers.

Riggleman, J.R., and I. N. Frisbee, *Business Statistics*, 3rd ed. New York: McGraw-Hill Book Company, 1951. Chapter 8 outlines steps for the selection and construction of an index number.

[10] An excellent discussion of bias in index numbers is found in Freund and Williams, *ibid.*, p. 371.

21

ELECTRONIC

DATA PROCESSING

Computers are proving to be workhorses for the decision maker, being used by business, government, schools, and research organizations. They can be segregated into two distinct classes, depending on the way in which they handle information. If information is used in the form of letters and digits, they are classified as *digital computers;* if it is used in the form of an electrical equivalent to physical variables, they are classified as *analog computers.* Everyone has been exposed to analog computers; even an automobile speedometer is a crude analog computer because it measures rate of speed.

The material in this chapter will be restricted to a discussion of digital computers. In addition, an introduction to binary arithmetic will be given, since it is basic to the language and operation of digital computers.

EARLY THINKING TOOLS

Early man could only count on his fingers; he had no means of recording the results of his counting. The invention of symbols enabled him to make records and relieved him of the effort of keeping everything in his head. The use of numbers led to the elimination of guesswork or trial-and-error methods to gain information in advance about quantity, distance, and time relationships. The discovery of mathematics was thus one of man's first tools for thinking.

Man first used a knotted string, then the abacus and "Napier bones" to move numbers around. Several types of machines, devices, and calculators were invented to speed up his manipulations. These developments led to the invention late in the nineteenth century of punched cards, which were a way for machines to "read" information; this brought the work of mechanical calculators into the area of automation.

The following chronological list identifies some dates and personalities responsible for developments leading up to the modern computer:

600 B.C.: The abacus was used by the Chinese.

A.D. 1617: John Napier, following his invention of logarithms, prepared a multiplication table on pieces of bone. More important was the fact that William Oughtred inscribed logarithms on slides of wood or ivory, creating the first slide rule.

1642: Blaise Pascal invented the first adding machine for use in his father's business. The machine used gears in much the same way as a simple adding machine does today.

1694: Gottfried Leibnitz, independently of Pascal, invented an adding machine, which could carry over a unit from one column to the next.

1786: J. H. Müller conceived the idea of an automatic calculator, but the technical difficulties of that day prevented him from producing an operating machine.

1812: Charles Babbage, sometimes referred to as the "father of computers," conceived the idea of the computer as we know it today. The work of Joseph Jacquard, who had recently controlled the threading of a loom by punched cards, led Babbage to envision the use of two sets of cards—operation cards and variable cards. Babbage began work on his automatic computer, known as a "difference engine," which was designed to build up mathematical functions automatically and to print the computed answers without human hands. However, the machine did not operate successfully until 1822.

It was in Babbage's more ambitious undertaking of an analytical engine, which he worked on until his death and never completed, that he tried to put into operation his idea of the modern-day computer. The engine would have been able to hold 1,000 fifty-digit numbers in its memory. Two different engines were finally built and were used in Sweden and England.

1890: Herman Hollerith invented punched-card methods of controlling calculators to complete the 1890 census of the United States.

1911: The first keyboard type of calculator was commercially built by the Monroe Company.

Much of the early development of automatic calculators was limited by the low level of technical facilities and by the use of electromechanical systems instead of the electronic systems of vacuum tubes and transistors of present-day computers.

DEVELOPMENT OF THE MODERN COMPUTER

Improved computer technology was found necessary during World War II. Many electronic developments used for weapons of war had an influence on the technology of the computer industry.

The major computer developments can be listed chronologically as follows:

1940: G. R. Stibitz and S. B. Williams, while working at the Bell Telephone Laboratories, built a small calculator using relays. This increased the speed of punched-card machine calculations by a factor of ten or more.

1944: Dr. Howard Aiken of Harvard University completed the Automatic Sequence Controlled Calculator. However, this machine was slow, because it relied on electromechanical operations.

1946: Dr. John Mauchly and J. P. Eckert designed ENIAC at the University of Pennsylvania. The Electronic Numerical Integrator and Calculator was the first true electronic computer. It counted by adding electronic pulses generated at the rate of 100,000 per second. This was the first time vacuum tubes were used in calculators.

1948: Eckert and Mauchly formed a company that improved on ENIAC. Their new machine, called BINAC, did not rely on wiring panels for each new problem; instead, it used internal programming. It also used diodes instead of vacuum tubes, and stored information with magnetic tape; this machine was faster than ENIAC.

1952: Commercial use of computers to solve business problems was made possible by UNIVAC I.

1956: A solid-state computer of the UNIVAC series was delivered to commercial users in 1956.

These are the most significant developments in computer technology that have led to present-day equipment. The trend toward increasing the speed of computers during this development is apparent. This emphasis has continued during recent years. The increased speed brought about by design improvements has even resulted in systems that utilize other computers to serve as input–output devices when conventional input–output methods are too slow.

The design of circuits for faster speed has had a significant effect on reducing the size of machinery. As the speeds of computers are increased and vacuum tubes are replaced by transistors, a reduction of computer size necessarily takes place. The space program's demands for miniaturization of computers in satellites has also had an effect on reducing the size of computers; current terminology even refers to microminiaturization.

BINARY EQUIVALENTS OF DECIMAL NUMBERS

There are two basic problems that must be solved before a computer can be designed, built, and operated. First, special symbols are needed to represent data in the computer, and second, a mathematically feasible numbering system must be employed that is compatible with the computer's technical machinery. Both of these problems can be solved simultaneously by a numbering system called *binary arithmetic*, which strangely enough is not basically different from the familiar decimal system.

Electricity is capable of only two basic states, on or off; since computers are electronic in nature, they also can reflect only two states. A magnetic material either is magnetized or it is not; a switch is on or off; an electric pulse is present or not present; a card or tape has a hole punched in it or does not. The main reason that some form of binary arithmetic is the basic system for computers is that it utilizes only two symbols, which represent the on and off conditions of a computer's circuitry.

The basic symbols used in any numbering system are called *admissible marks*. An admissible mark is nothing more than an element or basic symbol in a numbering or symbolic system. The letter "b" of the alphabet and the number "6" in the decimal-number system are admissible marks or characters for these systems.

The two states of a computer are usually given numeric symbols: 1 for on and 0 for off. In computer language, these two symbols or admissible marks are called *bits* (from the words *bi*nary dig*its*). Combinations of these bits form the various patterns that represent numbering systems, such as the binary, bi-quinary, and coded decimal systems commonly used in computers. The only admissible marks in binary systems are 0 and 1, while the admissible marks in the decimal system are 1, 2, 3, 4, 5, 6, 7, 8, 9, and 0.

The explanation of binary arithmetic and its rules of operation can be simplified by comparing it to the familiar decimal system. As a starting point, the decimal number 426 can be expressed in the following manner based on powers of ten. If

$$10^2 = 10 \times 10$$
$$10^1 = 10$$
$$10^0 = 1,$$

then

$$(4 \times 10^2) + (2 \times 10^1) + (6 \times 10^0) = 426$$
$$(4 \times 100) + (2 \times 10) + (6 \times 1) = 426$$
$$400 + 20 + 6 = 426$$
$$426 = 426.$$

Note that the left-hand factor inside each parenthesis shows the basic composition of the decimal or *base-ten* system. In this case, the 4, 2, and 6 represent the base-ten number 426 and were easily shown to equal it when it was expressed with its corresponding powers of ten. Note the descending powers of ten.

The rudiments of binary notation can be shown by starting with a small number such as 5, which appears as 0101 in binary:

$$(0 \times 2^3) + (1 \times 2^2) + (0 \times 2^1) + (1 \times 2^0) = 5.$$

The binary system is based on powers of two rather than on powers of ten. Note the descending powers of two in the expanded expression above. It can be shown that this expanded expression is equal to the decimal number 5, as follows:

$$(0 \times 2^3) + (1 \times 2^2) + (0 \times 2^1) + (1 \times 2^0) = 5$$
$$(0 \times 8) + (1 \times 4) + (0 \times 2) + (1 \times 1) = 5$$
$$0 + 4 + 0 + 1 = 5$$
$$5 = 5.$$

Again, note that the characters on the left within the parentheses form the binary 5, which is 0101.

Let us review this diagrammatically by comparing the decimal number 426 with the binary number 5:

The expansion of the decimal number 426 can now be represented as a binary number as follows:

The reader should evaluate this expanded expression to verify that it is equal to 426.

Some decimal quantities and their binary equivalents are listed as follows:

Decimal	Binary
1	0001
2	0010
3	0011
4	0100
5	0101
6	0110
7	0111
8	1000
9	1001
10	1010
11	1011
12	1100
13	1101
14	1110
15	1111
16	10000
...	...
426	110101010

Once the pattern of bits has been studied, an easy method of representing binary eqivalents can be developed by assigning "positional" values to the various bit locations. For instance, since 1, in binary, is an "on" state and zero is an "off" state, we could use a system of light bulbs with increasing wattage associated to ordered powers of two, as shown in Fig. 21–1. The wattage of the bulbs, proceeding from left to right, represents descending powers of two:

$$256 = 2^8$$
$$128 = 2^7$$
$$64 = 2^6$$
$$\cdots \quad \cdots$$
$$2 = 2^1$$
$$1 = 2^0.$$

When the on and off states of the array of bulbs are arranged as in Fig. 21–2, the decimal equivalent of the binary representation can be determined by merely adding the wattage of the bulbs in an on state. The number 5 would appear with bits in the first four locations as shown in Fig. 21–3.

It can be seen that any decimal number can be expressed in binary form; however, very large numbers are clumsy to handle in this form. Even the binary equivalent of 426 is cumbersome: 110101010 as opposed to 426 in decimal.

FIGURE 21–1. Representing binary equivalents by assigning positional values to "on" and "off" light bulbs.

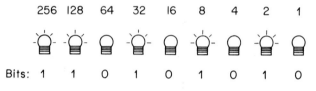

Decimal Equivalent: 256+ 128 + 0 + 32 + 0 + 8 + 0 + 2 + 0 = 426

FIGURE 21–2. Determining the decimal equivalent of the binary representation by adding the wattage of the bulbs in an "on" state.

Bits: 0   1   0   1

Decimal Equivalent: 0 + 4 + 0 + 1 = 5

FIGURE 21–3. Appearance of the number 5 in the first four locations.

One way that this awkwardness has been alleviated is by the use of a coded decimal system referred to as BCD (Binary Coded Decimal). In the BCD system, each decimal digit is represented by four bits associated with the positional values of 8, 4, 2, and 1. The decimal number 43 would therefore be represented by two sets of bits as in Fig. 21–4. The number 821 is shown in Fig. 21–5. The IBM 1620 computer is one of the computers that utilize the BCD system.

An alternative to the BCD system is the *bi-quinary* system. In this case, only two bits are necessary to represent any one-digit decimal number. The positional array of bits would be displayed on the console as shown in Fig. 21–6.

Binary units have only two possible bits, while quinary units have five. Only two bits are used to display a particular number—one binary and one quinary. In this case, the binary bits take on the values of 0 and 5, while the quinary bits represent the values 0, 1, 2, 3, and 4. It should be pointed out that the bi-quinary system is used mainly as external display on a computer console. The internal operation may still be basically binary, with extra circuitry

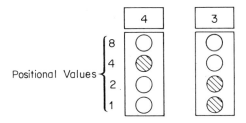

FIGURE 21–4.   Representing the decimal number 43 by the BCD system.

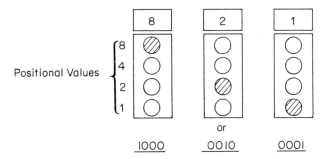

FIGURE 21–5.   Representing the decimal number 821 by the BCD system.

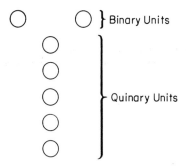

FIGURE 21–6.   Representing a one-digit decimal number by the bi-quinary system.

translating the number to a bi-quinary system. The positional values for each display are indicated in Fig. 21–7 for the decimal number 4 and in Fig. 21–8 for the decimal number 7. The number 7 would never be displayed as shown in Fig. 21–9, and the number 4 would never be displayed as shown in Fig. 21–10.

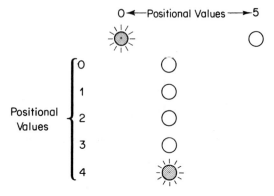

FIGURE 21-7.   Representing the positional values for external display and internal operation for the decimal number 4.

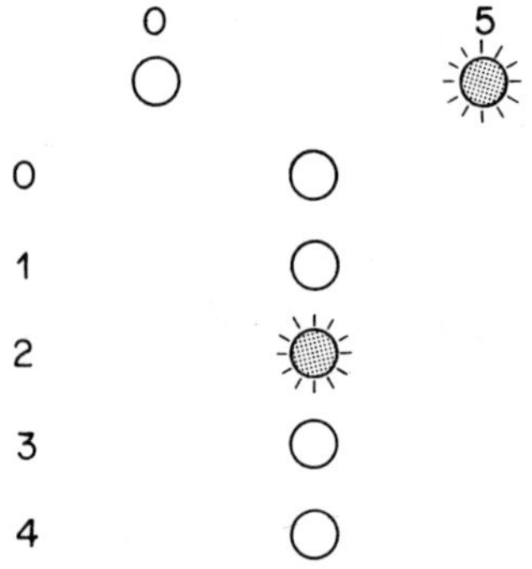

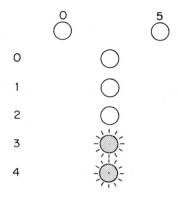

FIGURE 21-8.   Representing the positional values for external display and internal operation for the decimal number 7.

FIGURE 21-9.   Wrong display for decimal number 7.

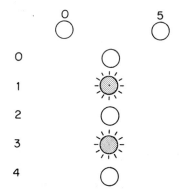

FIGURE 21-10. Wrong display for decimal number 4.

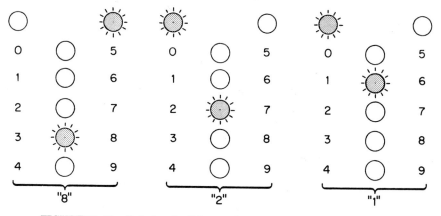

FIGURE 21-11. Indexing the lights on the console for interpretation of each decimal digit for decimal number 821.

The bi-quinary configuration renders a bit display that is referred to as an *even-parity condition*. Even parity means that an even number of bits must be displayed—in this case, one binary and one quinary bit.

Usually the lights on the console will be indexed as shown in Fig. 21-11 for easy interpretation of each decimal digit. The number 821, for example, would require three sets of lights, one for each digit. The operator reads under the appropriate binary bit (either the right side or the left side), observes the quinary bit being displayed, and reads the index number corresponding to the quinary bit that has been activated. The IBM 650 is a computer that uses the bi-quinary system for display purposes.

In summary, the two-state condition of digital computers requires a two-symbol language. The binary number system with its two admissible characters has played an essential part in the development and operation of digital computers. Furthermore, representation of decimal numbers by their binary equivalents causes little difficulty.

Once the binary number is understood, there remains the question of how mathematical operations are performed by the computer. Specifically, can the same basic arithmetic operations be performed with binary numbers as with decimal numbers? This question can easily be answered in the affirmative.

Some rules for adding, subtracting, multiplying, and dividing with binary numbers will be demonstrated next in order to indicate the essential elements of binary arithmetic. Knowledge of binary arithmetic also provides insight into the arithmetic operations of computers.

RULES FOR BINARY ARITHMETIC

Rules for Adding Binary Digits

The rules for adding binary digits are as follows:

$$0 + 0 = 0$$
$$1 + 0 = 1$$
$$1 + 1 = 0 \text{ with 1 to carry.}$$

Some examples of these rules are given next:

Decimal	Binary	
	$\boxed{8421}$	←Positional Values
2	0010	
+2	+0010	
4	0100	
9	1001	
+ 2	+0010	
11	1011	

The carrying over of a 1 bit should not be confusing, since the same procedure is used with decimal numbers. A carryover in decimal notation represents an increase of ten times the lower-order position; for instance.

$$\begin{array}{r} 10 \\ +90 \\ \hline 100 \end{array}$$

In binary arithmetic, a carryover represents a doubling of the lower-order positional value:

$$\begin{array}{r} \boxed{8421} \quad \leftarrow \text{Positional Values}\\ 0001\\ +0001\\ \hline 0010 \end{array}$$

Each 0001 indicates one one-value bit, while the 1 bit in 0010 is equivalent to two one-value bits. The binary number 0100 is equivalent to two two-value bits or four one-value bits. The opposite of the carryover rule, the borrowing of a bit, will be explained under the subtraction rule.

Rules for Subtracting Binary Digits

The rules for subtracting binary digits are as follows:

$$0 - 0 = 0$$
$$1 - 1 = 0$$
$$1 - 0 = 1$$
$$0 - 1 = 1 \text{ with one borrowed}$$

Here again, the rules are no different from the rules for decimal numbers, even to the procedure of borrowing from higher-order positions. An example follows:

Decimal	Binary
	$\boxed{8421}$ ←Positional Values
4	0100
−1	−0001
3	0011

Using this example, the borrowing of binary numbers can be diagrammed. Each binary 1 has a different decimal value depending on its position.

8	4	2	1	←——Positional Values
		1	1	
		(1)	1	
0	(1)	0	0	
−0	0	0	1	
0	0	1	1	

This is not different from the process of borrowing in the decimal operation:

$$
\begin{array}{cc}
\overset{2}{\underset{(3)}{\cancel{}}} & \overset{(10)}{0} \\
- & 9 \\
\hline
2 & 1 \\
\end{array}
$$

The 3 in the number 30 represents three 10's. One the of 10's is borrowed and nine is subtracted from it. This leaves a 1 in the units position and two 10's or a 20 in the tens position, resulting in 21. In the binary example, the number 1 in the four-value position of the upper number represents one four-value bit. When this number is borrowed by the position to the right, it becomes equivalent to two two-value numbers; when one of these is borrowed by the one-value position, it becomes equivalent to two one-value numbers.

Rules for Multiplying Binary Digits

The rules for multiplying binary digits are as follows:

$$
\begin{aligned}
0 \times 0 &= 0 \\
1 \times 0 &= 0 \\
1 \times 1 &= 1.
\end{aligned}
$$

These rules are the same as those for the multiplication of decimal numbers. This can be demonstrated by the following example:

Decimal	Binary
21	10101
× 8	× 1000
168	00000
	00000
	00000
	10101
	10101000

It is left up to the reader to verify the fact that the decimal equivalent of 10101000 is 168.

Rules for Dividing Binary Digits

Rules for dividing binary digits follow the rules of binary subtraction, since division is simply repeated subtraction. In the following example, for $\frac{32}{8} = 4$, division by repeated subtraction is demonstrated for both decimal numbers and binary numbers:

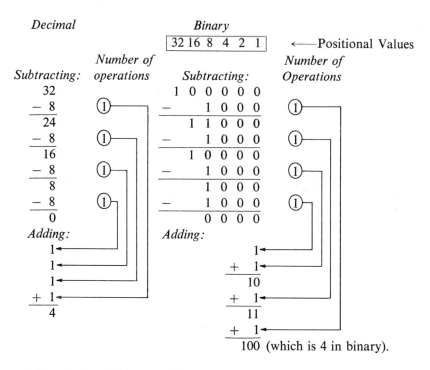

Decimal

Binary

| 32 16 8 4 2 1 | ←——Positional Values

| | *Number of* | | *Number of* |
| *Subtracting:* | *operations* | *Subtracting:* | *Operations* |

100 (which is 4 in binary).

A knowledge of binary arithmetic and its operations can provide an understanding and appreciation of the mathematical performance of computers within the environment of the two-state condition. With some understanding of a computer's binary language, the student is ready to be exposed to the concept of programming, which is the method for writing the instructions that direct a computer to perform the operations needed to solve a problem. The various approaches to programming computers will be explained in the next chapter.

BASIC COMPONENTS OF COMPUTERS

Awareness of the components of computers can give some insight into their operation and programming. The five components of a computer today are basically the same as those envisioned by Charles Babbage in the 1800's. They are diagrammed in Fig. 21–12. The relative importance of the components depends on the purpose or function for which the computer system is designed. A discussion of the basic components will be presented first, then a brief functional classification.

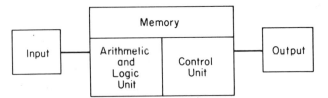

FIGURE 21–12.   Computer components.

Card Punched with Hollerith Code

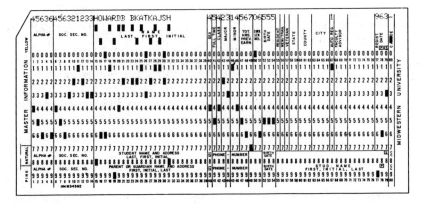

Example of a Student Registration Card

FIGURE 21–13.   Hollerith punched cards.

Input–Output Components

Input components are made up of devices that can be used to sense the information which has been placed on the various input media, such as

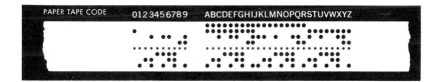

FIGURE 21-14.   Examples of input and output media.

punched cards, punched paper tape, and magnetic tape. Certain devices can scan magnetic-ink characters such as those inscribed on bank checks. Direct input of data can also be accomplished through the operation of console switches or by a typewriter mechanism. Examples of these commonly used input media are demonstrated in Figs. 21-13 and 21-14.

These same devices are used for the output of data and for the processed results, with the possible exception of the magnetic-ink-character scanner. However, there are a few additional types of output equipment. The most widely used is the *on-line* or *off-line printer*.

On-line equipment is directly connected to the computer, either physically or by cable hookup. Off-line equipment is not connected but can be utilized to interpret or display the computer's output media. Often a computer installation will not have an on-line printer; however, the card punch can be used as the on-line output device, and cards will be used in the off-line printer.

Actual Gas Company Statement

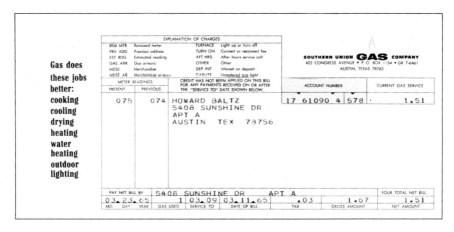

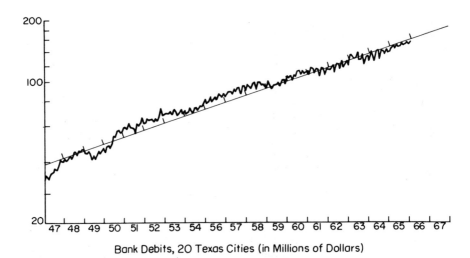

Bank Debits, 20 Texas Cities (in Millions of Dollars)

FIGURE 21–15. Examples of printed output.

Other specialized output equipment includes the *cathode-ray tube* (television tube) and the *plotter*. Plotters can display evaluations of mathematical functions on the familiar two-dimensional grid, or the contour lines of a surveyor's map can be drawn. Fig. 21–15 contains examples of outputs from a printer and a plotter. The gas bill shows a typical output from a printer, while the time-series chart of bank debits was produced on a plotter.

Memory

The most popular memory device used today is the *magnetic core*. Magnetic fields are generated by passing computer wiring through the center of these donut-shaped cores; the cores then store electronic bits generated by the magnetic fields. Another memory device is the *magnetic drum*. Magnetic reading and writing heads magnetize appropriate positions on the drum, storing electronic bits.

No matter what type of memory device is employed, it will be segmented in some manner so that the bits that are stored can be located easily. According to computer jargon, memory devices are "addressable." This means that coded information is placed at a prespecified location on a drum or within the core apparatus. It can then be retrieved by addressing the particular memory location.

The memory component can be thought of as analogous to a post office station and post office boxes. Information in the computer (the post office station) is stored in addressable locations in the same way that letters are placed in post office boxes. The box numbers are really "addresses."

A partial drawing of a hypothetical magnetic drum is displayed in Fig. 21–16 to clarify the storage concept. Earlier computers employed a similar drum that was capable of storing thousands of digits expressed in binary bits.

Investigation of the drum in Fig. 21–16 shows that stored in location number 1 (0001) is the number 9, represented by the bits for the binary number 1001. The drum locations in the boxes are specified in the upper left-hand corner of each segment. The read heads below the drum are magnetic devices for reading information from the drum; the positional values are provided for easy interpretation. Note that there are 2,000 memory positions for 2,000 digits. In the IBM 650, each of these 2,000 addressable positions would contain ten sets of binary bits instead of the four shown in Fig. 21–16.

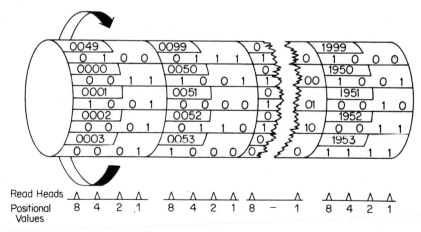

FIGURE 21–16.   A magnetic drum.

It must be mentioned here that the memory component retains the data to be used and the machine-coded instructions, which are also numeric in nature. More information on these instructions will be provided later.

Some computers are referred to as *fixed-length-word* computers, while others are called *variable-length-word* computers. As a comparison, the IBM 650, which utilizes a magnetic drum, is a fixed-length type because the data are all treated internally as ten-digit words. (For example, the number 12 is converted internally to 0000000012.) The operational instructions are also ten digits in length. On the other hand, the IBM 1620 computer, which is a magnetic-core machine, is a variable-length-word computer because its data can be stored in as few as two memory positions. (The number 12 would require only two positions.) However, the instructional commands are of a fixed 12-digit length. Other computers with cores may use both variable-length data and variable-length instructions.

Another auxiliary memory device that is widely used is the magnetic disk, which resembles a phonograph record. However, information is recorded and retrieved by magnetic means rather than by the conventional means of a phonograph.

The Control Unit

The functions of a computer's control unit can be compared to those of a control tower at an airport or a railroad switchyard. Incoming and outgoing planes are directed by the controlling station, and trains can be switched from track to track, depending on their ultimate destination. The computer also has a control unit that directs the flow of data and initiates the operation of the other components.

A computer control unit may function in two basic cycles: the instruction cycle, designated as the I cycle, and the execution cycle, classified as the E cycle. In the I cycle, a command is taken from memory and placed into a register, where it is divided into meaningful parts. In the E cycle, instructions are executed. The control unit also has a counter, an adding device that generates the address of the next instruction.

A look at one of the basic operating instructions employed in programming the IBM 1620 computer will illustrate a command structure in a variable-length-word machine. The instruction format for the 1620 computer consists of three main parts: the operation OP code, the P address, and the Q address. These are displayed in Fig. 21–17. The first two positions display the OP code, the next five contain an address of the computer memory, and the last five contain another address. The last five positions, however, can have other uses depending on the OP code.

Let us look at the instruction for addition, shown in Fig. 21–18. When the computer senses this instruction, the I cycle analyzes the OP code; the

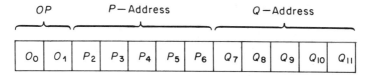

FIGURE 21-17. Instruction format for 1620 computer.

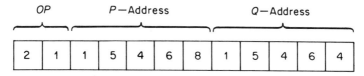

FIGURE 21-18. Instruction for addition for 1620 computer.

7	0	1̄	4	5	2̄	3	4	6	

| 15461 | 15462 | 15463 | 15464 | 15465 | 15466 | 15467 | 15468 | 15469 | Address Number of Memory Locations |

FIGURE 21-19. Memory appearance for numbers 14 and 234.

7	0	1̄	4	5	2̄	4	8	6	

| 15461 | 15462 | 15463 | 15464 | 15465 | 15466 | 15467 | 15468 | 15469 |

FIGURE 21-20. Memory positions after addition command is executed.

computer then is directed to execute the command by using the data located in the *P* and *Q* addresses. In this case, 21 directs the computer to add the number in the *Q* address to the number in the *P* address and place the result in the *P* address.

Let us assume that the data located in (or addressable by) 15464 and 15468 are the numbers 14 and 234 (shaded). This can be diagrammed in Fig. 21-19. The dash above the 1 and 2 in locations 15463 and 15466 is a signal to the computer that these two pieces of data are fields of two and three digits, respectively (14 and 234). After the addition command is executed, the memory positions appear as in Fig. 21-20. The result of adding 14 and 234 is 248, which is addressable at location 15468 (circled).

The Arithmetic-Logic Unit

The Arithmetic Section.   Sometimes, when the computer does its own arithmetic, this component is called the *processing unit*. It adds, subtracts, multiplies, and divides numbers. These four functions are handled by *registers* and *accumulators*, which serve as calculators in some computers; in others (specifically in the IBM 1620), the arithmetic operations make use of the *table-lookup method*.

The process which uses registers and accumulators needs little explanation, except that two different approaches may be used, the *parallel* approach or the *serial* approach. This is illustrated by the following example for addition:

Serial		Parallel
246		246
723		723
0009 ⟵ First Stage ⟶		0969
0069 ⟵ Second Stage		
0969 ⟵ Third Stage		

In the serial approach, the digits are added in separate stages. In the parallel approach, all digits are added simultaneously. The parallel approach is naturally much faster. The IBM 1130 computer is one of the less expensive computers that furnish parallel operation.

The speed of computers is very important to users. When computer technicians talk about speed, the units of time they discuss are not minutes or seconds but milliseconds, microseconds, and nanoseconds; these are

TABLE 21–1

ORGANIZATION OF ADD TABLE IN MEMORY UNIT

High-Order Positions of Address	Unit Positions of Address									
	0	1	2	3	4	5	6	7	8	9
0030	0	1	2	3	4	5	6	7	8	9
0031	1	2	3	4	5	6	7	8	9	0̄
0032	2	3	4	5	6	7	8	9	0̄	1̄
0033	3	4	5	6	7	8	9	0̄	1̄	2̄
0034	4	5	6	7	8	9	0̄	1̄	2̄	3̄
0035	5	6	7	8	9	0̄	1̄	2̄	3̄	4̄
0036	6	7	8	9	0̄	1̄	2̄	3̄	4̄	5̄
0037	7	8	9	0̄	1̄	2̄	3̄	4̄	5̄	6̄
0038	8	9	0̄	1̄	2̄	3̄	4̄	5̄	6̄	7̄
0039	9	0̄	1̄	2̄	3̄	4̄	5̄	6̄	7̄	8̄

equivalent to 1/1,000, 1/1,000,000, and 1/1,000,000,000 second, respectively. More recent technology has introduced 1/1,000,000,000,000 second as a time measurement.

The table-lookup method uses addition and multiplication tables similar to those learned in elementary school; the tables are stored internally in the memory unit. When two digits are added or multiplied together they generate an add table address. The answer is then "looked up" in the add table. A detailed explanation of this process will be illustrated next.

The add table is organized in the memory unit of the computer so that, in effect, its location and arrangement follow the pattern depicted in Table 21-1. This array of numbers is loaded into the respective memory positions as indicated in the following list. The bar or "flag bit" above some of the numbers is interpreted by the computer as a number 1 carried in the tens position; for example, $\overline{3}$ is 13.

Memory Location	Contents
00300	0
00301	1
00302	2
00303	3
00304	4
...	...
00310	1
00311	2
00312	3
...	...
00390	9
00391	$\overline{0}$
00392	$\overline{1}$
00393	$\overline{2}$
00394	$\overline{3}$

These same values are arranged in Table 21-1 by rows. Also, note that the contents of each memory location or address represent the addition of the two positions that are farthest to the right in each address number. For instance,

the content of location 00311 is 2 (1 + 1 = 2)

the content of location 00312 is 3 (1 + 2 = 3)

the content of location 00392 is $\overline{1}$ (9 + 2 = 11).

Let us now trace through the procedure the computer follows to generate the appropriate add table address and, consequently, the appropriate addition result. The following example demonstrates step by step the addition of the numbers 134 and 83:

Step 1:   The machine automatically inserts the number 003 into the three high-order positions of a special register because the add table is always located in storage positions 00300–00399.

Step 2:   In the special register, the computer inserts the 4 of the number 134 into the position immediately to the right of the 003. The register now contains the number 0034. Next the 3 of the number 83 is inserted just to the right of the 0034, giving 00343 in the special register.

Step 3:   The machine now transfers control and seeks the content in 00343, which is 7. This 7, which is the result of adding the units positions of 134 and 83, is then placed in the appropriate location for receiving addition results.

The first three steps can be illustrated by the schematic chart in Fig. 21–21.

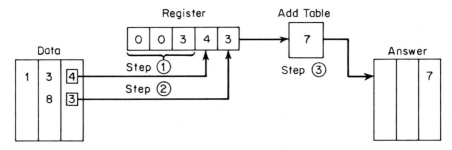

FIGURE 21–21.   Adding the numbers 134 and 83—steps 1, 2, and 3.

Step 4:   The computer repeats the procedure in steps 1–3 for the tens positions of the two input numbers. The 3 and 8 of the numbers 134 and 83 generate the address 00338, whose contents are transferred to the answer area. In this case, the number $\overline{1}$, which is 11, appears in the add table. The 1 of the units position is inserted in the tens position of the answer area, and the 1 of the tens position is saved as a carryover to the hundreds position. This step is summarized in the schematic diagram in Fig. 21–22.

Step 5:   The first three steps are again repeated, but on the hundreds position of the two numbers being added. This time, the 1 of the number 134 and the blank or 0 of the number 83 are placed in the special-address register, rendering the address 00311. The zero in the units position is changed to a 1 because of the carryover of the 1 from the previous step. This operation is clarified in the schematic diagram in Fig. 21–23. The proper answer, displayed in the answer area, is 217, since 134 + 83 = 217.

Numbers can be multiplied in a similar manner, using a special multi-plication table located in the storage section of the computer. Understanding

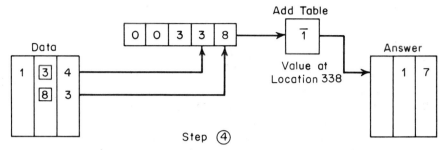

FIGURE 21–22.   Adding the numbers 134 and 83—step 4.

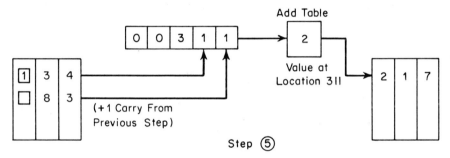

FIGURE 21–23.   Adding the numbers 134 and 83—step 5.

how the computer accomplishes addition and subtraction should give some insight into the other arithmetic operations. The logic capability of the computer will be introduced next.

The Logic Section. To understand the logic or decision-making mechanism, one must go back more than a hundred years to a development by a British mathematician named George Boole. Boole had the remarkable idea of applying mathematical laws to logic; he therefore constructed an algebra of logic. Boolean algebra takes many forms, but the form that eventually led to the electronic computer concerns itself with the fact that separate statements can be combined by mathematical rules to yield valid conclusions. For example, in the following series, statements 1 and 2 lead to statement 3:

1. If it is cloudy outside, then it may be raining.
2. If it is raining, then I will need my raincoat.
3. If it is cloudy, then I will need my raincoat.

For more than a century, this relatively abstract branch of mathematics seemed only suitable for parlor games. Then in 1938, an American scientist named Claude Shannon discovered that electrical switches had something in common with the propositions of Boolean algebra: a proposition is either true or false, just as an electrical switch is either on or off. Here, as in the binary arithmetic system, the two-state condition of computers is relevant.

Elementary electrical circuits are commonly divided into *parallel* and *series* designs; these designs form the basic circuitry for a computer's decision-making capability. No matter what type of advanced components a computer uses, each decision it makes depends on whether a switch is open or closed; Boolean algebra has become the tool computer designers use to organize decisions so that the computer can choose among the alternatives.

In Boolean algebra, only two operations are allowed, multiplication and addition. Multiplication corresponds to series-connected switches and addition to parallel-connected switches. The four possibilities of multiplication are illustrated in Fig. 21–24 by two switches connected in series. A 0 represents an open switch and a 1 a closed switch; alternatively, a 1 can be interpreted as true, and a 0 as false.

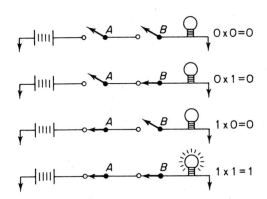

FIGURE 21–24. Multiplicative conditions of switches connected in series (Boolean algebra).

The four possibilities of addition with two switches connected in parallel are shown in Fig. 21–25, where the switches are labeled A and B. We can arrive at logical conclusions by merely testing for the flow of current. However, using the series design, we only can answer the basic question of whether switch A and B are both closed, while the parallel design allows us to determine whether switch A, switch B, or both are closed.

This operation can be transformed into a familiar card game to illustrate the importance of series and parallel circuits. When a spade is selected from a deck of playing cards, switch A is closed; switch B is closed when the card selected is a face card. If the switches are connected in series, the only time the light will go on is when the card selected is a face card from the suit of spades. This can be demonstrated by Venn diagrams in Fig. 21–26.

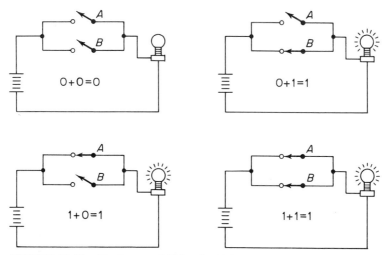

FIGURE 21–25. The four possibilities of addition with two switches connected in parallel (Boolean algebra).

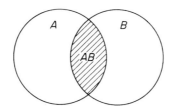

FIGURE 21–26. Venn diagram demonstrating operation of switches as a card game.

The circle *A* represents all the face cards in a deck of cards and *B* represents all the events corresponding to spades. Hence, the intersected area of *A* and *B* (the shaded area *AB*) represents face cards from the spade suit. If the switches are connected in series, the light will go on only when the intersection of *A* and *B* occurs—that is, when the card is a face card of spades. However, when the switches are connected in parallel, the light will go on when the card is any spade, any face card, or any spade face card. This is represented by the total areas of *A* and *B* in the Venn diagram (all three events).

It should be noted that series circuits correspond to the multiplicative rules of probability as well as to the multiplicative rules of Boolean algebra, while parallel circuits apply to the additive rules of probability as well as to the additive rules of Boolean algebra. The rules for binary arithmetic also follow these patterns. Of course, other combinations of circuits would establish the other logical conditions of a decision situation.

Students interested in further applications of mathematics to computer science should study Boolean algebra, set theory, and probability.

FUNCTIONAL CLASSIFICATIONS OF COMPUTERS

The basic functional uses of computers can be illustrated diagrammatically on the basis of the components that have already been outlined. Computers can be designed or adapted to handle all types of problems.

Problems can be oriented to two approaches: processing large volumes of data or computing complicated problems. In simpler terms, the two approaches involve processing large amounts of data with relatively few calculation requirements, or processing small amounts of data that demand relatively large computational activity. The first of these two situations can be illustrated by the diagram of the five computer components in Fig. 21–27.

In this case, enormous amounts of data must be handled rapidly; therefore, emphasis is placed on the input and output components. This problem is typical of those found in accounting, inventory control, and other business areas.

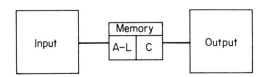

FIGURE 21–27.   Problem solving by processing large volumes of data.

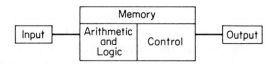

FIGURE 21–28.   Problem solving by computing complicated problems.

The other type of problem, which places demands on the memory, arithmetic, and control units, is illustrated in Fig. 21–28. This situation is typically encountered in the mathematical, statistical, and scientific fields. Of course, scientifically oriented or business-oriented computers are special-purpose machines. General-purpose computers would have greater balance between their components.

DIFFERENCES BETWEEN CALCULATORS
AND COMPUTERS

If a simple calculator is compared to a computer, two shortcomings of the calculator become quite evident. First, it requires continuous attention by an operator; and second, there are no mechanical or automatic ways to record results or to reset them into the machine so that a process can be automatically repeated or so that they can be used for subsequent calculations.

Calculators and computers differ in three ways:

1. The electronic computer carries a problem to completion because its data and instructions are stored.
2. The electronic speed of computers is faster than the electromechanical speed of calculators.
3. The computer is capable of making logical choices.

The significance of the computer rests with its capacity to store a sequence of commands or instructions. This concept of internal control is referred to as *stored programming*. Students who explore this concept can develop a powerful technique for research and application.

PROBLEMS AND PROJECTS

1. Using the references in this chapter or other references in the library, discover and explain the role that J. von Neumann had in the development of computers.

2. Write the binary equivalents for the following decimal numbers:

   a.   7.
   b.   16.
   c.   25.
   d.   783.

3. Display the bi-quinary equivalents for the following decimal numbers:

   a.   7.
   b.   16.
   c.   25.
   d.   783.

(*Hint:* Use a set of bits for each decimal number.)

4. Add the following binary numbers. Check your answer by deriving their decimal equivalents.

a.	1010	b.	0110	c.	0111	d.	010
	+1000		+1001		+0011		101
							+110

(*Hint:* Accomplish d. by pairs.)

5. Subtract the following binary numbers:

a.	1000	b.	1100	c.	101
	−0010		−0100		−010

6. Multiply the following binary numbers:

a.	0110	b.	1001	c.	11011
	× 111		× 011		× 1001

7. Display the bits in the binary-coded system for the numbers 2,14, and 843.

SELECTED REFERENCES

Adams, L. J., *Modern Business Mathematics.* New York: Holt, Rinehart & Winston, Inc., 1963. See especially Chapter 12 for a discussion of Boolean algebra.

Awad, Elias M., *Business Data Processing.* Englewood Cliffs, N. J.: Prentice-Hall, Inc., 1965. See Chapter 2 on the history and development of computers.

——— and Data Processing Management Association, *Automatic Data Processing, Principles and Procedures.* Englewood Cliffs, N. J.: Prentice-Hall, Inc., 1966. See chapters 1, 2, and 3 for a discussion of the history and development of computers.

Borko, Harold, *Computer Application in the Behavioral Sciences.* Englewood Cliffs, N. J.: Prentice-Hall, Inc., 1962. See Chapter 3 on the history and development of computers.

Chapin, Ned, *An Introduction to Automatic Computers*, 2nd ed. Princeton, N. J.: D. Van Nostrand Co., Inc., 1963. Chapter 9 discusses the history and development of computers.

Page, C. F., "Checking in Data Processing," *Instruments and Control Systems*, XXXVII (August 1964), 129–131.

Schmidt, Richard N., and W. E. Meyers, *Introduction to Computer Science and Data Processing.* New York: Holt, Rinehart & Winston, Inc., 1965. See Chapter 2, on the history and development of computers, Chapter 6 on binary arithmetic, and Chapter 7 on Boolean algebra.

Statland, Norman, "Fact, Fiction and Future," *Data Processing Magazine*, VIII (February, 1966), pp. 19–23.

Stibitz, G. R., and J. A. Larrivee, *Mathematics and Computers*. New York: McGraw-Hill Book Company, 1957. See Chapter 4 on the history and development of computers.

Swallow, Kenneth P., and Wilson T. Price, *Elements of Computer Programming*. New York: Holt, Rinehart & Winston, Inc., 1965. See Chapter 1 on the history and development of computers.

Wheeler, Gershon J., and Donlan F. Jones, *Business Data Processing: An Introduction*. Reading, Mass.: Addison-Wesley Publishing Co., 1966. See Chapter 12, "Choosing a Computer."

The following articles by Gilbert Burck are from a series in *Fortune* Magazine entitled *The Boundless Age of the Computer* (LXIX, Nos. 3, 4, 5, 6, 7, and 8).

Part I: The Boundless Age of the Computer (March 1964), 100–111, 230–232.
Part II: "On Line" in "Real Time" (April 1964), 140–145, 246–252.
Part III: "Machines That Man Can Talk With" (May 1964), 153–156, 149–198.
Part IV: "Assault on Fortress IBM" (June 1964), 112–116, 196–207.
Part V: "Management Will Never Be the Same" (August 1964), 124–126, 199–204.
Part VI: "Will the Computer Outwit Man?" (October 1964), 120–121, 162–172.

22

PROGRAMMING

Computer programming can be considered an art. The programmer must arrange a set of computer instructions in a sequence that will accomplish an assigned task; the ability to concentrate and the ability to reason in a logical manner are both essential traits.

The concept of programming distinguishes computers from other automatic machines. Other machines are designed to perform a limited number of inflexible tasks; their basic jobs or routines cannot be changed. The washing machine, for example, can be directed to perform an automatic sequence of operations and to provide the housewife with a selection of different types of washing cycles. Nevertheless, these cycles cannot be altered and new cycles cannot be inserted; the cycles are fixed by the mechanical construction of the machine.

A computer, on the other hand, can perform an unlimited number of tasks, and a changeable program can be stored in the machine (the computer) with a push of a button. It is not surprising that it was a woman, Lady Lovelace, who was probably responsible for suggesting the idea of changeable stored programming to Charles Babbage, because women for centuries have practiced the art of changing their minds. Perhaps this is why computers are always referred to as "she."

THE STORED-PROGRAMMING CONCEPT

The stored-programming concept can be illustrated with a hypothetical manual computer that we will call the shoe-box computer, because it is actually constructed of shoe boxes. A simple problem that involves adding and subtracting several numbers will be "programmed" for this computer.

The use of flow charts will also be illustrated in this section because this procedure is used by many programmers and has proved essential in preparing programs for most complex problems. Several problems will be introduced in flow-chart form; in the latter part of the chapter, a few of these will be translated into various computer languages.

The Shoe-box Computer

Before an electronic computer can perform the simple function of adding 1 and 1, someone must tell it what to do and how to do it by giving it instructions. The written instructions that are inserted into the computer are called the *program* or *routine*. The program is constructed in the form of a sequence of coded computer instructions that will obtain the solution to a given problem. Although the shoe-box computer is operated manually, it can provide a setting for the study of programming.

The problem that will be given to the shoe-box computer is that of adding two numbers, *A* and *B*, and subtracting another, *C*.

First, the manual computer must be visualized. A group of ten shoe boxes are placed in a straight row on a table as shown in Fig. 22-1. The boxes are numbered consecutively from 00 through 09. These numbers serve as the "addresses" of each box. Six slips of paper are placed in the first six boxes, those numbered 00 through 05. This is the first step in executing a computer program—placing the instructions in the computer.

The six slips of paper represent the routine (or program); each contains an instruction to be carried out by the computer. The six instructions are:

Address	*Instruction*
Box 00	PLACE (or read) the contents of the data cards in the boxes beginning with box 06.
Box 01	TRANSFER the number contained in box 06 to box 09.
Box 02	ADD the number contained in box 07 to the contents of box 09.
Box 03	SUBTRACT the number contained in box 08 from the number contained in box 09.
Box 04	PRINT on a card the contents of box 09.
Box 05	GO TO box 00 and execute the instruction contained there.

The second step is to have the data prepared on slips of paper and to place them so that they can be read into the computer at the proper time. Two sets of three cards each are prepared. The first three cards are printed with the numbers 44, 19, and 21, which represent values *A*, *B*, and *C*, respectively. The second set of cards is printed with the numbers 35, 14, and 27. The two sets now contain different values for *A*, *B*, and *C*.

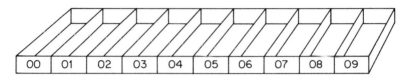

FIGURE 22–1.   Shoe-box computer.

The final step in solving this problem is to tell the computer to start. Since this is not an electronically powered computer, we must rely on manpower. Therefore, we will start by reading the instruction in the box numbered 00, then proceed from left to right, following each instruction as we come to it. This procedure is like a treasure hunt. We will now see if the shoe-box computer has been programmed accurately to give us the results of adding two numbers and subtracting a third; symbolically, the problem is to solve $A + B - C$.

When the start button is pushed, we are told to go to box 00 and follow the instruction located there, which is to place the first set of three data cards in boxes 06, 07, and 08. The numbers on the cards are 44, 19, and 21; they are placed in boxes 06, 07, and 08, respectively. We then proceed to the next address (box 01), where we are told to transfer the number in box 06 (the number 44) to box 09. Box 09 is the *accumulator*; it has access to either a Chinese abacus or other type of calculator that performs the necessary arithmetic operations.

After the number 44 is inserted into the accumulator, we proceed to the next address (box 02), where we find the instruction to ADD the number in box 07 to the contents of box 09 (the accumulator). Therefore, 19 (the number initially placed in box 07) is added to the number 44 which was placed in box 09 according to the previous instruction. As a result of this operation, box 09 now contains the number 63 (44 + 19).

The instruction in the next box, box 03, is to subtract the number contained in box 08 (which is 21) from the number in box 09. Box 09 will now contain the number 42, because $63 - 21 = 42$. Algebraically, we have computed $A + B - C$, where A was equal to 44, B was equal to 19, and C was equal to 21. The answer is $44 + 19 - 21 = 42$.

The instruction in the next box (box 04) directs that the contents of box 09 be printed on a card. This card will contain the number 42, our answer. The next address contains the instruction to GO TO box 00 and repeat the routine again, using the set of data cards that contains the numbers 35, 14, and 27. All previous data cards are cleared from the computer's memory. The execution of the routine should render an answer for $35 + 14 - 27$. The computer will continue to add two numbers and subtract a third until there are no more sets of data cards.

Flow Charts

A flow chart is simply a road map for the programmer that shows the logical steps required to solve a problem. There are two types of flow charts: the *general flow chart* and the *detailed flow chart*. A general flow chart of the problem used in the shoe-box computer is diagrammed in Fig. 22–2, and a detailed flow chart of the same problem is given in Fig. 22–3.

This problem does not require a very complex flow diagram; therefore, several other problems will be introduced to illustrate the use of the flow chart with different logical patterns.

The flow chart in Fig. 22–4 depicts the logical process of elimination for a "mind-reading" problem that can be executed on a computer. Although this is a very simple problem, the structure of the flow chart provides the basis for a routine that can be used to direct a computer to determine a number that has been chosen. After one of ten digits has been chosen, the computer is given the answers to the following three questions:

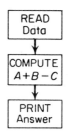

FIGURE 22–2.   General flow chart.

1. Is the number greater than 3?
2. When the number is divided by 4, is the remainder greater than 1?
3. Is the number odd?

Remember that when a number—say, 2—is divided by 4, the answer is not the fraction $\frac{2}{4}$; instead, the 4 goes into 2 zero times with a remainder of 2. The logic of the program is shown in Fig. 22–4. (The diamond-shaped figures are used to indicate a decision situation in the program. In this case, they represent the situation where the answers to the three questions above have been supplied.)

Let us now turn to a problem that has a more realistic application. This is the problem of calculating payrolls, which is being done more and more by computers. The purpose of this problem

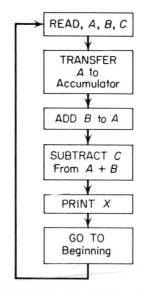

FIGURE 22–3.   Detailed flow chart.

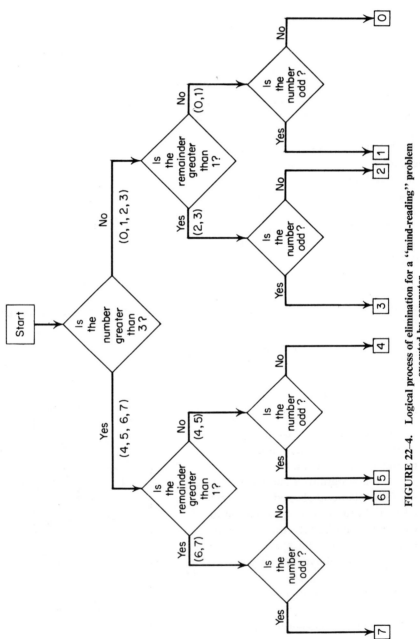

FIGURE 22-4. Logical process of elimination for a "mind-reading" problem executed by computer.

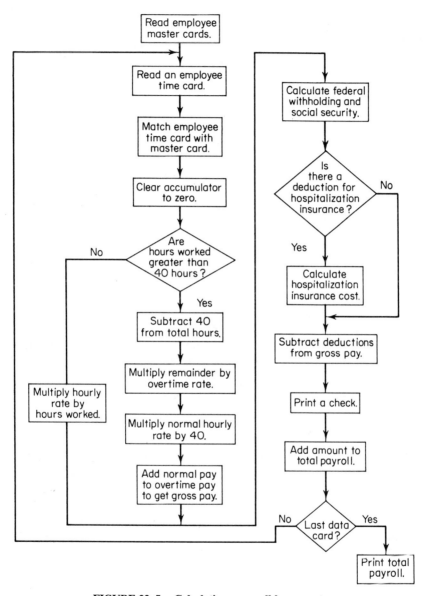

FIGURE 22–5. Calculating a payroll by computer.

is to calculate the amount of an employee's paycheck and the firm's total payroll. The flow chart is shown in Fig. 22–5.

The remainder of this chapter will be devoted to the introduction of some of the programming languages that have been written for computers. Several of the programs are based on the flow charts that have been illustrated in this section.

PROGRAMMING LANGUAGES

There are two basic types of programming languages: *machine-oriented* languages and *problem-oriented* languages. Machine-oriented languages appear, basically, in a strictly numerical coded form, as was illustrated in the previous chapter; for example, the instruction to add two numbers might appear in the form 210001407643. Problem-oriented languages usually appear in a more abbreviated grammatical form. For example, the instruction to add two numbers might appear as

$$Y = A + B$$

or, in the case of another problem-oriented language, it might appear as,

ADD A TO B TO GIVE Y.

Problem-oriented languages are easier to learn; they are used extensively by those who cannot devote a great deal of time to writing computer programs.

Several of the problems that were illustrated in flow chart form will be shown next in program form. The problems will be written in both machine-oriented languages and problem-oriented languages.

Machine-Oriented Languages

The instruction format for the machine language of the IBM 1620 was introduced in the previous chapter and several basic instructions were explained and illustrated. There is no way to explain machine language thoroughly enough in one chapter to make the reader a proficient programmer. However, two examples of programs written in machine language will be given so that the reader may become aware of the appearance of this language.

The first example describes several machine-language instructions that might be used to solve the problem given for the manually operated shoe-box computer—that is, $A + B - C$. The instructions are coded and can be briefly explained as follows:

OP Code	P Address	Q Address	Explanation
36	00006	00300	The OP code of 36 instructs the computer to read a card, because the 00300 located in

the Q address is the code for the card reader. We will assume that A, B, and C are only two-digit numbers; therefore, this instruction will place A in locations 00006 and 00007, B in locations 00008 and 00009, and C in locations 00010 and 00011.

26	00014	00007	The instruction with an OP code of 26 tells the computer to transfer the value of A, which is located in 00006 and 00007, to the three-digit locations of 00012, 00013, and 00014.
21	00014	00009	The OP code of 21 activates the circuitry necessary to add the two-digit number in 00008 and 00009 to the three-digit number in 00012, 00013, and 00014.
22	00014	00011	The numeric OP code 22 instructs the computer to subtract the number located in addresses 00010 and 00011 from the three-digit number located in 00012, 00013, and 00014.
38	00012	00400	The OP code of 38 tells the computer to write the answer located in addresses 00012, 00013, and 00014. The number 00400 of the Q address is the special notification that the answer is to be punched on a card.
49	00000	00000	This is the last instruction. The OP code of 49 is the signal to branch back to any location in the computer specified by the P address. In this case, the computer branches to address 00000, where the read instruction is located. The computer then proceeds to read the next data card and execute the series of instructions again. The computer will continue to read data cards and complete the calculations until it runs out of cards.

A few other incidental instructions are needed before this program can actually be executed. However, this partial program illustrates the most important instructions that are needed to solve the problem.

Another program can be illustrated that requires the use of machine instruction for multiplication. The OP code for multiplication is 23, and the result of the multiplication is placed at the special 20-digit location numbered 00080 through 00099. The multiplication problem is stated as follows:

The variables A, B, C, and X are five-digit positive numbers stored in the fields whose addresses are 00500, 00505, 00510, and 00515, respectively. Find $AX^2 + BX + C$.

We will assume that the data have already been read into the computer. Thus the program for calculating $AX^2 + BX + C$ is as follows:

23	00500	00515	This multiplies A times X.
26	00530	00099	This stores AX at 00530.
21	00530	00505	This adds B to AX.
23	00530	00515	This gives $(AX + B)X$.
26	00530	00099	This stores $(AX + B)X$.
21	00530	00510	This adds C to $(AX + B)X$, which is the answer.

A complete machine-language problem is listed in the Annex to this chapter. The necessary instructions for typing and executing the program with the console typewriter of the IBM 1620 are also given.

Problem-Oriented Languages

There are two types of problem-oriented languages: *assembly languages* and *compiler languages*. Instructions for these two types of languages will be helpful in indicating their differences.

One important fact which must be emphasized at this point is that a computer only "understands" machine-oriented languages. Therefore, if a program is written in the form of a problem-oriented language, the instructions must be "translated" into the corresponding machine-language instructions. However, this translation can be accomplished by the computer; the procedure will be explained in the final section of the chapter.

Assembly Language. If the problem which was introduced above $(AX^2 + BX + C)$ is written in an assembly language, it might appear as follows:

M	A, X
T	AX
ADD	AX, B
M	AX + B, X
T	(AX + B)X, ANS
ADD	ANS, C

These instructions operate in much the same way as machine-language instructions. For example, M stands for multiply, corresponding to the 23 operation code in machine language; T means transfer. Locations are given names, such as A, X, AX, and so forth, instead of numerical designations as was done in machine language. These six instructions correspond to the six machine-language instructions that were previously written for this problem.

Before the computer executes this assembly-language program, it must be instructed to translate it into the appropriate machine-language instructions; these might be the same six machine-language instructions shown previously, which were as follows:

$$
\begin{array}{lll}
23 & 00500 & 00515 \\
26 & 00530 & 00099 \\
21 & 00530 & 00505 \\
23 & 00530 & 00515 \\
26 & 00530 & 00099 \\
21 & 00530 & 00510
\end{array}
$$

Compiler Language. If the same problem $(AX^2 + BX + C)$ is written in the popular compiler language known as FORTRAN, which stands for *For*mula *Tran*slation, it will require only one instruction:

$$ Y = A*X*X + B*X + C. $$

(The asterisk indicates multiplication in FORTRAN.) This FORTRAN statement closely resembles the algebraic form of the problem. Hence, the name "problem-oriented language" means that the programmer writes the instructions for a program in a language that resembles the language of the problem rather than the language of the computer.

There is one main difference between an assembly language and a compiler language. Each assembly-language instruction is translated into a corresponding machine-language instruction, while each compiler-language instruction will probably be translated into many machine-language instructions; thus many machine-language instructions must be compiled to be equivalent to one FORTRAN instruction.

A compiler language known as COBOL is used in many types of business problems. COBOL is derived from the words *Common Business-Oriented Language.* If the problem of calculating $AX^2 + BX + C$ were written in COBOL, it might appear as follows:

MULTIPLY A TIMES XSQUARE TO GIVE AXSQUARE. MULTIPLY B TIMES X AND ADD TO C TO GIVE BXPLUSC. ADD AXSQUARE TO BXPLUSC TO GIVE RESULT Y.

No detailed explanation of COBOL will be given in this textbook because it is felt that FORTRAN is more appropriate for the types of quantitative problems introduced here.

An Example of a FORTRAN Program

We will now write in FORTRAN the simple problem of adding $A + B - C$ that was introduced with the shoe-box computer. No attempt will be made here to give a detailed explanation of FORTRAN instructions.

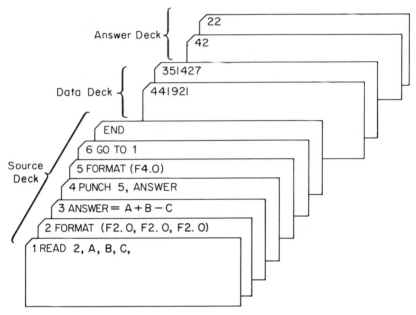

FIGURE 22–6.   An example of a FORTRAN program.

They are merely presented as an example of FORTRAN statements. The series of instructions may appear as follows:

1 READ 2, A, B, C
2 FORMAT (F2.0, F2.0, F2.0)
3 ANSWER = A + B − C
4 PUNCH 5, ANSWER
5 FORMAT (F4.0)
6 GO TO 1
END

Rules for writing FORTRAN statements are explained in the student manual, *Study Props*, that accompanies this textbook. Many other instruction manuals on FORTRAN are also avaliable.

These seven FORTRAN instructions can be prepared for computer input by keypunching them one per card; they are referred to as a *source deck*. This deck is followed by a deck of data cards.

As you may recall, two sets of three numbers each represented *A*, *B*, and *C* in our original shoe-box problem. The numbers constituting the first set, which were 44, 19, and 21, can be keypunched on one data card, and the second three numbers, which were 35, 14, and 27, can be keypunched on a second card. In this case, our so-called *data deck* will be composed of only these two data cards.

In processing this program, the source deck is placed into the computer's reading unit and the data deck is placed immediately after the source deck. The program will run repeatedly as long as there are data cards in the input hopper of the reading unit. In this case, the program is used only twice because there are only two data cards. Answer cards will be punched just a few moments after the source deck and the data cards are read into the computer. In this case, there will be only two answer cards. The keypunched cards for this particular program will appear with their punched information printed (or interpreted) on each card as illustrated in Fig. 22–6.

Processing FORTRAN Programs

It has been mentioned previously that compiler languages such as FORTRAN must be translated from a problem-oriented language into the machine language of the particular computer being used. This translation is

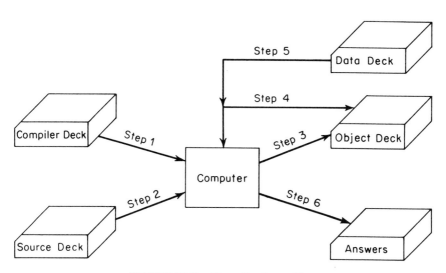

FIGURE 22–7. Skematic of compiling.

Step 1: The compiler deck is read into the computer; it is stored in the memory of the computer like any other program.

Step 2: The source deck (or program) is read into the computer and it is under control of the compiler deck which translates (or compiles) the machine language deck (called the object deck) from the FORTRAN deck (or source deck).

Step 3: The object deck is punched by the computer as if it were answers or output.

Step 4: The object deck is read back into the computer.

Step 5: The data cards are placed in the computer's reading unit immediately following the object deck.

Step 6: Moments later your answers begin to appear on punched cards.

performed by the computer under the control of a set of program cards referred to as the *compiler*. An explanation of the steps involved in processing a FORTRAN program (or any compiler language) is given in Fig. 22–7.

In many large computers, the third and fourth steps (generating the object deck and reading it into the computer) are eliminated because this step is accomplished internally and the object deck is stored directly into the memory unit.

One very important advantage of problem-oriented languages is that the computer can check for improper formulation of instructions during the compiling stage and can inform the programmer of any violations. This is helpful to programmers who must "debug" a program; programs rarely run correctly the first time.

One final point about programming is worth mentioning; that is, there is no way to be sure that a program is correct unless you know what the correct answer to the problem should be. The answers derived from a program must be tested against answers that have been determined by traditional manual methods. In very large and complex problems, it is usually customary for the programmer to check his program with a reduced amount of data that can also be handled manually.

ANNEX: A HANDS-ON EXERCISE FOR THE IBM 1620 COMPUTER

The following problem, which involves adding two numbers, can be executed on an IBM 1620 computer. The entire procedure is accomplished on the console typewriter; it is divided into five stages that are identified as follows:

> Stage 1: Clear the computer memory.
>
> Stage 2: Insert the add table into the memory.
>
> Stage 3: Type the program.
>
> Stage 4: Type the data.
>
> Stage 5: Receive the answers.

Each stage will be explained and demonstrated as it actually appears on the console typewriter.

Stage 1 (Clear the Computer Memory)

A simple instruction is typed on the console typewriter after the RESET and INSERT keys on the computer console are depressed. Thus the console typewriter can be used as an input device. The following 12 digit instruction is typed on the keyboard:

160001000000.

This instruction inserts zeros in all the memory positions of the computer.

In order for the computer to execute this instruction, the RELEASE and the START keys on the computer console must be depressed. The RELEASE key releases the typewriter and the START key initiates the instructions that were inserted. In this case, only one instruction was inserted. After a few seconds, the INSTANT-STOP key must be depressed to stop the execution of this particular instruction.

Stage 2 (Insert the ADD Table into the Memory)

Again, the RESET and INSERT keys are depressed. An instruction is typed as follows:

360030000100.

This is an instruction for reading the add table into 100 locations beginning with location 00300. After the read instruction is typed, the RESET and START keys are depressed again so that the add table can be typed on the console typewriter as data and read into the computer memory locations starting at 00300. Now the add table is typed as follows:

$$0123456789$$
$$123456789\bar{0}$$
$$23456789\bar{0}\bar{1}$$
$$3456789\bar{0}\bar{1}\bar{2}$$
$$456789\bar{0}\bar{1}\bar{2}\bar{3}$$
$$56789\bar{0}\bar{1}\bar{2}\bar{3}\bar{4}$$
$$6789\bar{0}\bar{1}\bar{2}\bar{3}\bar{4}\bar{5}$$
$$789\bar{0}\bar{1}\bar{2}\bar{3}\bar{4}\bar{5}\bar{6}$$
$$89\bar{0}\bar{1}\bar{2}\bar{3}\bar{4}\bar{5}\bar{6}\bar{7}$$
$$9\bar{0}\bar{1}\bar{2}\bar{3}\bar{4}\bar{5}\bar{6}\bar{7}\bar{8}$$

The bars above some of the numbers represent a 1 that is carried; for instance, $\bar{0}$ represents 10 and $\bar{1}$ represents 11. The bars are typed by depressing the key identified as FLAG on the typewriter before the appropriate number is typed. After these 100 numbers are typed, the RELEASE and START keys are depressed again.

Stage 3 (Type the Program)

The RESET and INSERT keys are depressed and the following three instructions are typed:

360010200100
360020100100
490010200000.

The RELEASE and START keys are then depressed. This causes the first instruction to be automatically read into computer locations 00000 through 00011. This was the instruction that directed the computer to read the program for adding two numbers into memory position, starting at 00102.

The second instruction is read into locations 00012–00023. This is the instruction that will read the two numbers to be added in locations 00201–00206 and 00207–00212, respectively. In this case, the two numbers to be added will be restricted to six-digit numbers.

The next instruction is a branch instruction that is read automatically into locations 00024–00035 as a result of typing them on the console typewriter. This instruction tells the computer to branch to location 00102 where the first instruction of the program will be located. After the RELEASE and START keys are depressed, the computer tranfers its control to location 00000. As you recall, this is where the start of these three instructions is located after the instructions have been typed. The first instruction (360010200100) prepares the computer and typewriter to type the program that will be inserted starting at position 00102. There are only three instructions for the simple addition problem; they are typed on the console typewriter as

210021200206
380020100100
490001200000.

The first instruction tells the computer to add the two numbers that will be read into positions 00207–00212 and 00201–00206. The second instruction tells the computer to read out the numbers in these same two positions. However, the answer will be found in locations 00207–00212 because of the instruction to add. The third instruction tells the computer to branch to location 00012, which contains the instruction for reading in the data (the two six-digit numbers).

It should be obvious that these three instructions are located in positions 00102–00113, 00114–00125, and 00126–00137, respectively. After these instructions are properly typed, the RELEASE and START keys are again depressed. This causes the computer to execute the second instruction of the first group (which is located at positions 00012–00023). The computer is now ready for stage 4, which is to read in the necessary data.

Stage 4 (Insert the Data)

The data for this problem must be two six-digit numbers. Each number is typed with a flag over the first digit—for example, $\overline{0}00002$ and $\overline{0}00004$. After these two numbers are typed properly, a *record mark* is typed. This is a special character which tells the computer that there are no more data for this field. It is marked on the typewriter with the symbol ‡. After the data and record mark are typed, they will appear as follows:

$$\overline{0}00002\overline{0}00004‡.$$

The RELEASE and START keys are again depressed. This allows the computer to read these two numbers and process them according to a program (in this case, the addition routine). In a few moments, the answers to the problem will be typed on the console typewriter.

Stage 5 (Receive the Answers)

The answer to this problem will appear on the typewriter as follows:

$$\overline{0}0000\overline{2}000006.$$

The answer, which is represented by the last six digits, is $\overline{0}00006$, because 000002 plus 000004 is equal to 000006. Now you are ready to insert (type) two additional numbers to be added; in a few seconds the answer will be typed on the console typewriter.

Let us now summarize the entire procedure step by step.

Depress: RESET and INSERT keys.
Type: 160001000000
Depress: RELEASE and START keys.
Depress: INSTANT-STOP key.
Depress: RESET and INSERT keys.
Type: 360030000100
Depress: RELEASE and START keys.
Type: 0123456789
1234567890
2345678901
3456789012
4567890123
5678901234
6789012345
7890123456
8901234567
9012345678

Depress: RELEASE and START keys.
Type: 360010200100
360020100100
490010200000
Depress: RELEASE and START keys.
Type: 210021200206
380020100100
490001200000
Depress: RELEASE and START keys.
Type: (for example) $\overline{0}00002000004\ddagger$
Depress: RELEASE and START keys.

The answer will appear as the last six digits of the following number:

$$\overline{0}00002\overline{0}00006$$

Type in another two six-digit numbers—for example,
$$\overline{0}01248\overline{1}12560\ddagger$$

Depress the RELEASE and START keys and you will have

$$\overline{0}01248\overline{1}13808$$

The last six digits, $\overline{1}13808$, comprise the answer.

Instead of typing in two new numbers, you can let the answer be treated as new data by simply depressing the RELEASE and START keys, this will provide the sum of the two numbers given above, 001248 and 113808; the new answer should be

$$\overline{0}01248\overline{1}15056,$$

since 001248 + 113808 = 115056.

PROBLEMS AND PROJECTS

1. Make a flow chart for a program to select the largest of three numbers. Call them *A*, *B*, and *C*.
2. Make a flow chart for a program to add positive numbers. Do nothing with zero, and print negative numbers.
3. Execute the example given in the Annex to this chapter.

SELECTED REFERENCES

Anderson, Decima M., *Basic Computer Programming: The IBM 1620 FORTRAN.* New York: Appleton-Century-Crofts, 1963.

IBM, *A FORTRAN Primer with Business Administration Exercises*, Manual No. C20-1605-O. New York: IBM Technical Publications Department, 1964.

Sprowls, R. C., *Computers—A Programming Problem Approach*, rev. ed. New York: Harper & Row, Publishers, 1968.

INDEX

Bonds, 265–66
Boole, George, 513, 514
Breach of contract, 15
Breakeven analysis, 201, 230–32, 258
Budgets:
 cash, 247–49
 long-run, 257
Bureau of the Census, 212
Business:
 evolution, 18–19
 financial needs, 243–72
 financial statements, 76–80
 fixed capital, 256–72
 objectives, 93
 operation functions, 95
 policies, 93
 role, 70–72
 working capital, 244–56
Business combinations, 80–87
 consequences of, 82–87
 horizontal, 82
 and market structures, 82–85
 nature of, 82
 nondirectional, 82
 objectives, 81–82
 principal methods, 80–81
 vertical, 82
Business Cycle Developments, 212
Business environment, dimensions of, 1–19
 economic, 1–11
 legal, 14–18
 social, 11–14
Business establishment, 70–87
Business ownerships:
 continuity, 75–76
 forms, 72–76
  compared, 74–76
 liability, 75

C

Capital:
 fixed, 243, 256–72
 management of, 243–72
 working, 244–56
Capital requirements, 76, 243
Carli, Giovanni, 274
Cash budget, 247–49
Cash flow, discounted, 264
Cash requirements (*see* Working capital)
Central tendency, measures of, 444, 446–51
Circulating capital (*see* Working capital)
Cohen, Kalman J., 219 *n*
Collateral-trust bonds, 266

Combinations, 371–74
Commercial credit, 253
Communication, 106–7
Competition, 10, 11, 81–82
 and game theory, 125–27
 imperfect, 199
 monopolistic, 83, 84
 pure, 83, 84, 227
Computers, 490–517
 analog, 490
 basic components of, 503–16
  arithmetic logic unit, 510–16
  control unit, 508–9
  input-output, 504–6
  memory, 506–8
 and calculators, 517
 digital, 490
 functional classifications of, 516
 history, 490–92
 shoe-box, 521–22
 (*See also* Programming)
Consumer behavior, 238–41
 Monte Carlo simulation, 239
 stochastic models, 238
Consumer Price Index, 475–76
Consumption spending, 44–47
Contracts, 15
Control, span of, 96–97
Controlling, 110–12
Corporations (*see* Business)
Cost analysis, 168–84
Cost-outlay line, 141–48
Cost-plus pricing, 229–30
Cost-push inflation, 58
Costs:
 average, 172–76
 estimating, 181–84
 fixed, 170
 long-run, 176–80
 marginal, 173–74, 205–9, 229
 operating, 170
 total, 171–72
 types of, 168–70
 variable, 170
Cost structure, 170–76
Counting techniques, 367–74
 without replacement, 369–74
 with replacement, 368–69
Cowden, Dudley, 470 *n*
Credit, 249–51, 265
 commercial, 253
 line of, 254
 long-term, 348
 short-term, 348
 and spending, 47
 trade, 253